D1338118

Works Councils

NBER Comparative Labor Markets Series
A National Bureau of Economic Research Series
Edited by Richard B. Freeman

Also in the series

David Card and Richard B. Freeman, editors
Small Differences That Matter: Labor Markets and Income Maintenance in Canada and the United States

Lisa M. Lynch, editor
Training and the Private Sector: International Comparisons

Rebecca M. Blank, editor
Social Protection versus Economic Flexibility: Is There a Trade-off?

Richard B. Freeman and Lawrence F. Katz, editors
Differences and Changes in Wage Structures

Works Councils

Consultation, Representation, and Cooperation in Industrial Relations

Edited by   Joel Rogers and
Wolfgang Streeck

The University of Chicago Press

Chicago and London

JOEL ROGERS is professor of law, political science, and sociology at the University of Wisconsin-Madison, where he directs the Center on Wisconsin Strategy. WOLFGANG STREECK is director at the Max-Planck-Institut für Gesellschaftsforschung in Cologne; at the time this book was written, he was professor of sociology and industrial relations at the University of Wisconsin-Madison.

The University of Chicago Press, Chicago 60637
The University of Chicago Press, Ltd., London
© 1995 by the National Bureau of Economic Research
All rights reserved. Published 1995
Printed in the United States of America
04 03 02 01 00 99 98 97 96 95   1 2 3 4 5
ISBN: 0-226-72376-3 (cloth)

Library of Congress Cataloging-in-Publication Data

Works councils : consultation, representation, and cooperation in industrial relations / edited by Joel Rogers and Wolfgang Streeck.
    p.   cm.—(NBER Comparative labor markets series)
    Includes bibliographical references and index.
    1. Works councils—Case studies—Congresses. 2. Comparative industrial relations—Congresses. I. Rogers, Joel. II. Streeck, Wolfgang. III. Series.
HD5650.W643   1995
338.6—dc20   95-13423
                                                       CIP

Relation of the Directors to the
Work and Publications of the
National Bureau of Economic Research

1. The object of the National Bureau of Economic Research is to ascertain and to present to the public important economic facts and their interpretation in a scientific and impartial manner. The board of Directors is charged with the responsibility of ensuring that the work of the National Bureau is carried on in strict conformity with this object.

2. The President of the National Bureau shall submit to the Board of Directors, or to its Executive Committee, for their formal adoption all specific proposals for research to be instituted.

3. No research report shall be published by the National Bureau until the President has sent each member of the Board a notice that a manuscript is recommended for publication and that in the President's opinion it is suitable for publication in accordance with the principles of the National Bureau. Such notification will include an abstract or summary of the manuscript's content and a response form for use by those Directors who desire a copy of the manuscript for review. Each manuscript shall contain a summary drawing attention to the nature and treatment of the problem studied, the character of the data and their utilization in the report, and the main conclusions reached.

4. For each manuscript so submitted, a special committee of the Directors (including Directors Emeriti) shall be appointed by majority agreement of the President and Vice Presidents (or by the Executive Committee in case of inability to decide on the part of the President and Vice Presidents), consisting of three Directors selected as nearly as may be one from each general division of the Board. The names of the special manuscript committee shall be stated to each Director when notice of the proposed publication is submitted to him. It shall be the duty of each member of the special manuscript committee to read the manuscript. If each member of the manuscript committee signifies his approval within thirty days of the transmittal of the manuscript, the report may be published. If at the end of that period any member of the manuscript committee withholds his approval, the President shall then notify each member of the Board, requesting approval or disapproval of publication, and thirty days additional shall be granted for this purpose. The manuscript shall then not be published unless at least a majority of the entire Board who shall have voted on the proposal within the time fixed for the receipt of votes shall have approved.

5. No manuscript may be published, though approved by each member of the special manuscript committee, until forty-five days have elapsed from the transmittal of the report in manuscript form. The interval is allowed for the receipt of any memorandum of dissent or reservation, together with a brief statement of his reasons, that any member may wish to express; and such memorandum of dissent or reservation shall be published with the manuscript if he so desires. Publication does not, however, imply that each member of the Board has read the manuscript, or that either members of the Board in general or the special committee have passed on its validity in every detail.

6. Publications of the National Bureau issued for informational purposes concerning the work of the Bureau and its staff, or issued to inform the public of activities of Bureau staff, and volumes issued as a result of various conferences involving the National Bureau shall contain a specific disclaimer noting that such publication has not passed through the normal review procedures required in this resolution. The Executive Committee of the Board is charged with review of all such publications from time to time to ensure that they do not take on the character of formal research reports of the National Bureau, requiring formal Board approval.

7. Unless otherwise determined by the Board or exempted by the terms of paragraph 6, a copy of this resolution shall be printed in each National Bureau publication.

(Resolution adopted October 25, 1926, as revised through September 30, 1974)

Contents

Acknowledgments

Work on this book would not have been possible without the support of a great number of institutions and, more important, individuals. Above all, Richard Freeman of the National Bureau for Economic Research convinced us to take up the subject in the context of his ambitious Working and Earning under Different Rules project—an effort whose scholarly excellence and practical importance we could not fail to note. Through him, we were happy to receive financial support from the Ford Foundation, which we used to assemble an international group of researchers and maintain a central project office at the University of Wisconsin-Madison. Room for this office was contributed by the University's Industrial Relations Research Institute.

Comparative institutional analysis requires extensive communication between researchers from different countries. In directing our project, we were lucky to be able to hold two project conferences. A first workshop took place in May 1991 in Madison, made possible by grants from the Washington Bureau of the Friedrich-Ebert-Stiftung and from the Hans-Böckler-Stiftung in Düsseldorf, a foundation maintained by the German Union Federation (DGB) and devoted to the study of co-determination. Dieter Dettke and Gerhard Leminsky, respectively, represented the two organizations and helped give us the confidence that our work would come to a good end. The conference was also attended by a number of representatives of American unions—in particular, James Cavanaugh (Wisconsin South Central Federation of Labor), Larry Cohen (Communications Workers of America), Jay Foreman (United Food and Commercial Workers), Peggy Kelly (Service Employees International Union), Charles McDonald (AFL-CIO), David Newby (Wisconsin AFL-CIO), Chris Schenk (Ontario Federation of Labour), and Denny Scott (United Brotherhood of Carpenters and Joiners)—whose comments and advice greatly improved our understanding of the problems of workplace representation in a North American setting.

One year later, the second project conference was hosted by the International Institute for Labour Studies at the International Labour Organization (ILO) in Geneva. We are still impressed with the unending attention to detail with which our friends at the Institute, in particular Werner Sengenberger and Duncan Campbell, helped make this conference as productive as it turned out to be. Conference participants also had the benefit of excellent comments on the draft papers from some of the leading experts on labor relations, who graciously took the time out of their busy schedules to contribute to our work. For their comments, we thank Robert Boyer, Duncan Campbell, Colin Crouch, Gerhard Leminsky, Charles McDonald, Bernd Marin, Werner Sengenberger, Tiziano Treu, and Kirsten Wever.

Finally, in running the central project office, we benefited from the support of three graduate students—Joohee Lee, Barbara Wootton, and Jooyeon Jeong—who successively served as project assistants, and Abby Coble, who assisted in final manuscript preparation.

I   Introduction

1 The Study of Works Councils: Concepts and Problems

Joel Rogers and Wolfgang Streeck

This book reports the results of one of several projects pursued within the research program Working and Earning under Different Rules, led by Richard Freeman of Harvard University and the National Bureau of Economic Research.[1] The Working and Earning program comprised a series of comparative studies of labor market institutions, income maintenance programs, and economic performance in the United States and other major OECD nations. It aimed to answer three large questions and to make the answers available to participants in policy debates in the United States (Freeman 1989, 5):

How do the distinctive labor market institutions and income maintenance schemes of advanced OECD countries work?

Which institutions offer fruitful guides to what the United States should (should not) do to improve its competitive position and economic well-being?

What explains the divergence of labor market institutions across OECD countries?

From the program's inception, works councils have been high on its list of research concerns. There are two reasons for this.

First, traditional forms of worker *representation*—whether the centralized bargaining and "political exchange" once characteristic of European countries or the more decentralized systems of collective bargaining characteristic of North America—are under pressure. This raises anew questions about how to provide workers with institutionalized representation at the workplace. In the

Joel Rogers is professor of law, political science, and sociology at the University of Wisconsin-Madison, where he directs the Center on Wisconsin Strategy. Wolfgang Streeck is director at the Max-Planck-Institut für Gesellschaftsforschung in Cologne; at the time this book was written, he was professor of sociology and industrial relations at the University of Wisconsin-Madison.

1. Other books arising from the program include Blank (1994), Card and Freeman (1993), Freeman and Katz (1995), and Lynch (1994); Freeman (1994) offers summaries of results from the different projects.

United States in particular, the continued decline of unionization—which now claims a bare 12 percent of the private sector workforce—has opened a yawning "representation gap" (Weiler 1990) that does not appear likely to be closed anytime soon by a simple revival of traditional unionism. Recognition of this gap has kindled new interest in alternative ways of providing "voice" for workers outside the traditional collective bargaining relationship. As works councils have in many countries historically provided representation to workers outside of formal collective bargaining, they provide a natural starting point to explore such alternative modes of worker representation.[2]

Second, councils appear capable of making an *efficiency* contribution to the performance of advanced industrial democracies, improving both individual *firm productivity* and the *effectiveness of state regulation* (economic or social) of firms. It is virtually definitive of councils, for example, that they increase and regularize consultation between management and workers. This may be thought to have several positive effects. By reducing information asymmetries between managers and workers, consultation can lead to more efficient labor contracts. By lowering the costs of information to both parties, it can facilitate adjustment to changed circumstances. By increasing trust between managers and workers, it can increase their willingness to engage in cooperative ventures, and with it increase the rewards that accrue to cooperation.[3] At a time when new forms of work organization—arising from the demands of shifting product markets and increased emphasis on "quality" production—place a premium on an unimpeded flow of information within firms and on cooperation among and between workers and managers, these potential effects have enormous appeal. In the United States, where the pace of adoption of advanced forms of work organization has been slow (Office of Technology Assessment 1990), that appeal is particularly pronounced.

The potential contribution of councils to effective regulation of firms is also evident. It is now well past cliché to observe that, to enhance competitive economic performance, government regulation of labor markets and working conditions needs to be "micro" as well as "macro." However fine, the regulation of fiscal aggregates and monetary policy is insufficient, for example, to assure an adequately trained workforce, rapid technology diffusion, or dynamically optimal levels of investment in research and development. To approximate these ends, considerable coordination and cooperation within firms—as well as among firms and between private firms and the state—is required. By pro-

2. To guard against misinterpretation in this highly charged area of current debate, we emphasize that the exploration of alternatives is not tantamount to the endorsement of those alternatives, or to rejection of that which they are alternative to.

3. Among others, see Freeman (1990), Freeman and Rogers (1993), Rogers and Streeck (1994), and, especially, Freeman and Lazear (chap. 2 in this volume). Note more generally the strong conclusion reached by Blinder and colleagues following their review of productivity-enhancing compensation schemes: "Whatever compensation scheme is used, meaningful worker participation, beyond labor representation in boards of directors, enhances productivity" (Blinder 1990, vii).

viding structured means of such intrafirm coordination, the thought goes, councils might help support government "modernization" policies in these areas.

What is true of economic regulation is true as well of fair labor standards, health and safety standards, and other "social" regulation of firm behavior. Directed to a large population of heterogeneous firms, such regulation in most cases cannot be effectively enforced through a state inspectorate or an army of "private attorneys general" bringing civil claims. Some on-the-ground monitoring and enforcement mechanism, rooted in the daily operation of firms, is also desirable. Many think that works councils might be just such a mechanism.

It bears emphasis, if only for its centrality to the U.S. discussion, that the availability of such local mechanisms might reasonably be expected to improve not only regulatory enforcement but the regulation itself. In the United States, the general absence of local monitoring and enforcement capacity has encouraged "command and control" regulatory programs. These, which are functionally adapted to the state inspectorate and private attorney general modes of enforcement that do exist, are widely criticized as overly broad, inflexible, and excessively process (as against performance) oriented. Councils are commonly involved in implementing social regulation, and then in ways that appear to favor regulatory styles simultaneously more exacting on outcomes and more flexible on means than is common in the United States. Here too, then, better understanding of their operation may be instructive for U.S. policy discussions.

It is not the purpose of this book to produce actual recommendations for policy in the United States. All that research can do is clarify the issues at stake. Framed by the basic questions posed by the Working and Earning under Different Rules program, contributors to this volume aim to improve the available knowledge of: the incidence, activity, and daily operation of councils in different settings; the contribution of councils to meeting representation and efficiency concerns (both private firm efficiency and the efficiency of the state or other collective regulatory effort); the precise institutional mechanisms that account for these effects; the comparative institutional advantage of councils (relative to other mechanisms) in producing those effects; and the conditions antecedent (e.g., in industrial relations systems and public policy) to parts or all of their production.

We begin this introduction by proposing an initial definition of works councils, broad enough to accommodate the diverse experiences of advanced industrial countries, and by suggesting a working typology of councils. We then proceed to explore the relations of works councils with, in turn, unions, employers, and states, mapping the main subjects that will be dealt with in the country studies and other subsequent chapters. Finally, we explain the general approach of the research and the organization of this volume.

1.1   Basic Definition and Initial Typology

We define *works councils* as *institutionalized bodies for representative communication between a single employer ("management") and the employees ("workforce") of a single plant or enterprise ("workplace")*. This is a very inclusive definition, but inclusiveness is needed to cover the great variation in what have historically been considered "council" forms and functions, at different times, in different systems. The following elaborations may be offered:

1. *Works councils represent all the workers at a given workplace, irrespective of their status as union members.* Where in addition to councils there are also unions claiming to represent workers, this raises the fundamental problem of determining the relationship between councils and unions—a problem that will occupy a central position in the studies in this book.

Where unions have strong "external," territorial organizations that engage in multiemployer collective bargaining, council-union relations are part of the vertical relationship between centralized and decentralized collective action of workers and between central and local joint regulation with employers. To the extent that (in addition) unions are, or try to be, organizationally present at the workplace, the relationship is (also) a horizontal one between representation of unionized workers through workplace union branches ("locals" and "sections") and representation of all workers through councils. In the typical European case, councils are in this way enmeshed in a complex triangular relationship with what are often called the "external" and the "internal" unions.

At stake in this relationship are questions of control—of the external union and centralized collective bargaining over works councils and internal unions and over joint regulation at the workplace, and of works councils or internal unions over workplace industrial relations with the employer. External unions, where they lay claim to central control over workplace bargaining, view the relationship between works councils and union branches above all in terms of its contribution to such control. Typically, central and external control seems to require a stable division of labor between external and internal industrial relations, and especially neutralization of the latter on subjects over which the former claim jurisdiction.

At the workplace, union-council relations differ in the extent to which councils and workplace unions are structurally independent from each other. At the one extreme, as in Italy, worker and union representation may be merged in one body. At the other extreme, as in Germany, councils may be clearly differentiated structurally from unions and created and sustained not by union action or governance but by a separate, legally based "works constitution."

To the extent that union and worker representation are structurally separated, one can speak of two "channels" of representation: a "first channel" operating through unions and collective bargaining—at the workplace, centrally, or both—and a "second channel" working through councils and "industrial democracy," "collective participation," or "joint consultation" at the workplace only. Structural separation of channels, however, does not preclude, and indeed may require, coordination between them. Organizationally, for example, works council election procedures typically favor union candidates, and especially candidates of large, "representative" unions. This enables union workplace organizations to penetrate the council system at least to some extent and to use it to promote union policies within the limits of whatever rules may govern councils as institutions.

Functionally, mature council systems provide for an elaborate division of labor between councils and unions, especially external unions. Just how functions are divided is strongly related, again, to questions of control, particularly over the wage bargain and the strike and more generally (of the external union) over the workplace. In Spain and Italy, where councils may negotiate wages and call strikes, external unions often find it difficult to make central wage bargains stick locally and to prevent local bargainers from calling strikes in pursuit of wage increases exceeding nationally negotiated rates. In Germany, by comparison, the legally institutionalized separation of channels excludes councils from wage bargaining and from calling strikes. With union workplace organizations effectively subordinated to councils, national union leadership has an effective monopoly on such functions. In return, works councils and the union workplace organizations that are involved in them are compensated with jurisdiction over a range of other, workplace-specific issues. In exercising this jurisdiction, however, their mode of operation is not through collective bargaining, but through legally based co-determination; and while they may exercise pressure, they do so not by threatening or calling a strike, but by taking the employer to mandatory arbitration or to the labor courts.

2. *Works councils represent the workforce of a specific plant or enterprise,* ***not*** *of an industrial sector or a territorial area.* Their counterpart is a single employer, not an employers' association. Industrywide councils, like wage councils in the United Kingdom, are thus not works councils in the sense of the definition used here.

3. *Works councils are* ***not*** *"company unions."*[4] Even as compared to a single-site, employer-dominated union, there is a distinction between works council representation of all workers in one workplace only and union representation—of union members at the workplace or of the common interests of workers across workplaces. Even "enterprise unions" in Japan, for example, tend to be affiliated to union federations covering more than one employer, weak as that affiliation may be.[5] By contrast, works councils are by definition single-employer institutions. And even under closed-shop company unionism,

---

4. We use this term in its generic international sense of "workplace-specific union." For consideration of the U.S. case, where what is traditionally meant by "company union" is approximated by what we call "paternalistic" councils below, see Rogers (chap. 13 in this volume).

5. Japanese company unions often create union-management consultation committees, kept separate from the union itself, for joint deliberation of production issues. If there were a Japanese equivalent to works councils, it would be these rather than the unions themselves.

there is usually a possibility of interunion competition, with workers joining an alternative union or management replacing the existing union with a "second" union. By contrast, works councils are by definition not voluntary associations but established institutions with a representational monopoly. Once established, workers cannot refuse to "join" them or to be represented by them. There is no exit from a works council other than changing one's place of employment.

4. *Being* **representative** *institutions, works councils also differ from management policies encouraging individual workers to express their views and ideas, as well as from new forms of work organization introduced to increase the "involvement" of workers in their work roles through decentralization and expansion of competence and responsibility in production tasks ("group work," "quality circles," and the like).* While works councils may make it easier for managements to implement work reorganization, they themselves are institutions outside the managerial line of authority (however decentralized) and differentiated from the functional organization of production. And while works councils make it easier for individual workers to speak up, as institutions of collective representation they typically aggregate the views of workers and transform them into a *common* voice of the workforce. If made at all, then, the "firm efficiency" argument for works councils is not based on their occupational competence but on their organization of representative communication between the employer and the workforce as a whole. Similarly, the "voice" argument is not identical with the argument for a decentralized work organization or for management being more accessible to individual workers.

5. *Representative communication between employers and their workforces may be of all possible kinds and may originate from either side.* Communication may be initiated and, in the limiting case, controlled by the employer, making the works council more like the "ear" than the "voice" of the workforce. At the opposite end of the continuum, it may mainly serve to express the collective interests of workers, with the employer obliged to listen. It may also involve an exchange of views and a dialogue leading to negotiations and, ultimately, agreement. Communication may or may not be on production issues, or on how better to cooperate in the pursuit of production goals and good competitive performance. It may be limited to information exchange, may entail consultation, or may end in negotiated co–decision making, or *co–determination.*[6]

Where council rights pertain only to *information,* managerial discretion is left largely intact, except that managements cannot avoid giving information. By contrast, *consultation* rights involve obligations for management to inform

6. Note here that whether a works council's relations with its employer are friendly or not is *not* part of our definition. Even where strikes are formally ruled out as a means of applying pressure, relations may well be highly antagonistic. And there is always the possibility, generally the case in industrial relations, that the law is not fully observed in practice.

the works council before a decision is taken, to wait for a considered response or counterproposal, and to take it into consideration when finally deciding. While this still leaves the decision to management, it may delay it. Finally, under *co-determination,* decisions can be taken by management only if they are agreed to beforehand by the council; in this sense the council can veto them, usually until the matter is resolved by an outside arbitration board.

6. *Works councils may (the usual case) or may not have legal status.* In the limiting case, they may be set up unilaterally or voluntarily by the employer, with the employer retaining the option of dissolving them if they do not perform to—paternalistic—expectation. Works councils may also be created or regulated by industrial agreement between unions and employers' associations at the sectoral or national level.

Typically, however, such agreements will in some way be encouraged or supported by legislation. In fact, *most council systems are more or less strongly legally institutionalized,* with legislation playing a facilitating role even in countries like Sweden and Italy where councils are primarily union based. Legal status usually affords works councils an institutional power base independent from both union and employer.[7]

7. *Works council structures vary widely across and within countries.* Representation may be categorically encompassing, with all employees in a given workplace being represented by one common body, or categorically differentiated, with different councils representing different groups of employees (e.g., blue-collar vs. white-collar workers). Councils may be functionally comprehensive, in the sense that all concerns of the workforce are represented by the same body, or functionally differentiated, with different councils serving different functions (e.g., health and safety councils, training councils, and productivity councils). Councils may or may not include management; in the limiting case, the employer may preside over council meetings.[8] And systems vary in the structure of the resource base supporting council operation—although in general works councils are not financed out of union dues, do receive some support from the employer, and are typically entitled to such support on a basis other than the employer's free and changeable will.

8. *Works councils are not the same as worker representation on company boards of directors.* This said, councils often coexist with such representation, and in such cases are closely related to it. In the German case, for example, "economic co-determination" through workforce and union representatives on the supervisory boards of large firms became closely linked in the 1970s and 1980s to the formally separate system of "workplace co-determination" through works councils. Largely the same people serve simultaneously on both

7. Of course, that base may also be weak, or the law may only be partly observed.

8. Even the German works council system, while otherwise organized on a strict workers-only basis, incorporates one institution that does include the employer: the *Wirtschaftsausschuß* (economic committee) to which the employer must reveal confidential information on the economic condition of the enterprise.

bodies, and works councillors use the information and access they get as board members to increase their effectiveness as works councillors.

On the basis of our definition, and as a very general classification, we distinguish three ideal types of works councils:

Paternalistic councils are formed by employers or governments to forestall or undo unionization. Often, such councils include or are presided over by the employer. Councils of this kind are (allowed to be) representative of workers to the extent that this is necessary to prevent independent expression of worker interests.

Consultative councils are set up to improve communication between management and workers through exchange of information and through consultation, in order to facilitate cooperation in production and thereby enhance the competitive performance of the enterprise or plant. Unlike paternalistic councils, the main function of which is "political," consultative councils are put in place primarily for economic purposes—in the belief that there are a range of production-related issues on which employers and workforces may cooperate to mutual benefit. While collective representation of workers is assumed to facilitate such cooperation, representation in the form of collective bargaining is seen as unable to raise the relevant issues, or as distorting them by placing them in an "adversarial" context. As a second channel of industrial relations supplementing collective bargaining, consultative councils respond to employer interests in worker "involvement" and to worker interests in the competitiveness of the firm that employs them and, perhaps, in an intrinsically rewarding utilization of their skills.

Representative councils are typically established through collective agreement or legislation giving the entire workforce of a plant or enterprise (again, unionized or not) some form of institutionalized voice in relation to management. Representative councils enable workers to assert distributional or general interests that the employer would not be willing to gratify for paternalistic or economic reasons alone. As a second-channel institution existing alongside unions and collective bargaining, they reflect a belief that workers have workplace-based interests that fail to be sufficiently represented by unions and collective bargaining and that require some form of worker "participation" in management in order to be realized. In this sense, the rationale for their establishment is "industrial democracy."

While consultative councils may be seen as supplementing the functional organization of the firm, representative councils—like, in a different way, paternalistic councils—are part of a firm's political system. Characteristically, representative councils have or claim rights, not just to information and consultation, but also to co-determination—or use other ways of intervening in the exercise of managerial prerogative, in pursuing worker interests.

Of course, ideal types rarely exist in pure form. All works councils have at least some representational function. And all, except possibly the most radical representative councils, serve some productivist consultative purposes. Indeed, the main problem in understanding works councils is to disentangle, for different historical periods and national contexts, their often densely interwoven paternalistic, consultative, and representative functions.

1.2   Works Councils and Unions

Union attitudes toward works councils differ widely across countries and have often changed dramatically over time within them. Indeed, union-council relations seem to have moved through all conceivable permutations, and then often in rapid succession—with councils alternatively supported and rejected by unions for both "left" and "right" strategic reasons.

Historically, works councils have been most prominent in the industrial relations systems of continental Europe. There, craft unionism, the natural organizational site of which was the workplace itself, was early blocked or absorbed by politically oriented industrial unionism, the natural organizational site of which was the national economy and polity as a whole. The success of political industrial unionism thus bred questions unique to it: How to deal with pressures for the representation of workers employed in a specific plant or firm, as distinguished from representation of all workers in a sector or country? How to add an internal to the external union organization? How to link the two?

It should be noted that the rise of political industrial unionism was due in part to the success of *employers* in preserving managerial prerogatives inside the firm—their *Herr im Hause* status—and not letting unions enter their workplaces. Often assisted by an authoritarian state, employers forced unions to seek bases and resources of power other than those found directly in the labor process. This encouraged the politicized model of union action, organized outside the workplace, that aimed either—in its moderate version—at sectoral or national collective bargaining and "political exchange" or—in its radical version—at the wholesale overthrow of the economic-political system.

In any case, having established itself as such, political unionism did not typically deploy its newly gained power to reverse the outcome of the battle over union presence at the workplace that it had lost in its formative period. In fact, political unionism came to hold deep suspicions about workplace organization and representation. These were regarded as a potential base for the assertion of the particularistic and economistic interests of workers—at odds with the objective of mobilizing broad, political, class-based solidarity across the boundaries of individual plants, enterprises, or, for that matter, occupations. Therefore, where remnants of craft unionism had survived employers' attacks, political unionism usually did its best to undo and absorb them in its more encompassing organizations.

There are two versions of the suspicion in which political industrial unionism holds workplace representation. For moderate unions trading wage and other restraints for political concessions on social welfare, employment, fiscal, and other policies, the workplace is a zone of potential *wildcat militancy*—excessive demands, unauthorized strikes, and overshooting settlements ("wage drift")—especially in prosperous firms. For militant unions engaged in political class struggle, the enterprise is a sphere of potential *wildcat cooperation* with the employer—workers acting on their narrow interest in the health and profitability of "their" firm and disregarding the interests of the working class as a whole.[9]

Industrial unions' typical fear of workplace-based particularism opened the possibility, and often indeed produced the reality, of an unlikely compromise between employers interested in protecting managerial prerogative and political unions keen on establishing a universalistic, class-based interpretation of worker interests. If on nothing else, employers wanting the freedom to run "their" workplace as they saw fit and unions seeking to build class solidarity for dealing with employers politically or abolishing them altogether could agree on neutralizing the workplace as a site of conflict—on avoiding workplace negotiations by recognizing each other as interlocutors at the industrial or national level and on helping each other prevent independent organization of worker interests at the workplace. It is this "negative convergence" of interests that has long been in the background of the politics of workplace representation in continental European industrial relations.

Of course, the problem with a peace formula like this was always that, as much as the neutralization of the workplace may have corresponded to both sides' first preference, it was bound to be unstable, making the resulting truce a permanently uneasy one. For unions, centralized and politicized as they may be, neutralization of the workplace inevitably means an *organization gap,* making it hard for them to recruit members, collect dues, and mobilize support for industrywide or national collective action. For employers, an unrepresented workforce may give rise to a *consultation gap,* precluding potentially productive representative communication between management and workers. For workers themselves, centralized unionism and collective bargaining may leave a *representation gap* regarding workplace-specific interests that cannot be adequately served at the industrial or national level.

Neutralization of the workplace thus creates an institutional vacuum that demands to be filled and that poses powerful temptations to invade it: for unions, to set up externally controlled workplace union sections; for employers, to organize consultative councils to improve productive performance or

9. Note that while the two problems may seem to be mutually exclusive opposites, the typical social democratic union faces them both in that it has to mobilize for conflict as well as accept compromise, making it as vulnerable to insurgent cooperation as to insurgent militancy. Instructive here is the use of the term "syndicalism" in the language of a union like IG Metall, the industrial union of German metalworkers. "Syndicalism" denotes any "plant-egoistic," workplace-specific articulation of interests in conflict with industrial union policy—be it ("militant") demands for higher wages and better conditions than negotiated at the industrial level or cooperation with the employer in contradiction of union policy. Conflictual or cooperative, syndicalism is the worst offense an IG Metall workplace leader can commit.

paternalistic councils to prevent union penetration or independent workplace organization; for workers, to form representative councils, cooperate with employer-controlled councils, or demand union workplace organizations; and for all of them, to invent and explore ever new strategies, alliances, trade-offs, compromises, and institutional hybrids to fill the vacuum. It is in this context that works councils have again and again surfaced in the industrial relations systems of continental Europe—as a way to fill the void left at the workplace by the always tenuous compromise between centralized political unionism and managerial prerogative.

Councils also emerged in the Anglo-American world of early, persistent, and hegemonic craft unionism. Here they were typically promoted by employers looking for interlocutors on behalf of their workforces that were more identified with the enterprise that employed them than with their occupation or with workers as a class. Unions, as a consequence, came to regard councils as instruments of employers designed to undermine them, and since they had been there first, they strongly preferred collective bargaining over any (other) form of "industrial democracy."[10] To the extent that defeating employers' works council initiatives required organizational effort and personal sacrifice, the experience of the struggle had a lasting impact on unions' attitudes toward councils in those countries and defined works councils ideologically in a way that long ruled out any accommodation with them.

In the politicized industrial relations systems of continental Europe, the matter was considerably more complicated, and ultimately generative of the broad variety of dual structures of workplace representation, and complex configurations of external unions, internal unions, and works councils, that one observes today. Emerging industrial unions often encountered council systems that had historically preceded them, either shop stewards in the craft union tradition or paternalistic councils set up by employers as a preventative measure against unionization.[11] Where this was the case, industrial unions had to absorb or abolish the councils in order to establish themselves as the principal representatives of worker interests. This happened, for example, in the German metalworking industry before 1914, where the socialist union had to find ways of integrating existing workplace representatives (often referred to as *Vertrauen-*

10. This history is not without ambiguity, however. In discussions in the United States in the 1920s, near the high point of the "American plan" of company unions, some observers sympathetic to unions (and even some unions themselves) looked more favorably on councils as a way of assuring at least some measure of representation in nonunionized settings and of providing unions with a foothold for organizing. A fascinating analysis, showing the openness of the U.S. discussion, is provided by Douglas (1921).

11. Councils had also been an early demand of workers. In Germany, the liberal Paulskirche Constitution of 1848, which never took effect, provided for legally regulated council representation of workers at the workplace. The difference from England in this respect is remarkable; in addition to the obvious differences in trade union strength, it seems to reflect different "cultural" perceptions of the firm: what in England appeared, and appears, to be a "nexus of contracts" was in Germany from early on regarded as an *institution*.

sleute) in its growing organization. The price for such integration was acceptance of some form of internal union organization, which however became increasingly closely tied into the external union. Other battles had to be fought with paternalistic, employer-dominated councils. Councils also emerged in other countries at the time, with some, for example in Italy, being established by employers and unions together to provide for orderly internal governance of large industrial workplaces.

During the First World War, mainstream European unions collaborated with their national governments in the war effort, achieving lasting gains in legal and political recognition at the price of growing opposition from their members. As external unions appeared to lose control over the shop floor, governments tried to help them close the widening representation gap by promoting various kinds of councils designed to give workforces narrowly circumscribed participation rights. Typically, however, it was the growing radical opposition to the war and to the meanwhile more or less established official unions that drew the support of the workers in the factories of the war economy. Especially after the Russian Revolution of 1917, which by its own Bolshevik description had been a self-consciously councilist (*soviet*) revolution, governments and unions in many European countries found themselves confronted by a revolutionary movement of "workers' councils" which saw itself as the basis of a new social order: a "producer democracy" based on direct worker self-government without employers, states, and, not least, trade unions.

In the immediate postwar period, mainstream unions and social democratic parties often joined forces with the remnants of the old regimes, in particular the army, to suppress the "syndicalist" councils—only to see the return of paternalistic councils a few years later or, as in Italy and Germany, to be done away themselves by their short-time allies, together with the liberal democracy whose victory over the syndicalist council project they had helped bring about.

A special development took place in Germany and was intensely watched elsewhere in Europe. Having broken the political backbone of the syndicalist council movement, the Social Democrats, led by the eminent labor lawyer Hugo Sinzheimer, institutionalized the defeated "workers' councils" (*Arbeiterräte*) as "works councils" (*Betriebsräte*) in the 1920 Weimar Constitution and the *Betriebsrätegesetz*, thereby laying the cornerstone for what later became the German Works Constitution (Arbeitsverfassung). Works councils, to be elected by all workers regardless of union membership, were given legal rights and responsibilities with respect to both representation of workers at the workplace and consultation and cooperation with management. In addition, they were made legally responsible for supervising the implementation of industrywide collective agreements and public legislation applicable to their workplace. Finally, they were barred from calling strikes, with wage bargaining explicitly reserved for the unions and employers' associations.

Sinzheimer's Arbeitsverfassung was an early attempt to address the problem of a potential representation gap at the workplace under centralized industrial relations, and to fill that gap in a way compatible with both industrial unionism and parliamentary democracy. It also took into account the demonstrated intensity of the demand of German workers for workplace representation—be it radical, cooperative, or both. The legislation of 1920 was to make it possible for unions and works councils to coexist with and benefit from each other, incorporating the councils in unionism in the same way that it incorporated the unions in the new democratic system—by granting them constitutionalized rights to self-governance while at the same time firmly establishing the primacy of the more encompassing over the more specific order. While councils were to be in charge of the workplace-related interests of workers, unions were to represent their general interests. While councils were to look after the productivist cooperative interests of workers as producers, unions were left free to represent the distributional conflictual interests of workers as consumers and citizens. Union control over the strike and the industrial agreement assured the precedence of general over special interests, and of pluralist conflict over productivist cooperation.

The legislation of 1920 was only the beginning of a long evolution, one never without tension. By the mid-1920s, many of the onetime "left" councils again behaved "right" (and often, for that matter, "yellow"). At the same time, the memory of the more ambitious demands of the postwar council movement lingered in German unions' project of economic democracy (*Wirtschaftsdemokratie*). In it, councils, either of workers alone or of workers and employers, were to be the principal agents of economic decision making. Operating both at the workplace and at the sectoral and national levels, their powers would extend to investment decisions and the setting of prices. With economic democracy aborted by the Nazis, Sinzheimer's design came to fruition only after 1945, when the less demanding "co-determination"—itself conceived as a "third way" between socialism and full-fledged capitalism—became the German unions' main strategic objective. Under co-determination, works councils gradually turned into the local infrastructure of a flexible system of shared, quasi-public, centralized governance of the employment contract.

The German case, precisely because it underwent so many twists and turns, impressively illustrates the ineradicable *ambivalence of unions toward works councils.* As is evident not only from this case but from others in continental Europe, councils may be all kinds of things to unions: employer-sponsored union substitutes, as well as vehicles of union recognition and union access to the workplace; radical syndicalist opposition to unionism and collective bargaining, as well as easily controlled internal representatives of the external union; agents of particularistic collaboration with the employer, as well as of particularistic militancy; supports for centralized bargaining, as well as vehicles of decentralization. As a result, depending on the circumstances, unions have preferred or accepted a vast variety of configurations at the workplace: from total absence of any organization at all, to more or less externally controlled workplace union sections, to works councils based on union rights, collective agreement, or special legislation—with or without rights to co-management.

1.3 Works Councils and Employers

Employers have been just as ambivalent as unions toward councils. Their overriding concern in workplace industrial relations has always been to protect their freedom to manage as they see fit. But employers are often also interested in their workers' cooperating with them, above and beyond the call of contractual duty, in a common pursuit of productivity, competitiveness, and profitability. To the extent that institutionalized consultation with workforce representatives may contribute to such cooperation, employers have eschewed the consultation gap in an unorganized workplace and have often inclined toward supporting some kind of council structure.

The problem is that such structure, once in place, may be hard to sterilize politically. While originally intended to be no more than consultative bodies, councils may be captured by workers seeking not just consultation on production matters, but a chance for articulating distributional interests different from the employer's. Councils may also be used by external forces, such as unions, as an entryway into the workplace, where they may insert themselves between employer and workforce. Institutional structures created to increase acceptance of managerial decisions may thus ultimately enable workers to contest such decisions, or to demand participation in them. For employers, the improved opportunities councils offer for collective communication may thus come at too high a price.

It is this dilemma—the danger that institutionalized consultation, set up to increase productivity, may undermine the managerial control that is the traditional means of increasing productivity—that explains why historically the attitudes of employers toward councils have been as diverse as those of unions. At various times and places, employers have promoted councils on their own and then abolished them when they became too independent—sometimes, as with syndicalist councils, in alliance with governments and unions. They have urged governments to introduce councils by legislation where unions threatened to penetrate the workplace. And where unions had already penetrated, they have tried to turn union workplace organizations into works councils, to get antiunion candidates elected in works council elections, to get unionized works councillors to carry the conflict between workplace-specific and general worker interests into the union itself, to isolate councils from the influence of external, full-time union officials, to break up unitary structures of workplace representation by introducing separate councils for white-collar or managerial employees, and to help external unions gain control over too independent councils—in ever changing alliances with workplace leaders, external unions, and governments of different political compositions.

Amid this variation and flux, however, there have been definite periods during which employers and unions agreed on councils of a certain kind and were jointly capable of assigning them a place in a common industrial relations system. One such period in Western Europe came immediately after World War II. At that time, employers had lost the capacity to support authoritarian alternatives to liberal democracy, just as communist and syndicalist tendencies among labor movements were more or less effectively suppressed by the American presence. Unlike the interwar period, there was no doubt that industrial relations in reconstructed Europe would be both labor inclusive and moderate—with employers recognizing unions and unions by and large accepting the role of employers. The pressing need for economic reconstruction, moreover, virtually forced unions and employers to work together in pursuit of economic improvement.

In this situation, unions and employers in most Western European countries agreed on supplementing centralized collective bargaining with workplace-based bodies for joint consultation. These consultative councils were insulated from distributive conflict and dedicated to improving economic performance; their power to negotiate local agreements, if recognized at all, was carefully circumscribed. Again, postwar consultative councils were in some measure a concession by labor to employers; they reflected union acceptance of the employer's right to manage, in exchange for employer acceptance of centralized collective bargaining. But they also responded to union needs for neutralizing the workplace as a condition for a centralized, universalistic, and egalitarian union policy.

Postwar consultative councils came in many different forms, depending on the specific political situation and the institutional traditions of their respective countries. Some council systems were created by national collective agreement between unions and employers—raising, and differently answering, the question of whether nonunionized workers were allowed to vote in elections or serve on councils. In other countries, councils were legally based, and some were equipped with incipient rights to co-determination that served as a reminder of continuing union doubts about unlimited managerial prerogative even in centralized industrial relations systems. These differences, as will be seen, were important in how council systems evolved later. But the commonalities are also of interest—the consensual recognition in many countries, in a situation of economic hardship, of a need for joint collective consultation at the workplace through special institutions that were not involved in the inevitable distributional conflict between employers and workers and that provided for productive cooperation within the broader context of that conflict.

Still, the contradictions and dilemmas of councils remained and were soon to surface again, for employers no less than for unions. For the former, even consultative councils raised the puzzling problems summarized in Alan Flanders's paradoxical observation that to retain control over the workplace, management might have to share it with the workers.[12] To be safe from encroachment on their power to manage, employers preferred councils to remain voluntary arrangements controlled unilaterally by themselves—neither legislated nor prescribed or regulated by collective bargaining. Legislation was welcome only insofar as it imposed legal limitations on councils—especially by subjecting them to a "peace obligation," requiring them to cooperate with the employer in good faith, and limiting their relations with unions—while similar obligations for employers, in particular those that might have detracted from their right to manage, were fiercely resisted and could be imposed by governments only in exceptional circumstances.

With the notable exception of the most strongly legally based council system—Germany's—consultative councils generally fell into disuse in Western European countries in the 1950s and 1960s. Of the many reasons for this, one surely was the general insistence by employers that councils only be consulted at their discretion, as they saw fit in the unrestricted exercise of their managerial rights. This was bound to result in a "trust gap" among workers who came to believe, in the absence of enforceable management obligations to consult or inform, that management turned to councils only if doing so served its own interests. Unions in particular came to regard councils at best as a management tool, and at worst as a device to cultivate company patriotism at their expense. Employers, for their part, expected councils not only to yield economic benefits but also to keep unionization at bay, without however allowing them to perform meaningful representative functions. As a result, both sides became disappointed and lost interest, and joint consultation systems gradually dried up, with industrial relations becoming increasingly identified with conflictual collective bargaining. For the unions this was just as well until the late 1960s when a wave of spontaneous worker unrest reminded them, too, of the dangers of a representation gap at the workplace.

Employer preferences for voluntarism—for works councils limited to receiving information without obligation for management to wait for their response, and certainly for consultation over co-determination: overinstitutionalized, obligatory sharing of management control—were not necessarily modified by the experience of the attrition of postwar joint council systems. Nor do they seem to have been diluted by the easily available observation that even legally based works councils such as the German ones, with a strong union connection and significant capacity to interfere with managerial decision making, may be compatible with high economic performance in competitive markets and may even outright contribute to it. While the limited capacity to promote confidence in voluntary information and consultation practices motivated exclusively by economic expediency or the employer's unilateral goodwill is one thing—making workers hedge against management defection in pursuit of short-term economic benefits—the fear of a loss in discretion and

---

12. Among other places, see Flanders (1975).

"flexibility" that is associated with more institutionalized representation is quite another. The history of works councils in postwar Western Europe demonstrates that, left to their own devices, employers find it exceedingly hard to resolve this dilemma.

One way in which employers have historically responded to the quandaries of representative collective representation is by trying to avoid it altogether and instead to base social relations at the workplace on nonrepresentative, one-to-one communication with individual employees. This approach, which reaches back at least as far as the "human relations" school of the 1930s, seems to have been rediscovered on a broad scale in the 1980s, when it came to be referred to as "human resource management." Recent interest among employers in reindividualizing the employment relationship seems to reflect both a growing economic payoff of improved communication between management and labor at the workplace and traditional management concerns about the unwelcome side effects of collective representation. Individualized human resource management seems to have progressed most where postwar consultative councils had faded away in the absence of a supportive legal framework, and where unions were either too hostile to serve as a conduit for workplace cooperation or too weak to defeat employer attempts to exclude them from a socially reconstructed workplace. Although human resource management is itself likely to be beset with dilemmas and contradictions—and probably with the same ones as its predecessors—its appearance does seem to pose problems even for strong unions and well-established works councils, which are hard pressed to find ways of establishing a role for themselves in the new methods of personnel management.

Human resource management may be seen as an attempt by employers to take the social organization of the workplace in their own hands. The strategy seeks simultaneously to avoid the political risks of a disorganized and thus potentially radical workforce, the economic costs of deficient communication, and the expense of relying on a potentially adversarial representative intermediary. There may, however, be economic, social, and political conditions under which management unilateralism, even in this most sophisticated of forms, fails to accomplish its objectives. Today, with the larger questions of capitalism, socialism, and democracy more or less settled, there are indications in many European countries of a possible renaissance of councils as a workplace-based infrastructure of productive cooperation alongside institutionalized conflict. According to some of the country studies in this volume, competitive market pressures for cooperation and consensus at the point of production may have become so strong that employers, for lack of a better alternative, may now be willing to accept representative institutional arrangements of labor-management cooperation, even if they involve a unionized works council making the joint pursuit of mutual economic advantage conditional on shared control over managerial decisions.

To the extent that this is indeed the case, there may today be a broad if silent movement in the industrial relations of advanced capitalist countries toward a new productivist covenant between capital and labor. Again, this appears in a rich variety of empirical manifestations—not always easily discernible, and inevitably beset with ambiguities, paradoxes, dilemmas, contradictions, and tensions that make it inherently precarious and dependent on constant renewal and reinforcement.

1.4   Works Councils and the State

In many European countries, liberal democracy was introduced only against the violent resistance of radical syndicalist council movements. The worker councils of World War I saw themselves as the foundation of a decentralized, direct-democratic *producer democracy* that had no need for a "state"—that is, for territorially based political rule with parties, parliaments, and bureaucracies alienated from the organization of material production.

Nowhere, of course, did syndicalist projects come close to realization. They were opposed not only by the old and new ruling classes but also by main-stream unions and social democratic parties, as well as communists.[13] Once firmly established after 1945, however, European liberal democracies could afford to treat works councils as one element among others of a new social order of production, and as part of a preferably self-governing system of indus-trial relations within which organized workers and employers were given broad freedom to regulate their affairs on their own.

With workers and unions strong enough to insist on free collective bar-gaining as an essential element of the "postwar settlement" between capital and labor, governments and legal systems tried to stay out of industrial rela-tions, as much as possible devolving to those immediately concerned the gov-ernance of a subject as politically explosive as the employment contract. The extent to which industrial relations came to be founded on "voluntarism" dif-fered between countries, in line with national traditions and specific political circumstances, although the tendency for governments to minimize their direct involvement was universal. But it also differed for types of institutions—with workplace representation, and particularly works councils, more likely every-where to be legally regulated or constituted than, for example, union organiza-tion or collective bargaining.

State intervention in workplace representation may amount to as much as full-scale legislative introduction of a second channel of industrial relations, as in Germany, or to as little as the minimalist prescriptions found in Italian or Swedish law. In all countries, however, workplace representation has a ten-dency to be less voluntaristically based than other industrial relations institu-tions. This is most likely the case because it touches on so many fundamental

---

13. Exemplary here was the policy of the Communists in the USSR itself, who immediately after 1917 subjected the Russian *soviets* to the iron rule of the Bolshevik party.

issues—from the exercise of property rights to the rights of workers to free association—that finding an acceptable solution for them may be too difficult for unions and employers acting on their own without support of formal law, and too important to the public order to be treated as a private affair.

For example, governments may be drawn into regulating workplace representation because of its effects on nonunionized workers, making it even less amenable than centralized wage bargaining to being construed as a bilateral matter between unions and employers. Also, employers may seek legal protection against worker or union interference with their right to manage, while unions may call for legislation against employers refusing to allow them onto their premises or, as in Sweden in the early 1970s, to agree to union-based "industrial democracy." And governments themselves may regard it as in the public interest to deploy legislation to help employers, workers, and unions, not only to insulate the workplace from distributive conflict but to institutionalize it as a site for productive cooperation.

In keeping with their general inclination to avoid direct entanglement in industrial relations, governments often prefer to wait for unions and employers' associations to regulate workplace representation by industrial agreement, or they pass no more than framework legislation to be filled out by supplementary collective bargaining at the enterprise or more typically national level. But even where unions and employers are able to agree on a structure of workplace representation, they may ask governments to pass their understanding into formal law—to make it binding on all workplaces in a country or sector regardless of membership in unions or employers' associations, or to strengthen the positive effects of representation on cooperation by providing them with legal backing. And governments may threaten to legislate if the "social parties" do not strike an acceptable agreement between themselves. In this way, governments may not just expedite but may even direct the negotiation of these parties, producing a result that is de facto far less "voluntaristic" than it looks.

If the terms of workplace-based representation are more likely to find legal expression, moreover, they are not often revised. Legislatures tend to stay away from the existing law, regardless of changes in political majorities or economic and organizational conditions. And rather than trying to accommodate new problems with new legislation, governments prefer to let the parties at the workplace make adjustments in practice, or to wait for legal innovation to come from the courts. This is so even in such countries as Germany, where the use of law in industrial relations is widely accepted. There, the Works Constitution Act of 1951 was revised once, in 1972, and has since remained basically unchanged—in spite of the change of government in the early 1980s to the Christian Democrats and regardless of the country's unification in 1990.

The extraordinary stability of the law on workplace representation reflects the technical complexities of the subject and the political sensitivity of reopening the political bargain underlying it, as well as the need of the parties to industrial relations for steadiness and predictability of the institutional conditions in which they interact. Together these factors seem to make works council legislation similar to constitutional law even where it is not, as in Germany, referred to as such.

Among the subjects of, direct and indirect, legal intervention in workplace representation, and in works council systems in particular, are:

1. *Creation of councils:* Typically works councils are not mandatory. Even the German Works Constitution Act requires a minimal initiative from workers or unions for a council to be set up, probably as a measure of perceived need and spontaneous support. Legal thresholds for council formation are, however, very low. Unions tend to be given special procedural privileges, and employers have no right to object, nor can they demand that an established council be rescinded.

2. *Election procedures:* Most countries regulate in law the voting procedure, the nomination of union and nonunion candidates, and the lengths of terms of council office, although in Italy all of these are left to the unions to determine unilaterally, and in Sweden most of them are. Unions are usually given certain privileges in nominating candidates, even where the procedure is not strictly union based, and large, "representative" unions with many votes tend to be advantaged in the allocation of council seats—reflecting a shared interest among unions, employers, and government in limiting the influence of "splinter groups."

3. *Council resources:* Universally, employers must defray the costs of councils. Typically, the number of paid hours council members can spend on their position is regulated in legislation, as are other rights of councils and their members—for example, to office facilities, training, and special employment protection. Legislation on these matters exists even in countries, like Italy, with otherwise highly voluntaristic council systems, presumably because a sufficient resource base is so essential for councils that it cannot be left to the discretion of employers. Nowhere do councils have to collect dues from workers, as unlike unions councils are not voluntary associations. Council resources are legally kept apart from union resources, although unions are everywhere more or less marginally, and more or less legally, subsidized by councils—and, less frequently, council activities may be subsidized by unions. In most countries, finally, unions, councils, or both may negotiate additional resources for councils above and beyond what the law prescribes.

4. *Relations between councils and unions:* Where councils are not legally defined as union bodies, the law typically sets unions and councils apart while at the same time establishing relations between them. Legislation on the latter is usually highly contested, involving such touchy issues as the right of councils to use union assistance (if necessary, against employer objections) and the right of unions, especially full-time union officials, to have access to councils (even over either council or employer objections). Other subjects of legal regulation may include the training of council members in union schools, the rights

or obligations of councils to consult with external unions before making major decisions, the participation of full-time union officials in council negotiations with the employer, the performance of union functions by council members, and again, the access of unions to council resources. In some systems, unions may have a legal right to initiate recall procedures against councils neglecting their duties, including the duty to cooperate in good faith with industrial unions and carry out the industrial agreement.

5. *Council rights and obligations:* National systems differ perhaps most widely in the extent to which rights and obligations of works councils are detailed in formal law—compare, for example, the German Works Constitution Act to the Italian Statuto dei Lavoratori. The matter is politically highly sensitive as it pertains to both the functional differentiation between unions and councils and the extent to which councils may infringe on managerial prerogative and, ultimately, property rights. Functional differentiation as well as co-determination require law, either legislation or, less likely, binding industrial agreements, and the more there is to be of them, the more law there will tend to be. To the extent that council rights are legally different from union rights and councils are formally independent of unions as organizations, rights are likely to be accompanied by obligations—for example, rights to information accompanied by obligations to preserve confidentiality, and rights to consultation and co-determination accompanied by obligations to observe industrial peace and to cooperate with the employer in good faith. Balancing the rights and obligations of councils is an exceedingly difficult task for legislation to accomplish, and therefore not easily taken on. Employers that violate council rights are typically subject to legal sanction, but so may be councils that fail to perform their obligations.

Some types of works councils, such as health and safety councils, may be set up by law directly and prescriptively in the context of regulatory legislation when governments need reliable instruments to enforce rules regulating employer behavior at the workplace. Tied to enabling legislation with particular goals, councils emerging in this context are functionally specialized and narrowly circumscribed in their jurisdiction. They may, however, accumulate tasks, or later be merged with similar bodies, or be chartered for other legislation, to realize administrative economies.

6. *Dispute resolution:* Where the law refuses councils recourse to the strike, it may compensate them with alternative means of power to exercise their rights and counterbalance the employer's powers of decision making. Typically, councils have legal standing to seek redress in courts if their rights are infringed on. Where councils have rights to co-determination and may use them to veto employer decisions, the law must in addition provide for efficient mechanisms to break a possible impasse—for example, arbitration committees with the power to make binding awards.

Both management and labor have at different times and in different circumstances called on government to regulate workplace representation to suit their special interests. Often legislative intervention was not much more than the imposition of one side's political will on the other, or at best the formalization of a compromise between the two that merely reflected a momentary balance of power. But a more creative role for public policy also seems possible, one that uses the state's unique capacity for authoritative institutional design to increase the certainty, and thereby expand the range, of mutually beneficial cooperation at the workplace. The way governments have done this is by introducing into the relations between the immediate participants externally enforceable obligations that make the continuation of cooperative behavior less sensitive to short-term fluctuations in goodwill or self-interest. Deployed in this way, formal law becomes a productive resource in its own right. By injecting a nonvoluntary, public dimension into arrangements otherwise prone to instabilities arising from defection, it stabilizes cooperative practices against defensive expectations of such defection. It is this potential contribution of legal-political intervention to long-term cooperation that would seem to be the most intriguing aspect of the role of the state in workplace representation today.

1.5   Method of Research and Organization of the Volume

This book surveys the recent experience with works councils in Europe and North America, with special attention to possible lessons from Europe for the discussion in the United States on alternative or supplementary forms of workplace representation. The present chapter has introduced the book's main concepts, explored the politics and institutional characteristics of works councils in relation to unions, employers, and governments, and outlined the history of works councils in Europe. The next chapter, which completes the introductory part of this volume, attempts to model the basic economics of works councils. It shows why councils may be expected to contribute to good economic performance.

Apart from the United Kingdom and Ireland, works councils are an established feature of the industrial relations systems of most Western European countries, and have increasingly become so in recent years. Part II of this book is therefore devoted to Europe, in particular to the economically advanced democracies of Western Europe, using them as a research site in an attempt to find general insights into the nature of works councils. There are six country chapters, each reviewing the history and present state of councils in a particular Western European country (chaps. 3 to 8), a chapter on supranational works councils in the European Community (chap. 9), and one on councils in Poland, an Eastern European country in transition to a market economy (chap. 10). The sequence of country chapters begins with Germany (chap. 3) and the Netherlands (chap. 4), two countries where works councils operate on a strong legal base. This is followed by a consideration of France (chap. 5) and Spain (chap. 6), two countries that have weaker, though also legally based, councils functioning in an environment of declining politicized multiunionism. Chapters 7 and 8 deal with Sweden and Italy, where councils are not prescribed in law but have developed out of cooperative relations between employers and strong unions. Part II concludes with a synopsis and synthesis of the European country studies (chap. 11).

The Western European country chapters loosely follow a common format. They all focus on the postwar period, and especially on developments in the past two decades of increased competition and intense economic restructuring. Each chapter describes the structure of its country's works council system, its organizational and legal base, the rights and obligations vested in it, its relations with unions, employers, and governments, and especially its impact on and response to economic change.

Understanding the subtleties of the institutional politics of work councils requires extensive description of institutional structures and political conditions, of the surrounding industrial relations systems, and of councils' historical development. Due to the low number of cases and limited cross-national comparability, most of the information used for comparison must be qualitative, including that bearing on councils' economic effects. Rather than applying rigorous statistical analysis, which is impossible and always will be, the discussion relies on the identification of parallel developments and common trends and is more concerned with understanding the range of possible variations and options than with developing deterministic causal propositions.

Part III deals with North America. Chapter 12 looks at joint health and safety councils in Canada, as an example of a council-like structure in a North American country. Chapter 13 recounts the story of futile attempts in the United States to institute union-independent workforce representation, places the United States in comparative perspective, and explores the implications of the Western European experience for current policy debates about labor law reform.

References

Blank, Rebecca, ed. 1994. *Social protection vs. economic flexibility: Is there a tradeoff?* Chicago: University of Chicago Press.

Blinder, Alan S. 1990. Introduction. In *Paying for productivity: A look at the evidence,* ed. Alan S. Blinder. Washington, D.C.: Brookings Institution.

Card, David, and Richard B. Freeman. 1993. *Small differences that matter: Labor markets and income maintenance in Canada and the United States.* Chicago: University of Chicago Press.

Douglas, Paul H. 1921. Shop committees: Substitute for, or supplement to, trade-unions? *Journal of Political Economy* 29(2): 89–107.

Flanders, Allan D. 1975. *Management and unions: The theory and reform of industrial relations.* London: Faber.

Freeman, Richard B. 1989. Working and earning under different rules: Labor market institutions, income maintenance, and economic performance in the U.S. and its major OECD economic partners. Research proposal submitted to the Ford Foundation. Manuscript.

————. 1990. Employee councils, worker participations, and other squishy stuff. *Proceedings of the 43rd annual meeting of the Industrial Relations Research Association.* Madison, Wisc.: Industrial Relations Research Association.

————. ed. 1994. *Working under different rules.* New York: Russell Sage Foundation.

Freeman, Richard B., and Lawrence F. Katz, eds. 1995. *Differences and changes in wage structures.* Chicago: University of Chicago Press.

Freeman, Richard B., and Joel Rogers. 1993. Who speaks for us? Employee representation in a non-union labor market. In *Employee representation: Alternatives and future directions,* ed. B. E. Kaufman and M. M. Kleiner, 13–79. Madison, Wisc.: Industrial Relations Research Association.

Lynch, Lisa, ed. 1994. *Training and the private sector: International comparisons.* Chicago: University of Chicago Press.

Office of Technology Assessment. 1990. *Worker training: Competing in the new international economy.* Washington D.C.: Government Printing Office.

Rogers, Joel, and Wolfgang Streeck. 1994. Workplace representation overseas: The works councils story. In *Working under different rules,* ed. Richard B. Freeman. New York: Russell Sage Foundation.

Weiler, Paul C. 1990. *Governing the workplace: The future of labor and employment law.* Cambridge: Harvard University Press.

2   An Economic Analysis of Works Councils

Richard B. Freeman and Edward P. Lazear

Students of councils . . . have leagues to travel before
producing parsimonious predictive models of council
behavior.

J. Rogers and W. Streeck

Although works councils are an important labor institution in Western Europe
and were introduced by many large firms in the United States in the 1920s,
economists have rarely studied their operation. The most recent article on
councils in a major economics journal was Paul Douglas's 1921 piece in the
Journal of Political Economy (*JPE*). In part, the neglect of councils reflects
economists' traditional unwillingness to look inside the black box of the firm
and lack of adequate theoretic tools to treat organizational issues. In part also,
it reflects the absence of empirical studies or observations that are needed for
parsimonious theorizing. Such neglect of works councils can no longer be justified. The precipitous fall in private sector unionism in the United States, declining unionism in the United Kingdom, and concerns about how different
labor relations systems fare in a global marketplace have renewed interest in
councils as a workplace institution. Economic theorists have developed tools
and models suited to analyzing how councils affect the internal operation of
enterprises and to determining the environments more or less conducive to
them.

   Do councils require external institutional mandating, as in most of Western
Europe, or can they be expected to arise from voluntary managerial decision
making? When will councils communicate productivity-improving information between workers and firms? What are the benefits and costs of giving
councils co-determination rights over some decisions? What can go wrong in

Richard B. Freeman holds the Ascherman Chair in Economics at Harvard University. He is also
director of the Labor Studies Program at the National Bureau of Economic Research and executive
program director of the Comparative Labour Market Institutions Programme at the London School
of Economics' Centre for Economic Performance. Edward P. Lazear is professor of human resource management and economics at Stanford University's Graduate School of Business, senior
fellow at the Hoover Institution, and a research associate of the National Bureau of Economic Research.
   This work was supported by the National Science Foundation and the Ford Foundation. The
authors benefited from comments at the NBER conference on works councils, in particular from
Robert Boyer.

a council setting and what arrangements might minimize the risk of poorly functioning councils?

To answer these questions, we model what works councils do inside firms.[1] Since councils are complex institutions, we develop a set of related models, each stressing a particular facet of councils, rather than try to encapsulate the entire institution into a single model.

The main results of our analysis are:

1. Neither employers nor workers have incentives to create voluntarily councils with the power to maximize social value.

2. Councils with rights to information reduce economic inefficiencies by moderating worker demands during tough times. Conversely, by assuring that firms use worker-provided information to benefit labor as well as the firm, councils increase the willingness of workers to communicate to management, raising social surplus.

3. Councils with consultation rights can produce new solutions to the problems facing the firm. This is more likely when both workers and management have relevant information that is unavailable to the other side. Its effectiveness depends on the amount of delay caused by the process.

4. Co-determination rights that increase job security should lead workers to take a longer-run perspective on firm decisions and thus invest more in firm-specific skills and give workplace concessions that enhance enterprise investment in capital.

5. The specific rules for selecting works councils affect their representativeness. Increasing council size raises the likelihood the council will reflect workers' views when there is a strong but not overwhelming majority on an issue but not when workers are evenly divided.

6. Workers with minority views and those who dislike their jobs are likely to run for council office, raising the specter of "maverick" councils dominated by small cliques. One way to reduce the first risk is to choose council members by jury-style random selection. A way to reduce the second is to limit the release time of workers for council work.

This paper has five sections. Section 2.1 gives our argument why councils must be mandated from outside. Section 2.2 examines the conditions under which council-induced communication from management to workers improves social well-being. Section 2.3 examines communication from workers to management and the voting rules needed for councils to be representative of the workforce. Section 2.4 examines the consultation and co-determination powers of councils. We conclude with some comments on the problems councils might face in a decentralized American or British labor system.

---

1. Our selection of issues is guided by the empirical papers in this volume and the interviews conducted by Richard Freeman and Joel Rogers in the winter of 1991–92 with management officials at various U.S.-owned subsidiaries and other multinationals having experience with works councils in Europe and with some union officials and works councillors, as well.

2.1   Works Councils: Mandated or Voluntary?

Most Western European countries mandate elected works councils in enterprises above some size and give the councils rights to information and consultation about labor and personnel decisions. Germany gives councils co-determination over some decisions as well. In contrast to plant-level unions, councils cannot call strikes nor negotiate wages, though they invariably use their power to improve the position of workers within the firm.[2] Their function, often specified in legislation, is to foster labor and management cooperation with the goal of increasing the size of the enterprise "pie." Most observers and participants believe that councils succeed in doing this (see the other papers in this volume), and most managers in the Freeman-Rogers interviews endorsed councils as a valuable part of the internal structure of the enterprise.

If works councils increase the joint surplus of the firm-worker relationship, why do countries mandate them instead of relying on firms to institute councils voluntarily?

Our answer is based on the proposition that institutions that give workers power in enterprises affect the distribution as well as amount of joint surplus. The greater the power of works councils, the greater will be workers' share of the economic rent. If councils increase the rent going to workers more than they increase total rent, firms will oppose them. It is better to have a quarter slice of a 12-inch pie than an eighth slice of a 16-inch pie. Formally, we show:

PROPOSITION 1. Employers will give worker institutions within the firm less power than is socially optimal and will fail to establish productivity-enhancing councils when there are high fixed costs to the councils. Analogously, workers will prefer more power than is socially optimal.

The argument is based on two relations. First, let x denote the amount of power or discretion given to the works council. The rent of the organization, R, depends on x. If workers are given no discretion, then $R = R_0$. With some worker discretion, decisions improve and R rises. If too much worker discretion is given, then rent falls because management does not have enough control over decisions. The detailed rationale behind these arguments is explored in sections 2.2–2.4 of the paper; the result is an $R(x)$ function that has an inverted U-shape. This is shown in figure 2.1A.

Denote the share of total rent that goes to workers as τ. The share τ also depends on x. It is a standard result of bargaining models (both Nash and Rubenstein)[3] that the share rises with bargaining strength. Thus, $\tau(x)$ is monotonically increasing in x. To start, then,

---

2. By our definition Spanish works councils, which can legally call strikes, are de facto local unions rather than works councils.

3. We are grateful to Peter Crampton for pointing this out.

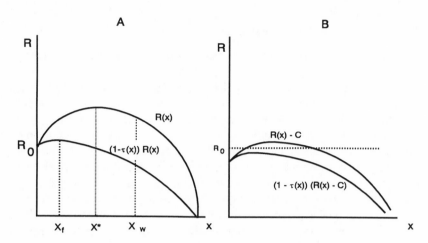

Fig. 2.1   *A*, Firm establishes weak council; *B*, firm establishes no council

(1a) $$R = R(x),$$

(1b) $$\tau = \tau(x).$$

Will the firm voluntarily establish councils with the socially optimal level of worker power? For a profit-seeking firm, analysis of optimizing behavior says "no." The firm will give less than x^* power to the council, where x^* is defined as the level of worker power that maximizes joint surplus. Formally, the profit-seeking firm will maximize

(2) $$[1 - \tau(x)] R(x),$$

which has the first-order condition

$$- \tau'(x)R(x) + [1 - \tau(x)]R'(x) = 0,$$

so that

(3) $$R' = \frac{\tau'(x)R(x)}{1 - \tau(x)}.$$

Since τ is increasing in x, the right-hand side of equation (3) is positive, which implies that $R' > 0$ at the firm's optimum point. The firm will choose a level of power for the council on the rising part of the rent-producing curve

4. The reader will notice that this contradicts the Coase theorem in which two parties to an arrangement are expected to attain the joint surplus through some means or other. By giving the two sides only one tool to produce the joint surplus and divide it, we have ruled out such an arrangement.

and will voluntarily give workers less power than $x*$.[4] This is shown in figure 2.1A, where x_f, the optimum point on the firm's profit curve, lies to the left of the social optimum $x*$. Given fixed costs to works councils—time and preparations for elections, meetings, reduction in work activity by elected councillors, and so forth—the firm may lose money at x_f, so that it will not establish councils at all, even though they raise the social product. This is shown by the curves $R - C$ and $(1 - \tau)(R - C)$ in figure 2.1B, which lie below the surplus in figure 2.1A by the fixed amount C. In this case the rent to the firm from establishing the council that maximizes its profits, $[1 - \tau(x_f)][R(x_f) - C]$, is less than R_0, the profit from no works council. Note that a council is socially preferred because $R - C > R_0$ for some values of x.

What about workers? If they could choose the amount of power for the works council, would they choose the socially optimal level? Workers who seek to maximize their share of the total surplus ($\tau(x) R(x)$) will, by symmetry with the analysis of the firm, fail to select the socially optimal point. Workers will choose a level of power that exceeds $x*$. They choose x_w in figure 2.1A, shortchanging the interests of capital.

The preceding analysis has implications for the existence and viability of works councils. It shows that management, on its own, will either fail to institute socially productive councils or give them less power than is socially desirable. If the government knew the R function, it could enact laws giving works councils $x*$ power. Absent such knowledge, the fact that the optimum level of power lies between the preferred levels of labor and management suggests that some average of the two sides' desires will move toward the social optimum. Whether the political bargaining mechanism institutes rules that are superior to the outcome of industrial bargaining remains an open question.

Mandating councils does not, however, necessarily mean that they will be developed at particular workplaces. Even in Germany, many (small) companies do not have councils. The condition for a company to introduce a council is that either the workforce or the firm sees a potential benefit. If each believes that instituting a council will cost it more than the benefits accruing to it, neither will go to the effort of introducing the council. Thus, there will be no council when the sum of worker and firm costs exceeds the total surplus created. This shows that a council will only be established when the benefits from the council exceed its total costs.

If it were possible to decouple the factors that affect the division of the surplus from those that affect the surplus, there would be an obvious way to establish the optimum division of power: the state (or some other outside party) could determine a rent-sharing coefficient and then allow firms and workers to choose the power to be given the council. With the division of rents fixed, the division of power that maximizes total profits also maximizes the amount each side receives. Such a decoupling of production and distribution of surplus is, however, unlikely. In most bargaining models, the division of rent depends on threat or reservation points that would be affected by changes in the authority given to works councils. In practice, managers in the Freeman-Rogers interviews took it as fact that councils used their power strategically to gain greater surplus for workers.[5] Still, this "solution" suggests that councils fit better in labor relations systems where pay and other basic components of compensation are determined outside the enterprise (essentially bounding divisions of the rent) than in systems where firms set pay, and may help explain why councils are found largely in economies with relatively centralized collective bargaining.[6]

Figure 2.1 can also be used to show why unions may oppose works councils. Reinterpret "joint surplus" to be the surplus that goes to workers, councillors, and union leaders, and think of τ as the share of rent that goes to the works council and workers and $1 - \tau$ as the share that goes to union leaders. Then, assuming the function that relates this joint surplus to x is also an inverted U, the result in equation (3) applies. Union leaders would choose a level of power for works councils that falls short of that maximizing overall labor surplus. Giving the council more power would benefit labor but would reduce the well-being of union leaders. This resonates with the fear German unionists had when they first opposed strong works councils, and with American unionists' worry that councils may substitute for unions—the issue Douglas addressed in his article. The possibility that councils benefit workers but not unions means that one cannot take unions as speaking for "labor" on this issue.

The analysis in proposition 1 illuminates the failure of employer-initiated councils in the United States in the 1920s. In that decade, many "progressive" firms instituted workers' councils or shop committees, to which they gave consultative rights but not access to company financial records. At their peak employer-instituted councils covered some 10 percent of the workforce in manufacturing, mining, transportation, and public utilities (Freeman 1990). While some firms introduced councils solely to prevent unionization, many believed councils were an efficient tool of management. Douglas, who supported unionism, reported favorably on councils in the *JPE*. The effort to "sell" councils by the Chamber of Commerce (1927), National Industrial Conference Board (1920, 1922), and other management groups also shows genuine commitment. But despite the enthusiasm with which firms formed councils, most abandoned them in the ensuing decade, as our analysis would lead one to expect. Some managements complained that workers did not truly cooperate, while workers complained that councils gave them no real power to affect deci-

5. In Germany, respondents gave cases in which councils would trade off their legal right to co-determine the timing of vacations or the need for them to gain the right to approve a social plan for redundancies for wages or benefits beyond those in the industry agreement.

6. There are several complexities that we do not address. A system that sets the level of compensation outside the firm and has no profit sharing might be viewed as giving councils no way to raise workers' well-being. In fact, in countries with relatively centralized bargaining, firms can pay wages above the central agreement, and stronger councils are likely to make gains in this way. But councils cannot push too far in light of the central agreement. In addition, with pay fixed, workers can still benefit from increasing the surplus if that means faster promotions and the like.

sions. Many firms withdrew the limited powers they had given councils and imposed unilateral wage and employment reductions when economic times worsened. These patterns highlight the problem of any employer-established council. As long as the firm is the ultimate authority, workers risk being caught in a "cooperate, defect" prisoner's dilemma solution when the firm sees the relation potentially ending. If the gains from councils, like other cooperative arrangements, are based on long-term benefits, economic changes that shorten horizons can readily undo a voluntarily established council. Finally, when the Wagner Act strengthened the chance for genuine unionism, some councils transformed themselves into unions, raising additional questions about the viability of council arrangements on the labor side.

2.2   Communication from Management to Workers

"The works council is for management a very important tool to inform employees of what is happening in the company. You cannot talk every day with 10,000 people." (manager in Freeman-Rogers interviews)

Economic theory recognizes that asymmetries in information between labor and management can produce inefficient social outcomes. Different levels of a firm's hierarchy can use private information opportunistically, possibly through coalitions against other levels of the hierarchy (Tirole 1986). Management may misinform workers about the situation of the enterprise when it sees workers' gains as owners' losses. Knowing that management can use information strategically, workers may disregard what management says even when it is truthful. Workers may fail to inform supervisors about ways to improve conditions for fear that the firm will use that information against them, say by reducing piece rates or speeding up assembly lines. Legal requirements that management disclose information to elected works councils raises the possibility that councils may help resolve the communication problem and raise rents. With access to information that will verify or disprove management's claims, a council can make those claims credible to the rank and file. In Western Europe management provides councils with detailed information about enterprises' financial and business plans and discusses with the council the substantive issues raised by this information.[7] While we know of no statistical study showing that council-facilitated information flows raise the joint surplus, many managers in the Freeman-Rogers interviews believed this, and econometric analysis of Japan's "joint consultation committees," which operate much like councils, shows a positive relation between committee effectiveness and enterprise profitability (Morishima 1991).[8]

7. The Freeman-Rogers interviews showed that large European firms obey the spirit as well as the letter of information and consultation laws. Note also that councillors receive some information on a confidential basis, so that it does not become known to competitors.

8. In the United States, Kleiner and Bouillon (1988) show that information does not in fact harm profitability.

We model the economic value of the council as a communicator from management to workers with the following simple situation. A firm and its workers decide on one workplace variable: the speed of work, which can either be fast (F) or normal (N). Workers view speed as bad and prefer a normal pace. They obtain utility U_N working at a normal pace and U_F working at a fast pace, with $U_N > U_F$. In addition, we assume that workers prefer to remain with the firm even at the fast pace, so that $U_F > U_0$, where U_0 is the utility from leaving the firm. In contrast to workers, firms view speed as good because their profits are higher when workers work at the fast pace.

Assume that the environment consists of two states: good and bad, with known probabilities p and $1 - p$. In the good state, firm profits are π_F when the workers work at the fast pace and π_N when they work at the normal pace, with $\pi_F > \pi_N$. In the bad state, profits are $\pi_B > 0$ when workers work at the fast pace but are negative when workers work at the normal pace, forcing the firm to shut down. Total surplus is larger in the good state than in the bad state and is larger in the bad state when work is fast than when the firm goes out of business. This highlights the fact that the major social loss occurs when the firm closes because workers do not accede to management's desire to work at the fast pace.

The problem for workers is that while they prefer to work at the fast speed in the bad state, they lack credible information about the state of the firm. They distrust what management says because management can lie about the state, getting them to work at the fast speed even in the good state and thus garnering more of the joint surplus. Assuming that management finds it profitable to act opportunistically (of which more in a moment) workers will ignore management claims and work at normal speed in all periods or at the fast speed in all periods.[9] Holding out for the normal speed when the firm is in trouble means the firm closes and workers receive utility U_0 instead of U_F. Acceding to fast speeds when the firm does well means that workers get less utility than otherwise. If workers hold out for U_N, p percent of the time they will be right, but $1 - p$ percent of the time they will be wrong and receive utility U_0. The expected utility from working at the normal speed at all times is

(4) $$EU_N = p\,U_N + (1 - p)\,U_0.$$

Alternatively, if workers work fast at all times, their expected utility is just U_F. Workers will choose between working at a fast or normal speed depending on the probability of the states and the expected utility of the alternatives. If they think the good state always prevails, they choose N. If they think the bad state always prevails, they choose F. Define p^* as the probability at which workers are indifferent between N and F: $p^*U_N + (1 - p^*)U_0 = U_F$, which yields

9. Under the conditions of the model that we describe shortly, firms have an incentive to lie about the state of the world, knowing that workers will choose an F or N strategy.

(5) $$p^* = (U_F - U_0)/(U_N - U_0).$$

The solution, p^*, lies between 0 and 1 since $U_0 < U_F < U_N$. Since p^* depends on utility levels, it reflects the situation and attitudes of workers, not the likely state of the firm. When p^* is low, workers can be viewed as being more "aggressive" in insisting on working at a normal pace rather than acceding to requests to work fast. When p exceeds p^*, workers will work at a normal pace; when p is less than p^*, they will work at a fast pace.

Differentiating p^* with respect to U_N, U_F, and U_0 shows that increases in U_N and U_0 reduce p^* while increases in U_F raise p^*. This implies that workers are more aggressive the greater the utility of working at a normal pace, the greater the utility of alternative opportunities (they do not mind losing their jobs if the alternative offers nearly the same utility as their job), and the lower the utility of working at a fast pace. Put differently, big differences between U_N and U_F and small differences between U_0 and U_F produce aggressive workers. Since differences between earnings inside the firm and outside will depend on specific human capital, seniority rules, and the like, (younger) workers with less specific training and seniority are likely to be more aggressive than older workers.

Table 2.1 analyzes the surplus going to workers and firms when workers know the actual state versus when they only know the probability. Panel A shows the surplus when they only know p. Here workers must choose a strategy

Table 2.1 **Surplus Produced and Distributed under Alternative Information and Gains from Full Information**

A. Workers Not Informed about State		
Utility to:	Choose N ($p > p^*$)	Choose F ($p < p^*$)
Workers	$pU_N + (1 - p)U_0$	U_F
Firm	$p\pi_N$	$p\pi_F + (1 - p)\pi_B$

B. Full Information	
Utility to:	N in Good Times/F in Bad Times
Workers	$pU_N + (1 - p) U_F$
Firm	$p\pi_N + (1 - p) \pi_B$

C. Change in Well-Being from Information		
	With Information	
Utility to:	Would Have Chosen N	Would Have Chosen F
Workers	$(1 - p) (U_F - U_0)$	$p(U_N - U_F)$
Firm	$(1 - p) \pi_B$	$p(\pi_N - \pi_F) < 0$
Society	$(1 - p) (U_F - U_0 + \pi_B)$	$p(U_N - U_F + \pi_N - \pi_F)$

of working at normal or fast speed in both states. By definition of p^*, if $p >$ p^* they choose N, whereas if $p < p^*$ they choose F. This yields one solution when $p > p^*$ and another solution when $p < p^*$. Panel B gives the surplus when workers have full information. In this case they work at normal speed during good times and at fast speed during bad times. This is the socially optimal situation, which produces average utility for workers of $p\ U_N + (1 - p)$ U_F and average profits for firms of $p\ \pi_N + (1 - p)\ \pi_B$. Panel C shows the change in surplus for workers, firms, and society between the two situations. If $p > p^*$ so that absent full information workers choose N in all states, the benefit to workers of full information is $U_F - U_0$ in the $1 - p$ of the time when the firm is in a bad state, the benefit to firms is π_B, and the social benefit is the sum of the two. In bad states information improves the well-being of all parties. If $p < p^*$ so that workers choose strategy F in all states, they lose $U_F - U_N$ in p of the time, while firms gain $\pi_F - \pi_N$.

The social benefit of information from management to labor is that it eliminates the danger that workers choose the N strategy in a bad state. The condition that $p > p^*$ shows that this is most likely to occur when a firm generally does well and workers are "aggressive." Since the firm does well, workers distrust the claim that it is in trouble, and if they are sufficiently aggressive, they will refuse to work at a fast pace in the bad state. Full information allows workers to respond flexibly, working at a fast pace in the bad state and at a normal pace in good states.

Since management as well as workers gain when work is fast in the bad state, we would expect management to endorse councils as a valuable tool for conveying "bad" news to workers. In fact, in the Freeman-Rogers interviews several managers volunteered worker responses to potential plant closings as examples of the benefits of councils to the firm. One manager said, "Councils are a very good communication channel, especially with regard to bad news. They are more credible than management." By contrast, in good times the information given the council benefits workers at the expense of management, and no manager cited the virtues of such redistribution as examples of useful councils.

How will the benefits of full information vary with economic uncertainty? In our model uncertainty is measured by p; it is highest at $p = .5$ and lowest at $p = 0$ or $p = 1$. Figure 2.2A graphs the social surplus created by full information as a function of p. When p is 0 or 1, there is no information problem, and the social value of council-provided information is nil. When p is 0, the workers know that the bad state always occurs, so there is no benefit to additional information: $p < p^*$ and workers will always work fast. When p is 1, workers know that the firm is always in the good state so that the plant will not close. Note that the value of information peaks when p is just a bit above (or possibly just below) p^*, not when uncertainty is highest.

One further refinement is needed to complete our analysis. If by opening its books to workers in bad times management can convince workers to work at a

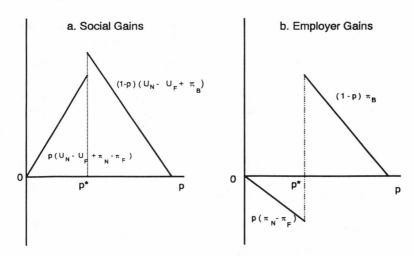

Fig. 2.2   Gains from information disclosure as a function of p

fast pace, the firm might be expected to do so, obviating the need for mandatory disclosure of information. But opening the books in the bad state tells
workers that the firm is in the good state at all other times, which loses the firm
the option of inducing workers to work at a fast pace in good times. The firm
will disclose its state voluntarily only when the expected benefits from keeping
the enterprise alive in bad times exceeds the gains from inducing workers to
work at a fast pace in good times. If the firm knows p but not p^* (a worker
characteristic), it will estimate the probability α that $p > p^*$ and will open its
books voluntarily when

$$(6) \qquad \alpha(1 - p)\pi_B + (1 - \alpha)p(\pi_N - \pi_F) > 0$$

as derived from firm net benefits in panel C of table 2.1.

The social value of opening the books is

$$(7) \qquad \alpha(1 - p)(U_F - U_0 + \pi_B) + (1 - \alpha)p(U_N - U_F + \pi_N - \pi_F),$$

derived from the last row of table 2.1. The difference between equations
(7) and (6) is the worker returns to the information, $\alpha(1 - p)(U_F - U_0) +
(1 - \alpha)p(U_N - U_F)$, which is necessarily positive. Since the firms' gains are
less than the social gains, the firm will voluntarily show workers their books
less frequently than is socially desirable.[10] This leads to

---

10. The firm's ability to commit to a nonrevelation strategy is key. Ex post, firms in bad states
want to show their books to workers. But doing so makes the absence of a report a signal that the
good state must hold. Firms may be able to commit to nonrevelation by hiring a third party to keep
the books. Alternatively, separating the human resource department from the accounting department and giving the latter incentives to withhold information from workers may solve the problem.

PROPOSITION 2. Requiring firms to disclose profit information has social value when firms will not voluntarily provide the information.[11]

Finally, since the social gains of full information depend on the differences in utility and in profits between maintenance and closure of the firm, which will reflect the extent of firm-specific investments in human and physical capital, council-created communication between management and workers will be especially valuable in firms with large firm-specific complementary investments. The prediction that full information will induce workers to be "less aggressive" in bad times also suggests that councils increase effort flexibility.

2.3   Communication from Workers to Management

"Councils give management a better idea of what employees are willing to accept. Things come up in discussion that management didn't know." (manager in Freeman-Rogers interviews)

Councils affect communication from workers to management by improving the incentives for workers to provide information to management and by filtering the information through the subset of workers on councils.

2.3.1   Incentives to Communicate

To see how works councils can increase the incentive for workers to communicate truthfully to management, consider how workers will respond to a management request for information about the compensation package: "How much wage would you give up for various amounts of a fringe benefit?" Assume that workers are divided between those who love the fringe, and who will accept a large wage reduction for it, and those who only like the fringe, and who will accept only a small wage reduction for it.

In figure 2.3, two sets of indifference curves are shown, corresponding to two types of workers. The convex solid curve, labeled K0, shows the points that provide the minimum level of utility to keep a worker who likes the fringe working at the firm. The convex dotted curve labeled V0 shows the points that provide the minimum level of utility to keep a worker who loves the fringe working at the firm. The bold, concave curves show the firm's isoprofit contours where movements to the southwest reflect higher profits.

If the firm knew that a worker loved the fringe, it would offer point S with wage W1 and fringe level F1 since this yields higher profits than any other feasible point. If the firm knew that a worker liked the fringe, it would offer point R with wage W0 and fringe level F0. Offering S to fringe-likers causes those workers to quit. The problem is that a fringe-lover can gain by telling the

11. This assumes that the real resource costs of disclosure do not exceed the social gain from disclosure. The real costs are auditing the books to ensure accuracy and training workers to read the books. There is also the risk that information revealed to workers may find its way to rivals who can use it to firms' detriment, which may or may not have social costs.

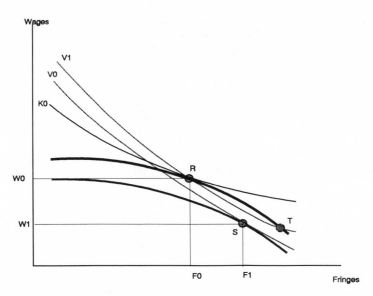

Fig. 2.3   Wages versus fringes

firm that he is only a fringe-liker since he prefers point R to point S. The result is that while the fringe-likers tell the employer their true preferences, the fringe-lovers do not, and the firm gets no information from what workers say. Surplus is lost because there are fringe/wage combinations preferred to R by both management and fringe-lovers. In the diagram, all points in the area bounded by points R and T and curve V1 and the corresponding isoprofit curve are Pareto improving. For workers to communicate truthfully with management, they need a say over how the firm uses worker-provided information—that is, a guarantee that management will not extract the full surplus. This establishes

PROPOSITION 3. Works councils that give workers some control over the use of information can enhance information flows from workers to management.

2.3.2   Representative Councils

Works councils are forms of representative government, giving rise to the question that faces any representative institution, "How well does the subset of the population (works councillors) reflect preferences of the population (workforce)?"

The following situation provides a way of analyzing this question. Suppose management chooses to paint an office blue or red and wants to pick the color preferred by the workforce. A majority, q, of the workforce prefers red, but management does not know this and relies on the council to convey worker sentiment. Assume, in the first instance, that councillors are a randomly selected subset of an odd number n of workers and that councillors give their own preferences in discussion with management. The probability that the council will fail to represent the majority is the probability that $(n - 1)/2$ or fewer prefer red. Let $f(x; n, q)$ be the binomial density function where there are n trials. Let q be the probability of a success defined as vote for red, and x be the number of successes in n trials. The probability that x will vote red is

$$f(x; n, q) = \binom{n}{x} q^x (1 - q)^{n - x},$$

and the probability that the council misrepresents workers is

$$\sum_{x=0}^{(n-1)/2} f(x; n, q),$$

that is, the probability that 0 vote red, plus the probability that 1 votes red, . . . , plus the probability that exactly $(n - 1)/2$ vote red.

The probability that the council misrepresents workers decreases as n rises and increases as q approaches .5. A large council is more representative and will communicate preferences more accurately when there is a large majority on an issue. A near-even split of workers raises the danger that the council will favor the minority. If a near-even split means that workers do not feel strongly about the issue, erring in favor of the minority may be relatively harmless. If workers feel strongly, however, a correct decision requires an assessment of the strength of preferences rather than a simple count.

To model the strength of preferences, let ΔU^* be the utility of red (versus blue) to red-lovers and ΔU be the utility of blue (versus red) to blue-lovers. The value of choosing red over blue is then $q \, \Delta U^* - (1 - q) \, \Delta U$. If this is negative, it would be better to choose blue despite the red majority. If blue fans can convey the strength of their preferences in council meetings, they may be able to sway management and the council to choose blue. If q is near 1, so that there is a large majority, or if red-lovers are nearly as committed as blue-lovers, the average weighted preference is unlikely to favor blue. Discussion is more valuable when the majority is a bare majority, and when the majority has weak preferences and the minority strong preferences.

At first blush, one might expect the optimal size of the council to be highest when the workforce is nearly evenly divided. If 51 percent prefer red and 49 percent prefer blue, a large sample is needed to assure that the minority does not hold the majority on the council. But the value of adding additional randomly selected councillors is actually smallest when q is near .5 or 1. To see this, consider the two extremes. If $q = 1$ every worker prefers red, so the probability of getting a blue fan on a one-person council equals the probability of getting a blue fan on a 1000-person council—zero. Similarly, if $q = .5$, the probability of a blue fan on a one-person council is .5. But the chance that any additional randomly selected worker prefers blue is also .5, so that the proba-

Table 2.2   **Probability of Blue Majority on Council Given That *q* Prefer Red**

q (1)	Prob. of Error $n = 1$ (2)	Prob. of Error $n = 3$ (3)	Prob. of Error $n = 5$ (4)	Error Difference $n = 3$ and 1 (5)	Error Difference $n = 5$ and 3 (6)
0.500	0.500	0.500	0.500	0.000	0.000
0.520	0.480	0.470	0.463	−0.010	−0.007
0.540	0.460	0.440	0.425	−0.020	−0.015
0.560	0.440	0.410	0.389	−0.030	−0.022
0.580	0.420	0.381	0.353	−0.039	−0.028
0.600	0.400	0.352	0.317	−0.048	−0.035
0.620	0.380	0.323	0.283	−0.057	−0.040
0.640	0.360	0.295	0.251	−0.065	−0.045
0.660	0.340	0.268	0.220	−0.072	−0.048
0.680	0.320	0.242	0.191	−0.078	−0.051
0.700	0.300	0.216	0.163	−0.084	−0.053
0.720	0.280	0.191	0.138	−0.089	−0.054
0.740	0.260	0.168	0.114	−0.092	−0.053
0.760	0.240	0.145	0.093	−0.095	−0.052
0.780	0.220	0.124	0.074	−0.096	−0.049
0.800	0.200	0.104	0.058	−0.096	−0.046
0.820	0.180	0.086	0.044	−0.094	−0.042
0.840	0.160	0.069	0.032	−0.091	−0.037
0.860	0.140	0.053	0.022	−0.087	−0.031
0.880	0.120	0.040	0.014	−0.080	−0.025
0.900	0.100	0.028	0.009	−0.072	−0.019
0.920	0.080	0.018	0.005	−0.062	−0.014
0.940	0.060	0.010	0.002	−0.050	−0.008
0.960	0.040	0.005	0.001	−0.035	−0.004
0.980	0.020	0.001	0.000	−0.019	−0.001
1.000	0.000	0.000	0.000	0.000	0.000

Note: Council size is given by *n*.

bility of blue is .5, independent of the size of the council. Table 2.2 illustrates the point. Column (1) gives the proportion of the workforce that likes red. Columns (2)–(4) give the probabilities that councils with one, three, and five members, respectively, will erroneously consist of a blue majority. Column (5) gives the decline in the probability of an error when council size is increased from one to three persons (the difference between cols. [3] and [2]). Column (6) gives the decline in the probability of an error when council size is increased from three to five persons (the difference between cols. [4] and [3]). At $q = .5$ or $q = 1$, a council of one is as good as a council of five: the decline in the probability of error is zero. When the proportion preferring red gets near .75, the value of a larger council reaches a peak: in columns (5) and (6) the incremental reduction in the error is largest when the proportion who favor red is between .70 and .80. Note further that the gain from going from one to three members is larger than the gain from going from three to five members. There are diminishing returns to adding council members.[12]

The logic is that information is very valuable when q is close to .5 but almost impossible to obtain by adding council members. At $q = 1$, the value of additional information is zero. In the area around $q = .75$, these two effects balance out: information is valuable and adding a new member contributes information. This demonstrates

PROPOSITION 4. Increasing council size improves the accuracy of information from workers when there is a strong but not overwhelming majority. Size adds little accuracy when the workforce is nearly evenly divided or unanimous over an issue.

Note finally that if, as many models of politics suggest, candidates' positions are close to the preferences of the median voter, majorities will generally be extremely small. For example, if 95 percent prefer red over green but workers are more ambivalent about red versus blue, then the final ballot is likely to be between red and blue, not between red and green. This equilibrating force, coupled with proposition 4, implies the surprising result that increasing the size of works councils may generally do little to ensure that the right decision is made.

2.3.3   Elected Councils and Minority Representation

Counsellors are not, of course, randomly selected from the workforce, but are, rather, elected according to rules that differ across settings. Some countries mandate separate election districts for plant and office workers. Some allow blue-collar workers to elect white-collar workers to represent them. In countries with multiple-union federations, different unions run slates under various proportional representation rules. Belgium restricts counsellors to workers on union election slates. Without analyzing actual voting rules, we show next how specific rules can affect the representativeness of councils.

At one extreme, consider the election of members chosen by workers at large. Suppose the rule is that workers vote for n persons from a ballot of z candidates and that the leading n candidates are elected. As before, q of workers favor red. If the z names were randomly chosen, then an expected qz individuals would, on average, prefer red, and the remaining counsellors would prefer blue. Workers favoring red would vote the "red slate," and as long as there are at least n candidates who favor red the council would be stacked with red-lovers: the minority gets no representation. The usual way to avoid such an outcome is proportional representation, based on ex ante criteria such as occupation, age, income, location, and sex, which may not reflect attitudes on

---

12. The formal proof of these propositions relies on the monotonicity of the binomial density function. The key ingredient is that the binomial is monotone increasing for $x < (n + 1)p$ and monotone decreasing for $x > (n + 1)p$.

the color question. Proportional representation is a partial but imperfect cure to the problem of guaranteeing minority representation on specific issues. If women and young workers have different preferences on some issues than older men in the same jobs, proportional representation along traditional factory/office or supervisory/nonsupervisory lines may not mirror those differences, suggesting the possible value of grouping by gender, age, and perhaps race in some countries.

An alternative way to obtain minority representation is to select councillors jury style. When councillors are selected randomly from the population, the minority is more likely to be represented in proportion to its numbers than when councillors are elected at large, or when the criteria for proportional representation are unrelated to attitudes. While a jury system produces minority representation, it has a disadvantage as well. When councillors are elected (and may run again), they are accountable to the workforce and thus may make a greater effort to find out what their peers want than a jury-style councillor.[13] And elected councillors may be more able than those chosen by a jury system.[14]

2.4   Consultation and Co-determination

"In the press shop the works council . . . made many concrete proposals . . . making sure there are sufficient racks . . . ensuring that a foreman is available to train new workers . . . (for) movement of personnel . . . to compensate for a faster-moving press line whose parts are in higher demand." (manager in Freeman-Rogers interviews)

All works council laws give councils consultation rights over some decisions. For example, management may be required to consider council suggestions about plant closing before proceeding with any action, although final authority still resides with management. In Germany councils have additional co-determination rights over some issues which require agreement by both sides before any action can be taken. (Compulsory arbitration is used on impasses.) Even when management has the final say, however, consultation rights give the council an influence on the firm's behavior. For one thing, consultation is costly: Management must spend time to prepare for and participate in council meetings. The potentially more important indirect cost is delaying decisions

13. What about alternatives to councils, such as votes (referenda) on issues? There are two advantages to using a council instead of general voting. First, as the management quote given at the outset indicates, it should be cheaper to canvas 10 representative workers than to survey an entire workforce. Second, votes do not register strength of preferences very well. Oral communication in the council setting may provide management with a better sense of how strongly each side's views are held.

14. If some randomly selected delegates do not want to serve, they could be given the right to name a substitute from the same group. The substitute would likely have similar views and might be chosen because he or she is a more able spokesperson.

until consultation is completed. Nearly every manager in the Freeman-Rogers interviews cited the time delay as a major drawback of consultations. The need for consultation may, in fact, eliminate some profitable options for firms that depend upon rapid responses to market opportunities.

When might consultation increase the enterprise surplus? How will co-determination, particularly over employment security issues, affect the social surplus and the firm's returns? There are four issues involved in co-determination. They are: the overlap of each party's information set, the relevance of nonoverlapping information, the delay caused by consultation, and the creativity that occurs during discussion. We model all four but deal least well with the last.

2.4.1 Council-Facilitated Consultation

Consultation can increase enterprise surplus when workers offer solutions to firm problems that management fails to see (vide the quotation at the outset of this section) and when management and labor together discover solutions to company problems that neither would have conceived separately. One necessary condition for either situation is that workers have some information that management does not have that is not conveyed freely when management simply asks. Workers must be able to suggest a better solution than that proposed by management.

For specificity, consider again the choice of color when management plans to paint the office red or blue and workers prefer red. The works council might suggest green, which (for whatever reason) maximizes enterprise surplus. This situation has the flavor of Koike's (1989) and Aoki's (1986) analyses of plant-level operations in which "unusual circumstances" or shocks occur at workplaces. Occurrences such as daily or weekly breakdowns of machines provide workers with opportunities to alter activities in ways that affect productivity. Key is that these occurrences cannot be foreseen or observed by management but can be exploited by workers.[15]

The essence of co-determination is teamwork. Management has information or thoughts that workers lack, and workers have information or thoughts that management lacks. By combining information and effort, new ideas are spawned and joint surplus is increased. Since teamwork is key, we model co-determination as analogous to playing a team sport. The metaphor we use is American football.

Suppose that only 30 seconds remain in the game and the team with the ball must score a touchdown to win. The best strategy is to throw a pass, but the

---

15. The color-green example differs from their cases, however, because the optimal solution when workers face unusual plant-level circumstances is for management to delegate to workers the authority to respond. Consultation rather than on-the-spot treatment of problems requires that management can also contribute to the solution, for instance by bringing other information to bear on the problem or by changing investments or coordinating activities that lie under its control. This is more likely when shocks have a pattern, permitting a general solution to the problem.

probability that the pass is completed depends on knowledge of whether the passer and receiver are right- or left-handed. It also depends on the type and distance of the pass thrown. Neither player knows the other player's hand preference and communicating this information to one another requires a huddle. The huddle communicates information and also allows passer and receiver to combine their thoughts on the type of pass that is best.

The huddle takes time, analogous to delay caused by the co-determination process. Suppose that if players stop to huddle, they have time for only one play in the remaining 30 seconds. If they do not stop to huddle, they will have $1 + j$ plays, so j is a measure of the time cost of co-determination.

If they huddle, the probability of completing a touchdown pass is β. There are two potential gains from the huddle. One is that players learn each other's hand preference. The other is that they may select a better play. If they do not huddle, each must guess the other player's hand preference and go with a traditional pass. If they both guess correctly, the probability of completing the pass is $\beta' \leq \beta$. The difference between β and β' is that without a huddle, there is no possibility of inventing a new play for the current situation. Thus, β exceeds β'. If passer or receiver guesses wrong about the other's hand preference, the probability of completing the pass is only ρ, with $\rho < \beta'$. Suppose that the world has γ right-handers with $\gamma > .5$. Then the best guess is that the other player is right handed. Thus, γ^2 of the time, both guesses are correct and the probability of a completed pass is β'. But $1 - \gamma^2$ of the time, they guess wrong, and the probability of a completed pass is only ρ.

The trade-off is that co-determination provides better information, creativity, and thereby expected output. The cost is delay. Delay in this case takes the form of sacrificing some plays.

If they huddle, the probability of a touchdown is simply β because only one play is run. If they do not huddle, the probability of a touchdown is

$$\gamma^2 [1 - (1 - \beta')^{1+j}] + (1 - \gamma^2) [1 - (1 - \rho)^{1+j}].$$

The first term is the probability, given that players guess correctly, of scoring a touchdown on at least one of the $1 + j$ plays (i.e., one minus the probability of failing on all $1 + j$ plays) times the probability that they guess correctly. The second term is the probability, given that they guess incorrectly, of scoring a touchdown on at least one of the $1 + j$ plays times the probability that they guess incorrectly.

It pays to huddle if and only if

$$\beta > \gamma^2 [1 - (1 - \beta')^{1+j}] + (1 - \gamma^2) [1 - (1 - \rho)^{1+j}],$$

or if and only if

(11) $$\beta - \gamma^2 [1 - (1 - \beta')^{1+j}] - (1 - \gamma^2) [1 - (1 - \rho)^{1+j}] > 0.$$

Initially, let us abstract from creativity and focus on coordination by assuming that $\beta' = \beta$, so that the huddle only serves to communicate hand preference. It is obvious that whether condition (11) holds depends on the values of the parameters. For example, if $\beta = 1$, $\rho < 1$, and $\gamma < 1$, the condition holds with certainty since the sum of the last two terms is always less than 1. If a huddle brings certain victory on one play, the strategy should be followed no matter how many plays are sacrificed.

However, if $\rho = \beta$, then condition (11) becomes

$$(1 - \beta) [(1 - \beta)^j - 1] < 0.$$

This situation is one in which there is no gain to communication because the information is useless. (Recall that we have temporarily assumed that there is no creativity, in that $\beta' = \beta$.) Knowing whether the passer or receiver is right or left handed has no effect on the probability that the pass is completed. A huddle only serves to reduce the number of plays that can be attempted, which decreases the probability of a touchdown.

There is no value to co-determination when the knowledge to be transferred has no effect on joint surplus. When $\beta' = \rho = \beta$, there is no relevant information communicated in a huddle, so there is no value to it. There is no point in having works councils meetings to discuss management and workers' taste in wine if wine is never served at work. So the first point is that the information sets must not only be different, but the union of the sets must yield higher joint surplus than the disjoint sets. Sharing information must be valuable, or it never pays to have co-determination.

Second, and related, note that

$$\partial/\partial\rho = -(1 - \gamma^2) (1 - \rho)^j (1 + j),$$

which is negative. As ρ falls, the expression in condition (11) rises. For a given probability of completion given full information, the value of the huddle increases as ρ falls. When ρ falls, the gains to communication rise because joint surplus is increased more by sharing knowledge.

The value of coordination is measured most directly by γ. Recall that γ is the proportion of the population that is right handed. Note that when $\gamma = 1$, equation (11) becomes

$$-[(1 - \beta) - (1 - \beta)^{j+1}] < 0$$

and

$$\partial/\partial\gamma = 2\gamma [(1 - \beta)^{1+j} - (1 - \rho)^{1+j}] < 0.$$

As γ increases, the assumption that passer and receiver are right handed is correct, and there is less need to coordinate. At the extreme, when $\gamma = 1$, there is no role for communication. Coordination of information is redundant. Independent analysis by passer and receiver results in the correct solution and avoids the delay of the huddle.

Discussion and co-determination are valuable when the information sets do not overlap and when that information is relevant. If γ were 1, information would be completely overlapping. If $\beta = \rho$ and $\gamma < 1$, information would not be common, but it would be irrelevant, having no effect on the probability of success.

In the workplace, the more different the relevant experiences of workers and management, the more likely that co-determination will be valuable. Sharing information is most likely to affect the probability that the job gets done when each side has independent, but relevant, information. If ex ante guesses are generally correct, there is little reason to waste time meeting. Further, even if inferences about the other side's characteristics are wrong, meetings are still valuable only when the information is relevant.

The Freeman-Rogers interviews provide examples in which worker suggestions produced more profitable outcomes for the firm and in which the interplay between management and labor proved useful. In one major enterprise, management told the works council that the enterprise had to save a certain amount of money to maintain an engineering facility. Devising a plan to provide the savings was left to the workers. Schemes that management thought were infeasible turned out to be feasible, presumably because management did not have an accurate reading of what could be done or of the sacrifice workers would make to save the facility.

These considerations do not mean, of course, that consultation is always useful. Benefits must be weighed against costs. Thus, we present the third formal result: As the costs of delay rise, co-determination becomes less valuable. Specifically,

$$\partial / \partial j = \gamma^2 (1 - \beta)^{1+j} \ln(1 - \beta) + (1 - \gamma^2) (1 - \rho)^{1+j} \ln(1 - \rho),$$

which is negative since $1 - \beta$ and $1 - \rho$ are both less than 1. The extreme cases are informative.

If $j = 0$, then no time is sacrificed by a huddle. In this case, equation (11) becomes

$$(1 - \gamma^2) (\beta - \rho) > 0.$$

It always pays to huddle if there is no cost and some potential benefit.

Also, evaluating equation (11) as j gets large,

$$\lim_{j \to \infty} \beta - \gamma^2 [1 - (1 - \beta)^{1+j}] - (1 - \gamma^2) [1 - (1 - \rho)^{1+j}] = -(1 - \beta) < 0.$$

As the delay cost becomes infinitely large, it never pays to huddle.

This may be one reason why it is important to have councillors who speak the same language as managers. If it takes too much time for an accountant to communicate with a machinist, it might be better to have the machinists elect an accountant as their representative. (Of course, this begs the question of how machinists communicate to their representative.) It also suggests a role for training councillors. American managers who do not spend time consulting with their workers or staff can make decisions faster than European or Japanese managers. But they lose the benefits of information from those below them in the organization and may find implementation of decisions more difficult.

Let us return then to the issue of creativity and abstract from coordination. We replace the assumption that $\beta' = \beta$ with the assumption that $\beta' < \beta$, the difference reflecting creativity that occurs in the huddle. To eliminate coordination difficulties, assume that all players are right handed. With $\gamma = 1$, equation (11) now becomes

$$(11')\qquad\qquad -(1 - \beta) + (1 - \beta')^{1+j}.$$

If $\beta = \beta'$, then equation (11') is clearly negative for $j > 0$. A huddle does not pay. But with $\beta < \beta'$, it is quite possible that the creativity generated in the huddle outweighs the delay cost. If $\beta' = 0$, the condition clearly holds and it pays to huddle; as β' goes to β, it does not. Define

$$\beta^* = 1 - (1 - \beta)^{1/(1+j)}.$$

Then for $\beta' < \beta^*$, it pays to huddle because the creativity effect outweighs the delay effect. For $\beta' > \beta^*$, a no-huddle offense dominates because the creativity gains do not outweigh the delay costs.

It can be shown as a general proposition, that

$$\beta^* > \beta/(1 + j).$$

The creativity effect is more important than the time effect. For example, if $j = 1$, the council meeting costs half of the firm's time. Even if the probability of success on a given try did not quite double with a huddle, it could still pay to huddle. For example, if $j = 1$, $\beta = .5$, and $\beta' = .29$, a huddle is worthwhile even though it increases the probability of success by less than 100 percent.

2.4.2   Co-determination, Worker Loyalty, and Investment in Skills

Few, if any, managements want to give workers co-determination over important decisions, particularly those relating to employment, conditions of work, and the like. Co-determination can greatly increase worker power. If workers have veto rights over hours worked, as in Germany, they possess a potentially powerful chip in bargaining over the division of rents. Indeed, outside of Germany, works council legislation accords co-determination rights only to decisions on which management is presumably neutral, such as the French-mandated expenditures on benefits that fall under the social fund. When does adopting the German model, which gives works councils rights over employment levels, employment patterns, and work conditions, improve worker surplus?

The German-style works council has the ability to enhance worker job security. The most important positive feature of additional job security is that it induces workers to take a longer-run view of the prospects of the firm. A consequence is that worker interests are brought more in line with those of owners.

The easiest way to model this is to add additional periods to our section 2.2 model (where workers choose how quickly to work) and to make the rewards to the worker in later periods depend on company well-being in earlier periods. Without a formal analysis, the logic is clear: workers who have job security place value on company profits because the profits are reflected in worker compensation in the future. Thus, one would expect workers in enterprises with strong councils to have greater loyalty to their firm and to be more eager to invest in firm-specific skills than workers in other firms. To the extent that there is underinvestment in firm-specific human capital (because no one side captures 100 percent of the returns), providing additional job security helps to alleviate the problem.[16]

2.5 Conclusion

Our analysis has shown that works councils are most likely to improve enterprise surplus when they have limited but definite power in the enterprise. We have attempted to illuminate situations in which the mandated information sharing and consultation can improve social well-being. Further, we have discussed the implications of choosing specific rules for electing councils. We have stressed that the social-welfare–maximizing council power lies between the amount of power management will voluntarily give the councils and the amount of power labor desires.

European countries with works councils give councils limited legal power but also restrict conflict over the division of rents through centralized wage-setting systems. By setting the bulk of pay packages at the industry level, leaving only modest potential increments for bargaining by firms, and by forbidding councils from using labor's main weapon, the strike, European labor relations systems limit councils' ability to increase labor's rents at the expense of the total surplus. On the other side, by setting pay in industry negotiations, unions and employer federations create a wage floor for workers that serves a similar function. The risk that lack of local bargaining power will allow employers to garner the bulk of enterprise surplus is reduced. Industry unions help, of course, to maintain this dual system by influencing the behavior of councils. When centralized wage setting precludes councils from spending time and effort on wage negotiations, they must focus their attention on other aspects of the work environment.

Would mandated councils work in a different labor relations system, for instance the decentralized wage-setting system of the United States or the United Kingdom? Because we have assumed that the internal operation of councils is determined outside the enterprise, our analysis does not adequately address this critical question about the potential portability of institutions across labor relations systems. In a U.S. or British labor relations system, with

16. See, e.g., Kennan (1979) and Hall and Lazear (1984).

decentralized wage setting, would councils, once established, turn into aggressive plant-level unions? Or might they become company-dominated quality-of-work circles and wither on the vine, as did the company-initiated U.S. councils of the 1920s? While our analysis does not answer these important questions even in the abstract, it does suggest the value of paying serious attention to the design of council-type arrangements that might best fit decentralized labor systems. There are potential net social gains from works councils. But to work best and gain those potential benefits, the rules governing councils must be carefully written to bound the power of labor and management and "fit" the broader labor system in which councils must function.

References

Aoki, Masahiko. 1986. Horizontal vs. vertical information structure of the firm. *American Economic Review* 76:971–83.

Chamber of Commerce. 1927. *Employee representation or works councils.* Washington D.C.: Chamber of Commerce.

Douglas, Paul. 1921. Shop committees: Substitute for, or supplement to, trades unions? *Journal of Political Economy* 29 (February): 89–107.

Freeman, Richard B. 1990. Employee councils, worker participation, and other squishy stuff. *Proceedings of the 43rd annual meeting of the Industrial Relations Research Association.* Madison, Wisc.: Industrial Relations Research Association.

Freeman, Richard B., and Joel Rogers. 1993. Who speaks for us: Employee representation in a nonunion labor market. In *Employee representation: Alternatives and future directions,* ed. Bruce E. Kaufman and Morris M. Kleiner, 13–39. Madison, Wisc.: Industrial Relations Research Association.

Hall, Robert, and Edward Lazear. 1984. The excess sensitivity of layoffs and quits to demand. *Journal of Labor Economics* 2:233–57.

Kennan, John. 1979. Bonding and enforcement of labor contracts. *Economic Letters* 3:61–66.

Kleiner, Morris, and M. Bouillon. 1988. Providing business information in production workers: Correlates of compensation and profitability. *Industrial and Labor Relations Review* 41:605–17.

Koike, Kazuo. 1989. Intellectual skill and the role of employees as constituent members of large firms in contemporary Japan. In *The firm as a nexus of treaties,* ed. Masahiko Aoki, B. Gustafsson, and O. Williamson, 185–208. Newbury Park, Calif.: Sage.

Morishima, Motohiro. 1991. Information sharing and collective bargaining in Japan: Effects on wage negotiation. *Industrial and Labor Relations Review* 44(3): 469–87.

National Industrial Conference Board. 1920. *A works council manual.* Research Report no. 26. Boston: National Industrial Conference Board.

———. 1922. *Experience with works councils in the United States.* Research Report no. 50. New York: Century.

Rogers, Joel, and Wolfgang Streeck. 1991. Works Council Project: Concept paper and research guideline. University of Wisconsin-Madison, February. Mimeograph.

Tirole, Jacques. 1986. Hierarchies and bureaucracies: On the role of collusion in organizations. *Journal of Law, Economics, and Organization* 2(2):181–214.

II The European Experience

3   Germany: From Collective Voice to Co-management

Walther Müller-Jentsch

3.1   Introduction

Works councils were not always as undisputed as they are today among trade unions and the great majority of employers. Already in the period of early industrialization liberal politicians and social reformers advocated bodies of workers representatives, called factory or workers' committees *(Fabrik-ausschüsse or Arbeiterausschüsse)*. In addition, some early social-minded employers relinquished some of their traditional prerogatives by setting up committees designed to air workers' collective views. Prussian state bureaucrats, too, conceived of workforce representation at the plant level as part of their general political program to modernize state and society, together with a vocational training system, an industrial code *(Gewerbeordnung)*, and a system of social insurance. But not until 1891 did the amended industrial code provide for optional workers committees, which were made obligatory in 1905 for the mining industry in the wake of extensive industrial strife. At that time the unions still opposed such institutions as—in the view of August Bebel, the leader of the Social Democratic party—mere "fig-leaves of capitalism."

During the First World War the unions and the Social Democratic party observed a policy of collaboration with the war government *(Burgfriedenspolitik)*. A special law (Gesetz über den vaterländischen Hilfsdienst) extended workers committees to all factories with more than 50 employees in industries of basic importance to the war economy. After the war, when works councils were legally established in the Weimar Republic in 1920, they were designed to preempt the revolutionary council movement. Being stripped of political functions, the *workers' councils* became industrial *works councils (Betriebs-*

Walther Müller-Jentsch is professor and holds the chair in co-determination and organization in the Department of Sociology at Ruhr-Universität Bochum.

räte). On the day the Works Councils Act was passed, a powerful demonstration of revolutionary workers and militant trade unionists marched to the Berlin parliament. Machine-gun fire violently ended the march, killing 42 demonstrators.

The political and economic turbulence of the Weimar Republic did not give the works councils a real chance to develop their potential. Because of their politically radical background, they were kept subordinate to a cooperative union movement that desperately tried to play its part in the reconstruction of a peace economy and the building of a social democratic society. At the time, the common goal of the legislator and of the employers and unions was the "unionization of the works councils." A thorough analysis of the period came to the conclusion that the legislator defined the works council as "an organ of the collective agreement" (Brigl-Matthiaß [1926] 1978, 15), primarily responsible for the supervision and implementation of the collective agreements negotiated between unions and employers' associations.

After the Second World War the dual structure of interest representation through unions and works councils was reinstitutionalized with the Collective Bargaining Act of 1949 and the Works Constitution Act of 1952. But the political situation was now completely different. This time the aim of the employers and of the legislature was not to bring a revolutionary council movement under union control, but to counteract a politically united union movement *(Einheitsgewerkschaft)* that advocated nationalization of basic industries and full codetermination in line with their anticapitalist Munich Program of 1949. What was on the agenda now was a neutralization of the works councils and their separation from the unions. When the conservative majority under Adenauer passed the Works Constitution Act in the Bundestag, it was against fierce opposition from the labor movement. The Deutscher Gewerkschaftsbund (DGB)— the national union confederation—spoke of a "black day in the development of democracy" in Germany. The unions objected especially to the denial of full parity of representation on the supervisory board (unlike in the coal and steel industries, where parity had been instituted in 1951, for all other industries only one-third representation was enacted), the tight limits on the councils' codetermination rights on economic matters, and regulations that kept the unions out of the workplace and insulated the works councils from their influence.[1]

When the Social-Liberal coalition under Chancellor Willy Brandt pushed ahead with its policy of social reforms, amendment of the Works Constitution Act in 1972 was a central objective. The employers saw an erosion of managerial prerogatives and spoke of a "trade union state" (Gewerkschaftsstaat) about to destroy free enterprise and strangle the economy. This was certainly a political statement which greatly exaggerated the fears of the employers. Although

---

1. After the battle was lost for the unions, a leading and influential union intellectual, Victor Agartz, drastically phrased the view of the Left: if the union movement still wanted to achieve its goals, it must chase the Bundestag into the Rhine (Pirker 1979, 282).

the works councils' co-determination rights on social and personnel matters were strengthened, co-determination was not extended to financial and economic matters. And although the access of the unions to the workplace and their links with the works councils were improved, the formal independence of the councils and their exclusive jurisdiction over interest representation at the plant level were not affected.

In the course of time, the industrial relations actors have learned to live with works councils; in fact, they have used and adjusted them in line with their goals. Unions had to accept and cooperate with a workplace institution that was not an integral part of their organization and had its own constituency. Employers had to accept that broad areas of managerial decision making had become an arena of joint regulation. The facts of industrial life forced management to change its style and become willing to cooperate with the works councils, whereas the councils had to learn the rules of co-management by transcending their collective-voice function and taking responsibility for productivity and economic success.

There are three main challenges to the status quo. The first is that works councils are now the pivotal institution of the German industrial relations system, their position vis-à-vis the union having been continually strengthened. What consequences will this have for the future role of unions within the dual system of interest representation? Second, the world of business is undergoing profound changes in market environment and production spheres. New networks of cooperation and producer-supplier relations, as well as joint ventures and transnational conglomerates, blur the demarcation lines of the traditional business unit which the law defined as the realm of the works council. What strains are put on the works council by the dual development of globalization on the one hand and decentralization on the other? Third, what will be the consequences for the works council if the new models of management-initiated direct participation at the workplace spread over the economy?

3.2   Institutional Base and Legal Rights

German works councils are representative, encompassing, and mandatory in the private sector (manufacturing and services). A different system of staff representation exists in the public sector, which provides for staff councils with somewhat fewer powers than works councils.

Works council members are elected by the whole workforce of establishments with five or more permanent employees. Companies with more than one establishment have central works councils, composed of delegates of the establishment-level works councils. A works council for a group of companies *(Konzernbetriebsrat)* is to be formed if requested by the works councils of subsidiaries employing at least 75 percent of the group's workforce. Wage earners and salaried employees are represented according to their numerical

Table 3.1   **Works Council Elections, 1965–90**

Year	Number of Establishments Participating	Elected Council Members	Percentage Female	Percentage Foreign
1965	23,813	142,672	11.0	–
1968	24,902	142,412	11.4	–
1972	29,298	173,670	13.5	2.2
1975	34,059	191,015	15.7	2.6
1978	35,294	194,455	17.1	3.1
1981	36,307	199,125	19.3	3.3
1984	35,343	190,193	20.0	3.1
1987	34,807	189,292	20.5	4.5
1990	33,012	183,680	23.5	4.6

Source: DGB.

strength. Employers and senior executives *(leitende Angestellte)*[2] are not represented by works councils. It is estimated that no more than 2 percent of all employees are *leitende Angestellte* in the sense of the law.

There are no official figures about the actual number of works councils. The DGB collects data on all establishments with an affiliated union present, and the Ministry of Labor regards the DGB figures as giving a fairly correct picture of the real distribution. According to the DGB, some 180,000 members of works councils were elected in more than 33,000 establishments in the 1990 elections (table 3.1). There are no exact figures on the number of establishments that are legally eligible to have a works council; hence, the percentage of eligible establishments and workers that are covered by the works council system can only be estimated, and it is believed that about 35 percent of establishments that could have a works council have one. Establishments without a works council are almost exclusively small firms with fewer than 100 or, more typically, fewer than 50 employees. The percentage of total employment covered by the works council system is therefore much higher than the percentage of establishments. It is estimated that about 70 percent of the eligible workforce is covered by works councils.

Data are also collected by the Deutsche Angestellten Gewerkschaft

2. *Leitende Angestellte* (senior executives, senior managers, or leading personnel, as the term is sometimes translated; the official translation of the Works Constitution Act speaks simply of "executive staff") are persons "who under their contract of employment and by their status in the company or establishment (1) are entitled on their own responsibility to engage and dismiss employees on behalf of the establishment or one of its departments; or (2) are endowed with general authority (power of procuration) or full power of representation or power to sign *(Prokura),* the latter also being important in relation to the employer; or (3) regularly carry out other duties which are important for the existence and development of the company or an establishment and fulfillment of which requires particular experience and knowledge, if, in doing so, they either essentially make decisions on their responsibility or substantially influence these decisions; this may also be the case with stipulated procedures, particularly those based on legal provisions, plans or guidelines and when cooperating with other executive staff" (Works Constitution Act, section 5(3)).

Table 3.2   **Union Representation on Works Councils, 1965–90 (%)**

Year	DGB A	DGB B	DAG and Others A	DAG and Others B	Nonunion A	Nonunion B
1965	82.7	–	4.3	–	13.1	–
1968	83.1	–	3.5	–	13.4	–
1972	77.6	–	3.5	–	18.9	–
1975	77.5	67.9	3.5	14.6	18.8	17.5
1978	78.1	58.6	3.8	18.1	18.1	23.3
1981	77.5	63.2	3.9	13.5	18.6	23.3
1984	77.4	63.9	3.6	10.7	19.0	25.4
1987	76.6	65.4	3.4	7.1	20.0	27.5
1990	76.3	69.3	3.1	5.6	20.6	25.1

Sources: A, DGB; B, IW.

(DAG)—a small union of white-collar workers—and by a research institute maintained by employers, the Institut der Deutschen Wirtschaft (IW). Both institutions, however, cover significantly fewer establishments than the DGB. The DAG survey extends only to some 7,000 establishments where the DAG has members and elected representatives. The IW survey is more reliable as it is based on quota sampling by size of establishment. The IW also gradually expanded its sample, from 4,528 establishments in 1981 to 14,644 in 1990. Since the DGB does not include establishments in which DGB unions are not present, it is biased in regard to council members' union affiliation and votes gained by DGB unions. Table 3.2 therefore presents the figures from both samples.

In eligible establishments that do not have a works council, three employees or a union represented in the establishment[3] can take the initiative to call a meeting, with the aim to set up an electoral board. Alternatively, a labor court can set up such a board on application from three employees or the union; in this case, an external union official can be delegated to the electoral board. Electoral board members enjoy the same legal protection against dismissal as works council members.

Works councillors have a term of office of four years. Prior to 1989 it was three years, and prior to 1972 two years. The extension of the time in office reflects the increasing professionalization of a works councillor's role. The number of council members varies with the number of employees; establishments with 100 employees have five members, those with 500 employees nine, and those with 1,000 employees 15 (table 3.3).

The larger the firm, the higher the number of full-time works councillors. Establishments with 300 to 600 employees must give full-time release to one of their nine works council members; establishments with more than 1,000

3. To be legally "represented" in an establishment a union need have no more than one member.

Table 3.3   **Legal Number of Works Council Members by Size of Establishment**

Size of Establishment (number of employees)	Council Members	Released Full-time
5–20	1	–
21–50	3	–
51–150	5	–
151–300	7	–
301–600	9	1
601–1,000	11	2
1,001–2,000	15	3
2,001–3,000	19	4
3,001–4,000	23	5
4,001–5,000	27	6
5,001–7,000	29	7–8
7,001–9,000	31	9–10
9,001–12,000	33	11–14
12,001–15,000	35[a]	15–18[b]

Source: Works Constitution Act, sections 9 and 38.
[a]Two further members for every additional 3,000 employees.
[b]One further member to be released for every additional 2,000 employees.

employees must release three members; and establishments with more than 5,000 employees must release at least seven members (table 3.3). Other, more favorable arrangements can be made by collective agreement between unions and employers' associations, or by a works agreement between works council and employer. Volkswagen, for example, has a works agreement that provides for the full-time release of all works council members.

The numerous and effective participation rights of German works councils are tied to a general obligation to cooperate with management in "a spirit of mutual trust" for "the good of the employees and of the establishment" (Works Constitution Act, section 2(1)). The council is required to negotiate "with a serious desire to reach agreement" (section 74(1)); "acts of industrial warfare" as well as "activities that interfere with operations or imperil the peace of the establishment" are inadmissible (section 74(2)). Works councils are also obliged to observe confidentiality of information. Matters defined by the employer as "trade or business secrets" may not be shared with the workforce. In fact, these rigid regulations can be and have been circumvented informally without resulting in legal action.

The works council's participation rights include:

1. *Co-determination rights on social matters,* including principles of remuneration, introduction of new payment methods, fixing of job and bonus rates and performance-related pay, allocation of working hours, regulation of overtime and reduced working hours, leave arrangements and vacation plans, and

the introduction and use of technical devices designed to monitor worker performance (section 87);

2. *Co-determination rights on personnel matters,* especially questionnaires and testing methods and guidelines for recruitment, transfer, up- and downgrading, and dismissals (sections 94 and 95);

3. *Veto rights on individual staff movements,* such as hiring, grading, transfer, and dismissal—this right, however, is limited to specified cases (sections 99 and 102);

4. *Information and consultation rights over personnel planning* and over changes in work processes, the working environment, and jobs; a full co-determination right only exists when these changes "are in obvious contradiction to the established findings of ergonomics" and prove to be "a special burden for the employees" (sections 90 and 91);

5. *Information rights on financial matters and alterations:* a standing committee of the works council, the finance committee *(Wirtschaftsausschuß)* must be informed by the employer "in full and in good time of the financial affairs of the establishment"; the same applies in case of planned changes "which may entail substantial prejudice to staff interests" (sections 106–12).

The information and consultation rights of works councils over the introduction of new technology were extended by the 1989 Works Constitution Act amendment. While the DGB wanted full co-determination, the law strengthened the consultation and information rights of both works councils and affected employees. Employers now must not only inform but also consult the works council in good time, so that its suggestions and objections can be taken into account (section 90(2)). The employer must also inform affected employees about planned measures and their effects on their jobs and formally discuss with them how their skills may be adapted to the future requirements. Employees are entitled to call in a member of the works council to the discussion (section 81(3)).

The works council has strong participation rights in the field of health and safety. Among them are: (1) information and consultation rights concerning working procedures and the working environment, as far as necessary for the prevention of accidents; (2) co-determination rights on "arrangements for the prevention of employment accidents and occupational diseases, and for the protection of health on the basis of legislation or safety regulations" (section 87(7)); and (3) rights of supervision with respect to a firm's compliance with applicable legal safety regulations.

The Work Safety Act (Arbeitssicherheitsgesetz) of 1973 requires certain firms to hire company physicians *(Betriebsärzte)* and professional safety staff *(Fachkräfte für Sicherheit)*. The law gives the works council co-determination rights on the appointment, dismissal, and task assignment of these personnel.

In general, works council participation rights are strong in social matters, less strong in personnel matters, and weak in financial and economic matters. The potential for works council intervention in managerial decision making decreases with the proximity to essential business decisions. This confirms the nature of the works council as a body designed to reconcile conflicts of interest between workforce and management. Councils can act as co-management directly on social affairs and personnel policy; in other matters they can only indirectly challenge managerial authority and the existing power relations at the workplace. For example, the council can hold up decisions on staff movements where it has veto rights, or it can withhold consent on overtime where it has co-determination rights, in order to obtain concessions on other issues.

Being subject to a general peace obligation, works councils cannot call strikes, but they may appeal to an internal arbitration board, called a *conciliation committee,* which is chaired by an outsider, or to the labor court.

There is no doubt that the works council is the most important and most effective institution of the German co-determination system.[4] Representation on the supervisory boards of large companies has mainly a supportive and supplementary function for the works council (Bamberg et al. 1987). Three-quarters of the elected workforce representatives on supervisory boards in firms under the jurisdiction of the 1976 Co-determination Act are also works councillors (Witte 1980). Being represented on the supervisory board enables the works councils of large companies to get more reliable information about economic matters and the firm's strategic goals.

The results of negotiations between the works council and management are laid down in "works agreements." In large enterprises there exist hundreds of works agreements which are sometimes extensive documents regulating the details of wage systems, working conditions, and the like. Works councils that do not negotiate works agreements are usually in a weak position. One of the rare studies on works agreements shows that 80 percent of firms with 200 or more employees had written works agreements in the early 1980s (Knuth 1982). More than four-fifths of them regulate issues on which councils have enforceable co-determination rights. However, among manufacturing firms

---

4. There are three different forms of representation at the board level in Germany: (1) equal representation in the coal and steel industry *(Montanmitbestimmung)* under legislation from 1951, (2) subparity representation in companies with more than 2,000 employees under the Co-determination Act of 1976, and (3) one-third representation in companies with 500 to 2,000 employees under the Works Constitution Act of 1952.

For the unions *Montanmitbestimmung* is the most important model of co-determination since it provides for full parity and uncontested union representation on the supervisory board. Also, one member of the executive board, the "labor director," is appointed solely by the supervisory board representatives of the employees. But coal and steel is a declining sector with no more than 30 companies and fewer than half a million employees. Subparity representation covers more than 500 companies with a total of about 4.5 million employees. It remains below full parity even though 50 percent of the supervisory board members are workforce representatives; this is because the chair, who is appointed by the shareholders, has a casting vote, and at least one employee representative must be elected from among *leitende Angestellte.* The third form of representation is the weakest and covers roughly 1,400 companies with about one million employees.

with more than 2,000 employees, 85 percent had formal bilateral regulations on matters not covered by legal rights to co-determination (Witte 1980).

In 1989 a special law was passed allowing *leitende Angestellte* (see n. 2) to elect separate representative committees *(Sprecherausschüsse der leitenden Angestellten)*. Neither the unions nor the employers' associations were in favor of a second legal representative body at the workplace. Regardless of their concerns about frictions between the two institutions, the Free Democratic party, junior partner in the coalition government, was able to gain the legislation as a boon for its client organization, the Union der leitenden Angestellte (ULA), which had lobbied for separate committees since the 1960s. The ULA represents some 48,000 middle managers, roughly 10 percent of the total, mainly in the chemical, metal-manufacturing, and electrical industries.

The first elections to the new *Sprecherausschüsse* took place in 1990. Election may be held in establishments with at least 10 eligible voters if requested by a majority of these. A survey by the IW covering 568 committees with 2,854 members reports a turnout of 88 percent. More than 80 percent of those elected did not stand as candidates of a trade union or professional association, and only 3 percent of the elected members were women (Niedenhoff 1991).

3.3   Works Councils and Unions

As legal institutions works councils are formally independent of unions and have their own constituency, being elected not by union members only but by the entire workforce of an establishment. Nevertheless, most works councillors are loyal union members with close ties to their union. In practice unions and works councils depend on each other. Unions supply works councils with information and expertise through educational courses or furnish them direct advice through union officials. Works councils, in turn, are pillars of "union security": union members are usually recruited by works councillors who are, contrary to the legal provisions, often regarded as workplace union representatives.[5] This makes the works councils indispensable for the unions and adds to their power vis-à-vis union officials and headquarters. That power, in turn, is checked by the fact that election and reelection to a works council usually depends on being nominated on a trade union list.

The majority of works council members are elected on lists of unions affiliated to the DGB, although in some industries members of DGB unions make up only a minority of elected works councillors (table 3.2). Establishments with a majority of DAG or unorganized works councillors are usually found in the banking and insurance, retail, catering, hotel, and food processing industries. There are also some big companies in the computer and media industries, such as Siemens, IBM, Nixdorf, and Bertelsmann, with low union density of

---

5. IG Metall, the German metalworkers' union, estimates that 97 percent of all new members are recruited by works councillors.

about 10 to 15 percent—which, however, does not necessarily imply that union members are in the minority on the works council.

As to the different bargaining domains of unions and works councils, the activities of the latter generally relieve the unions of the representation of local and sectional interests. Grievances and local disputes are also usually settled by the works council in such a way that the union is relieved of the representation of particular group interests, allowing the union to concentrate on common interests, for example, higher wages and shorter working hours. Recent developments have brought about a modification of this general pattern of the division of labor between the two institutions as traditional demarcations have become blurred.

During the 1960s and 1970s it was usual for works councils in large companies to negotiate informally with management about additional wage increases after conclusion of an industrywide wage agreement, although this practice was not authorized by the law. Matters settled in collective agreements can legally be regulated by works agreements only if the collective agreement expressly authorizes supplementary work agreements by an "opening clause."

As early as the 1970s, important collective agreements on working conditions and new technology made use of opening clauses, by mandating supplementary works agreements to allow for the flexible implementation of general, industrywide rules. The two most prominent examples were the 1973 collective agreement on "humanization of work" in the metal industry and the 1978 agreement on new technology in printing. Both laid down general rules on working conditions that were to be worked out in detail by works councils and management in supplementary works agreements. This tendency toward local co-determination complementing and supplementing union bargaining at the industry level increased with the flexible working hours policy of the 1980s. More than 10,000 works agreements were negotiated in the metal industry after the 1984 settlement that followed the strike for the 35-hour workweek. The downside of this is that works councils increasingly complain about the burdens imposed on them, demanding an extension of the services provided to them by the unions and more full-time works councillors. Unions, however, are short of staff for delivering extensive advice to works councils on their local activities.

In principle, a stable coalition between works councils and external unions has developed on the basis of a division of labor in the representation of interests that has been characterized by Streeck (1979) as a "contradictory unity." Its stability requires that a sufficient number of loyal trade unionists are elected as works councillors. For this reason the results of the council elections are of primary importance for the unions. Challenges may come from two sides: from competing unions and unorganized groups mobilizing protest votes and from oppositional groups within the trade union itself that demand a more militant or, to the contrary, more moderate policy.

As to the first possible challenge, DGB-affiliated unions have been success-

Table 3.4   **Union Representation on Works Councils by Industry, 1990 (%)**

Industry	DGB	DAG and Others	Nonunion
Metal manufacturing	81.1	2.2	16.7
Chemicals	85.5	1.3	13.2
Construction	72.2	0.6	27.2
Retail, banking, and insurance	55.8	9.9	34.3
Mining and power generation	96.1	1.8	2.1
Food, drink, and tobacco	78.4	1.2	20.4
Textiles and clothing	82.6	0.9	16.5
Printing and publishing	76.3	3.2	20.5
Wood and plastics	83.1	0.2	16.7
Agriculture	52.9	2.8	44.3
Leather	82.7	1.0	16.3

Source: DGB.

ful in filling works council seats with their own members (table 3.2): according to union sources more than three-quarters, and according to the employers more than two-thirds, of all elected works councillors belong to a DGB union, showing a much higher rate of unionization among works councillors than among workers. Only two unions, in the retail, banking, and insurance sector and in the agricultural sector, have to concede large numbers of council seats to competing unions and unorganized groups (table 3.4).

Support for internal union opposition is quantitatively marginal. Alternative union lists are typically presented by active *Vertrauensleute* or militant union dissenters in large companies. They usually demand a break with "social partnership" and support more democratic nomination and election procedures. Since the early 1970s, challenges of this kind have emerged in large establishments of the automobile, steel, shipbuilding, and chemical industries. In several cases, oppositional trade unionists have scored spectacular successes. In a few establishments, foreign workers have also challenged the official union lists following complaints about underrepresentation.

On average in a large establishment, four or five lists of candidates compete at the works council election: two from the respective DGB-affiliated unions— one for the blue-collar constituency and the other for the white-collar group[6]— a DAG list for white-collar workers, a list of "independent" nonunion candidates, and sometimes a list from the Christian Union Federation (Christlicher Gewerkschaftsbund), a numerically unimportant splinter organization.

Officials of unions represented in an establishment have legal rights of access to the establishment and may attend works council meetings after giving

---

6. The Works Constitution Act treats blue-collar and white-collar workers as separate groups, each of which elects its council members by separate secret ballot. It is also possible, however, to hold a joint election if this is approved by a majority of each group. This is the usual practice in two-thirds of the establishments with works councils.

notification to the management. They must also be invited to attend council meetings if requested by one-fourth of the members of the council.

Unions also have their own representational body at the workplace, at least in the most important industries and establishments. This is called the *Vertrauensleutekörper,* the assembly of elected or appointed union stewards *(Vertrauensmänner* or *Vertrauensfrauen).* Usually union stewards are elected by the union members in a department or work group of between 30 and 50 workers. Their functions are limited and mostly include services for the organization, such as information and instruction for union members, recruitment, and the distribution of union material. Stewards are also expected to support the unionized works councillors. In many cases, *Vertrauensleute* are both the messengers of the works council and the mouthpieces of work groups. In cases of conflict with the employer, they function as informal organizers of industrial action.

In the past IG Metall and other unions tried to build up the *Vertrauensleute* as a counterweight to the *Betriebsräte,* causing rivalry and conflict between the two. In the late 1960s and early 1970s, there were strands of internal union opposition with militant *Vertrauensleute* as their backbone. Especially in IG Metall and IG Chemie (the chemical workers' union), rank-and-file activists organized unofficial strikes, opposed established works councils,and became the representatives of discontented groups among the membership. But the rivalry between *Vertrauensleute* and *Betriebsräte* ended with a victory for the latter. This was due to the firm legal establishment of the works councils and, not least, their strategic position for the recruitment of union members. Today it is no longer control but support of council activities that unions expect from *Vertrauensleute.* Since most unions have made the unionized works councillors ex officio members of the *Vertrauensleutekörper,* in most establishments the executive committee of the *Vertrauensleute* is dominated by works councillors.

In recent research covering 33 establishments with more than 300 employees in the North Bavarian engineering industry, Schmidt and Trinczek (1991) distinguish three typical patterns of division of labor between unions and works councils:

Works councillors of *type A* (fewer than 20 percent) see themselves primarily as union activists and more as representatives of the working class as a whole than of a particular workforce. Their loyalty to the union is nearly unshakable, many of them simultaneously holding office in union committees on the local, regional, or national level. Whenever the union calls for industrial action, they lend their support by initiating warning strikes and imposing overtime bans. Recruiting new union members is a job of great importance for them, but even stronger emphasis is placed on safeguarding and supporting the organization and activities of the *Vertrauensleute,* whose resolutions are loyally respected.

Works councillors of *type B* (about one-half of the sample) consider the interests of the workforce and the firm to be just as important as those of the union. In principle, while being loyal members of their union, they always look for possibilities for compromise and mediation between conflicting demands. Where compromise seems impossible, they side with the workforce. Unlike type A, they are not strongly committed to the union line on warning strikes and overtime bans. But they do take seriously the recruitment of new union members, regarding it as a duty to the union in return for its services. Considerably less priority is given to supporting the *Vertrauensleute.*

Works councillors of *type C* (roughly 30 percent) have an instrumental orientation toward the union. They have no ideological barriers against attending educational courses offered by employers or "independent" institutions. For them, the interests of the workforce, or even the firm, come first since the firm's prosperity is seen as the fundamental basis of their policy. Often they complain about the union's poor knowledge of the particularities of their situation and about the one-sidedness of the union's political orientation. Low union density in their establishments is a comfortable argument for them to back their claim of being representatives of the whole workforce and not of a union. No special effort is invested in union recruitment, and little support is provided for *Vertrauensleute* activities.

3.4   Works Councils and Employers

German works councils are elected by and composed of employees only. They meet with the employer at least once a month. The employer bears all the costs of a council's activities. According to a survey by the IW, the average cost of the works constitution, including council elections, conciliation committees, and labor courts, amounts to DM 440 per employee per year. The bulk of this (DM 285) pays for the day-to-day activities of the works councils (Niedenhoff 1987b). In large companies, works councils have not only their own offices but also secretarial staff, and sometimes even expert staff with university degrees.

All companies with more than 100 permanent employees must set up a finance committee *(Wirtschaftsausschuß)*. Its members are appointed by the works council, and it may also include senior executives. Its monthly meetings are appointed by the works council, and it may also include senior executives. Its monthly meetings are attended by the employer, who must inform the committee in full and in good time of the financial affairs of the establishment and their implications for employment and long-term personnel policies.

A survey of 315 works councils in the printing, publishing, electrical engineering, and ceramics industries shows what councils regard as the most important matters they must deal with; respondents could choose three out of a list of nine items (table 3.5). A cluster analysis divides the councils in three groups with typical clusters of priorities: (1) *traditional tasks*—34 percent of the councils mention personnel matters, classification into wage grades, and health and safety as their main set of activities; (2) *rationalization measures*—38 percent of the councils concentrate on technical change and further educa-

Table 3.5   Main Tasks of Works Councils

Tasks	Percentage of Councils
Personnel matters	68
Technical change	47
Health and safety	44
Classification in wage groups	42
Working hours	33
Overtime	26
Further training	15
Initial vocational training	9
Social benefits	7

Source: Hans-Böckler-Stiftung (1992).

tion; and (3) *working-time questions*—28 percent are mainly concerned with questions of working hours and overtime.

The three groups do not seem to correlate with structural variables like economic sector, size of company, or recent changes in employment level. It seems rather that each firm's specific conditions determine a council's main tasks. Plausibly, technical change often evokes activities for further training, and managerial efforts to attain greater flexibility call for council action on working time.

Overtime is a very important issue. Works councils usually do not refuse their consent when management wants employees to work longer; many employees like the extra pay. Since overtime is subject to co-determination, however, works councils frequently use it for package deals to get concessions from management on other matters. If a workforce reduction is in the offing, councils usually do not agree to overtime unless management reveals its plans and offers a "socially acceptable" solution. Sometimes councils ban overtime during wage negotiations if their union calls for it. In some industries, especially those organized by the metalworkers and the printers, most councils follow their union's line not to extend working time into the weekend; this does not preclude occasional extra Saturday shifts in manufacturing and regular Sunday shifts in newspaper editing and printing.

Legally mandated cooperation with the employer does not exclude conflict and disagreement, but in most cases cooperation and trust between works council and employer prevail. Employers' acceptance of the works council and its tasks has generally increased, and the uncertainties and resistance raised by the amendment of the Works Constitution Act in 1972 has largely disappeared in subsequent years. This is the general finding of a panel study investigating the labor relations of some 60 manufacturing firms between the mid-1970s and the early 1990s. The earlier survey (Kotthoff 1981), carried out shortly after the 1972 amendment, revealed a rather negative picture of works council relations with management. Effective interest representation was found in only one-third of the establishments, while the in the others works council activities were classified as poor and insufficient. Fifteen years later, the follow-up study (Kotthoff 1993) showed a picture that had changed remarkably for the better: now in two-thirds of the establishments Kotthoff found effective interest representation. Improvements in labor relations have taken place in most establishments. Even under the stress of economic recession and pressures for industrial restructuring, the works constitution had become widely accepted as the most important piece of machinery for conflict resolution. Kotthoff concludes that management has come to accept what he calls the "spirit of co-determination."

Kotthoff's findings are confirmed by a recent study using qualitative interviews with 111 senior managers (Eberwein and Tholen 1990). No fewer than 96 percent of those interviewed had a positive attitude toward the activities of the works council. Managers valued in particular the council's collective voice function (table 3.6). Some even expressed the opinion that, "if the works council did not exist, it had to be invented."

Quite frequently, managers consciously take advantage of the confidence the works council commands among the workforce, asking it to share responsibility not only in difficult personnel matters but also for policies and strategies aimed at more ambitious goals. The advice given to employers by their research institute, the IW, is to consider the works council as a "factor of production" and as serving essential functions as an agent of information and communication. It saves time and money to cooperate with the works council as a partner and thereby improve the working atmosphere (Niedenhoff 1990).

If a company goes through economic difficulties, works councils usually cooperate with necessary adjustment measures. Among the most common ways of coping with slack demand is employment reduction by jointly approved early retirement schemes or financial incentives for voluntary redundancies. Tolerated and sometimes even supported by the works council, management in some mass production industries may also offer foreign workers from outside the European Community financial compensation for giving up their jobs—in the 1980s in addition to the incentives provided under the 1983

Table 3.6   **How Managers See the Works Council**

Response	Percentage of Managers
Important for management as a partner for discussion	50
Important for the representation of the interests of the workforce	29
Important for conveying information between management and workforce	11
Used as part of the personnel department	6
Useless, even damaging	4
Total	100

Source: Eberwein and Tholen (1990).

legislation to encourage foreign workers to return to their native countries. It is also true that, at times, works councils agree to temporary employment contracts for new hires if they fear a reduction of the workforce in the near future.

In general, works councils do not oppose management policies for the modernization and rationalization of production; in fact, they support such policies if they are convinced that they can improve the firm's potential for economic survival and success and if they are assured that two essentials are met: no involuntary dismissals and no wage reductions subsequent to internal redeployment (Kern and Schumann 1984). The way in which work organization and the production system were rationalized and modernized in German firms has improved the acceptance and strengthened the position of the works council in many companies. Although it is difficult to measure the economic effects of the works council, it is widely regarded as an important factor in accounting for the high productivity of German industry, contributing by creating and consolidating social consensus.

The 1972 amendment of the Works Constitution Act gave works councils information and consultation rights on changes in work processes, the work environment, and job design. A survey of 30 engineering companies showed that over 90 percent of the works councillors and over three-quarters of the managers were satisfied with the legislation (Kreikebaum and Herbert 1990). Although it does not offer strong participation rights, its practical relevance is highly appreciated by both sides, even though many works councillors would prefer full-blown co-determination rights in these matters.

There is no single pattern of labor relations across industries as far as rationalization and restructuring processes are concerned. Kern and Schumann (1984) found a number of differences between the automobile, machine tools, and chemical industries. But these are differences only of degree and in the intensity of information, consultation, and cooperation. In the chemical industry, the works councils regard themselves as partners of management and do not interfere in its modernization strategy; their activities are centered on social matters and health and safety questions. In the automobile industry, works councils are much more involved in the modernization of the production system. Their role has become strongly professionalized, and works councillors are very self-confident; they are also able to extract comprehensive information from management. The basis of cooperation in this industry is a broad understanding that the restructuring of production and the labor process must serve a double goal: to increase productivity and product quality on the one hand and to improve working conditions on the other. Finally, in the machine tools industry, labor-management relations are mostly based on informal arrangements, with management playing a leading role; works councillors are less professionalized and less informed. Nevertheless, as Hildebrandt and Seltz (1989) maintain, a pattern of high-trust labor relations prevails in this industry, at least in the Baden-Württemberg region where their research was conducted and where the industry's most important firms are located.

Unfortunately, there has been no systematic research about the relations between *foreign* employers and managers and their works councils. It seems that American and British managers especially find it difficult to understand the German co-determination system. If they try to ignore it and enter in guerilla warfare with the works council, they sooner or later have to "face the facts of life." Since the respective union pays special attention to such cases, foreign firms usually cannot avoid the formation of a works council. Ultimately, they have to come to terms with the reality of an institutionalized workforce representation system endowed with legally enforceable participation rights. Some foreign employers have decided to delegate this matter entirely to their German personnel directors, leaving them complete freedom in dealing with the works council.

As in several other countries, new forms of employee involvement and participation have been introduced in Germany as part of a more sophisticated approach to human resource management. Still, German-style "participatory management" continues to differ from the Anglo-American pattern in that it does not try to displace or erode institutionalized workforce representation, but rather is complementary to it. Quality circles and teamwork are the two main models of management-led employee participation. Quality circles are problem-solving groups aimed at improving personal work behavior and motivation as well as labor relations at the workplace. Work teams aim at improved utilization of workers' abilities and experience, and at improved informal social relations among employees (Malsch 1989; Beisheim, Eckardstein, and Müller 1991).

If some unions and works councils first rejected management-led participation, especially quality circles, today their position has changed. Now, union and works council representatives often go so far as to regard them as a first step toward "co-determination at the workplace." Since the mid-1980s several works agreements on quality circles have been signed specifying the circles' composition, procedure, and agenda, as well as the role of the works council in their governance. A first content analysis (Breisig 1991) of a small sample of works agreements on quality circles covered various big companies in the automobile and chemical industries. As a rule these companies have large blue-collar workforces and high union density rates. In other firms, quality circles and similar arrangements were established unilaterally by management because works councils were either uninterested or opposed.

The few available figures on quality circles indicate that they have greatly expanded during the 1980s. A group of researchers (Antoni, Bungard, and Kübler 1990) interviewed the personnel departments of the 100 largest companies (measured by sales) in 1985–86 and 1989–90. In the latter period, they found that quality circles and similar problem-solving groups had been established in 50 percent of the companies, as compared to 40 percent in 1985–86; another 11 percent were planning to establish them. Quality circles are to be found in production (38 percent of the firms), marketing (12 percent), R&D

(12 percent), and personnel and training (10 percent). Companies with quality circles had had them for eight years on average and still thought highly of them. Opposition to quality circles comes primarily from middle management; works councils were reported to be the least opposed. The latter finding is confirmed by Kotthoff's follow-up study, in which he noticed resentment of quality circles only among weak works councils. Strong works councils were found to be self-confident enough to accept a role in the institutionalization and regulation of quality circles.

As to teamwork, companies in the automobile industry in particular are profoundly restructuring production and work organization. Alarmed by the MIT study (Womack, Jones, and Roos 1990), which showed large productivity gaps with Japanese and even American automobile producers, nearly all German companies have started or are planning to introduce teamwork. Most ambitious of all is Opel, the German subsidiary of General Motors, which originally planned to involve all its employees in teamwork by the end of 1992. Daimler Benz (Mercedes) intends to restructure production work more gradually and to introduce teamwork for roughly 50 percent of the direct workforce by the mid-1990s. Volkswagen, which has an extended network of quality circles, called VW-Zirkel, started with semiautonomous working groups in some smaller establishments and is now on the brink of introducing this type of work organization at one of the six production lines in their main plant, Wolfsburg. In most companies, management and works councils have signed works agreements on teamwork providing for extra time for team discussions, the possibility for teams to elect a group spokesperson, and better pay for more integrated and more flexible work tasks.

The question of initial and further vocational training is of paramount importance not only for the economic success of the firm but also for the market situation and earnings prospects of its employees. German unions have always paid close attention to initial vocational training and have recently intensified their activities on further training. Unions played an active part in the modernization of the vocational training system in industries like building and construction and mechanical and electrical engineering (Streeck et al. 1987). Several unions have also negotiated collective agreements on further training and retraining that, according to Mahnkopf (1990, 7), serve as "a substitute for the lack of [legal] co-determination rights" in this area.

In Germany, apprenticeship training is regulated by the Vocational Training Act of 1969. Most apprentices, who account for roughly 65 percent of each age cohort, spend three years in a program that involves three or four days per week of on-the-job training and one or two days of education in a public vocational school. Training is administered by "chambers of commerce and industry" or "chambers of artisans," with compulsory membership of all employers and legally mandated participation of "employee delegates"—mostly unionized—who have a say in all training-related matters. Works councils also participate in the governance of the training system, as the law gives them consultation rights on the establishment and equipment of training facilities and co-determination rights on the implementation of training programs and the appointment and removal of full-time training staff. In addition, councils supervise the employer's compliance with all applicable training regulations, in the same way in which they monitor compliance with other rules and statutes.

Works council participation rights in further training are still more extensive, partly because of the weaker legal regulation in this area. (It has already been mentioned that the unions try to fill this gap with collective agreements.) Under the Works Constitution Act, works councils have co-determination rights on the content and procedure of retraining and further training and on the selection of trainees; special employment contracts for trainees also need the consent of the works council. As Streeck et al. (1987, 21–22) point out, works councils as a rule take their participation rights seriously. Most works councils of larger firms have set up special training committees (*Bildung-sausschüsse*). According to a survey of 315 works councils in four industries, training committees are found rarely in firms with fewer than 300 employees, but frequently in firms with more than 1,000 employees (table 3.7).

Works council training committees deal mostly with matters of apprenticeship training. For them this field is more manageable than the less structured and "newer" area of further training. Works councils are often not competent enough and lack the time to get into the subject deeply, and they need and expect more advice from their union. This, however, does not mean that they regard further training as a negligible matter or are unaware of its increasing relevance for survival and success in product and labor markets. In their daily activities, councils emphasize the general need for expanding opportunities for further training on and off the job, and they encourage workers to keep their qualifications up to date. They also negotiate with management on release from work for training and on the kind of training measures to be provided to specific groups of employees (Kühnlein and Kohlhoff 1991, 134). Discussions between works councils and managers on training-related questions are frequent; in the survey mentioned above, 80 percent of works councils reported

Table 3.7   **Works Councils with Training Committees by Size of Establishment, 1989–91 (%)**

Size of Establishment (number of employees)	Percentage of Councils
Up to 300	12
301–600	45
601–999	63
1000–1999	77
2,000 or more	88
All works councils	56

Source: Hans-Böckler-Stiftung (1992).

such talks. Written agreements, however, are less frequent: only 40 percent had negotiated works agreements on training matters, and the density of formal regulation was found to be unevenly distributed between industries (table 3.8).

In the 1960s and 1970s most unions negotiated "protection against rationalization" agreements. These were basically defensive, providing for financial compensation if retraining measures for workers threatened by redundancy were not possible. Since the late 1970s some unions—among them those representing metalworkers, printers, construction workers, and chemical workers—have fought, and sometimes even struck, for collective agreements taking a more forward-looking approach. The most extensive regulations of this kind are contained in an agreement for the metal industry in Baden-Württemberg (the famous Lohn- and Gehaltsrahmentarifvertrag I). The agreement commits the employer to ascertain regularly the establishment's skill needs, given ongoing and future technological and organizational changes, and to consult once a year with the works council on the matter. The works council for its part is to assess the training needs from the perspective of the workers and is entitled to discuss the results and its related proposals with the employer. Subsequent to this, the employer must put forward a skill development plan *(Qualifikationsplan)* for the establishment.

Three and a half years after the agreement had been signed, a research team found that there was still a considerable discrepancy between rules and reality: two-thirds of the managers and three-quarters of the works councils were not aware of the existence of a *Qualifikationsplan* (Bahnmüller, Bispinck, and Schmidt 1992, 347). Still, the general conclusion suggested by the body of existing research is that unions and work councils know the increasing necessity of further training for firms and employees and that they want to participate more actively in this expanding field but need more competence, time, and experience.

Table 3.8   **Works Agreements on Training Matters by Industry, 1989–91 (%)**

Industry	Percentage of Firms
Printing	44
Electrical engineering	49
Ceramics	17
Publishing	17
All works councils	40

Source: Hans-Böckler-Stiftung (1992).

3.5   Works Councils and Workers

Being representative bodies, works councils are influenced by their constituents mainly through the selection of their members.[7] The high turnout at council elections (table 3.9) shows that workers are keenly interested in their results. A comparison with other elections reveals that turnout in council elections is second only to the general national election (Niedenhoff 1987a). In the late 1950s and 1960s participation oscillated around 75 percent; in 1975, after the amendment of the Works Constitution Act, it jumped to over 80 percent; and in 1990 it fell again by several percentage points (table 3.9). As a rule, participation among blue-collar workers is slightly higher than among salaried employees, and the drop in turnout in 1990 was less significant for the former group.

The Works Constitution Act stipulates that wage earners and salaried employees must be represented on the works council according to their relative numerical strength (section 10). Nothing, however, is said about the representation of women and foreign workers. Both groups are clearly underrepresented, although their shares in works councils seats have slightly increased recently (see table 3.1). The traditional social profile of works council members is male (about 80 percent) and native German, with a standard full-time employment contract as a skilled worker or as a supervisory and technical staff member. In fact, for some of its members, the works council serves as a career ladder for political and professional advancement. Experienced council members may either move on to political office in a party, a union, or a local council or change over to a management job. The latter is more likely among white-collar works councillors. Some recent studies recognize that white-collar employees have become more accepting of collective interest representation through the works council—a pattern that has been observed especially in high-tech enterprises (Kotthoff 1992).

A problematic relationship continues to exist between works councils and foreign workers. Of a representative sample of the foreign population in Germany (Friedrich-Ebert-Stiftung 1981, 1986), only one-third of the foreign workers regarded the activities of their works councils as satisfactory. Works councils were perceived as unfamiliar with the problems of foreign workers, and as mainly representing the interests of the German workforce or the employer. In fact, foreign workers generally run a higher risk of redundancy than German workers. Their rate of unemployment is higher, and dismissals are twice as frequent as among German workers (Jaeger 1989). Studies about employment reduction in the automobile (Dohse 1976; Dombois 1982) and the steel and coal industries (Schäfer 1985) found that under the threat of mass

---

7. Councils are, however, legally required every three months to call a "works meeting" of all employees, to which the council must report on its activities.

Table 3.9   **Turnout at Works Council Elections (%)**

Year	Percentage Turnout
1959	73.4
1962	76.2
1965	73.9
1968	73.5
1972	72.1
1975	79.1
1978	81.3
1981	79.9
1984	83.7
1987	83.3
1990	78.4

Source: IW.

redundancies the works councils do not actively oppose, and often tacitly approve, "soft" discriminatory measures aimed at filtering out foreign workers from outside the European Community, especially if this can help them avoid redundancies among German workers.

3.6   Outlook

Co-determination, we said at the outset, is a learning process; more precisely, it is a process during which individual and corporate actors learn to take into account the strategies and goals of their counterparts and thereby modify their own strategies and goals. The practices, rules, and institutions that emerge from their antagonistic, competing, or joint actions differ from their individual goals; they are the combined result of all the various actors' intentions. In this sense, the industrial relations system can be understood as an institutional order that is—partly tacitly and partly explicitly—negotiated and adjusted to changes in the balance of power and in environmental conditions.

In the German case, the dual system of interest representation was shaped over more than half a century during which its actors, institutions, and levels of rule making changed in their relevance and function according to the prevailing constellations of economic, political, and social forces. The strains of contemporary changes in the world economy and in the organization of production have not only not destroyed the dual system but have confirmed its stability and flexibility. Nevertheless, certain remarkable institutional changes and shifts have occurred.

Today, the position of the works council is much stronger than it was in the 1950s and 1960s. In response to economic and technological change, the major German unions have developed a coherent workplace strategy *(Betriebspolitik)* under which they try to attain qualitative objectives—on matters like work organization and training—through the works councils. The links between works councils and unions are today largely ones of mutual support; only a minority of works councillors regard themselves as union agents. While the ties between unions and their members are becoming looser, the relationship between works councils and unions seems to be growing closer. If, as can be expected, the tendency toward a "disaggregation of industrial relations" (Crouch 1986) continues, the responsibilities of the works councils will continue to expand; this, in turn, will increase the demand for union support and expertise. The unions of the future will, therefore, be less bargaining machines than support organizations for the works councils.

After a period of skepticism of and opposition to employer-sponsored participation and involvement schemes, many works councils now actively cooperate with the kind of human resource management that usually accompanies comprehensive restructuring of production. If the rationale for this is that works councils will increasingly move into the role of co-manager, two other developments could reinforce this. One is the gradual change in the composition of works councils in favor of technical staff and salaried employees. Their professional interests and attitudes are more easily reconciled with managerial goals. The other, ironically, is the transformation in East German companies. Since there is no tradition in East Germany of open conflict, the works councils that replaced the old workplace union committees *(Betriebsgewerkschaftslei-tungen)* have difficulties finding their new role as "conflict partner," particularly since the struggle for economic survival drives them into collaboration with management to a much higher degree than their colleagues in the West.

As is widely known, the German industrial relations system is highly formalized and representative, with industrial unions and works councils accustomed to acting on behalf of the workers *(Stellvertreterpolitik)*. Today these traditional actors face the emergence of work groups and production teams. While previously participation, co-determination, and collective bargaining were exclusively the business of representative institutions, now, with a larger space for more actors and a greater variety of patterns and coalitions, centrifugal tendencies are likely to become more effective. Sooner or later the structural characteristics of the German model may be modified, and the dual system might give way to a triple system, with sectoral bargaining between trade unions and employers' associations, enterprise negotiations between work councils and management, and direct participation by work groups with elected team leaders. As a result the highly formalized and strongly representative model may be softened and weakened. And there is no guarantee that the integration of the formal and representative institutions with the emerging decentralized and more informal structures will succeed.

Following major changes in the division of labor in the world economy, businesses have adopted a global perspective. Multinational mergers and joint ventures and the restructuring of the logistical chain between producer, supplier, and distributor threaten to undermine the participation rights of works councils set up for spatially unified business units within a national territory.

How can a works council exercise participation rights in an establishment for which the relevant decisions are made elsewhere? It is true that efforts are made to set up multinational European works councils, but so far their participation rights are much weaker than those of German councils and more like those of German finance committees *(Wirtschaftsausschuß)*, which have information and consultation rights only. As far as the new logistics is concerned, there are discussions about adjusting the co-determination system to the new networks between producer, supplier, and distributor. In some cases working parties of the various works councils have been created to look into the problems.

Finally, the challenge of German unification is putting the established system under considerable stress. The transfer of institutions and the extension of organizational domains from the West to the East has proceeded with fewer frictions than expected. But industrial relations practices cannot be transferred so easily. The handling of industrial disputes, labor law cases, and joint conflict management demand experience and skill, which were not cultivated under the authoritarian Communist regime. It is true that the "social partners" played a major role in the transformation from a command economy to a social market economy and in the process built something like a new *Arbeitsgemeinschaft.*[8] The social and economic problems that demand to be solved may, however, exceed their capacities. Both sides may thus feel permanently tempted to abandon their joint understanding and return to adversarial strategies.

It is also true that the old *Betriebsgewerkschaftsleitungen* in East German workplaces have been replaced by works councils. But their activities greatly differ from those of their counterparts in the West. Works councils in the East are above all concerned with the economic survival of their firms and collaborate closely with a management that must still learn its proper role. Also, many foreign investors acquiring companies from the government privatization agency, the Treuhandanstalt, lack experience with the German co-determination system. It is still likely that in the long run, the outcome in the East will gravitate toward the strong pattern of the West. But it is quite possible that the East will not end up simply as a copy of the West and that the copying will not leave the original untouched.

References

Antoni, Conny Herbert, Walter Bungard, and E. Kübler. 1990. Qualitätszirkel und ähnliche Formen der Gruppenarbeit in der Bundesrepublik Deutschland: Eine Bestandsaufnahme der Problemlösungsgruppen-Konzepte bei den 100 umsatzgrößten Indus-

---

8. The close coalition between organized business and labor after the defeat of the old regime in the First World War.

trieunternehmen. *Mannheimer Beiträge zur Wirtschafts- und Organisations-psychologie* 1:18–52.

Bahnmüller, Reinhard, Reinhard Bispinck, and Werner Schmidt. 1992. Betriebliche Personalpolitik, Weiterbildung und betriebliche Interessenvertretung: Erfahrungen aus der Metallindustrie. *WSI Mitteilungen* 45:338–48.

Bamberg, Ulrich, Michael Bürger, Birgit Mahnkopf, Helmut Martens, and Jörg Tiemann. 1987. *Aber ob die Karten voll ausgereizt sind . . . ? 10Jahre Mitbestimmungsgesetz in der Bilanz.* Cologne: Bund.

Beisheim, Margret, Dudo von Eckardstein, and Matthias Müller. 1991. Partizipative Organisationsformen und industrielle Beziehungen. In *Konfliktpartnerschaft: Akteure und Institutionen der industriellen Beziehungen,* ed. Walther Müller-Jentsch, 123–38. Munich: Hampp.

Breisig, Thomas. 1991. Betriebsvereinbarungen zu Qualitätszirkeln: Eine Inhaltsanalyse. *Die Betriebswirtschaft* 51(1):65–77.

Brigl-Matthiaß, Kurt. (1926) 1978. Das Betriebsräteproblem in der Weimarer Republik. In *Die Betriebsräte in der Weimarer Republik 2,* ed. Reinhard Crusius, Guenter Schiefelbein, and Manfred Wilke. Berlin: Olle & Wolter.

Crouch, Colin. 1986. The future prospects for trade unions in Western Europe. *Political Quarterly* 57:5–17.

Dohse, Knuth. 1976. Ausländerentlassungen beim Volkswagenwerk. *Leviathan* 4(4):485–93.

Dombois, Rainer. 1982. Beschäftigungspolitik in der Krise. In *Wohin läuft VW? Die Automobilproduction in der Krise,* ed. Reinhard Doleschal and Rainer Dombois, 273–90. Reinbek bei Hamburg: Rowohlt.

Eberwein, Wilhelm, and Jochen Tholen. 1990. *Managermentalität.* Frankfurt am Main: Frankfurter Allgemeine Zeitung.

Friedrich-Ebert-Stiftung. 1981. *Repräsentativuntersuchung '80.* Bonn: Forschungsinstitut der Friedrich-Ebert-Stiftung.

———. 1986. *Repräsentativuntersuchung '85.* Bonn: Forschungsinstitut der Friedrich-Ebert-Stiftung.

Hans-Böckler-Stiftung, ed. 1992. *Zur Situation der Aus- und Weiterbildung in der Druckindustrie, der Elektroindustrie, der fein Keramischen Industrie sowie im Verlagswesen.* Umfragen unter Betriebsräten, no. 75. Düsseldorf: Hans-Böckler-Stiftung.

Hildebrandt, Eckart, and Rüdiger Seltz. 1989. *Wandel betrieblicher Sozialverfassung durch systemische Kontrolle?* Berlin: Edition Sigma.

Jaeger, Rolf. 1989. Ausländische Arbeitnehmer, Betriebsräte und Arbeitsrecht. *Der Betriebsrat* 3:65–68.

Kern, Horst, and Michael Schumann. 1984. *Das Ende der Arbeitsteilung?* Munich: Beck.

Knuth, Matthias. 1982. Nutzung betrieblicher Mitbestimmungsrechte in Betriebsvereinbarungen. *Die Mitbestimmung* 28(6):204–208.

Kotthoff, Hermann. 1981. *Betriebsräte und betriebliche Herrschaft.* Frankfurt am Main: Campus.

———. 1992. Qualifizierte Angestellte in high-tech-Betrieben erobern den Betriebsrat. In *Organisation von Dienstleistungsarbeit,* ed. Wolfgang Littek, Ulrich Heisig, and Hans-Dieter Gondek, 179–98. Bonn and Berlin: Edition Sigma.

———. 1993. Wandel und Kontinuität betrieblicher Interessenvertretungsstrukturen: Eine Folgestudie, DFG-Abschlußbericht. Manuscript.

Kreikebaum, Hartmut, and Klaus-Jürgen Herbert. 1990. *Arbeitsgestaltung und Betriebsverfassung.* Berlin: Duncker & Humblot.

Kühnlein, Gertrud, and Angelika Kohlhoff. 1991. *Bildungschancen im Betrieb: Unter-*

suchungen zur betrieblichen Weiterbildung in der chemischen Industrie. Berlin: Edition Sigma.

Mahnkopf, Birgit. 1990. Training, further training and collective bargaining in the Federal Republic of Germany. Report for the OECD. Manuscript.

Malsch, Thomas. 1989. Flexibilisierung der Massenproduktion in der Automobilindustrie und ihre arbeitspolitischen Gestaltungsperspektiven. In *Trends betrieblicher Produktionsmechanisierung,* ed. Leo Pries, Rudi Schmidt, and Rainer Trinczek. Opladen: Westdeutscher Verlag.

Niedenhoff, Horst-Udo. 1987a. *Betriebsratswahlen. Die Betriebsräte bis 1990.* Cologne: Deutscher Instituts-Verlag.

————. 1987b. *Kosten der Mitbestimmung.* Cologne: Deutscher Instituts-Verlag.

————. 1990. Der Betriebsrat als Produktionsfaktor. In *Die Zusammenarbeit mit dem Betriebsrat,* ed. Horst-Udo Niedenhoff. Cologne: Deutscher Instituts-Verlag.

————. 1991. Die Sprecherausschußwahlen 1990. Beiträge zur Gesellschafts- und Bildungspolitik, no. 162. Cologne: Deutscher Instituts-Verlag.

Pirker, Theo. 1979. *Die Blinde Macht: Die Gewerkschaftsbewegung in der Bundesrepublik,* vols. 1 and 2. Berlin: Olle & Wolter.

Schäfer, Hermann. 1985. *Betriebliche Ausländerdiskriminierung und gewerkschaftliche Antidiskriminierungspolitik.* Berlin: Express Edition.

Schmidt, Rudi, and Rainer Trinczek. 1991. Duales System: Tarifliche und betriebliche Interessenvertretung. In *Konfliktpartnerschaft: Akteure und Institutionen der industriellen Beziehungen,* ed. Walther Müller-Jentsch, 167–99. Munich: Hampp.

Streeck, Wolfgang. 1979. Gewerkschaftsorganisation und industrielle Beziehungen. In *Sozialer Wandel in Westeuropa,* ed. Joachim Matthes, 206–26. Verhandlungen des 19. Deutschen Soziologentages in Bamberg 1982. Frankfurt am Main: Campus.

Streeck, Wolfgang, Josef Hilbert, Karl-Heinz van Kevelaer, Friederike Maier, and Hajo Weber. 1987. *Steuerung und Regulierung der beruflichen Bildung: Die Rolle der Sozialpartner in der Ausbildung und beruflichen Weiterbildung in der BR Deutschland.* Berlin: Edition Sigma.

Witte, Eberhard. 1980. Das Einflußpotential der Arbeitnehmer als Grundlage der Mitbestimmung. Die Betriebswirtschaft 40:3–26, 541–59.

Womack, James P., Daniel Jones, and Daniel Roos. 1990. *The machine that changed the world.* New York: Rowson.

4 The Netherlands: From Paternalism to Representation

Jelle Visser

4.1 Introduction

There are three main reasons why the Dutch works council presents a case of comparative interest. First, we can study three different councils in the same country. Like Italy, the Netherlands displays discontinuity in the tasks, function, and organization of employee representation in firms. The mandatory works council of 1950 was designed as a channel of communication between employer and employees and was embedded in a paternalistic view of labor-management relations. The law of 1971 gave the works council a dual role: representation of employee interests was added to the task of contributing to the optimal functioning of the firm. The reform of 1979, finally, removed the employer from the council's chair. Advisory and co-determination rights were broadened, and a larger array of legal instruments was placed in the council's hands. In short, the Dutch case presents us with an opportunity to study the effects of institutional reform within the relatively invariant structural, institutional, and cultural context of one country.

The second reason for a closer inspection of the Dutch case is that it allows us to evaluate the impact of institutional intervention under adverse economic conditions. The 1979 reform came on the eve of what became the worst economic and employment crisis since 1945. How did the new "employee-only" works council assert itself? What was its contribution in defining and defending employee interests? How did the new council affect the performance of Dutch businesses?

A third point of interest derives from the contrast with Germany. In their current forms, works councils in the two countries are rather similar in their strong institutionalization and legal facilitation. The systems of industrial rela-

Jelle Visser is senior lecturer in sociology at the Universiteit von Amsterdam.

tions in the two countries are also quite comparable. Collective agreements are negotiated between trade unions and employers' associations at the level of industrial branches and take precedence over local (firm-level) agreements, though there are now more exceptions to this situation in the multinational firm sector in the Netherlands. But unlike the German union movement after 1945, Dutch unions did not overcome their ideological and religious divisions, and in most firms and industries we find three or more unions. Moreover, since the decline in overall union density from nearly 40 percent in the mid-1970s to 25 percent at the end of the 1980s, the Netherlands constitutes a case of weakening unionism, if not union weakness. In particular, in manufacturing, where the German density rate is double the Dutch rate, we should be able to evaluate the differential impact of weak and divided unionism on the functioning and effectiveness of what is otherwise a similar institution.

In addition, the coincidence of the council reform of 1979 and the severe decline in unionization invites a closer inspection of crowding-out effects. Do statutory works councils, by offering publicly available, free protection, replace trade unions as private associations of workers? Does voting for union candidates in works councils substitute, in the minds of workers, for membership in trade unions? Does management try to substitute unions for councils? Are there examples of unions that, by having access to mandatory works councils, find it easier to organize particular groups of workers?

I start with an overview of the legal and organizational aspects and then, after a brief historical digression, proceed with an analysis of the changing relationship between councils and employers. Next, I focus on variations in influence among works councils and discuss the "logic of exchange" between management and council. This is followed by a closer look at the organizational and contextual variables explaining these differences. Additional attention is given to the interaction with trade unions. The question of whether the role of the council in collective bargaining has been enhanced in the context of decentralized industrial relations and human resource management will be addressed next. The final section is devoted to an evaluation of the costs and benefits of works councils for employees, management, trade unions, and society.

4.2   Tasks, Rights, and Organization of the Council

4.2.1   Consultation, Co-determination, and Monitoring

Under the Works Council Act of 1979 (Wet op de Ondernemingsraden),[1] works councils have three main rights: consultation, co-determination, and

---

1. I follow the latest available English edition: Ministerie van Sociale Zaken en Werkgelegenheid (SZW—Ministry of Social Affairs and Employment), Works Council Act (The Hague, May 1990).

monitoring. When and how these rights apply, and how conflicts must be resolved, is carefully specified. The main rights of the council read as follows:

Consultation (Section 25)

"The entrepreneur shall give the works council the opportunity to tender advice on any proposed decision" in the case of transfer of control of (parts of) the enterprise; control, mergers, or takeovers of other enterprises; termination of operations or plant closure; significant reduction, expansion, or change of activities; major changes in the organization or division of powers within the enterprise; change in the location of production; employment or lease of temporary staff; major investments; major capital loans; and assignments given to outside consultants or experts on any of the above issues. Council advice is also needed on proposals concerning the dismissal or appointment of members of the board of supervisors. The right of consultation in case of mergers, takeovers, and use of outside consultants does not apply if one of the firms involved is located outside the Netherlands.

Co-determination (Section 27)

"The entrepreneur shall require the approval of the works council for every proposed decision by him to lay down, amend, or withdraw" a regulation as referred to in article 1636j of the Civil Code;[2] pension insurance, profit-sharing, or savings schemes; arrangements of working hours and holidays; job assessment; health, safety, and welfare at work; rules concerning hiring, firing, and promotion; staff training; staff assessment; industrial social work; job consultation; grievance handling; and the position of young workers. The obligation to ask approval "shall not apply if and insofar as the substance of the matter in question has been regulated for the enterprise in a collective agreement."

Monitoring (Section 28)

"The council oversees the compliance with the regulations, by collective agreement, public statute or otherwise" concerning the terms of employment and the health, safety, and welfare of workers. The council is also required to oversee the implementation of the law and to promote general public policy objectives with respect to job consultation, employee involvement, prevention of discrimination, equal treatment of men and women, and integration of handicapped persons in the enterprise.

4.2.2 Consultation Procedures, Information, and Sanctions

In 1979, while removing the employer from the council's chair, the legislative officials took great care to specify proper consultation procedures between

2. This refers to general rules of conduct for employees and to terms of the contract of employment not covered by collective agreement.

employer and council in order to prevent a radicalizing impact on labor-management relations. Accepting the council's main function of representing employee interests, the law clearly discourages overt expression of conflict and promotes a *problem-solving approach* through improved communication and mutual accommodation of interests.

Employer and council must meet within two weeks if either party so demands. A minimum of six consultations *(overleg-vergaderingen)* is required every year. The council is not allowed to publish its advice or disapproval without prior consultation with the employer. Neither must the employer reject the council's advice, objection, counterproposal, or initiative without discussion with the council. Council and employer will together determine the agenda and decide who will chair the joint meeting. The law further prescribes that the employer, or the board of directors, will designate a permanent and fully mandated representative for these consultations (the so-called *overleg-bestuurder*).

Under section 31, "the entrepreneur is obliged to provide, in good time, the works council and its committees with all the information that they reasonably require in order to perform their work," in particular, at least twice a year, with data on the firm's financial and economic position, its long-term strategies, and its social and personnel policies. The council may engage an outside expert at the firm's expense to check financial statements or develop counterproposals. In the case of major changes involving matters under section 25, the employer must seek the council's advice "at a time which will allow it to have a significant impact on the decision," and the council "shall be furnished with a list of reasons for the decision, its expected consequences for the employees of the enterprise, and the measures proposed in response" to these. This information shall be given in writing.

If there is disagreement, the law wants to ensure that all avenues for conflict avoidance are exhausted. At least one consultation meeting between the council and the employer must take place before a conflict can be taken to external authorities. In particular, if the council wants to advise against a proposed decision covered by section 25, or wants to withhold approval under section 27, it may do so only after the matter has been discussed in a formal meeting with the entrepreneur. The works council must specify its reasons in writing.

In the case of council objection, the employer "shall be obliged to postpone implementation of his decision with one month" unless the council agrees to a shorter delay. In the meantime, the council may lodge an appeal with the Company Law Chamber of the Court of Appeal in Amsterdam, "on the grounds that the entrepreneur in weighing the interests involved could not in all reasonableness have arrived at his decision." The court can order the employer to rescind his decision and may prohibit the entrepreneur from carrying it out. In the case of a co-determination issue under section 27, the council's position is stronger, although the legislation has stopped short of giving the council a right of veto. Decisions that have not been given council approval are invalid, but the employer may appeal to a cantonal court. The court can grant permission if it deems the council's refusal "unreasonable" or if the proposed decision "is based on important organizational, economic, or social considerations."

Finally, the council does not have to wait until the employer asks its advice. Under section 23 of the law, the council may take the initiative and "submit proposals on which it considers consultation desirable." The employer is obliged to consider the proposal in a formal consultation meeting. Oddly, the law does not specify sanctions if the firm ignores a council initiative.

4.2.3   Further Legislation Regulating Dutch Firms

Several other laws should be mentioned to describe the legal and institutional context in which Dutch firms operate (for a full treatment of Dutch business law see Schuit et al. 1988). Under Dutch company law, a limited liability company above a certain size must have a board of supervisors. Board members are appointed by the shareholders through a system of "controlled co-optation." Unlike German workers, Dutch workers have no representation on the supervisory board. However, the works council is entitled to give its advice on any appointment, may veto a proposed appointee, and may suggest alternative candidates. Company staff and union officials are excluded from positions on the board. The board's main power is the appointment and dismissal of the board of directors, which is the actual management of the firm and the firm's legal agent.

A typical feature of the Collective Dismissal Notification Act of 1975, the nonstatutory Code of Conduct for firms of the same year, and certain sections of the Civil Code is the role given to the unions in addition to the rights vested in works councils. The firm must notify the union of collective dismissals affecting 20 or more employees. To encourage negotiations and the development of a "social plan," the director of the Regional Manpower Service must wait at least one month before granting permission for the dismissal, unless unions and management agree otherwise. Unions may, but need not, involve the works council in these negotiations. The Code of Conduct concerning company mergers was developed by the tripartite Social Economic Council and is supervised by one of its committees. Trade unions are to receive prior information, under conditions of secrecy, and must be involved in the drafting of a social plan. They will also help define the involvement of the works council, as required under section 25. Trade unions can also appeal to the Company Law Chamber for an independent audit of the firm's finances, condition, and operations if they have legitimate reasons to suspect gross misconduct and other remedies have failed.

The latest piece of relevant legislation, increasing the council's monitoring tasks, is the Health, Safety and Welfare at Work Act, which was phased in between 1981 and 1990. The act specifies certain requirements for working conditions that must be met in the workplace. Dutch works councils are functionally comprehensive, and monitoring adherence to health, safety, and welfare regulations is among their tasks. They may, however, transfer rights in this area to special committees, except the right to start legal proceedings. According to a survey of the largest private sector union, the Industriebond FNV (IB FNV), there are some 700 health and safety committees in the about 1,000 industrial firms with 50 or more employees that the union organizes (IB FNV 1990). Their main task is to draw attention to hazards at work and find methods of prevention. Dutch works councils, or health and safety committees, have no authority to stop dangerous work processes. This decision can only be taken by the state's labor inspectors, following a request from the works council. It remains to be seen whether the law will be effectively enforced, but one may expect legal effectiveness to increase through the involvement of the councils and health and safety committees, given the advantages of a customized and negotiated application of general norms. Union and firm training of health and safety committee members has increased in recent years.

4.2.4   Domain and Coverage

The Works Council Act applies to all firms with 100 or more employees. In 1981 a new law regarding worker participation in small firms was enacted, extending the obligation to create works councils, but with restricted rights,[3] to all firms with between 35 and 99 employees working at least one-third of a full-time working week. Also, this Small Enterprise Participation Act places employers with very small firms, between 10 and 34 employees, under the obligation to organize at least an annual consultative meeting. These laws apply to the private sector, including subsidized activities or activities under public control (e.g., railways or hospitals). The sizes of the domains of the various laws is shown in table 4.1. The General Civil Servants Statute regulates the participation rights of civil servants and public employees, including the election of departmental committees in local and central public administration and public utilities, with special statutes for the police, the military, and educational institutions.

This chapter is only concerned with the "hundred-plus" councils, in firms and establishments with 100 and more employees. Even so, variation in size and organization is large, from 100 employees to the around 90,000 employees of the largest private firm in the Netherlands, the Post and Telecommunications Office (PTT). In 1990, the hundred-plus councils covered 55 percent of all employees in the private sector, accounted for 55 percent of national output, and represented 50 percent of the value added of all private businesses (Economisch Instituut voor het Midden- en Kleinbedrijf [EIM] 1990). Of the 4,500 hundred-plus firms in which works councils are mandatory, almost one-third are in manufacturing, accounting for about two-thirds of total manufacturing employment.

---

3. E.g., the right of advice is restricted to decisions on major changes in location, organization, or employment that affect at least one-quarter of the workforce. No obligation exists for the employer to delay decisions for at least one month in case of disagreement.

Table 4.1   **Works Council Laws and Firms Covered**

Law	Firm Size (number of employees)	Number of Firms	Number of Employees	Percentage of Employees
1971/1979	100+	4,500	2,500,000	55
1982	35–99	11,000	750,000	18
1982	10–34	31,000	700,000	17
None	1–9	205,000	550,000	16
None	0	305,000	–	–
Total		560,000	4,500,000	100

Sources: Centraal Bureau voor Statistiek (CBS—Central Bureau of Statistics), *Statistisch Zakboek 1992* (The Hague, 1992); and data provided by the EIM.

Note: Table reports rounded figures (January 1991) for private sector excluding agriculture. Employees are those working a minimum of 15 hours per week.

4.2.5   Coverage

Under Dutch law, employers must set up a council, and no prior initiative of employees, trade unions, or third parties is required. The employer may, however, ask for an exemption, which can be granted for a maximum of five years after hearing the trade union(s) as representative(s) of the workers. Law enforcement is a task of the state and is entrusted to a Labor Inspectorate. Looise (1989) calculates that works councils exist in 83 percent of the hundred-plus firms and for 87 percent of the employees in firms of this size. In firms with 35 to 100 employees, coverage has risen from 20 percent in 1981, when works councils were still voluntary in such firms, to 41 percent of the firms and 45 percent of the employees in 1985. Coverage in the small-firm sector has since stagnated at around 50 percent (Van der Heijden 1991). In our survey, conducted in May 1991, 19 percent of the workers in small establishments (those with fewer than 35 employees) reported the existence of consultation meetings or councils, compared with 82 percent of the workers in larger establishments. Coverage increases with establishment size, reaching 95 percent of employees in establishments with 1,000 or more employees (van de Putte, Visser, and van Rij 1991). Least covered in small and large firms are employees in commercial and financial services (Teulings 1981; Huiskamp and Risseeuw 1988); within the small-firm sector, coverage is lowest in construction, in family firms, and in services employing mainly low-skilled workers (Dekkers, Calhoen, and Andriessen 1989).

Since we are dealing only with hundred-plus firms, firm size cannot be the only explanation for the differences in council coverage shown in table 4.2. Teulings (1981) found a large difference in council coverage between firms (91 percent) and establishments (31 percent). This difference is most clearly present in financial institutions.

Table 4.2   **Employees and Works Councils by Sector for Firms with 100 or More Employees**

Sector	Share of Employment (%)	Share of Councils (%)	Councils per 10,000 Employees	Employees per Council
Manufacturing	38	43	25	400
Construction	5	7	29	340
Transport	4	4	23	430
Commerce	24	21	19	540
Finance	16	4	9	1,120
Health, etc.	18	19	23	430
All	100	100	22	452

Sources: Labour Inspectorate, *Registratie enquete instelling ondernemingsraden 1984* (The Hague: SZW, mimeograph); author's calculations.

Note: Figures are for private sector excluding agriculture. $N = 3,627$.

4.2.6   Multiplant Firms and Council Organization: Some Examples

The law is flexible as to whether firms with several plants should set up more than one council. Before the latest amendment to the law, in April 1990, the minister was to decide in case of disagreement. Current law encourages self-regulation with the possibility of taking matters to court. As a rule, council organization follows the structure of the firm. If the firm is centralized, one works council with an extensive committee structure may suffice;[4] in a decentralized or multidivisional company, or in a holding company, each establishment usually has its own works council. Together they elect the divisional councils, from which a central works council is elected. Between 10 and 15 percent of all works councils in the Netherlands are group or central works councils.

Examples of a very elaborate council structure are found at PTT and at multinational firms like Philips, Unilever, and AKZO.[5] Many large banks, insur-

4. One difference between a works council and a committee is that the council can be a legal party and sue the employer.

5. PTT was privatized in 1989. It has a holding company structure with five subsidiaries, of which the Post Office, with 60,000 employees in 5 districts, and Royal Dutch Telecom, with 30,000 employees in 13 districts, are the most important. In 1991 PTT had 22 works councils (one for each district, one for each of the three smaller subsidiaries, and one for the holding company), supported by an extensive committee structure. There were two group works councils, one for Telecom and one for the Post Office, elected by and from the works councils. Together with the works councils of the other subsidiaries and the council of the holding company, they elect the central works council. The result is that individuals may be member of three councils. The central works council meets every week and meets with management every two weeks, and also meets in a number of study groups. Members of the central works council spend most of their working time on council business. In total, works councils at PTT involved some 1,500 members, or one councillor for every 63 employees. Philips, which currently employs about 45,000 employees in the Netherlands, had in the late 1980s 80 works councils in its Dutch establishments, 10 divisional councils, and one central works council.

ance companies, the Dutch railways, and the national airline, KLM, have only a works council at headquarters. In April 1990, demands to decentralize council organization at the Amsterdam-Rotterdam Bank (with 11,000 employees and two councils) and at the railways (28,000 employees and one council) were rejected by the employers. In his last decision on the matter, the minister supported the employers' point of view. Of the major multinational firms, Philips is most critical of indirect elections of the central works council since voting alliances of union members in the works councils at the establishment level tend to produce a union majority in the central councils. In the 1992 works council elections Philips will implement its plan to abolish the divisional councils, and the members of the central works council will be chosen in direct elections.

Another bone of contention is the separation of national and international activities. Employees working in the international departments at Philips headquarters in Eindhoven are not represented by the central works council. They have a works council of their own with almost no union representation. The central works council argues that this denies it access to the strategic center of the firm and that it must deal with managers of Philips Holland, who have insufficient authority. Management argues that if it included the international division under the central works council, it would have to apply a similar council structure to its Belgian, German, Italian, and other employees. After its short-lived and unhappy experiment with an international works council in the early 1970s, Philips is adamant in its opposition to European works councils. Other Dutch multinationals appear to share this view (e.g., Unilever) and have also rejected European councils (Visser and Ebbinghaus 1992).

4.2.7   Works Council Elections

Regular elections of their members by and from the workforce is an important source of strength for councils. As a rule, elections take place every three years, but since 1990 council and employer may agree that elections are to be held every two or every four years. All mandates are renewable. Unlike in France, Spain, and Germany, works council elections in the Netherlands are not synchronized and are scheduled differently in each firm. Hence the public visibility of these elections is small.

Turnout averages about 75 percent (Koene and Slomp 1990), but the average conceals considerable variation among firms. Teulings (1981) found that in 40 percent of the council elections turnout had been 90 percent and more, in 30 percent between 70 and 90 percent, and in 30 percent less than 70 percent. Huiskamp and Risseeuw (1988) report that in half of the 444 councils in their survey, conducted in 1988, turnout had been over 77 percent. In our survey of May 1991, 55 percent of all "permanent" employees in the private sector said that they had voted in the "most recent elections," 26 percent had not voted, 16 percent said that there had been no elections (because of lack of candidates), and 4 percent had not (yet) been eligible to vote. This translates into a turnout of 68 percent of the eligible workforce, excluding the firms with no elections but including elections in smaller firms with 35 to 99 employees.

Dutch works councils are categorically encompassing and include blue-collar workers as well as clerical, technical, and managerial staff. There are no guaranteed seats for any functional group, but elections are frequently organized on a departmental or functional basis. The franchise extends to all employees who have worked in the firm for at least six months; council and management may agree to include employees who work for the firm but are not directly hired by it. Council members must have worked at least one year with the firm. The size of the council increases with employment, from 7 council members in firms with 100 to 199 employees, to 9 for up to 399 employees, 11 for up to 599 employees, 13 for up to 999 employees, and 2 more with each 1,000 additional employees until a maximum of 25 members is reached. Larger numbers are possible by mutual agreement. The average Dutch works council has between 9 and 10 members (Teulings 1981; Heijink 1986; Koene and Slomp 1990).

The Dutch works council is a firm and not a union institution. Among the firm's permanent employees, union and nonunion members have the same rights. However, with respect to electing council members, the law gives recognized trade unions a slight advantage. A "union list" of council candidates is automatically recognized. Members of nonrecognized unions or nonunionized workers must collect a minimum of 30 signatures from among the firm's employees before they can present a list of candidates. Recognition is automatic for any union affiliated with one of the major confederations, but nonaffiliated unions may be recognized in certain industries or firms.

4.2.8 Facilities and Rights of Council Members

Protection of council members, exmembers, and candidates is another major source of council independence. The employer must ask special permission from the cantonal court if he wants to dismiss any of the above, and protection is given for two years after membership on the council. Council members are granted paid leave for meetings, training, and preparation. The number of hours and the amount of other facilities, such as office space and secretarial assistance, are to be arranged between council and employer. The council is entitled to hire experts at the employer's expense and may have a budget of its own. The council can constitute itself as a legal party, represented through its elected president, and may sue the employer. Legal expenses are to be paid by the employer, within negotiated limits and only after prior notification. Works councils cannot be held liable for the costs of legal proceedings.

The law guarantees a minimum of 60 paid working hours or five days of time off per year per council member. A representative survey of works councils in the mid-1980s showed that the average council member used 27 hours per month for council activities (Looise and Heijink 1986; Looise and de Lange 1987). About half of these were working hours paid by the employer. Council presidents spend 37 hours on average, of which half are compensated, though in larger firms with over 500 employees it is not unusual to find a full-time council president. The average council meets 10 to 11 times per year; in addition, it consults seven times per year with the employer. Just over half of the councils had office space and the support of a typist; one-third had also the support of a staff secretary and their own budget, averaging 30,000 guilders ($18,000) per year in 1985; one-fourth had an additional budget for hiring experts, though fewer councils had actually engaged expert advisers. Three out of four councils received regular training, about five days per year, organized and paid through the Joint Training Board for Works Councils, which is funded by employers. It goes without saying that these averages may be misleading since we are dealing with firms having from 100 to 90,000 employees, though measured by establishment the variation is smaller.

4.3 Changing Relations with Employers

In 1979 the legislature found it hard to disown the Dutch legacy of vertical corporatism in which the employer, as "head of the enterprise," was also chairman of the works council. After years of preparation and political horse trading, a compromise was found in which the emancipation of the council was tightly knit into a tissue of consultation. The employee-only council, with increased rights and authority, became firmly embedded in a highly formalized set of rules which privilege compromise and problem solving over bargaining and articulation of conflict. A brief historical overview will help explain the complexities of current law and practices.

4.3.1 Paternalistic Councils

The works councils of 1950 satisfied in all but one aspect the ideal type of the paternalistic council as defined by Rogers and Streeck (chap. 1 in this volume). They were not designed to encourage the independent expression of worker interests, but "to contribute, with due recognition of the autonomous function of the employer, to the best functioning of the enterprise" (Act of May 4, 1950). A representative role for the council elected members on behalf of their constituency was excluded because representation was seen as the sole prerogative of trade unions, and because it would have contradicted the view of the firm as a community.

The 1950 works councils legislation did not, however, result from employer or state initiatives to forestall union organization in the workplace, even though it did have that effect. The act was part and parcel of an institutional framework of organized consultation with which labor and capital tried to break with the prewar past. From the viewpoint of organized labor it was the least important ingredient of the postwar compromise, the basic component of which was the recognition of trade unions as a legitimate party at all levels of decision making above the firm, in exchange for unions' acceptance of management's right to manage and an undertaking to refrain from union activity in the firm (Windmuller 1969; Visser 1992a).

The idea of social partnership was embodied in the joint Foundation of Labor, which was pivotal in the execution of statutory wage policy between 1945 and 1963. Pessimism about the viability of European economies and of democracy abounded, and there was widespread distrust of conflict and market solutions. The works councils of 1950 were only the third layer in a neocorporatist framework, at the top of which stood the tripartite Social-Economic Council, and in the middle a bipartite industry board, or product board, in each industry. The unions believed that this arrangement, a compromise inspired by Catholic social thought, would give them sufficient influence in socioeconomic decision making. In their view, *überbetriebliche Mitbestimmung,* to use the German expression, exercised through representative organizations of employees would make interest representation at the firm level redundant. Moreover, the unions were anxious to defend their newly gained right to collective bargaining. If indeed the council of 1950 was an embodiment of paternalist ideology, unions were part of this ideology.

It is characteristic of the spirit of the 1950 legislation that it placed all firms with more than 25 employees under an obligation to set up a works council without ever mentioning sanctions against employers who did not comply. The philosophy behind this striking omission was that cooperation with unwilling employers would be useless (Fase 1969, 28). The fact of the matter is that until the early 1960s few employers felt a need to install works councils. The unions kept complaining about lack of cooperation of employers but suffered equally from lack of enthusiasm among their members, in spite of large educational campaigns (Smid, Sprenger, and Visser 1979). In the course of the 1960s more councils were established, but now the unions began to worry about "wildcat cooperation" between council and management. The variable best explaining the presence of a works councils was the existence of a modern personnel or labor relations department, which at the time were proliferating in Dutch industry (Buitendam 1979). As might be expected, firm size was the contingency that explained most of this variation (Drenth and van der Pijl 1966; Lammers 1968). Predictably, the factor highlighted in later studies was the age of the council itself: the longer it had existed, the more established its position, the more active and sophisticated its use of rights (Hövels and Nas 1975; Andriessen, Drenth, and Lammers 1984).

In neglecting the firm as an arena of interest representation the unions had miscalculated, though it took almost two decades before this became evident. With the exception of a few sectors—agriculture, retail, catering, and food production being the most prominent—the industry boards remained insignificant. But increased international activities, vertical integration, and horizontal mergers of firms followed the opening of European markets with the creation of the European Economic Community in 1958, and decisions on capital investment, mergers, takeovers, and firm location were increasingly taken by management and owners of capital without any input from workers. This became painfully clear in the merger wave of the mid- and late 1960s, which was followed by an upsurge in plant closures. To check tendencies of wildcat cooperation among the councils, as well as in response to growing criticism from an increasingly radical membership, trade unions in metal engineering began to organize networks of "trusted members" in the firm, similar to the *Vertrauensleute* in West German industry. The unions also encouraged the practice, emerging in these years, of organizing so-called preparatory sessions of elected works council members prior to the official works council meeting chaired by the employer.

4.3.2   Dual Councils

The new Works Council Act of 1971 did little but adjust the law to reality. It raised the threshold for councils to firms of 100 or more employees and recognized the preparatory sessions of the worker members of the council. But it also left the employer in the council's chair. Works councils were now given a dual mission: they were to "organize consultation with and representation of the firm's employees . . . in the interest of the optimal functioning of the firm" (Works Council Act of 1971). The consultation rights of councils were strengthened, and council members gained protection against dismissal and were offered training and other facilities to be paid for by the employers out of a common, industrywide fund. Employers who ignored or curtailed the council's rights had to face legal sanctions. The number of councils rose rapidly: from 48 percent of all hundred-plus firms in 1972, to 75 percent in 1974, to 85 percent in 1975, more or less the percentage today (all figures based on Labor Inspectorate reports).

From the start the new dual councils, paternalist and representative at the same time, came under pressure. In 1973, during a major strike in the metal industry over narrowing the pay differential between white- and blue-collar workers, a number of works councils, as well as union members on the councils, had attempted to play a conciliatory role between union and management, just as their dual mission seemed to demand. It was against this background that the more radical unions started to press for reform and began to play with the idea of shop steward representation and the replacement of works councils with union plant committees. This antagonized employers and put pressure on the government to reform the works council into a body of employee representation.

First proposals for a council without the employer were drafted in 1976, when the Labour party was still the major party in a center-left coalition government. Council reform was one of the initiatives meant to attract support for the government's policy of wage restraint (Flanagan, Soskice, and Ulman 1983). However, the proposals encountered heavy resistance from the right while not arousing much enthusiasm from the union left. Employers' organizations and a lobby of major multinational firms warned the government not to proceed with its plan to create an independent works council. In 1977 the government fell, a new center-right coalition government was formed, and after no more than two years Parliament voted the 1979 reform into law.

4.3.3   Representative Councils

The 1979 reform was a compromise between those who wanted to keep the employer in the council, though not necessarily as its chairman, and those who envisaged the works council as an instrument subject to worker control. The first position was defended by the employers' federations, major multinational firms, and the Christian Federation of Trade Unions (Christelijke Nationaal Vakverbond [CNV]). The CNV and employers disagreed, however, on enlarging the council's co-determination rights and on parity representation on the board of supervisors. The largest union federation, the Federation of Dutch Trade Unions (Federatie Nederlandse Vakbeweging [FNV]), and in particular its affiliate in the chemical, metal, and textile industries, the IB FNV, wanted stronger worker rights, though not necessarily through the statutory works council, which was sometimes portrayed as a competitor to the union. Employers remained set against the reform until the last minute, predicting a radicalization and polarization of Dutch industrial relations.

From the point of view of its intended effects the 1979 reform was a success. Research based on surveys, case studies, and interviews is univocal in showing that the works councils have become an established institution, that council-employer relations have become more professional, and that there was no polarization of interests, or much less than had been expected (Teulings 1981, 1985; van Vuuren and Koopman 1986; Looise and Heijink 1986; Looise and de Lange 1987; Pool et al. 1988; Pool, Koopman, and Mijs 1991). In short, fears that the independent council would radicalize Dutch labor relations at the workplace proved unwarranted. Today, many employers see the works council as a necessary and in some cases useful platform without which the restructuring of work organization—the major issue of the 1980s—would probably have been less easy. With few exceptions and some reservations management has discovered that it can live with the current law (Interviews with managers from major multinational firms and with staff at the Ministry of Social Affairs and Employment).

Of the main multinational firms in the Netherlands (Shell, Unilever, AKZO, and DSM Chemicals), Philips is clearly the most unhappy with current legislation. In a report in 1988 its director of industrial relations complained that works council members lacked expertise, indulged in unnecessary procedures, and were insufficiently representative. They also attracted unwelcome and negative press attention, and too much time and energy was wasted on meetings. Philips has never hidden its preference for a return to the situation before 1979 or even 1971, when the council was mainly a tool of management. Works council members at Philips, on the other hand, complain that local works councils are confronted with plant managers who have no authority and lack sufficient information on strategic decisions. According to union representatives, this problem is also felt in other large multiplant companies, especially in subsidiaries of foreign firms. It must be added that unions at Philips are weak and represent only between 15 and 20 percent of the employees. Management prefers to deal with full-time union officials, does not want an internal role for the union, and strongly resists a unionized works council.

4.3.4   As Works Councils Mature

It is safe to say that the position of the works council has strengthened with regard to agenda setting, information rights, use of independent expertise, and legal redress in conflict. It is interesting in this respect to compare the results of two representative surveys, one conducted two years after the 1971 act (Hövels and Nas 1976) and the other six years after the 1979 reform (Heijink and Looise 1986; Looise and de Lange 1987). The 1973 survey showed the employer in full control. As chairman of the council he determined its agenda, often refusing to discuss issues prepared by the elected members. The latter depended almost exclusively on information released by the employer during the meeting. In 1985, by comparison, it was found that in just 1 percent of the cases the agenda of consultation meetings was unilaterally set by the employer, in 19 percent by the works council without apparent employer influence, and in 80 percent by a bilateral committee or in informal meetings between the president of the council and the director designated to represent the firm.

Changes in the type of issues handled by councils are another indicator of the increased importance of works councils after 1979. In 1973 less than half of the councils assigned importance to financial information or issues related to the firm's internal organization (sec. 25 subjects on which consultation with the council is now required). In 1985, 90 percent of the councils attached importance to such issues. This does not mean that council members are satisfied with their influence in these matters. Nearly half the works councils indicated that information on economic, financial, and technical issues is obtained only after management has made its decision. Late involvement and insufficient information is also reported for social and personnel issues; here one out of every four councils complain about management's failure to provide sufficient information.

Teulings (1985) has emphasized that the reform of 1979 has professionalized the works councils and promoted the development of a small "works council industry" with its own journals, information and training services, experts, and organizational consultants. The supply of resources outside the firm, partly maintained through public intervention, has reduced the councils' dependence on management. This may well be related to the declining propensity of councils to employ "radical" methods of action, as reported by Teulings (1989). Fewer councils apply "unionist" power instruments, like demonstrations during lunchtime, sit-ins, work-to-rule, or work stoppages. Instead, more councils tend to use "milder," "internal" forms of protests, for instance, appeal to an "authoritative" third party, such as an industry board, a court, or a public official, rather than mobilizing workers. Councils also voice protests in a staff paper, rather than in a newspaper.

This deradicalization may reflect several developments: the onslaught of the economic recession in the early 1980s, the weakening of unions, fatigue among council members and workers, but also a process of learning and more skillful use of bargaining sanctions by the stronger and previously more militant councils. The latter explanation appears to be favored by Teulings (1989, 94) who interprets the instrumental rather than expressive use of sanctions as a sign of the advancement of a "fairly rational, calculative approach" among leading works councils. Once established, these councils tend to prefer bargaining over recourse to third parties, whereas for councils still fighting for recognition and attention, appeal to outside support, through the law or via extralegal action, remains important. This view is consistent with the finding that in recent years a growing number of works councils have negotiated a "covenant," which regulates individual employment contracts. According to Van der Heijden (1991) this can be taken as an indicator of the maturation of the works councils, with the latter emerging as players in their own right.

Comparing the results of their 1985 survey with the *Industrial Democracy in Europe (IDE)* study of 1976 (*IDE* 1981; Andriessen et al. 1984), Looise and de Lange (1987, 268) conclude that "the level of influence of the works councils has increased in all areas of decision making." But they also note the existence of a "participation paradox": involvement in decision making is strongest toward the end of the decision-making process, in the implementation stage, when the probability of impact on the outcome is smallest. This had also been one of the main findings in 1976. Ten years later a majority of managers and council presidents agree that the council is only involved in the last stages of decision making. Ten to 20 percent agreed that the council is involved in all stages, and about the same number responded that the council is not involved in any part of the decision-making process at all.

It is generally acknowledged that late council involvement diminishes the chance for councils to influence decisions, as well as for beneficial outcomes such as job security, legitimacy for the decision itself, speedy implementation, and employee satisfaction. Late involvement is also associated with longer waiting times for the council to present its advice or approval (Looise and de Lange 1987; van Vuuren and Koopman 1986; Heller et al. 1988). However, in a replication of their 1976 study a decade later, the *IDE* researchers also found that the role of the works council in strategic decisions, especially in firm or plant restructuring, had increased. Does this indicate that the participation paradox is receding?

4.4 A New Logic of Exchange

The first half of the 1980s were difficult years. Plants closed, unemployment soared, union membership declined, real wages fell, social benefits were lowered, and eligibility rules tightened (Visser 1990). A conservative political and cultural climate emphasized the virtues of a "no-nonsense" management of cost efficiency, competitiveness, and rewards for efforts. Organizational change seemed driven by its own logic, fueled by market forces, international competition, and technological innovation. In the light of these developments, it may seem surprising that works councils increased their influence over some aspects of management behavior. How do we explain this "growth against the tide" (Looise 1989)?

4.4.1   The Weight of Formal Institutions

Law matters. Contrary to their initial hypothesis that the current economic, political, and technological climate would diminish the role of works councils, the *IDE* researchers found that in the mid-1980s the "relative weight of the formal institutions had increased" (Pool et al. 1988, 54). This was best visible in the area of strategic decision making, and more true for metal engineering than for the service sector, such as hospitals and insurance (Pool et al. 1991). Apparently, the strengthening of consultation rights under section 25 had made management seek to involve the council earlier, especially where the council could delay the implementation of decisions. This is most clearly the case with firm and plant restructuring, followed by work planning and the arrangement of working hours—which must be negotiated under section 27, with the council having something close to a veto right. More than half of management requests for advice were related to organizational adjustments and layoffs. Two out of five requests for council approval were related to changes in working hours, following a major central agreement between unions and employers in late 1982 (Visser 1989).

Some works councils succeed in using their stronger position on operational decisions in the human resources area as leverage to gain access to earlier and more strategic stages of management decision making. The main sanction against noncooperative employers is to cause delay, for instance, by lodging a court appeal. Teulings has compared the ability of councils to delay the labor process of management with the unions' ability to interrupt the labor process of workers. Councils may trade their consent to speedy implementation of operational decisions for earlier information and some degree of influence on strategic decisions.

This logic of exchange, based on "conflictual cooperation," is present in only a minority of councils. In less than 10 percent of all cases, management and works council representatives agree that the council plays a significant role in strategic decisions. Table 4.3 shows that only a minority of councils lodge a formal protest if management fails to consult the council; most limit themselves to symbolic protest. Teulings (1989) reports a similar finding in his survey of 63 works councils in 1986. Two-thirds of the councils had never put forward an initiative, and less than 20 percent claimed to have obtained full information. Councils are more inclined to insist on their information rights on social and personnel than on economic and financial issues, just as manage-

Table 4.3   **Response of Works Councils to Employer Refusal to Heed Council Advice (%)**

| | Advice | | |
Response	Consultation (Section 30)	Co-determination (Section 27)	Initiative (Section 23)
No reaction	15	10	22
Expression of regret	72	45	55
Threat of action	5	16	15
Appeal to third party	7	22	8
Formal legal steps	1	7	0

Source: Adapted from Looise and de Lange (1987, 15).

ment is more forthcoming with information on the former than on the latter kinds of subjects. Clearly, the tougher sanctions under section 27 elicit more caution and cooperation from management.

The council's ability to delay the labor process of management in restructuring contrasts with its much weaker position on new technology. To begin with, section 25 does not mention technology and automation as an issue on which consultation and information is mandatory. Moreover, the link between technological choice and the redesign of work organization is often vague and may be traceable only ex post facto. The *IDE* researchers observe that in technology decisions the legal position of the council is ambiguous, that expertise is often lacking, and that management is reluctant to involve the council in this kind of strategic choice (Pool et al. 1988). Indeed, explicit reference to automation and technology in section 25 is one of the proposals for legal reform that have been considered by the Social Economic Council in the past two years. Divisions between employers and unions have prevented a unanimous opinion, and new legislation is therefore unlikely. The weaker position of the council on technological and major financial decisions is also reflected in worker opinion. Workers assign more influence to works councils on issues like "job security" and "fair treatment" than on "automation" or "financial decisions" and are also much more positive about the council's contribution in the first two cases (van de Putte et al. 1991).

4.4.2   The Council's Role in Reorganization: Some Examples

Some of the councils that have advanced into strategic decision making are found at major manufacturing firms, for instance, at NedCar, a joint venture of Volvo and Mitsubishi, at Daf Trucks, and at Hoogovens, a steel manufacturer. These firms underwent major organizational changes in the 1980s. At NedCar the works council was able to trade its agreement to a new *kanban* organization for early information on strategic business plans and the appointment of a "trusted member" to the firm's board of supervisors. In the recent case of the Dasa (in effect, Daimler Benz) takeover of the aircraft manufacturer Fokker, the central works council played a prominent role at all stages of the negotiation process and succeeded in obtaining guarantees for airplane production and employment remaining in Holland. It is significant that management informed the central works council the day after Fokker and Dasa had signed their "operational agreement," before the minister of economic affairs, who is the main shareholder of Fokker, and before the unions. Three days later the council presented management with its counterproposals. In the three weeks that followed before the definite takeover decision, the council closely cooperated with the unions and the chairman of the parliamentary committee for economic affairs. The council met twice with the minister and strengthened his hand in the negotiations (*Niewe Rotterdamse Courant-Handelsblad,* September 4, 1992; Interviews).

How many councils exploit their opportunities for bargaining in this way is not known. The Fokker case is probably exceptional and reflects the technological, political, and symbolic importance of the country's only airplane manufacturer. The downsizing of another industrial champion, Hoogovens, has attracted similar attention. In September 1992, the firm proposed to lay off 2,500 workers, including for the first time since 1945 involuntary dismissals. While accepting the need for further cost cutting and downsizing, unavoidable in the face of cheap imports from Eastern Europe and the European Community's ban on public subsidies, the unions and the central works council were quick to reject the proposal and vetoed any forced dismissals. The next step will be a compromise with further cost-cutting reorganization, an extensive social plan cushioning layoffs, and no or very few forced separations.

In this context, developments at Philips should also be mentioned. As part of its "Operation Centaur," intended to refocus the firm on its core activities and develop a leaner and more market-driven organization, Philips has in recent years reduced its workforce in the Netherlands from 70,000 to 45,000, partly by selling some divisions and business units and partly by restructuring and layoffs. Within the constraints of the law, management has worked mainly with the unions and kept the central and local works councils at bay. An important factor is that the company has always been able to avoid forced dismissals. For access to an unorganized and intimidated workforce, management has increased its use of "direct communication," with televised speeches by the director-general and feedback discussion groups.

A case with interesting implications, especially for the application of Dutch law to foreign-based multinational firms, is the closure of the Amsterdam plant of the British-American Tobacco Corporation. Batco Amsterdam is a small and very modern facility with between 200 and 300 employees, profitable, with an active works council and a comparatively high level of union organization. In the late 1970s Batco International, based in London, decided to close the plant in Amsterdam and relocate production to its plant in Brussels. After an appeal lodged by the trade unions, the Company Law Chamber, in a rare "audit procedure," ruled that this decision was unjustified. The court argued that as a result of failing to consult properly with the unions and the works councils, management had not given sufficient weight to social as compared to economic interests. The verdict sent a shock through the Dutch business community; some argued that the judges had placed themselves in the chair of the entrepreneur. Batco rescinded its decision and even built a new, though smaller, production facility in Amsterdam.

In 1989, however, Batco International decided for a second time that the Amsterdam plant must be closed and work relocated to Brussels. Council and unions were doing everything possible to keep the plant open. Failing other efforts, the council lodged another appeal with the Company Law Chamber arguing that, according to expert opinion, there were no sound economic reasons for the decision and that consultation had been insufficient. This time, however, the court let management have its way, stating that consultations had taken place and that in the final analysis it was not the council but management that is responsible for weighing social against business interests. According to legal experts, the new verdict indicated not only that Batco had learned how to discharge its obligation to consult but also a shift in legal doctrine (Koning 1991). In another case, in 1985, the court had ruled that while a foreign multinational firm is fully entitled to direct its subsidiary, this cannot take away rights and obligations under Dutch law. In the 1989 Batco case, however, the court took a different view, observing that a Dutch subsidiary is bound by the business strategies of its proprietor firm unless this constitutes an unreasonable infringement of rights under Dutch law.

4.4.3   Variations across Firms

The 1979 reform increased the resources and the overall influence of works councils, but its equalizing impact remains to be seen. Works councils differ very much in their level of activity, use of legal rights, readiness to protest and appeal employer decisions, and propensity to engage in extralegal or militant action. A persistent finding in all surveys of the 1980s is that about one-third of all councils make full use of their legal possibilities, meet frequently with management, employ bargaining tactics, and do not shy away from reliance on legal sanctions or pressure tactics if need be. An equally large proportion rarely invoke their rights. Management failure to consult and perfunctory council discussions are a frequently observed phenomenon (Teulings 1989).

Strong councils have made better use of the possibilities of the 1979 reform than weak councils and have increased their lead over the latter. In the early 1980s, some councils were quick to perceive and make use of the new opportunities, while others behaved as if no change had occurred or made at best ritualistic use of their newly acquired rights (Teulings 1985). This is probably the best explanation why the works councils grew apart, in terms of their levels of activity and their effectiveness. Learning by imitation should increase the equalizing effects of the law in the future.

According to Teulings, the main determinant of council effectiveness was support from the union and, in particular, a council majority of FNV members. Councils with an FNV majority—about one-third of all councils—made more use of their legal and extralegal opportunities. FNV-dominated councils were more likely to be found in manufacturing, construction, and transport than in public or private services, more in large than in small firms, and more in establishments with production workers than in offices or white-collar environments. In the larger manufacturing firms it is not uncommon that the main FNV union organizes a union plant committee that monitors the works council (see section 4.5.3 below). Effectiveness was measured by the degree to which the council evaluated its influence on management decisions as "considerable," enabling it to achieve a different outcome than originally proposed or intended by management. This included the possibility of management anticipating council opposition.

Looise and de Lange reject the claim that union organization or a particular majority corresponds with more active use of legal rights and greater influence on management. Like Pool et al. (1988), they stress firm size, the existence of a personnel department, the age of the council, and its relations with its constituency and external union officials as the main causes of differences in council performance. The first and last of these factors correlate with the level of unionization and the presence of a union plant committee. Unfortunately, the number of cases are too small to estimate the impact of unions while holding some of these factors constant.

What is at stake in these debates is the dynamics of power and exchange between management and the works council. Teulings argues that the council's ability to delay decision making is decisive for bringing about a process of "political bargaining" in which management trades information and consultation for cooperation with and legitimation of its decisions. The *IDE* researchers argue that retreat to a legalistic position is the main management response to radical or militant councils: information is of poor quality, and consultation takes place only if it is enforceable under the law (Pool et al. 1988, 53); a case in point is Philips. Looise and de Lange (1987, 268–69) also argue that cooperative councils have a better chance of gaining access to the early and more important stages of decision making, whereas councils that insist on formal rights are confined to dealing with the implementation of decisions. As early as the 1960s, Dutch organization sociologists argued that cooperative councils were more effective and had more influence than conflictual councils (Lammers 1968).

But why would management "give away power" if not under pressure? De Man and Koopman (1984) argue that management cooperation can be explained by management's desire to increase worker commitment, as well as its need to gain acceptance for decisions. The works council, then, serves as a "sounding board" for preparing major strategic shifts, with communication through the council making it unnecessary for management to reach each individual worker through line managers. Also, communication through the council may inspire greater confidence among workers. For this contribution the council may receive compensation in terms of earlier involvement in management choice. My own view is that the cases of works councils that seem influential without ever having applied sanctions and without any trace of union support—as observed in the software sector, at IBM, or in certain financial institutions—are explained by high and stable profit levels, high public visibility, and resulting needs for legitimation, as well as management desire to keep the firm union free. "Cooperation without conflict" may well end if a drop in profitability requires a revision of the firm's employment policy.

4.5   Unions and Councils: Friends or Foes?

4.5.1   Absence of a Tradition

To understand the relationship between trade unions and the works council in the Netherlands, we need to recall some historical facts about Dutch trade unions. The first point is the absence of a craft tradition in a union movement that emerged late in the nineteenth century. With few exceptions Dutch unions originated outside the firm and were relatively centralized. The division of the Dutch labor movement in three ideological and religious currents (socialist, Catholic, and Calvinist), each enveloped in emergent political movements striving for full political citizenship, promoted further centralization (Harmsen and Reinalda 1975).

Second, unlike Germany there was no council tradition in the Netherlands. Neither in the upheaval following the First World War, in which the Netherlands remained neutral, nor in the years after the Second World War was there a council movement among workers. Nor had there been a council organization in the 1870s when the first groups of (skilled) workers began to organize trade unions. In 1874 a Calvinist brewer organized his employees into a "factory council"—or "core committee" as it was then called—but few if any Dutch employers appear to have imitated this high-minded example of what seems to have been benevolent paternalism (van Haren 1985).

It is true that there were attempts to lure workers into employer-dominated councils after unions had organized and became more aggressive in asking for collective agreements. In 1907 the metalworkers union brandished the "core committees" as "obstacles to the development of worker organizations . . . against the interests of the workers." The union warned its members "not to take part in elections or to join such bodies" (van der Berg 1924, 58–59). The attempts to head off the development of true union representation with paternalistic works councils were, however, bound to fail. After the establishment of collective agreements around the First World War, employer-initiated works councils were no longer a threat to unions, and employers lost interest. Some hundred factory councils, of little relevance, appear to have lingered on into the 1920s (van Haren 1985; Hueting, de Jong Edz, and Ney 1985).

4.5.2   Union Ambiguity

After 1945, Dutch unions conceded the workplace to the employer. Not that unions had much influence in the workplace when they made this concession, given the absence of a craft tradition. Windmuller (1969, 402) was probably right when he wrote that "the neglect of the plant as a place of activity was also very much the result of a sober appraisal of the power distribution between management and labor." Moreover, the social democratic union movement in particular held a deeply felt conviction that works councils would fuel *Betriebsegoismus,* to use the German expression, and become the springboard for company- rather than industry-based forms of solidarity, undermining sectoral multiemployer agreements and ultimately jeopardizing the equalizing logic of action of the industrial union. In the first decade after the war, competition with nonrecognized communist unions, which did particularly well in the first works council elections in the metal and shipbuilding industries in Amsterdam and Rotterdam, added to the sense of uneasiness (Harmsen and Reinalda 1975; Hueting et al. 1985).

Starting in the metal industry, unions began to organize a network of plant representatives in the late 1960s, and a decade later similar initiatives were taken in the service sector. Originally, this overlapped with the organization of preparatory meetings of elected council members. In the union that most actively pursued the new strategy, the Industriebond NVV (now IB FNV), the plant committee had the task of monitoring the behavior of elected council members and screening the union list of council candidates. This was resented by council members and created many tensions in the union. In the course of the 1970s the union became more radical and favored a workers' control strategy, which met with hostility from employers and with skepticism by most other unions.

In quantitative terms, the new approach seemed successful. By the end of the decade the IB FNV reported that it had organized 574 plant committees, compared to around 1,000 works councils in its domain. These committees covered about half of all establishments where the union had at least 25 members (IB FNV 1979). However, the quality of these committees was often very poor. Only one-third or one-fourth of these committees were really active; their protection against employer retaliation was modest as many employers refused to grant recognition; they were highly dependent on, and often abandoned by, union district officials; and in most cases they sought in vain for a role that was not yet occupied by external union officials or, indeed, by the works councils (van Vliet 1979). Also, the union was never fully committed to a workers' control strategy and never contemplated a devolution of power over collective bargaining or strikes, which remained firmly in the hands of union officials supervised by the union's central office. Still, the development and radicalism of the plant committees did contribute to the 1979 reform insofar as it rallied conservative support in Parliament for a stronger works council as the lesser evil.

Soon after the reform, the unions adjusted their strategy. In 1980, the IB FNV announced that "under the present circumstances, the works councils seem to offer more possibilities than union action through the plant committees or the district officials" (IB FNV 1980). Especially in the recession of the early 1980s, with its plant closures, restructurings, and layoffs, the plant committees had a difficult time. Left alone by district officials who were fully absorbed by negotiations over layoffs and social plans, leading members resigned or sought refuge in the works council. With its enhanced powers, the council seemed to have at least a legal grip on the problem, if only because it had access to information on business plans, mergers and takeovers, reorganization, and relocation of firm activities. Not least, its members had protection against dismissal and were entitled to basic facilities.

A bill to offer some protection and facilities to union plant representatives was presented in 1981, but a few years later was shelved and has recently been withdrawn. The unions never made it an important issue. Currently, most collective agreements provide some guarantees to union representatives in the workplace, but always less than the protection and support which council members are assured. In the late 1980s IB FNV restated its policy that plant committees should play a supportive role for the works council. There are even more committees than in 1979, but still only one in four is truly active (IB FNV 1988), and fewer still have a true role in decentralized bargaining (van Rhijn and Huiskamp 1989).

In conclusion, partly in response to the institutional strengthening of the works council and partly under pressure from the shift from sectoral to firm-level decision making among employers, Dutch unions have adopted the works council as an additional instrument for the defense of worker interests. In this section I have highlighted the turns in the policies of the IB FNV because it is the leading union in the field, had considerable influence on legislation, and had to make the largest adjustment after the reform of 1979. Christian and white-collar unions always had a more positive attitude toward the works council, and unions outside the manufacturing industry had been slower to start plant committees.

4.5.3   Weak and Divided Unionism

Between 1945 and 1975 the overall level of unionization in the Netherlands averaged a stable 40 percent of all wage and salary earners. In the 1980s aggregate union density dropped by more than 10 percentage points—from about 37 percent in 1979 to 25 percent in 1989—partly reflecting a wider definition of employment, including part-time jobs held mainly by women. The decline signifies a substantial weakening of the union presence in nearly all occupations and industries. Private sector density is currently down to about 18 percent; even in manufacturing only one in four workers is member of a union, and in financial and commercial services fewer than one in ten. Within Western Europe, the Netherlands now has one of the lowest union density rates, after France and Spain (Visser 1991b).

The union decline has multiple causes. Unemployment reached double digits in the first half of the 1980s; employment in manufacturing and construction and among blue-collar workers contracted sharply. Between 1982 and 1986 unions had to accept a substantial loss in real wages. Social security benefits were cut. When the center-right government pulled away from customary incomes policies and employers shifted their attention to the firm, the highly centralized Dutch unions were left to their own devices and suffered (Visser 1990). Generally well staffed, though mainly specialized in participation in macroeconomic and social security policy networks at the national level, the main federations and private sector unions have been forced to lay off staff and restructure their internal organizations. Traditionally, unions have been poor in servicing members in firms.

The power of Dutch unions is further impaired by ideological divisions. Historically, Dutch unions were divided into a social democratic, a Catholic, and a Protestant union movement, with a syndicalist (later communist) and a liberal fringe. After 1945, in spite of the failure to reunify the union movement, there was a high degree of interunion cooperation. In the 1970s a new attempt to unify all currents failed and led to increased tensions between the FNV, which combined the social democratic and Catholic unions, and the remaining Protestant center, the CNV, which attracted the membership of a number of Catholic public sector unions. A third federation, MHP, was formed in 1974 of white-collar unions and staff associations. FNV and CNV unions organize on an industry basis, often combining several industries in one union in order to obtain economies of scale. FNV unions represent about 60 percent of all union members, CNV unions some 20 percent. In the Netherlands there exists no doctrine of "exclusive jurisdiction." Unions that are affiliated to the FNV, the CNV, or the MHP are automatically granted recognition at the industry or firm level, irrespective of actual membership. Of course, membership levels and union strike capacity do carry weight in bargaining with employers.

The consequences of union pluralism are several: interunion competition, especially over objectives and policies (member poaching is rare), diminished bargaining power and fragile strike coalitions, competition over works council representation, and attention to the needs of the marginal rather than the median worker. In the context of this paper it should be stressed that multiunionism makes it unlikely that works councils, even where they are highly unionized, will become the extended arm of a union.

4.5.4 Social Profile and Unionization of Works Councils

The social profile of works councils members in the Netherlands is traditional: male (83 percent), standard employment contract, full-time job, long job tenure (15 years on average), and skilled (49 percent, compared with 18 percent unskilled or semiskilled, and 33 percent supervisory and technical staff). The comparative figures for the labor force are 67 percent male, 5 to 10 percent in flexible employment, 20 to 30 percent in part-time jobs (of which 80 percent are held by women), 8 to 10 years of job tenure, 40 percent unskilled and semiskilled, 40 percent skilled, and 20 percent supervisory and technical staff. As can be expected, works council members are also on average older and have more years of general education or vocational training. The social profile of union membership lies somewhere between that of council members and of the workforce as a whole.[6] I do not know of data on the representation of ethnic minorities and immigrant workers.

In contrast with the sharp decline in union density in the 1980s, the unions maintained their position on the works councils (table 4.4). Two-thirds of all works council seats are occupied by union members. FNV members outnumber CNV members by a stable ratio of 3.5 to 1, which corresponds to their relative strength in private sector membership. The unionization rate of works council members, at 64 percent, exceeds that of employees in the private sector—18 percent—by a large margin. The most appropriate comparison, of course, is with the employees eligible to vote in works council elections in hundred-plus firms. In our 1991 survey, we measured a union density rate of 39 percent of employees in such establishments (van de Putte et al. 1991).

Among eligible workers, turnout is higher among union members. In our recent survey of FNV and CNV members, 72 percent indicated that they voted "always," 11 percent "usually," 3 percent "occasionally," and 14 percent "never." Eighty-six percent said they had voted in the last election (Klandermans et al. 1992). The fact remains that a large number of nonmembers vote for union candidates, and an even larger proportion would do so if given a chance. In many firms, the absence of a sufficient number of union members prevents the presentation of a union list. Even among union members, 25 percent indicated that there had been no union list in their firm, and 16 percent said they could not tell since they had given their vote to personally known candidates irrespective of union membership (van de Putte et al. 1991).

One of every four councils experiences difficulties with finding candidates, and another 37 percent report problems, although less than 3 percent of seats remain vacant. Problems are most severe where unions are absent or scarcely visible, that is, in smaller establishments and firms, and in firms in commercial and financial services (Looise and de Lange 1987; Huiskamp and Risseeuw 1988). The problems include negative impact on prospects of promotion in the firm, lack of cooperation from the employer, and excessive demands on one's leisure time (Acampo, Kunst, and Soeters 1987). In a survey of council members commissioned by the CNV, 24 percent of members that had ended their council activities mentioned that membership had held up their career. But it was also found that council members tend to be longer with the firm and to have already exhausted their possibilities of internal promotion (CNV 1986).

Can we interpret the support for union candidates in works council elections as a vote of confidence for the unions, despite the declined propensity of work-

---

6. CBS, *Enquête beroepsbevolking* (Quarterly Labor Force Sample Survey) (The Hague, 1986); census data for 1985–86.

Table 4.4   **Union Density**

Federation	All Employees			Private Sector			Works Councils		
	1980	1985	1990	1980	1985	1990	1980	1985	1991
FNV	21	17	15.5	19	15	13.5	43	40	41
CNV	6	5.5	5	4	3	2.5	7	10.5	11
Other	8	6	5	3	2.5	2.5	18	14	12
Total union	35	28.5	25.5	26	21.5	18.5	68	64.5	64

Sources: J. Visser, DUES database; calculated from Teulings (1981) and Looise and de Lange (1987); Visser (1991b).

ers to become members? Does the disparity indicate a free rider problem, in that voting for a union-backed council member, presumably making the council more effective while not making the voter share in the costs of union organization, is a rational response of calculating employees? In our survey we asked whether respondents thought that the works council made the union redundant and whether voting for a union list is a substitute for membership. An overwhelming majority rejects the first statement; less than one in ten respondents agreed strongly. Those that felt it was enough to vote for a union list were more numerous, 30 percent; but 55 percent disagreed with this proposition, and 14 percent were not sure. In short, some crowding-out does seem to occur. The real problem, however, is that Dutch unions, given their internal divisions and their long absence from the workplace, find it hard to activate mechanisms of social punishment for free riders privatizing public goods. The comparison with Belgium, where works councils were introduced later and have remained secondary to recognized union shop representatives (Visser 1991a), and Germany, where DGB unions hold a virtual monopoly of representation, is instructive.

4.5.5   Union Politics on Works Councils

On about one-third of the councils the FNV has a majority. This has not changed much during the membership crisis of the 1980s (table 4.5). On the basis of their survey, Huiskamp and Risseeuw (1988) found similar proportions in 1988. On about 25 percent of the works councils no FNV member is present, while on just under 20 percent there are neither FNV nor CNV representatives. An FNV majority is more likely in manufacturing, construction, and transport. In commercial services more than half of the works councils have a nonunion majority.

Surprisingly, the proportion of works councils with a nonunion majority has declined between 1980 and 1985, from 34 to 25 percent, in contrast to the trends in union membership. This probably reflects the lesser "staying power" of unorganized council members. Council members without the support of a union are less likely to complete their tenure on the council and are less likely

Table 4.5   Majorities by Union (% of councils)

Majority Federation	All Councils		Establishment Councils (3)	Central Works Councils (4)
	1980 (1)	1985 (2)		
FNV	35	35	35	47
CNV or other	7	13	13	5
Nonunion	34	25	36	16
No majority	26	25	17	32

Sources: Calculated from Teulings (1981) and Looise and de Lange (1987).

to run a second time. A survey among former council members in 1986, commissioned by the CNV, indicated that almost one in four council members did not complete their terms.

Table 4.5 (cols. [3] and [4]) also shows that the likelihood of a union majority, and an FNV majority in particular, increases on central works councils. This is the result of indirect elections with lower-level councils each choosing one delegate, who is likely to come from the largest group or the group that is most effective in coalition building. The 1980 works council election at Philips can serve as an illustration. On the 91 councils at the establishment level the FNV union gained 33 percent of the seats, in the 20 divisional councils its share rose to 40 percent, and on the central works council it achieved a majority of 52 percent. Unions representing managerial and technical staff are also overrepresented on central works councils; within the FNV, the skilled manual and white-collar component increases with council level. The reverse is true for women. Fifteen percent of the elected members of establishment works councils were women, and there were still 33 women among the 330 divisional council members; none, however, was left on the central works council. Nonunion members occupied 44 percent of the seats on establishment councils, but only 11 percent on the central works council. This goes some way toward explaining the preference of management for direct election of the central works council.

Regular contact with its voters and with the external union contributes to the council's level of activity. Again, a picture of great variation emerges. About 40 percent of the councils organize regular meetings with their electorate or have office hours during which council members can be consulted. Another 40 percent limit themselves to providing information, through a staff paper or a bulletin or billboard, and 20 percent do not have any contact, active or passive, with their voters. Most works councils (79 percent) report "contact with the union," but the majority of these contacts are ad hoc. Forty-three percent report the existence of a union plant committee, but only 24 percent of the councils have regular contact with it (Looise and de Lange 1987). The presence of a union plant committee is most likely in manufacturing, and the likelihood increases with the size of the establishment. Union plant committees exist in 60 percent of the largest firms (more than 1,000 employees); in manufacturing this proportion rises to 90 percent. The proportion of firms with a union plant committee is 50 percent among medium-sized firms (400 to 1,000 employees) and decreases to 28 percent in firms with fewer than 400 employees (van Rhijn and Huiskamp 1989).

Works councils with an organized constituency and structured contacts with the external union pursue and guard their rights more vigorously. This does not imply that they are more adversarial or reject a larger proportion of management proposals. They may rather be better prepared and behave in a prudent and calculating way, especially when they have regular contacts with union officials; or indeed management may behave differently toward them and involve them on a more regular basis. This would sustain the conclusion that works councils do not substitute for trade unions. If well organized, with good full-time staff and effective internal organization, unions can help create effective works councils. As a result, works councils may be rather ineffective when unions are ineffective, although in many firms this is yet to be tested.

4.5.6   Works Councils and Collective Bargaining

In the 1980s virtually all Dutch businesses restructured their activities, often making accompanying heavy cutbacks in staff. The first motive was to restore cost efficiency and profitability; later, general demands for working-time reduction required new ways of organizing work teams and time schedules. In addition came new ideas about leaner organization and human resource management: flatter hierarchies, reintegration of staff and line functions, marketlike transactions between organizational units, employee involvement, and productivity- and quality-related reward structures. From being championed for its own sake, worker participation became a means to improve productivity and product quality; in the words of a leading Dutch sociologist of organization, participation is now promoted for functional rather than structural reasons (Lammers 1974).

It is not yet possible to estimate the full impact of these changes, but undoubtedly the importance of the firm as an arena in labor relations has increased. Sectoral multiemployer agreements on wages, hours, and related conditions remain important in metal engineering, construction, printing, the dairy industry, agriculture, banking, insurance, and hospitals and health care institutions, to name only the most important. But there is also a tendency to make application of these agreements more flexible and allow better tailoring to the conditions in individual firms. Company agreements have always been predominant in the international sector of the Dutch economy (Philips, Shell, Unilever, AKZO, DSM, PTT, and KLM) and are also typical for firms in the rapidly expanding sector of professional and business services, though many of these firms offer only individual contracts.

Collective bargaining below the firm level, in individual plants or workshops, is rare. Industrywide agreements tend to set minimum rather than standard terms, but the differences are often small. Unions, in particular affiliates of the FNV, seem attracted to a "second round" in the negotiating process, after framework agreements have been reached at the industry level; but the leading employers' federation in the metal and electronics industry has rejected this since two bargaining rounds would, in its words, inevitably lead to two pay rounds. The General Employers' Association (AWV), which is not itself involved in bargaining and instead assists individual firms, is more disposed to a two-tier bargaining system. Both the sectoral and the general employers' associations agree that industry-level agreements have still a function to serve, but they want leaner agreements with narrower coverage and scope, allowing for more individual contracts and reversing the trend toward adding ever newer subjects such as pay compensation systems, training, health, job security, facilities, and so forth.

The unions are reluctant to accept a larger role for the works councils in decentralized collective bargaining. They favor a more restrictive reading of section 27.3 of the Works Council Act—which prohibits the council from renegotiating matters already dealt with by collective agreement—to the effect that councils should be allowed to renegotiate matters under agreement only if asked to do so by the contracting parties. In 1990 the Foundation of Labor, in which the central employers' and union organizations work together, surprisingly issued a recommendation to revise the law in this direction. Employers saw a chance to restrict the scope of co-determination, whereas the unions wanted to forestall an erosion of their prerogatives. This manifestation of opportunism led to protests among works council members and the union rank and file, and the proposal has not been heard of since. After almost two years, the Social Economic Council, whose advice on works council reform was invited by the government, still does not know what to do and is hopelessly divided. A change of the law in either direction—reducing or expanding the bargaining responsibilities of works councils—is improbable.

Dutch employers seem not quite ready to concede works councils a greater bargaining role. In 1985 the parliamentary leader of the Christian Democratic party, who was later minister of social affairs and employment (1990–94), proposed increasing the role of the council in decentralized wage bargaining, causing a storm of protest from the unions, especially from the FNV. But employers did not embrace the idea either. The general position of their associations, and the actual behavior of most employers, is to keep works councils out of wage bargaining. According to a representative sample among Dutch firms by Huiskamp and Risseeuw (1988), only 6 percent of all works councils were actually involved in collective bargaining. It must be recalled that, unlike trade unions, works councils cannot legally call a strike.

The role of the works council is different in firms not covered by an industry or company collective agreement. This is often the case in the subsidiaries of American firms, especially but not only in computer firms, software houses, and consultancy and accountancy firms, and also at Dow Chemicals. Not all American firms stay outside the employers' federations, however, and collective agreements may also be absent in Dutch-owned firms. In these cases management sometimes negotiates a "covenant" with the council. In a recent court case[7] the unions demanded nullification of such a covenant signed between the works council and an employer who had refused to negotiate with the unions. The court rejected this request, arguing that under Dutch law unions do not hold the exclusive right of employee representation in collective bargaining. While works councils cannot renegotiate a collective agreement signed by unions, where the emperor is not present he loses his rights. If unions fail to organize or gain a collective contract because the employer refuses recognition, works councils are free to negotiate alternative arrangements. Covenants lack the juridical infrastructure of the collective agreement, do not receive public protection, and are not legally binding on individual contracts between employer and employee (Doup and Van der Heijden 1991).

The long-term implications of this ruling remain to be seen. Elsewhere I have argued that in Dutch industrial relations the traditional, highly centralized, and patterned model of industrial relations is being eroded by strong centrifugal pressures (Visser 1992b). The 1980s witnessed the emergence of a *terra nova* of large and small firms connected to volatile international markets and engaging in innovative work organization and labor management practices. Many new and expanding firms in emerging sectors, such as business services, computers and information processing, and small-scale engineering and design, are nonunion. If management discovers that individual contracting is less than optimal, especially in such areas as training, job evaluation, and company benefits, its natural partner is the (nonunion) works council. It would be premature to argue that in this case the council becomes a union substitute, since there was no union to begin with. The question is rather whether councils in this case preempt union organization and make the organizing task of unions more difficult. I have no direct evidence either way, but one might speculate that the road to union organization may well go *via* works councils. As a next step, employees, if they feel they need stronger negotiators, may vote for candidates who have the support of unions.

4.6   Evaluation: Costs and Benefits of Works Councils

What do works councils contribute to the economy, the performance of firms, and the welfare of workers? What costs in terms of time, money, production losses, or otherwise are associated with works councils, and who is paying them? Do councils benefit only insiders? Do they lower employment levels by raising the threshold for employment? Do councils help management and

---

7. *Dienstenbonden FNV/CNV v. Grabowski & Poort,* May 19, 1992.

employees negotiate more efficiently and accelerate adjustment to changing technological and international conditions?

The data needed for drawing a complete social, political, cultural, and economic balance sheet of the works council is lacking. Recently, van Hees (1993) explored the impact of works councils and unions on labor costs, quality and speed of decision making, conflict resolution and social peace, management quality, wage inequality, and the use of external resources in Dutch firms. However, his was a qualitative study based on a discussion of one case in particular, and he made no distinction between the impact of the union and that of the works council. To my knowledge there exist no empirical studies on the effect of Dutch works councils on firm profitability or productivity, over time or across firms. Generalization from case studies is not without problems: all surveys show that council practices vary a great deal, although the legal structure of constraints and opportunities is the same. On the other hand, while managers and works council presidents disagree on many aspects of council performance, on one point they agree: works councils have improved the quality of decision making, and works council legislation has penalized hit-and-run styles of management.

Of course this comes at a cost: decisions take longer and require more preparation, paperwork, and meetings, and this is often perceived as an increase in rigidity. Other costs include time off and training for council members, as well as expert advice and other resources that must be paid for by the employer. For a firm of 500 employees, I hazard an estimated cost of 2 percent of the annual wage bill, taking into account paid leave, meetings, facilities, and the council's budget. This does not include the hours management spends on consultation and preparation. The benefit for the firm is greater legitimacy and better acceptance of painful decisions, especially on organizational adjustments. Time "wasted" on preparation may be time saved on implementation, more efficient bargaining, and less conflict. But the largest benefit may well be higher worker commitment, which may survive even painful adjustment processes.

The benefits for workers are more security and fairness, with few or no costs attached. With some sense of fairness in decision making and increased employment security, the acceptability of decisions will rise. Works councils, if they actively use the opportunities offered by the law, will ensure that due consideration will be given to the social and employment consequences of decisions, and that forced dismissals or layoffs will be used only as a last resort. If there must be forced separations, the firm must come forward with a social compensation plan, which usually offers better terms than existing social security and unemployment insurance provisions. Because of the high costs involved, employers will have an incentive to think of something better than returning redundant workers to the external labor market. In exchange, employees will have less reason to oppose alternative options which may entail changes in tasks, job loads, skills, or working hours for themselves.

It is tempting to attribute some of the membership decline in the 1980s to a crowding-out of unions by works councils. Under multiunionism it is difficult for unions to conquer the workplace through control of the council. We have shown some evidence that workers do perceive *voting for union candidates* as a substitute for *union membership.* However, few workers see *the works council* as a substitute for *the union,* and most workers believe that both institutions are needed to be effective. This suggests that Dutch unions suffer from a free rider problem that they cannot solve without either improving their services to members or reinforcing social norms of solidarity through plant organizations of their own.

On the other hand, voting may be a first step toward greater involvement in the union, and unions may find it easier to organize councils than disaggregated workers. There are no indications that employers use councils against unions. Most firms prefer to bargain with unions rather than with works councils. But there are also firms that have excluded unions, insist on non-union membership as a condition of employment, offer individual employment contracts only, and entertain a rather cozy relationship with the council. At the same time, we also witness a formalization of relations in these very firms, through quasi-collective agreements ("covenants") which may well prove an intermediate step from individual contracting to full-blown collective bargaining.

We may, finally, look at the costs and benefits of works councils from a societal point of view. I have found no evidence that works council legislation has scared away businesses or lowered investment and employment in the Netherlands. Less conflict, higher worker commitment, and more investment in training may be seen as advantages. Statutory works councils cast the safety net for workers wider than unions, though they need the help of unions under adverse conditions. Works councils also assist in the enforcement of health and safety legislation, the protection of handicapped and disabled persons, equal opportunity, and so forth, where the law explicitly assigns a monitoring task to them. Councils may well deepen the bite of legislation on firms, but as local enforcement agents, trained in weighing conflicting interests, they may also help find customized and flexible solutions.

My overall conclusion is that, even under weak and divided unionism as currently exists in the Netherlands, works councils do make a positive difference. Despite the economic recession and severe union decline, councils have achieved an established position in Dutch industrial relations. They contribute to the quality of managerial decision making and help trade flexibility in work organization for employment security. This beneficial outcome is not always achieved, and in fact much variation is found in what works councils actually do. Some are sleeping and have never been tested, and others would fail if they were, but some—probably a minority—have become active players. Where councils have achieved an active role, this was often because of support from an organized constituency and the union; but there are also examples of works councils that owe their position to employers realizing a functional need for consultation. Above all, works councils, having been strengthened as an institution of employee representation in 1979, have cushioned the impact of economic adversity and union decline on firm-level labor relations in the Netherlands during the 1980s.

References

Acampo, J., P. Kunst, and J. Soeters. 1987. OR-lidmaatschap en loopbaanperspectief. *Tijdschrift voor Arbeidsvraagstukken* 3(4): 37–49.

Andriessen, Jan H. T. H., Pieter J. D. Drenth, and C. J. Lammers. 1984. *Medezeggenschap in Nederlandse bedrijven: Verslag van een onderzoek naar participatie- en invloedsverhoudingen.* Amsterdam: North-Holland.

Buitendam, Arend-Jan. 1979. *Personeelsafdelingen in de Industrie.* Groningen: Konstapel.

CNV (Christelijk Nationaal Vakverbond). 1987. OR-lidmaatschap, loopbaan en verloop. Report prepared by Rijksuniversiteit Limburg. Utrecht: Christelijk Nationaal Vakbverbond. Mimeograph.

Dekkers, H., P. T. Calhoen, and J. H. T. H. Andriessen. 1989. *Medezeggenschap in kleine ondernemingen (35–100 werknemers).* Tilburg: Instituut voor Sociaal-Wetenschappelijk Onderzoek.

de Man, Herman, and Paul L. Koopman. Medezeggenschap tussen ideologie en bedrijfsspraktijk. M&O: Tijdschrift voor organisatiekunde en sociaal beleid 38(6): 471–80.

Doup, Anneke C. B. W., and Paul F. Van der Heijden. 1991. Medezeggeschap per convenant. The Hague: Organisatie voor Strategisch Arbeidsmarktonderzoek.

Drenth, Pieter J. D., and J. C. van der Pijl. 1966. *De Ondernemingsraad in Nederland.* The Hague: Sociaal Economische Raad.

EIM (Economisch Instituut voor het Midden- en Kleinbedrijf). 1990. *The state of small business in the Netherlands,* rev. ed. Zoetermeer: Economisch Instituut voor het Midden- en Kleinbedrijf.

Fase, Wim J. P. M. 1969. *Medezeggenschap in de onderneming.* Haarlem: Algemene Werkgeversvereniging.

Flanagan, Robert J., David W. Soskice, and Lloyd Ulman. 1983. *Unionism, economic stabilization and incomes policies: European experience.* Washington D.C.: Brookings Institution.

Harmsen, Ger, and Bob Reinalda. 1975. Voor de bevrijding van de arbeid: Beknopte geschiedenis van de Nederlandse arbeidsbeweging. Nijmegen: Socialistiese Uitgeverij Nijmegen.

Heijink, Jan Z. 1986. Het functioneren van de ondernemingsraad. Namens: Tijdschrift voor vertegenwoordiging en bestuur 2: 56–57.

Heller, Frank A., Pieter J. D. Drenth, Paul L. Koopman, and Vaklo Rus. 1988. *Decisions in organizations: A three-country comparative study.* London: Sage.

Hövels, Ben W. M., and Peter Nas. 1976. Ondernemingsraden en Medezeggenschap. Nijmegen: Instituut voor Toegepaste Sociologie.

Hueting, Ernst, Fritz de Jong Edz, and Rob Ney. 1985. *Naar groter eenheid: De geschiedenis van het FNV.* Amsterdam: van Gennep.

Huiskamp, Rien J., and R. J. Risseeuw. 1988. *Ondernemingsraad en arbeidsvoorwaarden: Een onderzoek naar de rol van de OR bij het tot stand komen van de primaire arbeidsvoorwaarden.* Amsterdam: Economisch-Sociaal Instituut-Vrije Universiteit.

IB FNV (Industriebond Federatie Nederlandse Vakbewiging). 1979. *De Industriebond-FNV in het bedrijf.* Amsterdam: Industriebond Federatie Nederlandse Vakbewiging.
————. 1980. *Verder Kijken.* Amsterdam: Industriebond Federatie Nederlandse Vakbewiging.
————. 1990. *VGW in profiel.* Amsterdam: Industriebond Federatie Nederlandse Vakbewiging.
IDE. (Industrial Democracy in Europe). 1981. Oxford: Clarendon.
Klandermans, Bert, Sharda Nadram, Bas van der Putte, Coen van Rij, Wim Saris, Gerite van der Veen, and Jelle Visser. 1992. *Participatie in vakbonden: Een opiniepeiling onder CNV- en FNV-leden.* Amsterdam: Nederlands Instituut voor Markt- en Maatschappij Onderzoek.
Koene, Anneke M., and Hans Slomp. 1990. *Medezeggenschap van werknemers op ondernemingsniveau: Een onderzoek naar regels en hun toepassing in zes Europese landen.* The Hague: VUGA.
Koning, Frank. 1991. Rechtspraak medezeggenschapsrecht. *Sociaal Maandblad Arbeid* 46(3): 171–84.
Lammers, Cornelis J. 1968. De ondernemingsraad als beleidsinstrument: Sociologische beschouwingen naar aanleiding van enkele onderzoeks-resultaten. *Mens en Onderneming* 22(1): 24–43.
————. 1974. Self-management and participation: Two conceptions of democratization of organizations. *Organization and Administration Sciences* 5(4): 17–33.
Looise, Jan C. 1989. The recent growth in employees' representation in the Netherlands: Defying the times? In *International handbook of participation in organisations,* vol. 1, *Organisational democracy: Taking stock,* ed. C. J. Lammers and G. Szell, 268–84. Oxford: Oxford University Press.
Looise, Jan C., and F. G. M. de Lange. 1987. *Ondernemingsraden, bestuurders en besluitvorming.* Nijmegen: Instituut voor Toegepaste Sociologie.
Looise, Jan C., and Jan Z. Heijink. 1986. *De OR en zijn bevoegdheden. Interim-rapport OR-onderzoek.* Nijmegen: Instituut voor Toegepaste Sociologie.
Pool, Jan, Pieter J. D. Drenth, Paul L. Koopman, and Cornelis J. Lammers. 1988. De volwassenwording van de medezeggenschap: Invloeds-verhoudingen in de jaren tachtig. *Gedrag en Organisatie* 3(1): 36–57.
Pool, Jan, Paul L. Koopman, and A. A. Mijs. 1991. Invloed en medezeggenschap na tien jaar no nonsensemanagement: Een replicatiestudie in drie bedrijfstakken. *Tijdschrift voor Arbeidsvraagstukken* 7(2): 54–66.
Schuit, Steven R., Marcel Romyn, Gerrit H. Zevenboom, and Michael W. den Boogert. 1988. *Dutch business law: Legal, accounting and tax aspects of doing business in the Netherlands.* 3d ed. Kluwer Law and Taxation. Deventer: Kluwer.
Smid, Gerhard, Wim Sprenger, and Jelle Visser. 1979. *Vakbondswerk moet je leren.* Amsterdam: Socialistische Uitgeverij Amsterdam.
Teulings, Ad. 1981. *Ondernemingsraadpolitiek in Nederland: Een onderzoek naar de omgang met macht en conflict door de ondernemingsraad.* Amsterdam: van Gennep.
————. 1985. Prominenten en volgers: Recht, macht en invloed van ondernemingsraden op de besluitvorming. *Tijdschrift voor Arbeidsvraagstukken* 1(1): 51–64.
————. 1989. A political bargaining theory of co-determination. In *The state, trade unions and self-management: Issues of competence and control,* ed. G. Széll, P. Blyton, and C. Cornforth, 75–101. New York: de Gruyter.
van der Berg, G. 1924. *De medezeggenschap der arbeiders in de particuliere onderneming.* Thesis, University of Amsterdam.
Van der Heijden, Paul F. 1991. De volwassen ondernemingsraad. *Sociaal Maandblad Arbeid* 46: 692–98.
van der Putte, Bas, Jelle Visser, and Coen van Rij. 1991. *De vakbond in het bedrijf.* Amsterdam: Nederlands Instituut voor Markt- en Maatschappij Onderzoek.

van Haren, Ivo. 1985. *De geschiedenis van de medezeggenschap in Nederland.* Deventer: Kluwer.

van Hees, Bert. 1993. *Bedrijfsmatige aspooten van vakbonden en ondernemingsraden.* Louvain/Apeldoorn: Garant.

van Rhijn, I. A. W., and Rien J. Huiskamp. 1989. *Vergelijkende analyse van vakbondsgroepen in bedrijven.* Amsterdam: Economisch-Sociaal Instituut-Vrije Universiteit.

van Vliet, G. E. 1979. *Bedrijvenwerk als vorm van belangenbehartiging.* Alphen a/d Rijn: Samson.

van Vuuren, C. V., and Paul L. Koopman. 1986. Medezeggenschap door de ondernemingsraad nieuwe stijl. *Tijdschrift voor Arbeidsvraagstukken* 2(1): 50–62.

Visser, Jelle. 1989. New working-time arrangements and policies in the Netherlands. In *Current issues in labor relations: An international perspective,* ed. Alan Gladstone, Russell Lansbury, Jack Stieber, Tiziano Treu, and Manfred Weiss, 229–52. New York: de Gruyter.

———. 1990. Continuity and change in Dutch industrial relations. In *European industrial relations: The challenge of flexibility,* ed. Guido Baglioni and Colin Crouch, 199–243. London, Newbury Park, New Delhi: Sage.

———. 1991a. Employee representation in West European workplaces: Structure, scale, scope and strategy. Paper prepared for the 3d European regional congress of the Industrial Relations Research Association.

———. 1991b. Trends in trade union membership. In *Employment outlook July 1991,* 97–134. Paris: Organisation of Economic Co-operation and Development.

———. 1992a. The coming divergence in Dutch industrial relations. In *Labor relations in a changing environment,* ed. A. Gladstone et al., 251–66. New York: de Gruyter.

———. 1992b. The end of an era and the end of an system. In *Industrial relations in the new Europe,* ed. R. Hyman and A. Ferner, 323–56. Oxford: Blackwell.

Visser, Jelle, and B. Ebbinghaus. 1992. Making the most of diversity? European integration and transnational organization of labor. In *Interests organization and the European Community,* ed. J. Greenwood, J. Grote, and K. Ronit, 206–37. London: Sage.

Windmuller, John P. 1969. *Labor relations in the Netherlands.* Ithaca, N.Y.: Cornell University Press.

5   France: From Conflict to Social Dialogue?

Robert Tchobanian

Works councils are required by law in France. They are part of a mixed system of worker representation in the workplace, which includes union locals. The actual place and the role of the works council has long been contested between employers and trade unions, and this has reduced the impact of councils on company life. During the 1970s, the growing crisis in the labor market, the decline of Taylorism, and companies' emerging human resource policies exacerbated the conflict. Meanwhile, the industrial relations system underwent major changes due to new laws and economic and social transformations. Are the works councils now becoming the focal point of a more active social dialogue? And is such change possible at a time when the influence of unions on the workforce is sharply declining?

The characteristics of the French system require works council activities to be analyzed within the wider framework of industrial relations and its evolution, keeping the councils' history in mind.

5.1   Legal Framework of Workplace Representation

Collective worker representation at the workplace level is a mixed system bringing together elected bodies and trade unions. Its purpose was redefined in 1982 with the Auroux reforms, named after the minister of labor of the time. It is within this framework that the place of works councils in France will be examined.

Robert Tchobanian is a senior research fellow at the Centre National de la Recherche Scientifique at the Laboratoire d'Economie et de Sociologie du Travail, Aix en Provence.

5.1.1   Systems of Workplace Representation

In 1990, there were approximately 19 million workers in France, according to general census figures. National and local government workers are represented under special rules. The law regulating worker representation at the workplace level mainly affects the private and competitive public sectors, which at the end of 1990 employed about 14 million workers.

The complexity of the workplace representation system required by law varies with firm size. No internal representation system exists for firms with up to 10 employees. In firms with 11 or more employees, personnel delegates (*délégués du personnel*), elected by all employees, are required by law. In companies and establishments with a workforce of 50 or more, there are in addition enterprise committees (*comités d'entreprise ou d'establissement*), whose members are elected in the same way. These companies have also a health and safety committee (*comité d'hygiène, de sécurité et des conditions de travail*— CHSCT), which is named by the elected enterprise committee and the personnel delegates.

Trade unions may set up union locals at the workplace by naming union delegates (*délégué syndical*) to the management. Unions have a legal right to name union delegates in companies with more than 50 employees. In smaller firms, the personnel delegates can be named union delegates for their term of office, unless a more advantageous system is created by industrial agreement.

The distribution of workers by size of establishment shows the worker populations represented by the different arrangements (table 5.1). For companies and establishments with 50 or more employees, which employ approximately half of the workforce in the private and competitive public sectors, the representation system is made up of four bodies: personnel delegates, the enterprise committee, the health and safety committee, and union delegates. Personnel delegates, enterprise committees, and health and safety committees all perform functions of works councils; they are part of a mixed representation system which also includes the trade unions.

Table 5.1   **Employment in the Private and Competitive Public Sectors by Size of Establishment, 1990**

Size of Establishment (number of workers)	Number of Workers	Percentage of Workers
1–9	3,338,986	24.1
10–49	3,973,647	28.7
50–199	3,175,644	22.9
200–499	1,614,070	11.7
500 or more	1,744,701	12.6
Total	13,847,048	100

Source: UNEDIC 1991.

The enterprise committee comes closest to the definition of a works council (see Rogers and Streeck, chap. 1 in this volume). All employees of the firm are represented, not just the union members. The committee is involved in the economic and organizational life of the firm. In terms of the typology proposed by Rogers and Streeck, the enterprise committee is a representative council, its rights being defined by law. In particular, the enterprise committee engages in three kinds of activity:

1. It manages the funds provided by the firm for social and cultural activities for the employees and their families. These can be considered indirect wages, the allocation of which is decided by the enterprise committee.

2. It is entitled to receive information and offer advice on "the firm's organization, management, and general functioning."

3. It may negotiate agreements on profit sharing (the distribution of part of the company's annual profits to the employees) and financial participation.

Enterprise committees meet every month. Meetings are chaired by the head of the firm; a secretary is elected from among the members. Committees are entitled to 0.2 percent of a firm's total payroll to cover their operating expenses, and each member is entitled to limited paid release from work, not counting the time spent in committee meetings. Depending on the size of the firm, commissions are set up in which individual employees may be asked to assist the enterprise committee. Economic training is to be provided to the elected members to prepare them for their mission. A certified accountant helps the members understand the company's accounts. Under some conditions, the enterprise committee may also obtain advice from an outside expert on the introduction of new technology.

In companies with several establishments, each with its own enterprise committee, a central enterprise committee exists to deal with problems common to the entire company. Likewise, companies that are part of a group of companies have a group committee. Where all of these provisions are applied, the enterprise committee, rounded out by the health and safety committee for questions of occupational hazards, is the representative body with the best access to information and the strongest technical means for influencing the firm's economic and social life and its consequences for the employees.

The situation of the personnel delegates is more complex. They are responsible for presenting the employer once a month with all individual and collective grievances concerning the application of legal or contractual rules. They also present any demands aimed at changing these rules. Thus, their role is similar to that of the trade unions. Before 1982, they were often the main place of union expression before management. Personnel delegates do not, however, have bargaining rights; these belong to the union locals. Their role appears to be on the decline today.

Union locals, and the union delegates who represent them to management, play a more general role. Legally, they are in charge of "defending the material and moral interests" of the workers. This includes organizing union life within the firm, for example, collecting dues and convening union meetings. Coordinating the activities of union members in works councils is another general prerogative of union locals. Like the personnel delegates, the union delegates are responsible for representing workers' individual and collective grievances. But their true representative role lies in the area of collective bargaining. Union delegates can bargain with management and sign company or plant agreements. The 1982 legislation makes it obligatory for management to bargain locally on matters like wages, working hours, time schedules, and worker participation ("expression") at regular intervals. Like elected representatives, the union delegates are protected against dismissal, and the firm pays them for a certain number of hours spent on union activities.

Finally, there are links among the enterprise committee, the health and safety committee, the personnel delegates, and the union delegates. The personnel delegates may transmit employee demands to the enterprise committee and the health and safety committee. During their monthly meeting with management, they may be assisted by a union delegate. Union locals may send representatives to the enterprise committee and thus receive all information provided to its elected members. The enterprise committee and the health and safety committee sometimes deal with the same problems. The union locals typically try to coordinate the activities of the different bodies. For certain questions, enterprise committee consultations may be carried out in conjunction with negotiations conducted by the union delegates. During elections of personnel delegates and enterprise committees, the first round of voting is open only to the lists of the unions present at the workplace. Nonunion candidates may run only in a second round, which is called if there are no union lists or if these did not obtain the votes of the majority of the employees.

Even though it is complicated, this system seems relatively balanced, giving space to elected bodies representing all employees, as well as to union representation. But it is also the result of a long historical process. The place of workforce representation in the company, and the place of the unions within such representation, was until recently more a question of power and the result of mutual distrust between employers and unions than one of stable rules of joint regulation.

5.1.2 Historical Formation of the Representation System

The present system is the result of an accumulation of representative bodies that appeared at various stages in the history of the French industrial relations system and that are the expression of sometimes contradictory choices regarding the levels of collective bargaining, the role of union activity in the plant and the company, and the proper place of elected employee representation.

Before 1936, employee representation at the workplace was not required by law. Collective bargaining existed at the industry level. The company was not a place of bargaining, nor was there internal worker representation. Works councils had existed in a variety of forms since the middle of the nineteenth century (e.g., health and safety delegates in coal mines, works councils in the armaments industry during World War I, and paternalistic councils in individual companies). But all attempts at legislation on a broader basis failed because of distrust between employers and unions (Andolfatto 1992). In 1936 the employers, faced with many strikes, proposed that representatives responsible for expressing workers' demands be elected by all workers within each establishment, regardless of union membership. Acceptance of the institution of personnel delegates was an employer concession made in a crisis to keep unions themselves out of the workplace. A law on collective bargaining that same year confirmed that bargaining was to take place mainly on the industry level.

Enterprise committees were created in 1945, in a period of relative social consensus after the end of World War II. Enterprise committees were to play a role in the operation of the establishment. They were to be given information and to be consulted, so as to improve the dialogue between management and labor. However, the representative trade unions obtained a monopoly over candidacies in enterprise committee elections, just as in the elections of personnel delegates. A 1951 law reaffirmed the centralization of collective bargaining at the industry level.

After the severe social conflicts of 1968, a law was adopted entitling unions to set up locals at the workplace. Very few workers need to be unionized for a local to come into existence since all that is required is the designation of union delegates by external unions. From 1968 on, personnel delegates, enterprise committees, and union delegates coexisted without any clear division of their tasks. A law adopted in 1971 made it possible to negotiate collective agreements at the company level. However, while union locals were set up in large numbers, workplace bargaining did not develop widely.

This was one of the reasons why in 1982 the new leftist government proposed the Auroux reforms. Their purpose was to reform industrial relations, and particularly representation at the workplace, by linking them to the major changes that were under way at the time. Employers and unions together had made the system inoperative. Their traditional positions must be analyzed for a better understanding of what was at stake with the Auroux reforms and how they were actually applied. Special attention must also be paid to the economic situation of the 1970s, especially to the crisis of Taylorist forms of work organization.

5.2   Workplace Industrial Relations before the 1980s

Traditional French industrial relations assigned little significance to the workplace. Despite the existence of personnel delegates and enterprise committees, employers as well as unions preferred to avoid social dialogue at this level. Employers have traditionally been suspicious of union activities at the workplace. The position of the works councils is a result of this attitude.

5.2.1 Employer Strategies

Neutralizing the Workplace in Industrial Relations

French employers have always tried to protect their discretion in managing their companies by limiting union intervention and, more generally, any regulation imposed from outside. Personnel delegates and enterprise committees are representative bodies instituted by law; they may therefore limit the employer's autonomy. Moreover, they came into being at times when political and social events had weakened the power of employers.

French employers and their organizations have consistently strived to neutralize the individual company as a place of collective bargaining, resisting direct union intervention in its functioning. This explains in large part why bargaining was centralized at the industry level (Sellier 1961). Industrywide wage agreements set minimum wages, thus regulating the labor market to a certain extent by limiting competition among companies. Other contractual provisions standardize general employment conditions. On the other hand, industrywide agreements almost never affect work rules. Centralized collective bargaining therefore offers two advantages for the firm: agreements are not very restrictive at the workplace where they are actually applied, and the organization of work and the firm is not affected since these are matters that cannot be regulated in industry-level negotiations. Employers thus avoid union control over the very heart of company life.

Thus, the company remains in the hands of the employer. Taylorization in industry illustrates this. It began between the two world wars and went together with the development of large industry. This rationalization of production was undertaken without the unions being able to influence organizational choices or to control their effects on the workers (Ribeill 1984). Work rules imposed on the workers were determined exclusively by management initiative and the hierarchy in conceiving tasks and controlling their execution. Similarly, the social organization of the company was the result of unilateral decisions made by management.

The neutralization of the firm as a place of bargaining weakens the presence of the unions at the workplace. The traditional position of French employers toward works councils is related to this. In a paternalistic strategy, works councils can be used to limit union influence. But proposed works council legislation has often been designed to allow for a measure of "workers' control" (Hordern 1988). The personnel delegates, as set up in 1936, can be considered as combining these two concepts. By accepting them, employers were able to avoid direct union representatives. But the activity of the personnel delegates was one of relaying grievances and demands. They contested employer decisions and were soon perceived as indirectly carrying out union activities. Employers therefore always tried to limit their role.

Employer attitudes toward the enterprise committees are more complex. Enterprise committees were created after the war when unions were strong. They appeared after experiments with worker participation in the management of some factories at the time when France was liberated. Enterprise committees did have some effect on company organization and, in this respect, were a threat to the employer's authority. On the other hand, they came into being during a time of relative consensus and economic reconstruction. Moreover, they were not decision-making bodies but bodies of information and consultation. Also, the fact that the head of the company chaired the enterprise committee made it easier to integrate them into the life of the company. Employers have therefore always favored the enterprise committees over the personnel delegates, and even more over the unions. At the same time, employers never made an effort to turn them into a more dynamic place for dialogue, and neither the employers nor the unions have tried to change their mutual relations through the enterprise committees (Montuclard 1963). In practice, enterprise committees have therefore often done no more than manage the company's social budget. Toward the end of the 1960s, however, new horizons began to open up for works councils.

The 1970s: The Strategy of Direct Participation

The development of French industry after 1950 entailed a high degree of Taylorization linked to mass production. Assembly lines and jobs requiring little training became common. The strikes of 1968 brought to light deep resentment among workers, particularly related to working conditions. The employer organization, the Conseil National du Patronat Français (CNPF—National Council of French Employers), for the first time had to accept union locals at the firm level. In the early 1970s, strikes over the organization of work became frequent, and workplace-level bargaining appeared necessary for dealing with the new quality of working life problems that had appeared (Reynaud 1968). But employers still refused to expand bargaining at the workplace.

In particular, union locals were accepted only under social pressure. Employers considered them foreign bodies introduced into the workplace and tried to limit their role to organizing union activities. A 1974 report studied the effects of the 1968 legislation on the relationship between enterprise committees, personnel delegates, and union delegates (Bachy, Dupuis, and Martin 1974). It showed that company management preferred informal over formal relations with employees, and relations with the elected representatives of all workers over relations with the union locals. In addition, the enterprise committee, dedicated to dialogue, was preferred over the personnel delegates, who expressed worker demands. The traditional suspicion of union activities was found to persist, and social dialogue with union-dominated works councils was limited.

It would seem that the social conflicts associated with a Taylorist system of organization should have modified employer attitudes. Conflicts in Taylorist factories were often spontaneously initiated by the workers themselves, and an established bargaining machinery could have helped prevent uncontrollable social outbursts. The unions, however, found it difficult to define offensive strategies in these areas, given their traditional reticence toward adopting a position on the operation of the firm. In 1975, an economywide, "interoccupational" agreement signed by the CNPF and the minority unions stressed the need to improve working conditions while confirming that responsibility for this lay with the employers. No machinery was set up to enforce the agreement, however, and very few clarifying industry or company agreements were signed.

In subsequent years, companies began to develop their own social policies in response to the effects of Taylorism, without negotiation and often without even consulting the works councils: new forms of work organization, opportunities for workers to express their interests directly, changes in work schedules, communication policies, dialogue with supervisory and managerial staff, and so forth. At its 1977 and 1980 annual congresses, the CNPF presented summaries of these experiments, proposing to all firms a new, unilateral model for active social relations at the workplace.

This model was based on the direct mobilization of the workers themselves. Direct participation enabled the employer to limit union influence and thereby limit bargaining at the workplace. It also reduced the role of the legally required works councils. For example, employer-worker committees on safety and working conditions gave workers the opportunity to participate in improving safety at work. But they were acting in an area for which two legal commissions connected with enterprise committees already existed. Through social policies of this kind, employers reintroduced nonrepresentative forms of communication, using problems in working conditions to reassert control in managing the company and its human resources. A 1975 survey of company executives showed that the majority were still against bargaining and preferred increased direct participation (Bunel and Saglio 1979).

This is regardless of the fact that works councils, especially in the form of enterprise committees, would have seemed well suited for assisting with these new practices. In some cases, organizational innovations had actually been discussed with and were overseen by the enterprise committee. In 1973, the introduction of variable working hours was legally authorized, contingent on prior consultation with the enterprise committee. Certain public subsidies to firms for the improvement of working conditions also required an enterprise committee opinion. Furthermore, under the law the enterprise committee must be presented with an annual assessment of the impact of a company's activities and projects on working conditions. However, firms generally carried out their innovative projects without the elected representatives. A survey published by the CNPF in 1980 spent only a half a page out of 410 pages on enterprise committees and personnel delegates (CNPF/CODESE 1980).

This attitude can be explained by the influence of the unions on the works councils. Moreover, the CGT and the CFDT, the unions most strongly represented on works councils, had at the time a strategy of conflict rather then aiming at agreement. The employers, in turn, demanded the elimination of the union monopoly on candidacies in the first round of enterprise committee and personnel delegate elections. Through their unilateral social policies, employers wanted to limit both legally and union based intervention to issues covered by the law or to bargaining outside the firm. A different type of dialogue, established directly with the employees, was to be used for dealing internally with most social questions. In a way, these were "paternalistic" works councils (Rogers and Streeck, chap. 1 in this volume) created by the employer. But their very success raised the question of the relationship between them and legally required worker representation.

At first, companies wanted to protect their autonomy in areas traditionally beyond union control. But economic difficulties and the loss of competitiveness of French industry gave rise to new needs for social and organizational flexibility. At the end of the 1970s, the CNPF asked that centralized regulation be reduced in favor of regulations decided upon within the company, but without accepting the unions as bargaining agents at that level. Who was to be the employer's bargaining partner was unclear. An interoccupational agreement reached in 1981 linked a reduction in working hours to greater flexibility in the organization of company time schedules. But the CNPF refused to negotiate time schedules with the union locals and recommended that managements discuss the subject with the enterprise committee. The CFDT, the second-largest union, which had signed the agreement, demanded that bargaining rights be explicitly accorded to the unions alone. The Auroux reforms took these difficulties into account, along with other needs, in redefining the levels and actors involved in social dialogue at the workplace.

5.2.2 Union Attitudes before the Auroux Reforms

Employer distrust of works councils before the Auroux reforms is explained mainly by union policies and their influence on elected representatives. In turn, the strong position of the employer within the workplace explains the attitudes of the unions. It is difficult to describe the latter in short because of the variety of unions in France and the differences between them. The base of the French union movement lies outside the company. There are four union confederations that are open to all workers: the Confédération Générale du Travail (CGT), the Confédération Française Démocratique du Travail (CFDT), the "Force Ouvrière" (FO), which broke away from the CGT in 1947–48, and the Confédération Française des Travailleurs Chrétiens (CFTC). Managerial staff can also join the Confédération Générale des Cadres (CGC). Here we will primarily deal with the traditional "mass and class" unionism in industry, which, under the influence of the CGT, stresses a working-class worldview. This model exercised a certain hegemony in the union movement, as confirmed by election results. For example, 50.8 percent of the votes in the enterprise committee elections of 1966 went to the CGT, and only 19.1 percent to the CFDT. The positions of these two unions can be used to describe union attitudes toward enterprise committees and personnel delegates up to the end of the 1970s.

Union Workplace Organization and Fears of Integration

Attempts to organize union activities within the company always met with resistance from employers. Perhaps works councils could have been used as an institutional means of indirectly increasing union influence. But the traditional weakness of the unions at the workplace explains their hesitation and their preference for a strategy of conflict. Union strategy on works councils was long defined by this conflictual stance.

The situation is similar for collective bargaining. Industry-level negotiations leave the individual firm autonomy and thus give power to the employer. Company-level bargaining should therefore have been a major union goal. In fact, union attitudes were not that simple. Up until 1982, company bargaining was rarely used and was considered more a phase in the general conflict process than a means of obtaining a lasting collective agreement. Its general use was considered risky. Because union presence differed from one company to another, bargaining at the company level would have been less favorable for less well organized workers. There was also a risk of company egoism, and possibly even of competition among employees. Centralized bargaining, on the other hand, created a minimum level of protection that could then be improved in more prosperous companies. Unions also lacked the human, material, and conceptual resources to carry out effective company-level bargaining. The situation was more balanced at the industry level where the union was represented by full-time leaders.

On the other hand, industry-level agreements were unable to impose effective restrictions on employers. They were therefore regarded as a point of departure for union activists at the workplace, who had to use all available means to obtain improvements. This was the goal behind the mobilization of workers during conflicts. Strikes and demands were used for constant "harassment" of management. Within the model, results obtained through collective bargaining or strikes are no more than "social armistices" which hold until the unions have built up enough strength to challenge management again. Strikes are not a weapon related directly to formal collective bargaining since company-level conflict and industry-level bargaining are often unconnected. Rather, strikes are to mobilize the workers, many of whom are not unionized, and to strengthen the position of the workers within the firm. Unions are not organized by occupational groups, even though they consist mainly of skilled workers, since they aim at representing all workers whatever their job or category. They therefore do little to influence work rules (Eyraud 1983).

French unions' approach to the company is determined by this model of union action. The organization of work and the management of the firm are considered to be inevitably defined by the power of the employer. For the workers, it is therefore more important to control the consequences of the organizational choices made by the employer than to influence these choices themselves. The introduction of Taylorist principles was seen as confirming this analysis. In practice, French unions have left the company a free hand in organizing the workplace. This "Fordist social compromise" does not imply the absence of social conflict; in fact, conflict is at the very center of union activity. But it coexists with a tacit understanding that leaves company organization to the company itself and focuses union activity mainly on the distribution of income and other material benefits. The result is very low union involvement in the governance of the workplace.

The ideologies of each of the two major unions contributed to this outcome. The CGT, which is Marxist, sees socialism as the solution to the contradictions of capitalist management. Involvement in a firm's economic decision making under the present system is regarded as dangerous. The CFDT, in turn, advocated socialist self-management in the 1970s. But this never translated into concrete demands, even though the CFDT was highly critical of Taylorist principles. Thus, works councils provide unions with an indirect but institutionalized presence, and they may be used to increase union influence within companies and with the workers. They are not, however, considered instruments of intervention in the organization of the firm and of work. Moreover, union pluralism often leads to union competition at the workplace, which stifles innovative initiatives.

The cases of the personnel delegates and the enterprise committees are, however, quite different. The personnel delegates deal with demands and grievances, which corresponds directly to the union model of action. Once a month, the personnel delegates have the right to express demands, and management is required to meet with them. While the monthly meetings between the personnel delegates and management were designed for individual grievances to be presented, this is rarely the case (Bonafe-Schmitt 1981). The personnel delegates' main activity is to present general union demands, which are raised anew at each meeting. Given that they are often accompanied by union representatives, personnel delegates are actually a union delegation that meets with the employer. Indeed during strikes, the personnel delegates use their meetings with the employer to articulate the demands of the unions in order to help obtain the desired results. This is not really formal bargaining since there is no agreement but only employer concessions. The institution of the personnel delegates also enables the unions to make their demands known to the employees, despite the hostility of the employers, and personnel delegates do play a role in representing individual grievances, which is often done more informally. Through these interventions, the personnel delegates have managed to bring together formal action, mainly by raising collective demands, and informal influence with respect to individual employee needs. To reduce the number of demands expressed through this channel, management in the 1970s reinforced the contacts between workers and the company hierarchy and created opportunities for direct expression of worker interests.

The enterprise committees are in a different position. Created at a time when large sections of the French union movement demanded that employees be given a role in the management of the firm, enterprise committees never had more than advisory status. While there had been plans to institute arbitration in case of disagreement, this did not materialize, and unlike their German counterparts, enterprise committees were not given powers of co-determination, although they did obtain rights to accounting and organizational information. Their activities therefore remained of little importance, except during the period immediately after the war; and the unions did little to change this. After 1948, the CGT warned against the dangers of class collaboration inherent in enterprise committee policies that were not directly unionist. This corresponded to union fears of getting involved in management in the absence of conflictual conditions. As a consequence, the number of enterprise committees declined until the mid-1960s.

The 1970s: Trade Unions Facing Company Social Policies

The creation of workplace union organizations enabled the unions, especially the CGT and the CFDT, to attempt to coordinate their activities with those of the elected works councils. A growing number of enterprise committees were set up in this period, not only because of the new presence of the unions but also because some companies tried to use the committees to limit the role of the union locals. The position of both the CGT and the CFDT was to make the union local the center of the representative system at the workplace, with the enterprise committee and the personnel delegates serving as sources of information and general institutional resources. Reality in the companies, however, was much more varied. The actual structure of representative systems, especially the relationship between the works councils and the union locals, was determined by the interaction between employers and unions and their respective strength. Three main situations could be found in the beginning of the 1970s (Martin 1976). In the first, in which the unions were weak, both actors favored normally functioning elected bodies despite their small influence. In the second, in which the employer was opposed to bargaining with the unions, unions coordinated their activities with the works councils, which in fact expressed the union position. And in the third, in which union presence was strong and management preferred a single bargaining partner, the union local was predominant.

The relationship between elected works councils and union structures cannot be explained simply by existing legal provisions. The interaction between the social actors and the context of this interaction played a predominant role. Conflict over the rules of the game (the procedural rules) became more important than maximizing the benefits of representation (the substantive rules).

Union difficulties toward the end of the 1970s illustrated the effects this had on the role of the representative bodies.

At the beginning of the 1970s, rising social conflict and growing unionization appeared to ensure that a new balance would be reached, with greater union influence. Union locals were rapidly set up: while in 1970, 27.5 percent of all establishments with 50 employees or more had at least one union local, in 1978 this figure had increased to 58.4 percent. And yet, at the end of this period, company social policies had undermined the stability of the workplace representation system as well as of collective bargaining. Faced with this situation, the unions began to examine new strategies.

The employment crisis is often presented as the main cause of the difficulties faced by the unions after 1977. Declining employment in major industries took away social pressure and limited the benefits obtainable through union action. The result was a decline in union membership. But other factors also contributed, among them the union's response to company participation practices (Tchobanian 1990). New forms of work organization, direct employee expression, and flexible work schedules were often denounced by the unions simply because these ideas came from the employer. Union locals were unable to intervene through negotiation or enterprise committee consultations. Fear of agreeing to technical solutions that might benefit the company while not increasing the unions' conflictual power led the latter to denounce practices that the employees often approved. The lack of any real debate among unions on changed work practices and new needs of workers contributed to union decline.

Employee expression is an area in which the rising difficulties were easily observed. The CFDT had demanded it since 1973, but in a form that linked it to union action. The other unions were less sure. Finally, it was the employers who created opportunities for expression, in a form that corresponded to their needs and competed with the unions, and especially with the personnel delegates. For the unions, denouncing these practices to the workers was no longer enough. The evolution of a new attitude was most striking at the CFDT, which in 1978 accepted union-independent employee expression, provided that it was negotiated at the workplace with the union locals. Less conflictual union policies were offered in exchange for recognition of the union's presence at the workplace. At that time, the CNPF rejected the CFDT's propositions, only to find them later included in the Auroux reforms.

The Auroux reforms tried to fulfill two needs. The role of the unions, which were faced with considerable difficulties at the workplace, was reasserted. In addition, the reforms tried to promote continued and intensified structural change in response to new economic constraints. While unions were assigned a legitimate role within the company, they were expected to accept major changes in their practices.

5.2.3   The Auroux Reforms: The Search for a New Industrial Relations System

In 1982 the Auroux reforms redefined the collective rights of workers. Union locals obtained the right to annual negotiations on wages and the organization of working hours; the involvement of the enterprise committee in company activities was strengthened; the health and safety committee was created; and the right to direct and collective "expression" was instituted for employees. The purpose of the reforms was to rationalize representation at the workplace and define its relationship with collective bargaining on the one hand and the social and human resource policies of management on the other. The role of the unions as the employers' most important counterpart was confirmed—unions alone can negotiate for the workers—but the enterprise committee and the health and safety committee were given legal capacities to intervene in the organization of the company. As for the right to direct expression, union locals had to react to the practices of direct participation developed by companies. The reforms tried to modernize collective representation by reinforcing the importance of union action but at the same time favored dialogue on the new problems facing companies. Their goal was to decentralize industrial relations to a certain extent while changing the logic behind them (Eyraud and Tchobanian 1985).

The Auroux reforms were proposed by a newly elected leftist government, but they continued previous reform efforts by the French state. Since 1968, the state had made several attempts to strengthen collective bargaining and social dialogue in the regulation of labor relations. The 1971 reform had permitted company bargaining, and the enterprise committee obtained supplementary rights in the areas of working conditions and social information, for example, a right to an annual "social assessment" in firms with more than 300 employees. In 1975, a study group described social relations in French firms as poor and called for de-Taylorization of work organization and recognition of unions as part of the firm (Sudreau 1975). The Auroux reforms gave these policies a more concrete form while keeping in mind changed economic and social conditions. The organizational rigidity of French companies, their declining competitiveness, the use of new technologies, and the growing number of small and medium-sized firms all had to be taken into account. The crisis of the French trade union movement, its political divisions, and the negative attitude of employers toward unions were other important factors.

The CFDT was the union most involved in the reforms. Obligatory negotiations at the company level, the right of workers to direct expression, and the use of experts in assessing new technologies were all part of a new strategy that the CFDT had tried to develop since 1978. The CGT adopted a more critical position. While it approved of the new rights, it criticized the lack of means to ensure that they were applied in the best interest of the workers; its strategy remained attached to conflict. The FO, for its part, rejected company-level bargaining, fearing for the stability of bargaining at the industry level, and regarded direct expression as a threat to collective representation. The employers denounced the reforms as creating new constraints on firms. They also objected to the requirement of dialogue with the unions at the workplace since this reversed the deregulatory effects of the neoliberal social policies of the 1970s—despite the fact that the law did provide for greater legal and contractual flexibility.

Employer hostility and union distrust could have made the reforms fail. They had been introduced in the hope that changes in the legal framework would change the behavior of the actors. Ten years later, some changes are striking, such as the increase in company-level bargaining (Caire 1992; Goetschy and Rozenblatt 1992). Other parts of the reforms, such as the provisions for employee expression, have failed, at least for the time being.

5.3 The Auroux Reforms and Works Councils

The Auroux reforms appear to have affected the works councils least. The only new elements were the creation of health and safety committees and the strengthening of the role of enterprise committees in economic matters. Worker participation in management, or "co-supervision" on the board of directors or board of trustees, was limited to two representatives designated by the enterprise committee who would have only an advisory role. However, works councils were strongly affected indirectly by innovations in their environment and their new links to collective bargaining and the representation and participation of employees. Before 1982, no legal framework existed that would have required the actors to define these relationships clearly. For example, direct employee participation, as developed by the employers, touched on an area—the organization of work and social relations at the workplace— that was traditionally outside the influence of works councils or union workplace organizations. Likewise, since company-level bargaining was not obligatory, works councils did not necessarily have to take it into account. Three modes of social regulation could be found side by side: management initiatives, works council rights to dialogue, and union intervention. The Auroux reforms encouraged the actors to coordinate the three procedures, giving works councils a central position at the crossroads of the systems of collective action of workers (especially union action, where unions were present) and of social relations set up by the company (especially direct employee participation).

5.3.1 Difficulties Facing the Personnel Delegates

In 1988, only 43.3 percent of eligible establishments had personnel delegates. The rate was even lower, 36 percent, in establishments with fewer than 50 employees, where personnel delegates are the only legally required representative body. Moreover, the rates have been on the decline since the mid-1980s (table 5.2).

Table 5.2   **Workplace Representation by Size of Establishment**

Size of Establishment (number of workers)	Percentage of Establishments with Personnel Delegates	
	1985	1988
11–49	39.5	36.1
50–99	63.4	55.3
100–499	82	78.1
500–999	96.9	95.4
1000 or more	97.3	98.8

Source: Ministry of Labor, Employment, and Professional Training, *Dossiers statistiques du Travail et de l'Emploi,* 1990.

Even in large companies, personnel delegates are negatively affected by changes in the functions of the representative bodies. A recent study has shown that their actual activity is often very limited (Tchobanian 1992). Company-level negotiations have increased the role of the union delegates. Although personnel delegates are generally elected, their main activity, the presentation of grievances, has long been connected with union practices of confrontation and struggle. As a result, their position has been diminished by the institutionalization of negotiations and the strengthening of the union delegates.

The crisis of the personnel delegates is an indicator of the crisis of union strategies based on conflictual demands. The falling number of union activists and the trend toward deunionization is another factor. Union locals prefer enterprise committees and union delegates, with their important role in dialogue with management, over the personnel delegates. In addition, the social policies of employers and the new direct participation practices have diminished the often informal role of personnel delegates in handling individual employee grievances. Personnel delegates have thus been reduced to their institutional role, which is less apparent to workers. Worker attitudes also seem to have changed, with workers having become more reticent about having a representative express their grievances for them. Personnel delegates were well adapted to blue-collar workers; they seem to be less accepted by the new categories of skilled workers, technicians, and engineers.

5.3.2   Enterprise Committees and Social Dialogue

The Auroux reforms strengthened the enterprise committees. Statistics confirm that enterprise committees are found in the vast majority of companies with 50 or more employees. According to the ministry of labor, 79 percent of eligible establishments held enterprise committee elections in 1990. This percentage is slightly higher than in the early 1980s. Approximately five million employees are represented by enterprise committees. Health and safety committees are also frequent; they exist in 65 percent of eligible establishments.

Enterprise Committees and the Economic and Social Life of the Company

The law describes the enterprise committee as responsible for the "collective expression of the employees" on decisions about the "management, the economic and financial development of the company, the organization of labor and production techniques." The law requires that committees be periodically informed on a variety of subjects. Before management makes major decisions on economic, technological, organizational, or social matters, it must consult the enterprise committee. For example, the committee must be consulted on such issues as mergers, transfers, or the purchase of subsidiaries; on collective layoffs for economic reasons; on workforce training projects; and on the introduction of new technology. As a rule, management cannot make a final decision without consultations, but it is not required to take the enterprise committee's view into account. Through the information it receives and the consultations to which it is entitled, the committee can express the interests of the workers, monitor the operation of the firm, and help the local unions act with full knowledge of the facts.

To be able to influence the life of the company effectively, the enterprise committee must have competence and means of action. The law provides for economic training for elected representatives, an operating budget, and periodic information. Studies have shown that these arrangements vary. Many small companies provide neither economic training nor an operating budget, and elected representatives do not always recognize the importance of these (Le Maître and Tchobanian 1992). Moreover, representatives are often ignorant of their rights, especially when they are not union activists (Cam 1991). In general, employers do provide economic and social information, for example, on the firm's economic activity and finances, technological choices and related investments, workforce structure, pay, and human resource policies. This information, however, is not always adapted to the needs of committee members. A study of 47 small and medium-sized companies in 1989 showed that the information provided by management is often limited (Henriet 1990).

Another study, which covered 200 companies, found three typical situations (Harff and Henriet 1988). In the first, the enterprise committee is not given the information to which it is entitled. Management refuses to incur the expense, and the elected representatives do not apply pressure to enforce their rights. In the second situation, management provides the information required in compliance with the law but does not worry about its usefulness. The committee contents itself with the fact that the legal requirements are met, without trying to use the information. This situation is characterized by its formalism. In the third case, one or both parties try to use the committee's rights to develop more dynamic practices. For example, management may try to make committee members and union representatives understand the economic constraints that the company faces or may use the enterprise committee to transmit information to the workforce about company operations. Workforce representatives can then try to use this information to benefit the workers. The second situation was found to be the most common one.

Consultation is a case in point. Enterprise committees must be asked for their advice on all major company projects. Consultation is obligatory on employment, working conditions, working hours, the economic status of the company, and technological change. Through compulsory consultation, the enterprise committee can contribute to social dialogue at the workplace alongside the formal negotiations conducted through the union delegates. Consultation is more intensive where management sees the benefit of including the employees and their representatives in its social strategy and unions try to monitor the management of the company. In firms above a certain size, commissions supporting the enterprise committee can be created. In some areas, the enterprise committee may seek the help of an outside expert (e.g., a certified accountant or an expert on technology and work organization).

The influence of enterprise committees on personnel management seems more developed (Harff and Henriet 1988). On dismissals, the enterprise committee can call in an expert to help it make economic and organizational proposals so as to reduce the number of layoffs. In most cases, however, the enterprise committee is informed only after the decision has been made. Its intervention will therefore usually be limited to trying to negotiate a social assistance plan. Consultations with the enterprise committee on economic matters often seem to be merely formal. Employers must provide information on financial results, and an accountant paid by the company may be called in to assist the committee. A study of enterprise committees in large companies showed that almost half of them used this opportunity (Cohen 1986).

The influence of enterprise committees on work organization and technological change is a more recent development. Enterprise committees must be consulted on a company's workforce training programs. A 1970 interoccupational agreement and a law require firms to have a budget for the vocational training of their employees; this was confirmed by another agreement and new legislation in 1991. Enterprise committee consultations are required on both the preparation and the implementation of training programs. A recent study found that in approximately 80 percent of cases consultations actually took place. However, in less than 30 percent were enterprise committees, or their training commissions, involved in the preparation of a training plan at all stages. Thus, consultation usually means that workforce representatives are allowed to express their views on a decision made by management, but not that they can influence the decision itself.

Enterprise committee consultations on new technologies illustrate this. They were mandated in 1982 when the significance of the technological changes under way was realized. In the 1970s, the CFDT had strongly criticized the direction of technical change and the methods used in effecting it (CFDT

1977). The introduction of computer technology, with its effects on the organization of work, led enterprise committees and union locals to make technological and organizational counterproposals. Enterprise committee consultation procedures were instituted where "major" installations of new technology are planned. Legally, the enterprise committee must be informed at least one month prior to the meeting in which its advice is to be given. In companies with at least 300 employees, it can with the agreement of the employer call on the assistance of an expert, paid by the employer. If no agreement is reached, the enterprise committee may ask the courts to decide.

Many difficulties have appeared in the application of these consultation rules. A study of 83 cases in which enterprise committees called an outside expert found that the result of the expert's intervention is strongly related to general management acceptance of enterprise committee involvement in technological matters. In a conflictual context, expert advice has little influence on the ongoing project (Lochouard 1990). Company projects have usually already been firmly defined before the enterprise committee is invited to give its opinion. Activities of enterprise committees concerning the social consequences of technological changes, especially with respect to employment and working conditions, are more easily accepted by employers than intervention in the project itself, which is usually rejected in defense of managerial discretion over work organization and investment. Technological experts are therefore rarely called (Cam and Chaumette 1989). An overall evaluation in 1986 found fewer than 200 cases in which experts had been used (Carre and Valenduc 1991).

Enterprise Committees and Indirect Wages

Enterprise committees are often accepted by the workers mainly for the services they provide. Most important, they manage the company's social budget. They sometimes also play a role with respect to benefits unrelated to wages, for example, company health insurance plans or the management of the company restaurant. In addition, enterprise committees may negotiate financial participation agreements. Committee involvement in defining and managing a firm's indirect wages increases the variety of situations that exist in firms. Some enterprise committees concentrate on managing the social budget at the expense of their more representative role.

Managing the social budget is the only area in which the enterprise committee is in the position of decision maker, within the limits of the budget provided by the employer. There is no legal definition of the kind and amount of resources the enterprise committee may control. A study on establishments with more than 500 employees found a wide range of situations, from the absence of any social budget to one amounting to 5.45 percent of total payroll (Dufour and Mouriaux 1986). In most cases, the social budget varies between 0.5 and 1.5 percent of payroll. Managing these often large amounts can take up a major share of the enterprise committee's time. While this is not really a representative activity, and could better be described as a paternalistic one, it often determines the enterprise committee's image among the workers, and therefore the outcome of future elections.

The enterprise committee's role in negotiating financial participation for employees is an exception to the principle of union monopoly over negotiations. Financial participation entails the sharing of part of a company's profits with the workforce, based on results. By negotiating a formal agreement, a special tax status can be obtained for the amounts distributed. This provision, which was legislated in 1986, has been very successful. More than 10,000 agreements were in effect in 1990, and almost two million employees received on average an additional 3.2 percent of aggregate remuneration in their respective companies. Financial participation agreements enable the firm to vary wages with economic activity. They also sometimes include incentives; in 1990, 7.5 percent of existing agreements linked profit sharing to productivity. Both the enterprise committee and the union delegates may negotiate agreements on profit sharing; in certain cases, these have to be ratified by two-thirds of the employees in a referendum. In this area, therefore, the separation of functions between enterprise committees and union locals is not clearly defined.

Enterprise committees also play a de facto role in areas not foreseen by the law. For example, employees sometimes use the enterprise committee rather than the personnel delegates to seek redress of grievances. Likewise, enterprise committees may conduct informal (or de facto) collective bargaining with management; this happens in about one-third of the cases in which compulsory negotiations with unions locals do not take place. Also, formal bargaining with the unions is sometimes preceded by discussions with the enterprise committee. Finally, the enterprise committee is the principal representative of the workforce where no unions are present. The relative importance of different enterprise committee activities varies greatly from one company to another. The fact that enterprise committees exist in the vast majority of companies with over 50 employees is therefore not in itself enough to appraise their actual role. This is defined by which kind of enterprise committee activity is dominant, and by the committee's position in the firm's entire workplace representation system.

5.3.3   Company-Level Bargaining and Works Councils

Mandatory workplace bargaining did not mean obligatory contractual agreement. For opposite reasons, employers and, in part, unions were against negotiating at this level. Nevertheless, the number of company or establishment agreements increased quickly: 2,067 were signed in 1982, 5,165 in 1985, and 6,750 in 1991. In that year, 2.5 million employees were covered, about three-quarters of whom worked in companies with a workforce of 500 or more, amounting to nearly one in five employees that were at all covered by collective bargaining. In addition, between 1983 and 1986 more than 4,000 agreements regulating employee "expression" were signed. The French collective bargaining system appears to have greatly decentralized over the past 10 years, the low union presence at the workplace explaining why only a minority of employees are covered by the system.

The subjects covered in company-level bargaining are mainly wages and working hours, for which the law requires annual negotiations. In 1990, 58 percent of company agreements dealt with wages, and 38 percent with working time. Other subjects were classification (5 percent), employment (3 percent), and training (2 percent). Company-level wage settlements make it possible to get closer to real wage variations, sometimes specifying precise methods of wage determination. Some agreements provide for general raises, while others are more individualized. In 1990, 32 percent of company agreements provided, at least to some extent, for individualized wage increases. Wage negotiations at the workplace seem to have become acceptable to employers since they are closer to the employees. Local unions, on their part, have come to accept elements of individualized pay increases, partially calling into question the traditional importance of seniority in wage setting.

These changes affect the works councils. In traditional industry-level bargaining, wages paid at the workplace were often very different from those defined in the industrial agreement, the employer being free to do what he wanted. It is true that workplace unions could express their wage demands through the personnel delegates, with the industrywide agreement and conflictual worker mobilization as arguments. In this way, unions had some influence on wages, even without formal negotiations. Company-level negotiations, however, make union action at the workplace legitimate, although their real effect is still being discussed. For some, the traditional weakness of unions at the company level limits their ability to influence wages significantly. A study of company-level bargaining has shown that in most cases, no more than two bargaining sessions are held and union negotiators do not usually have the necessary training. Except in large companies, workplace negotiations on wages are not comparable to industry-level negotiations, sometimes leading to an agreement that simply accepts formally the employer's offer without any real bargaining. Conceivably, wage demands presented at personnel delegate meetings were more effective than most company bargaining.

Company-level negotiations on working time and work schedules were another factor that changed the balance between centralized collective bargaining and the works councils. Major changes have taken place in the positions of the social actors on this question. The unions were on the defensive in this area. The employers, while they wanted greater flexibility in work schedules and in the rules governing overtime pay, first were against decentralized bargaining, but then realized the advantages of being able to depart locally from general legal or contractual rules. In 1985 the employers demanded that negotiations be held mainly at the company level, while the unions wanted industry-level agreements. But in 1990, there were already 1,025 company agreements on adapting work schedules to fluctuations in economic activity or extending the use of equipment by having employees work successive shifts or on weekends.

During the 1970s enterprise committees had progressively acquired a regulatory role on working hours. The creation of a new level of bargaining reduced their influence in this area. Enterprise committees are still being consulted on hours, and studies show that they continue to play a part, although often an informal one. Just as for wage negotiations, company bargaining on working time formalizes regulation and thereby limits the importance of dialogue with the works council. Moreover, negotiations give rise to differences between unionized and nonunionized companies since in the latter working-time agreements, made with the enterprise committee, have no legal status.

Other topics negotiated at the company level are not legally mandated, except for the organization of the right of expression. Only a few agreements, signed in the largest firms, deal with these matters. Usually their subjects are linked to human resource management, such as classification, training, working conditions, organization of work, and employment. These areas are strongly affected by the technological, economic, and organizational transformations that companies are undergoing at the present time. The negotiations extend social dialogue to areas that had traditionally been dealt with by management alone, or only at the industry level. An example is an agreement at Renault covering skill requirements, mobility, career planning, and work involvement, as affected by the reorganization of the firm.[1]

The prerogatives of enterprise committees and health and safety committees in these areas were reaffirmed. Enterprise committees have gained a particularly important role with the obligatory consultations on the introduction of new technologies. The committees must be informed of the entire project, on its organizational aspects as well as its social consequences. Collective bargaining, by comparison, covers the effects of technological change on employment, classification, and career prospects of individual employees. Consultations with the enterprise committee on the organization of work and negotiations with the unions on a social plan regulating its consequences for workers are two aspects of an identical process of cooperation for change. Enterprise committees have no powers of co-determination on organizational matters, and employers are free to ignore their views. But, by coordinating their activities with company bargaining, enterprise committees can increase their influence on the employer's organizational and technical decisions.

Initially, company-level negotiations dealt mainly with matters that had previously been bargained at the industry level. Under a trade-off, employers accepted collective bargaining at the workplace and unions accepted more flex-

---

1. The importance of these matters for workplace bargaining is rising. A study of about 300 agreements on classification, vocational training and employment that were signed in the first half of 1991 shows that 60 percent of the agreements applied to companies or establishments with fewer than 500 employees. Agreements signed at the largest companies addressed a wide range of issues, while those at smaller companies were limited to specific, individual points.

ible rules. To this extent, formal company agreements may have weakened the more informal dialogue that used to take place with the works councils, without giving them a new role. On organizational and human resources matters, however, company bargaining remained limited mainly to large companies. This is where a new balance between negotiations with the unions and dialogue with the works councils had initially seemed possible. Recent "modernization agreements" (see below) are aimed at this.

5.3.4   Direct Employee Participation

The development of direct employee participation was one of the reasons for the Auroux reforms. Legislators recognized the importance of such participation for the economic and social modernization of companies. But they did not want participation to compete with collective representation, through works councils or unions, as it had in the 1970s. For this reason, the way in which the employees' right of expression is exercised, both directly and collectively, must be negotiated at the workplace between union locals and employers.

Employee expression is situated at the crossroads between collective representation and social relations organized by the company. Its legal institutionalization pursued objectives that could have been uncomfortable to both employers and unions but also had the potential to overcome the deadlock at the workplace and lead to a more dynamic situation. Several projects have studied company-level bargaining, the implementation of agreements, and the follow-up by management and personnel delegates on the subject of employee expression.[2]

Employers were opposed to the law because it required them to negotiate modes of expression with the unions. The CNPF considered employee expression part of the internal organization of the relation between the company and its employees. Among the unions, the FO rejected the law, in the fear that expression would compete with collective representation. Negotiations, however, often produced agreement. Between 1983 and 1986, over 4,000 agreements on direct expression were signed. Their implementation, however, was disappointing. "Expression groups" often held only a few meetings. Most of them were content with presenting grievances to management, making it impossible for direct expression to find its own place in relation to other channels of representation. In 1989, an assessment by the Ministry of Labor indicated that the majority of employees subject to the legislation on expression were indeed covered by collective agreements on its implementation. But more qualitative analyses show that in many cases, the agreement was no longer applied. The attempt of the Auroux laws to place social relations at the workplace into a negotiated framework has failed.

There are several reasons for this. One is competition from "quality circles,"

2. Many of these are summarized in Martin (1989).

which during the period emerged in over 3,000 firms. Quality circles are unilaterally created by management, normally after informing the enterprise committee, and are often given the means to resolve problems on their own. In some cases, they were intentionally set up to limit the impact of expression. But it is also true that workers have often taken more interest in quality circles than in expression groups. Through quality circles, workers can have a direct impact on their workplace, while expression is typically limited to the defensive presentation of demands and grievances to the employer.

In addition, the failure of employee expression was caused by inability of the unions to develop a consistent position on the relation between expression and collective representation. A study of about 100 locals of the CFDT, the union behind the Auroux legislation, showed a wide diversity of union practices (Tchobanian 1989). Some branches had not signed any agreement, mainly because they refused to allow groups to be led by middle managers. Most often, agreements were simply aimed at guaranteeing the greatest possible freedom of expression, treating the latter as a democratic right belonging to employees and different from union rights. Local unions came in only to transmit employee demands to management. In other cases, unions adopted a more conflictual strategy, using the right of expression to mobilize workers for union demands. Only rarely did expression groups cooperate with the enterprise or health and safety committee to inform their activities and help prepare their consultations with the employer. It is only in these infrequent cases that expression groups help improve the effectiveness of collective representation, notably on the adoption of new technologies.

Since the 1970s, it has often been pointed out that the personnel delegates were most vulnerable to direct employee participation. Indeed, weakening the personnel delegates was one of the goals of the employers' new social policy. With the right of expression, workers can express their demands directly, and personnel delegates lose control of some of the problems that they had been in charge of handling. By favoring freedom of expression rather than acting on concrete problems, unions increase the difficulties of the personnel delegates without safeguarding the future of the right of expression. Union strategy has often been more supportive of democratic expression at the workplace than of workers' participation in company life.

Enterprise and health and safety committees have sometimes played a different part. The former have used their rights regarding work organization and technology to include individual employees in their work, thus avoiding competition and creating complementary relations between the collective position they represent and the employees who contributed their know-how to its development. The right of expression does raise the wider question of the place of individual employees in works council activities. Depending on the size of the firm, enterprise committees may form special commissions that include nonmembers. On matters like technological change, direct involvement of employees in the work of works councils is often recognized as useful even by employers (du Roy 1989). Also, through their consultation rights, enterprise committees may present their views on other participatory practices, such as quality circles, so as to optimize their usefulness to the workers.

5.4   A New Balance for Workplace Representation?

The aim of the Auroux reforms was to improve coordination between the various representative bodies at the workplace. The changed balance between the social partners and the new problems to be dealt with through social dialogue motivated these reforms. But the actual representation system and the place of the works councils in it continue to differ from one company to another. Beyond the legally required system, new models of representation, better adapted to present problems, are still being sought.

The Auroux reforms tried to create a new balance by reaffirming the central role of the unions in worker representation. In part they seem to have succeeded. The CNPF no longer rejects the representative role of unions at the workplace. But the low level of union presence and the wide variety of economic and social situations in different firms lead to wide differences in systems of workplace representation from one company to another.

5.4.1   Weakening Union Presence in Workplace Representation

Union presence may be measured by the proportion of companies and establishments with at least one union local. In 1989, 51 percent of all establishments with over 50 employees, and 70 percent of employees in such establishments, were in this situation. Four years earlier, in 1985, these figures had still been 57 percent and 76 percent, respectively (table 5.3). In smaller establishments, union presence is much less common. Most employees, in other words, do not have union representation at the workplace. Given union pluralism, workers have a choice between unions, depending on their ideological posi-

Table 5.3   **Union Influence by Size of Establishment**

Size of Establishment (number of workers)	Percentage of Establishments with Union Delegates		Percentage Votes for Nonunion Candidates in Enterprise Committee Elections		
	1985	1989	1979	1985	1989
50–99	41.7	35.9	48.2	56	61.7
100–199	63.4	57.1	35.9	40.1	45.3
200–499	83.6	77.7	18.5	20.7	25.5
500–999	93.6	89.4	7.3	9.4	13.5
1000 or more	96.6	92.3	2.0	2.1	2.8

Source: Ministry of Labor, Employment, and Professional Training, *Dossiers statistiques du Travail et de l'Emploi.*

tions or their view of what unions should do for them. Yet only a minority of workers are unionized.

Union weakness is not new, but since the middle of the 1970s the number of union members has dropped sharply (Bibes and Mouriaux 1990). Union membership density in France seems to be the lowest of all Western developed countries and has been falling faster than everywhere else (Visser 1991; Chang and Sorrentino 1991). The CGT, the most important union in manufacturing, has lost more than half its members during the 1980s, as has the CFDT. The crisis of the CGT is continuing, while the other unions have recently had small increases in density. Total union membership is today estimated at around 10 percent in the private sector. Paradoxically, French unions are at their weakest at a time when they have more opportunity than ever to intervene directly at the workplace.

The crisis of the unions affects the position of the elected employee representatives. To be fully effective, the system created by the Auroux reforms requires the presence of strong unions. Their absence or weakness affects the actual impact of the reforms. Company collective bargaining needs workplace union organizations, as formal agreements with the enterprise committee or the personnel delegates have no legal standing. The problems of the French union movement are not only low union membership but also lack of support from workers in general, as indicated by the results of enterprise committee elections (for a general overview, see Bouzonnie 1991).

Over the last 15 years, the distribution of votes among the different unions and nonunion candidates changed dramatically (table 5.4). The most important trend was the continuous decline of the CGT vote. Mainly based among blue-collars workers and advocating class unionism, the CGT is today in a deep crisis. However, the other, more reformist unions were unable to take advantage of this, resulting in the second trend, a rise in the vote for nonunion candidates. The union monopoly in the first round of enterprise committee and per-

Table 5.4   Results of Enterprise Committee Elections (%)

Union	1976–77	1978–79	1980–81	1982–83	1984–85	1986–87	1988–89	1990–91
CGT	39.8	36.8	34.5	30.7	28.6	27.0	25.9	22.7
CFDT	19.6	20.5	21.8	22.4	21.1	21.3	20.9	20.2
FO	9.2	10.0	10.6	11.5	13.3	12.8	12.4	12.2
CFTC	2.9	2.9	3.0	3.5	4.4	4.3	4.2	4.0
CGC	5.4	6.3	6.1	6.8	6.7	6.7	6.1	6.5
Other unions	6.7	5.1	4.7	4.7	5.4	5.5	5.6	5.6
Non unions	16.5	18.5	19.3	20.5	20.6	22.5	24.9	28.7
Total	100	100	100	100	100	100	100	100

Source: Ministry of Labor, Employment, and Professional Training, *Dossiers statistiques du Travail et de l'Emploi.*

Note: Results for 1985–89 include the French National Railroad Company, which is strongly unionized.

sonnel delegates elections normally should help establish a strong union presence among elected representatives. But in the 1989 enterprise committee elections, nonunion candidates obtained 26.4 percent of the votes, making them "the largest union in France." By comparison, the CGT obtained 25.1 percent, the CFDT 21 percent, and the FO 11.2 percent. This decline in union influence is particularly strong in small and medium-sized establishments, as shown in table 5.3. Little by little, a dual system has come into being. In large companies, works councils and union locals work together. In many small and medium-sized companies, unions are not present, making company-level bargaining impossible. Some employers want a reform to unify the various bodies, to enable them to negotiate with nonunion, elected representatives.

5.4.2   Actual Structures of Workplace Representation

Presence or absence of union locals leads to two models of workplace representation. In addition, where unions exist, the links between the different representative bodies may fit several types. One source of difference is the frequent de facto grouping of representative bodies around the enterprise committee, especially where there are no personnel delegates. In establishments with between 50 and 200 employees, the enterprise committee is often the only, or at least the most active, representative body. Moreover, workplaces differ in the way in which the representative bodies interact, especially in the links between union locals and enterprise committees. A study of 41 companies (Le Maître and Tchobanian 1992) found four main types of interaction. In the first, activities do not overlap. Each body plays its own role, the enterprise committee concentrating on the management of the social budget and the union generally not getting involved in the life of the company, except for annual bargaining. In the second type, the enterprise committee is dominant despite the presence of a union. The employer's desire to use it for dialogue, lack of interest in this on the part of union locals, and the weight of its activities make the enterprise committee the most influential representative body. This does not diminish the company-level negotiations carried out by the union delegates. But since these are limited to wages, they are of no consequence for other representative activities.

In the third type, works council activities are coordinated by the union locals, which use the enterprise committee's legal rights to information and consultation. The enterprise committee becomes a union instrument, but with its own place and role in areas such as the organization of work. Finally, in the fourth type, the union locals dominate all representative bodies, using the personnel delegates or the enterprise committee to put forward union demands regardless of their legal functions. Including those situations where no unions are present, then, there are at least five possible types of interaction between the representative bodies.

The purposes to which the representative system is thus put differ according to the actors present and their modes of action. Three kinds of representative activity are allowed in the system as defined by the law: the raising of demands, centered around the activities of the personnel delegates and union pressure; joint regulation, centered around negotiation and consultation; and the provision of benefits and indirect wages, especially the management of the social budget. All three exist in all workplaces, but the actors, and in particular the unions, tend to place different emphasis on them. The traditional situation stresses the raising of demands. Negotiations were nothing but a pause in the conflictual process, making it impossible to develop a joint definition of the rules. Neither the employers nor the unions really wanted a negotiated procedure for regulating the workplace.

With the Auroux reforms, periodic bargaining became an independent function aimed at establishing a joint definition of rules. This may be strengthened by enterprise committee consultations, which sometimes may attain a dominant position. This was one of the implicit goals of the Auroux reforms. In reality, however, joint regulation remains restricted to a few well-defined themes, and indirect wages often take up most of the activity, especially at the enterprise committee level. The distribution of companies among the three types depends on several, often interdependent factors. The logic of the actors partially explains the choice of models (Reynaud 1989).

Some employers consider representation as nothing more than a legal constraint. Others try to use the representative bodies for internal communication. They prefer the enterprise committee for its closer contact with the employees. Employers may also want to formalize their human resource management methods by agreement with a partner. Agreements are signed by the union delegates, while the enterprise committee is consulted for the implementation. Employers' attitudes appear to have changed during the 1980s. Some are concerned about the decline in union membership and the risk of uncontrollable demands by workers. Such employers increasingly accept the idea that economic, technical, and organizational transformations must be accompanied by social dialogue.

Three main attitudes are found on the union side. The CGT, attached to conflictual unionism, seeks control over the works councils to ensure that a "union logic" prevails at the workplace. Thus, union delegates are assigned great importance, the personnel delegates are maintained as a tool for expressing grievances, and the enterprise committee must not be used for collaboration with the employer. There is, however, a debate in this union on the kind of unionism needed at the present time. Class unionism remains the ideological reference, but some CGT leaders want to devote a greater share of the union's activities to work reorganization. The CFDT, for its part, would like workplace representation to have influence on management's organizational choices. While the local union branch decides on its goals and strategies, the enterprise committee must be free to perform its distinct role, particularly in consultation. Similarly, the health and safety committee should have an impact on safety and working conditions, questions that are very important to the CFDT. For these reasons, the goal of the CFDT is union coordination of the works councils and a joint definition of rules through negotiation and consultation. The other unions generally leave the enterprise committee free to do what it wants, with the result that it spends most of its time managing the social budget. The CGT and the CFDT each publish a journal for their enterprise committee representatives, which gives policy directions and describes models of action in line with the unions' strategies. The CFDT's position, now resolutely reformist, has shown a major transformation since the 1970s.

The position of the workers themselves is harder to determine. Their expectations concerning the representative bodies in the workplace have rarely been studied. As to unions, workers express low motivation to participate in their activities yet have great expectations regarding their outcomes (Beauville 1989). Concerning enterprise committees, worker attitudes do not necessarily contribute to expanding their role in consultation. Workers know the enterprise committee first and foremost for the material benefits it provides. In committee elections, these strongly affect workers' choices. Since election results indicate the relative strength of unions in the workplace, the activities of enterprise committees on indirect wages are an important factor in interunion competition. It is important to note that by voting, nonunionized employees may influence the unions' position at the workplace, thereby affecting the legitimacy of union activities.

In recent years, the relationship between workers and their representatives has widely been perceived as problematic. Deunionization is not the only concern. Human resource management has often become more individualized, while the personnel delegates are on the decline. Neither the unions nor the works councils have much direct influence on day-to-day personnel management, although the capacity to make a difference for workers' daily experience at the workplace is of highest importance for the legitimacy of representative bodies (Hassenteufel 1992). At the same time, new forms of collective activity, aimed at the defense of particular occupational groups, are making their appearance. This can be seen in the "coordinations" that have sprung up to compete with the unions. The occupational interests of these groups, which are concerned with employment and work organization, are difficult for the unions to represent. The enterprise committee could help by including employees from these categories in its work, or by taking the initiative on employee expression and offering this more participatory form of representation as an alternative to traditional mobilization through conflict.

5.4.3   A New Role for Works Councils?

The Auroux reforms had contradictory results. While the institutional space for representative bodies was expanded, the decline of the unions threatens the future of the industrial relations system. Probably, the legal framework defined in by the reforms has not yet had its full effect. Company-level negotiation could be extended in the future to subjects of a more qualitative kind (Lagrande

1990). Several large companies have signed agreements in recent years on employment and skills, work organization, and human resource development. Consultations with the enterprise committee could become an effective instrument for implementing such agreements, provided the attitudes of the actors change. Several proposals have been put forward to promote this, two of which redefine the jurisdiction of representative bodies, in particular the enterprise committee.

The first proposal deals with the workplace representation system in small and medium-sized companies. The law is often not effective in these because union delegates and personnel delegates do not exist. The Center of Young Leaders (CJD) has suggested that a *conseil d'entreprise* (company council) be created. This would be a single elected body combining the rights of all existing bodies. While joining the functions of the enterprise committee and the personnel delegates is not difficult—it will be legally possible after 1994—this is different for the union delegates. The CJD has proposed that the union delegates be designated from among the elected representatives. The *conseil d'entreprise* would thus have twofold legitimacy: as a mixed body, it could negotiate like the union delegates and would be consulted like the enterprise committee. The proposal tries to safeguard company-level bargaining in spite of declining union presence, preventing the emergence of a dual system of industrial relations in which unionized companies would be better able to engage in social dialogue than nonunionized, usually small firms.[3] A single works council system for small companies would make for a more active social dialogue.

The second idea tries to improve the coordination among representatives bodies. A number of economywide, interoccupational "modernization agreements" signed in 1988 and 1989 promote development of advanced methods of human resource management as part of economic restructuring, addressing questions of technological change, working conditions, working hours, and equal opportunity. The idea was that economic modernization cannot succeed without social modernization. This was the conclusion of a report submitted to the government in 1987 by the head of a major company (Riboud 1987). The report emphasized that the modernization of the French economy must be carried out in cooperation with employees, enterprise committees, and unions; that the social consequences of modernization must be anticipated; and that measures must be taken to preserve employment and improve the content of work.

The interoccupational agreement on technological change specifies the place of social dialogue in the change process, providing for three negotiating levels. Interoccupational agreements lay down general procedures and themes,

---

3. Small firms are where most new jobs are being created. In 1974, nearly 36 percent of all jobs in the private or competitive public sectors were in establishments with more than 200 employees; in 1990, this figure had dropped to 24 percent.

mandating proactive plans concerning employment, requiring that attention be paid to qualification and training, and defining the role of information and employee participation. Industry-level agreements provide more details in these areas, depending on the special characteristics of each industry. For example, an agreement signed in the chemical industry defines the roles of the enterprise committees and the union delegates in case of major technological transformations. The enterprise committee is to be consulted on the project as a whole. Having to deal with difficult technical matters, it needs information, the means to analyze it, and the time required to produce informed advice. Technology experts are mentioned among the resources the committee may need. The union delegates are promised that negotiations will be held on the social consequences of technical change. None of these elements is really new; in fact, they correspond to the spirit of the Auroux laws. But the agreement recognizes the importance of social dialogue and shows that enterprise committee and union delegates have their distinct but related functions.

Some company-level agreements also deal with procedures to regulate change and its consequences. A recent agreement in the Pechiney group clarifies the place of dialogue in changes in work organization. The goal is to set up a system of anticipatory, proactive management by getting the enterprise committee involved early. The union delegates are informed, and training concerning changes in work organization is planned for them.

Agreements like these redefine the various representative bodies by promoting a new interpretation of the idea of bargaining. The government has called this "negotiated modernization." It includes not only formal bargaining but the entire social dialogue related to modernization at the workplace: negotiations with the unions, consultations with the enterprise committee, and involvement of workers and the management hierarchy. The logic of the Auroux reforms can be seen here. Attitudes among unions and employers differ widely on this. While the CFDT signed the agreements, the CGT has not. The FO is torn between its fear of becoming involved in management and its interest in controlling the social consequences of change. Positions among employers are just as varied. The employer confederation signed the interoccupational agreements, but so far they seem to have been applied only in the largest companies.

5.5 Economic Effects of Works Councils

One of the goals behind the creation of enterprise committees was to involve employees in the economic life of the company. Likewise, the Auroux reforms were meant to favor cooperative change at the workplace and to contribute to economic progress through social dialogue. Their economic effects are difficult to assess, however, as the economic efficiency of representative bodies is strongly linked to the market conditions faced by firms.

5.5.1   Costs and Advantages

It is relatively easy to determine the direct costs of enterprise committees. These consist of wages for the elected representatives during the time spent on enterprise committee activities, other operating costs paid by the employer, preparation of the information supplied to the enterprise committee, meetings, and so forth. Some firms try not to exceed 50 employees to avoid these expenses. On the other hand, in many firms enterprise committees receive more resources than required by law, and several recent agreements even provide financial assistance to the unions present in the companies. In both cases, these expenses help set up structures of joint regulation. The legal requirements are perceived as a burden by some companies, while others go beyond them; their personnel management strategies are different.

The same observations can be made about the social budget. The sum of all social budgets managed by enterprise committees and equivalent bodies in the competitive public sector has been estimated at 15 billion francs. However, these can hardly be considered a pure expense. A study of large companies has shown that absenteeism is lower in companies with larger social budgets. Similarly, profit sharing, which is a supplement to normal wages that sometimes reaches significant proportions, is linked to the economic results of the company or to productivity. This seems to increase economic efficiency, although the effect is difficult to establish.

Similar considerations apply to human resource management and work reorganization. Through its right to information and consultation, an active enterprise committee can make a firm seek higher qualifications, make greater efforts in occupational training, and implement career planning and internal mobility. In some cases, such measures run up against management strategies driven by market conditions, which prefer lower wages, less recognition of special skills, and the use of fewer permanent workers. In such firms, legally required training expenses, subject to enterprise committee consultations, are considered a burden unrelated to the firm's needs. In other cases, management strategy is already aimed at the development of human resources in response to economic conditions, and enterprise committee pressure has different economic consequences.

During the time of high growth up to the mid-1970s, industrial employment increased strongly in France under Taylorist principles using a low-skill workforce. The human resource choices of that period were compatible with fast growth. Today, however, companies often lack skilled workers. Part of their workforces, who were trained in the Taylorist era, are not able to adapt to new skill requirements. Performance is reduced, and unemployment due to failure to adjust is on the rise. An evaluation of the economic benefits of enterprise committees therefore cannot be separated from economic and market conditions. The enterprise committee's intervention can help make management adopt and apply new policies. But such intervention is possible only because it has become possible to go beyond Taylorism. Demands that used to be considered costs are now often considered investments in skills and adaptability. Social dialogue can help make such investment choices easier.

5.5.2   Works Councils and De-Taylorization in French Companies

Taylorist principles have been contested for over two decades. But the resulting practices have not been uniform. Schematically, three phases can be identified. After 1968, the social crisis of the Taylorist organizational model led firms to try to improve the quality of working life, the goal being to respond to the workers' new expectations and to increase their motivation to work. In the late 1970s, French industry had lost in competitiveness, and the economic crisis began to be seen as lasting. Companies began to look for more flexible employment and work organization (Boyer 1988). Finally, in the mid-1980s, structural solutions were sought and a new paradigm of flexible production emerged as an alternative to Taylorism (d'Iribarne 1989).

That new paradigm has several dimensions: total quality management, just-in-time production, group work, and so forth. Technical change alone was not felt to be enough; it had to be part of a wider modernization strategy that included human resource development. A study of companies with 50 or more employees in 1989 showed that managers anticipated skill shortages for 60 percent of their respective workforces. Facing unstable markets, firms look for higher work skills and workers more adaptable to future changes. Training, flexible work schedules, and human resource management in line with the firm's environment became central factors in enterprise restructuring (Bechet and Huiban 1992; Stankiewicz 1988).

The place of the works councils in this development depended on the nature of change and the attitudes of the social actors. The priority of the quality of working life policies of the 1970s was to restore dialogue with employees. They were also often used to destabilize collective representation, including the enterprise committee. Redirecting its activities toward company organization was not facilitated by this, despite encouragement by the government. The flexibility policies that started in the late 1970s were better suited for applying the new system created by the Auroux reforms, especially when it came to negotiations on working hours.

In general, worker expression seems to provide a framework for transforming the relationship between employees and the management hierarchy on the one hand, and between employees and their representatives on the other hand. Enterprise committees and health and safety committees would seem ideally suited to help improve union procedures for worker participation in the life of the company. But in this respect the results have been disappointing. The economic effects of enterprise committees can therefore be considered mainly in terms of the "negotiated modernization" of the production system, dealing with new technologies, training, and proactive employment and skills management.

In principle, one might compare the practices of companies with enterprise committees to those of others without them. But enterprise committees exist mainly in medium-sized and large companies. It would therefore be better to distinguish between different types of enterprise committees with different practices. This information, however, exists only in unquantified, monographic form. Enterprise committees whose activities are coordinated by the unions appear better adapted to influencing choices made by management (Le Maître and Tchobanian 1992). For example, the CFDT has developed a "skills network" for use by enterprise and health and safety committees in dealing with the effects of computerization, ergonomic analyses, and training practices. Likewise, management choices may strongly affect the place of the enterprise committee. Personnel planning may be conducted together with the enterprise committee, depending on the goals and methods of management (Gadille 1992). Similarly, the intervention of a technology expert will have very different effects depending on whether it is imposed on the employer or is the result of company-level negotiations.

Another way of analyzing the economic impact of enterprise committees is to look at differences between firms in human resource management and its evolution in recent years. Vocational training provided to employees is an example of a link between social dialogue and human resource management. Training is both human resource policy and the result of institutional pressures. However, while the enterprise committee has to give advice on a firm's "training plan," occupational training has always been more widespread in large companies than in small ones and has always been used more by skilled workers than by others. Moreover, these differences have increased since the mid-1980s. More than ever, larger companies today consider training a necessary step in the adoption of new organizational models (Podevin and Verdier 1989), increasing the gaps that have always existed between firms.

Training effort may be measured by training expenditures as a percentage of total payroll. Table 5.5 shows the differences between firms of different size over time. The ratio of employees getting training in 1990 was 7 percent in establishments with 10 to 19 employees, and 53 percent in establishments with 2,000 employees or more. Small companies create the most jobs, but they also use the greatest number of unskilled workers. Large companies, on the other hand, have reduced their workforces but attach more importance to skills (Echardour and Maurin 1992). Two alternative approaches to personnel management can be observed, one leading to a flexible relationship with the external labor market, the other managing a stable group of employees with growing skills. Companies with enterprise committees and union delegates are generally in the second category, although it is difficult to demonstrate a causal relationship.

The results show that when works councils exist in small firms, they are not strong enough to ensure that human resource development strategies are implemented. Larger units seem to be needed to accomplish this. In fact, the

Table 5.5   **Vocational Training Expenditures of Firms as a Percentage of Total Payroll (%)**

| | Size of Establishment (number of workers) | | | | | |
Year	10–19	20–49	50–499	500–1999	2000 or More	Total
1974	0.66	0.86	1.11	1.45	2.59	1.63
1982	1.00	1.10	1.33	1.81	3.06	1.96
1989	1.30	1.43	2.02	2.92	4.67	2.89

Source: Centre d'Etudes et de Recherches sur les Qualifications (CEREQ—Center for Research on Education, Training, and Employment) *CEREQ-Bref* (Paris, 1991).

objectives of further training, and the resources to be used for it, are periodically negotiated at the industry level so as to affect the training policy choices of small firms. Likewise, the government provides financial encouragement and technical support for reorganization of work and proactive employment management in small firms. Works councils are then mobilized for implementing the new policies.

In general, the economic effects of French works councils with respect to the adoption of a post-Taylorist work organization cannot be studied apart from external conditions. The goal for the future is to make it possible for most employees to influence the human resource policies adopted by their employers.

5.6   Conclusion

Works councils in France vary widely from one firm to another. The complexity of the legal framework makes this inevitable. But high variation is also the result of changes in the environment of works councils. In particular, the decentralization of collective bargaining has tipped the internal balance of the industrial relations system toward the company level, making works councils, in particular the enterprise committees, more influential than ever.

The new importance of company-level bargaining and of enterprise committees proves that the Auroux reforms did help unions and employers change their relations. At the same time, as developments at the company level have become crucial to the future of industrial relations, unionization has rapidly declined. The growing number of firms without union representation has led to the emergence of a large nonunionized sector. Joint regulation in this sector is increasingly rare. In particular, new practices in human resource management have raised the problem of how either works councils or unions may intervene in the organization of work.

How can a system of decentralized industrial relations be developed in a country with weak unions? Can the mixed representation system, consisting of unions as well as elected workforce representatives, be maintained in small companies? Will the differences in union strategies continue to grow, or can they be reconciled? The Auroux reforms tried to deal with these problems by setting up a new legal framework for increased social dialogue. But today, 10 years later, basic problems remain.

References

Andolfatto, Dominique. 1992. *L'univers des élections professionnelles.* Paris: Les Editions Ouvrières.

Bachy, Jean-Paul, François Dupuy, and Dominique Martin. 1974. *Représentation et négociation dans l'entreprise.* Paris: Centre de Recherche sur les Sciences Sociales du Travail.

Beauville, Claire. 1989. L'entreprise, le syndicalisme et l'adhésion: Etudes d'opinion. *Revue de l'IRES* 1:91–109.

Bechet, Marc, and Jean Pierre Huiban, eds. 1992. *Emploi, croissance et compétitivité.* Paris: Syros.

Bibes, Geneviève, and René Mouriaux, eds. 1990. *Les syndicats européens à l'épreuve.* Paris: Presses de la Fondation Nationale de Sciences Politiques.

Bonafe-Schmitt, Jean-Pierre. 1981. L'action du délégué du personnel en matière de réclamations individuelles. *Droit Social* 9–10:627–47.

Bouzonnie, Huguette. 1991. Audience syndicale. *Liaisons sociales* 10995:9–85.

Boyer, Robert. 1988. *The search for labour market flexibility: The European economies in transition.* Oxford: Clarendon.

Bunel, Jean, and Jean Saglio. 1979. *L'action patronale, du CNPF au petit patron.* Paris: Presses Universitaires de France.

Caire, Guy. 1992. *La négociation collective.* Paris: Presses Universitaires de France.

Cam, Pierre. 1991. Le droit à la lumière ou les ambivalences du savoir, *Travail et Emploi* 43:9–21.

Cam, Pierre, and Patrick Chaumette. 1989. L'expertise technologique du comité d'entreprise. *Droit Social* 3:220–28.

Carre, Dominique, and Gérard Valenduc. 1991. *Choix technologiques et concertation sociale.* Paris: Economica.

CFDT (Confédération Française Démocratique du Travail). 1977. *Les dégats du progrès: Les travailleurs face au progrès technique.* Paris: Le Seuil.

Chang, Clara, and Constance Sorrentino. 1991. Union membership statistics in 12 countries. *Monthly Labor Review* 114 (December): 46–53.

CNPF (Conseil National du Patronat Français)/CODESE. 1980. *Amélioration des conditions de vie dans l'entreprise: Expériences et réalisations.* Suresnes: Hommes et Techniques.

Cohen, Maurice. 1986. Le fonctionnement et le financement des comités d'entreprise. *Revue Pratique de Droit Social* 495:209–18.

d'Iribarne, Alain. 1989. *La compétitivité: Défi social, enjeu éducatif.* Paris: Presses du Centre National de la Recherche Scientifique.

Dufour, Christian, and Marie Françoise Mouriaux. 1986. *Les comités d'entreprise: quarante ans après.* Dossiers de l'IRES, no. 4. Paris: Institut de Recherches Economiques et Sociales.

du Roy, Olivier. 1989. *Gérer la modernisation.* Paris: Editions d'Organisation.

Echardour, Annick, and Eric Maurin. 1992. La gestion de la main d'oeuvre par les entreprises. *INSEE Première* no. 179. Paris: Institut National de la Statistique et des Etudes Economiques.

Eyraud, François. 1983. Principles of union action in the engineering industries in Great Britain and France. *British Journal of Industrial Relations* 3:358–76.

Eyraud, François, and Robert Tchobanian. 1985. The Auroux Reforms and company level industrial relations in France. *British Journal of Industrial Relations* 2:241–59.

Gadille, Martine. 1992. L'apprentissage par les entreprises de la gestion prévisionnelle de l'emploi. *Travail et Emploi* 51:70–85.

Goetschy, Janine, and Patrick Rozenblatt. 1992. France: The industrial relations systems at a turning point? In *Industrial relations in the new Europe,* ed. Antony Ferner and Richard Hyman. Oxford: Blackwell.

Harff, Yvette, and Bruno Henriet. 1988. Evolution du rôle et des interventions économiques du comité d'entreprise. *Droit Social* 2:166–74.

Hassenteufel, Patrick. 1992. Institutions et pratiques dans l'établissement. *Revue de l'IRES* 8:9–40.

Henriet, Bruno. 1990. L'information du comité d'entreprise: une pratique encore imparfaite. *Droit Social* 12:874–79.

Hordern, Francis. 1988. *Naissance d'une institution: Du contrôle ouvrier aux délégués du personnel, 1880–1939.* Cahiers, no. 1. Aix en Provence: Institut Régional du Travail.

Lagrande, François. 1990. *Nouvelles relations de travail, pratiques contractuelles et perspectives.* Paris: L'Harmattan.

Le Maître, Annick, and Robert Tchobanian. 1992. *Les institutions représentatives du personnel dans l'entreprise: Pratiques et évolutions.* Paris: La Documentation Française.

Lochouard, Didier. 1990. Les expertises nouvelles technologies et prévention des risques graves. *Travail et Emploi* 43:22–28.

Martin, Dominique. 1976. Les systèmes de négociation et de représentation dans l'entreprise. *Droit Social* 3:99–101.

———. ed. 1989. *Participation et changement social dans l'entreprise.* Paris: L'Harmattan.

Montuclard, Maurice. 1963. *La dynamique des comités d'entreprise.* Paris: Centre National de la Recherche Scientifique.

Podevin, Gérard, and Eric Verdier. 1989. *Formation continue et compétitivité économique.* Collection des études, no. 51. Paris: Centre d'Etudes et de Recherches sur la Qualifications.

Reynaud, Jean-Daniel. 1968. L'avenir des relations professionnelles en Europe Occidentale: Perspectives et hypothèses. *Bulletin de l'IIES* 4:76–106.

———. 1989. *Les règles du jeu, l'action collective et la régulation sociale.* Paris: A. Colin.

Ribeill, Georges. 1984. Les organisations du mouvement ouvrier en France face à la rationalisation. In *Le Taylorisme,* ed. Maurice De Montmollin and Olivier Pastre. Paris: La Découverte.

Riboud, Antoine. 1987. *Modernisation mode d'emploi.* Paris: Union Générale d'Editions.

Sellier, François. 1961. *Stratégie de la lutte sociale.* Paris: Les Editions Ouvrières.

Stankiewicz, François, ed. 1988. *Les stratégies d'entreprises face aux ressources humaines: L'après-taylorisme.* Paris: Economica.

Sudreau, Pierre. 1975. *La réforme de l'entreprise (Rapport du comité d'étude).* Paris: La Documentation Française.

Tchobanian, Robert. 1989. Des sections syndicales et le droit d'expression des salariés.

In *Participation et changement social dans l'entreprise,* ed. Dominique Martin. Paris: L'Harmattan.

——. 1990. Amélioration des conditions de travail, jeu des acteurs, et transformation des relations professionnelles. In *Les systèmes de relations professionnelles,* ed. Jean-Daniel Reynaud et al. Lyon: Editions du Centre National de la Recherche Scientifique.

——. 1992. Activité de représentation dans l'entreprise et rapports aux salariés: Quelques problèmes actuels. *Revue de l'IRES* 8:75–104.

UNEDIC (Union Nationale pour l'Emploi dans l'Industrie et le Commerce). 1991. *Rapport d'activité 1990.* Paris: UNEDIC.

Visser, Jelle. 1991. Trends in trade union membership. In *Employment Outlook, July 1991,* 97–134. Paris: Organisation for Economic Co-operation and Development.

6   Spain: Works Councils or Unions?

Modesto Escobar

6.1   Introduction: Industrial Relations in Spain

In Spain works councils are legally defined as unitary bodies for the representation of workers at the workplace. The law also regulates the existence of union sections inside the firm. In this sense, there is a dual system of worker representation in Spanish labor relations. However, in contrast to many other systems, the "second channel" of interest representation is especially salient in relation to the unions, which control the works councils and implement their policies at the firm level through them. One of the main questions that the Spanish case raises is precisely whether and to what extent it is possible for a union to pursue its policies effectively by means of an institution with union and nonunion duties. Another important question concerns the implications of a council representation system in a country with two main unions divided along ideological and political lines: the socialist Unión General de Trabajadores (UGT—General Union of Workers) and the communist Comisiones Obreras (CCOO—Workers' Commissions).

Historically there has been a succession of very different labor relations systems in Spain. Since the 1930s, the country has experienced four different combinations of unionism and works councils: free unionism without works councils during the Second Republic (1931–39), neither free unions nor works councils under fascism (1939–53), works councils without free unionism (1953–77), and both free unions and works councils (1977 to the present).

Modesto Escobar is professor of sociology at Universidad de Salamanca and a research associate at the Center for Advanced Study in the Social Sciences of the Instituto Juan March de Estudios e Investigaciones.

The author thanks Robert Fishman, Pedro Luis, and Juan Carlos Rodríguez for their comments, which have improved this chapter, and Elisa Arévalo and Pamela Aguilar for their help. He also thanks the Institute Juan March, whose facilities made this research possible, and its former director, Victor Pérez-Díaz, who introduced the author to the field of industrial relations.

Works councils were first discussed in 1921 when the Institute for Social Reforms, a government advisory body, inspired by the creation of works councils in Germany in 1920, proposed the introduction of industrial cooperation councils, through the Law on Employment Contracts that was being debated at the time. However, unions and employers, both represented in the institute, took very different positions, and the project did not succeed (Borrajo 1975; Cabrera 1987; Soto 1989). However, it returned during the Second Republic in 1931, when a parliamentary commission approved the creation of unionized "intervention councils of workers" in all nonagricultural firms with a workforce of more than 50. Again, employers opposed the project, and it failed to get the approval of the Republican parliament (Borrajo 1975; Cabrera 1983).

During the Spanish Civil War many firms were expropriated. Revolutionary works councils led by the anarchist National Confederation of Labor (CNT) and, in some cases, by the socialist UGT confiscated enterprises and imposed a collectivistic production regime in agriculture and industry, especially in Republican regions such as Catalonia, Aragón, and Valencia (Girona 1987; Bosch, 1987; Casanova 1988).

The industrial relations system changed dramatically in the first phase of Francoism (1939–58), when it came to be based on "corporations." Unions were outlawed, with the exception of an official syndicate which both employers and workers were forced to join. Through this "vertical union," the state controlled labor relations on the assumption that there was no basic conflict between the interests of employers and those of workers. Wages and working conditions were regulated by governmental decree, and the hierarchical organization of the firm was established under a set of statutes called *ordenanzas laborales.* However, the official union was unable to control the regulation of production in every firm, as its activists were not numerous enough to be present in every workplace. For this reason, restricted works council elections were introduced, to legitimize the vertical union and to ensure the effective implementation of the *ordenanzas laborales.* This explains why the law on *jurados de empresa,* the first form of legally based works councils in Spain, was passed as early as 1947, long before the economic liberalization program of the late 1950s.

The second period of the Franco regime (1958–75) was characterized by economic liberalization. The autarchic economic strategy was replaced with an opening toward international markets. Labor repression was loosened through the introduction of a controlled system of collective bargaining in 1958 that gave negotiating rights to the already existing works councils and paved the way for the emergence of semiclandestine unions (Maravall 1978; Foweraker 1989; Balfour 1989). The state tried to control the system by reserving for itself the right to veto the candidates in works council elections, approve agreements between employers and workers, and impose compulsory arbitration if the two sides did not come to an agreement (Amsden 1972).

During the transition to democracy the main reforms in industrial relations were aimed at granting bargaining autonomy to employers and workers and making the Spanish industrial relations system similar to that of other Western European countries. Free unions and employers' associations were admitted, and most of the mechanisms of state intervention in this area were dismantled. Works councils had their name changed from *jurados de empresa* to *comités de empresa*. Their compulsory presence was extended from enterprises with more than 50 to those with more than 10 employees, although in the smallest firms they were called *delegados de personal* (staff delegates). Also, state control over the electoral system was abolished, and workers and unions were given the right to present freely selected lists of candidates. Furthermore, unions were given certain competitive advantages in council elections over nonunion lists, and councils became worker-only bodies, no longer including the employer as they had under Franco. Finally, their cooperative functions were deemphasized in favor of representative functions, without detracting from the employer's right to manage.

There was a general conviction that works councils were institutions that should be allowed to survive in the context of a democratic industrial relations system. More problematic was their function in relation to unions. At the beginning of the transition, union workplace organizations were not legally recognized, putting many functions in the hands of the works councils, including firm-level negotiation and the organization of strikes. The bargaining role of unions inside the firms was not recognized until the Ley Estatuto de los Trabajadores (LET—Workers' Statute) of 1980.

At the same time, the new democratic labor legislation eliminated the representation of workers on the boards of enterprises, which had existed since 1962 and had provided for one worker for every six employer representatives. This is explained by union rejection of participation in a minority position in the management of private firms, as well as by employer resistance to parity on company boards. Unions were, however, eager to participate in the management of public enterprises. Participation was implemented in two stages: first, via union representation in public regulatory institutions and, second, with the introduction of union representation on the boards of public enterprises by an agreement in 1986 between UGT and the National Institute of Industry (INI), which is the holding company for Spanish public enterprises.

Simultaneously, a new union system emerged in the course of the democratization of Spanish institutions. To understand Spanish works councils better, it is necessary to sketch the main features of this system. First, the Spanish model of unionism may be labeled one of *representative duopoly*. In response to the multitude of union names that were registered immediately following the opening of the Register of Union Organizations in 1977, legal mechanisms were devised to insure the predominance of majority unions, similar to the French and Italian concept of "most representative" worker organizations. In contrast with these cases, however, works council elections, which are held nationwide every four years within a period of three months, are used to establish the representativeness of the unions. This has resulted in small unions losing representative status unless they are strictly concentrated in one sector or geographical area.

Representative duopoly in Spanish unionism has a number of exceptions, the most important ones being regionally based unions. In the Basque country, the Christian Democratic Solidarity of Basque Workers (ELA-STV) fills the largest number of council seats. The same holds in Galicia for the Nationalist Union of Galician Workers (INTG), now known as the Galician Inter-Union Coalition (CIG). As a consequence, both have achieved the status of representative unions in their regions as well as for national-level collective bargaining. In addition, in individual enterprises there often are minority unions with more than 10 percent of elected councillors, giving them the right to negotiate collective agreements. Among these are the socialist autonomous Union Sindical Obrera (USO), the anarchist General Confederation of Workers (CGT), which exists mainly in Catalonia, the Independent Union Confederation of Civil Servants (CSIF) in public administration, and various company unions or nonunion lists that arise where the majority unions are weak, or where there are charismatic leaders that are not integrated in those organizations.

A second feature of Spanish unionism is its *political dependence.* As in all southern European countries, the major unions are linked with political parties and are typically subordinate to them. The relationship of the UGT with the Partido Socialista Obrero Español (PSOE—Spanish Socialist Workers'party) is rooted in the origins of the two organizations. The UGT was set up by PSOE activists. During the tenure of its first general secretary, Pablo Iglesias, the top leadership was the same for both organizations. After Iglesias's retirement in 1918, the leadership was divided between Francisco Largo Caballero and Julián Besteiro, although each of them was on both the PSOE and UGT executive committees.[1] In the Second Republic the two leaders disagreed fundamentally on economic and political matters, leading to deep division among the party and union rank and file during the Civil War (Gillespie 1988, 35–52).

Both Largo Caballero and Besteiro lived in exile until the beginning of the 1970s, a time when younger leaders emerged in Spain. Most prominent among them were Nicolás Redondo, from the Basque socialist movement, and Felipe González. The 1973 UGT congress in Toulouse, France, marked the ascent of Redondo to the top leadership of the union. After Redondo relinquished his role in the party at the 1974 congress in Suresnes, Felipe González, leader of a Sevillian group of socialists, was named the new secretary general of the PSOE, with an executive committee composed of domestic leaders.

Until 1985, Redondo and González worked together without major frictions. Their common goal was the growth of their respective organizations, which

---

1. At the end of the 1920s, "of the eleven positions in each of the two executive committees, eight were held by officials who were in both committees, and the five who were in control of daily decision-making were the same in both organizations" (Tuñón de Lara 1985, 257).

they could achieve only through mutual assistance. The PSOE, the main opposition party from 1977 to 1982, formed a common front with the UGT against the government of the Unión de Centro Democrático (UCD), a coalition of many small parties. In the first years of the Socialist government, the UGT took advantage of its good relations with the government to improve its position in competition with CCOO. However, the PSOE's program of economic stabilization was bound to conflict with the desire of the UGT to protect working-class interests. The new law on retirement benefits, the project for industrial restructuring, the liberalization of labor markets, the priority given to the fight against inflation, low wage increases, and high unemployment caused a progressive deterioration in the relationship between the party in government and the unions. The schism began with Redondo's vote in Parliament against the new pension law and continued with the resignation of the UGT leadership from the Socialist parliamentary group; it climaxed in a general strike in December 1988 that paralyzed the country in protest against the government's economic policy.

The CCOO, on its part, which had emerged spontaneously from worker activism under Francoism, was used by the Partido Comunista de España (PCE—Communist party) in its fight against the dictatorship from within its institutions. Although originally the union was a politically independent organization committed to the struggle for working-class interests and accepted in its core not only independent members but also activists from other parties (Ariza 1976), at the beginning of the 1970s all major executive positions were held by PCE members. After the transition, however, the CCOO also gained more independence, although for very different reasons than the UGT—not because of differences in political strategy, but because of the PCE's political weakness. As long as the party was strong, it used the union as a platform for its political objectives. However, when the PCE lost almost its entire parliamentary representation in the 1982 elections, the union recovered the political initiative.

Third, Spanish unions are *organizationally weak,* having together with France the lowest membership figures in Western Europe. Today, approximately 10 to 15 percent of the employed wage-earning population is affiliated to a union (Escobar 1991). Membership density reached its peak in 1978 with approximately 40 percent and declined to a little more than 20 percent in 1981. In the manufacturing industry, too, surveys have periodically shown a declining tendency since the end of the 1970s. In 1978, 42 percent of industrial workers were *not* affiliated to a union. In 1980, this proportion increased to 60.7 percent, and in 1984, it reached 75.4 percent (Pérez-Díaz 1985, 1992).

This dramatic decline has several explanations. The euphoria of the transition was associated with rapid but unstable growth in the desire to participate in public life, principally through neighborhood associations and workers' associations. There also was an initial belief that union members would have advantages over nonmembers—this was disappointed by the unions' inability to gain favorable agreements for their members at a time of economic crisis. Spanish unions also failed to offer attractive services to their members. In addition, the economic crisis with high unemployment did not favor stable membership, nor did the evolution of the economic structure, especially the growth of the service sector, of the black market, and of new forms of business organization. The membership decline reached its bottom before the general strike of 1988. The strike seems to have resulted in a progressive absolute increase in membership, tracing the simultaneous growth in employment. According to the UGT, between 1986 and 1989 its membership grew from 333,000 to nearly half a million, a 44 percent increase (UGT 1989, 53). In the CCOO there was a 33 percent increase between 1984 and 1989, from 375,000 also to about half a million.

Membership figures do not adequately reflect the power and influence of Spanish unions, however. Support for unionism, as reflected in voting behavior in council elections, must also be taken into account. At the beginning of the transition, three-fourths of industrial workers were in favor of unionism. In a 1980 survey 47.8 percent showed no support for any union organization, and in 1984 the same segment had declined to 41.2 percent, despite the continuing decline in membership (Pérez-Díaz 1992). In 1988, 43.5 percent did not sympathize with any union (Instituto de Estudios Sociológicos [IDES] 1989), and in 1991, with a differently worded question, 62.4 percent of the workers responded in this way (Escobar 1991). The data seem to indicate growing disenchantment with unionism during the mid-1980s and early 1990s.

The weakness of Spanish unions is especially visible in their organizations. The low number of full-time staff working for the UGT—less than 100 people in 1989—the low number of elected officials, and the poor training of its activists impinge on the union's effectiveness. Unlike their Western European counterparts, Spanish unions are very young. After 40 years of illegality, they had to build their organizations in a short period of time. Fifteen years, mostly of economic crisis, are not enough to create the organizational infrastructure of effective union activity. Organizational weakness is particularly evident in the shortage of financial resources. Spanish unions keep their dues low to avoid further loss of members. This forces them to cut costs, though at the same time they must offer services to their members. As a consequence, unions have to turn to other sources of revenue. In particular, the state became the big benefactor of the unions in the mid-1980s, mainly as a result of the law requiring restitution of union property confiscated by the Francoist regime—a law that was especially advantageous to the UGT.

It is also true, however, that Spanish unions have considerable mobilizing capacity. In part this is the result of the experiences of the working class under Francoism. During Franco's last 20 years, worker organizations were illegal; it was, therefore, impossible to build a formal network of union activities. However, by allowing collective negotiation, the regime gave union leaders the opportunity to learn to mobilize workers in adverse conditions of police control and semi-illegality of strikes.

This has produced three major forms of union mobilization: sectoral or enterprise strikes, general strikes, and demonstrations. Strikes at the sectoral or enterprise level are the main way of promoting union demands. They take place either during the negotiation of collective agreements or when employers do not adhere to an agreement. The majority of work days lost results from this type of conflict. During the 1980s, industrial conflict was more frequent in Spain than anywhere else in Europe—it was slightly higher than in Italy. Conflict was most intense in the four years from 1976 to 1979 (table 6.1), during the transition period, when workers mobilized for demands pent up from the time of the dictatorship and the unions acted to establish their presence and prove their power.

The main indicator of the unions' mobilizing capacity is the effectiveness of their strike calls, which can be measured by the percentage of workplaces or workers that join a strike. Since 1986, the first year for which reliable data are available, the effectiveness of strike mobilization with respect to workplaces has normally been above 70 percent, and with respect to workers it

Table 6.1   **Macroeconomic Indicators, 1975–91**

Year	Unemployment (%)	Inflation (%)	Growth (%)	Strikes[a]
1975	4.0	16.7	1.1	–
1976	4.9	16.7	3.0	12,593
1977	5.7	22.8	3.3	16,642
1978	7.4	20.2	1.8	11,551
1979	9.1	16.7	0.2	18,917
1980	11.8	13.7	1.8	6,178
1981	14.6	12.0	−0.3	5,154
1982	16.5	13.8	1.2	2,788
1983	18.1	11.6	1.8	4,417
1984	20.9	10.9	1.9	6,358
1985	21.9	8.5	2.3	3,223
1986	21.5	10.5	3.8	2,279
1987	20.5	5.9	5.6	5,025
1988	19.5	5.7	5.2	6,843
1989	17.3	7.0	4.8	3,685
1990	16.3	7.3	3.7	2,443
1991	16.3	6.9	2.4	4,421

Sources: Instituto Nacional de Estadistica, *Contabilidad Nacional de España* (Madrid: Ministerio de Hacienda, Secretaria General Tecnica, various years); Instituto Nacional de Estadistica, *Encuesta sobre Población Activa* (Madrid, various years).

[a]Working days lost, in thousands.

exceeded 75 percent every year. In 1986 it even reached 94 percent of a total of one and three-quarter million workers called out to strike.

General strikes may be called for subnational geographical areas. During industrial restructuring, several general strikes took place in localities such as Sagunto and Reinosa, whose main industrial plants were closed, and in regions like Asturias and Murcia. Since the beginning of the transition, only five general strikes have been called for the entire country. The first was called by the CCOO against a wage freeze and for amnesty, freedom, and democracy. At the time the UGT had not yet held its first congress and did not participate in the call to strike. The second general strike was called by the short-lived, Coordinating Committee of Union Organizations (COS), which included the UGT, CCOO, and USO, against the referendum for political reform and in support of a joint platform of Socialist, Communist, and other centrist or leftist parties. The third followed the attempted coup d'état of 1981 led by Colonel Tejero and was called only by the CCOO, as was the strike in 1985 against the Retirement Pension Law. Next was the general strike of 1988, called by the two majority unions against the Socialist government's economic policies, which was a complete success for its organizers. Finally, in 1992 the CCOO and UGT called for a four-hour general strike, with less success, against a governmental decree cutting unemployment benefits and proposed legislation regulating strikes.

6.2   Spanish Works Councils since Democratization: The Political and Economic Setting

Works councils played an important role during the transition to democracy (1975–78). For the 1975 elections of *jurados de empresa,* the CCOO promoted in many firms so-called *candidaturas unitarias y democráticas* (CUD—democratic unitary lists), with candidates belonging to different illegal parties or unions which had been in opposition to the Franco regime. The anarchists and the Socialists of the newly founded UGT, for their part, opposed participation in these elections.

The CUD were successful in some sectors of the economy and in certain geographical areas. Balfour (1989) has reported documents, found in the headquarters of the police in Barcelona, that include a chart of the election results in that province. Sixty-nine percent of the elected delegates belonged to the CUD. Among them, police classified 44 percent as *red* (*sic*)—and of these, 9 percent as *good* (*sic*) and 22 percent as *bad,* many of the latter being members or sympathizers of clandestine organizations with a "criminal" record or at least a personal file in the police archives. In some places an alternative to representation by *jurados de empresa* was organized by the workers. This system consisted mostly in nonstanding committees elected in mass meetings; it disappeared after the first democratic works council elections in 1978.

The initial period of the transition was marked by high political mobilization and strong demands for higher wages. Works councils whose members belonged to an opposition party or union played an important role in mobilizing workers in favor of one of the two paths to democracy that were discussed at the time. Two main political options were available (Maravall and Santamaría 1986): *reforma* (reform) and *ruptura* (breakup). The former entailed a smooth process of democratization that preserved some elements of the old regime; the latter favored more rapid change through the formation of a provisional government. Most local labor leaders endorsed the second choice and mobilized for it (Fishman 1990). The confrontation between the two models resulted in the adoption of a compromise path to democracy, called "negotiated reform" and backed by the two main leftist parties, the PSOE and PCE. Works councils and workers, backed by the semi-illegal unions, also managed to obtain high wage increases during this period, in a time of international economic crisis.

Nineteen seventy-seven was a key year in the transformation of labor relations in Spain. Unions were legalized under a pluralist model, against the policy of the CCOO, which tried to build a unitary union structure. Two governmental decrees were issued clarifying the rules of industrial relations, one regulating collective bargaining and the right to strike and the other establishing worker representation through *comités de empresa* and the rules for the first democratic works councils. In addition, the first attempt to deal with the economic crisis through social pacts was made, although the first pact included only the main parties with parliamentary representation, ranging from the moderate right to the Communists (Pactos de la Moncloa).

The second period (1978–85) in the evolution of industrial relations in the young Spanish democracy was one of social as opposed to political concertation. After the Moncloa Pacts, the first two accords were reached between the peak employers' organization, the Confederación Española de Organizaciones Empresariales (CEOE), and the Socialist UGT. While the CCOO tried to rely on direct mobilization of the workers, the UGT engaged in negotiation with employers, offering moderation in exchange for union recognition at the workplace. At the national level, wage increases were agreed, together with the contents of the coming legislation on industrial relations, the Workers' Statute. One result were new confrontations at the enterprise and provincial levels between the two main unions, with the UGT willing to negotiate wage raises within the limits set at the national level and the CCOO trying to mobilize workers to obtain more, at least in firms not suffering from the effects of the crisis. This led to a debate about the structure of collective bargaining in which the CCOO defended an articulated form of negotiation, under which agreements at lower levels could improve on the national agreement, while the UGT and CEOE favored the extension of the national agreement to all lower levels of bargaining, except in situations of economic crisis.

Bilateral social concertation between the UGT and CEOE broke up for two reasons: the danger of a breakdown of democracy, as evidenced by the unsuccessful coup d'état of 1981, and the worsening of economic conditions, manifested mainly in high unemployment. These two factors made the CCOO join social concertation, leading to the National Agreement on Employment that was signed in 1981 by the government, the CEOE, and the Socialist and Communist unions. Two years later another agreement followed, negotiated by the CEOE, UGT, and CCOO, without the signature but with the approval of the Socialist government. The two agreements reduced the conflict between the unions but generated tensions inside the CCOO that led to a decline in its membership and its representation on works councils, in favor of the UGT. At the time, social concertation seemed to be effective in controlling inflation and labor conflicts; it was, however, unable to improve employment (table 6.1).

In 1985, the UGT, but not the CCOO, signed together with the employers and the Socialist government a national agreement that ended the period of centralized collective bargaining and income policies (Espina 1990). All pacts had focused on industrial relations outside the firm, giving a salient role to the peak union organizations at the expense of works councils and other local union structures (Giner and Sevilla 1984; Roca 1987; Zaragoza 1988; Pérez-Díaz 1992). At the workplaces, a deep division developed between the two unions' sections, with the CCOO accusing the UGT of following and implementing government policy, and the UGT accusing the CCOO of supporting Communist party opposition to the Socialist government. After the CCOO had won the majority in the two first works council elections, the UGT, backed by the Socialist party, won the majority of seats in 1982.

During the period of social concertation, the Socialist government promoted a tough plan to restructure several sectors affected by the crisis. While the UGT took a moderate position on this, the CCOO adopted a strategy of countermobilization. Works councils, under pressure from the rank and file, tried to defend the current level of employment and negotiate the best possible conditions for layoffs. The Socialist government also tried to make labor markets more flexible, amending the chapter on employment of the Workers' Statute to open the way for new forms of employment contracts. While this was to increase employment and facilitate the creation of new jobs, it resulted in the segmentation of the workforce and the creation within workplaces of two kinds of workers with different interests, raising new problems for the works councils.

In its dealings with unions, in its first period the Socialist government backed the UGT. Legislation was passed that gave union sections a seat on works councils and the right to be recognized by employers. In addition, measures were taken to support unions financially in a way that favored the UGT. After Spain's accession to the European Community in 1986 and as a result of a restrictive monetary policy that raised interest rates, foreign capital increasingly flowed into Spain, mainly benefiting the financial sector but also resulting in key companies being sold at low prices.

A new period began after 1985, when the expectations of UGT leaders that the government they supported would pursue social democratic policies were finally disappointed. This gave rise to tensions and estrangement between them and the Socialist party. The first strains were related to the government's policy of industrial restructuring, but the issues that led to the greatest tensions were a pension reform designed to reduce public expenditure, various measures to increase labor market flexibility—like the Decreto sobre Empleo Juvenil (Decree on Youth Employment) that was the immediate cause of the successful general strike—and more recently the reduction of unemployment benefits.

After the mid-1980s, macroeconomic concertation no longer took place. The UGT argued that it was time that workers benefited from economic growth and business profits, which were to a large extent due to wage moderation during the democratic transition. The government, for its part, absolutely refused to make concessions, arguing that a wage increase was incompatible with the objectives of low inflation and competitiveness in the European Common Market. The employers' association, the CEOE, closed ranks with the government, while the CCOO, given the Communist party's political weakness, tried to forge an alliance with the UGT in an attempt to weaken the Socialist party's base among workers. As a consequence, wage negotiations had to take place at the regional, provincial, or firm level, where the UGT and CCOO tried to obtain increases above the wage raise proposed by the government. In the public sector, no agreement was possible and conflicts increased; in the private sector, employers, in a context of economic recovery, were willing to concede wage increases as long as they could assure social peace, and perhaps in order to divide the unions and the government.

The effects on works councils of this new economic and political scenario were dramatic. The UGT and CCOO became more likely to take similar positions in negotiating with employers, especially with public firms, while at the same time enjoying greater autonomy from central unions and no longer being restricted by peak-level negotiations. In 1991 and 1992, national unions refrained from issuing general wage guidelines for their members on negotiating committees, and unionized workforce representatives began to negotiate high raises in exchange for collaboration with employers trying to adapt their enterprises to more open markets, subsequent to the integration of Spain into the European Community.

6.3 Legal Regulations

The structure, composition, election, duties, and rights of Spanish works councils are highly regulated, mainly through the Workers' Statute approved by Parliament in 1980, at the end of the transition period. The statute permits further regulation by formal or informal collective agreements and is complemented by a large number of court rulings resolving conflicts of interpretation between employers and employees (Rodríguez-Sañudo 1988; Martín Herrero

1991; Albiol 1992). The rights conferred by the Workers' Statute to the works councils are the following:

Information rights: The employer must inform the works council at least quarterly of the economic development of the sector and the firm's production, sales, and employment prospects. The council must also be informed annually of the balance. In joint-stock companies, the employer must provide the council with all the documents he distributes to shareholders. Works councils must also be regularly informed on other topics, such as the level of absenteeism, work accidents, and occupational diseases. A posteriori, the works council must be given information on all sanctions imposed on workers for offenses. Finally, councils are empowered to review all written contract forms, and since 1990 employers must give councils an abstract of every new employment contract, with the exception of those for senior management.

Consultation rights: Although the Workers' Statute reserves the management function for the employer, works councils have the right to be heard on matters such as reduction of working time, redundancies, job reorganization, functional and geographic mobility of workers, training programs, introduction or revision of systems of work organization or supervision, and changes in the incentive system and job evaluation. These are important resources for works councils in influencing management decisions. The Workers' Statute specifies that in cases of redundancies and major changes in work organization, management must obtain authorization from the public authorities unless an agreement is reached with the works council.

Legal action rights: One of the most important functions works councils perform in Spain in monitoring the implementation of labor legislation and collective agreements. For this purpose, they have the right to take judicial or administrative action against employers and can take them to court for not observing legal regulations regarding not only the works council itself, but also the entire workforce.

Negotiation rights: From the legal reintroduction of collective bargaining in 1958, at a time when unions were banned, works councils have been entitled to negotiate collective agreements at the enterprise level. They have retained this right, while unions must meet certain criteria to be entitled to bargain.[2] The scope of the bargaining rights of Spanish works councils includes wages, working time, union rights, and any other labor questions.

Right to strike: While works councils in other European countries typically have no legal recourse to the strike, Spanish councils do. The right to strike is usually exercised while negotiations are taking place, during conflicts over the interpretation of collective agreements, or to bring pressure to bear on other employer decisions not regulated by law or industrial agreement.

---

2. They need recognition from the employer. Alternatively, they must, either alone or together with other organizations, have more than 50 percent of the representatives elected in the sector or region for which negotiations are held.

Right to manage the social funds of the firm: Almost every big firm in Spain has a special fund to promote the social welfare of the workers. The money is used to make low-interest loans, to subsidize the education of the children of workers, and to organize sports competitions, parties, and clubs. According to the law, these funds must be co-managed by the works council together with the employer.

Complementing their rights, Spanish works councils have the following obligations: to collaborate with management in maintaining and increasing productivity, to inform the workers on all matters related to the firm's labor relations, and to observe confidentiality on all information their members receive in their capacity as workforce representatives. The law requires the employer to provide works councils with resources, in particular adequate office space and notice boards and paid time off for performance of representative functions, depending on the number of employees in the workplace. Council members also enjoy special protection from dismissals.

Spanish works councils are elected by a firm's entire workforce. However, in firms with more than 250 employees, they also include directly appointed union delegates that have the same rights and obligations as the other members, except that they are not allowed to vote. The number of council members depends on the size of the plant. The Workers' Statute makes the workplace the basis for the election, but the definition of "workplace" is left unclear. Different locations and sizes of a firm's plants gives rise to conflict between workers and employers in delimiting works council constituencies. Workers and unions try to increase the number of elections in order to have adequate organizational structures in each single workplace, while employers prefer to hold common elections for all plants in order to minimize the costs of council representation. Table 6.2 shows the legal number of council members by size of workplace.

Table 6.2	Legal Number of Works Council Members by Size of Workplace		
Size of Workplace (number of employees)	Number of Council Members	Number of Union Representatives	Paid Hours per Council Member
6–30	1		15
31–49	3		15
50–100	5		15
101–250	9		20
251–500	13	1	30
501–750	17	1	35
751–1000	21	2	40
1001–2000	23	2	40
More than 2000	25–75[a]	3–4[b]	40

[a]Starts at 25, plus one for every 1,000 additional workers, up to a maximum of 75.

[b]Three for workplaces with fewer than 5,000 workers, and four for larger workplaces.

A firm with three plants in the same province, each with 200 employees, could either agree to set up three works councils with 9 members each, or have only one works council with 17 members, which means that it would have to pay for 10 fewer representatives. A good example of the possible consequences of reorganization of constituencies is the Spanish National Railways, which before the 1986 elections reduced the number of constituencies from 134 to 51—one works council for each province, except for Madrid with four and Barcelona with two—and the number of representatives from 1,947 to 1,139 (Ferner 1988, 94).

Although the entire workforce of a plant or firm has the right to vote, the law divides the elections in workplaces with more than 49 employees into two "colleges," one for technical and administrative staff (or white-collar workers) and the other for skilled and unskilled (blue-collar) workers. The Workers' Statute makes it possible to establish a third college for middle management by collective agreement. This, however, has only rarely been done: in the 1990 elections, only 8,143 voters were classified in the third college (excluding the Basque country; UGT 1992). The objective of the division is to assure the proportional representation of each group of workers where one of them constitutes a minority. Unions or workers can call elections every four years. Works councils are not compulsory unless there is an initiative to form one, either from a representative union or from the majority of the workers in a plant or firm. Most works council elections take place within a period of three months, so that the results can be used for granting unions representative status at the territorial or functional level above the individual firm. Where several unions or groups of employees schedule an election, the first initiative has priority over later ones. In the 1990 elections, the CCOO, being a representative union at the national level and thus having the right to call elections everywhere, scheduled elections in more than 200,000 workplaces. Its strategy was to hold elections as early as possible in the three-month period in those firms in which it expected to win a majority and delay elections to the end of the period in firms that it might win. In this way, the campaigns of the rival unions would not jeopardize its victory in "CCOO firms," while a good CCOO campaign might influence the results in the others. However, all this strategy led to a harsh confrontation between the two main unions and mutual charges of electoral fraud during the three-month election period.[3]

6.4   Presence and Composition of Works Councils

From the first democratic elections in 1978, the number of workplaces where works council elections are held within the three-month period has increased, especially after 1986 (table 6.3). This can be attributed to growing

---

3. Even after the elections, there were mutual accusations of fraud. This is the reason the government did not publish the official results until one year after the end of these elections.

Table 6.3   **Official Results of Works Councils Elections**

Year	Workplaces Participating	Workers Participating	Representatives Elected
1978	61,850	3,821,839	193,112
1980	61,049	3,419,914	164,617
1982	53,601	2,987,933	140,770
1986	70,812	3,159,778	162,298
1987[a]	1,432	997,522	13,065
1990	109,133	5,443,283	237,261
1990[a]	2,123	1,181,533	15,375
1990[b]	107,010	4,261,750	221,886

Source: Ministerio de Trabajo y Seguridad Social (MTSS 1992).
[a]Public administration only.
[b]Excluding public administration.

competition between the two main unions, as well as to new legislation in 1985 that gave unions more rights in the workplace and confirmed that the "representativeness" of a union depended on the election results. According to the law, a union is representative at any level if it obtains more than 10 percent of council seats at the national level, or more than 15 percent at the regional level. Furthermore, since the 1977 Moncloa Pacts, unions and employers' associations have the right to participate in state agencies such as the National Institute for Unemployment (INEM), the Health National Institute (INSALUD), and the National Institute for Social Services (INSERSO), with union positions being allocated in proportion to the election results.[4] Moreover, the Socialist government began to support unions financially in proportion to the number of works council seats they held.[5]

It is difficult to determine precisely the number of firms with a works council since statistically firms are defined as organizational units paying into the social security system, which may not be coterminous with the constituencies of works councils. In 1989, when there were about 20,000 units of this type with more than 50 employees, about 14,000 works council elections were held in workplaces of this size. The number of workers in these firms was about four million, while the electorate included about three million. An approximate calculation shows that about 75 percent of the workers in firms with more than 50 employees had the opportunity to vote for a council, and that roughly 70 percent of the workplaces in this category have at least one works council.

4. In every province, unions are entitled to three representatives in every state agency with provincial offices. A union that obtains a majority of works council seats in all provinces would thus have 100 representatives in just one agency.

5. Between January 1986 and June 1989, the UGT, the union with the highest income from subsidies, received 2,127 million pesetas from the government, out of total union revenues of 5,202 million pesetas (UGT 1989, 158).

All in all, the 109,133 works councils officially counted in the 1990 elections represented an electorate of 5,443,000 workers. Since there were more than nine million wage earners in Spain at the time, about 60 percent of Spanish workers were thus represented by staff delegates or works councils. This figure could in fact be somewhat higher because some elections do not take place within the three-month period[6] or are not included in the official results because of procedural problems.

Another source of evidence on the diffusion of works councils are surveys. In the 1984 survey directed by Pérez-Díaz, only 10 percent of the industrial workers in enterprises with more than 500 employees, and 50 percent in enterprises with fewer than 25 employees, answered that there was no works council in their firm. The overall results for the six sectors studied (metals, textiles, building, mining, chemicals, and food processing) showed that 23 percent of the workers did not have council representation in their workplace. Workers employed in public firms in those sectors were less likely not to be represented by a council (8 percent), and the same holds for workers in multinational firms (12 percent). In private Spanish firms, 27 percent of the workers had no works council representation.

The legal regulation of works councils in Spain also pertains to the election process. In workplaces with fewer than 50 workers, voters can vote for between one and three candidates. In larger workplaces voters must choose between lists. Each list is composed of a ranked set of candidates belonging to the same union. The system gives the union section the power to nominate the candidates and makes it very difficult for nonunionized workers to run for election, although this is possible provided a potential candidate manages to obtain a minimum number of signatures from workers. Also, any group of workers may be legally registered as a union and in this case would not have to collect any signatures. This explains the picturesque names of some unions that won seats in the 1990 elections.[7]

A problem with the closed-list system is that a union may not have enough members in a workplace to fill a list. The result is that in some nonunionized firms, union lists include not just union members but also sympathizers, generally the former at the top and the latter at the bottom. In fact, there is evidence that a significant number of council members elected on union lists are not actually union members. In a survey of representatives and members of the UGT, 24 percent of the works councillors were not members, 5 percent had quit the union after the election, and of the 71 percent unionized council mem-

6. E.g., a firm studied for this project, with about 10 thousand workers, held elections a year before the general elections since its first elections had been outside the official counting period and it followed the four-year rhythm established by the law.

7. E.g., Sociedad Obrera: La Marítima Terrestre (Worker Society: The Terrestrial Navy), Asociación de Mandos Intermedios de Tubos Reunidos (Association of the Intermediate Command of the Joined Tubes), and Asociación de Personal Encuadrado en la Tercera Categoría de ENDESA (Association of Staff in Third Category of ENDESA).

bers 22 percent had joined only after the election (Bouza 1989). Although data on the other main union in Spain are not available, it is likely that the percentage of nonmembers among CCOO works councillors is even higher, as a result of the greater openness of this union to nonaffiliated workers.

The official election results (table 6.4) show a high and increasing share of works councillors elected from among union candidates. While in the first free election 18 percent of elected councillors were nonunion candidates, in 1990 this figure had declined to less than 5 percent, and the two main unions won almost 80 percent of council seats. These results confirmed the Spanish model of biunionism, with the exception of two autonomous regions: the Basque country, where a nationalist Christian Democratic union won more than 37 percent of the seats, and Galicia, where a nationalist leftist union won more than 23 percent.

While the two main unions interpret the election outcomes as a victory for the class-oriented labor movement, others, such as the USO, CGT, and CNT, point to the electoral mechanism, complain about fraud, and blame political and governmental intervention. As a matter of fact, the electoral rules—for example, excluding from works council seats candidates from lists with less than 5 percent of the vote—favor big unions with the ability to present lists in a large number of workplaces.

Table 6.5 reveals interesting voting patterns. Although on the whole the UGT was the winner, with 42.6 percent of the vote, in workplaces with more than 49 employees the CCOO was more successful (39.8 percent vs. 37.0 percent). The main difference between the two unions is found among skilled and unskilled workers, where the CCOO is clearly favored. Also, small unions and nonaffiliated candidates get most of their votes among technical and administrative staff, while more than one-half of the votes for the UGT come from workplaces with fewer than 50 workers.

Another aspect of the unionization of Spanish works councils is the extent

Table 6.4   **Works Council Elections: Distribution of Seats by Union (%)**

Year	UGT	CCOO	USO	ELA	CIG	CSIF	Other Unions	Nonunion
1978	21.7	34.4	3.9	1.0	–		20.9	18.1
1980	29.3	30.9	8.7	2.4	1		11.9	15.7
1982	36.7	33.4	4.6	3.3	1.2		8.7	12.1
1986	40.9	34.5	3.8	3.3	0.7		10.0	7.6
1987[a]	23.1	24.2	–	–	–	24.9	27.8	–
1990	42.0	36.9	2.9	3.2	1.5	2.6	7.1	3.8
1990[a]	26.9	28.4	0.9	2.0	1.8	19.4	18.2	2.4
1990[b]	43.1	37.6	3.0	3.2	1.5	1.4	6.4	3.9

Source: Ministerio de Trabajo y Seguridad Social (MTSS 1992).

[a]Public administration only.

[b]Excluding public administration.

Table 6.5   Works Council Elections, 1990: Distribution of Votes by Union and Employee Category

Union	Total	Workplaces with Fewer than 50 Employees	Workplaces with 50 or More Employees			
			All	First College[a]	Second College[b]	Third College[c]
UGT	1,292,545 (42.6)	719,300 (48.5)	573,245 (37.0)	424,587 (38.0)	145,679 (34.4)	2,979 (35.4)
CCOO	1,201,275 (39.6)	585,156 (39.5)	616,119 (39.8)	409,134 (36.6)	204,807 (48.4)	2,178 (25.9)
CIG	44,993 (1.5)	25,565 (1.7)	19,428 (1.3)	12,437 (1.1)	6,948 (1.6)	43 (0.5)
Nonunion	107,506 (3.5)	43,082 (2.9)	64,424 (4.2)	53,185 (4.8)	10,927 (2.6)	312 (3.7)
Other unions	379,092 (12.5)	108,211 (7.3)	270,881 (17.5)	215,010 (19.3)	52,970 (12.5)	2,901 (34.5)
Total[d]	3,030,947 (100.0)	1,482,755 (100.0)	1,548,192 (100.0)	1,116,858 (100.0)	422,921 (100.0)	8,413 (100.0)

Sources: UGT (1992) from Ministry of Labor and Social Security data. Basque country results not included.

Note: Table reports absolute numbers with percentages in parentheses.

[a]Technical and administrative staff.

[b]Skilled and unskilled workers.

[c]Middle management.

[d]Percentages do not add up to 100 due to missing data.

Table 6.6   **Works Council Elections, 1986: Composition by Union of Councils Representing More than 500 Workers**

Composition	Number	Percentage
UGT present	437	82.3
CCOO present	412	77.6
UGT only	30	5.6
CCOO only	306	5.6
UGT and CCOO only	232	43.7
UGT and others	37	7.0
CCOO and others	12	2.3
UGT, CCOO, and others	138	26.0
Neither CCOO nor UGT	52	9.8
Total	531	100.0

Sources: Ministerio de Trabajo y Seguridad Social (MTSS 1987); Instituto de Estudios Superiores de Administracion (IESA, in preparation).

to which the two main unions are present on them. As no such data are as yet available for the 1990 elections, we must look at the 1986 results. Of the 11,653 councils for which results were computed, 7,602 had at least one UGT representative, and 6,944 had at least one CCOO member. Of the 531 works councils representing more than 500 employees, only 9.8 percent had neither a UGT nor a CCOO representative, and 55.0 percent included only UGT or CCOO representatives. Works councils with only UGT (5.6 percent) or only CCOO (5.6 percent) members were difficult to find in this segment (table 6.6).

6.5 Works Councils at Work

While there are more than 100,000 works councils in Spain, not all of them work properly. For example, according to the survey of UGT representatives and members (Bouza 1989), almost 60 percent of works councils in workplaces with fewer than 30 employees do not use their paid release time. In the remainder of this paper, seven firms in the metal sector are studied in depth.[8] In four of the firms (A, B, C, and D) the works council had negotiated a legally recognized collective agreement; the other three (X, Y, and Z) were covered by the provincial agreement negotiated by the unions and the sectoral employers' association. Three of the firms had a high level of unionization of more than 50 percent, two a medium level of 15 to 50 percent, and the other two a low level of less than 15 percent (table 6.7; see the appendix for more details).

In the seven case studies, all works councils in firms with more than 150 employees have important functions to perform, and they perform them effectively. One indicator of their activity is the frequency of their meetings. During

---

8. In each firm, two works council representatives and the manager dealing with the works council were interviewed.

Table 6.7   **Firms Studied**

	Union Density		
Agreement	High (>50%)	Medium (15%–50%)	Low (<15%)
Firm-level	A, B	C	D
Sectoral	X	Y	Z

the period of observation, the number of meetings ranged from one per month to one per day. The rule for big, highly unionized firms is once a week; in medium-sized, less unionized firms, once a month. Meetings are more frequent when industrial agreements are being negotiated, when the employer takes an unpopular initiative, or when a problem arises.

Unlike the *jurados de empresa* that preceded them, works councils do not include management; however, in some meetings management representatives may be present, either to give legally prescribed information or at the request of the workers, for example, when they want to raise demands or express disapproval. Councils with more than three members usually have a functional division of labor. Under the law, a works council with five or more members must designate a president and a secretary. In general, the president is the leader of the majority union. The position of secretary tends to go to the leader of the second-strongest union, unless there is a large majority for the first union, or a lack of trust between the main unions in the workplace.

In addition to the positions of president and secretary, there are other functions that are distributed among council members. The council may set up subcommittees on special matters and sometimes is forced to do so by law or collective agreement. In all firms under study, there was a health and safety committee, instituted by law in 1971 with a majority of seats held by managers; its structure is presently under revision. Also, in six of the seven firms there was a commission referred to as "productivity, production, time study methods," or simply the "parity commission," the latter referring to the fact that it was composed of the same number of delegates from management and workers. Other standing committees were concerned with employment and job assignment and the administration of social funds. Moreover, the works council may create temporary and task-specific committees, for example, to negotiate a collective agreement with the employer, to implement a signed agreement, or to lead a strike. Other committees are formed in response to employer initiatives on working-time reduction or job regulations. It must be emphasized that membership in the committees reflects the strength of the different unions at the workplace. Works council members are assigned to the different committees by their unions.

The main functions performed by Spanish works councils are the following:

Negotiation at the firm level: This is one of the main functions assigned to works councils by legislation. Works councils have a legal right to negotiate formal agreements. In practice, this is exercised not by the works council as a whole, but by a committee selected from among its members. This committee is legal if it represents at least one-half of the council members. This means that in a firm where one union has an absolute majority of the works council seats, its union section has the right to negotiate agreements directly with the management. The normal situation, however, is that the bargaining committee includes both of the two largest unions, frequently together with a third partner.

Firm-level negotiations are usually held by plant. But there are also multiplant agreements that involve more than one works council. In this case, the main role is played by an interplant works council, the creation of which requires a collective agreement. In two of the three enterprises with more than one plant, the collective agreement was negotiated by the interplant work council. Company D, with more than 20 plants in Spain, had not recognized an interplant council because management was not willing to assume its costs. According to the Ministry of Labor, of the 3,137 firm-level agreements, more than 10 percent are negotiated at the interprovincial level, which implies the inclusion of members of several works councils. More than one council may also have been involved in some of the other agreements, to the extent that firms have more than one plant within a province.

Works councils may also reach semi-informal agreements with the employer. Agreements of this kind are written and signed by both sides but are not registered with the public authorities. They are usually improvements on the sectoral agreement signed by the employers' association and the representative unions at the sectoral level. Under the Workers' Statute, they determine the month in which bonuses are paid and the holiday periods. But they also often regulate wage increases and working hours; in fact, in the three firms studied that had no formal firm-level collective agreement, there were semi-informal agreements on these matters.

Works councils may negotiate on everything, including wages. The only exception to this was under the social pacts signed by the main national unions, when unionized works councils were charged with implementing at the workplace the conditions negotiated by their peak organizations. The unlimited right of works councils to negotiate gives the Spanish collective bargaining system an anarchic character. In the case of public enterprises, the agreement reached at the national railway company, RENFE, usually serves as a guideline for other agreements. Often, however, works councils begin to negotiate wage increases after a sectoral agreement has been signed, usually trying to exceed it. It is true that in recent years, firm-level agreements show lower rates of wage increase than agreements at the industry level. This is explained by other improvements, for example, in the level of employment or in working conditions, that can be more easily attained at the firm level. Also, sectors without firm-level agreements have lower wages, and the effect of union intervention is to reduce interindustry wage differentials.

Control of managerial decisions: Their legal prerogatives, their facilities, the protection enjoyed by their members, their legitimacy derived from being elected by the whole workforce, and the support they receive from the external unions often enable Spanish works councils to prevent managers from acting against the rights and interests of the workers.

First and foremost, works councils watch over the legality of management policies and their implementation. As firms are highly legally regulated in Spain, a council can threaten to take the employer to court or to go to the labor administration. This is particularly important in health and safety matters, where the employer's majorities on the respective committees make it difficult for conflicts to be resolved inside the firm. Spanish works councils are also involved in the public regulation of labor markets, which includes control over temporal contracts, overtime, and mass dismissals. An empirical study in Catalonia showed that 72 percent of the works councils in the sample had appealed to the courts or to the labor administration in the preceding year. Of the works councils in firms with more than 500 employees, all had done so (Crespán and Falguera 1991).

Second, works councils participate in the governance of the internal labor markets of Spanish firms. They have a voice in promotions and generally do not favor functional or geographic mobility (Alós-Moner and Lope 1991). Both issues are of strong interest to workers. Works councils and unions can use this as a basis for clientelistic practices, which can transform a plant into a de facto closed shop in situations where there is a dominant union. In addition, when the number of short-term contracts increased in the late 1980s, demands for transforming these into permanent contracts were increasingly placed on the agenda of the negotiations between works councils and employers.

Third, Spanish works councils may have an important role in the introduction of new technologies and in major changes in work organization. As such changes may affect the level of employment or the content of jobs, councils take a close look at employer initiatives in these areas and often impede them.

Cooperation with management: Apart from the management of a firm's social fund, the most important issue on which Spanish works councils tend to collaborate with the employer is productivity. As raising productivity makes it possible to increase wages, councils tend to support almost any measure that stimulates production. A related topic is absenteeism, which was very high in Spain during the 1970s, and which works councils helped to fight by agreeing to the introduction of special bonuses.

Very rarely do works councils collaborate with management on improving the organization of work. It is commonly accepted among Spanish workers that this is a managerial matter. However, works councils that are independent from external unions have sometimes contributed to improving supervision at work, especially in firms with low entrepreneurial authority (Iriso 1992). Also, in company X the president of the works council, who belonged to one of the two main unions, became the production director of the plant, and the leader of the rival union was promoted to foreman.

6.5.1 Works Councils and Employers

The introduction of works councils in 1953 was not welcomed by employers whose power over their workers was very high at the time. Works councils could be seen, at least in theory, as an instrument with which the official union could improve the working conditions of its members. A few years later, after the economic liberalization, employers began to see works councils as potentially improving the efficiency of their enterprises, and as a means of coupling wage increases to productivity growth. At the same time, works councils paved the way for free, and at first illegal, unions. The most important of these was the Communist CCOO, making employers and the state again seek to put unionism under some form of control.

During the democratic transition, employers, unionists, workers, and politicians shared the conviction that works councils were an institution that should be included in a democratic organization of industrial relations. Employers feared, however, that the CCOO would establish a monopoly over worker representation. Organized employers therefore promoted a pluralist union system and supported workers organizations other than the CCOO. There are reasons to believe that in the first works council elections, employers backed the UGT especially, which attracted the vote of the moderate workers with its bargaining rather than mobilizing strategy.

The agreement between the UGT and the CEOE in 1979, which paved the way for the Workers' Statute, recognized the important role of works councils at the workplace. At the same time it allowed for the organization of internal unions, which was the main weapon of the UGT against the CCOO, and thus gave a bargaining role to the unions even at the firm level. The CEOE accepted this by signing a national agreement on workplace union organization, which favored the UGT, in exchange for social peace at the workplace in a moment of economic crisis and political transition. Five years later, with a Socialist government backing the UGT while holding an absolute majority in Parliament, the Organic Law of Union Freedom confirmed the union sections by law.

In a survey of 608 employers in seven industrial sectors accounting for 70 percent of Spanish industrial workers, 29 percent called industrial relations in their firm "excellent", and 60 percent "tolerable" (Pérez-Díaz 1985). Seventy-eight percent expressed trust in their workers, and 43 percent in their works councils; only 8 percent distrusted the latter. Internal union sections were viewed with less favor. Only 50 percent of the employers had a good opinion of them, whereas 25 percent had a bad one; 53 percent recognized their knowledge of the firm, but 51 percent criticized their ideological stance. Even more respondents lacked confidence in the external unions, which were seen as politicized (65 percent) rather than as promoting the interests of the workers (27 percent).

When managements take unpopular measures, works councils become crucial because they can mobilize the workforce easily. Employers have learned that it is better to announce such measures in advance to the works council. This may delay implementation because, inevitably, negotiations ensue; however, if managers take decisions without previous information, the council can mobilize resistance and thus make implementation even less likely.

Still, in general the strategy of Spanish employers seems to be to reduce the role of the works council to the minimum. Employers prefer to manage the workforce through a hierarchical line of command, unless they are forced to do otherwise by legal regulations. Union strength in a firm also influences the role the works council is allowed to play. Another factor that affects the behavior of the employer toward the council is the extent to which the different union forces are in agreement. When unions are united the works council may take a leading role, while when they disagree the union sections become more important. In company B, where there was fundamental agreement between the two main unions, the works council was stronger than the union sections. In companies A and X, employers had to deal with the union sections because of high interunion conflict, while in companies D and Z, with weak unions, works councils again played the leading role.

Strategies of employers in relation to works councils thus vary from firm to firm. The following, nonexclusive classification can be suggested:

1. The role of works councils can be minimized, in particular by refusing them the right to negotiate by abiding by the sectoral industrial agreement. This can easily be done in small or medium-sized firms without a tradition of collective bargaining, for example, in companies X, Y, and Z.

2. A collaborationist union can be promoted in order to keep other unions out. This is possible only where there is no previous union presence, and there were no examples of this in our sample.

3. Employers can offer to cooperate with unionized council members, granting them involvement in the organization of production and participation in exchange for improvements in efficiency. This is possible in medium-sized firms where external unions have no control over their affiliates, or in some enterprises with foreign capital (companies X and Z).

4. Employers can try to divide the council by signing agreements with the least conflict-oriented group of representatives and thus reducing the popularity and support of the others. This strategy requires a strong division between unions, as was usually the case in the period of national industrial agreements not signed by the CCOO. Company A belongs in this category, although the Socialist union in this case is more radical than its Communist opponent.

5. Employers can take an aggressive position in negotiations on one specific subject, at the risk of a strike and in the hope that this will prevent other issues

from being negotiated, which would reinforce the position of the employer. This pattern was found in companies C and D.

6. Employers can accept the demands of unionized works councils on wages and hours to avoid a strike. This attitude prevailed in companies C and D during the late 1980s. A strategy like this is possible only in prosperous sectors or in periods of expansion.

In public firms, works councils play a more active role, usually advised by external union officials in negotiating collective agreements at the firm level. Public sector managements have recently adopted a more confrontational stance toward works councils, under pressure to contribute to government objectives such as the reduction of inflation and public expenditure and the restructuring of publicly owned enterprises. In public administration, however, negotiations take place only with unions; works councils, called *juntas de personal* instead of *comités de empresa*, play only a minor role.

6.5.2 Works Councils and Unions

As pointed out above, the election system based on closed lists makes running candidates easier for a big union than for independent and small unions. Today almost 80 percent of Spanish works councillors belong to one of the two main unions. The remaining 20 percent is due to three factors. First, in some regions there are strong nationalist unions, especially in the Basque country and in Galicia. Surprisingly, there is no similar union in Catalonia, probably because of the independence and nationalism of the Catalan section of the CCOO, called Comisiones Obreras Nacionalistas de Cataluña, and the high proportion of immigrant workers from other Spanish regions. Second, in the public sector a coalition of independent unions usually wins more than a quarter of the works council seats. And third, in some firms there are groups of independent workers, leftist or rightist, with a charismatic leader trained in one of the main unions before resigning from it.[9]

Apart from works councils, the other legal mechanism of workplace representation in Spanish firms is the union section, defined as the group of workers affiliated to a given union. The union section functions as the extended arm of the union at the workplace. It has a number of legal rights, such as to distribute information to the workers, bargain collective agreements if bargaining is not conducted through the works council, and be given physical facilities for performing its activities. Also, in workplaces with more than 250 workers, each union section is entitled to be represented by one union delegate on the works council, with voice but without the right to vote. In workplaces with more than 5,000 workers, the number of union delegates increases to up to four.

---

9. An example is Pablo Rodríguez, the main leader of the Union Platform in the Municipal Transport Authority of Madrid. After gaining a high wage agreement, he won an absolute majority in the works council while the CCOO and UGT lost all their previous council members.

Given that works councils appeared in Spain earlier than the present unions, one might say that the latter have absorbed them. Yet, contrary to the German case, in Spain two unions compete for representative space at the workplace, which turns the council into an arena of interunion competition where unions discuss and, perhaps, agree on their strategies inside a workplace.

The opinion of the main Spanish unions on the two forms of representation are rather different. The CCOO defends the councils as a representative body that defends the rights of the workers. Works councils are viewed as expressing the interests of the rank and file under the guidance of the labor movement. The UGT on its part stresses the danger that a works council may lose sight of workers' general interests and may defend only the interests of the employees of a given firm. For this reason, the main actor in the negotiation of collective agreements should be the union section, inspired and led by the external union which provides the correct analysis of the situation and pursues the right policy for the working class as a whole.

The two positions were very different at the beginning of the democratic transition, when the CCOO wanted a unitary union built up from below, in which the CCOO-dominated works councils would have played an important role in articulating a confrontational policy at the firm level. The UGT, by contrast, sought recognition with a moderate strategy of negotiation (Zufiaur 1985). Since the general strike of 1988, the two unions have followed a unitary strategy, seeking common platforms at levels above the individual firm and, less frequently, at the firm level and trying to develop more similar conceptions of what a union is or must be. "Far from pushing the works council and the union section against each other, we have to think about how we can enable union policy to penetrate inside the firm" (CCOO 1992).

As a consequence of the long debate between the unions, the views of the workers on the two institutions are divided. In a survey conducted in mid-1988, 25.7 percent of workers answered that the best voice for them at the workplace was the works council, 18.3 percent mentioned the union sections, 14.5 percent (but only 3.8 percent in firms with more than 500 workers) mentioned management, and 10.8 percent mentioned mass meetings (IDES 1989). Union members favor works councils at a higher rate than nonmembers (33.3 percent). What is even more important is that, in spite of the different positions of their unions, there is no major difference in the views of CCOO and UGT members. Workers in firms with more than 49 employees are more in favor of works councils as a mechanism of voice (33.2 percent) than workers in small firms. But, again, CCOO and UGT members or sympathizers are more in favor of works councils than workers belonging to or inclined toward other unions.

The main problems external unions face today are their low presence in some sectors of the economy, in small and medium-sized enterprises, and in the black economy; the autonomy of internal unions due to the strong position of unionized works councils at the workplace; and the lack of organizational resources on the part of the main union federations, which increases the internal unions' autonomy.

There is no legal regulation of the relationships between union sections and works councils. However, there is a pattern of low participation of workers in union activities (Tezanos 1982; Equipo de Investigación Sociológica [EDIS] 1983; IDES 1989; Bouza 1989; Alós-Moner and Lope 1991; Pérez-Díaz 1992; Iriso 1992). Where there is a small union section, its principal members are at the same time the works council leaders (Lope 1991). Almost without exception, the leader of the internal union has the most powerful position in the representative system of the firm. While in small firms there may not be enough union members to fill all council positions, in unionized firms there is no division of functions: those who are on the executive committee of the internal union also represent the whole workforce on the works council (Alós-Moner and Lope 1991).

As the organization of Spanish unions is based on both geographical and sectoral lines, internal unions and works councils may have relations with different kinds of external unions. Works councils located in the main city of a province are likely to have links to industrial unions, while councils in small localities are typically connected to local unions unless their industrial sector is very important in the area. Usually, however, it is the industrial union that supplies the internal union with information and from which works councillors expect help in performing their tasks, such as legal services, training, or programmatic guidance.

Nevertheless, the relationship between members and works councillors on the one hand and the external union on the other is rather loose. In the survey of UGT affiliates, 40 percent of their works council representatives had not been to the external union office in more than a month, and the rate of participation of council members in elections to external union bodies was only 50 percent. Recently, external unions have tried to improve contacts with their representatives by offering them training courses, which according to the survey have been attended by 46 percent of UGT council members. However, works council membership means active participation in union activities and in this sense performs an important training function for the external unions. The majority of present union leaders come from the works councils of important firms, meaning that councils lose their main leaders to the external unions (Fishman 1990). Other losses occur because the external unions' small organizational resources force them to sometimes use elected works council members with paid release time for work at the external union office.

The level at which collective bargaining is conducted for a particular enterprise is a key factor in the relationship of its works council to the external union. In a firm under a provincial or national agreement, the works council watches over the implementation of the agreement and needs the external union to strengthen its power in relation to the employer. One reason why independent or local unions are usually not well regarded by workers is that they are less able to do this. On the other hand, where the contract is negotiated at the firm level, works councils are of greater importance and have more autonomy. In this case, the relationship with the external union depends on the extent to which the company agreement corresponds to the union's recommendations. If there is correspondence, members of the works council are likely to be invited to take part in sectoral or regional negotiations above the enterprise level. Otherwise, there is either growing autonomy of the internal union or a split, with a subsequent loss of union membership.

Firms with works councils have higher union membership than firms without them. But this is a spurious association. Workplaces with councils are larger. In fact, it is likely that the Spanish works council system reduces union membership because the collective agreements negotiated by the council are extended to everyone in the firm. Union members enjoy no instrumental advantage. The election procedure explains why there is a minimum number of members in unions that want to be representative. Once this level is attained, unions usually have little interest in increasing their membership.

6.5.3   Works Councils and Workers

As we have seen, while union membership among works councillors is high, rates of union affiliation in Spain are very low in general. This raises the question of the legitimacy of Spanish works councils. A good indicator for the acceptance of works councils among Spanish workers is election turnout. In 1986, 79.8 percent of those eligible to vote voted in the works council elections; in 1990, this share had declined slightly to 74.0 percent. Another indicator is the way workers evaluate works councils. In Pérez-Díaz's survey of six industrial sectors in 1984, one-quarter of the workers interviewed did not have a works council, one-tenth did not answer the question; 45 percent evaluated their council as satisfactory, and less than 20 percent found it unsatisfactory. Excluding workers without a works council, 60 percent of the respondents were satisfied with their councils, while 36 percent were not. The survey also offers evidence on what workers expect from works councils. With respect to who should negotiate with the employer, less than 10 percent answered that it should be the unions, while more than 60 percent assigned this function to an elected committee. That is, workers tend to accept the negotiating role of the works councils.

Regarding workforce participation through works councils, respondents were asked who decided and who should decide a range of issues in their firm, such as working time, work organization, employment practices, investment, and sales. Possible answers were management only, management after consulting with workers, and management and workers together by agreement. The results show that the only aspect that is negotiated is the time schedule, though even here 40 percent of the workers think that this is decided by the employer alone. At the same time, workers feel that, with the exception of investments and sales, all decisions on matters in the survey should be subject to agreement between the "two sides."

Another important aspect of the relationship between works councils and workers is communication between them. In principle, one may distinguish three possible patterns: (1) an informative relationship, with information flowing from the works councils to their constituents, (2) a representative relationship, where information flows from the workforce to the employer through the work council, and (3) mediation by the works council between employers and employees.

Works councils give information to workers mainly through mass meetings. The Workers' Statute establishes a maximum of six mass meetings per firm every year, at which council members can give information. When the works council is negotiating with the employer, it can call more than one mass meeting in a two-month period. Attendance varies over time and between firms. It is difficult to call a mass meeting in a nonunionized workplace, except in periods of negotiations over wages or employment. In companies D, Y, and Z, attendance at mass meetings was low, apart from special circumstances when more than 70 percent attended. In companies A and B, works councils regularly used the lunch breaks to inform the workforce. Mass meetings enjoy a high degree of legitimacy, in spite of certain perceived shortcomings. In the 1984 survey, more than 90 percent of workers agreed with the statement "Mass meetings are essential for the workers to discuss and solve their problems," and 85 percent with the sentence "In mass meetings one gets information and can discuss, but only a few know the problems and dare to speak up." Unionized workers are better informed than nonunionized ones because of better informal relations with plant union leaders and because of special mass meetings for union members only.

Representation, of course, is at the core of the functions of Spanish works councils and plays a central role in negotiations with the employer. A unionized works council represents at least two sets of interests: those of the union and those of the workers that have elected it to improve or defend their working conditions. There may also be conflicting interests among the workforce itself. Two main cleavages can be distinguished in Spanish firms in the 1990s: technicians versus manual workers and temporary employees versus employees with an indefinite contract.

The main mechanism that works councils and union officials use for defining the interests they represent is the negotiating platform. This is a catalog of demands, written independently by each union or group of workers with representation on the works council and to varying degrees taking into account the recommendations of the external unions and the demands and problems of the employees in the firm. Internal unions are essentially autonomous in defining their policies; in 1991 the two main union confederations stopped giving specific recommendations for wage increases to sectoral federations and workplace union sections. Union sections use different procedures to develop their platforms: they may simply take over the recommendations of their external union, may modify them in line with the views of the local leadership, may sound out the views of rank-and-file activists at the workplace, or may even incorporate the demands of nonunionized workers individually expressed through an informal survey or at a mass meeting.

An alternative, reflecting the recent tendency of the two main union confederations to act in unison, is to write a common negotiating platform. Where this is done, and no union proposes an alternative, the works council takes the lead. Otherwise, platforms developed by the different unions may be unified later, with the unions' works council representatives negotiating a compromise or all workers in a mass meeting voting for a common position to be presented to the employer (Lope 1991). Workplace leaders prefer unified platforms in the belief that they make it easier to extract concessions from the employer.

The most critical moment in the negotiation process arises when the negotiating committee begins to talk to management. Negotiations are accompanied by a continuous flow of information from the committee to the works council, and from there to the workforce. Keeping the workforce informed serves several functions: it mobilizes the support of the workers—who may be asked to go on strike—and makes known the distinctive policies and strategies of the different unions and other groups, in an effort to obtain votes in the future.

Divisions between unions complicate the negotiations. A union may, for example, quit the negotiating committee, making it impossible for the committee to meet the legal requirement of representation of at least 50 percent of the works council members. Unions may also remain on the negotiating committee but refuse to sign the agreement; this will leave unfulfilled the requirement that 60 percent of the committee members must give their consent. To prevent interunion conflict of this kind, referendums are increasingly used on issues on which the two leading unions disagree.

A third, less important function of works councils is their mediating role between employers and workers. Conflicts between the two are sometimes resolved by calling in a works council member, without appealing to a court. Council members both have a closer relationship with management than other workers and are respected as leaders by the workers. They may therefore be in a good position to help resolve everyday conflicts between the employer and individual employees. Sometimes the employer uses the works council to relate information to a worker or a group of workers, and more often workers use the works councils for communicating problems to management. This is more likely to happen if workers are affiliated to a union because their union leader is very likely also a works council member or union delegate. However, nonunionized workers may also find it easier to solve their problems by talking to their representatives than to their superiors. This may be another source of the clientelism of unions at the workplace, serving to recruit members and, more important, to obtain votes.

6.6   Conclusions and Future Prospects

Spanish industrial relations are becoming decentralized. After the mixed success of the social pacts, employers' associations and unions are favorably disposed toward enterprise-level negotiations, letting rank-and-file union members take the leading role.

Works councils in Spain are not an alternative to unions, nor do they stand in opposition to unions. Their main function in the Spanish industrial relations system is to be an arena in which divergent union policies can be confronted and may be joined. This is because there are not clear boundaries between union and works council functions. While the former do try to take over the latter, the existence of another union that competes to represent the workers is an unsurmountable obstacle. Only if the present unity between the two main Spanish unions lasts can the importance of works councils be expected to increase.

In Spain, it has been unusual for works councils to contribute to the restructuring of companies and to help in increasing internal flexibility. The reason is that Spanish councils are highly unionized, and unions face other problems, such as bargaining over wages and hours, regulating working conditions, and surviving in competition with rival unions, as well as dealing with unemployment and developing social services and the welfare state. At the same time, because of works councils' special conditions and their relative autonomy from the external unions, employers and workers may be developing a relationship of trust mediated by councils. In such instances, councils may contribute to improving efficiency through productivity agreements with employers based on a positive-sum game within individual firms.

Appendix
Firms Studied for This Paper

Company A is a 40-year-old firm with three main plants located in three different provinces. It belongs to the automobile sector and has frequently changed ownership. Although it was heavily affected by the economic crisis, it survived because of state funds. Nevertheless, in the last 10 years it has reduced its workforce by half.

The plant studied has around 3,000 workers. Its works council includes 25 elected members and seven union delegates (four representing the UGT and three the CCOO). Union density, at 70 percent, is very high by Spanish standards. While the UGT has more members because of its strong position among clerical workers, the CCOO remains the main union among direct production workers and in the last works council elections received the highest number of votes. There are also four council members from an enterprise union backed mainly by technicians and clerical workers.

The firm has a collective agreement that covers all three plants. It is negotiated by the interplant council, complemented by plant-level bargaining conducted by local works councils. The latter are also in charge of the implementation of the agreement. Relations between works councils and employer were good when the firm was still a public enterprise. Since privatization, however, there has been less communication, and the works council complains about insufficient information on the restructuring process.

The CCOO and UGT have gone through different stages in their relationship. At the time of the study there were in an intense battle with each other. Interunion conflict had made it necessary to submit the collective agreement for the preceding year to a referendum of the workforce, with the UGT taking the more radical position—mainly on the restructuring of the firm and on mobility and redundancies—and losing.

Company B is a multinational automobile firm. Unlike company A, it has not undergone a loss of employment or change of ownership. Although it has several plants in Spain, its main factory is outside Madrid, with 10,000 employees working in different nearby plants that have only one works council. The council consists of 40 members. The CCOO has one representative more than the UGT, and there is a third union, the anarchist CGT, with five representatives. The works council also includes 20 union delegates, half of them belonging to the UGT and the others to the CCOO and CGT. This reflects the UGT's higher membership; the CCOO, however, obtained more votes in the elections.

The firm does not have an interplant works council. There is only one collective agreement for a two-year period. The negotiators for the workers are drawn from the works council; they are assisted by experts from their unions. Council members were highly satisfied with the last agreement; they had won a high wage increase and had been able to convert a large number of temporary employment contracts into permanent ones. Apart from wages, the most important concern of the unions is employment. Much attention is paid to monitoring the firm's subcontracting activities in order to avoid labor market segmentation.

Relations between council and management were smooth at the time of the study, although there had been conflicts in the past when the unions had been more radical. A works council delegation, composed of the president, the secretary, and one delegate of every union, meets frequently with the personnel director. Interunion relationships are more complicated. Since the late 1980s, the UGT and the CCOO have been working together because of the existence of a common adversary, the anarchist sympathizers who prefer an alternative model of industrial relations based on decisions of the rank-and-file. Before that time, however, the two main unions did not always have the same views, and some collective agreements were signed by the UGT only; within the

CCOO, there had been a history of factions and resignations that ended with a victory for the moderates.

Company C has more than 3,000 employees. The firm belongs to the telecommunications sector and was owned by the state until it was sold to a multinational company. There are two works councils, one for six plants in the province of Madrid and another for a special category of workers based all over the country. The first council has a CCOO majority, while the second is dominated by the UGT. A third, right-wing union also has representatives on both councils. There is also a joint works council with 13 members, drawn from the two directly elected councils, that negotiates those parts of the collective agreement that are common for the two halves of the firm. Union density is around 20 percent.

In the five years before the study the firm's good economic situation led to an increase in its labor force through temporary contracts. However, future prospects are less good, and in spite of union opposition temporary workers are not being reemployed. The works councils supervise the implementation of the collective agreement, especially with respect to working conditions and employment. Relations with management used to be paternalistic but are now changing. A number of unpopular measures were taken that were contested by the works councils with the backing of the workforce. Interunion relations have also been changing. Lately, interactions between the UGT and the CCOO have been cooperative, reflecting the new unity of action at the peak level; inside each union, however, there are different views about this.

Company D is a multinational computer company with 20 plants in Spain. The firm once had more than 2,000 employees but has reduced its workforce by 20 percent in three years, almost exclusively by not reemploying temporary workers. Economic problems remain, and greater employment reductions are envisaged.

In each of the 20 workplaces there is a works council, except in plants with fewer than 50 workers; these have between one and three staff delegates. No interplant works council exists; there is, however, a coordinating committee that negotiates a collective agreement for all workers whose plant is not covered by an agreement of its own.

Union density and union strength in the firm are low, apart from the production plant. While there is a UGT majority in the latter, all other works councils are dominated by the CCOO. There are also a few independent works councillors. Recently, negotiations on employment reduction have been taking place, assisted by officials from the external unions. Relations with management are very poor, and lack of trust is common on both sides. There is also disagreement between the unions on redundancies and negotiation procedures.

Company X is a medium-sized firm with a long history of strong unionism and a number of takeovers, after having been originally a family-owned business. When research was in progress, there was an intense period of negotiations aimed at saving the firm from bankruptcy. The works council has fewer than 10 members, all of whom are from the two main unions, with a slight majority for the CCOO. There is no formal collective agreement; the firm follows the provincial agreement for the metal sector, with specific improvements negotiated formally with the works council but de facto with the two union sections separately.

Parts of management and the works council maintain good relations in an attempt to solve the crisis of the enterprise. Workers and unions, mainly the CCOO, are willing to make concessions in order to save the firm. However, there is a tradition of interunion rivalry that makes collaboration with management difficult. In the present crisis, as in many other firms, external union officials join the negotiations to assist the works council.

Company Y is a medium-sized firm that produces metal furniture. It has more than 500 employees, a majority of whom are low-skilled direct production workers. The firm's economic situation was good at the time of interviewing. Union density, at 25 percent, is high by Spanish standards. Half of the union members belong to the CCOO, the other half to the UGT. In the last council elections there were three lists of candidates, the third submitted by a group of independent workers who won five seats. A short time later, however, all but one of them had joined the CCOO.

The strategies of the UGT and CCOO are very similar. As with many other works councils, the unions try with some success to defend existing working conditions, but it is very difficult for them to obtain improvements. Up to the time of research, the council had failed to get a formal collective agreement for the firm and had been unsuccessful in getting indefinite contracts for a large number of temporary workers. Its main weapon was its control of overtime. Union sections did not work properly, and their functions were completely in the hands of the works council.

Company Z is a medium-sized firm with about 200 workers producing telecommunications equipment. It is owned by foreign capital and uses flexible methods of production, with high functional mobility. Union density is less than 10 percent. The works council consists exclusively of women, although women make up only 30 percent of the labor force. Only one list was presented at the last election, under the name of the UGT; however, it included one CCOO member and a few independent workers. The council's main activities are to police irregularities, especially with respect to health and safety conditions and redundancies. The council sometimes uses help from the external union to solve problems with management.

References

Albiol, Ignacio. 1992. *Comités de empresa y delegados de personal.* Bilbao: Deusto.
Alós-Moner, Ramón, and Andreu Lope. 1991. Los sindicatos en los centros de trabajo.

In *Las relaciones laborales en España,* ed. Fausto Miguélez and Carlos Prieto. Madrid: Siglo XXI.

Amsden, Jon. 1972. *Collective bargaining and class conflict in Spain.* London: London School of Economics.

Ariza, Julián. 1976. *CCOO.* Barcelona: Avance.

Balfour, Sebastian. 1989. *Dictatorship, workers and the city: Labour in greater Barcelona since 1939.* Oxford: Clarendon.

Borrajo, Efrén. 1975. *Introducción al derecho español del trabajo.* Madrid: Tecnos.

Bosch, Aurora. 1987. Las colectivizaciones: estado de la cuestión y aspectos regionales. In *La Segunda República: Una esperanza frustrada,* ed. Josep Fontana et al. Valencia: Alfons el Magnànim.

Bouza, Fermín. et al. 1989. *Perfil, actitudes y demandas del delegado y afiliado a UGT.* Madrid: Fundación Largo Caballero.

Cabrera, Mercedes. 1983. *La patronal ante la II República: Organizaciones y estrategia (1931–1936).* Madrid: Siglo XXI.

———. 1987. Las organizaciones patronales ante la conflictividad social y los Jurados Mixtos. In *La Segunda República: Una esperanza frustrada,* ed. Josep Fontana et al. Valencia: Alfons el Magnànim.

Casanova, Julián, ed. 1988. *El sueño igualitario: Campesinado y colectivizaciones en la España republicana, 1936–1939.* Zaragoza: Institución Fernando el Católico.

CCOO (Comisiones Obreras). 1992. *Documentos aprobados en el 5º Congreso Federal.* Madrid: Confederación Sindical de CCOO.

Crespán, Javier, and Miguel A. Falguera. 1991. Huelga, empresa, y servicios esenciales, hoy: Reflexiones sobre la situación de España. *Ayer* 4: 235–54.

EDIS (Equipo de Investigación Sociológica) 1983. *La elecciones sindicales, 1982.* Madrid: Fundación Friedrich Ebert.

Escobar, Modesto. 1991. Afiliación y movilización sindical en España. Paper presented at conference held at Universidad Internacional Menéndez Pelayo, Sevilla.

Espina, Alvaro. 1990. *Empleo, democracia y relaciones industriales en España.* Madrid: Ministerio de Trabajo y Seguridad Social.

Ferner, Anthony. 1988. *Governments, managers and industrial relations: Public enterprises and their political environment.* Oxford: Blackwell.

Fishman, Robert M. 1990. *Working-class organization and the return to democracy in Spain.* Ithaca, N.Y.: Cornell University Press.

Foweraker, Joe. 1989. *Making democracy in Spain: Grass-roots struggle in the south, 1955–1975.* New York: Cambridge University Press.

FTN (Fomento del Trabajo Nacional). 1981. Ante la negociación colectiva el empresario debe estar antento a CCOO. *Horizonte Empresarial,* March: 27–32.

Gillespie, Richard. 1988. *The Spanish Socialist party: A history of factionalism.* Oxford: Clarendon.

Giner, Salvador, and Eduardo Sevilla. 1984. Spain: From corporatism to corporatism. In *Southern Europe transformed,* ed. Allan M. Williams. London: Harper and Row.

Girona, Albert. 1987. La responsabilidad obrera en el colectivisimo industrial valenciano. In *La Segunda República: Una experiencia frustrada,* ed. Josep Fontana et al. Valencia: Alfons el Magnànim.

Hawkesworth, Ricard, and Lluis Fina. 1987. Trade unions and industrial relations in Spain: The response to the economic crisis of the 1980s. In *Trade unions and the economic crisis of the 1980s,* ed. William Brierley. Aldershot: Gower.

IDES (Instituto de Estudios Sociológicos). 1989. *Estudio sociológico sobre las orientaciones, actitudes y demandas sindicales de los trabajadores españoles.* Madrid: Centro de Investigaciones Sociológicas.

Iriso, Pedro L. 1992. Trabajadores y sindicatos: Las relaciones industriales en los centros de trabajo. Ph.D. Thesis, Universidad Complutense de Madrid.

Lope, Andreu. 1991. *Els treballadors: Actituds associatives i acció sindical a l'empresa: El cas d'un centre productiu del metall.* Barcelona: F. Jaume Bofill.

Maravall, José M. 1978. *Dictatorship and political dissent: Workers and students in Franco's Spain.* London: Tavistock.

Maravall, José M., and Julian Santamaría. 1986. Political change in Spain and the prospects for democracy. In *Transitions from authoritarian rule: Southern Europe,* ed. Guillermo O'Donell, Phillip C. Schmitter, and Laurence Whitehead. Baltimore: Johns Hopkins University Press.

Martín Herrero, Pedro. 1991. *Jurisprudencia del Estatuto de los Trabajadores.* Madrid: Ministerio de Trabajo y Seguridad Social.

MTSS (Ministerio de Trabajo y Seguridad Social). 1987. *Elecciones sindicales de 1986.* Madrid: Ministerio de Trabajo y Seguridad Social.

———. 1992. Elecciones sindicales de 1990. Madrid: Ministerio de Trabajo y Seguridad Social.

Pérez-Díaz, Victor. 1985. Los empresarios y la clase politica. *Papeles de Economía Española* 22:2–37.

———. 1993. *The return of civil society.* Cambridge: Harvard University Press.

Roca, Jordi. 1987. Neocorporatism in Post-Franco Spain. In *Political stability and neocorporatism,* ed. Ilja Scholten. London: Sage.

Rodríguez Sañudo, Fermín. 1988. Jurisprudencia reciente sobre la actividad del comité de empresa. *Revista Española de Derecho del Trabajo* 36:621–33.

Sauto, Jose F. 1992. Aplicación de técnicas multivariantes al análisis de la representación sindical en los comités de empresa de la Comunidad Autónoma de Madrid: Análisis de segmentación y modelos *log-lineals.* Universidad Complutense de Madrid. Typescript.

Soto, Alvaro. 1989. *El trabajo en la España contemporánea (1874–1936).* Barcelona: Anthropos.

Tezanos, José F. 1982. *Crisis de la Conciencia Obrera?* Madrid: Mezquita.

Tuñón de Lara, Manuel. 1985. *El movimiento obrero en la historia de España.* Madrid: Sarpe.

UGT (Unión General de Trabajadores). 1989. *Memoria de gestión del XXXV Congreso Cofederal.* Madrid: Unión General de Trabajadores.

———. 1992. *Las elecciones sindicales de 1990.* Madrid: Comisión Ejecutiva Confederal de Unión General de Trabajadores.

Zaragoza, Angel, ed. 1988. *Pactos sociales, sindicatos y patronal en España.* Madrid: Siglo XXI.

Zufiaur, José M. 1985. El sindicalismo español en la transición y la crisis. *Papeles de Economía Española* 22:202–34.

7   Sweden: Joint Councils under Strong Unionism

Göran Brulin

7.1   Introduction

In Sweden there are no workplace-based arrangements for the representation of employees *independent* of trade unions. There is no second channel providing voice for employees outside the traditional union-employer bipartite system, as this would not be compatible with the "Swedish model" based on collective bargaining. This model implies strong trade unions at both the local and central levels. While the emphasis is on the latter, the model does not preclude strong enterprise- and plant-level employee participation practices. Local union bodies, white- and blue-collar, take part in extensive co-determination procedures, in addition to wage bargaining. The Act on Co-determination at Work provides a general instrument for these procedures, giving local union bodies a participative role somewhere between information exchange and consultation on the one hand, and negotiations and collective bargaining on the other (Iseskog 1990, 76). The absence so far of sanctions in the event of conflict limits the significance of co-determination procedures. Nevertheless, the impact of the act on cooperative practices at the plant level should not be underestimated.

Swedish trade unions have always been skeptical of council arrangements, regardless of their form. With very few exceptions, council-like institutions have historically been rejected. Various arrangements similar to works councils do exist but are not independent of the unions. The latter are strongly present at the workplace, and both the white- and blue-collar unions have workplace sections. Works council co-determination has been viewed as a threat to the

Göran Brulin is professor of industrial relations at the School of Business of Stockholm University and a research associate of the Swedish Institute of Work Life Research.

The author thanks Stan Edlund of the Swedish Center for Working Life and Kathleen Thelen of Princeton University for their comments on an earlier version of this paper.

legitimacy of the collective bargaining system, and as a potential source of greater labor market inequality. The aim of the unions has therefore always been to ensure that all council forms were safely founded in collective agreements. It may, however, be questioned whether this policy can be maintained.

Although the Swedish model is characterized by regulation at the central level, there is no absence of monitoring and enforcement arrangements at the workplace. Co-determination councils, health and safety committees, and board representatives ensure that rules are observed. However, these are all part of the bipartite system. Some arrangements are also functionally linked to corresponding public institutions. For example, the health and safety committees are supported by the National Board of Occupational Safety and Health, and the development of co-determination is supported by the Swedish Work Environment Fund.

Those workplace arrangements in Sweden that resemble works councils should rather be labeled *informal joint councils*. Projects for industrial democracy in Sweden were originally based on joint consultative bodies. Joint councils (*driftsnämnder*) were launched in the 1920s by the Industrial Democratization Commission as the means to democratize Swedish industry. But the proposals were never realized. After the Second World War joint councils were introduced through collective agreement between the largest unions, the LO and TCO, and the main employers' association, the SAF. In the mid-1970s they were replaced by a co-determination system based on collective bargaining. That system is now being transformed into a system of consultation and participation arrangements.

Today, council-like arrangements emerge at an increasing rate in Sweden for practical reasons. They are required or regulated by formal law; typically they are joint employer-union creations that rest on industrial agreement and the Co-determination Act. There is no legal basis for council-like arrangements in Sweden, with the exception of the health and safety committees which are mandatory joint councils.

7.2   Institutional Foundations of the Swedish Model

The Swedish model of industrial relations, characterized by a highly centralized bargaining system and strong social parties independent of the state, is rapidly changing. This section gives an account of the institutional foundation of the Swedish model, with special attention to works councils and co-determination.

7.2.1   Structure of Swedish Labor Market Organizations

Collective bargaining has always been the core institution of the Swedish model.[1] Pay bargaining is normally conducted at three levels. First, there are

1. For a comparison between the Swedish model and other industrial relations systems, see Bratt (1990). For a thorough account of Swedish labor laws, see Edlund and Nyström (1988).

negotiations between the central organizations of business and labor, followed, second, by negotiations and formal agreements between member unions (sometimes cartels of unions) and employers' associations at the industry level, and, third, by company and workplace-level negotiations between employers and workplace union sections on the application of the agreement. The most important functions of the collective agreements are to maintain industrial peace and determine a floor for wages and working conditions, as employers cannot offer their employees conditions inferior to those laid down in the collective agreement.

This whole system is now under great pressure and may be abolished. A rising number of strikes and lockouts, mainly among white-collar workers and public employees, has brought the system into disrepute. Growing wage drift during the 1980s also eroded the legitimacy of the system. New forms of work organization, new methods of rationalizing production, and new payment systems put additional pressure on the model. On the other hand, the social partners accepted a national income policy agreement for 1991 and 1992, thereby preserving and temporarily increasing the centralism of the Swedish model.

Apart from collective agreements on wages and working conditions that are concluded for a limited period, a number of permanent agreements have existed for many years. In 1938, the main employer and worker organizations, the SAF and the LO, reached the so-called Saltsjöbaden Agreement, which codified negotiating procedures and the handling of disputes. There are also several *cooperation agreements,* most of them concluded in the 1940s between the SAF and the LO. Some of these were terminated in conjunction with the passage of the Act on Co-determination at Work in 1976. The act was supposed to be supplemented by a central agreement on co-determination; it was not until 1982, however, that the Agreement on Efficiency and Participation was actually signed.

The dominant central union organization is the Swedish Confederation of Unions for blue-collar workers (LO). It was formed in 1898 and has 24 member unions which together organize more than two million workers. (The population of Sweden is 8.4 million.) The largest member unions are the Local Government Workers Union, the Metalworkers Union, the Union of State Workers, the Retail Workers Union, and the Building Workers Union. The LO has urged several of its affiliated unions to amalgamate to make the negotiating system work better. In the fall of 1991 a planned amalgamation of three industrial unions failed.

The main organization for white-collar employees is the Swedish Confederation of Unions (TCO) with more than one million members. Organizational density among salaried employees is almost as high as among blue-collar workers. The largest of the TCO's 21 member unions is the Union of Salaried Employees in Industry. Next are the Local Government Salaried Employees Union and the Government Salaried Employees Union. The Swedish Union of Foremen and Supervisors withdrew from the TCO in 1980 but returned in 1985.

There is a third central organization with 25 member unions, the Central Confederation of Professional Unions (SACO). Its largest member unions are the National Union of Teachers and the Union of Graduate Engineers. Other strong SACO unions are the physicians' union and the union of lawyers. The SACO is organized along professional lines. Historically, its member unions were, with a few exceptions, divided by occupation rather than by industry (Lundh 1991, 2). The LO was reorganized according to the industrial union principle at the beginning of the twentieth century, whereas the TCO has both professional and industrial unions.

To coordinate and centralize bargaining, unions form "negotiating cartels." In the private sector a cartel may involve unions from different central organizations, in particular the TCO and SACO. As the significance of the central bargaining model is decreasing, so is that of the cartels.

The dominant private sector employers' association is the Swedish Employers' Confederation (SAF). It was formed in 1902 in reaction to the creation of the LO. Its largest member associations are the Swedish Engineering Employers' Association, the Retail Employers' Association, the SAF General Group, and the Building Employers' Association. There are plans for a radical reorganization of the SAF, aimed at amalgamating its 36 member associations into seven to nine negotiating groups to improve services to member companies while at the same time enabling affiliation fees to be reduced.[2] The SAF believes that the division between blue- and white-collar workers and the occupationalism of the SACO are antiquated, arguing that a modern production organization requires only one category of employees—referred to as "co-workers"—and individualized employment relations. The breakdown of the old Swedish model and the need for new structures are also illustrated by the fact that the Metalworkers Union and its counterpart on the employer side have in recent years preferred to conclude their agreements ahead of the LO and SAF.

The Swedish public sector is large compared to most other OECD countries, employing about one-third of the Swedish workforce. Public sector unions won full rights to negotiate and strike in 1966. There are three employers' organizations covering the public sector, the State Employers' Negotiating Agency (SAV), the Swedish Association of Local Government Authorities, and the Swedish County Councils Association.

7.2.2   Cooperation Agreements

The Saltsjöbaden Agreement codified a structure that made possible increasingly comprehensive collective regulation of working conditions. It was followed by cooperation agreements on special subjects. One of these was joint councils; others were vocational training and safety and health. In 1992, the

---

2. For further information, see *European Industrial Relations Review,* no. 217 (February 1992).

last remnant of the Saltsjöbaden spirit, the cooperation agreement on safety and health, was renounced by the SAF.

The Joint Councils Agreement, concluded in 1946, was a compromise in the ongoing debate on industrial democracy. The spirit of Saltsjöbaden that had ended the adversarial industrial relations of the 1920s made the unions accept the idea of joint councils, in line with international efforts to establish works council systems after the Second World War. While the LO had proposed joint councils at all levels of the enterprise, which were to include white-collar workers, the system that was finally accepted was almost identical with that proposed by the SAF. Joint councils were formed only at the company or plant level, and the TCO was excluded (Johansson 1989, 268).

While the mission of the joint councils had been to solve problems and enhance rationalization at the firm and plant level, they increasingly came to be viewed by the unions as a potential threat to worker solidarity across enterprise borders. There was also a fear that they might compete with the unions. In negotiations with the SAF, the LO had argued that its representatives would refuse to cooperate with nonunionized workers within a works council system and that therefore the workforce representatives on the joint councils should be elected exclusively by union members (Johansson 1989, 273). The result was the formation of joint councils based on collective agreement between the LO and SAF.

A short time later, the TCO and SAF concluded their own Joint Councils Agreement. Unlike the LO, the white-collar unions accepted the absence of formal connection between the union and the joint councils. Because the white-collar unions were weak at the time, employers were able to insist that all white-collar workers, not only union members, would have the right to vote in the joint council elections and to serve as council members. When at the end of the 1950s the white-collar unions had grown in power, this arrangement was ended and a new agreement gave the white-collar unions the same rights as the LO, excluding nonunionized workers from the joint councils (Nilsson 1985, 146).

The position of the joint councils was weak. The purpose of the agreement was to provide employees with information about matters such as work organization and investment. The joint councils also had a consultative function, although management retained the power to make all final decisions. The unions felt they had no real power on the joint councils and wanted the councils to have a stronger impact on management decision making. When the agreement was revised in 1966, "a provision was added to the effect that an employer wishing to do so could delegate his decision-making powers in certain limited fields to the joint councils" (Edlund et al. 1989, 10).

Yet evaluations of the councils differed. Carlsson (1966, 98), then the LO's education director, gives a positive picture of the system, although he acknowledges that the activity and significance of the councils varied a great deal:

As they are consultative institutions the result depends, to a large degree, on the parties' ability to co-operate; if one of the parties is unwilling, it is probable that the activity will be only formal. And even when the parties are aware of the importance of co-operation they must in addition have the ability to get satisfactory results. They must also learn to regard the enterprise from the viewpoint of the council, instead of regarding it only onesidedly. So far, there is a difference between the work done by the worker representatives on the councils and the work on the board of the local union section. The borderline is not always clear, and is defined by tradition and practical adjustments. There is, of course, always close contact between the workers representatives in the works council and the union section; as a rule the chairman or another union leader is also a works council member.

One may add that as an LO representative, the author somewhat underestimates the impact of the TCO representatives in the joint councils.

The revision of the agreement did not satisfy the unions. At the end of the 1960s, the LO complained that there was no co-determination machinery in Sweden and, in particular, no bodies corresponding to German works councils (Hauser 1971, 11). Swedish councils were said to exist only by virtue of collective agreement, and their chief function was no more than to "provide for an exchange of views and consultation on matters of common interest." In the absence of sanctions for noncompliance with the agreed procedure, Swedish councils in practice often failed to allow for satisfactory co-determination. The LO concluded that it was necessary to secure a better balance of power between the two sides by extending the right to negotiate to all matters at all levels where decisions are taken and by creating a general obligation for the employer to negotiate. "In other words, the employer should be compelled to enter into negotiations at the time when he takes a decision, and not, as has been the case up to now, only when implementing a decision already taken, usually only at the direct request of the unions. In important decisions which are likely to have adverse social repercussions which are difficult to correct at a later stage, the unions should also have a right of veto" (Hauser 1971, 18).

In the beginning of the 1970s the LO still hoped to revitalize the joint council system. Arne Geijer, the president of the LO, argued that the union movement should stick to its role as an independent, external, and primarily claim-making party, again expressing the LO's fear of collusive entanglement through works councils. But Geijer continued that there was also room for much closer management-union cooperation inside the firm: "Work councils must be given a proper picture of their companies' true situation. The most logical development would be for the councils gradually to take on responsibility for questions of long-term planning" (1971, 5).

In subsequent years, however, joint councils gradually came to be regarded as inadequate by the unions. Janérus (1989), a secretary in the LO industrial democracy department, argued that the launching of joint councils in Sweden had been a mistake. The introduction of the solidaristic wage policy in the mid-

1950s had made the role of the joint councils unclear. The emerging Swedish model driven by central bargaining, solidaristic wage policy, and structural rationalization measures above the plant level had, according to Janérus, made the council system redundant. As unions perceived rationalization, in line with the theories of LO economists like Meidner and Rehn, as an objective force above the realm of the local plant, the joint councils lost their mission.

7.2.3 Works Councils and Labor Law Reforms of the 1970s

The official report of the commission that investigated the labor laws and launched the Co-determination Act (Arbetsrättskommittén 1975, 16) states as a general principle that all questions touching upon the employment relationship should be open to co-determination proceedings based on negotiation. Unions are given a right to be informed, and a primary obligation is created for employers to negotiate on any matter before carrying out major changes.

The committee's original proposal (Arbetsrättskommittén 1975, 39) provides for possible co-determination procedures through a works council set up by the local parties. Two different procedures were suggested to regulate the formation of a works council. According to the first, councils were to be set up on the initiative of either a union or the employer. According to the second, a works council could be created only on union initiative. Neither of these suggestions was finally accepted. The act that finally passed Parliament was based on the view of the LO and TCO representatives of the commission.

The representatives of the unions rejected the creation of a legal right for the employer to initiate works councils (Arbetsrättskommittén 1975, 945). In a dissenting opinion, the union representatives agreed that unification of different employee organizations at the plant level was desirable. This, however, should not be imposed by works council legislation. Instead, it was to be left to the parties themselves—that is, the different unions and the employer—to organize co-determination on the basis of the negotiation principle. Co-determination through legally based works councils was said to be suited only for countries with comparatively weak unions; the strong Swedish unions would not benefit from it, and the parties should be free to develop co-determination procedures on their own without legal guidance.[3]

7.3   Legislated Reform

In 1977 the Joint Councils Agreement was superseded by the Co-determination Act. Unions in Sweden as well as in other countries had become radicalized at the end of the 1960s. Union leaders came under increasing pressure from the rank and file and began to demand reforms at the workplace. Unrest in the labor market and more frequent unofficial strikes forced the

---

3. It is widely believed that at the time the Swedish unions were also motivated by a desire to create a more radical co-determination system than the German *Betriebsräte* system.

unions to seek legislative solutions when negotiations with the SAF did not yield substantive results. The Social Democratic government, closely allied with the LO and eager to stay on good terms with the TCO, was prepared to push union demands through Parliament. Legislation of this kind on industrial relations matters represented a major deviation from the Saltsjöbaden model.

Most of the existing labor legislation was introduced in the 1970s, including legislation on co-determination, workforce representation on boards of directors, and health and safety. These laws, as well as subsequent agreements between the social partners, have shaped the procedures for cooperation and co-determination in Sweden. There are no alternative bodies to the unions for the exercise of co-determination. It is only the unions at the local and central levels that are the legal representatives of the organized employees, collectively and sometimes individually. Nonunionized employees are only indirectly represented.

7.3.1 Health and Safety Committees

There is, however, one exception to the normal negotiation and bargaining procedures. On health and safety matters, employees in workplaces with more than 50 workers are represented by safety representatives on joint health and safety committees. The Work Environment Act obliges safety representatives to act for *all* employees, unionized and nonunionized. Representatives are, however, appointed by the union, in line with the basic premise of Swedish industrial relations that workers are represented by unions.

Health and safety protection is regulated by law and, in addition, by special agreements between the unions and employers' associations. The law determines both substantive measures of health and safety protection and the rights and obligations of safety representatives. Responsibility for the working environment, including measures of a preventive nature, rests primarily with the employer. The Work Environment Act has recently been sharpened, forcing the employer to take a comprehensive view of health and safety matters and work organization.

Compliance with work environment legislation is supervised by a central authority, the National Board of Occupational Safety and Health, on which the social partners are represented.[4] The board maintains regional bodies, the labor inspectorates, which also include representatives of the social partners. It is empowered to elaborate the rules of the Work Environment Act by issuing general implementation orders of a binding nature, some of which carry penal sanctions. In special cases, the labor inspectorate can issue an injunction to secure compliance with work environment regulations.

The fact that there are special health and safety committees causes certain problems. The co-determination system greatly overlaps the health and safety

---

4. Representation of the social partners may be canceled by the present, nonsocialist government. In February 1991, the SAF decided to withdraw from all government boards.

system, as matters involving work safety issues are also covered by co-determination (Brulin and Victorin 1992, 157). For example, the work environment agreement between the SAF and the LO-PTK[5] gives employees in the covered sector a majority on health and safety committees, with employee representatives recruited proportionally from the different unions according to their strength at the workplace. Decisions are made by majority, but committees should seek consensus first. Decisions with financial implications for the company require unanimity (Edlund and Nyström 1988, 72). The special rules for the SAF and LO-PTK sector are based on the Co-determination Act.

7.3.2   Act on Board Representation

In 1972 the Act on Board Representation for Employees in Joint Stock Companies and Cooperatives was passed after long and divisive discussion. The act was revised in 1976 and 1988. According to the new Worker Directors Act, employees of companies with more than 25 workers are entitled to appoint two members to the board of directors, and three members in companies where more than one occupational group is present. Worker directors have the same rights as other board members (Edlund and Nyström 1988, 46). At non-unionized companies, of which there are very few, the law prescribes elections. Normally, worker directors are appointed by the unions.

The purpose of the act was to give employees both information and influence on the company. Workforce representatives are always in the minority and may not take part in discussions relating to negotiations with the unions. There had been concerns in the 1960s that worker representatives would be torn between loyalty to the enterprise and loyalty to their fellow employees. "These misgivings, however, were dispelled once an extensive program began to unfold for the development of employee participation, board representation being just one of several instruments, which meant that it could be used and controlled more adequately" (Edlund et al. 1989, 16). Generally, board representation has come to be regarded as a means of keeping the union informed, rather than of directly influencing corporate decision making.

In 1990 the subject of divided loyalties returned when many of the workforce representatives had become "owners." Rapid development of equity options systems and employee share ownership had begun to blur the distinction between workforce and shareholder representatives on boards of directors. The broad recruitment of union members added to this, in that many of the managers of personnel departments have a union background (Gehlin and Nilsson 1985) and quite a few supervisors have been active members of an LO union section before advancing in their careers (Larsson 1984, 117). The scope and implication of this "mix" of roles are unknown.

---

5. PTK is a white-collar negotiating cartel of the TCO and SACO unions.

7.3.3   Shop Stewards Act

Another arrangement that has supported decentralization of industrial relations and closer contacts between unions and employers at the workplace is the Shop Stewards Act of 1974. The act entitles elected workplace union officials to a "reasonable" amount of paid leave from work to discharge their union duties and keep in touch with the members. Paid leave also gives workplace union officials an opportunity to get involved in informal joint committee activities.

Full-time shop stewards are, however, becoming a problem for the legitimacy of the unions, the fear being that they might lose contact with other workers. The choice of a shop steward at the Kiruna/LKAB local of the Mineworkers' Union not to take full-time leave for union duties, challenging an established behavior among union officials that has recently been much debated in the union journals, was given great public attention in the fall of 1989.

7.3.4   Co-determination System

As stated before, one purpose of the co-determination legislation was to avoid forms of co-determination similar to works councils. Democratization of working life was supposed to take place inside the bipartite system, strengthening the role of formal negotiations and producing collective agreements. Nearly all aspects of the employment relationship are therefore in principle open to co-determination proceedings. Yet, the right to negotiate has to some extent been limited, in that negotiations are supposed to be cooperative. Also, while the unions are given an opportunity to influence decision making in the hope that the two sides will arrive at consensus, the employer still has the final decision.

The Co-determination Act of 1977 was strongly opposed by employers, and it took a long time before supplementary collective agreements specifying the intentions of the act were signed. Many observers believe, however, that the employers have benefited from the co-determination system and from the obligation it imposes on them to negotiate. Negotiations often influence the unions as much as they influence the employer, if not more (Blomquist 1982). Smart employers turn the negotiations into a continuous seminar on the economic situation in general, and that of the firm in particular. Union representatives sometimes feel that they are being held hostage by the co-determination procedures. Also, legal provisions for sanctions in the event of employer noncompliance are weak and diffuse. Disputes are supposed to be settled by the parties at the industry level, and some procedural matters may be brought to the Labor Court or, in the private sector, to an arbitration board. An employer who has failed to inform the unions in time may be fined by the Labor Court. If he has informed them, however, it is very hard for the unions to change his decision.

In general, the act is seen as providing for information and consultation rather than co-determination in a strict sense. A comparison of the Swedish co-determination system with the German works council system concludes that "the local union's right to be consulted on various issues does not include an obligation that management also reach agreement with the union. And in this respect the rights of German works councils—on a narrow range of questions that are subject to full co-determination and conciliation—are perhaps stronger" (Thelen 1991b, 212). This crucial point was not changed by the collective agreements concluded on the basis of the Co-determination Act.

Yet, the act should not be evaluated only on its formal merits. It has changed the climate for co-determination, and there are reasons to believe that the cooperative culture at many Swedish workplaces is related to it. James Fulcher goes as far as to argue that the act "comprehensively changed the legal framework of plant-level industrial relations by abolishing the employer's rights, institutionalizing worker influence, and ending the superior legal position of the employers. It would be no exaggeration to say that it challenged the capitalist relations of production" (1991, 267).

The intention of the legislators was that the Co-determination Act should be supplemented by central agreements and, subsequently, by agreements at the local level, in line with the traditional Swedish model. In 1978 a central co-determination agreement was concluded for the national government, followed by one in 1980 for local government. It is symptomatic that agreements were concluded first in the public sector, and that these agreements were quite detailed and oriented toward bipartite negotiations. Negotiations in the private sector were more difficult. Private employers did not want an agreement that emphasized negotiations because they regarded direct participation by individual employees as equally important. The private sector co-determination agreement was more in line with management preferences. Its emphasis on efficiency and the parties' respective responsibility for productivity constitute in many respects a break with the 1970s.

7.3.5   Agreement on Efficiency and Participation

The 1982 Agreement on Efficiency and Participation between the SAF and the LO-PTK states that "the forms of participation and co-determination shall be adapted to local circumstances at the workplace. The local parties have a joint responsibility for developing suitable participation and co-determination practices." On request by one of the local parties, the employer and the local union organization are to negotiate an agreement on the way in which co-determination shall be exercised. According to the central agreement, there are three possible forms of co-determination: (1) negotiations between the company and its local unions in accordance with the Act on Co-determination, (2) "line negotiations," under which union representatives participate at the various levels of the company's line organization, and (3) creation of "bipartite participation and information bodies." According to the central agreement, local agreements must clearly indicate which form of co-determination is chosen. The central agreement also stipulates that when co-determination is exercised in accordance with locally agreed practice, the primary obligation to negotiate and the responsibility to provide information in accordance with the Act on Co-determination must be observed. In reality, very few local agreements were concluded, although the local parties often act as if they have a local agreement. Joint consultative bodies are created for dealing with a particular problem or union representatives are inserted in the ordinary line of management, for example, in semiautonomous work groups, without this having been regulated by local agreement. Arrangements of this kind are viewed by both parties as "bipartite participation and information bodies" or "line negotiations," although they have no formal legitimation. The juridical status of these arrangements is therefore unclear.

In the early 1980s co-determination procedures were much more formalized and conducted through negotiations, especially in the public sector. Increasingly, however, practices in national and local government seem to be approaching those in the private sector (Edlund et al. 1989, 28). Practices that have developed from the Agreement on Efficiency and Participation between the SAF and the LO-PTK have in this way gradually become norms.

Since the passing of the act and the signing of the central agreements, informal participation has become more frequent, partly as a consequence of the agreements and partly in response to new requirements in production. Bipartite negotiations and co-determination bodies are increasingly being bypassed (Edlund et al. 1989, 67). Assured of influence at the general, joint-consultation level, unions have for the most part sanctioned these developments. The new ways of rationalizing production favor informal participation, for example, project group organization or semiautonomous work groups. In some workplaces, the emerging informal structures have been formalized.

Paradoxically, the Co-determination Act that superseded the Joint Councils Agreement now supports arrangements similar to joint councils. Co-determination oriented toward negotiation and collective agreement is replaced with information and consultation arrangements in joint bodies along the line of management. The new forms of co-determination are not entirely independent of the Co-determination Act since local unions have recourse to the act as a legal support in discussions with management. If cooperation in the new informal bodies is not satisfactory, unions may demand negotiations based on the procedures of the act. But this is becoming increasingly unusual.[6] A recent study on the implementation of the Co-determination Act concludes that management opposition to the act has mellowed considerably, and that the unions consider the act as having been effective in its attempt to provide co-determination: "In fact, management has joined hands with the union in ad-

6. After the Co-determination Act had been passed, the LO and the TCO/SACO negotiation cartel, PTK, concluded an agreement on Union Coordination on Co-determination. Similar agreements have been concluded between unions in other sectors. Interunion cooperation made it possible to negotiate the Agreement on Efficiency and Participation.

justing to the changes brought about by the Act, and has not considered this change detrimental" (Dokras 1990, 214). In recent years, Dokras notes, the act has been criticized for not providing the unions with what it had promised. Dokras's study, conducted mainly through expert interviews, claims to disprove this:

> If rapid technological change alters the way in which work will be conducted in future, the Act provides the proper avenue to structure the consequent change in industrial relations. By stressing the negotiation element in codetermination, the Act has paved the way for better industrial relations by avoiding the path of conflict and by giving the unions a say in almost all matters concerning the workplace, and also other changes the next decade will bring for Swedish industry.

7.4   Recent Trends in Swedish Industrial Relations

Swedish industrial relations are changing. The center of gravity has moved to the local level. Flexible joint council forms of employee representation, ad hoc or permanent, have gained significance. An important factor in this are new methods of rationalizing production (Brulin and Nilsson 1991a, 328). The globalization of the Swedish economy, the ongoing internationalization of Swedish enterprises, and a divided front among employers are also changing the traditional Swedish model (Lundberg 1985), and the change of government and the very deep recession have played a part as well. Unemployment is now rising, although from a very low level. The crucial test for the Swedish model is whether unemployment can be kept down. Even the nonsocialist government that came to power in September 1991 has promised to do everything possible to avoid an unemployment crisis similar to that affecting the rest of Europe. But it has also pledged to abolish the employee investment funds and change the labor laws to promote a more individualized employer-employee relationship.

7.4.1   New Forms of Work Organization and Participatory Structures

Sweden is still one of the most affluent countries in the world. Swedish firms have become world leaders, building competitive advantage through continuous upgrading. In this, the Swedish industrial relations environment served as a source of challenges and pressures, fostering high-quality management and productive employer-employee relations. The competitiveness debate in Sweden has for the last few years been preoccupied with taxes, wage levels, exchange rates, interest rates, and inflation. Recently, however, more dynamic factors have been considered. Sölvell, Zander, and Porter (1991, 215) argue that "in the long run, high productivity and high wages require . . . upgraded factors of production, increasingly sophisticated customers, strong clusters of supporting and related industries, and tough rivalry. With these pressures and challenges, Swedish firms will be driven to invest in advanced manufacturing technologies and better products, and to move into less price-sensitive market segments, thereby upgrading competitive advantage and gaining the ability to pay higher wages." As an additional factor one may add new forms of work organization and corresponding arrangements for employee and employer co-operation, as the new methods to rationalize production require the involvement of employees at various levels in the reorganization of the labor process (Produktivitetsdelegationens betänkande 1991, 82).

The Co-determination Act gives unions the right to be informed and obliges the employer to negotiate any changes that are of importance for union members. In practice, this is often conducted in bipartite participation and information bodies called "co-determination councils." The unions are informed about planned changes in the organization of production. In case of a major change, a joint council is set up to make the change process smoother. For minor changes, a project group is created. Joint councils and project groups are often formed on an ad hoc basis, and their members represent a broad range of functions and roles. Very often the employer himself wants some sort of union representation. But he also often requests that the individual not just represent the union but also have a professional view.

Co-determination councils and the various bodies set up by them function as integrated representation and consultation councils. Almost all employees are given representation through their union; the density of union organization is very high, about 80 percent. Still, these are not primarily negotiating bodies. Sometimes disputes within co-determination bodies may be channeled into the negotiation system. But often the unions, having been consulted or informed in a proper way, in the end must accept a employer's decision. There are also workplaces where employee representation is weak. Here the unions get only a minimum of information, in line with the act and the central agreements, and the employer does not let them take part in the planning and monitoring of change processes. At the same time, some employers that used to oppose the co-determination procedures increasingly use them to set up consultative councils to improve communication between management and employees on production issues.

7.4.2   Capital Rationalization and Service Management

A new management strategy is replacing Taylorism in the most progressive Swedish enterprises, aimed at "modernizing" the organization of industrial production. Taylorism is succeeded by more market-oriented, flexible, decentralized, and integrated forms of organization, including arrangements for communication, participation, and co-determination. The core message of the new management strategy is that to be successful, an enterprise must develop strong motivation among its employees. For this, employees must have a part in the organization of their work. Flexibility is the catchword of the new strategy. "Hard" control systems are supplemented with "softer" methods, such as quality circles, deliberately developed corporate cultures, and charismatic leadership. Through computerized information systems, top management is able to control more independent subunits, which often operate as profit centers at different levels of a "flattened" corporate hierarchy (Sandberg et al. 1992, 271).

The new forms of work organization are not developed in a vacuum. The Swedish manufacturing industry is undergoing a paradigmatic change toward "capital rationalization," pioneered by firms like Asea (ABB) (Björkman and Lundquist 1987, 61). To speed up the throughput of products, one of the main goals of capital rationalization, the organizational design is changed. Since complex hierarchies inhibit a smooth flow of production, capital rationalization encourages decentralization of responsibility and authority. In particular, group work and job rotation are used to speed up the flow of products through the organization.

If capital rationalization constitutes the core of the new management strategy in manufacturing, "service management" (Normann 1984) is its equivalent in the service sector. In service management, image and culture are deployed as management tools. Client-oriented work organization and effective communication with and between employees are used to help achieve consistent quality of service. "Internal marketing" is viewed as equal in importance to external marketing. The leaders of a service organization are to "market" the organization not only to its customers but also to its personnel. According to the service management concept, the most important component of the service system is the staff at the front-line who meet the customer at the "moment of truth."

Do the new methods of rationalizing production favor works council—like structures of participation? It is too early to make a final evaluation of the impact of the new management concepts on communication, participation, and co-determination. The tendencies and reports are contradictory. The Swedish debate on productivity, work organization, and workplace democracy is much affected by the international debate, and especially by the Japanese example. Skeptics expect that the new rationalization methods will turn into a "super-Taylorism" actually inhibiting dialogue and participation. The Swedish discussion now highlights the negative aspects of Japanese "lean production," especially that it makes workers work not only smarter but also much harder and that workers are encouraged to discuss limited productivity-related problems while otherwise performing very standardized and monotonous work tasks.

Three Swedish researchers, after a visit to nine Japanese transplants in the U.S. automobile industry, report a "quasi-military factory regime" (Berggren, Björkman, and Hollander 1991, 4). Although Japanese management talk about small-group activities, job rotation, quality circles, a high level of communication, and so forth, the factories were found to be characterized by discipline and punishment, not at all illustrating a break with the Taylorist paradigm of work organization. Workers are tightly controlled, and operators are trained to become their own time-and-motion study experts to speed up production.

Suggestions for improving the production process are encouraged. But any deviation from standardized procedures is forbidden.

Other researchers and management consultants argue to the contrary that workers in Japan, although there is no legal framework for worker participation in management, are "vocal about management, and joint consultation between labor unions and the company at the enterprise and plant level is remarkably widespread" (Koike 1987, 319). According to the *kaizen* method (Imai 1986) of improving production, now becoming very popular among Swedish managers, communication-oriented and cooperative labor-management relations are decisive in improving productivity. Two main features of the new production model—the "pull system" and employee involvement—might well be labeled post-Taylorist in certain ways. Also, the new emphasis on task uncertainty and worker responsibility does constitute a break with Taylorist rationalization methods (Brulin 1993, 5).

7.5   The Swedish Experience: A Scattered Picture

Many Swedish firms, convinced of the importance of improving communication between management and unions, are today setting up joint council arrangements. An extreme case is the management-union advisory board of the president of Volvo. Another arrangement that is becoming increasingly common are management-appointed joint project groups, like those at Alfa Laval, that work on rationalization and work reorganization. Such groups are primarily supposed to take a professional view, but they are also acting as union representatives.[7] New rationalization concepts, especially capital rationalization and service management, are behind the creation of participatory arrangements that, in some respects at least, are in opposition to the Swedish model. Codetermination, based on collective bargaining, is now being transformed into joint consultation and participation, reducing the importance of negotiations and in the long run perhaps weakening the bipartite system.

7.5.1   Informal Participation

At Ericsson in Söderhamn, a leftover from the postwar joint council system was transformed into a "plant council," corresponding to the Co-determination Act, which replaced the old central agreement on joint councils. There are two main differences between the old joint council and the new plant council. Today, the council's agenda is set jointly by management and union representatives, while in the past, it was determined solely by the employer. Also, the working committees are jointly appointed. The main purpose of the plant coun-

---

7. According to the final report, "PRO-VISION," from Alfa Laval in Lund, and interviews in 1990 with the members of the companies' research group (Mariette Lagerberg, Lars-Erik Nilsson and Bengt Nilsson).

cil meetings, however, is still to inform the unions, primarily on economic issues.

At the same time, a new cooperative culture developed at the plant, either because of the Co-determination Act or as the result of pressing needs for corporate renewal. In the mid-1980s, parts of the production process were reorganized through joint management and union efforts (Brulin 1989, 85–98). Plant management conceded the local union a role in this process, although only unwillingly: the experts on computerized manufacturing did not want organizational solutions from below, supervisors resisted change in their traditional role, and management at different levels did not want to make additional effort.

In the early 1990s management began to perceive the traditional supervisors as part of the problem. Computerized manufacturing had not solved as many problems as it had promised, and the plant still had to improve flexibility, cut lead times, and speed up the throughput of products. In addition, something had to be done about bad working conditions, especially repetitive and monotonous jobs.[8] Today, management accepts employee and union representation in the change process. For example, an initiative from a local representative of the metalworkers' union who works in final product testing, to integrate testing and assembly work, was strongly supported by management (Interview, February 1992). Working hours have been set aside and groups set up to carry out the initiative. Despite criticism from supervisors, the union representative became the informal project leader since he had the professional competence and knew how to reorganize production in line with both rationalization and work development requirements.

The workplace section of the metalworkers' union has one representative for each of the plant's 40 departments, keeping an eye on the numerous local wage schemes. There are also representatives of the white-collar unions, as well as a special body for health and safety matters that has union and employer representation. Under the plant's participation regime, all of these might play an active role in managing change to the extent that they have competence and are motivated. The employer needs facilitators in the change process and is apparently prepared to accept union influence in the reorganization. However, he does not want to have such influence regulated in formal agreements. Although the central co-determination agreement among the labor market parties recommends that the local parties conclude local co-determination agreements, none has been concluded in Söderhamn.

7.5.2 Formal Agreements

Co-determination practices may differ even within the same enterprise. This applies, for example, to Saab Automobiles AB (Brulin and Nilsson 1992b). At

---

8. Workplace program for Ericsson Telecom AB, Söderhamnsfabriken, Söderhamn, written by Stig Wernersson, January 15, 1992.

Saab, representatives from the unions representing the firm's numerous workplaces and plants have formed a "contact group," which handles codetermination issues common to Saab as a whole. The group has 15 members, 8 from the metalworkers' union and 7 from the three white-collar unions. One of its objectives is information exchange, another the formation of a unified union voice. The group appoints three employee representatives to the company's board of directors. It also appoints a five-person group for negotiations with the employer on common co-determination issues. Wages and working conditions are excluded from its agenda. Still, according to one of its members, it is a weakness of this group that, when the chips are down, the unions do not speak with one voice on co-determination matters and are not able to settle their own conflicts before negotiating with the employer (Interview, October 1991).

Below the central Saab level the unions conduct co-determination procedures at each plant, sometimes jointly and sometimes individually. At the company's worldwide distribution center in Nyköping, the metalworkers' local union section has been very active, and local management has been imaginative. Jointly, they have moved away from hierarchical and Taylorist forms of organization, and an encompassing change program is currently being carried out that will create a work organization based on continuous learning in semiautonomous work groups, supported by a new pay system. Union involvement in the process is highly informal. A project group was formed in the fall of 1989 with representatives from management and the blue-collar union. The formal status of this group is hard to define. Co-determination, if conducted in a way different from the negotiation procedure envisaged by the act, must be regulated by agreement. Neither at the retail center nor at Saab centrally has such an agreement been concluded, with the result that the project group has no formal status. Nevertheless, the group has negotiated three agreements that together constitute the local action program for rationalization and work development. Formally, two of these agreements, on work organization and on training, were reached through co-determination negotiations; the third agreement, on the new pay system, was negotiated through normal collective bargaining on wages and working conditions.

Before and after concluding the agreements, many questions were handled informally through other channels, in an interplay between formal negotiations and informal communication. Informal procedures have, however, been facilitated by the Co-determination Act and by the industrial agreement on wages and working conditions. The latter recommends that local parties create pay systems that encourage job satisfaction and productivity and ensure high wages over a long period. If no agreement can be reached, pure piece-rate or time-based pay systems are to be used. This section replaces a previous one recommending that local parties install piece-rate pay systems whenever possible, to support a Taylorist organization of work.

It is worth noting that cooperation at Saab is not an expression of complete harmony. What is important is that the parties depend on each other. So far, blue-collar workers appear to have been the winners. The supervisors have been unenthusiastic, although they admit that changes are needed. White-collar workers are losing jobs due to new technology and therefore have not been deeply involved in the change program. The interesting question is whether the cooperative culture will survive a more aggressive management. Remarkably, the former president of Saab Automobiles, the General Motors director David Herman, seems to have easily adjusted to participatory Swedish practices. When he arrived in Sweden in early 1990, his first question was reported to have been "Co-determination, what the hell is that?" Later he noted several times in public that the unions had been constructive partners in reorganizing the production process at Saab and in reshaping the firm: "Saab has succeeded in reconstructing the enterprise on its own. We have reduced the workforce by a third. At the same time productivity has risen dramatically, and turnover and absenteeism due to short-time illness have begun to decline fast. We could never have done this in such a short time without the partnership of the strong Swedish unions. Naturally there have been conflicts but weaker unions would not have helped, on the contrary."[9] Herman's opinion concerns only the local level and co-determination at the firm level. He has been more doubtful about the central bargaining system.

7.5.3 Public Sector

The public sector is also rapidly changing its work organization and co-determination procedures. Local agreements in each county or at the workplace replace central co-determination agreements, which until 1992 had covered all local government authorities and all county councils. This is just one step in a general decentralization process.

Tengblad, Joelsson, and Wilhelmsson (1991, 120) have studied joint development projects within the government sector. Their conclusion is that the parties at the national level must decentralize co-determination procedures and act as facilitators of *direct* co-determination and participation at the workplace rather than as negotiating parties. The study argues that instead of conducting co-determination negotiations over the heads of the staff concerned, it is their responsibility to create a culture of cooperation at the workplace. Where the parties have succeeded in creating a local cooperative culture, the bipartite system functions as a development force in organizational change, creating better jobs and more efficient organizations.

The Swedish co-determination system seems to be quite dynamic. As new methods to rationalize production and organize work are practiced, co-determination seems to adjust easily. More fundamental institutional change, such as privatization or total reorganization, may still create considerable ten-

---

9. "Facket en partner, inte en motståndare: Saab-chefen vill avliva myten om fordelen med ett svagt fack," *LO tidningen,* no. 42 (October 18, 1991).

sion. The reorganization of the National Employment Training Board with 5,000 employees has been accompanied by heavy conflict, and at various times the co-determination system more or less ceased to function (Brulin and Nilsson 1992b). It seems that the change of the Training Board AMU from a government authority to a profit-oriented company and, among other things, the abolition of seniority-based wages and salaries caused tensions that were too strong for the co-determination system to contain. There were even unofficial strikes among the teachers at some regional centers. Co-determination in the new organization is more decentralized and has regained legitimacy. At some centers co-determination procedures have evolved into council forms, whereas the significance of co-determination has diminished at others.

7.6   Future of the Swedish Model

The SAF concludes from recent trends to decentralize enterprise organization and restructure work organization that the Swedish model must be abolished. Employer representatives have resigned from all corporatist bodies at the national and sectoral levels. The chairman of the SAF, Ulf Laurin, argues in a book entitled *Farewell to Corporatism* that it is time for individual employers themselves, in each firm, to set wages and conclude local agreements on working conditions suited to their special needs and circumstances (1991, 9–18). The SAF program "Free Markets and Free Choice" is based on the assumption that the trend will be toward a free market economy, with individualization, decentralization, and internationalization as its main characteristics.

Today, the SAF's member associations, instead of the SAF itself, are in charge of collective bargaining on wages and other conditions of employment. The intention is to hold all negotiations at the company level, individualize the employment relationship, and limit the impact of the bipartite negotiation system. According to the SAF, it is the companies themselves that are best able to set wages that reward good performance and greater competence that increases productivity and stimulates economic growth. The SAF is celebrating its first 10 decades with a book entitled *The Rise and the Fall of the Swedish Model: The Employers and Industrial Relations during Ten Decades* (De Geer 1992).

According to the SAF, the significance of institutionalized systems for co-determination and participation is diminishing, in Sweden and elsewhere. The SAF recognizes that single-status collective agreements ("coworker agreements," or *medarbetar avtal;* see below) and the new work organization may create pressures for works councils, from both employers and employees. But such pressures should be dealt with locally firm by firm. Production problems can be handled in the line of management or in semiautonomous work groups, and if the problem at hand demands it, a project group may be set up. But the SAF sees no need for a formalized or institutionalized co-determination system.

The nonsocialist government is trying to change the structure of unionism, for example, by rescinding the tax exemption for union dues, raising the penalties for unofficial strikes, and taking unemployment insurance under state control, making it obligatory, and increasing worker copayments from 5 to 30 percent. A committee was appointed to review all labor laws (Kommittédirektiv 1991, 118), with special attention paid to the effect of the Swedish application for membership in the European Community. Overlaps between codetermination bodies and the health and safety committees will also be reviewed. The main issue, however, is who should be the legal subjects of labor law, the employer and the individual employee or the employer and the union. The Swedish industrial relations system is built on collective agreements and labor laws that give unions, as representatives of the employees, legal rights to be informed and to act. Individualization of these rights would fundamentally change the Swedish model.

The majority of LO and TCO member unions recognize the pressures exerted by the new work organization and rationalization methods for more decentralized participation systems. They have concluded that it will no longer be possible to implement a solidaristic wage policy, the very core of the Swedish model, through central bargaining—although some unions have gone so far as to ask for state income policies or to demand a general strike as means of preserving the centralism of the Swedish model. As a result of the decentralization process, the centralist negotiating cartels of the TCO and SACO have been or are about to be disbanded. Individual unions have strengthened their positions and are trying to individualize their services to their members. Both the LO and TCO argue that, while issues will increasingly be handled in semiautonomous work groups and in the line of management, collective bargaining should remain the basis of employment relations, hoping to channel the pressures towards decentralization into the traditional collective bargaining system.

To modernize the Swedish model and at the same time protect the strong position of Swedish unions, top union officials must improve their knowledge of work organization, so as to be able to support their local bodies in their activities for further work development. To be able to prevent rapid increases in wage differentials as a result of firm-specific wage systems, unions must also develop national job classification systems compatible with new enterprise job evaluation schemes. Refined wage statistics are also needed. These are essential instruments for preventing the "Japanization" of Swedish industrial relations (Brulin and Nilsson 1991b, 75–76).

Swedish unions are changing strategy toward a solidaristic work policy carried out at the workplace. Their aim is to participate in the reorganization of the labor process and turn it to the advantage of wage earners while also contributing to productivity growth (Mahon 1991, 311). The concept of work development catches the change from a solidaristic wage policy to a solidaristic work policy. Work development is a way for local union bodies to create a work organization without repetitive jobs where employees are trained for better and more productive work tasks. Work development is to be supported by new pay systems that reward high and broad skills within a team organization.

In parts of Swedish industry, progressive management and workplace unions seem to cooperate quite well in accordance with these ideas, simultaneously rationalizing production and creating better jobs. At such workplaces, an infrastructure of co-determination is created in support of joint work development. The program of the metalworkers' union to modernize the Swedish model and make it compatible with the demands of competitive and flexible production has served as a guide for the union movement. According to the program, a new compromise at the firm level may revolve around a constantly learning work organization built on semiautonomous groups with the authority to request better tools, machines, and organizational design. Such groups must be supported by a participatory infrastructure that is flexible and less oriented toward bargaining (Swedish Metalworkers' Union 1989).

7.6.1 Coworker Agreements

The aim of Swedish employers today is to have one consolidated collective agreement regulating co-determination, wages, and working conditions for all employees of a given plant, with "single-status" workplaces representing a first step toward single unionism. ABB Service in Sweden has been a pioneer of "coworker agreements" applying to both blue- and white-collar workers. Pressures to move toward consolidation of collective bargaining have been created, not so much by the transaction costs of divided bargaining procedures or by increasing interunion competition and demarcation disputes, but by changing production requirements—the fact that a vertical division of labor between different categories of workers, with its correspondingly divided union organizations, no longer fits modern production methods.

Unlike Britain where single unionism has been put on the agenda by the politicians (Bratt 1988, 166), in Sweden it is the employers that have been very active on this issue. In fact, the needs that result from changing work organization are recognized by worker representatives as well as by employers. The latter are primarily interested, not in single unionism, but in single-status or one-category employees—although in the long run the two are hard to separate. In principle, the unions have been positive toward the idea since it is in line with their productivity-oriented policies. In practice, however, it has been hard for employers to obtain single-status agreements. In the mid-1980s an effort was made at the Volvo Uddevalla plant, but it failed after resistance from the national unions. The metalworkers' union in particular questioned whether assembly work at Uddevalla was really going to be interspersed with white-collar work to such a degree that it required a one-category employee with a single-status agreement.

The dilemma for the blue-collar and white-collar unions involved is that the jobs of their members are now becoming more and more integrated due to the new work organization. Employers have become more aggressive, and local unions understand the possible productivity gains and prospects for work development. At ABB Service work organization has been totally changed by the "T 50" project, which aims at cutting all lead times in half and doubling the speed of product throughput. Semiautonomous work groups were set up which were initially composed of all categories of workers, from operators organized by the metalworkers' union to professional engineers organized by the Union of Graduate Engineers. A condition for this form of organization to function, however, is that different categories of workers are eventually merged in one category (called "coworkers") with individually determined salaries. The ABB agreement gives the local parties at each ABB Service workplace the freedom to negotiate their own working-time regimes. Coworkers also have extra pension benefits beyond the public pension schemes and the supplementary pension plan created by central agreement.

One of the most interesting parts of the ABB coworker agreement concerns co-determination. As in many other cases, the local parties at ABB Service acted as if they had a local agreement on efficiency and participation. But since no such agreement existed, the old co-determination councils and joint project groups had unclear legal status. Now the coworker agreement will function as a local efficiency and participation agreement (Malm and Pihlgren 1991, 91), giving the local parties wide co-determination options in an arrangement similar to a works council system. Local unions are to set up joint local bodies for coworkers at each plant. These will appoint employee representatives interacting with management in what will in the future will be a joint council. Various working committees will be composed of both worker and employer representatives. At some companies it has been proposed that nonunionized workers should also have the right to appoint representatives to the local body for coworkers.[10] This would constitute a dramatic change in Swedish industrial relations, implying a development toward works councils not only for union members but for all employees.

The coworker agreement at ABB Service is closely watched by management at ABB headquarters and the rest of Swedish industry. According to leading representatives of the Swedish Engineering Employers' Association, there will be coworker agreements everywhere by the mid-1990s. The chief executive of ABB, Percy Barnevik, hopes to conclude coworker agreements for all parts of ABB in Sweden, encompassing 30,000 employees, in the near future.[11] Coworker agreements are likely to weaken the bipartite system oriented toward negotiations. The aim of the employers is to conclude coworker agreements at the firm or plant level that supersede the industry-level agreements between the union and the employers' association. This will make the unions' struggle for solidaristic wage policy and work development vastly more difficult.

10. Svenska Industritjänstemannaforbundet (Union of Salaried Employees in Industry) (1992, 3).
11. Speech by Percy Barnevik at the conference A Changing Working Life arranged by the ILO and the Swedish Work Environment Fund, October 1, 1991.

Today, it is still the central agreement that applies if there is a conflict between local and central agreements. But as time passes and coworker agreements become more common, the legitimacy of central agreements may diminish. As working conditions become more firm specific and local codetermination methods are improved, it will be harder for the central unions to uphold a common wage earner interest. One suggestion discussed by a government commission investigating the productivity problems in Swedish industry was to make it legally impossible to have more than one collective agreement for a firm or workplace.[12] An obvious response by the vertically divided unions would seem to be to unify their organizations to meet this challenge locally and nationally, not least since they themselves have so strongly criticized the Taylorist organization of work. However, historical reasons, among other things the close connection between the LO unions and the Social Democratic party, as well as the LO's solidaristic and collectivistic wage policy have been major obstacles to a restructuring of the union movement.

7.7   Concluding Remarks: Influence from the European Continent

Employers and employees agree that the old joint council system failed because of certain traits of the old Swedish model, in particular solidaristic wage policy and structural rationalization. These were dealt with above the individual firm in central bargaining and corporatist institutions at the meso- and macrolevels, stripping the councils of their mission. According to an LO representative, hardly anybody misses the joint councils and they should be viewed as an interlude (Janérus 1989, 167). However, the weakened hegemony of solidaristic wage policy and the declining significance of structural rationalization from above may create opportunities for new joint consultative and councillike arrangements at the workplace, although these bodies will hardly ever be mandatory.

Neither the Ministry of Labor nor the SAF nor the LO believes that Sweden's application for membership in the European Community will change the Swedish industrial relations system. The LO and TCO hope that the "social dimension" of the Internal Market will be realized, although they do not believe that it will affect the Swedish labor market since the floor it will create will in all likelihood already have been reached and exceeded in Sweden. Concerning the European Company Statute, both the LO and TCO view the possibility of selecting a co-determination system in line with a tradition built on collective bargaining as a major advancement for the Scandinavian countries. The official at the LO in charge of European Community matters argues that works councils are alien to Sweden and does not regard the former joint councils as works councils in a strict sense since they had no legal backing. They

12. *LO tidningen,* no. 43 (October 27, 1991).

should rather be seen as products and parts of the collective bargaining system (Interview, October 21, 1991).

The SAF for its part views the "social dimension" and the various participatory arrangements proposed in the European Company Statute as expressions of German influence on the European Community that will, however, hardly be realized. The SAF used to favor some sort of works council arrangement when it hoped to prevent the Co-determination Act. In the early 1970s a special department at the SAF kept an eye on the issue both domestically and internationally. Today, there is no longer interest in works councils at the SAF.

The breakdown of centralism in industrial relations and Taylorism in work organization presents labor everywhere with both opportunities and risks. In light of the employer offensive in Sweden to get the workforce to speak with one voice through coworker agreements, there is reason to make comparisons with German co-determination and to ask whether works councils may provide a buffer for unions, making their adjustment to the new rationalization methods easier. In Thelen's words, "works councils have emerged as critical actors as plant bargaining becomes an increasingly important locus of conflict and compromise in West Germany's dual system" (1992a, 14). German unions today aim at implementing a set of centrally defined goals through a decentralized mechanism. The works council has become an important instrument in IG Metall's strategy to appropriate the kind of ability to reorganize production that employers want when new technology and work organization are introduced. Thelen shows how German unions and employers have concluded industrial agreements that charge works councils and individual employers with negotiating the specific extent and form of flexibility within centrally defined parameters (1992a, 14).

Swedish unions have not yet found instruments and strategies to handle the post-Taylorist challenge. They were, however, very successful in preventing representation outside union control. One expression of their strength was their ability to limit the spread of quality circles. In the early 1980s Swedish employers, especially in large firms, tried to introduce quality circles and related methods to improve productivity, creating union fears that they were trying to build up a new participatory infrastructure beyond union influence. In the second half of the 1980s, the quality circle movement receded, not least as a result of union protests and resistance.

Nevertheless, the change in management strategy demands more from unions than just rejection. Decentralization must be handled in a new way if unions are to provide their members with real influence on work reorganization, beyond minor information and consultation procedures and independent of the goodwill of the employer. A dual system may be able to facilitate a response to such a daunting challenge. If Swedish unions cannot find ways of influencing the new management strategy at the plant level, they will lose much of their credibility. Time-honored antipathy to council-like arrangements at the workplace must be superseded by a new vision of a co-determination and participation structure in harmony with modern work organization and rationalization methods.

According to a radical interpretation, the Co-determination Act, in combination with the other labor laws and the wage earner funds, represents a challenge to the capitalist organization of work, and in this compares favorably with the German works councils (Hyman 1989, 213). Swedish institutions are claimed to enable unions to develop an autonomous position in the capitalist system and in relation to the individual employer. The problem, however, is that procedures oriented toward negotiation and based on bipartitism are weakened when employers make radical experiments with work organization that question the legitimacy of unions. Negotiation procedures are not suited to the smooth handling of production questions, and it is hard to mobilize interest among union members in negotiating on such matters.

Swedish unions may lose control of the rapid reorganization of the labor process, and also of wage setting, as employers make work reorganization an integral part of a decentralized wage formation model. Today it may be asked whether Swedish unions would not stand stronger if they had a more formalized co-determination system at the workplace, one less dependent on negotiations. A quasi-constitutional system or an extended version of the old joint councils may conceivably suit the present situation better. As long as Swedish unions are not capable of restructuring their own organizations, workers need more formal backing from central unions, or legal backing from the state, to unify their voices at the workplace and to ensure that participation does not become completely employer-controlled as, for example, in Japan.

References

Arbetsrättskommittén. 1975. *Demokrati på arbetsplatsen: Förslag till ny lagstiftning om förhandlingsrätt och kollektivavtal.* Stockholm: Statens Offentliga Utredningan.

Agreement on Efficiency and Participation. 1982. Stockholm: SAF-LO-PTK.

Berggren, Christian, Torsten Björkman, and Ernst Hollander. 1991. *Are they unbeatable? A report from a field trip to study transplants, the Japanese owned auto plants in North America.* Ann Arbor, Mich.: Labor Studies Center.

Björkman, Torsten, and Karin Lundquist. 1987. Work relations, capital accumulation, technological and social change. In *The Multiparadigmatic trend in sociology,* ed. Ulf Himmelstrand. Uppsala: Uppsala Universitet.

Blomquist, Marta 1982. *Vem bestämmer medbestämmandet?* Stockholm: Arbetslivscentrum.

Bratt, Christian. 1988. *Thatcher och det nya facket: 80-talets förnyelse av brittiskt arbetsliv.* Stockholm: Norstedts.

———. 1990. *Labour relations in 18 countries.* Stockholm: Svenska Arbetsgivareforeningen.

Brulin, Göran. 1989. *Från den "svenska modellen" till företagskorporatism: Facket och den nya förtagsledningsstrategin.* Lund: Arkiv.

————. 1993. Vers un nouveau modèle productif dans la Suède. In *Vers un nouveau modèle productif?* ed. Jean-Pierre Durand. Paris: Syros.

Brulin, Göran, and Tommy Nilsson. 1991a. From societal to managerial corporatism: New forms of work organization as a transformation vehicle? *Economic and Industrial Democracy* 12(3): 327–46.

————. 1991b. *Mot en ny svensk modell.* Stockholm: Rabén & Sjögren.

————. 1992a. *Det nya AMU: Arbetslag, Marknad och Utvecklade partsrelationer.* Stockholm: Institutionen för Arbetsvetenskap, Tekniska Högskolan.

————. 1992b. PM om rationalisering och arbetsutveckling vid SAAB Automobile Distribution. Stockholm: Institutionen för Arbetsvetenskap, Tekniska Högskolan.

Brulin, Göran, and Anders Victorin. 1992. Improving the quality of jobs: The Swedish model. In *New directions in work organization: The industrial relations response.* Paris: Organisation for Economic Co-operation and Development.

Carlsson, Bo. 1966. Industrial relations at the local level in Sweden. *Co-existence* 4(4): 91–98.

Carlzon, Jan. 1989. *Moments of truth.* New York: Harper & Row.

De Geer, Hans. 1992. *The rise and the fall of the Swedish model: The employers and industrial relations during ten decades.* Chichester: Carden.

Dokras, Uday. 1990. *Act on co-determination at work: An efficacy study.* Stockholm: Almqvist & Wicksell.

Edlund, Sten, Inga Hellberg, Tore Melin, and Birgitta Nyström. 1989. *Views on co-determination in Swedish working life.* Lund: Juristförlaget.

Edlund, Sten, and Birgitta Nyström. 1988. *Developments in Swedish labour law.* Stockholm: Swedish Institute.

Fulcher, James. 1991. *Labour movements, employers, and the state: Conflict and co-operation in Britain and Sweden.* Oxford: Clarendon.

Gehlin, Jan, and Tommy Nilsson. 1985. *Tjänstemannen, facket och yrkesrollen.* Stockholm: Arbetslivscentrum.

Geijer, Arne, ed. 1971. *Industrial democracy in the seventies.* Stockholm: Landsorganisationen.

Hauser, Urs. 1971. Co-determination or shop floor democracy. In *Industrial democracy in the seventies,* ed. Arne Geijer. Stockholm: Landsorganisationen.

Hyman, Richard. 1989. *The political economy of industrial relations: Theory and practice in a cold climate.* London: Macmillan.

Imai, Masaaki. 1986. *Kaizen: The key to Japan's competitive success.* New York: McGraw-Hill.

Iseskog, Tommy. 1990. *Att medbestämmandeförhandla.* Stockholm: Aktuell Juridik; distributed by Allmänna Förlaget.

Janérus, Inge. 1989. Företagsnämnderna: En parentes. In *Saltsjöbadsavtalet 50 år: Forskare och parter begrundar en epok 1938–1988,* ed. Sten Edlund et al. Stockholm: Arbetslivscentrum.

Johansson, Anders, L. 1989. *Tillväxt och klassamarbete: En studie av den svenska modellens uppkomst.* Stockholm: Tiden.

Koike, Kazuo. 1987. Human resource development and labor-management relations. In *The political economy of Japan,* vol. 1, ed. Kozo Yamamura and Yasukichi Yasuba. Stanford: Stanford University Press.

Kommittédirektiv. 1991. *Översyn av den arbetsrättsliga lagstiftningen.* Stockholm: Statens Offentliga Utredningan.

Larsson, Tor. 1984. *Industrins furirer: Studier rörande den sociala innebörden av förmansskapet inom svenska företag.* Uppsala: Uppsala Universitet.

Laurin, Ulf. 1991. Farväl till översåtligheten. In *Farväl till korporatismen.* Stockholm: Svenska Arbetsgivareforeningen.

Lundberg, Erik. 1985. The rise and fall of the Swedish model. *Journal of Economic Literature* 23(1): 1–36.

Lundh, Crister. 1991. *The crisis of the Swedish model: Recent trends in collective bargaining in Sweden.* Lund: Lund Papers in Economic History.

Mahon, Rianne. 1991. The Swedish working class in the 1990s: Advance or retreat? *Economic and Industrial Democracy* 12(3): 295–325.

Malm, Lars, and Marianne Pihlgren. 1991. *Medarbetare i service: Ett förändringsprojekt inom ABB i Sverige.* Stockholm: Pihlgrens Förlag.

Nilsson, Tommy. 1985. *Arbetare eller tjänstemän? Om ny teknik, arbetsorganisatoriska förändringar och fackliga gränsdragningsproblem i svensk verkstadsindustri.* Lund: Arkiv.

———. 1990. *Bonus för tjänstemän: Lönar det sig? Stockholm: SIF (Union of Salaried Employees in Industry).*

Normann, Richard. 1984. *Service management: Strategy and leadership in service business.* New York: Wiley.

Produktivitetsdelegationens betänkande. 1991. *Drivkrafter för produktivitet och välstånd.* Stockholm: Statens Offentliga Utredningan; distributed by Allmänna Förlaget.

Sandberg, Åke, et al. 1992. *Technological change and co-determination in Sweden.* Philadelphia: Temple University Press.

Sölvell, Örjan, Ivo Zander, and Michael E. Porter. 1991. *Advantage Sweden.* Stockholm: Norstedts.

Sturmthal, Adolf. 1964. *Workers councils: A study of workplace organization on both sides of the Iron Curtain.* Cambridge: Harvard University Press.

Swedish Metalworkers' Union. 1989. *Solidarisk arbetspolitik för det goda arbetet.* Conference Report. Stockholm: Metallindustriarbetarförbundet.

Svenska Industritjänstemannförbundetl (SIF) (Union of Salaried Employees in Industry). 1992. Co-worker agreement—what the local union should be aware of when the parent company wants to conclude such an agreement. Stockholm: SIF.

Tengblad, Per, Lena Joelsson, and Lars Wilhelmsson. 1991. *Effektivt inflytande: Försök med fördjupat medbestämmande i statsförvaltningen.* Stockholm: Statens Arbetsgivarverk.

Thelen, Kathleen A. 1992a. The politics of flexibility in the German metalworking industries. In *Bargaining for change,* ed. Miriam Golden and Jonas Pontusson. Ithaca, N.Y.: Cornell University Press.

———. 1991b. *Union of parts: Labor politics in postwar Germany.* Ithaca, N.Y.: Cornell University Press.

8   Italy: The Costs and Benefits of Informality

Ida Regalia

8.1   Introduction: Historical Overview and Glossary

Clarity, unequivocality, and rationality are certainly not the main virtues of Italian political culture. This applies in particular to the industrial relations system. Turning to our topic, we have first to distinguish between different workplace-based representative institutions and to disentangle a puzzling knot of different names referring to the same realities and, vice versa, of identical labels attached to rather different entities.

A full historical review must go back as far as the very beginning of the twentieth century, when the earliest demands for permanent "internal commissions" of workforce representatives began to spread. In a period when union organization and the consolidation of the Socialist party were only beginning and the labor movement was deeply divided along craft boundaries (Gompers 1910, 162), the formation of ad hoc worker committees in the larger manufacturing establishments of Milan and Turin to coordinate industrial action and negotiate with management is a rather well-documented practice (Barbadoro 1973); similarly, it is well documented that attempts were soon made to transform the temporary commissions in permanent, and recognized, ones, entitled to give voice to workers' grievances and control the implementation of the first contracts.

In a collective agreement signed at Pirelli in Milan as early as 1902, provision was made for the formation of a permanent worker representative committee of nine members to be elected by all workers. Four years later, at the Itala car manufacturing plant in Turin, this was followed by what is usually considered the first agreement on the introduction of a *commissione interna* (internal

Ida Regalia is professor of social sciences at the University of Turin.

A first draft of this paper benefited from comments by Tiziano Treu, to whom the author expresses her thanks.

commission).[1] It was only during the First World War, however, that representative bodies elected by union members became a consolidated institution in major workplaces, supported by the government and recognized by employers in exchange for industrial peace and union commitment to the production goals of the war economy (Bezza 1978). After the war, in a period of social unrest during which the Socialist party and the General Confederation of Labor (CGDL) experienced a steady increase in their following, the organizational form of the internal commission, supported by the trade unions, was widely adopted.

Simultaneously, however, a new radical movement arose for the introduction of works councils consisting of shop delegates (*commissari di reparto*) elected by all workers. The main purpose of these councils, in which the internal commission was to play the role of an executive committee, was to give voice to the workforce as a whole. At the same time, as theorized by Antonio Gramsci, they were to form the first level of a "new order" based on workers' direct involvement in and assumption of responsibility for production. While they had a strong productivistic and—as one might say today—rather cooperative nature, they were looked upon with a mix of suspicion and hostility by union leaders, especially outside Turin,[2] who did not support them actively and who finally let them be swept away in 1920. In 1925, the union-controlled internal commissions were also abolished[3] when the fascist corporations were given official recognition by the peak employers' association, and the CGDL was dismantled.

After the Second World War, the following historical forms of worker and union representation at the workplace must be distinguished:

1. The *commissione interna* was reintroduced in 1943 in a new form. This is the representative body which best fits the definition of a works council (Rogers and Streeck, chap. 1 in this volume): it is plant-based, different from the unions, and not entitled to enter into collective bargaining or call a strike, and its functions range from consultation with the employer to controlling the implementation of collective agreements signed by the external unions, in a perspective of cooperation within the social system of the enterprise. It is worth emphasizing that internal commissions were reintroduced as early as in 1943, through a national agreement between representatives of what soon

1. It is worth noting that this commission differed from that at Pirelli in that it consisted only of union members. The agreement was a success for the metalworking union (FIOM), which obtained the recognition of a closed shop. However, the agreement never went into effect (Antonioli and Bezza 1978).

2. CGDL leaders at the time supported a strategy of "workers' control," to be accomplished through the initiative and under the leadership of the union rather than the "spontaneous and irresponsible" efforts of the unorganized (Bezza 1978; Spriano 1971).

3. Nota bene, however, that recent historical research has shown that influential employers such as Agnelli at Fiat in Turin would have preferred to continue working with their *commissioni interne* to settle grievances (Bezza 1978). With the consolidation of the fascist regime, this did not happen. But the fact sheds light on the cooperative nature of the institution in those years.

afterward would become the national union and employers' organizations, in a period of worker unrest. As a result, at the fall of fascism the internal commissions came into existence before free unionism could be officially restored, which is why initially they were given bargaining rights at the plant level and broad powers of intervention as worker representatives as well as connecting institutions between the workforce and the external union (Vais 1958).

Subsequently, the rights and functions of the commissions were revised several times: in 1947, soon after the official reconstitution of the—initially unitary—general confederation of labor, the Confederazione Generale Italiana del Lavoro (CGIL), in 1953 after the division of the union movement along ideological lines and the formation of two other confederations, the Confederazione Italiana Sindacati Lavoratori (CISL) and the Unione Italiana del Lavoro (UIL), and finally, in 1966, in a period of decline of the institution. Each time the revision was instituted through a national agreement between the union confederations and the peak employers' association and never by law. Briefly, the process of normative readjustment can be described as a sequence of moves on the part of the external unions: as soon as they had recovered their strength (Craveri 1977), they sought, first, to gain full control of the commissions and, subsequently, after the consolidation of multiunionism, to reduce the prerogatives of the elected bodies and make space for direct union initiatives at the workplace.

Independent of their formal definition, however, up to the late 1960s the internal commissions, which continued to be supported by the CGIL as a general representative institution for all workers, in many workplaces represented and defended the workers vis-à-vis the employer. They did this in an environment of growing union weakness and rivalry, in which the unions remained substantially absent at the plant level despite repeated attempts since the mid-1950s to set up their own workplace union sections (Treu 1971).[4]

In quantitative terms, it has been estimated that by the mid-1960s about 3,000 internal commissions with about 15,000 representatives had been in office and active for nearly 20 years (Accornero 1976). Qualitatively, it is hard to assess their true relevance because their situation seems to have differed case by case, and a full historical account has not yet been produced. In any case, in the early 1970s the internal commissions were de facto[5] and abruptly replaced by other representative institutions, in a period of grass-roots mobili-

---

4. It was left open at the time whether union sections, whose introduction was strongly supported especially by the CISL, should be more like German *Vertrauensleute* or union locals in the U.S. tradition. In any case, in the political debate of the 1960s it was a common view that the Italian labor movement was weak because of the absence of a formal and recognized union organization at the workplace.

5. The national agreement on the internal commission was never officially rescinded, so it might be considered still in force in spite of the major changes that occurred in the 1970s. In fact, in the late 1980s the reintroduction of internal commissions was demanded by the radical opposition to official trade unions in a few large plants such as Alfa Romeo in Milan.

zation and protest during which they were labeled as "old," "bureaucratic," and "ineffective."

2. The workplace union representations (*rappresentanze sindacali aziendali* [RSA]), which were legally introduced by the Workers' Statute of May 1970. Article 19 of the law allows workers from the "most representative" unions—a phrase left undefined[6]—to form workplace-based union representations. The law does not regulate their structure or operation, although it confers a number of rights on them and entitles them to organizational resources. As a consequence, the RSAs, which eventually replaced the older form of works council, the internal commission, took different forms and names in different workplaces.

3. The most widespread form of workplace union representation today may be referred to in English as a works council, although it has different names in Italian: *consiglio di fabbrica, consiglio dei delegati, consiglio d'azienda,* even *comitato di base* in the early 1970s, and also, in a broad sense, RSA. Councils of this kind arose in the late 1960s and early 1970s independent of and before the Workers' Statute, in a period of worker mobilization and social protest and as an unexpected outcome of union initiatives experimentally undertaken to gain control over the movement. Soon after the law was passed, the unions that had previously promoted the councils had to decide how to combine the legal mandate, vague as it was, with the rather different—and highly diversified—reality that had emerged from the protest.[7] Very often, for organizational reasons and to get access to the benefits offered by the law, the new councils, or some of their members, were designated vis-à-vis the employer as union workplace representations, or RSAs, although they defined themselves as factory or works councils.[8]

The same term, then, RSA, can mean three different things: workplace-based union stewards, or union representatives, more similar to a union local than to the German *Vertrauensleute;*[9] those works councillors who, after having been elected by all workers, are designated by the external unions as their representatives in the workplace; and the full works council as such. The reason for this confusion is the coincidence in the early 1970s of several factors:

6. In the 1970s the concept was generally understood to refer to the three main union confederations, the CGIL, CISL, and UIL. During the 1980s, however, this became less obvious, as various forms of sectional organizations (COBAS) or of "autonomous" unions not affiliated to the three confederations drew growing support from workers.

7. E.g., while the law provided for an equal and limited number of representatives to be assigned to each "most representative" union, factory councils were being set up as a heterogeneous aggregate of union members and unorganized workers, in most cases without any list of union candidates being presented (Romagnoli 1976; Regalia 1978).

8. In 1970 when the peak employers' association, Confindustria, conducted a study on the diffusion of works councils, it was unable to find out what was really going on because of the terminological confusion (Confindustria 1973).

9. In this case, no works council exists. This is the most common situation in some service industries, which were least affected by the collective protest movement of the late 1960s and early 1970s.

the success of a protest movement demanding militant, "direct" forms of worker involvement and participation rather than representation (Pizzorno 1978; Tarrow 1990) and thus the introduction of large, informal, participatory committees at the workplace; the passing of new legislation that conferred a number of rights on trade unions and their, not yet existent, organizations at the plant level; and the new activism of the previously weak trade unions trying to seize the opportunity of the moment and make use of the new law to grow stronger, in a perspective of organizational reunification.

The terminological ambiguity, then, was the result of a discrepancy between the law, which was intended to support union representation, and the social movement, which by its very nature looked with suspicion on any form of representation. But it also corresponded to an ambiguity in the character of the representative institution itself. In 1972, after an experimental period, the factory council was officially defined by the three union confederations as a workplace-based institution of *worker and union* representation[10] (Regalia 1978). The Italian councils that were set up in the 1970s therefore fit the basic definition of a works council less well than the internal commissions that preceded them because they are considered, by the unions, the workers, and the law, to be union organizations *also,* allowing them to engage in collective bargaining, call strikes, and generally perform union functions.

While this twofold nature is also reflected in the electoral procedures and in the composition of councils, what should be emphasized in addition is the high informality of the system. When the unions opted in favor of the councils in 1972, they announced that they would soon issue a broad framework regulating the councils' operation. This they were never able to do, at least until recently. One might say that for a long time the unions were not really interested in proceeding further with the legitimation of the councils and the formalization of their rights and duties since this would have increased either the councils' autonomy or the unions' own involvement in the workplace. Put differently, the dual and ambiguous nature of the councils was tolerable as long as it was possible to avoid defining their functions and prerogatives clearly.

To sum up, as a representative institution at the workplace, Italian councils are ambiguously denominated, receive rights and resources from a law that was devised for another kind of representation, and were long considered by the unions as union organizations without, however, any formal regulation of their structures and functions. In spite of all this, the councils enjoyed unexpected vitality, are widely diffused, and played a major role in plant-level industrial relations not only in the 1970s, but also later during the 1980s, although then their appreciation by the unions started declining for a number of reasons.

10. This is analogous to a formal merger between the German *Betriebsräte* and *Vertrauensleute*.

8.2   Changing Functions of Works Councils in the 1970s and 1980s

Unions hoped the works councils that replaced the internal commissions in the early 1970s would offer a way of reconciling the different and conflicting needs of having the whole workforce as well as the external unions represented at the plant level, with both functions being performed by the same institution. The questions that were debated in the early 1970s were whether works councillors should respond first to the workers who had elected them or to the external union, or unions, and whether the works council should be considered more similar to the postwar *commissione interna,* given that representatives were elected by the entire workforce, or to a workforce union organization, in light of the fact that it was recognized by the unions as a RSA in the legal sense (Romagnoli 1976; Regalia 1978; Accornero 1992). For those in favor of dual-channel representation, the question was what kind of second channel was to be added, with different unions giving different interpretations of the existing situation. The problem was solved, or better *circumvented,* by postulating that councils should respond to both workers and unions and that they had both *commissione interna*–like and unionlike aspects.

Certainly, this was a compromise solution, one intended to be a temporary answer to workers' widespread demands for more union democracy and to the unions' diverging positions on how to deal with these demands. And it was a solution whose rationale cannot be fully understood without taking into account the widespread labor mobilization and union organizational weakness from which it originated—which implies that the particular formula cannot easily be transferred elsewhere.[11]

When commenting on the consequences of the ambivalent, dual nature of Italian works councils, observers generally turn their attention to the incongruities that may derive from it, the unions' inability to fully control the councils, and the councils' precarious balance of forces and functions (see recently Accornero 1992, chap. 5). The unions themselves have repeatedly devoted much effort to devising regulations—and especially electoral rules, as we shall see—to institutionalize the councils more firmly, although with limited success because of their own divisions and rivalry. However, inadequate attention has been paid to the fact that this same ambivalence may prove—and in fact often did prove—to be an advantage and an unforeseen resource as well, in that it allows continuous adjustment to changing internal and external pres-

11. Even in Italy, as already mentioned, the councils had little success in industries where unions were already relatively strong at the workplace and workers had not joined the mobilization, e.g., banking and insurance or in the public service sector. Note that these are also the areas in which "autonomous" unionism had a longer tradition, which prevented the unions from reaching pacts like the one in 1972 that established the unitary federation of CGIL-CISL-UIL and at the same time gave legitimacy to the councils. The problem, however, is not one of manufacturing vs. services, as there are service areas (e.g., large department stores, fast-food chains, and the like) in which works councils have been successfully introduced (Regalia 1990).

sures. More specifically, precisely because of their less than unambiguously defined character the councils can preserve a certain amount of union control in periods of worker unrest and provide for a measure of uninterrupted union activities at the workplace in periods of recentralization of industrial relations and collective bargaining, or even of conflict between the confederations.

Seen this way, it is possible to reinterpret the recent evolution of works councils as a history of shifting equilibrium among the functions they perform.[12] According to existing research, we can broadly distinguish three periods:

1. The first period, up to the mid-1970s, was characterized by high levels of worker unrest within a context of economic expansion. The newly created councils succeeded in gaining massive support from the workers, who saw the councils as a stable and easily available reference channel for their participation in the labor movement and also as a way to counterbalance the employer's discretionary powers in the organization of work. At the same time, being recognized as union representatives, the councils enabled the external unions to enter workplaces and extend their influence there as never before. Moreover, as soon as they were de facto entitled to represent the workers vis-à-vis the employer, the councils became fundamentally important for the aggregation, selection, and redefinition of worker demands, thus making it easier for the unions to gain control of protest. As a result, a successful prolonged campaign of decentralized collective bargaining at the plant level was possible, which in turn reinforced the popularity of the representative bodies and more generally the following of the unions among the workers. This is a period in which union membership figures continued to rise as a by-product of the mobilization and of successful collective bargaining, reaching their highest point among active workers in 1977 when the three union confederations together organized 49 percent of the total labor force.

2. The second period, from about the mid-1970s to the mid-1980s, was one of recentralization of collective bargaining and of macroeconomic concertation policies. It ended in 1984 in a dramatic break between the three confederations at the national level over the reform of the wage indexation system (*scala mobile*), under conditions of high unemployment and inflation. Usually this period is seen as one of deep crisis and of decline of the councils. Yet, in light of recent research, it seems more appropriate to speak of a period of pragmatic readjustment to a changing context. In line with the new situation, more emphasis was placed on the internal organization and the rights and obligations of the councils themselves, and more attention was paid to the individual needs and demands of the workers and the day-to-day activities of regulating working

12. Differences may also be found between industries or regions. Regalia (1984) records the more pragmatic approach of the councils in the chemical industry in comparison with councils in metalworking, or the more "optimistic" climate in the then more recent councils of the southern regions in comparison to the older councils in the North.

conditions; even some kind of collective bargaining continued to be carried on at the shop floor or plant level (Regalia 1984; Negrelli 1987).

The outcome was institutional change according to local needs and circumstances, often without much support from the external unions, and with differences in local cultures, in political traditions, and in the relations with individual employers playing an important role. In this way, a continuing union presence could be ensured at the workplace, in spite of heightened competition among the external unions,[13] and conditions were created for the development of new patterns of industrial relations at the plant level.

3. The third period, which lasted from the mid-1980s to the early 1990s, was characterized by increasing initiatives by employers at the workplace to gain worker consent and to mobilize commitment to productive goals, within a context of economic expansion but also of increased market competition and growing needs for more flexible use of work. In this situation, especially where they continued to command a large following among workers and sufficient support from external unions, the councils started performing the rather new task of collective representation vis-à-vis the employer, inside a more consensual pattern of labor relations at the shop floor. The wide diffusion of formal agreements and informal understandings at the plant level in recent years (Baglioni and Milani 1990) and the growing propensity of employers to involve council leaders directly in various aspects of the management of production (Regalia and Ronchi 1988–92) are indicators of a changing situation in which the councils are growing stronger.

In conclusion, we can summarize the functional evolution of Italian works councils in the two decades since the Workers' Statute by observing that from the beginning councils appear to have performed *representative functions:* first with strong support from the external unions, later because of their established presence and their support from the workers. *Consultative functions* were then increasingly added after the early 1980s. Moreover, in the ongoing Italian debate on works councils (for recent references, see Accornero 1992; Della Rocca 1989), observers have devoted much more attention to the councils' dualism of worker and union representation than to their relationship—and possibly even closeness—to employers. In the 1970s this might have been jus-

---

13. When in 1984 the unitary federation of the three main confederations broke apart because of differences on macroeconomic policy, the CISL and UIL tried to withdraw their recognition from some of the councils. There were different reasons for this: the prerequisite of unitary trade unionism on which the factory councils had been based had faded away; the CISL, and especially the UIL, stood to gain from a redistribution of the resources provided by law to the RSAs, and the councils tended to side with the CGIL rather than with the other organizations on macroeconomic policies and on the question of the *scala mobile.* For a period in 1984, a movement of autonomously convened councils, which received only tepid support from the CGIL, rose to protest against the national unions. Evidence shows, however, that at least in the northern industrialized regions, the actions of the CISL and UIL were not very effective, not only because of the CGIL's continuing support for the councils, but even more because of the workers' appreciation of the institution and the emerging need of employers to have a counterpart to deal with at the workplace.

tified by the often open antagonism between the social parties. However, since the early 1980s this omission can only be explained by cultural and political bias. One might even go so far as to say that in recent years, many councils were to a large extent sustained by a growing managerial need to find effective and not too expensive ways to obtain greater and more active worker consent. This fits well with the growth in councils' consultative functions that has been observed by many researchers.

8.3   Works Councils in Practice

8.3.1   Institutional Base

Italian councils developed as one of the possible forms, and indeed the most common form, of workplace union representation, or RSA, under the Workers' Statute. The statute applies to operating units, both plants and subsidiaries, of industrial and service firms with over 15 employees and of agricultural enterprises with over 5 employees.

Council formation is voluntary, in the sense that it is not statutorily prescribed. While it is legally supported, it requires a specific initiative, either by the "most representative" unions acting together or by employees in conjunction with the external unions. Very often in the 1970s, workers gathered in a plant meeting to form a council that afterward received official union legitimation. Later, in the 1980s, it sometimes happened that workers in nonunion workplaces such as fast-food outlets or private television studios organized a council and then called on the external unions to legitimate their initiative (Regalia 1990). Employers have no active role in the formation of councils, and insofar as councils are simultaneously RSAs, can be taken to court if they interfere with the process.[14]

There are no specific legal regulations to which unions must conform, and actual practice has changed many times since the early 1970s. This does not apply, however, to the implicit, unwritten, but highly effective rule that any decision concerning the formation of representative institutions at the workplace must be taken jointly by all "most representative" unions present.

Because of the informal and voluntary features of the system, there are no official statistics available. It is clear, however, that works council coverage is wide, except for areas where councils were never really introduced, such as agriculture, the public sector in general, and some of the private service industries.[15] According to union data, in the early 1980s some five million employees

14. Of course, this does not mean that attempts at interference were not made. In the late 1970s, when the author was doing field research in a southern region, a shoe factory with some hundred employees was much talked about because the employer had up to then resisted the introduction of a council and had threatened to shut down the plant.

15. The reasons for this are to be found in the less militant and unitary tradition of the confederations there and in the deeply rooted presence of independent, "autonomous" unions. One might

were represented by over 32,000 councils consisting of 206,300 worker representatives. This means that, excluding agriculture and the public sector, about 50 percent of the workforce in manufacturing and private services was represented by councils. Since in Italy a high proportion of employees work in small firms where the introduction of a RSA either is not legally provided for or is particularly difficult, the percentage is even higher when restricted to those workers that can be organized.

Many believe that the councils nearly disappeared after the collapse of the unitary federation of CGIL-CISL-UIL in 1984, and union statistics have never been brought up to date. Recent empirical research, however, reveals a rather different picture. Data from a panel study by Federmeccanica, the employers' association of the metal industry, show that councils, referred to as "RSAs" or "factory councils," existed in all responding firms at the time of the first survey, and in 97 percent of firms in the second wave, with all firms without councils having fewer than 100 employees (Mortillaro 1984, 1986). According to research by the Centro di Studi Sociali e Sindicali (CESOS), the research institute of the CISL, which studied a national sample of workplaces in the manufacturing industries in 1988, unitary forms of worker representation were established in 81 percent of firms with 20 to 99 employees, and in 96 percent of firms with more than 100 employees (Squarzon 1989). Similarly, according to the annual Instituto di Ricerche Economiche e Sociale (IRES) Lombardia survey on industrial relations in the manufacturing sector in Lombardy, which has been carried out since 1987, works councils appear to exist almost without exception in all workplaces with more than 50 employees (Regalia and Ronchi 1988–92).

8.3.2   Structure

Only employees sit on the councils, which represent all workers, unionized or not. The law does not specify the mechanisms for the formation of a council (or, technically speaking, a union workplace representation), leaving them entirely to union decisions or negotiation. According to, rather unspecific, union regulations (Bergamaschi 1986) and to custom, councils are typically established by ballot, or sometimes by a show of hands, on the basis of "homogeneous groups" of workers from the same shop, department, or office, without formal presentation of competing lists of candidates. Traditionally, the density of representation is high, with about one representative for every 40 to 50 workers, which may give rise to very large bodies. In the 1980s, however, a trend toward a slight reduction in council size can be observed.

In principle, then, councils are categorically encompassing bodies that are internally structured in such a way as to represent the structure of the workforce. In practice, however, blue-collar workers are overrepresented. This is

---

add that in the public sector, there was also less managerial attention to productivity, efficient work organization, and worker involvement.

not, as many believe, primarily a consequence of electoral practices, but is the outcome of a lower propensity among white-collar workers to seek office: for fear of being set back in their careers because of lower identification with the unions, and as a result of a diffuse uneasiness with an office whose content is widely perceived as vague and undefined. Council seats that should be occupied by white-collar representatives therefore often remain vacant.

According to union regulations,[16] council elections should be held every two or three years. As a matter of fact, in the 1980s, rivalry among the unions made it impossible in many plants (and especially in the historical strongholds of traditional working-class unionism, such as Fiat) to call elections for some time. Existing councils thus remained in office—sometimes with partial elections held to replace resigning council members—until new general elections could be held. Toward the late 1980s, however, the situation appears to have been less precarious. According to the CESOS survey of 1988, elections had been held in the two years before the survey in 48 percent of the small, 72 percent of the medium-sized, and 66 percent of the large plants in the sample. To these another 37 percent, 18 percent, and 30 percent, respectively, could be added where elections had taken place in the preceding two years, meaning that in about 90 percent of the cases there had been a general council election within a four-year period in the late 1980s.[17]

Elections are held on the employer's premises during working time. The Workers' Statute specifies a small minimum number of representatives that the "most representative" unions are entitled to appoint or to have elected. Generally, however, the councils are larger than the legal minimum. Unions therefore either negotiate better conditions with management, so as to have all their *delegati* recognized as statutory "union representatives," or designate some of the elected workers as their representatives. In the early 1970s especially, this allowed unions to exercise some kind of a posteriori control over the electoral results (Regalia 1978, 1984). An official list of elected and appointed councillors must be sent by the unions to the employers' association, which subsequently informs its member firm. In this way representatives acquire the legal status of RSAs and become entitled to the legal rights provided to union workplace representations under the legislation.

Candidates are not subject to any particular eligibility requirement, not even that of being union members. Unions have of course always exerted pressure in favor of their members and have urged elected nonmembers to join. While originally the unions abstained, at least officially, from direct intervention in the elections, with time they developed techniques—such as majority rules, limited or multiple voting, and the formation of informal lists of candidates

16. Unlike the postwar internal commissions, there is no formal regulation of election procedures by collective agreement, not to mention by legislation.

17. These results are consistent with those of the annual IRES Lombardia report (Regalia and Ronchi 1988–92).

(Regalia 1984)—to increase both the councils' representative capacity and union control over them. In the early 1980s the practice of organizing some kind of preselection of candidates had been widely adopted. Later, many of the unions affiliated with the three confederations jointly established detailed rules for council elections. From the extreme informality of its origins, the electoral process has thus become much more formalized, although this tendency is limited both by each organization's potential veto right and by the low propensity especially among white-collar workers to run for office.

The great majority of elected representatives are unionized. In the early 1980s, according to the results of a national survey of works councils, nonmembers were found in about 40 percent of the councils. In practice, however, this meant only that there were no more than two or three nonaffiliated council members on each council, generally among the white-collar representatives (Regalia 1984, 67). In the late 1980s, according to data from the IRES Lombardia survey on workplace industrial relations, nonmembers on the average never amounted to more than 8 or 9 percent of councillors, with a declining trend: in the 1990 survey, which focused on medium-sized and large firms with over 300 employees, to which the external unions traditionally pay particular attention, only 2.5 percent of all councillors were not union members (Regalia and Ronchi 1988–92).

In addition, it must be remembered that the unions from the beginning maintained their right to appoint a small number of council members directly if they considered this necessary for them to be sufficiently represented.[18] This made the establishment of the council subject to internal negotiation, external pressure, and ad hoc readjustment, which is the price to be paid for competing unionism (Regalia 1978, 1984). The great majority of the councillors are, however, elected by the workforce. According to the IRES Lombardia survey, in 1988 only 1 percent of the council members in small firms, 6 percent of those in medium-sized firms, and 8 percent in large firms had been appointed by the external unions.

Councils are usually functionally comprehensive. Where joint permanent or ad hoc committees exist with management, their members are usually selected from among the councillors (Negrelli and Treu 1992). Depending on the size of the council, an executive committee with responsibility for negotiation and day-to-day activities is appointed—as a rule it includes the leaders of the different unions. Other council members may be assigned specific tasks, such as the representation of women and young workers or of high-skilled technicians, health and safety matters, technological innovation, and so forth.

In multiestablishment companies, a coordinating committee, whose members are selected from the councils of the individual plants, may be appointed.

18. Obviously, the possibility of appointing members to the council is exercised more often by the weaker or less militant unions. At least until recently, it was less common among the unions affiliated with the CGIL.

In practice it normally consists of the members of each plant's executive committee. While in the mid-1970s coordinating committees were widely established, many of them later fell into disuse, either because of the decline in collective bargaining at the plant level or, on the contrary, in reaction to what came to be considered excessive coordination of union negotiating strategies in a more and more diversified environment.

Works councillors are entitled to meet on the employer's premises during working time. There are no legal norms regulating the size and composition of councils or the frequency of meetings. The law does, however, assign union workplace representations a certain number of hours per year, depending on plant size, to devote to their activities. A council's yearly endowment in hours can be spent on internal meetings, meetings of the union branches, and conferences with local government institutions, but also on participation in union training programs. On the request of the council, full-time union officers as well as internal or external "experts" may participate in council meetings.

8.3.3   Relation to Unions

As has been pointed out, Italian councils represent both workers and unions. In the 1970s when the councils derived their legitimacy primarily from the workers—although the unions had helped establish them—unions strove to get full control of the councils. Subsequently, in the early 1980s, when the councils appeared to be unequivocally unionized even as their role seemed to be diminishing, unions lost interest in them. Recently, new attention is being paid to them insofar as employers are showing an increasing interest in involving worker representatives in some day-to-day decisions on the management of work.

Unions are represented on the councils both through elected union members, who make up the great majority of councillors, and additional, directly appointed activists not elected by the workers. The latter arrangement is the main organizational device through which multiunionism is accommodated. The form of external representation has been the subject of continuous bargaining among the three confederations, resulting sometimes in new rules but more frequently in ad hoc agreements—the most obvious option, changing the system, is unavailable because of worker support for the councils. In the late 1980s various proposals for electoral reform were made by the national unions in an effort to increase their shares among the representatives. The main proposal was a dual election system, with some councillors elected, as before, by all the workers while the others, equally divided between the three organizations, would be elected separately by each union's members, or directly appointed by the unions (Regalia 1992). This solution, however, which after some experimentation was adopted in 1989 as a formal reform proposal, was soon set aside as it met with widespread resistance.

Union officers may attend council meetings, and council leaders are normally elected by union congresses to union bodies. Union officers also participate in the councils' most important meetings with management, especially those in which information on company strategy is disclosed and discussed and collective bargaining is conducted. Data from the IRES Lombardia survey of large and medium-sized firms indicate that in 1989 union officers participated always or nearly always in negotiations with management on workplace issues in about two-thirds of the cases in which such negotiations were held (Regalia and Ronchi 1991).[19]

In the 1980s there was an increasing tendency even in the manufacturing sector toward establishment of separate workplace organizations for individual unions.[20] Up to now, however, these have maintained a very informal, voluntary status, avoiding direct competition with the councils, which generally have the same leaders. Also, according to the CESOS study, their diffusion appears to be still rather limited.[21] External unions provide the councils with a number of services, such as legal advice and assistance and training programs; they may directly finance the councils after they have used up the yearly allowance of hours for their activity provided by the employer.

Cooperation between internal and external unions is by no means without friction. One source of conflict is the changing and blurring boundary between the respective spheres of activity, which reflects the poorly institutionalized structure of Italian industrial relations, as well as the unions' preference for informal, adjustable demarcation of their and the councils' relative competences. It must be remembered that Italian councils, unlike German *Betriebsräte,* have the right in their legal capacity as union workplace organizations to negotiate agreements at the plant level—which, however, they usually do only together with the external unions—and to call workers out on strike. Moreover, councils sometimes serve as channels for worker protest against the national unions' macroeconomic policies or prevent the implementation of unpopular agreements at the workplace.

19. Nonparticipation of unions in negotiations does not necessarily mean loss of union control over workplace activities. On the contrary, it may indicate high trust between the "internal" and "external" unions (Regalia 1984).

20. As already mentioned, this is common in service industries where RSAs are often formed as single-union organizations. Recently even the CGIL, the largest and most militant confederation, which most strongly resisted the introduction of formalized single-union organizations at the workplace in order not to weaken the councils and divide the representation of the workforce, has been setting up its own committees, mostly in the service industries or where the councils do not function properly because of the limited commitment of the other organizations.

21. Squarzon (1989, 165) found the following percentages of firms (by size) with single-union workplace organizations for the three confederations:

Confederation	Small	Medium-sized	Large	All
CGIL	6.4	10.3	28.3	13.1
CISL	6.5	14.3	39.1	17.0
UIL	3.2	6.2	24.1	12.1

In the late 1980s there was a trend toward decentralization of collective bargaining, resulting in thousands of agreements signed at the plant or company level. In Lombardia, for example, over 2,000 agreements were signed between 1987 and 1988, and about 8,000 in the whole country (Baglioni and Milani 1990). Not only did this not happen against the will of the unions, but on the contrary it was the result of an explicit union strategy to regain control over the shop floor, or at least to increase the unions' visibility after a period of centralized policies. It also met with widespread interest among employers in negotiating more flexible work rules and involving union representatives in the day-to-day management of the workplace. In most cases such agreements were signed at the plant level, very often with assistance from the unions, and generally without any formal presence of employers' associations (Baglioni and Milani 1990; Regalia and Ronchi 1988–92).

In the short term, Italian unions face the classical dilemma for a representative system between suppressing internal opposition and providing channels for it. In the long term, however, there is no doubt that the existence of the councils helped unions increase their membership in periods of worker unrest, and defend their position in periods of distress.

8.3.4   Relation to Employers

Italian councils consist of workers only. Sometimes, however, temporary joint committees are created with management for specific purposes, such as studying new systems of job classification in the 1970s or defining the criteria for performance-related wage increases in the 1980s. Permanent joint committees are still exceptional in Italian industrial relations. A few examples can be found, however, in publicly owned manufacturing and service companies (Negrelli and Treu 1992).

Whether councils are perceived as more adversarial or more cooperative than unions has changed over time. By and large, councils were perceived as more adversarial in the 1970s, while employers tend to see them as more cooperative in the 1980s, according to several case studies (e.g., Regini and Sabel 1989). In recent unpublished research directed by Marino Regini on managerial strategies of labor regulation, managements of large firms characterize relations at the workplace as consensual and cooperative. The issue here is not primarily whether a particular council can be considered more or less cooperative: in Italy especially, where the industrial relations system is only weakly institutionalized, the style of the interactions between the parties will vary a lot according to the balance of power.

Generally, where there are both a strong union presence and economic conditions that require high work flexibility and worker involvement, councils are more likely to be fully recognized by the employer and to be involved in some kind of cooperation. This is shown by data from the IRES Lombardia annual survey on the day-to-day management of work, which roughly measure the

Table 8.1   **Council Involvement[a] in Day-to-Day Management by Plant Size**

Subject	Small	Medium	Large
Yearly calendar and vacations	84.0	94.8	97.3
Overtime	38.2	57.8	70.8
Internal mobility	20.8	50.3	70.4
Technological and organizational change	13.9	50.0	60.0
Training for blue-collar workers	16.5	41.2	63.1
Training for white-collar workers	11.7	14.4	45.0

Source: IRES Lombardia survey, 1989 (Regalia and Ronchi 1990).

[a]Measured as percentage of discussions in which council is involved.

Table 8.2   **Formal and Informal Workplace Agreements by Subject, 1989**
                         (% of firms with such an agreement)

Subject	Formal Agreement	Informal Understanding
Economic and labor market perspectives	56.2	13.8
Hiring	14.9	29.5
Redundancies	17.1	6.4
Remuneration	70.5	21.3
Working hours	82.9	73.4
Health and safety and environment	53.3	34.0
Job classification and occupational development	51.4	36.2
Work organization and internal mobility	38.1	38.3
Company welfare services	53.3	38.3

Source: IRES Lombardia survey, 1990 (Regalia and Ronchi 1991).

Notes: Figures are for firms with more than 250 employees. In 1989, formal agreements existed in 64.2 of the firms covered, and informal understandings in 57.2 percent.

extent of factual recognition of councils by employers (table 8.1). Information from the same source details the subjects that are jointly dealt with through formal or informal negotiation[22] at the plant level (table 8.2).

In Italy, unlike in Germany or, more recently, in France, employers are not legally obligated to consult, negotiate, or take joint decisions with the union workplace organizations on any of the issues mentioned, except for some aspects of labor market regulation. Research findings can thus be interpreted as indicating a rather unexpected and perhaps unintended pattern of continuous interaction between the parties, which is equivalent in practice to a recognition of the importance of institutionalized workforce representation in the manage-

22. By "informal negotiation" we mean bargaining activity that leads, not to a formally signed agreement, but to a less official mutual understanding. In large and medium-sized firms at least, such practices, typically involving the council rather than the external unions, are not a substitute for formal negotiation but a supplement to it. Their function is similar to that of consultation (Negrelli and Treu 1992) insofar as they make possible experimentation with new solutions or help with the implementation of formal agreements.

ment of production, and which is in sharp contrast to the official positions of both the external unions and the employers' associations.

Drawing again on the IRES survey, this impression may be reinforced by data on the frequency and regularity of the formal contacts between managements and councils (table 8.3), revealing a scenario of widespread and increasingly formalized tight interaction. That this is not merely a peculiarity of the more developed northern regions such as Lombardy is indicated by similar findings from a national study of large state-owned companies (Negrelli and Treu 1992).

To sum up, there are reasons to believe that the role of the councils may be enhanced by employers' interest in using their consultative functions as way of increasing worker commitment and consent. This seems to hold especially in periods of change, such as technological innovation, reorganization of work, or introduction of total quality management. This, however, is by no means the general situation. Especially in workplaces where the unions were less strong in the 1980s, or were highly divided, employers often excluded councils and unions and attempted to build direct contacts with workers. Fiat was long the best and most important example of this. Recently, however, from about 1989, the strategy of the largest Italian private company appears to have changed, in connection with the announced introduction of a total quality management project. A collective agreement on new industrial relations in the workplace was signed, and collective bargaining at the establishment and company levels, involving the external unions together with the internal worker representatives, was resumed.

The effects of these recent trends on the influence and power of the external unions are presently under debate. Some unions, such as the metalworking union affiliated to the CGIL, have asked for co-determination rights to be formally recognized by employers, and much emphasis is being placed on the goal of industrial democracy. Generally, Italian unions, both inside and outside the workplace, appear less opposed to the challenge of innovation and high-

Table 8.3   **Frequency and Regularity of Interaction between Management and Works Council in Medium-Sized and Large Firms, 1986 and 1988 (%)**

	1986		1988	
Interaction	Medium	Large	Medium	Large
At least one formal meeting per month	48.3	72.0	39.5	77.3
Regular preestablished meetings	38.6	43.2	40.1	54.4
Agreements on joint verification	67.9	76.5	87.8	97.8
Regular information on				
Economic perspectives	74.0	77.8	72.9	84.6
Occupational perspectives	74.8	82.4	72.4	91.0

Source: IRES Lombardia survey, 1987 and 1989 (Regalia and Ronchi 1988, 1990).

quality, flexible production than unions in other countries. This is related to their ideological commitment, which has often made them emphasize long-term, "political" objectives rather than immediate practical targets. It also has to do with the limited time available in the 1970s to build up a full system of union-controlled work rules. A long productivistic cultural tradition, especially within the CGIL, also plays a role.

In any case, the powers of Italian councils vis-à-vis the employer are to a large extent linked to their unionlike nature. Because the council is also representative of the unions, it can be reliable in the long term, making it worthwhile for the employer to pay the costs of involving it in aspects of his decisions and of negotiating with it. Councils, for their part, need the support of the unions, not just to be recognized as union workplace representatives but also to be a valuable counterpart for the employer.

8.3.5   Relation to the State

We have already mentioned the great importance of the Workers' Statute in helping the councils emerge and consolidate in a situation that had previously been characterized by union weakness at the workplace. We have also pointed out that the law had been designed to strengthen the unions, so that its provisions required a certain amount of interpretation and adaptation. This incongruity, however, helped the unions maintain control over the councils by giving them the possibility of withdrawing recognition from them as union workplace representatives. While this did happen in the 1980s, it was less frequent than one might have expected, at least in the manufacturing sector.

Other legal provisions which indirectly support the councils are to be found in the special legislation on the Cassa Integrazione Guadagni—a wage guarantee fund during layoffs—or in laws on industrial restructuring, requiring employers to disclose information to workplace unions or external unions as a condition of access to public subsidies. At the regional or local level, there are many examples of meetings and consultations of council leaders with local authorities. In the 1970s contacts between local governments and councils were frequent because of the advantages, both practical and symbolic, that accrued from them to both parties (Regalia 1984, 1988).

Some of this seems to have continued into the 1980s. According to the 1990 IRES Lombardia industrial relations survey, councils in 36 percent of the large and medium-sized firms had contacts with local political institutions in the preceding year, dealing not just with traditional unemployment and labor market problems, but more often, in over 50 percent of cases, with health and safety and ecological issues (Regalia and Ronchi 1991).

In the mid-1970s projects for a territorial extension of the councils beyond the workplace were much debated. But they remained largely experimental. Even in the industrial districts of the "Third Italy" (Bagnasco 1977), where the unions had become particularly strong (Trigilia 1986), councils appear to be well rooted only within the workplace (Perulli 1989; Trigilia 1989). At present, the introduction of new forms of territorially rather than workplace-based council-like representative bodies, with specific competences on labor market issues, has been envisaged in some regional and national collective agreements signed by the unions and the employers' associations of the small industry and the artisanal sector. While their formation is still in a very early and experimental stage, they might well prove to be a good way of enhancing worker representation in small firms.

8.3.6   Relation to Workers on the Shop Floor

In the last 20 years works councils have gained strong support from the workers. This is illustrated by the high participation in council elections, even in periods of union rivalry and membership decline. Among blue-collar workers, voter turnout is regularly between 70 and 80 percent, at least in areas with a consolidated union tradition such as Lombardy (Regalia and Ronchi 1988–92). In moments of particular importance, such as the Fiat elections in 1988, it can be still higher.[23] The opportunity to establish their council seems to be highly appreciated even by young workers with no union experience.

Council elections are often the first step toward the unionization of a new plant. Usually, the council is seen by the workers as their close-at-hand union, where information and assistance can be easily obtained. Councils are legally entitled to convene worker meetings during working time; the Workers' Statute establishes a minimum of 10 paid hours per year per worker for this, an amount that may be increased through collective agreement.

Recently, worker involvement programs and employer strategies of direct communication with individual workers have become widespread. However, they do not necessarily affect the status and performance of the councils in a negative way. Research shows that the outcomes may vary considerably according to a number of factors; on the whole, however, neither party seems to view innovative personnel management as a challenge to the internal unions. Usually, the council is informed; sometimes works councillors even participate in the programs, although they are often keen to criticize their effectiveness.

Issues, targets, and addresses of the new managerial practices on the one hand and of collective action on the other tend to be at least partially differentiated, which accounts for a degree of "peaceful coexistence" between the two regulatory principles (Negrelli 1992; Turati 1992; Regalia and Ronchi 1988–92). In fact, changes in the organization of work, such as the introduction of semiautonomous work groups, decentralization of decision making, and increased job rotation, are likely to have positive effects even on the councils, at least where they are rooted in a consolidated tradition, since in periods of organizational change their importance as channels for worker voice and internal two-way communication is enhanced.

---

23. Exact data are not available because of the high degree of informality that is still characteristic of the system.

It is always possible for a council to be taken over by the dissatisfied, and this may sometimes lead to the emergence of radical organizations. This is an inevitable outcome of the Italian legal framework, under which the rights to strike and free association are vested in single individuals. On the whole, however, there can be no doubt that worker radicalism is more likely to be found where councils are absent—as in the public service sector where the COBAS developed in the 1980s (Bordogna 1992).

8.3.7   Efficiency Effects

While exact data are not available, the administrative costs of councils for employers are not low. The Workers' Statute provides for eight hours per month of paid release time for each council member, and better conditions are generally created by negotiation. Moreover, in plants with over 200 employees the council is entitled to a permanent room, which generally includes telephone facilities and other services. Apparently, however, this is not a topic of complaints, at least not openly. Although managements rarely ask for a council to be formed, they do not find it too costly once it has been introduced.

Some of the reasons for managerial acceptance of councils may be gleaned from research on other subjects. In a number of in-depth interviews with personnel managers, the following positive functions of councils were identified: they facilitate internal communication at lower cost than separate managerial channels and programs, they help settle individual and collective grievances, and they operate as a feedback mechanism on the operation of middle management, for example, with regard to promotions. One manager commented that, "if councils didn't already exist, one should invent them" (Interview with the author).

Case studies of industrial readjustment in the 1980s have shown that the existence of active and well-rooted councils made innovation and reorganization of production easier for firms while making the management of redundancies and changes in work practices less traumatic for employees (Regini and Sabel 1989). In recent discussions with the author, personnel managers of multiplant companies pointed out their preference for strong and even militant councils that are the undisputed leaders of the workers, as compared to representative bodies that are weak and poorly supported. In the former case, joint decision making, through consultation or collective bargaining, would lead to much more reliable and therefore in the end more efficient outcomes, while in the latter case, apparently more convenient results might easily turn into a bothersome waste of time.

8.4   Conclusions

It is not easy to draw clear conclusions from the Italian experience with works councils. Because of the dual nature of the councils as worker and union representative bodies, much depends on the perspective one takes. For the councillors themselves, the system's indeterminacy with respect to rights and rules of behavior must make it appear very ambitious, a model that can never be fully realized, with a large and lasting gap between expectations and reality. A sign of this is the high level of dissatisfaction found in all interviews with works councillors since the early 1970s. From the perspective of the external unions, the system probably appears too much in flux, not sufficiently uniform and too difficult to control. Employers probably have the least doubts, as evidence shows that the councils are generally accepted by managements as a matter of fact, and as a somewhat informal but effective reality with which it is better to seek accommodation.

From a factual and functional point of view, however, it may be precisely because of their twofold nature and limited regulation that councils appear to be a successful—that is, flexible and adaptive—institution, one that is especially adequate in periods of changes in unions' and employers' strategies and behavior. First, being legally supported but not legally regulated, councils have been largely protected from employer retaliation (unlike the postwar internal commissions that depended much more on the employers' goodwill), while at the same time being able to function quasi-experimentally. Over time, this allowed them to adjust both to situations of collective movement and protest and to more stable conditions, as well as pragmatically to accommodate multiunionism. Moreover, it is important that the model requires only a small initial organizational investment, allowing even a few workers to take the initiative to set up their representation by calling for general elections and asking the unions to legitimate the results.

Second, insofar as they represent both workers and unions, Italian councils are a borderline case, providing for something more than single-channel and something less than dual-channel representation. In other words, Italian councils give voice to all employees while enabling the unions to maintain ultimate control over workplace activities. This is why the councils never replaced the unions, and why they are generally perceived by the workers as the nearby "internal" union.[24] And this is also why the councils did not turn into company unions either. In fact, one unexpected consequence of Italian multiunionism might have been to prevent collusion between councils and employers at the expense of workers or unions.

Third, that councils' functions remained largely unspecified added flexibility and adaptability to the system. As a consequence, councils became, rather than a tool dedicated to specific and circumscribed purposes, a permanent opportunity to be used by the parties, continuously available for information disclosure, consultation, or negotiation as required by changing circumstances. In

24. But it is also true that, because of multiunionism, councils only rarely acted openly on behalf of the unions in recruiting members. Proselytism and membership campaigns are usually not organized by the councils, but by the unions working through their rank-and-file workplace leaders—who in most cases happen also to be elected councillors (Regalia 1984).

fact, the Italian experience is likely to show that, once councils have been legally introduced with a minimum of legitimation from workers and unions, their success depends on both sides seizing a few crucial issues to develop and work out, so that a learning process about the mutual advantages of continuous interaction between the parties may begin.

In conclusion, the Italian case may be seen as an extraordinary example of the possible virtues of informality and soft regulation in the field of workplace industrial relations. At the same time, however, the costs of the system must also be considered in terms of blurring boundaries between councils' and unions' respective powers and prerogatives, of procedural uncertainty, and of unpredictability in the parties' behavior. In fact, such costs have been growing in the last decade for all actors involved—most perhaps for the unions because of their increasing need to control their workplace organizations in a period characterized by new and "cooperative" decentralization of industrial relations, in an environment of renewed competition among union confederations.

A recent protocol agreement, signed in March 1991 by the three union confederations in a joint effort to reform workplace representation—the latest of many previously unsuccessful attempts—confirms this uneasiness. The project, while slightly changing the name of the councils to "unified union representations" (*rappresentanze sindacali unitarie* [RSUs]), preserves the dual nature of the representative bodies. However, while elections continue to be open to all workers, they are to be on the basis of lists of candidates presented by the union confederations or other groups as long as they are recognized as independent unions and can show the support of at least 5 percent of the workers eligible to vote; also, the council is to be considered a union institution. All council members are to be elected through secret ballot; however, while 67 percent of the seats will be assigned to the competing organizations in proportion to their obtained votes, the remaining 33 percent will be equally divided among the unions affiliated to the CGIL, CISL, and UIL, so as to guarantee minimum representation of each confederation. Moreover, for the first time an attempt has been made to define more clearly the powers, prerogatives, and functions of internal unions with respect to external unions. The agreement tries to consolidate the dual nature of workplace representation, offer a general solution to the question of how to accommodate a more fragmented and competitive multiunionism, and reduce the system's functional uncertainty.

Implementation of the agreement appears to have met with widespread resistance. Many observers are more and more persuaded that it is not possible to reform the Italian system of workplace representation without some kind of further, although preferably "soft," legislative support reducing the range and complexity of voluntary decisions: support that might take the form either of a legislated minimal definition of the councils' structure and operation or of some kind of legal facilitation of industrial democracy.

8.5 Postscript

This presentation and discussion of the Italian experience was completed by the end of 1992. But, in a period of steady, continuous transformation such as the one Italian politics and society are facing in the early 1990s, a brief updating of the story already looks appropriate at the beginning of 1994.

In July 1993 a fundamental tripartite national agreement between the major union confederations, the employers' associations, and the government was signed, which explicitly and formally reorganized the general framework for wage determination and collective bargaining. The agreement is the outcome of two years' hot negotiation and was submitted to the workers' approval through a nationwide ballot campaign. On the one hand, it introduces a kind of soft income policy and, on the other, defines for the first time the competences, subjects, actors, and timing of a two-level collective bargaining system where a backbone of industrywide agreements is supplemented by the substance of company/plant-level negotiation on nationally specified issues.

Because of the latter feature, a better definition and organization of workplace-based representative institutions was required to give more certainty and reliability to collective bargaining at the plant or company level. A study committee of independent experts was therefore appointed by the Ministry of Labor and in October 1993 finally produced a draft legislative project on worker representation in workplaces and on union representativity in general.

The proposal is a legally based works councils system whose members are *all (and exclusively)* elected by the workers by secret ballot on the basis of lists of candidates presented by the union confederations or other groups that can show minimum support from workers eligible to vote, and whose *collective bargaining* as well as representative and consultative (and possibly co-determination) *functions* are to be recognized, although only *within the limits set by industry agreements* and in accordance with the external unions. It is also suggested that, at least during a transition period, collective bargaining be performed by a negotiating team, one-third of whose members are directly appointed by the unions, proportionately to their electoral share, to safeguard the voice and the role of the unions; the requirement of a large and qualified majority for the approval of company or plant agreements (without which a ballot is required) should help ensure decisions that can be effectively implemented.

Up to now the proposal, which has not yet been formally presented or discussed, has been informally greeted with concern by the interested organizations—especially by the employers' associations, which want a stronger role for the unions and seem to prefer softer arrangements that are not legally binding. As an indirect outcome, in December 1993 a national collective agreement on the whole matter was finally, and rather quickly, signed by the three union confederations and the major employers' associations, through which the union protocol agreement of March 1991 on the introduction of the RSU (see above) received substantial legitimation by both parties.

Thus, after a 30-year period of informality since the last collective agreement on the *commissioni interne* in 1966, the workplace representation system is again regulated by collective agreement. On the one side, the devised solution conforms to the practice of recent decades, as the dual nature of the representative bodies has been preserved, as already discussed; but on the other hand, the system appears to be a little less informal and uncertain than in the recent past because of the employer contractual recognition of the representative system and of its functions.

However, this does not necessarily mean that the matter has been settled. On the contrary, new demands for a clearer and more universal arrangement, legally based, which may give better voice to all occupational categories are spreading. And it is very likely that the story will soon continue with a new chapter.

References

Accornero, Aris. 1976. Per una nuova fase di studi sul movimento sindacale. In *Problemi del movimento sindacale in Italia: 1943–1973*, ed. Aris Accornero. Milan: Feltrinelli.

———. 1992. *La parabola del sindacato: Ascesa e declino di una cultura.* Bologna: Mulino.

Antonioli, Maurizio, and Bruno Bezza, eds. 1978. *La Fiom dalle origini al fascismo: 1901–1924.* Bari: De Donato.

Baglioni, Guido, and Rinaldo Milani, eds. 1990. *La contrattazione collettiva nelle aziende industriali in Italia.* Milan: Angeli.

Bagnasco, Arnaldo. 1977. *Tre Italie: La problematica territoriale dello sviluppo italiano.* Bologna: Mulino.

Barbadoro, Isidoro. 1973. *Storia del sindacalismo italiano: Dalla nascita al fascismo.* Florence: La Nuova Italia II.

Bergamaschi, Miriam. 1986. *Statuti dei consigli di fabbrica.* Milan: Angeli.

Bezza, Bruno. 1978. Il sindacato di massa tra riorganizzazione capitalista e fascismo. In *La Fiom dalle origini al fascismo, 1901–1924,* ed. Maurizio Antonioli and Bruno Bezza. Bari: De Donato.

Bonazzi, Giuseppe. 1984. La lotta dei 35 giorni alla Fiat: Un'analisi sociologica. *Politica ed Economia* 15(11): 33–43.

Bordogna, Lorenzo. 1992. Nuove organizzazioni non confederali. In *Gli attori: I sindacati, le associazioni imprenditoriali, lo Stato,* ed. Giuliano Urbani. Turin: Giappichelli.

Confindustria. 1973. *Le rappresentanze dei lavoratori in fabbrica.* Rome: Tip. Failli.

Craveri, Angelo. 1977. *Sindacato e istituzioni nel dopoguerra.* Bologna: Mulino.

Della Rocca, Giuseppe. 1989. I consigli di fabbrica: Vent'anni di dispute con il sindacato italiano. *Prospettiva sindacale* 20(73/74): 54–66.

Gompers, Samuel. 1910. *Labour in Europe and America.* New York and London: Harper.

Mortillaro, Felice. 1984. *Sindacati e no.* Milan: Sole 24 Ore.

———. 1986. *Aspettando il robot.* Milan: Sole24 Ore.

Negrelli, Serafino. 1987. La contrattazione della flessibilità. *Prospettiva sindacale* 18(66): 7–20.

———. 1992. Relazioni industriali e relazioni interne nelle piccole, nelle medie e nelle grandi imprese. In *Le attività: Contrattazione collettiva, consultazione/concertazione, contrattazione politica,* ed. Tiziano Treu. Turin: Giappichelli.

Negrelli, Serafino, and Tiziano Treu, eds. 1992. *Le scelte dell'impresa fra autorità e consenso.* Milan: Angeli.

Perulli, Paolo. 1989. Il distretto industriale di Modena. In *Strategie di riaggiustamento industriale,* ed. Marino Regini and Charles F. Sabel. Bologna: Mulino.

Pizzorno, Alessandro. 1978. Le due logiche dell'azione di classe. In *Lotte operate e sindacato: Il ciclo 1968–1972 in Italia,* ed. Alessandro Pizzorno et al. Bologna: Mulino.

Pizzorno, Alessandro, Emilio Reyneri, Marino Regini, and Ida Regalia. 1978. *Lotte operate e sindacato: Il ciclo 1968–1972 in Italia.* Bologna: Mulino.

Regalia, Ida. 1978. Rappresentanza operaia e sindacato: mutamento di un sistema di relazioni industriali. In *Lotte operaie e sindacato: Il ciclo 1968–1972 in Italia,* ed. Alessandro Pizzorno et al. Bologna: Mulino.

———. 1984. *Eletti e abbandonati: Modelli e stili di rappresentanza in fabbrica.* Bologna: Mulino.

———. 1990. *Al posto del conflitto: Le relazioni di lavoro nel terziario.* Bologna: Mulino.

———. 1992. Le rappresentanze sindacali nei luoghi di lavoro. In *Gli attori: I sindacati, le associazioni imprenditoriali, lo Stato,* ed. Giuliano Urbani. Turin: Giappichelli.

Regalia, Ida, and Rosella Ronchi. 1988–1992. Le relazioni industriali nelle imprese lombarde. Annual Reports. IRES Papers nos. 14, 20, 24, 31, and 34. Milan: Instituto di Ricerche Economiche e Sociale.

Regini, Marino, and Charles Sabel, eds. 1989. *Strategie di riaggiustamento industriale.* Bologna: Mulino.

Romagnoli, Guido. 1976. *Consigli di fabbrica e democrazia sindacale.* Milan: Mazzotta.

Spriano, Paolo. 1971. *L'Ordine Nuovo: E i consigli di fabbrica.* Turin: Einaudi.

Squarzon, Corrado. 1989. I consigli dei delegati vent'anni dopo. *Prospettiva sindacale* 20(73/74): 151–71.

Tarrow, Sydney. 1990. *Democrazia e disordine: Movimenti di protesta e politica in Italia, 1965–1975.* Bari: Laterza.

Treu, Tiziano. 1971. *Sindacato e rappresentanze aziendal.* Bologna: Mulino.

Trigilia, Carlo. 1986. *Grandi partiti e piccole imprese.* Bologna: Mulino.

———. 1989. Il distretto industriale di Prato. In *Strategie di riaggiustamento industriale,* ed. Marino Regini and Charles F. Sabel. Bologna: Mulino.

Turati, Carlo. 1992. Impresa, persone e sindacato: I risultati di una ricerca. In *Le attività: Contrattazione collettiva, consultazione/concertazione, contrattazione politica,* ed. Tiziano Treu. Turin: Giappichelli.

Vais, Marco. 1958. *Le commissioni interne.* Rome: Riuniti.

9   The European Community: Between Mandatory Consultation and Voluntary Information

Wolfgang Streeck and Sigurt Vitols

9.1   Introduction

Attempts to develop legal instruments for workforce participation at the European Community level, either to harmonize national industrial relations systems or to extend participation regimes to multinational companies, go back as far as the early 1970s. The period was one of union strength throughout Europe in the wake of the 1968 and 1969 strike wave, and of ascendancy of social democratic parties in EC member states, most notably in West Germany. Industrial democracy at the workplace and in the enterprise had come to be widely perceived as an indispensable condition for social consensus within a union-inclusive bargained economy, with shared responsibility for full employment at acceptable rates of inflation. Also, expectations for the future of the European Community were generally optimistic, based on a widespread belief in growing market integration more or less inevitably requiring and bringing about political and institutional integration.

One consequence of the rise of social democracy in an increasingly international Europe was the agreement among the EC heads of state and governments at their first summit in October 1972 to endow the European Community with the beginnings of a welfare-state-like social policy. Prominent among the objectives of the so-called Social Action Programme were Europe-wide information, consultation, and co-determination rights for workers at the workplace. In subsequent years the Programme slowly worked its way through the EC legislative machinery, with little success, and even less as time passed. With the change in political climate at the end of the decade, EC social policy was effectively abandoned as European integration ground to a halt. Indeed, it had

Wolfgang Streeck was at the time this was written professor of sociology and industrial relations at the University of Wisconsin-Madison. Sigurt Vitols is a research fellow at the Science Center Berlin for Social Research.

contributed heavily to this event in that it had created strong hostility among business against the European Community, most of all for its attempt to impose legally binding obligations on Europe's powerful multinational corporations to inform and consult with their workforces across national borders.

When in the mid-1980s the Single European Act and the Internal Market project relaunched the integration process, the European Commission tried to attach to it a new, less ambitious version of the Social Action Programme, referred to in EC jargon as the "Social Dimension of the Internal Market." Very little of this, if any, has yet found its way into EC legislation (Streeck 1995). Mandatory workplace representation was again proposed, and again not achieved. With the Maastricht Treaty and its aftermath, the European Community seems less likely than ever to acquire a meaningful capacity for legislation on social matters.

The difficulties for EC action on worker participation are many. To begin with, European employers have always been firmly opposed to any EC social policy that went beyond the proclamation of nonbinding general principles. European legislation on workplace representation in particular was and is unconditionally rejected. It is important to note that this position is shared even by employers, such as the German ones, who in their own countries have long successfully operated under legally instituted participation regimes.

Publicly, European employers never objected to participation per se. As early as the 1970s, European business associations argued that worker participation was part and parcel of good management and was already being widely practiced on a voluntary basis. Rather than imposing it by legislation, the European Community was urged to let participation grow on its own, arranged spontaneously and voluntarily at the local level between managements and their workforces in line with the specific and diverse business conditions and organizational traditions of individual workplaces. This insistence on voluntarism has remained nonnegotiable up to the present: having no interest in EC social policy other than in preventing it, European employers never had to consider accepting formal participation rights in exchange for union or EC concessions on demands of their own.

European unions, in turn, have a history of unsuccessful attempts to bargain with multinational companies through international company committees and sectoral union federations (Levinson 1972; Northrup and Rowan 1979; Grahl and Teague 1991). In the early 1970s, they had come to regard EC legislation on worker participation as welcome and, indeed, indispensable assistance for their international organizing activities, in that it promised to force multinational companies to enter into at least some kind of industrial relations at the European level. Getting such legislation enacted was, however, a different matter. EC political institutions are structured in such a way that interests in affirmative supranational government lack suitable points of access to its decision-making machinery. For example, EC legislation is passed, not by an elected parliament, but by the Council of Ministers in which each member state has one vote and which on important issues decides only by unanimous vote.

Producing what is in effect domestic legislation through international diplomacy and intergovernmental negotiations is awkward, not only because normally one member government is enough to prevent proposals being enacted. In addition, partly reflecting the European Community's lack of a responsive political system and partly prolonging it, unions suffer from endemically weak organization at the European level, their organizational base having always been and remaining the various national industrial relations systems. It is true that, to some extent, the same conditions affect organized business. The difference is, however, that while labor has a positive interest in European social policy, business has only a negative one. As a consequence, institutional weakness and deadlock at the EC level, while a liability for labor, is an asset for business. Where the institutional cards are stacked toward nondecisions, interests that require decisions are likely to suffer defeat regardless of effort, while interests served by nondecisions can often expect to prevail even though or precisely because they are unwilling or unable to play.

National governments, for their part, came to find European-level workforce participation more and more intractable. Initially, in the years after the strike wave, there seems to have been wide tacit acceptance of a need to harmonize national participation arrangements along the lines of the "German model," which was generally regarded as the most advanced way of achieving labor peace. Subsequently, however, more traditional concerns again became dominant, in particular the preservation of the sovereignty of member states and the integrity of national industrial relations systems, including the role of national governments in mediating the balance of power between capital and labor. Harmonization of national systems through a transfer of legislative authority to the Community thus lost its political appeal.

This left the possibility of supranational legislation applying only to multinational companies. Just as by EC-wide harmonization, the integrity of national industrial relations systems may also be impaired by large firms using their multinational organization to evade national obligations, not least workforce information and consultation requirements. Provided it can be confined to transnational actors that have grown beyond the reach of national systems and threaten to upset the balance of these systems from the outside, supranational regulation, rather than undermining national control, may in fact help restore it, making supranationalism potentially acceptable even and precisely to sovereignty-conscious nation-states.

Increasingly, however, national governments also responded to the decline since the late 1970s of union power and worker militancy and to growing business pressures for restoration of managerial prerogative. The election of a Conservative government in Britain in 1979 provided business interests and their political allies throughout Europe with energetic leadership and vastly reduced the prospects of legislative initiatives on worker participation at the EC level. Also, the emerging new domestic agendas in member states after the end of the social democratic decade found the Community's lack of a supranational domestic policy fortuitously congenial. Bent on deploying the sovereignty of the nation-state to increase that of managements and "market forces," European governments began to perceive the absence of supranational regulation not as a threat to the stability of national regulation but as helpful for the achievement of national objectives of deregulation—including more "flexibility," "decentralization," and an expanded space for "voluntary" instead of mandated cooperation between capital and labor.

A prominent topic in the European debates of the 1980s and 1990s on worker participation was the diversity of national industrial relations systems within the European Community. British accession to membership in 1976 vastly added to that diversity, but other factors worked in the same direction (Streeck 1992). Short of harmonization of national systems—which itself must become more difficult as national differences increase—growing diversity magnifies the technical problems of designing supranational regimes for transnational actors that fit equally well with all constituent national systems without causing unanticipated changes in them. For example, while mandatory European works councils for multinational companies with rights to co-determination would fit the German system, they may not sit equally well with existing Italian institutions. Not only would they favor German over Italian worker representatives serving on the same multinational works councils, but they would also strengthen forces in Italy, among employers or unions, that would like to move the Italian system closer to the German system. Especially if motivated by a desire to restore the integrity of national regimes, Europe-wide participation statutes for multinational companies must be drafted so as to be simultaneously meaningful for workforces and neutral with respect to the national systems in which companies operate—a task the Commission found increasingly vexing.

As the 1970s passed, the preservation of the diversity of national industrial relations systems slowly achieved the status of a normative objective in its own right. This extended well into the ranks of supporters of EC social policy legislation, qualifying and complicating their position and limiting their mobilizing capacity at critical moments. National diversity was first invoked as a value by the Left as European unions became uneasy about the emerging hegemony of the "German model," both in draft EC legislation and in the internal politics of European union confederations. The relative success at home of the German system in the difficult 1980s, especially from a union perspective, did little to defuse the resistance, which presented itself as deeply committed to nationally distinctive ideas of solidarity and union democracy; to different concepts of the political and economic responsibilities of unions, the role of employers, and the proper relationship between capital and labor; and to alternative views of the state and of the need for unions to remain independent from it. While the ideological debates about such issues as these have receded in recent years, the tendency of European unions to defend their national institutions against supranational interference, including institutions that would seem to have worked comparatively less well for them, appears as strong today as ever.

Institutional nationalism among nationally organized unions is not necessarily irrational, even in an increasingly international economy. Opportunities for political influence at the EC level are untested and weak at best, and developing them requires time and risky investment of scarce political and organizational capital. By comparison, European unions are well established in their respective national welfare states, which they have helped build and together with which they have grown. Externally caused institutional change in national systems is bound to upset the standard operating procedures and vested interests of large numbers of organizations and officials. Reluctance to take this lightly does not preclude recognition of the need for a supranational response to economic externalities that threaten the integrity of national systems as much as, and in the long term more than, institutional externalities. Organizing such a response, however, raises severe collective action problems that are exacerbated by inevitable uncertainty about the costs and benefits of supranationalism for national actors, with respect to both the domestic power balance and the distribution of influence in the new supranational institutions. The result is unstable, oscillating preferences and weak commitments, with unity among national union movements at the European level inversely related to the probability of proposals being passed into law.

The internal inconsistencies in the position of European unions on workplace participation did not escape the attention of the employers, who were often able to show that legislative initiatives had only shallow union support. Early on, European employers, with the full cooperation of their German colleagues, joined European unions in the struggle against the German model identified with any strongly normative European-level legislation on workplace representation. Later employers pledged themselves, just as to voluntarism, decentralization, and local democracy, to Europe-wide preservation of institutional and cultural diversity—in the act championing previously deplored practices like workplace bargaining, state abstention from industrial relations, and multiunionism as "historically grown" elements of "national culture" worth preserving for their own sake, and offering unions coalitions at the national level to defend national institutions against supranational meddling. It is remarkable that such cultural conservationism went together with another, quite different justification for opposition to supranational regulation: that "market forces" should be left free to weed out the less economically competitive national regimes and bring about Europe-wide convergence to market-driven "best practice."

During the 1980s domestic policy making in the Community came under the control of an ever more self-confident *coalition between nationalism and neoliberalism*. For a time, the alliance between the two was personified by Margaret Thatcher and her vigorous simultaneous defense of British national sovereignty against "French multinational bureaucrats," and of the "free market" against "socialism" creeping in through the Brussels back door. But in fact this was far more than a personal or national idiosyncrasy. In the constellation of decision procedures and policy areas that defined the relaunched integration process, and in the interaction between national politics, international relations, and economic interests inside the developing EC polity, defending a country's sovereignty in the councils of Europe and defending the freedom of "market forces" in the integrated European economy had come to be *one and the same thing*—inextricably intertwining the objectives of liberal nonregulation of the integrated economy and of nationalist defense of state sovereignty, and allowing opponents of an interventionist EC social policy freely and opportunistically to switch from a nationalist to a neoliberal frame of reference and back, in support of identical substantive demands.

With the failure of the Maastricht Treaty to unseat the dominant EC coalition, the second defeat of Europe-wide legislation on workplace participation seems a foregone conclusion. The next section of this paper traces the various attempts of the Community to create mandatory workplace rights for workers and discusses their present status. The paper then looks at the proliferation of voluntarily instituted European works councils in some multinational firms in the late 1980s and early 1990s, at the time when the battle over the "social dimension" was under way. While voluntary councils are sometimes regarded as intermediate steps toward mandatory councils in EC law, it is argued here that what one sees in Europe today may in fact be what one gets: an uneven pattern of weak and unilaterally withdrawable company-specific participation regimes growing in the empty spaces between competing national and supranational jurisdictions.

9.2   EC Legislation on Workforce Participation in European Firms

Beginning in the early 1970s, the Commission of the European Community took a number of legislative initiatives on legal participation rights for workers in European firms. Emerging from different policy contexts and based on a variety of articles of the Treaty of Rome—the de facto EC constitution—none of these were successful. Works councils or similar arrangements figured in some proposals but not in all.

Workforce participation became a concern for the European Community in three contexts: (1) the "harmonization" of national systems of company law, (2) the development of supranational, "European" company law, and (3) the creation of legal rights for workers vis-à-vis management to information and consultation.[1]

1. In the 1970s the European Community regarded differences in national systems of company law as "restrictive conditions on the freedom of establishment within the Community" (article 54 of the Treaty of Rome), deriving from this a mandate to pursue "approximation and harmonization" of such systems. The classical EC instrument for harmonization is a "directive," which once

1. The following draws in particular on various editions of the *European Industrial Relations Report (EIRR)*, especially no. 207 (April 1991): 23–27; Addison and Siebert (1991); Hall (1992).

enacted obliges member countries to rewrite their laws in accordance with it. In pursuit of harmonization, the Commission drafted a number of directives on company law, one of which—the famous "Fifth Directive"—deals with the governance structure of public limited-liability companies. The original draft was issued in 1972. Inspired by the then Social-Liberal German government, which was preparing legislation to strengthen company-level co-determination in Germany, the draft proposed to prescribe a two-tier board system with an obligatory supervisory board that would include employee representatives.

The 1972 draft directive never got close to enactment. In 1983 the Commission presented a revised version, which raised the minimum size for companies falling under the statute from 500 to 1,000 employees. More important, it offered firms and national legislators a choice among four alternative models of workforce participation in company governance: (1) the two-tier board system of the first draft, with one-third or one-half of supervisory board members coming from among the workforce, (2) a single board with employee representatives as nonexecutive members, (3) a company-level representative body of employees only (something akin to a works council without, however, being so called), and (4) any other participation structure provided it was collectively agreed upon between employer and workforce. The draft tried to ensure that access to information and rights to consultation and co-determination were the same regardless of what model was selected.

2. In addition to harmonizing national company law, the Commission also proposed to create a European Company Statute. Firms would be given the option to incorporate under that statute, as an alternative to incorporation in national company law. A firm incorporated as a "European company," or *Societas Europea,* would have the advantage of being ipso facto considered incorporated in all EC countries, making it unnecessary for it to seek incorporation in different national legal systems. The first draft of the statute was presented in 1975 and required European companies to have a supervisory board that included employee representatives with full rights to information and co-determination, as well as a European works council. This combination of company- and workplace-level co-determination was the closest the European Community came to a wholesale adoption of the German model.

Like the Fifth Directive, the European Company Statute got stuck in the legislative process, and in 1989 a revised draft was presented. The major change was that the draft dropped the German dualism of supervisory board and works council representation and instead offered firms the same menu of alternative arrangements as the 1983 revision of the Fifth Directive. Concerning the rights of worker representatives, while the 1975 draft had emphasized co-management and co-determination, especially via the supervisory board, the 1989 version emphasized information and consultation, again moving closer to the Fifth Directive in its revised form.

3. It was only relatively late that workforce participation came to be dealt with as a matter of labor law in a narrow sense, in competition with EC initia-

tives on company law or, more precisely, in response to their lack of progress. In 1980 the then commissioner for social affairs, Henk Vredeling, issued a broadly written draft directive on information and consultation rights for workforces, which came to be known as the "Vredeling directive." The initiative drew on article 100 of the Treaty of Rome, which requires "approximation" and "harmonization" of legal provisions in member states "as directly affect the establishment or functioning of the common market." Politically, it tried to follow up on two directives that had recently been passed under the Social Action Programme, the Collective Redundancies Directive of 1977 and the Transfer of Undertakings Directive of 1979. Both provided for workforce information and consultation in connection with the specific events they addressed (Addison and Siebert 1991). The Vredeling directive can be seen as an attempt to extend the information and consultation rights enacted for firms undergoing economic restructuring to firms in all economic circumstances— thereby bypassing the legislative deadlock on company law and bringing workforce participation within the ambit of EC social policy proper.

The 1980 Vredeling draft was largely agnostic on structural matters. While it specified in great detail a wide range of *information* on financial, economic, and employment issues to which workforces were to be regularly entitled, and in addition established legal *consultation* rights on any decision likely to have "serious consequences" for employee interests, it followed the example of the Collective Redundancies and Transfer of Undertakings directives by assigning the exercise of the new rights to "existing employee representatives by law or practice." Another defining feature of the draft was that it focused on companies with subsidiaries, and on the access of workforces in branch plants to information held by management at headquarters—and perhaps strategically withheld from local management. In fact, the draft's main thrust was to make it impossible for local management to excuse itself from obligations to inform and consult on the grounds of centralization of information and decision making in the parent company or at company headquarters.

In trying to create legal obligations for firms relative to their workforces in subsidiary plants, the draft directive simultaneously addressed three situations: where both headquarters and subsidiary are located in the same EC country, where the headquarters is based in a different EC country than the subsidiary, and where it is located outside the European Community. While the first situation is relatively easily covered by national legislation (although the directive would have constructed a "harmonizing" common floor for all national systems), the second suggests itself as a classic case for supranational regulation of transnational relations and externalities, given that the law of the country with the subsidiary is likely to find it difficult to govern the behavior of a headquarters located on foreign territory. The third situation also raises the question of exterritoriality, but in the relation between the European Community and third countries.

The draft Vredeling directive met with unprecedented hostility from business, European and extra-European (DeVos 1989). In part, this may have been because of the high specificity of the information and consultation rights stipulated by the draft. Nonetheless, it is hard to see how the substance of the directive justified the fierce battle that ensued. Very likely, that battle was more over the Social Action Programme as a whole and over the European Community's continued, somewhat time-lagged pursuit of a social democratic agenda, in spite of the accession to power of conservative governments in Germany and Britain and the rising themes of supply-side economics and "Eurosclerosis." It is also possible that business was so profoundly disturbed by the prospect of European labor law acquiring the capacity to regulate the internal affairs of multinational corporations that it felt the threat must be disposed of once and for all. In any case, although the Commission in 1983 watered down its draft significantly—by limiting its jurisdiction to firms with at least 1,000 employees and reducing the range and frequency of the information to which workforces would be entitled—it was unable to save its proposal. Under heavy fire from business and with a British veto certain, the Council of Ministers declined in 1983 to vote on the revised directive and has since failed to take the matter up again.

The defeat of Vredeling marked the end of the Social Action Programme, and indeed of the attempts of the 1970s to endow the European Community with a welfare-state-like social policy. It also documented the exasperation of business with the post-1970s European Community, as well as its new clout in EC politics. When after years of stagnation European integration was relaunched in the mid-1980s, the designated vehicle for this was the Single Market program with its deregulatory thrust. It was only several years later that the Commission returned to social policy in its attempt to add a social dimension to the increasingly integrated European economy. In this context, workforce participation reappeared on the European Community's legislative agenda.

After long preparation, the Commission in 1990 issued a draft Directive on European Works Councils, as a successor or substitute for the Vredeling directive.[2] Like the latter, the 1990 draft is about workforce information and consultation rights, it originated in the Social Affairs directorate, and it invokes article 100 of the Treaty of Rome. It also contains essentially the same rights for workers as the second, weakened version of Vredeling (*EIRR*, no. 207 [April 1991]: 27). However, unlike Vredeling the new directive specifies a structural arrangement, "European works councils," in which workforce information and consultation rights are to be vested.[3] Also, while Vredeling made specified information and consultation arrangements obligatory for firms be-

2. Indeed, the new draft was often referred to in Brussels jargon as the "son of Vredeling." The text can be found in *EIRR*, no. 206 (March 1991): 29–32.
3. But it also gives management and labor at the company level the choice to set up alternative structures by collective bargaining.

yond a certain size, the new draft requires that workers, unions, or management take the initiative in order for a European works council or an equivalent mechanism to come into being; at least in principle, this leaves the possibility of consensual nonapplication of the law.[4] And finally, the 1990 draft is to apply only to "undertakings or groups of undertakings" that have at least 1,000 employees *and* are significantly present, with establishments or group of undertakings employing 100 workers or more, in at least two EC countries.[5]

Works councils, then, have appeared in a number of Commission drafts on workforce participation: as an alternative to board-level representation in the 1983 draft of the Fifth Directive, as a supplement to it in the 1975 draft of the European Company Statute, and again as an alternative in its 1989 version. The presently pending European Works Councils Directive differs from all of these in that, among other things, the works councils it proposes are to exercise information and consultation rights only; are to be formed exclusively at the headquarters of multinational companies; and unlike, for example, the proposed European Company Statute, are not to be elected through a common procedure, but are to consist of delegates from local plants elected by local workforce representatives or workforces in accordance with national law and practice.[6]

9.3   Politics of the 1990 Draft Directive

The draft European Works Councils Directive of 1990 was an attempt to steer clear of the political conflicts and dilemmas that had destroyed Vredeling and stalled the progress of European company law. Particular care was taken to accommodate the desire of national governments and union movements, to protect the integrity and diversity of national industrial relations systems, and to preempt employer complaints about supranational regulations failing to take into account "the variety of information and consultation procedures evolved by companies to suit their particular circumstances" (Hall 1992, 9; see also Tyszkiewicz 1992).

1. While the first European proposals for legislation on workforce participation covered *all firms* above a certain size, the Vredeling draft applied only to *firms with subsidiaries*. However, although its language included both national

4. The requirements for triggering the creation of a European works council or some other information and consultation mechanism are, however, easy to fulfill.

5. According to Sisson et al. (1992), the directive would affect about 880 EC-based firms with a total of 13.5 million employees, and large parts of an additional 280 multinational companies based outside the European Community. Of the EC-based firms, 332 are British, and about one-half of the non-EC companies have a significant British presence. This helps explain the British government's prominent role in the resistance to the legislation.

6. It is not clear, and has hardly been discussed, how the proposed European works councils would fit into the workforce participation provisions of the Fifth Directive and the European Company Statute, and especially how the menus of options the revised drafts are offering will.

and multinational firms, its principal targets were *multinational companies* with their ability to use the exterritoriality of their headquarters to avoid legal obligations in the host countries of their subsidiaries. During the legislative process the Commission proposed to confine the directive to multinational companies only, in an attempt to divide the opposition from business (DeVos 1989). This was countered by the claim that exempting national firms would place a disincentive on internationalization. The 1990 draft disregards this point at its own peril, probably to placate national governments by keeping interference with national industrial relations at a minimum and limiting itself to the management of externalities and transnational relations.

The new draft also remains exposed to objections from non-European multinational companies, especially American and Japanese, that it proposes to make law with exterritorial applicability outside the European Community. At the bottom of this is, again, a problem of competition. To avoid giving non-European multinationals an advantage over European multinationals, the Vredeling directive tried to subject the former to the same obligations vis-à-vis their European subsidiary workforces as the latter. Lacking better means, Vredeling proposed legally to designate a non-European company's largest plant in the European Community as its headquarters for the purposes of compliance with European information and consultation requirements. In addition to forceful opposition from the American Chamber of Commerce in Brussels and a legion of American business lobbyists, this caused diplomatic interventions by the United States and Japan against what was claimed to be an attempt to extend European law to American and Japanese corporate citizens operating in their home countries. It has been argued that this contributed heavily to Vredeling's defeat (DeVos 1989). The present, successor draft takes the same approach to exterritoriality and is therefore likely to generate the same opposition. Excluding non-European multinationals from its ambit offers no solution, however, as it would again raise the issue of fair competition.

2. Under both the Fifth Directive and Vredeling, participation provisions were to be *obligatory* for all firms that fell under the proposed legislation. This is different for the European Company Statute, in that incorporation under European law was always intended to be the voluntary decision of the individual firm. In this sense, the participation provisions under European company law are *optional*. The draft directive of 1990 makes having a European works council, or an alternative information and consultation arrangement, a little less than fully obligatory by requiring triggering activities that must originate inside the company.

3. The first proposals on workforce participation were highly *prescriptive* in that they laid down detailed legal rules that firms were required to follow. Later versions, beginning with the second draft of the Fifth Directive in 1983, offered firms a *menu* of alternative rules and structures among which they were to be free to choose. The 1990 European Works Councils Directive also takes this approach by giving firms the option of selecting alternative mechanisms

for information and consultation, to the extent that they fulfill certain minimum requirements. Like the triggering procedure, this responds to business demands for "flexibility." But it also accommodates reservations among European unions about works councils, whether politically or nationally motivated, and allows national unions without a works council tradition to seek more expedient arrangements with European multinationals based in their countries.

4. While originally EC legislation sought *direct legal regulation* of workforce participation rights and structures, the 1983 draft of the Fifth Directive was the first to include a *collective bargaining option* allowing firms and unions to negotiate their own solutions.[7] This approach was always popular with unions less comfortable than, in particular, German unions with legislated, as distinguished from bargained, rights. The draft European Works Councils Directive assigns bargaining a prominent role in three respects: the triggering of works council formation, the determination of the representative structure that is to exercise workforce information and consultation rights, and the exact definition of those rights. By empowering collective bargaining in this way, the draft directive dissociates itself from a "second-channel" concept of industrial democracy and abandons previous ambitions to reform national industrial relations systems into this mold.

5. Much of EC legislation, proposed or enacted, tried to promote *harmonization* of rules and procedures across countries. The Vredeling directive was partly an exception to this in that it gave (albeit "harmonized") information and consultation rights to a *variety* of national mechanisms of workforce representation. Its 1990 successor diverges even further from harmonization.[8] While it suggests building a unified representative structure at multinational headquarters—the European works council—council members are to be selected according to very different national practices. Moreover, the limitation of the draft to multinationals, leaving national firms untouched; the—remote—possibility of having no information and consultation system at all; the menu character of the directive; the strong role for collective bargaining, making it possible for almost anything in the directive to be rewritten; and the draft's unquestioning acceptance of the legitimacy of existing national representation arrangements together amount to a strong endorsement of national and company variety and document the extreme reluctance on the part of the European Community to interfere with existing arrangements.[9]

---

7. Analytically, this is different from a menu-type directive that offers a set of alternatives for firms to select from.

8. In this it concurs with the second draft of the European Company Statute, which, while offering firms a menu of choices, also allows countries to limit those choices by national law to two or just one of the models in the directive. Countries may in this way preserve "national diversity" by shielding "their" firms from potentially uncomfortable forms of co-determination or by insulating established national practices from external, supranational pressures for change (Hepple 1990, 313).

9. "Indeed the approach adopted is essentially the *mutual recognition* of the different national systems of employee representation as the appropriate channels for the nomination of members of the European Works Council" (Hall 1992, 8).

The Commission's new strategy in drafting the 1990 directive was only partly successful. More than its predecessors, the draft managed to reassure unions outside Germany that it was not another attempt to export the German model to the rest of the European Community. Moreover, it spared European union confederations the embarrassment of having to choose between nationally and ideologically sacrosanct principles like union-based and second-channel forms of workplace representation, legally mandated co-determination and voluntary collective bargaining, and bargaining at the company and sectoral levels. But while unions remained united behind the proposal, employers continued to be adamantly opposed, insisting that information and consultation in multinational European firms can come about only case by case and voluntarily.[10] Governments, for their part, never even discussed the draft in the Council, neither before the Maastricht Treaty when passage would still have required unanimity and a British veto was certain, nor in the two turbulent years after.

9.4 Defeat of the Social Dimension

The move from harmonization to accommodation of diversity, and from prescriptive to "flexible" forms of legislation, is also visible in the evolution of the other proposals on workplace representation and corresponds to a general change in the late 1980s in the EC approach to social policy that we have elsewhere described as "neovoluntarism" (Streeck 1992, 1995): an emerging commitment to a decentralized regulatory regime with a preference for "soft" over "hard" law, and "private" over "public" order, operating under a "variable geometry" of participants that are protected from central intervention by ample opportunities for "opting out," as well as by a general presumption of precedence of both local traditions and market forces over universal normative regulation.

The ideological underpinning for neovoluntarism was provided by a laissez-faire reinterpretation of the social Catholic principle of "subsidiarity." Initially, subsidiarity was introduced by the embattled Commission in its desperate search for a formula for a mutually acceptable division of powers between the European Community and its member states. Like its original, the EC version asserts the priority of "self-regulation" by "smaller social units" at "lower levels" of political organization and civil society. But traditionally, subsidiarity also implied a capacity, and indeed an obligation, for the central state to ensure that the outcomes of self-regulation were compatible with general norms of social justice. Typically, this involved public "subsidies" to weaker social groups, often in the form of legal and institutional support to enable them to look after their own affairs or to assert themselves in relation to better-endowed

---

10. A concise summary of the position of UNICE, the European peak association of employers, is given in *EIRR*, no. 207 (April 1991): 27, to the effect that allegedly the draft "takes no account of national legislation, employers' authority, the autonomy of the 'social partners,' and economic necessities."

adversaries. This, in turn, required a state strong enough not to have to take the existing distribution of power and collective action capacity in civil society for granted, and capable of reconstituting private autonomy as a devolved mandate for socially balanced and responsible self-governance.

The defeat of the Commission's federalist welfare-state-building project was reflected in a gradual reinterpretation of subsidiarity in EC discourse. Step by step, subsidiarity came to mean simply that nothing should be regulated by the European Community that could "as well or better" be regulated at lower levels of governance. But what is better or as good may depend entirely on one's interests and objectives. Reduced to a technical formula empty of normative content, subsidiarity was increasingly invoked by the Commission's opponents in their effort to obstruct the development of supranational state capacity as a formula for legitimating whatever either nation-states or the empirical distribution of market power had decided, not decided, or decided not to decide. In this way, subsidiarity turned into yet another version of liberalism.

It was in the early 1990s, before and after the signing of the Maastricht Treaty, that the harsh political realities reflected by the European Community's new subsidiarity formula became visible. In principle, the treaty should have made passage of worker participation legislation easier. The Single European Act of 1986 had introduced "qualified majority voting" among member states on the Council for measures "which have as their object the establishment and functioning of the Internal Market" (article 100a). However, "the rights and interests of employed persons" were excepted from this and could, as before, be decided only unanimously. The exception here, in turn, was "improvements, especially in the working environment, as regards the health and safety of workers" (article 118a), which came under qualified majority voting. In 1990, the Commission rejected suggestions to introduce the European Works Councils Directive as a health and safety measure, or to base it on article 100a on the grounds that information and consultation rights affected competition in the Internal Market (Hall 1992). Passage of the draft at the time of its presentation therefore required unanimity of the Council.

There was, however, hope that this would soon change. The intergovernmental conferences that eventually produced the Maastricht Treaty were expected to agree on a package of institutional reforms that would significantly enhance the political capacities of the European Community. In the social policy area, the Commission's central proposal was to extend qualified majority voting to a range of subjects beyond health and safety, thereby improving the chances of social dimension proposals, including workplace representation, being passed into law.

As it turned out, qualified majority voting could be made to apply only among 11 of the 12 member states, with Britain gaining permission from the others to dissociate itself from EC social policy entirely. Substantively, the social policy agreement signed by the Eleven amended the Treaty of Rome to extend qualified majority voting to five subjects, including "information and consultation of workers." Another category of issues, however, among them "representation and collective defense of the interests of workers, including co-determination," continued to require unanimous decisions, if only among the Eleven. While Britain can no longer prevent the other countries from acting on them, any one of the others can, if willing to play the "British" part.[11]

Treaty ratification came only at the price of additional formal commitments to laissez-faire subsidiarity. Even apart from these, the treaty as signed made it anything but easy for meaningful social policy legislation to be passed, even among the new "social policy community" of the Eleven. The British "opt-out" raises a host of technical and "constitutional" questions that are so forbiddingly complex that they will likely stall any nontrivial legislative initiative. Not only will the jurisdiction of the European Court of Justice over social policy legislation passed by the Eleven be challenged. More important, to the extent that the Eleven may try to impose participation regimes on firms in their countries, these may appeal to the Court or the Commission against what could be construed as a competitive disadvantage against British firms, as these would remain unaffected while continuing to enjoy unlimited market access throughout the European Community. In particular, if the Eleven were to pass a works councils directive, British multinationals, while in all other respects corporate European citizens, would technically have to be treated as exterritorial in the same way as American or Japanese multinationals—which would re-create inside the European Community the same problems that helped defeat the first Vredeling proposal.[12]

Various observers have expressed the expectation that the "co-decision procedure" instituted by the Maastricht Treaty may make EC legislation on workforce participation easier to achieve. Under the Protocol on Social Policy, EC legislative powers on social policy matters, again only for the Eleven, may be jointly exercised by the European peak associations of business and labor, allowing in principle for a corporatist devolution of law making to organized social groups (Streeck 1994). It is hard to see, however, why European employers, having successfully prevented passage of a works councils directive in the Council, should agree to it being passed through tripartite bargaining. Usually,

11. Company law, such as the Fifth Directive or the European Company Statute, remains entirely outside the scope of the Protocol on Social Policy and thus continues to be subject to unanimity among all 12 EC members.

12. Like American firms, firms with headquarters in Britain that did not want to have a multinational works council or to comply with information and consultation obligations could refuse to obey "foreign" law and ask their government to protect them, and itself, from intrusion by a foreign government. To avoid writing unenforceable and technically illegal law for "foreign" citizens acting in "foreign" countries—i.e., multinationals based and incorporated in Britain—the Eleven would have to designate the largest subsidiary of a British multinational in the Eleven countries as its "headquarters" liable under "Eleven" law. As has been noted above, this problem is far from trivial given the large number of British or British-based firms potentially affected by the draft directive.

constructive participation of employers in corporatist political exchange, far from being a substitute for union strength or interventionist state capacities, presupposes at least one of the two, so employers can accept negotiated settlements as a "lesser evil" compared to industrial conflict or direct state intervention. Where, as in the European Community, both unions and state capacities are weak, institutionalized functional representation is much more likely to be used by employers to prevent regulation—which is exactly what UNICE has announced it will do with its newly formalized participation rights.[13]

Faced with protracted employer opposition, the Commission may ultimately give in and refrain from formal legislation once again. This would certainly not be a break with the trend of the past decade. Quite to the contrary, full adoption of a voluntaristic approach would be in line with the long-term evolution of EC social policy, as signified especially by the nonbinding status of the "Social Charter" and the successive rewriting of proposed participation legislation to conform to an ever more liberally interpreted "subsidiarity" principle. Ultimately, unmitigated reliance on voluntarism would probably be no more than a realistic recognition by the European Community of its vanishing prospects of ever acquiring the capacity to impose binding social obligations on Europe's most powerful corporate citizens, or to assist a nationally fragmented European civil society in organizing a collective response to the spread of transnational markets and organizations.

9.5   Rise of Voluntarism: "European Works Councils" in Multinational Firms

Since the mid-1980s a number of European multinationals and their workforces have agreed to set up supranational workforce information and consultation arrangements, usually referred to as "European works councils." By the end of 1991, 18 of the 100 largest European multinationals in manufacturing had either established a European works council or were planning to do so in

---

13. After an initial discussion, the Council of Ministers in the fall of 1993 forwarded the draft directive, with minor changes, to the social partners under the co-decision procedure. Hopes are being expressed that the procedure will conclude in the winter of 1994, when under the German presidency there might be an opportunity for council legislation to be passed. Considerable caution is advised, however. This will be the first time the procedure will be used, and since there is as yet no agreement on how it is to operate, all sides will be anxious not to create unfavorable precedents. More important, UNICE insists that deliberations among the social partners must start from a tabula rasa and must not be limited to the Commission draft, as amended by the Council; the unions, to the contrary, want a swift discussion after which the draft is to be returned to the Council. In particular, they reject the view of the employers that the procedure amounts to a mandate to find a "negotiated" solution. Substantively, UNICE offers to accept a works councils directive on the condition that it provides for negotiated solutions on a company-by-company basis, without a statutory fallback option in case no agreement can be reached. In practice, this would make European works councils depend entirely on employer discretion. (Footnote added at the time of the final revision of this manuscript in January 1994.)

the near future.[14] Two companies had two councils each,[15] making for a total of 20 European works councils.

The morphology of the 20 European works councils that were established by 1991[16] reflects their voluntary character and the absence of normative legislation. Voluntary European works councils are highly diverse in their organizational structures; their diversity reflects national differences; at the same time, they all have in common that as European-level bodies, they are union based and terminable at will by either side; and they are strictly limited in their functions, especially with respect to their capacity to interfere with managerial prerogative.

1. Only 8 of the 20 councils rest on a formal agreement between management and labor. In four companies, council operation is based on informal verbal understandings; in another two, meetings are organized and worker representatives invited at management initiative. A number of councils include management, and some are chaired by employer representatives, while the others are worker-only bodies. On 11 councils, workers are represented exclusively by company employees; 2 others consist entirely of full-time union officials; the rest include both (table 9.1).

Diversity extends also to the selection of council members. In two firms, each union organizing workers at a national subsidiary is given one seat. In other cases, seats are allocated to countries according to their percentage in the company's workforce, with delegate selection governed by national practice; if there is multiunionism in a country, the national quota is divided up in proportion to unions' relative strength. There are no simultaneous, companywide,

14. The data used for this study is based on a survey of the experience with European works councils of the 100 largest multinational manufacturing companies in Europe. This makes the present study the one with the highest number of cases under investigation. Other studies include Northrup, Slowinski, and Campbell (1988), which covers three companies; Gold and Hall (1992), which reports on 11 companies with 13 councils; European Trade Union Institute (1991), which looks at 13 councils at 12 companies; and Myrvang (1991), which is concerned only with Scandinavian firms.

15. Two European works council-type bodies went into operation at Thomson in 1986, one involving unions affiliated to the European Metalworkers' Federation (EMF), the other involving employees chosen to represent the different national workforces. Under a recent agreement the two councils will be merged in 1993. BSN set up a European Consultation Committee for its food and drink division in 1987, and a European Information Committee for its glass division in 1990.

16. Information on the companies and on existing or planned European works councils was gathered through a mailed questionnaire. Supplementary data was drawn from reports in the business and industrial relations press, from companies' annual reports, and from previous studies. Particularly useful sources were the studies by Myrvang (1991) and by Gold and Hall (1992). Northrup and Rowan (1979) provided information on international union activities in 39 of the 100 firms during the 1960s and 1970s. In addition, a small number of interviews were conducted with representatives of both labor and industry. (For a description of the method used in selecting firms and respondents, see appendixes A and B). The sample includes a number of companies based in the United States, Sweden, and Switzerland in addition to those based in EC countries. These companies were included because they are large employers within the European Community and would be subject to European works council legislation.

Table 9.1   Composition of European Works Council (EWC) Delegations

Type of Delegation	Number of EWCs
Union officials	2
Employee representatives	11
Union officials and employee representatives	5
Management invitation	2
Total	20

direct elections of European works councils; as a result, members of the same council may have different terms of office and are likely to have been selected in very different ways.

2. Many of the differences between European works councils are related to their companies' country of origin. The very existence of European works councils seems conditioned by a company's national industrial relations system. Of the 18 companies in our sample that have European works councils, no fewer than 17 have their headquarters in countries with some kind of works council or industrial democracy legislation: 6 in France, 5 in Germany, and 4 in Sweden (table 9.2).[17] And while U.S.- or U.K.-based companies make up 41 percent of the sample and include some of the largest European multinationals, none of them have a European works council.

National origin is also reflected in the institutional structure of European works councils. In three of the four Swedish-based multinationals, works councils are essentially meeting sites for shop stewards and union workplace officials, with part of the meetings devoted to a presentation by management on the company's economic situation.[18] This arrangement is in keeping with the union-based construction of workplace representation in Sweden. Similarly, at French companies councils are joint management-labor committees, while at German multinationals they are made up solely of workforce representatives, again mirroring national industrial relations systems.

Furthermore, national factors influence the degree to which multinational information and consultation arrangements are formalized. At least five of the

17. The remaining company is Nestlé, which is based in Switzerland. Nestlé is said, however, to enjoy a close relationship with the French state and French banks, as illustrated by the recent Perrier takeover. It is also reported that the European works council at Nestlé originated in an agreement between the German food workers' union (Gewerkschaft Nahrung-Genuß-Gaststätten) and the president of Nestlé Europe (Gold and Hall 1992, 22).

18. In one case, the council is de facto a world union council organized by the International Metalworkers' Federation. The fourth Swedish-based company has what could be called a second Swedish variant of European works councils, which includes representatives of the white- and blue-collar union federations from each of the Scandinavian countries in which the company has operations. This version, which involves the direct appointment of a limited number of union representatives, first appeared at a small company outside our sample in 1989; Scandinavian unions have seen the case as a precedent for spreading union involvement at the multinational group level throughout Scandinavia (Simonson 1991).

Table 9.2   **Home Countries of Multinational Companies (MNCs) in the Sample**

Country	Number of MNCs with EWCs	Number of MNCs in Sample	MNCs with EWCs (%)
France	7	16	44
Germany	6	22	27
Sweden	4	6	67
Switzerland	1	6	17
United Kingdom	0	29	–
United States	0	12	–
Netherlands	0	4	–
Italy	0	2	–
Belgium	0	2	–
Luxembourg	0	1	–
Total	18	100	18

six German councils have been or will be established under a formal agreement signed by the two sides or by a supervisory board resolution.[19] The European works council at Bayer has been set up under an agreement negotiated between the national chemical workers' union (IG Chemie-Papier-Keramik) and its counterpart employers' association (Bundesarbeitgeberverband Chemie) on the structure and functions of Europe-wide works councils in the chemical industry; the same agreement will govern the councils at BASF and Hoechst. By contrast, in France where collective bargaining is less widely accepted, only four of the nine councils are based on formal agreement; two were established by an exchange of letters; one, by verbal informal agreement; and two, in keeping with the paternalistic traditions of French management, by management invitation to individual employees.

3. Regardless of considerable differences in this respect between national industrial relations systems, all European works councils are exclusively union based, always involving national unions and sometimes, in addition, European union federations. In all firms, with the exception of the two attendance-by-invitation arrangements, the national unions organizing the various subsidiaries control the selection of delegates, and this also applies where delegates are employed by the company and are not full-time union officials. In fact, existing European works councils more resemble international union committees for multinational companies than works councils proper. While they share with the latter that their expenses are paid by the employer, they have no union-independent legal or organizational resources that would enable them to function as a second channel of representation.

The union-based character of European works councils is closely related to the absence of legal intervention and regulation at the EC level, helping make councils acceptable to national union movements that lack positive experience

19. Information on the sixth German European works council is missing.

with legally based workplace representation. But union hegemony also seems welcome to German unions, which in their own system require elaborate legal and organizational provisions to protect their primacy over independently resourced works councils and to prevent these from succumbing to "enterprise patriotism." Present European-level practice ensures that it is unions and not national, or supranational, works councillors that dominate European works councils. In fact, in the German-based companies in our sample, it was because of union efforts that European works councils came into existence, with both the metalworkers' and the chemical workers' unions having to put pressure, not just on management, but also on domestic works council members.[20]

Voluntarism and the union-based status of European works councils imply that councils can be terminated at any time by either side. In practice, of course, termination is less likely to issue from unions than from employers, for whom it constitutes a forceful sanction against councils overstepping their bounds. A widely visible precedent for this was set by the Dutch electronics manufacturer, Philips, one of the pioneers in the voluntary establishment of workforce information arrangements involving union representatives from foreign subsidiaries. Between 1967 and 1972, Philips held four formal meetings on Europe-wide issues with workforce representatives from its European plants. A fifth meeting, however, was canceled by the company, and no further meetings were called, apparently because the unions, under the leadership of the EMF, were planning to demand a multinational collective agreement on reduction of working hours without loss of pay, as well as harmonization of redundancy rules (interview; Northrup and Rowan 1979, 145–50). Today, Philips is among the most vocal opponents of the draft European Works Councils Directive.

4. The high diversity that characterizes the structures of voluntary European works councils is not, however, found in their functions. Only one of the 20 councils in the sample—that at Volkswagen—has rights, not just to information, but also to consultation. With impressive uniformity, the functional domain of voluntary European works councils falls short of the draft directive in that it is limited to the exercise of voluntarily conceded and unilaterally withdrawable information rights. While some firms claim that council meetings do involve two-way communication, with employee representatives having an opportunity to express their views, there are no explicit consultation rights in these cases, and councils are pure information bodies.[21] Topics on the

---

20. These members may have preferred not to share their influence on company management at headquarters with unionists from foreign countries and officials from international union confederations.

21. In a number of French firms (Bull, Elf Aquitaine, Thomson, and Pechiney), management claims that an ongoing "dialogue" and exchange of viewpoints is occurring, and the BSN European works council in its food and drink division has established a "program of joint work" on a number of industrial relations issues; in none of the French cases, however, do worker representatives have a formal right to consultation (Gold and Hall 1991, 28–29).

agenda of European works council meetings include the company's general financial situation, changes in its organization, rationalization plans, mergers and acquisitions, training and retraining policies, as well as general marketing, production, and investment strategies (table 9.3). Typical border-crossing issues, however, such as employee mobility between countries and allocation of work between plants, are surprisingly infrequent. In even fewer cases are traditional subjects of collective bargaining discussed; for example, wages are mentioned only once, the exception again being Volkswagen, and vacations and working time only twice.[22]

Volkswagen, of course, has long been the privileged site for the powerful German metalworkers' union, IG Metall, seeking and gaining breakthrough industrial agreements. That it today has the most advanced European works council arrangement is therefore not surprising.[23] Nor is it out of the ordinary that IG Metall and the EMF are together using the Volkswagen model to push for extension of consultation rights to all European works councils—as well as for the resources necessary for such rights to be meaningfully exercised (more frequent meetings, the right for unions and worker representatives to initiate meetings, preparatory meetings for workforce representatives, and facilities for these to remain in contact with each other). It is at this point, however, that all other European employers take exception (Gold and Hall 1992). And while in Germany advances made at Volkswagen can in principle be transferred to other employers through subsequent collective bargaining with an industrywide employers' association, no such mechanism exists at the European level, and nothing suggests that it may in the foreseeable future.

It is with respect to formal consultation rights that the emerging reality of voluntary European works councils refuses most conspicuously to fit the proposed EC legislation. *The difference between mandatory and voluntary workplace representation is the difference between information and consultation rights, and information rights only.* Consultation seems available to workforces only as a result of public intervention, even though it involves no more than minimal interference with managerial prerogative.[24] The study of European

22. The agenda of European works council meetings was the most difficult item on which to get complete information. Many of the companies returned their questionnaires incomplete, and press reports on the content of discussions tend to be sketchy.

23. Although the company was less than enthusiastic about having to be the avant garde again. For a time, management at Volkswagen cooperated with what was in effect a European workforce information arrangement, while refusing to call it a European works council or to sign a formal agreement on it. This reflected its experience in Germany, where the company has often come under fire from other employers that had to fall in line with precedents won by Volkswagen's strong union and, especially, works council. Nota bene that even at Volkswagen, the consultation rights of the European works council are limited to cross-border shifts in production and investment (Gester and Bobke 1992, 8).

24. To be sure, even the draft directive never comes close to creating rights to co-determination, i.e., to the—however limited—power sharing at the workplace that has come to be associated with works councils in countries like Germany and the Netherlands. Even more than consultation, co-determination is unlikely to emerge from negotiated agreement under a voluntaristic framework.

Table 9.3   Agenda Items at European Works Council Meetings

Item	Number of Times Mentioned
Company's economic/financial position	7
Rationalization plans	7
Changes in company organization	7
Production and sales	6
Acquisitions and mergers	6
Investment programs	5
Location of new plant	5
Training and retraining	5
Health and safety	5
Marketing strategies	4
Plant cutbacks or closures	4
Employee mobility between countries	3
Manufacturing and work methods	3
Employee benefits	3
Allocation of work between plants	2
Working time	2
Vacations	2
Language training	1
Wages	1

works councils confirms that if workforce participation is to include "voice," that is, is to be more than "ear," it must be based on more than the withdrawable goodwill or volatile sense of expediency of employers, or the conjuncturally sensitive market power of unions. Works councils that are to provide workers with more than information rights very likely require backing by public power.[25]

9.6   Sources of Voluntarism

There are conflicting views on the relationship between the emergence of voluntary European works councils and the legislative proposals of the European Commission. One position, compatible with optimism on the eventual evolution of a federal European social welfare state, sees voluntary councils as preparing the way for mandated councils (Hall 1992). Contrary to this is the belief that voluntary councils may potentially make formal legislation unnecessary or defuse political pressures for it. Both views are present among unions

25. Words are not important—unless they hide important distinctions and obscure crucial issues. Note that many German unionists object to the term, "European works council" since the arrangements to which it refers lack the legally enforceable rights German works councils have. Interestingly, German employers, knowing what real works councils are and how constraining they can be, do not like the term either. Bayer, e.g., insists on calling its council "Bayerforum" or "Euroforum," where "forum" is to emphasize that the council's only function can be the exchange of information.

as well as employers. Interestingly, while a majority of European union leaders hope that voluntary councils will *expedite* future legislation, many employers seem to expect that they will *substitute* for it. The ironic result is a developing convergence between employers and unions on the desirability of voluntary European works councils, for opposite strategic reasons.

It is not hard to see why European unions should today be willing to seek voluntary European works councils. In the 1970s, they had consistently argued that voluntary arrangements for workforce participation in multinational companies were not enough and that binding normative regulation, through either collective bargaining or supranational legislation, was indispensable. Later, however, they found the legislative road to European works councils closed by the apparently invincible coalition of European employers and the British government. Essentially, pressing for voluntary councils in the hope that these would get them closer to mandated ones was all that was left to them. There also was a need for European-level union officials to define a promising project for themselves that they could present to their national constituents. Not least, an important benefit that even voluntary European works councils do deliver is subsidized international communication between unions in multinational companies; for most unions, the costs of travel and translation for meetings at the European company level are prohibitively high.

While unions seem to have little to lose from voluntary European works councils, it is less clear why employers should have agreed to them. Voluntary alternatives to mandatory information and consultation arrangements in multinational firms have always figured prominently in the rhetoric of European employers. In the 1970s, employers argued that they were already voluntarily observing various international codes of good conduct for multinational firms—such as those developed by the ILO and the OECD—that included rules on workforce information; formal EC legislation was therefore unnecessary (DeVos 1989; Teague and Grahl 1991). This position was vulnerable to being periodically discredited by instances of manifest disregard of codes, sometimes found in the firms of the very same national or European employer spokesmen designated to sell voluntary compliance to the public as an alternative to legislative regulation. Later, survey studies showed a high percentage of large European firms, including some based in Britain, claiming that they had on their own introduced procedures for workforce participation or were thinking of doing so because of their expected economic benefits. Still, it was only during the battle over the social dimension that voluntary European works came to be *en vogue*.[26]

Two explanations are commonly offered for this, a political and an economic one. The former considers employer agreement to voluntary European works

---

26. No fewer than 11 of the 15 companies for which a council founding date is known established their councils after the passage of the Social Charter and the circulation by the European Commission of its proposed European Works Councils Directive.

councils as an attempt to preempt supranational legislation. Circulation of the draft European Works Councils Directive is believed to have given rise to disputes among employers on whether voluntary European works councils could be presented to a potentially prounion European legislator as a superior alternative to mandatory councils or whether they might have the unwelcome side-effect of legitimating legislation in the future, making it more difficult for companies to argue that councils are dangerous to their economic health. Firms that have agreed to European works councils would have done so because they have come to accept the first of the two positions.

If valid, a political explanation of voluntary councils would indicate that the European Community had in the late 1980s developed a credible capacity to threaten international companies with prescriptive legislative intervention unless they complied with EC policy on their own. What is more, the European Community would have succeeded in breaking up the solidarity of European employers, making some of them subject themselves to regulations that future legislation could then spread to all. In this, the European Community would have been able to apply political power to business in a way that in the past was typically associated with advanced nation-states.

An explanation of voluntary councils by anticipatory compliance of employers with potential European legislation would seem to be supported by the timing of council formation.[27] On the other hand, only a very small number of firms actually did set up councils, and all except one refused to allow them rights to consultation, as opposed to just information—in clear defiance of EC policy. Moreover, given the firm lock that employers had established on EC social policies in the 1980s, it is hard to see how the Commission would have been able to get formal legislation passed if companies had closed ranks and refused to introduce councils voluntarily as a lesser evil. Indeed, one might wonder why European employers did not have more confidence in their ability to defeat the 1990 draft as soundly as its predecessor; their political position had certainly not deteriorated since 1984. It is also not clear why European employers, if preempting legislation by voluntary arrangements was such an effective tactic, did not use it earlier to combat the much more threatening Vredeling draft.[28]

Economic explanations regard voluntary council formation as a response to economic efficiency imperatives derive from basically two factors: changes in companies in response to internationalization and new demands on labor relations in "post-Fordist" workplaces. The assumptions that inform such accounts

27. There are also examples of firms explicitly motivating their acceptance of European works councils by the expectation that this may forestall EC legislation. Specifically, this is said to apply to the French companies Rhone-Poulenc and St. Gobain (Gold and Hall 1992). Also, the German chemical industry is reported to have signed its European works councils agreement with the German chemical workers' union primarily to avoid EC legislation (Lamparter 1991, 75).

28. Explaining councils as a device to preempt EC legislation also fails to account for the presence of European works councils in Swedish firms. Sweden is not an EC member and would not be affected by a potential directive.

are summarized by Northrup et al.: "Complex issues pertaining to human resource management, arising in the 1980s and expected to continue into the 1990s, point to the need for labor and management to co-operate in exchanging information and ideas. The introduction of new technology, the restructuring of industry and the efforts to unite Europe provide the framework for extended union-management consultation in the years ahead where the parties desire it and find it helpful" (1988, 540).

Politically, economic-functionalist explanations imply that workplace representation comes about on its own if required by economic conditions and does not need legislation. The fact that voluntarily instituted councils have only information and no consultation or co-determination rights simply means that only the former and not the latter are economically efficient; if the latter were, they too would have been instituted voluntarily.

Assuming that firms undergoing internationalization experience increased needs for multinational communication with their workforces, efficiency explanations seem to be supported by the coincidence of council formation with the wave of cross-border mergers and acquisitions in Europe in the second half of the 1980s that was an intended consequence of the Internal Market program.[29] None of the presently existing councils on which we have a founding date was formed before 1986, the year the program was launched. Also, most of the restructuring was concentrated in a few sectors, with chemicals and food processing alone accounting for half of all intra-EC mergers and acquisitions (Kay 1991, 360), and multinational companies in such sectors appear to be more likely to have European works councils (table 9.4).[30]

There are, however, reasons to question the logic of managerialist accounts for council formation. Again, the number of firms that avail themselves of the presumed economic benefits of European works councils remains small. Perhaps more important, while few employers disagree with the notion that a "modern enterprise" exposed to unpredictable markets and using fast-changing technology requires the "active involvement" of its workforce, to what extent this includes information or consultation rights for workforce representatives at the supranational level is far from obvious. Employer pronouncements on the subject support the impression that workforce involvement, to be justifiable

29. In the industrial sector, the number of national mergers and acquisitions, involving large companies in one EC country, more than doubled (from 101 to 214) between 1984 and 1988. The number of cross-border mergers within the European Community almost quadrupled (from 29 to 111) in the same period (Kay 1991, 360). The process extended beyond the borders of the European Community to neighboring European countries, with companies based in Switzerland and Sweden especially eager to expand their presence inside the European Community.

30. The agreements at BSN and Thomson, in which management is said to have sought union involvement in anticipation of major restructuring programs, are cited as examples of management interest in the efficiency advantages of European works councils (Northrup et al. 1988, 525). More recent interviews indicate that, on the whole, managers seem to hold positive views about their experiences with European works councils and about their efficiency contribution (Gold and Hall 1992).

Table 9.4   Multinational Companies and European Works Councils by Industry

Primary Industrial Branch	Number of MNCs	Number of MNCs with EWCs	MNCs with EWCs (%)
Rubber products	3	1	33
Electronics	7	2	29
Computers	4	1	25
Chemicals	17	4	24
Metals and metal products	15	3	20
Industrial and farm equipment	5	1	20
Petroleum refining	5	1	20
Building materials	5	1	20
Motor vehicles and parts	11	2	18
Food, drink, and tobacco	14	2	14
Forest products	1	0	–
Publishing and printing	2	0	–
Scientific and photographic equipment	1	0	–
Aerospace	3	0	–
Pharmaceutical	5	0	–
Soaps and cosmetics	2	0	–
Total	100	18	18

by managerial efficiency concerns, would above all have to be production or workplace centered. Production-related decisions in multinational firms, however, are often, and perhaps increasingly, made locally. If workforce involvement is to be limited to such decisions, it must not be centralized. Moreover, while local involvement may, if well managed, remain focused on common interests in high productivity and competitiveness, centralization entails the risk of discussions extending to more adversarial subjects, such as finance and investment. From a managerial perspective, not only do workers have no special expertise to contribute in these areas, but involving workers in them is also likely to give rise to conflicts or delay urgent decisions and thereby frustrate the very purposes of "involvement." Not least, centralized information requirements may force a company to keep managerial functions centralized even if economic needs would demand devolution to local decision makers.

9.7   A National Theory of Supranational Works Councils

If neither EC politics nor economic efficiency pressures can account for the spread of voluntary European works councils, a better explanation may be one that takes off from their structural diversity, functional weakness, and uneven national distribution. In this view, voluntary supranational works councils are rooted in diverse national political and institutional conditions, especially the power and access to political and legal resources of national unions and employers. While on the surface "European," they are in reality the products of nationally different government policies, legal systems, industrial relations practices, union strategies, managerial power structures, and the like.

A national theory of supranational works council formation does not have to claim that supranational politics is without influence. However, rather than explaining the appearance of voluntary European works councils as a preemptive response to European legislation, it emphasizes its simultaneity with the change in European social policy toward voluntarism—a change which reassured employers that there will precisely *not* be an activist European legislator waiting to exploit voluntary councils for legitimation of legislative intervention. That is, employers have agreed to voluntary European works councils, not because these are necessarily economically efficient or provide protection against European-level social policy activism, but because they have become unlikely to precipitate statutory enactment. Given, not the strength but, on the contrary, the weakness of European welfare state federalism, employers felt confident enough by the end of the 1980s to accommodate whatever *other* political pressures there may have been for European works councils, the possible costs of accommodation having become so small as to no longer justify the costs of resistance.

Above all, pressures and incentives for firms to agree to supranational works councils grow out of the politics in and around national industrial relations. While national legislation cannot be used directly to set up supranational councils, bargaining power derived form it can. In countries with strong union and council rights, worker representatives may have enough power to make internationalizing firms extend council arrangements to the multinational level. As multinational management becomes increasingly differentiated from home-country national-level management, access to the former for national-level works councils may depend on the formation of a supranational council. With the growing importance of such access for national interest representation, national works councils may become willing to expend political capital on making management agree to supranational works councils, even though these involve sharing influence with workforce representatives from foreign subsidiary plants. Concerns over this among home-country works councillors should be lower in countries where councils are well established and well resourced, making it unlikely for them to be outcompeted by foreign council members more knowledgeable in council operations. Moreover, subsidiarity and the absence of supranational legislation make it possible for home-country councils to design supranational councils close to their domestic tradition, further cementing their hegemony on the council. Not least, limitation of supranational councils to information functions may reassure home-country councils endowed under national law with consultation or co-determination rights that the influence of foreign councillors will not exceed theirs.

Unions, for their part, should be more comfortable with works councils in countries where they have had time to learn to live with councils and control them. In fact, European works councils, as we have seen, make it possible for unions in countries with strong national works councils to insert themselves directly in the international industrial relations of large firms, which might otherwise be controlled by management and works councils alone. Management in countries with strong works councils may have their own reasons to find voluntary supranational councils attractive, not least as a means of counterbalancing the national council in the home country with workforce representatives from foreign plants with sometimes different interests.

The spectacular growth of European works councils in large French-based multinationals would seem to require a special, although again nation-specific explanation. While works councils do have some legal rights in France, union confidence in them as a channel of representation is low, and union control over councils is precarious due to multiunionism. Like French industrial relations in general, however, works councils in France are highly politicized. National as well as supranational works councils are often used by management and moderate unions, especially the CFDT, to isolate the largest union, the CGT, which has close links to the Communist party.[31] There also seems to have been pressure from the Socialist government on large companies that were either nationalized or otherwise had close relations with the state, to set up voluntary European works councils. In part, this was in pursuit of an international agenda of support for the European social dimension.[32] But the policy also had a domestic aspect in that the government seems to have hoped for external reinforcement of its less than successful legislative efforts to strengthen workplace representation in France itself.

For a quantitative assessment of the relative contribution of economic and national political and institutional factors to the voluntary establishment of European works councils, the companies in the sample were coded on four independent variables:[33]

1. *Strength of works councils in a company's home country.* Countries in which works councils have strong rights are Germany, the Netherlands, and Sweden; countries with weak legal rights for councils are Belgium, France, Italy, and Luxembourg; and countries without legally mandated councils in-

---

31. Among the European works councils in the sample, this applies in particular to those at BSN, Thomson, and Pechiney. At the former two companies, the existence of two European works councils instead of just one has its origin in complicated maneuvers to minimize CGT influence. In general, French companies tend to make arrangements for European works councils either with the CFDT or a European union federation to which the CGT is not affiliated, either way excluding the CGT from participation.

32. This is most obvious in the public declaration on the agreement at Elf-Aquitaine, which described the firm's new European works council as the embodiment of the spirit of the proposed EC directive on workforce information and consultation.

33. Since the companies included in the analysis are the universe of the 100 largest manufacturing companies in Europe and not a random sample of a larger universe, generalization of the results would strictly speaking be affected by the problem of sample selection bias (for a discussion see Berk 1983). The pattern of European works councils that we are aware of in service sector firms or in smaller manufacturing companies does not, however, conflict with the main conclusions of this paper.

clude Switzerland, the United Kingdom, and the United States. Two dummy variables were created, CD1 and CD2, which were coded for, respectively, weak and strong works council rights in home countries. Under a national political model of voluntary works council formation, the probability of a company having a European works council should covary with the strength of works council rights in the company's home country. CD1 and CD2 should therefore have positive signs, and CD2 should have a larger coefficient than CD1. Under an economic efficiency model, home-country legislation would not be expected to make a difference.

2. *French Socialist party influence.* Qualitative accounts and interviews with experts and participants offer strong indications that the French government urged state-owned multinational companies in the second half of the 1980s to establish European bodies of workforce representation, in anticipation and support of EC legislation. Companies in the sample were coded according to their country of origin, with French companies receiving a score of 1 on a dummy variable, FRANCE.

3. *Concentration of production.* Multinational companies vary widely with respect to the diversification of their product range. For the purposes of this study, companies are considered to have highly concentrated production if more than 75 percent of their employment is in their main product area, defined at the two-digit SIC level. This is the case with 52 of the 100 companies in the sample. Of the remaining 48, 38 have between 50 and 75 percent of employment in their main product area, and 10 are even more diversified. A variable, CONC, was created on which the 52 highly concentrated companies received a score of 1, and the rest a score of 0.[34]

An economic explanation of voluntary works councils would expect the probability for a company to have a European works council to increase with the concentration of its production, given that concentration is likely to increase the degree to which production is centrally coordinated. Concentration would also appear to increase a company's potential gains from international rationalization, placing a premium on effective mechanisms for information and consultation. A highly diversified company, by comparison, which in the limiting case simply buys up profitable plants without attempting to integrate them into a synergetic production structure, would derive fewer gains from rationalization at European level and may not wish to have worker representatives at multinational level inquire into its buying and selling strategies. Under an economic efficiency explanation, CONC should therefore have a positive sign. Since a firm's degree of productive concentration is not likely to be affected by its home-country's politics and industrial relations system, the alternative model would predict that it has no influence and that CONC will not be significant.

---

34. Division of the sample into three instead of two groups makes no difference for the statistical results.

4. *Internationalization of employment.* All companies in the sample are multinationals. But some have only marginal international activities while others are highly internationalized and significantly exposed to several countries' laws and practices in setting their industrial relations policies. To determine the impact of internationalization on voluntary works council formation, companies were grouped in three categories: those with more than two-thirds of their employment in their home country (low internationalization); those with between one-third and two-thirds of their workforces in their country of origin (medium internationalization); and those with less than one-third of employment there (high internationalization). The dummies INT1 and INT2 were coded 1 for, respectively, medium and high internationalization.

An economic efficiency model would suggest functional needs for supranational workforce information, consultation, and representation to increase with a firm's internationalization. While companies with limited foreign operations will tend to impose home-country practices on their foreign subsidiaries, companies with a high number of such subsidiaries will have difficulties doing so and will tend to allow them to follow local practices. As a firm's internationalization increases even further, it may need to develop a common "identity" and set of practices that are not reducible to those of any one of the countries in which it operates. A European works council could play an important role in facilitating a supranational, company-specific personnel policy. To the extent that the establishment of European works councils is driven by functional-economic imperatives, therefore, INT1 and INT2 would be expected to have positive and high coefficients, with the coefficient for INT2 larger than for INT1.

A nationally driven political-institutional model, on the other hand, would make the contribution of internationalization to voluntary European works councils dependent on favorable institutional conditions in a company's home country.[35] But as the number of countries involved increases with internationalization, the "reach" of home-country political and institutional resources might decline and unions may face growing collective action problems, reducing their ability to coordinate their interests among themselves. Moreover, the more internationalized a company, the less certainty there is for unions in its home country that they will be the dominant forces on a possible European works council; as a result they may be less willing to spend political capital on bargaining for one. The political model, then, might predict the coefficient for INT2 to be smaller than for INT1.[36]

35. The same conditional effect might be expected for productive concentration. Ideally, this possibility would have to be tested using interaction terms. However, in our sample the correlation between some of the original variables and the interaction terms formed with them is too high to allow results to be significant.

36. Internationalization and concentration may be correlated with company size. A control variable, LSIZE, defined as the natural logarithm of the size of a company's total workforce in thousands, was therefore included in the analysis. LSIZE is not an essential variable for either of the two models, although both would probably expect large size to increase the probability of having a European works council.

Table 9.5   **Expected Results According to the Political and Economic Methods**

Variable	Political Explanation	Economic Explanation
1. Strength of works council	CD1, CD2 > 0; CD2 > CD1	Not significant
2. France	FRANCE > 0	Not significant
3. Concentration	Not significant	CONC > 1
4. Internationalization	INT1, INT2 > 0; INT1 > INT2	INT1, INT2 > 0; INT2 > INT1

Note: Independent variables: CD1, weak works council rights in home country; CD2, strong works council rights in home country; FRANCE, company based in France; CONC, more than 75 percent of employment in main product area; INT1, 33 to 66 percent of employment in home country; INT2, less than 33 percent of employment in home country.

The independent variables and their signs and relationships expected under the modified political model and under the economic model of voluntary works council formation are summarized in table 9.5. Since the dependent variable—absence or presence of a European works council—is categorical in character, logistic regression is ideally suited to measure the impact of the independent variables.

The first model tested (model 1 in table 9.6) includes all independent variables. A striking result is that the coefficient for concentration is not significant. The internationalization variables are significant at the .05 and .01 levels, respectively, and are both positive. The fact that the coefficient for INT2 is slightly larger than that for INT1 would seem to lend some support to the economic as opposed to the political model.

Of further note is the large positive coefficient, significant at the .01 level, of the strong co-determination variable CD2, in line with the expectations of the political model. Neither the weak co-determination variable CD1 nor the French multinational variable FRANCE are significant; however, these two variables have very large estimated coefficients with opposite signs due to the high correlation between them.[37]

Comparison of the χ^2 statistics of models 1 and 2 shows that the concentration variable CONC may be dropped without loss of explanatory power.[38] The significance, order of magnitude, and signs of the other coefficients remain the same as in model 1.

Testing the assumption that French Socialist government influence rather than the presence of weak co-determination rights is behind the growth of European works councils in French multinationals, model 3 drops CD1 from the analysis. Comparison of the χ^2 statistic of model 3 with that of model 2 shows that this may be done without significant loss of explanatory power. As a result,

37. This reflects the large number of French-based companies (16) in this category, compared to companies based in Luxembourg, Belgium, and Italy (5), the other countries with weak works council rights.

38. The difference of 0.722 is below 2.706, the threshold for acceptance at the .10 level of significance for one degree of freedom.

Table 9.6   **Logistic Regression Coefficients for Presence of European Works Council, on Selected Independent Variables**

Independent Variable	Model 1	Model 2	Model 3
CD1	−14.519	−14.731	
	(0.008)	(0.008)	
CD2	3.812	3.652	3.765
	(3.249)***	(3.205)***	(3.294)***
FRANCE	18.600	18.7948	4.317
	(0.010)	(0.010)	(3.543)***
INT1	2.786	2.697	2.695
	(2.441)**	(2.381)**	(2.380)**
INT2	3.348	3.341	3.531
	(2.567)***	(2.592)***	(2.781)***
CONC	0.632		
	(0.868)		
LSIZE	0.741	0.705	0.700
	(1.694)*	(1.621)	(1.600)
Constant	−10.323	−9.700	−9.844
	(3.719)***	(3.716)***	(3.772)***
Log-likelihood	−26.380	−26.766	−27.254
Degrees of freedom	7	6	5
χ^2	41.519	40.747	39.771
N	100	100	100

Note: Numbers in parentheses are T-ratios.
*Significant at .10 level.
**Significant at .05 level.
***Significant at .01 level.

both CD2 and FRANCE have significant and positive signs, as predicted by the national political model; the coefficients of the internationalization variables INT1 and INT2 remain significant and positive.[39]

Overall, the results offer evidence for the overriding importance of national political and institutional factors in the formation of European works councils. Concentration of company production, a key variable for any economic model, was found not to contribute to the rise of European works councils. While internationalization does make a contribution to voluntary council formation, and apparently in a linear fashion as predicted under an economic efficiency model, this effect may in reality be conditional on home-country institutions and may thus be fully compatible with the political model.

Nota bene that the impact of national political and institutional conditions

39. Testing the three models with a reduced sample containing only the 45 companies that returned usable answers to the mail survey yields substantially the same results. A possible alternative to model 3, which involves dropping FRANCE instead of CD1, would technically also be acceptable relative to model 2; however, its relative fit was not as good as that of model 3. This is in line with the qualitative evidence that it is state pressure, and not weak domestic works council rights, that drives the developments in French companies.

would be even stronger were it not for the "Dutch anomaly," that is, the absence of European works councils at all four major Dutch manufacturing companies despite the existence of strong national works council legislation. In part, this may be accounted for by the experience at Philips, described above, and by the fact that two of the four firms, Royal Dutch-Shell and Unilever, are in part British. But there is also the possibility that in a small country such as the Netherlands whose large multinational companies inevitably have a very high share of employment abroad, unions are more ambivalent than elsewhere about sharing representation with what would almost inevitably be a majority of foreign representatives.

9.8 Summary and Conclusion

The growth of voluntary European works councils is best accounted for, not by common European factors such as economic integration or the politics of the social dimension, but by national conditions in companies' home countries, especially with respect to the political, institutional, and legal resources of labor. Governed by a logic of national diversity, voluntary European works councils, while on the surface "European," are products of national union strategies, industrial relations practices, legal systems, and government policies. The fundamental fact about them that any theory must accommodate is their highly skewed national distribution, which rules out political or economic explanations that would apply to all large European companies regardless of their national base.[40]

The voluntary adoption of European works councils by large multinational firms is unlikely to signal or precipitate statutory enactment of workforce information, consultation, and co-determination rights in EC law. Nor will voluntary councils contribute to the development of an integrated European industrial relations system with interrelated and coordinated arenas of joint regulation at the supranational, sectoral, and enterprise levels. The analysis in this paper suggests that the functional weakness and structural unevenness of present European works councils are there to stay. Voluntary European works councils are not works councils in a technical sense, but de facto international union committees for large companies, set up by managements and unions as a low-cost response to some of the consequences of the internationalization of the European economy. Far from providing or preparing supranational gover-

40. While not collected systematically, available information on developments since 1991 supports the conclusions offered in this paper. European works councils are reportedly being established at Volvo and at Thyssen AG, i.e., a Swedish-based and a German-based company. Information on companies outside the sample is also consistent with the analysis, in that European works councils exist or are being set up in German-based (Allianz, Tengelmann, Schmalbach-Lubecka, and Grundig) and French-based (AGF) firms. Functionally, all these councils are limited to the exchange of information. For a textbook case study of national political resources accounting for supranational workforce participation arrangements in multinational firms, see the case of Europipe (*EIRR*, no. 213 [October 1981]: 12ff).

nance of employment relations at the European level, European works councils seem to do no more than create interfaces within large companies between national industrial relations systems, which as such remain separate and exposed to the potentially destabilizing effects of regime competition in a border-crossing integrated market.

A theory that accounts for voluntary European works councils by national political and institutional differences can account not just for their skewed distribution and nationally imprinted structures but also for the tensions and conflicts between national unions over and within them. For example, in Britain works councils are usually regarded as instruments of "joint consultation" (Marginson 1992), which is in sharp contrast to the German view of councils as organs of co-determination. Since joint consultation is considered paternalistic by many British unionists, the prospect of European works councils not becoming "real" works councils does not appear threatening to them; British unions see their promise rather in being potential agents of enterprise-based collective bargaining (Hall 1992; Sisson, Waddington, and Whitston 1992). European works council legislation, if ever to come forward, would be expected by them to do no more, but also no less, than provide a form of statutory support for union recognition.[41] German unions, on the other hand, conduct collective bargaining *not* at the company but at the industrial level. For them it is vitally important that company-level industrial relations remain defined as *something other than collective bargaining,* above all in large firms whose presence in industrywide bargaining units is essential for the mobilization of strong bargaining power (Streeck 1991). That is, were European works councils to become collective bargaining agents, German unions would feel threatened; but were they to become co-determination bodies, British unions would find themselves dragged into "joint consultation." As a result, European works councils will likely be neither.

Another implication of voluntarism, and of European works councils coming about as an outgrowth of national conditions in a company's home country, is that supranational representation of workers and unions in foreign subsidiaries depends on the interests and power resources of home-base industrial relations actors. Without legislation, subsidiary unions are deprived of voice if home-country unions prefer not to push for supranational representation, or design it so that their privileged influence is preserved. Due to differences between countries in economic internationalization, industrial organization, and industrial relations, divisions of interest and strategy between home-country and subsidiary unions may come to be reflected in divisions between national union movements. For example, Italian unions are home-country unions for only a small number of large European multinationals (see above, table 9.2); for the vast majority of European multinational companies operating in Italy,

---

41. The hope apparently is that European legal provisions would then somehow radiate into the British domestic system, restoring conditions that existed there before Thatcher.

they organize subsidiary workforces. Under a voluntarist representation regime, what voice they may have depends largely on the goodwill and bargaining power of unions and works councillors in other countries. But while this should dispose them favorably toward European-level legislation, their own, Italian system of workplace representation is not legally based, and national resistance to legal regulation is strong.

British unions, on the other hand, organize the home base of many European multinationals, potentially enabling them to tailor international representative arrangements to their interests. But British multinationals are often highly internationalized. Even if British unions had the power to make them agree to European works councils, significant influence would therefore be exercised on the councils by unionists from other countries. British unions also have no experience with council-type workplace representation and often lack a workplace-based structure to which a multinational works council could be linked.[42] By comparison, foreign council members, especially from German or French subsidiaries, are likely to be well resourced and skilled. To the extent that this would make British unions reluctant to press for European works councils, the consequence would be disenfranchisement of workforces in the European subsidiaries of British firms.

Generally, the slow and uneven growth of works councils in European multinational companies demonstrates the dependence of council-style workplace representation on union and legal support. Works councils come into existence if demanded by strong unions or made mandatory by an interventionist government. In an international setting like the European Community, where unions are weak and legislation is absent and unlikely to come about, councils grow, if at all, out of constituent national systems, to the extent that national unions and legal regulations manage to extend their reach into the international arena. Even so, as long as they are not directly supported by supranational law, the councils that result remain functionally weak.

Employers' rhetorical recognition of the importance of collective communication with workforces notwithstanding, voluntarily instituted works councils remain limited to the exchange of information and are refused formal consultation rights, let alone rights to co-determination. Resistance to legally binding mandates for supranational workplace representation is offered even by employers that in other settings declare themselves comfortable with mandated works councils entitled to consultation and co-determination. Employer preferences for voluntarism seem resistant to experience, and certainly to theoretical reasoning on the economic efficiency advantages of mandated institutions. Very likely, this is because voluntarism leaves employers an exit option should matters become tough, and because, unlike unions and worker representatives,

---

42. In nonunionized companies, the present draft directive would require international representatives to be directly elected by the entire workforce—something that may appear to British unions as setting a dangerous precedent for dual-channel representation or even union substitution.

exit from participation regimes increases rather than reduces their control over decisions. Moreover, voluntarism in supranational settings seems to be a political resource even and especially for employers who in their national systems operate under legal regulation: to the extent that they have the possibility of moving subjects out of mandated national into voluntary supranational participation, the balance of power in national industrial relations is shifted in their favor.

Voluntary participation at the supranational level is acceptable to business as long as it remains an alternative to, instead of an intermediary step toward, a replication of national social democracy. Potentially even contributing to a softening of national regimes, supranational voluntarism leaves multinational firms the freedom to do what they want while sparing them the hazards of an anomic absence of all institutions. Under voluntarism, when everything is said and done, it is those in stronger market or hierarchical positions who decide how much symmetry and equity between themselves and others is symmetrical and equitable, and how much participation is reasonable and efficient. This advantage is not easily given up.

Appendix A
Sample and Sources of Information

The sample for this study consists of 100 of the largest European multinational corporations in manufacturing. The goal was to cover the 100 manufacturing firms with the largest number of employees in Europe, including companies based outside of the European Community and Europe. However, since standard lists, as provided by the *Financial Times* or *Fortune,* do not break down employment by country or region, they offer only approximations. A list of the 25 largest European manufacturing employers, compiled by Labour Research, was supplemented by a selection of European-based corporations included in the 1989 Fortune 500 international list. In this list, rank is based on annual sales, and manufacturing companies are defined as companies deriving at least 50 percent of their sales from manufacturing or mining. Companies based in mining as well as companies known to be limited to only one country (such as the large state holdings in Italy and Spain) were excluded from the sample.

From the various national and international business directories, which vary widely in the quantity and quality of the information they provide, a list was compiled of the names and addresses of the directors of the companies' international industrial relations, employee relations, or human relations departments. When this information could not be found, the names and addresses of the chief executive officers were used. Where these were not available either, the generic identification, "personnel director," at the company's European headquarters was used. A four-page questionnaire was mailed to the 100 ad-dresses, with a request that it be returned within six weeks. A follow-up letter was sent to those that had not responded within that period. Forty-five valid responses were received; an additional 17 companies sent replies declining to participate.

The questionnaire itself, in addition to asking for information on the person who filled it out, requested basic data about any existing arrangement for infor-mation, consultation, or negotiation with employee representatives on a multi-national basis. If such an arrangement existed, respondents were asked which countries were covered, how many workforce representatives there were and how they were selected, which unions (if any) were involved, how often meet-ings were held, what subjects were discussed at the meetings, whether meet-ings were just informational or also involved consultation or negotiation, whether any written agreements had been reached, how many of the company's employees in the European Community were covered, and whether separate provisions had been made for different categories of workers (e.g., white-collar and blue-collar workers). Companies that did not currently have a works-council–like arrangement were asked an open-ended question about whether establishing one was being contemplated or planned for the future, and whether one had been tried in the past and discontinued.

Other sources of information were used to supplement the survey responses. These included publications like the *European Industrial Relations Review, Industrial Relations Europe,* and the *Financial Times,* as well as publications from the European Trade Union Institute and two recent studies of multina-tional information and consultation arrangements in European multinationals (Gold and Hall 1992; Myrvang 1991). In addition, interviews were conducted with union and business representatives and EC officials.

Appendix B
Companies Included in the Sample

ABB Asea Brown Boveri*	Bertelsmann	Ciba-Geigy
Aerospatiale	BICC	Cockerill Sambre
Akzo	BOC Group	Continental*
Alcatel Alsthom	Bosch, Robert	Courtaulds
Allied-Lyons	British Aerospace	Daimler-Benz*
Alusuisse	British Steel Corp.	Dalgety
Arbed	British Petroleum Co.	Dow International
Associated British Foods	BSN*	Electrolux*
BASF*	BTR	Elf Aquitaine*
BAT Industries	Bull Group*	Exxon
Bayer*	Cadbury Schweppes	Feldmuehle Nobel
Bayerische Motoren Werke	Caterpillar Overseas	Fiat
(continued)		

Ford of Europe, Inc.	MMM (3M Europe)	Salzgitter
General Motors	Monsanto Europe	Sandoz
General Electric Co.	Nestlé*	Siemens
GKN	Nobel Industries	SKF*
Glaxo Holdings	Pechiney*	SmithKline Beecham
Grand Metropolitan	Peugot	Consumer Brands
Guinness	Pfitzer	Solvay & Cie
Hanson	Philips	STC
Henkel	Pilkington	Sulzer
Hoechst*	Pirelli	Tate & Lyle
Hoesch	Proctor & Gamble	Thomson Electronics*
Hoogovens Groep	Rank Xerox Ltd.	Thorn EMI
Huels	Reed International	Thyssen
IBM Europe	Renault, Regie Nationale des	Trelleborg*
ICI	Usines	Unigate
Krupp, F. GmbH	Rhone-Poulenc*	Unilever
l'Air Liquide	RMC Group	United Biscuits
l'Oreal	Roche Group (Hoffman-La	Usinor Sacilor
Lafarge Coppee	Roche)	Veba Oel
MAN	Rolls-Royce	VIAG
Mannesmann	Royal Dutch/Shell Group	Volkswagen*
Metallgesellschaft	Saint-Gobian*	Volvo
Michelin & Cie		

Note: An asterisk (*) denotes the presence of a European works council.

References

Addison, John T., and W. Stanley Siebert. 1991. The social charter of the European Community: Evolution and controversies. *Industrial and Labor Relations Review* 44(4): 597–625.

Berk, Richard A. 1983. An introduction to sample selection bias in sociological data. *American Sociological Review* 48:386–98.

Campbell, Duncan C. 1989. Multinational labor relations in the European Community. *ILO Report* 27:7–14.

DeVos, Ton. 1989. *Multinational corporations in democratic host countries: U.S. multinationals and the Vredeling proposal.* Dartmouth: Aldershot.

European Trade Union Institute. 1991. Vertragliche Vereinbarung über Informations- und Konsultationsrechte der Arbeitnehmer in europäischen multinationalen Unternehmen und die Auswertung der Praxis. Documentation for the ETUI conference on Multinationals, Maastricht, September 26–27.

Gester, Heinz, and Manfred Bobke. 1992. Europäischer Binnenmarkt und betriebliche Mitbestimmung der Arbeitnehmer. Manuscript.

Gold, Michael, and Mark Hall. 1992. Information and consultation in European multinational companies: An evaluation of practice. Luxembourg: Office for Official Publications of the European Communities/European Foundation for the Improvement of Living and Working Conditions.

Grahl, John, and Paul Teague. 1991. European level collective bargaining: A new phase? *Relations Industrielle* 46(1): 46–73.

Hall, Mark. 1992. Legislating for employee participation: A case study of the European

Works Councils Directive. Warwick Papers in Industrial Relations, no. 39. Industrial Relations Research Unit, School of Industrial and Business Studies, University of Warwick.

Hepple, Bob. 1990. European labor law: The European communities. In *Comparative labour law and industrial relations in industrialized market economies,* 4th rev. ed., ed. R. Blanpain, 293–316. Deventer and Boston: Kluwer.

Kay, Neil. 1991. Industrial collaborative activity and the completion of the internal market. *Journal of Common Market Studies* 29:347–62.

Lamparter, Dietmar H. 1991. Sprung über die Barrieren. *Management Wissen,* October: 74–81.

Levinson, Charles. 1972. *International trade unionism.* London: Allen & Unwin.

Marginson, Paul. 1992. European integration and transnational management-union relations in the enterprise. Industrial Relations Research Unit, University of Warwick. Manuscript.

Myrvang, Gunnar. 1991. Information and consultation rights in the Nordic countries: Experiences and perspectives. Report for the Nordic Foundation for Industrial Development.

Northrup, Herbert R., Duncan C. Campbell, and Betty J. Slowinski. 1988. Multinational union-management consultation in Europe: Resurgence in the 1980s? *International Labour Review* 127:525–43.

Northrup, Herbert R., and Richard L. Rowan. 1979. Multinational collective bargaining attempts: The record, the cases, and the prospects. Wharton School Industrial Research Unit, University of Pennsylvania.

Simonson, Birger. 1991. Scandinavian group trade union collaboration: An argumentation analysis. Working Paper no. WP/91/64/EN. Dublin: European Foundation for the Improvement of Living and Working Conditions.

Sisson, Keith, Jeremy Waddington, and Colin Whitston. 1992. The structure of capital in the European Community: The size of companies and the implications for industrial relations. Warwick Papers in Industrial Relations, no. 38. Industrial Relations Research Unit, School of Industrial and Business Studies, University of Warwick.

Streeck, Wolfgang. 1991. More uncertainties: West German unions facing 1992. *Industrial Relations* 30:317–49.

———. 1992. National diversity, regime competition and institutional deadlock: Problems in forming a European industrial relations system. *Journal of Public Policy* 12(4): 301–30.

———. 1994. European social policy after Maastricht: The limits of "social dialogue." *Economic and Industrial Democracy* 15 (May): 151–77.

———. 1995. From market-making to state-building? Reflections on the political economy of European social policy. In *Prospects for social Europe: The European Community's social dimension in comparative perspective,* ed. Stephan Leifried and Paul Pierson. Washington, D.C.: Brookings Institution.

Teague, Paul, and John Grahl. 1991. The European Community social charter and labour market regulation. *Journal of Public Policy* 11(2): 207–32.

Tyszkiewicz, Zygmunt. 1992. UNICE: The voice of European business and industry in Brussels: A programmatic self-presentation. In *Employers' associations in Europe: Policy and organization,* ed. D. Sadowski and O. Jacobi, 85–101. Baden-Baden: Nomos Verlagsgesellschaft.

10   Poland: Councils under Communism and Neoliberalism

Michal Federowicz and Anthony Levitas

10.1   Introduction

Employee councils in Poland progressively wrested from the Communist state the juridical rights to hire and fire managers; to control wages, profits, and investments; and to veto decisions over the sale, transfer, or privatization of their firms' assets. Paradoxically however, when Communism finally collapsed and the juridical rights of the councils became fully realizable in practice, many of the people who had earlier fought for them turned against them. This essay examines the history of the struggle to create works councils under Communism as well as the more recent attempts by the post-Communist state to radically reduce or eliminate their powers.

The first section traces how paternalistic councils evolved under Communism into the co-owners of state industry. We argue that as in other countries the development of councils in Poland can only be understood within the dual context of social pressures for greater shop floor democracy and economic pressures for greater flexibility at the point of production. In Poland, however, these generic pressures were intensified and transformed by the hypertrophized Taylorism of the Communist project, and by the often brutal attempt to organize the polity as if it were a single centrally planned organism. The economic and political difficulties that this project encountered meant that periodically

Michal Federowicz is associate professor of sociology at the Institute of Philosophy and Sociology of the Polish Academy of Sciences, Warsaw. Anthony Levitas is a graduate student in the Department of Political Science at the Massachusetts Institute of Technology and associate director of the Resources Development Foundation's International Public Finance Program in New York.

The authors thank their colleagues at the Gdansk Institute of Market Economics, particularly Janusz Dabrowski, Kazimierz Kloc, and Jan Szomburg. Without their work, past and present, this essay would not have been possible. The authors' judgments, however, in no way represent those of the Institute and are, for better or worse, their own.

elements within the Party promoted the creation of councils either as a way to legitimate Communist power on the shop floor or to improve the flexibility of the economy as a whole. At the same time, when workers or others sought to use the councils as vehicles of either industrial democracy or enterprise autonomy, they were immediately repressed for posing fundamental challenges to the Party's control over the social division of labor.

Over time, this cycle of invention and repression turned the councils into one of the principal institutional locations of a larger struggle between the state and society. On both sides of this struggle the economic and political rationales for supporting plant-based forms of worker representation became so intertwined that by the mid-1980s they were inseparable. Paradoxically, this fusion of economic and political rationales meant that when Communism finally collapsed in Poland, the same reformers who had earlier fought for the councils now abandoned them: once the councils had fulfilled their political role in helping to destroy the old regime, all ideas about their past or future economic significance were forgotten.

The second part of the essay examines the current nature of Polish labor relations and the ebb and flow of the state's struggle against the councils. We argue that post-Communist reformers have understood the challenge of systemic transformation in terms of creating "normal" economic institutions in which labor and capital have clearly defined and distinct social roles. This vision of normality has helped turn the government's privatization programs and its efforts to improve the structure and performance of state enterprises into frontal attacks on plant-based forms of worker representation. These attacks not only fly in the face of the successful patterns of post-Fordist industrial relations that seem to be emerging elsewhere, but have proved counterproductive. Worse, they have helped squander the knowledge, experience, and organizational capacities embedded in the councils and thus weakened one of the few institutions that might have served as a bridge between the nation's past and its future.

The third and concluding part of the essay situates the history of Polish works councils in a larger comparative framework and briefly speculates about their future development.

10.2   Polish Works Councils in, under, and against Communism

The cumulative effects of World War II destroyed prewar patterns of industrial governance in Poland. The Nazi extermination of the Jews, their almost equally genocidal policies against the Polish upper classes, and Yalta's movement of Poland's borders 100 miles west left the vast majority of Polish enterprises without owners and managers (Golebowski 1965, 12–22). As the German army retreated, spontaneously created "factory committees" (*komitety fabryczne*) or "plant councils" (*rady zakladowe*) took control of most enterprises, tracking down dismantled machinery, repairing factories, and restarting production. The councils were generally organized by skilled workers or white-collar employees and depended on high degrees of worker initiative and cooperation.[1]

Initially, the Communist-dominated Government of National Liberation supported the formation of the councils and accorded them wide competencies, including the power to name managing directors. In part, the Communists supported the councils because they feared that without them, control of the shop floor would pass either to the socialist-dominated trade unions or to former owners. Most important, however, the Communists realized that for the moment there was little practical alternative. Between January 1944 and the spring of 1945, the councils were the dominant force within enterprises.[2]

In May 1945, however, the newly established government began to exert its authority. The Ministry of Industry declared that it had the right to hire and fire managing directors and that managers, while they had to consult with the councils, were responsible for firm policy. The trade unions were given control over nominations to the councils, and a set of branch-based "operational groups" were empowered to establish production profiles and output targets for important firms. For the Communists, union control over the councils and state control over production profiles and output targets marked the beginning of their Leninist socioeconomic project: politically, all forms of labor representation were to be transformed into "transmission belts" of the Party, and economically, a single, unified state apparatus was to control the production and exchange of all goods (Kloc 1992, 41–49; Zukowski 1987, 26–39).

Within the postwar state the two "junior" partners of the governing coalition—the Polish Socialist party and the Polish Peasant party—struggled to maintain their practical and ideological independence from the Soviet-backed Polish Workers party. Both sought to distinguish themselves from the Communists by advocating a three-sector economy in which private property would exist alongside state and cooperative industries. And both stressed that the socialization of the means of production represented a higher form of human development than mere nationalization. Nonetheless, and despite their emphasis on socialization of productive relations, neither party made a concerted effort to defend the councils (Kloc 1992, 49–60). This political failure, while unlikely to have radically altered subsequent events (Malara and Key 1952; Coutouvidis and Reynolds 1986; Polonsky and Drukier 1980) is worth consid-

1. The best general account of the council movement in Poland through 1981 is Kloc (1992). For the immediate postwar period, see pp. 16–40. See also Zukowski (1987, 12–35). In general, Kloc tends to stress the worker origins of the councils, while Zukowski stresses their instrumental political invention.

2. For the early differences within the Polish Communist party and between Moscow and Warsaw over economic issues, including the councils, see Polonsky and Drukier (1980, 73–85). On the relationship of the councils to the struggle between the Socialist and Communist parties, see Coutouvidis and Reynolds (1986, 176–90). See also Kloc (1992, 20–43) and Zukowski (1987, 17–20).

ering because it highlights the principal forces that later converged to regenerate the council movement.

Despite the insistence of the Socialist and Peasant parties on a three-sector economy, and their high regard for cooperative industry, both recognized a large role for the state sector and placed great hopes in economic planning. For the Socialists in particular, the issue was not over planning per se, but over how to insure that plans were democratically formulated. The party thus proposed the creation of a third house of Parliament devoted solely to the construction of national plans and together with the Peasant party proposed that "socialized boards of directors" be interposed between firms and the planning apparatus to reduce the dangers of bureaucratization. These boards were to be composed of state, union, and consumers' representatives and were to name factory directors (Jedruszczak 1983, 5–75; Golebowski 1965, 24–47; Kowalik 1984, 5–55; Korbonski 1965, 20–49).

But although the Peasant and Socialist parties worried about nondemocratic planning and about the bureaucratic control of firms, they were less interested in direct participation of workers in the management of enterprises. Some of this ambivalence toward worker (co-)management was the result of Socialist strength within the trade union movement, and many saw the Communists' initial support for the councils as part of a larger attempt to monopolize power. Indeed, in late 1944, the Socialists agreed to centralize the administration of the unions, hoping that this would allow them to use their power more effectively. As it turned out, centralization only made it easier for the Communists to transform the unions into transmission belts of the Party (Kloc 1992, 119–59, Zukowski 1987, 26–40).

More important, the Socialists' ambiguous attitude toward the councils reflected their own lack of clarity about the exact relationship between planning and the socialization of the means of production. If the state was going to plan production for the nation as a whole or for key sectors of the economy, it would have to be able to tell firms what to produce and in what quantity. If so, then it was not clear what the boundaries of enterprise autonomy, let alone worker control, could or should be. If, on the other hand, workers or enterprises were to define the basic parameters of their performance, it was not clear what the content of economic planning really was. As the Soviet economist Kritsman put it, "For an economy to be anarchic it is sufficient for there to be a multiplicity of (independent) subjects" (Ellman 1979, 79).

Between 1944 and 1949, the Socialists' faith in planning—doubts notwithstanding—won out in practice over their continued ideological emphasis on the virtues of socializing the means of production. Indeed, despite their repeated conflicts with the Communists over the construction of plans, they supported the state's effort to expand its administrative control over enterprises. Thus, leading Socialists such as Oskar Lange, Michal Kalecki, and Czeslaw Bobrowski backed on economic grounds the reduction of the councils' powers, the state's right to name factory managers, the widening of managerial competencies, and most important, the development of a unified system of economic administration.[3]

Ideological and practical debates between the Socialist and Communist parties, and within them, became moot in 1949, when Moscow began to openly dictate Polish policy. The Socialists were forced officially to join with the Communists to create the Polish United Workers party, and the Communist movement itself was purged of its nationalist leadership. The three-sector model, already under siege, was officially discarded, and forced collectivization began. The State Planning Commission was given absolute authority to construct comprehensive national plans which were to be implemented through a (theoretically) unified chain of command. State planners formulated aggregate material flows and financial balances for the entire economy. These balances were then broken down on a sectoral basis and distributed to some 20 branch ministries. The ministries in turn drew up targets for the 200-odd "central administrations" that directly supervised firms. The central administrations determined production targets, investment funds, wage norms, and prices for firms. They also named managing directors (drawn from Party lists) and assigned firms their suppliers and buyers (Brus 1986, 3–40; Najduchowska 1964, 79–103).

Within firms, union and council jobs became subject to Party approval, and the managerial, consultative, and wage-setting roles of organized labor disappeared. The principal task of unions and councils became enforcing labor discipline and promoting socialist work competitions. At least partially to facilitate the fulfillment of these functions, the unions were given control over shortage commodities and allowed to determine access to training programs, health facilities, vacation spots, and most important, housing. In return for maintaining shop floor discipline the workforce was promised a share of the expanding economic pie (Kloc 1992, 164–204; Zukowski 1987, 35–54). These promises were not honored. While production skyrocketed, living conditions stagnated during the early 1950s. Communist trade unionism became a parody of its Western, Fordist counterpart.

As elsewhere, the Polish Communists believed that economic growth primarily depended on the production of producer goods. Thus, they directed investment to heavy industry at the expense of light industry and set the prices of producer goods low relative to those of consumer goods. This price policy insured a bigger bang for every zloty invested in heavy industry, while simulta-

3. On the ambiguous attitudes of leading Socialists toward central planning and its relationship to workers' councils, enterprise control, and "decentralization," see Bobrowski (1983, 145–90). Bobrowski was director of Poland's first Planning Bureau and the number-two man in the state economic administration in the immediate postwar years. His good working relationship with Hillary Minc, the economic tsar of Polish Stalinism—and an excellent planner—is particularly interesting. See also Drenowski (1976, 9–45), Kalecki (1982, 100–105), Osiatynski (1982), and Kowalik (1987, 1988). For an excellent treatment of the "decentralization—market socialism" problem, that focuses on Oscar Lange, see Lavoie (1985).

neously creating a system of forced savings for consumers. During the early 1950s, forced savings and low wages made it possible for the state to use more than 30 percent of the GDP for investment purposes. Extraordinarily high investment levels in turn generated extremely high growth rates as surplus agricultural labor was mobilized for industrial purposes. At the same time, rapidly expanding industrial employment, stable prices, and low levels of consumer goods production generated the chronic shortages associated with repressed inflation (Landau and Tomaszewski 1985; Brus 1986; Muller 1985).

The shortages produced by excessive and sectorally skewed investment rates were further compounded by the structure of the planning system. The (theoretical) unification of the economic apparatus, and the attempt to internalize all transactions within the state, meant that planners were never sure whether the failure of firms to perform as expected was the product of bad plans, the internal operation of firms themselves, or the failure of suppliers to provide the enterprises in question with the needed inputs. Unable to assess firm performance and constantly afraid of shirking, the state set taut plans in an effort to force enterprises to make maximum use of their resources. Firms, in turn, defended themselves against high plan targets by hoarding labor and materials and by understating their productive possibilities (Kornai 1985; Berliner 1956). Macroeconomically, this vicious circle manifested itself in constant shortages of basic goods. Microeconomically, it entailed the sweating of workers by the trade unions who supposedly represented them and the constant replacement of managers by a state that assumed their malfeasance.

In 1956, spurred by the succession crisis in Moscow following Stalin's death and by social unrest at home, the already embattled regime began a public discussion of economic reform. In May, the Party convened the Second Congress of Polish Economists. For the first time in seven years the relationship of planning to the "laws of supply and demand" and to enterprise autonomy were publicly debated. Despite sharp disagreements over "decentralization" and the use of market forces in planning, almost all the economists involved in the debate understood the issue of enterprise autonomy as being distinct from the question of industrial democracy (Montias 1962, 253–307).

In June, however, workers of the prestigious Cegielski Works changed the terms of the debate by taking to the streets to protest stagnating living standards and the Party's dictatorial control of the shop floor. The violent suppression of these demonstrations radicalized workers elsewhere. But instead of engaging in street demonstrations, workers began to organize themselves into independent factory committees. At the FSO Car plant in Warsaw, insurgent party activists demanded that democratically elected workers' councils (*rady robotnicze*) be made responsible for the administration of firms. Their demands were picked up by regionally based Party reformers and by reform economists. Both groups now began to connect economic decentralization and the marketization of planning with industrial democracy (Kloc 1992, 131–49; Zukowski 1987, 54–69).

By the fall, workers' councils had emerged in important coal mines, ship-yards, steel works, and textile mills. Now, however the councils were often formed without the help of local Party activists. Indeed, increasingly they arose despite Party and trade union efforts to suppress them. Sensing the threat posed by the councils, the Party leadership moved to contain the spontaneous seizure of factories by promising plant-based forms of worker representation and other reforms. Talk and half-measures, however, failed to stem the tide of social protest, and in October 1956 the Stalinist leadership of the Party was ousted. Wladyslaw Gomulka, head of the Party's erstwhile nationalist faction, was returned to power from prison. Boldly defying the Soviets, and hoping to satisfy demands at home, Gomulka declared that the country would now embark on a "Polish Road to Socialism."

In a series of hastily prepared decrees the new leadership called for the creation of workers' councils in all state enterprises. The councils were given the right to veto personnel decisions made by the state and to review firms' annual plan targets. Enterprises were allowed to retain a small percentage of their "profits"[4] in newly created "plant funds" (*fundusze zakladowy*), and the councils were given control over them in order to pay bonuses and to make small social investments. At the same time, the Party reduced the number of plan targets from 20 to 8 and modestly expanded the juridical autonomy of enterprises. Seventeen councils were granted extraordinary powers on an experimental basis so that the workable boundaries of decentralization could be tested. Finally, a wide range of other reforms were promised (Lipinski 1957; Sturmthal 1964, 119–40).

While the Party discussed reform, workers took matters into their own hands. Before electoral procedures for the councils could be specified, workers elected them on their own. By May 1957, the vast majority of the 3,300 councils that had emerged had been spontaneously created. Throughout the spring they hired and fired managers without the approval of the state and developed their own competitive tests to screen applicants. They also reorganized the administrative structure of firms, modified production profiles, introduced bonus systems, and altered supply networks. Most important, they demanded that they be recognized as the "sole authority within firms," and that the central administrations be liquidated and replaced by democratically elected branch councils. Indeed, despite the firing of managers, the councils' attack on the central administrations won them the support of many factory managers fed up with the state's intervention into their daily operations. Harking back to the earlier ideas of the Socialist party, council activists called for the creation of a third house of Parliament to construct plans and to coordinate the economic activities of firms at the national level (Kloc 1992, 148–77; Lipinski 1957, 3–44; Sturmthal 1964, 126–37).

Like the Socialists before them, however, even radical supporters of the

---

4. It is worth noting that it was completely unclear what the concept of profit meant in practice.

councils did not reject the framework of central planning and continued to recognize the state's right to determine prices, investments, major material flows, and basic wage rates. Thus, despite the desire of council activists and economic reformers to replace the central administrations with democratically elected branch councils, neither had a clear answer to the question of how firm autonomy was to be squared with central planning. Indeed, while reformers wanted firms to have greater control over wages and prices, and to extend the role of the market, they feared the inflationary effects of independent wage setting and rejected a system "of spontaneous price-formation beyond the control or influence of the state."[5] Moreover, in practice, while the councils were in constant conflict with the state's economic apparatus over the boundaries of their own autonomy—wanting to sell to whomever they pleased at prices of their own choosing—they frequently turned to these same organs to insure that other firms supplied inputs according to plan (Lipinski 1957, 3–44; Kloc 1992, 149–69).

Ultimately, however, it was not the theoretical or practical shortcomings of the councils that undid them. Instead, the Party quickly came to see them as a profound political threat, denouncing the movement's "anarchosyndicalist tendencies" and warning that "group property" could only lead to the rebirth of capitalism.[6] In the spring of 1957, the Party reasserted control of managerial appointments and made efforts to insure that state economic decisions were binding. Somewhat later, the unions were given control over the electoral lists to the councils, and in 1958 a new institution, the "conference of worker's self-management" (konferencja samorzadu robotnicego—KSR) was created. The KSRs formally assumed the remaining powers of the councils and were run by a troika composed of the factory director, the head of the plant Party organization, and the chief union steward. With their creation, plant-based forms of labor representation returned to the paternalistic patterns of the past.

Between 1958 and 1970, the economic system changed little. The Party, however, had learned to set less ambitious investment targets and to devote greater resources to the production of consumer durables so as to avoid the radical imbalances of the Stalinist years. But plan modesty did not end the cycle of hoarding, shortages, and bureaucratic intervention that came with the system as a whole. Indeed, as the productivity gains made possible by placing surplus agricultural labor into brick lines dried up and investment rates dropped, the growth rate steadily declined.[7]

In 1967, the Party attempted to reverse this trend by launching a program of

---

5. Quoted in Sturmthal (1964, 129). See Montias (1962, 263–307) for a fuller discussion of the price problem, as well as the works cited in n. 11, particularly those relating to Michal Kalecki and his work.

6. For a classic statement of this position, see Minc (1967).

7. On the political economy of the 1960s and Gomulka's strategy of selective development, see Brus (1986, 71–139), Landau and Tomaszewski (1985, 246–83), and Jezierski and Petz (1988, 259–77).

"selective development." "Archaic" industries were to be phased out and replaced by more "modern" ones, with the cost of the shift being paid for through increased labor discipline and higher consumer prices. In 1968, the government began cutting the wages of skilled workers and scaling back certain industries, among them shipbuilding. In December 1970, when the Party announced consumer price hikes, workers on the coast took to the streets. As in 1956, they were fired on by the military as they marched toward the Party headquarters. And as before, state violence did not immediately end resistance. But unlike in 1956, workers demanded not workers councils but the creation of an independent union: having seen their efforts to transform the regime through plant-based institutions undermined, workers now sought to link themselves in an organization that extended beyond the boundaries of individual enterprises.[8]

The Party tried to preempt these demands by ousting Gomulka and instituting an economic program that used large amounts of Western credit to simultaneously raise wages, consumption, and investment. For four years the economy boomed. By 1976, however, increasing shortages, massive financial imbalances, and a skyrocketing foreign debt forced the state to once again raise consumer prices (Landau and Tomaszewski 1985, 274–307; Muller 1988). The ensuing strikes were suppressed, but amazingly the investment boom continued almost through the end of the decade, forcing a repeat of the now well-scripted scenario in August of 1980. This time, however, and after 10 years of organizational struggle, workers forced the regime to recognize the independent trade union "NZZ Solidarnosc."

The emergence of Solidarity reopened the question of plant-based forms of worker representation. Paradoxically, however, it was the Party that first placed the issue on the table. For hard-liners, councils seemed to provide a way to split the labor movement. For reformers, they offered the promise of both replacing the disintegrating central planning system with some other way of coordinating the economy and trading a modicum of shop floor control for the social support necessary to undertake austerity measures.

Solidarity was initially unenthusiastic about the Party's offer to revive the councils and its attempt to involve the union in assuming some of the political burdens of austerity. During the first eight months of its existence, the union limited its economic proposals to demanding the redirection of expenditures from heavy industry and the military to consumer durables and social programs. Indeed, the union explicitly declined a more direct role in the formation of economic policy, repeatedly declaring, "we do not want to govern, we just want to control."

By the spring of 1981, however, the union's position on both economic reform and the councils began to shift. At the national level, the country's geopo-

---

8. For the origins of the demand for independent trade unions and its relationship to the history of the councils' defeat, see in particular Laba (1986) and Goodwyn (1991, 102–35).

litical situation left the union's leadership painfully aware that it could not pursue a reform strategy based on free elections. Thus, the national leadership was faced with the choice of entering into a coalition with a Party it could not trust or of finding a way to alter the structure of social power without openly calling into question the basic principle of one-party rule. Not surprisingly, the movement preferred the latter strategy, and its leaders began to talk in terms of creating a self-managed civil society that would progressively wrest "social space" from the state, but without directly challenging the Party's political monopoly (Michnik 1985, 133–55; Ost 1990).

At the local level, workers discovered that while the union increased their bargaining powers, the strike remained their only real weapon to change shop floor relations. With time, activists, exhausted by strikes, transformed the factory committees of the union into permanent negotiating bodies. These committees tried to throw out managers and to define procedural rules and jurisdictional competencies so that shop floor disputes did not inevitably end in strike threats. This de facto creation of works councils was, in turn, quietly supported by the union's national leadership, which felt increasingly vulnerable to the Party's accusations that constant strikes were destroying the economy (Jakubowicz 1989b; Lewandowski and Szomburg 1984; Norr 1984; Kloc 1992, 178–222; Zukowski 1987, 174–97).

Finally, the union realized that simply redirecting budgetary flows would not solve the country's economic problems. As in 1956, reform economists argued for the decentralization of economic decision making and for increasing the role of the market. Their demands, however, were more radical than before, calling for dismantling the entire planning apparatus and the creation of autonomous, self-managing, and self-financing firms. Firms were to be free to choose their own suppliers and buyers, set most of their own prices, make many of their own investments, and choose their own managers. In turn, the state's planning capacities were to be reduced to controlling interest rates, making key investments, and setting the prices of basic goods. By the summer of 1981, these economists had entered into an alliance with the union's most developed factory committees to form a network of 17 large enterprises located in each of the nation's major administrative districts. This network, or Siec, promoted the councils within the national union and aided other factories in forming their own councils.[9]

As the movement grew, the national union's position on works councils changed. Politically, the councils seemed to allow the union to wage war on the nomenklatura system of industrial appointments while leaving the principle

9. On the mix of economic and political motives behind the formation of Siec, see Chodorowski (1991) and Balcerowicz (1980). By the fall of 1981, and prior to the legislation that eventually mandated the creation of the councils, some several hundred had already emerged spontaneously. See Jaworski (1985).

of one-party rule unchallenged at the national level. Organizationally, they promised a way to institutionalize local conflicts, thus relieving the union of having to call strike alerts over every dispute. And economically, they gave the union a positive program that seemed to fall within the politically permissible parameters of the system as a whole.

In September 1981, the Sejm passed legislation changing the law on state enterprises and mandating the creation of employee councils (*rady pracow-nicze*) in all state firms. The legislation was an uneasy compromise between the union and the government. Both sides came to the negotiating table mixing political and economic rationales. Party hard-liners saw councils as a way to split the labor movement, while many unionists hoped to use them to destroy the Party's control of managerial appointments. Not surprisingly, the most contentious issue was over how much power the councils would have over managerial selection. Nonetheless, both within the union and the Party people supported the councils because they thought the councils could serve as the foundation for a profound economic reform. Indeed, without these voices it is inconceivable that the final legislation would have been passed.

The new legislation empowered democratically elected employee councils to fire managers and to veto hiring decisions made by the ministries. The councils were made the ultimate authority within firms, and the middle levels of the state's economic apparatus were to be abolished. Council approval became necessary for all the strategic decisions of the firm, and councils were given the right to review enterprise documents and contracts. Firms were to retain after-tax financial earnings, make their own investment and wage decisions, and choose their buyers and suppliers. Some price- and wage-setting powers were to be retained by the state, and the state reserved the right to reduce the powers of the councils in a limited number of "strategically important" firms. The size of the councils was to be determined by the firms themselves, and councils were to be directly elected by the workforce every two years. Each council named a smaller presidium whose president could not hold union or Party positions (*Ustawa* 1981a, 1981b).

In December 1981, two months after the passage of the legislation, martial law was declared and both Solidarity and the about 3,000 existing councils were suspended. In the spring of 1982, however, the councils were allowed to resume work, though the law on self-management was amended to give the state greater discretionary powers (*Ustawa* 1983). At first, the clandestine leadership of Solidarity argued against participation in the councils, believing— like Party hard-liners—that the councils would split the labor movement. Instead, the underground tried to organize a general strike to relegalize the union. As the prospect of a general strike receded, and after the regime reinvented, in 1983, the official unions that had collapsed with the birth of Solidarity, the underground's position on the councils softened. Without ever officially sanctioning participation, local activists were left to do what they thought best.

Increasingly, they ran for office in council elections arguing for what was called "the Spanish road" to industrial reform.[10]

Contrary to the councils elected in 1981, many of those that emerged in 1983 and 1984 were created without the real interest of workers and were in practice controlled by management. By 1985, however, in the second round of statutorily required elections, more and more firms followed the legal rules. In 1986, 6,400 of the country's 9,000 state firms had enterprise councils, while another 5,600 councils functioned at the plant or divisional level.[11] In most of these firms the councils acted as institutional substitutes for the outlawed union, focusing on wages and working conditions and on limiting the official union's abuse of their control over social services (Gesicka 1989). In a small, but extremely active group of firms, including many large and important enterprises, the councils attempted to exercise the full range of their managerial powers. As in 1956, they demanded the right to organize themselves across firms and actually held two national conferences before the Party stepped in.

Throughout the 1980s, the most active wing of the council movement attempted to extend the self-management system to the entire economy. These efforts failed, but they helped prevent the reassertion of centralized economic power. Stronger internal resistance and weaker external control pushed and pulled firms toward a vaguely defined autonomy that was periodically violated by the haphazard interventions of the center. Sometimes independence was achieved as workers and managers joined to keep firms within the self-management system. And sometimes firms increased their effective autonomy by agreeing to become "strategic enterprises" but demanding from the state investment funds or other privileges. In many firms, the councils became the arena for personal power struggles between different factions of management, and in most, their activities were limited to controlling pay schemes, dividing year-end "profits," and regulating the disposition of social funds. Indeed, over the course of the decade, council activists were often drawn into the political intrigues necessary to win resources for their enterprises and frequently came to adopt a managerial view of firm survival. This both eroded the link between the councils and the workforce and embedded the councils in the traditional power structure of the enterprise.

Nonetheless, relations between firms were more and more left to the firms themselves, while managers increasingly faced the workforce without the strong support of the Party. Rising shop floor pressure and declining central control intensified collusion between labor and management over wages, pushing up inflation and increasing shortages. Inflation rose only in part because the state was printing money. In addition, firms effectively printed money

10. For the history of the employee councils during the 1980s and their (ambiguous) relations to the underground union, see Jakubowicz (1989a) and Osiatynski, Pankow, and Federowicz (1985).

11. In all, some six million workers were employed in firms with councils. Fifty-four percent of council members were blue-collar workers, 27 percent economists, engineers, and technicians, and 19 percent line managers (Ruszkowski 1985).

themselves by buying from each other on credit and deferring payment.[12] As the situation deteriorated, the Party tried to jump start the economy by opening up the property regime.[13]

Firms under new property forms used their privileged regulatory status to raise wages and prices, further accelerating inflation. Experimentation with property rights increased the incidence of outright theft of state assets by government officials. By late 1988, this "propertization of the nomenklatura" had become a politically explosive issue.[14] In August 1988, workers once again went on strike demanding pay increases and the relegalization of Solidarity. As talks with the state began in early 1989, the union's factory committees re-emerged, in turn often forcing new elections to the employee councils. Moreover, many previously dormant councils now began to exercise their legal prerogatives in an effort to combat the managerial appropriation of state assets. In June, partly free national elections were swept by candidates nominated by Solidarity's national Citizen's Committee. Finally, in August 1989, after two months of parliamentary crisis, Solidarity was invited to form a government.

10.3   Employee Councils in, under, and in the Face of Post-Communist Neoliberalism

But the Solidarity that formed the government no longer was—if it ever was—simply a union. Nor was it a labor party. Solidarity's political structure was a loose coalition of deeply divided elites. Their divisions, however, had more to do with past tactical differences than with clearly articulated visions of a future social order. Indeed, virtually all of them described the goals of the victorious opposition in terms of a "return to normality": the creation of a parliamentary democracy with a "normal market economy" and a "normal European" property order.

Moreover, most of the country's leading economists agreed that real reform depended on the rapid privatization of the state sector. This consensus marked a profound movement away from the "third road" ideas that many of these same economists had implicitly or explicitly expressed in earlier years. Indeed, the most aggressive architects of Poland's neoliberal transition strategy came

---

12. On the microeconomics of inflation during the 1980s and the emergence of the so-called *zatory platnicze* (arrear backlogs), see Lipowski (1988) and Beksiak, Kawalec, and Malczewska (1990). For the classic statement of the relationship between inflation and shortage in socialist economies, see Kornai (1985).

13. Entry barriers for émigré-owned private businesses were lowered, and restrictions on the handicraft sector loosened. Managers were allowed to use a 1935 commercial code that had never been invalidated to form, nominally private, joint-stock companies out of state firms. And in 1988, the Ministry of Finance decided to experimentally transform the property status of a few enterprises. See Rostowski (1989).

14. There is no full account of the extent and nature of this process. The best empirical material can be found in the prosecutor general's report on the abuse of state property (*Prokuratura Generala* 1990). See also Levitas and Strzalkowski (1990).

from the same circles that had spearheaded the employee council movement within Solidarity during the 1980s, particularly those associated with Siec.[15]

This rejection of "market socialism" by those who had fought for the councils can only be understood in light of the history we have sketched. As we have argued, in the 1940s and 1950s the councils were seen as a way to break the Party's monopoly of political and economic power and thereby to make possible more rational planning. In the early 1980s, the vision was extended, and the promise of the councils became synonymous with the elimination of both central planning and the Party's control of industrial life. Indeed, throughout both periods, the political and economic motives for supporting the councils were so intertwined as to be inseparable.

During the 1980s, however, this linkage became unstuck. First, the Party itself attempted to save the economy by legitimizing new property forms, weakening the ideological constraints that had earlier bounded economic discussion. Second, the progressive collapse of the Party as a coherent institution suggested at least to some that the councils were no longer particularly useful battering rams against the system. And third, and perhaps most important, the (partial) decentralization of the economy brought about by the reforms of 1981 seemed to have had frightening inflationary consequences. Indeed, the poor performance of both the Polish and once "model" Yugoslav economies convinced economists that the failure of Communism had less to do with the single-party state than with the nature of socialized ownership itself: as long as enterprises did not have owners interested in maximizing profits for personal gain, the employees of state- or collectively owned firms would spend more on wages and ill-considered investments than was rational.

Indeed, by the time the Communist party finally collapsed, ideas about plant-based forms of worker representation had come full circle: if, over the previous four decades, the arguments used to support councils had fused economic and political rationales, then at the moment when the councils no longer were useful as weapons in the struggle against the Party, reform economists not only jettisoned their previous economic arguments but stood them on their heads. Now, not only was privatization necessary, but virtually all forms of worker influence on firm behavior came to be considered obstacles on the road to "normality." It is within the context of this profound suspicion of all forms of worker control that Poland's neoliberal reform strategy must be understood.

This strategy presented the transition to a market economy as a sequential process composed of three elements; stabilization, privatization, and industrial

---

15. The list of former self-management advocates in the ministries is long. To name a few: Leszek Balcerowicz, Marek Dabrowski, and Stefan Kawalec at the Ministry of Finance; Janusz Lewandowski, Tomasz Gruszecki, Tomasz Stankiewicz, and Jan Szomburg at the Ministry of Ownership Change. Most see their earlier advocacy of self-management simply as the best political and economic compromise available to them under "really existing socialism." Other advocates of self-management have remained more true to the idea of workers' control. They have also been among the most active critics of their former allies.

restructuring.[16] Stabilization was to free prices, radically tighten fiscal and monetary policy, and open the country to new private businesses and foreign goods. Taken together these measures were to introduce demand barriers into the economy, forcing state firms to reduce costs, change production profiles, and find new markets. Stabilization, however, was to be followed rapidly by privatization because reformers believed that without private owners empowered to choose investments and profits over wages, the spending patterns of state enterprises would continually threaten macroeconomic equilibrium.[17] By extension, reformers argued that it was a mistake to attempt to restructure state enterprises before privatization since this amounted to little more than throwing good money after bad. Thus, on the one hand, reformers planned to expose state firms to precisely the market forces that they assumed would eventually overwhelm them. On the other hand, they saw little point in trying to help state firms adjust to those forces so long as they remained socialized entities. Indeed, the entire reform strategy conceived of state firms in general and worker-run firms in particular as something of an enemy, an enemy that had to be first outflanked by the development of the private sector and then rapidly conquered through privatization.

After two years in operation this strategy is now (in mid-1992) encountering increasing difficulties (Schaffer 1992b; Blanchard and Berg 1992; Dabrowski, Federowicz, and Levitas 1991a). The growth of the private sector, while dynamic, has been insufficient to absorb the losses sustained by the state sector. Output remains about 20 percent lower than in December 1989, while unemployment has climbed to above 12 percent of the active labor force (Johnson 1992; Coricelli and Revenga 1992; Freeman 1992). The fall in both production and employment has occurred without a significant number of bankruptcies, despite the fact that close to half of all state firms are now operating near or in the red. Inflation remains high, and centrally imposed wage controls are breaking down. Moreover, declining tax revenues and increased social insurance costs have left the state facing a profound fiscal crisis (Schaffer 1992a). Finally, the government's ultimate weapon of reform privatization has yet to be successfully wielded in battle (Dabrowski et al. 1992; Berg 1992; Levitas 1992).

Despite the country's increasing economic problems, reformers continue to defend the overall soundness of their basic strategy. Indeed, they claim that the collapse of the state sector only demonstrates the fundamental weakness of

16. See Council of Ministers (1990). The plan broadly paralleled and was clearly influenced by the ideas of Jeffery Sachs. Nonetheless, the domestic origins of the strategy should not be underestimated. See Sachs (1989) and Sachs and Lipton (1990).

17. Some participants in the debate, however, were so pessimistic about the adjustment capacities of state firms that they argued that privatization should precede stabilization. For an extremely cogent statement of this position, see Hinds (1990a, 1990b). Hinds recognizes the autonomy that the "self-managed firms" have acquired and proposes a combination of massive, rapid privatization prior to stabilization, and reassertion of state control over the rest of the sector during stabilization. He does not, however, fully recognize the degree to which Polish firms had acquired control over the very decision to be privatized.

socialized property and underscores the need for rapid privatization. In the following, we argue on the contrary that the government's extremely pessimistic assessment of the adjustment capacities of state firms in general, and of council-run firms in particular, has been something of a self-fulfilling prophecy. In fact, the government's adversarial conception of the state sector and its frontal attack on the councils have not only been costly but have undermined one of the few social and economic institutions that might provide a workable bridge between the past and some unknown, but more viable future.

We make this argument at four different levels. First, we argue that the adjustment patterns of council-run firms have been both extremely varied and generally rational. Second, we point out that the government's assumption that all council-run firms were structurally flawed, and therefore not worth helping, meant that the state could neither see nor act on the differences between them. As a consequence, the economy as a whole lost the potential growth of at least some state firms. Third, we argue that many of the weaknesses of council-run firms lie beyond their governance structures and that contrary to expectations strengthening management by eliminating the councils has not improved firm performance. In fact, it may actually worsen it. And finally, we show how the state's hostility toward the councils has hampered privatization itself and that privatization in general has succeeded only where the councils have been allowed to lead the process. To make our case it is necessary to look more closely at the structure and functioning of council-run firms during 1989–91.[18]

With the relegalization of Solidarity in April 1989, factory committees of the union reemerged in the vast majority of industrial enterprises. Unlike in 1980, however, workers did not return en masse to Solidarity. Nor did they completely abandon the official trade unions revived in 1983. Instead, in a typical firm, 20 to 35 percent of workers rejoined Solidarity, while another 20 to 35 percent remained in the Ogolnopolskie Porozumienie Zwiazkow Zawodowych (OPZZ).[19] In some firms, the relegalized factory committees of Solidarity immediately forced the election of new employee councils. In most firms, however, the election of new councils took place in May 1990 with the

18. In the following we rely primarily on a series of empirical studies conducted by the Gdansk Institute of Market Economics since January 1990. Unless otherwise indicated, the information contained in the following is based on the quantitative and qualitative study of 50 state manufacturing enterprises. Interviews were repeated quarterly and conducted individually with managers, unionists, and employee council members. Respondents are asked about firm finances, wage and employment policy, production and sales, industrial relations, privatization, and future prospects. Statistical information bearing on these subjects was obtained. The enterprises are located in 10 different *voviodships*. Nineteen firms operate in large industrial centers of more than 500,000 inhabitants, 10 in cities of 100,000–500,000, and 21 in towns of less than 100,000. The sample population is not statistically representative. Dabrowski, Federowicz, and Levitas (1991a, 1991b, 1991c).

19. In both cases, real union membership is hard to establish because the payment of dues is highly irregular. OPZZ membership rates are inflated by large numbers of pensioners who remain in the union to gain access to various social assets. Since 1990, union density has probably declined by a few percentage points.

normal expiration of statutory terms of office. In virtually all firms, the newly elected councils attempted to assert their legal rights over the disposition of firm assets, lest managers steal them in the chaos of the transition.

Not surprisingly, the councils frequently moved to fire managing directors. By the end of 1990, approximately 30 percent of all managing directors were new, and by the end of 1991 some 40 percent were.[20] Contrary to reformers' expectations, however, organized labor did not blindly strike out at managers for their past political allegiances or for the immediate hardships caused by stabilization. Indeed, during the first and most painful months of reform, surprisingly few industrial conflicts were over wage issues. Instead, they centered on managerial capacities to adjust to the new environment: ironically, managers were often fired for failing to reduce employment and to streamline the operation of their firms fast enough.

Moreover, managerial change and the extension of council power in general facilitated rather than blocked enterprise adjustment. Deep organizational reform was almost always associated with the appointment of new managing directors. New managers were more able than old ones to make changes in the operation of their firms.[21] Overall, about a third of the firms we examined made comprehensive efforts to reform their sales, employment, financial, and production structures, while the adjustment patterns of the rest could be classified as shallow. Where reform was limited, failure was generally the product of passivity on the part of both management and labor, and not the result of open warfare. Where reform was actively blocked by one side or the other, management was as often responsible as the councils or the unions.

While Solidarity members tend to dominate the councils, the councils are not simple extensions of the union. Disagreement between the councils and Solidarity over managerial selection and firm policy is common.[22] In 1990, some councils were more "workerist" than their local unions, while others supported radical restructuring plans against more traditional union policies. In 1991, the tendency seems to be that the councils are more interested in firm survival while the unions are more interested in wages and employment. This is the result, in part, of the increasingly white-collar nature of the councils and, in part, of rank-and-file pressures on the union to adopt more militant positions.

Despite hostility between the unions at the national level, locally they tend to work together, presenting common positions to management on most issues. Solidarity is the more influential union and even when in the minority is taken more seriously by management. Solidarity is also more aggressive both in pur-

20. While exact data is lacking, most of these new managers probably were employed earlier in the firms they now run.

21. This, however, was not always the case, and more than 25 percent of newly elected managers initiated only limited reforms.

22. In a few firms, councils that were expected to vote out managers did not do so after examining the firm's accounts and surveying prospective replacements.

suing enterprise reform and in blocking it. In contrast, the OPZZ—despite its radical rhetoric at the national level—seems to adapt itself to the policies of the dominant local force. As the economic situation has deteriorated, both unions have found themselves chasing wildcat strikes.

In small and medium-sized firms, unions and the councils frequently compete with each other over firm policy. In general, competition has facilitated adjustment by making one or another group more inclined to take a long-term perspective on firm survival. In a few cases, organizational competition has generated leapfrogging wage and employment demands. But this seems to be exceptional. In most firms, there are enough actors aware of the need for structural reform to insure that management has at least some allies for change. In small and medium-sized firms, more than half of the "deep" or "significant" reforms were made before the onset of financial problems, indicating a capacity for strategic foresight. In all these cases, cooperation between management and labor was critical.

In large enterprises, the often daunting social consequences of radical reform have inclined both organized labor and management toward caution, if not passivity. In these enterprises, both sides are often painfully aware that even the most dramatic cutbacks will do little to ensure firm survival without the arrival of new resources. Not surprisingly, comprehensive reform in large firms was rare and, in general, began only after financial reserves had been exhausted. In some highly visible, heavy-industrial firms, the unions have demanded the elimination of the councils and the renationalization of the firm. Unable to win pay increases from the councils, or disturbed by the slow pace of reform, unions felt they would do better negotiating directly with the government in a renationalized setting.

In sum, the overall picture of the adjustment efforts of council-run enterprises is mixed. On the one hand, approximately two-thirds of the firms we examined made only limited attempts to adapt to the new environment. Everywhere people complained that decisions were taken too slowly and that too much time was spent in meetings. Managers often claimed that their hands were tied by incompetent councils or that they would be fired if they really made radical changes. For their part, council members argued that managers often lacked the skills necessary to save firms and that if it was possible to hire better management they would have already done so. Council-run firms have also become more willing over time to exceed centrally imposed wage norms even as profits have declined.

On the other hand, at least one-third of all state enterprises made radical changes in the way they do business. Councils and unions were either the leading forces of change or crucial partners to it. Moreover, the weakness of adjustment efforts elsewhere has not been the result of open conflict between labor and management, despite their mutual recriminations. Instead, passivity is more often the product of confusion in the face of huge and very real structural difficulties. The fact that most firms initially resisted raising wages when profits were high, and only began to overshoot wage norms when profits fell, suggests that wage maximization is related to the bleakness of enterprise prospects and not to squandering of development possibilities that wage restraint might in theory facilitate.[23]

Despite the generally rational reaction of council-run firms to the stabilization program, and the efforts of many to adjust to the market, reformers continue to insist that firms are simply waiting for the financial discipline of the state to break down and for the era of easy money to return. Thus, the government has declined to aid state firms in restructuring their operations prior to privatization, and substantial amounts of international funds earmarked for industrial restructuring are being held back until firms are privatized.

More important, the government's hope that stabilization and open markets would force bad firms into bankruptcy while allowing good firms to get loans from commercial banks has proved painfully naive. The number of bankruptcies has been small, and banks continue to lend to marginal enterprises. Capital has not been redirected to dynamic firms, and new investment loans have virtually stopped. Worse, firms that are making dramatic adjustment efforts are often refused credit while the loss-making enterprises around them still get it.

The paralysis of the banking system is not simply the product of incompetence. State bank portfolios are swamped with the bad debts of a relatively small number of huge industrial loss-makers (Boguszewski et al. 1993). Given the banks' undercapitalization, foreclosing on these firms would essentially mean bankrupting themselves. Moreover, even if they could afford to absorb the losses, the banks are essentially being asked to bear the burdens of the past lending patterns of the Communist state. Not surprisingly, they have been reluctant to do so without assurances that the state will help absorb these costs (Brainard 1991; Hinds 1990a, 59–64).

For its part, the state has been reluctant to get involved, insisting that the market alone must determine the allocation of capital.[24] This reluctance to help redirect capital to dynamic firms before privatization, and to engage in the politically messy business of rewriting bad debts, has helped turn the state's extremely pessimistic assessment of the socialized sector's adjustment capacities into a self-fulfilling prophecy. In the process, the economy has been deprived of the potential growth represented by well-run but capital-constrained state firms.

The costs of the government's hostility to state firms in general, and council-run ones in particular, are best exemplified by the practice of privatization to date. As we have noted, by the early 1980s the councils had acquired the legal right to control decisions about the disposition, transfer, or sale of firm assets.

23. It should be added that the share of wages in firms' overall costs is relatively low (though rising), making it unlikely in most firms that savings on wages would provide a real source of investment capital.

24. Finally in 1993, the government began developing a plan to write off some of the bad debts burdening the banking sector.

Throughout the decade, these rights were both contested and constrained by the Party, and most councils eventually lost their dynamic and independent character. Nonetheless, as Communism finally collapsed, two forces pushed the councils to exercise a fuller range of their managerial powers. First, the struggle against the "propertization of the nomenklatura" and the disorganization of the post-Communist state left the councils as the sole institution capable of preventing managers from appropriating assets. And second, stabilization— if it was to be achieved through market mechanisms—required firms, and by extension councils, to be free to determine their contractual relations and to set prices.

Post-Communist reformers, afraid of the consolidation of council power and hoping to privatize state firms as quickly as possible, immediately announced an ambitious plan to sell off state firms. To do so, the government argued, firms had to be commercialized first. This procedure was to entail turning firms into capitalized joint-stock companies of the Treasury. As joint-stock companies, firms were to replace their councils with boards of directors to which management would be responsible and on which the state would have the dominant voice. In short, commercialization was renationalization by another name.[25]

The government intended to sell firms, once commercialized, on the open market, in the belief that the only rational way to allocate property rights was to let the market decide.[26] In early 1990, 20 "good" firms whose councils had agreed to commercialization were selected for the public offering program. The state quickly discovered, however, that even with the full cooperation of employees, preparing firms for auction and setting opening stock prices was a lengthy procedure that often involved restructuring the firm itself. Moreover, the fall in disposable income that came with stabilization made it clear that even if many firms could be prepared for sale, multiple offerings would push stock prices "toward zero."[27] In fact, only 17 successful public issues were

25. In public, the Ministry of Finance argued that commercialization was simply a necessary prerequisite for its ambitious program of public offerings. In private, it hoped that the power to commercialize firms at will would give the state insurance against the presumably perverse behavior of council-run firms. In return for giving up control of their enterprises, employees were promised the possibility of purchasing a maximum of 20 percent of stock at preferential prices, as long as the sum total of preferences did not amount to more than a year's average wages. It is fair to say that the government feared worker ownership about as much as it feared worker control. Not surprisingly, the government did not propose that within privatized firms some more modest form of plant-based worker representation replace the employee councils.

26. For the assumptions and activities of the Agency for Property Transformation, see Gruszecki (1990) and Jasinski (1990). The government hoped that by offering the stock of good firms at low prices the state could generate a cycle of self-reproducing investor confidence that would make possible the rapid sell-off of the state sector.

27. The initial plans to sell off firms on the open market were formulated in an extremely inflationary environment. Market sales not only had an air of normality about them but also seemed to be a useful tool in fighting inflation. Stabilization devastated the political and economic logic of these plans as ridiculously low stock prices would allow a very select and suspect group to acquire state assets at bargain basement prices. See Kawalec (1989).

carried out between January 1990 and June 1992 (Berg 1992; Gruszecki 1990; Levitas 1992).

In the spring of 1990, as the problems with public offerings became palpable, the draft legislation on privatization was debated in Parliament. Council activists opposed giving the government the right to commercialize firms at will. Significantly, they were joined by others who, while not enamored of the councils, argued that the slowness of public offerings meant that mass commercialization would entail the recentralization of economic power. As the tenuous boundary between the state and "its" firms dissolved, the state would once again be responsible for running the entire economy.[28]

Not surprisingly, the idea of giving away state assets became more attractive. Giveaways seemed to lessen the constraints imposed on privatization by shallow markets and hard-to-establish stock values, while taking the ownership question out of an arena in which only firms and ministries had something at stake. Stocks would be given to citizens, regardless of their workplaces, through intermediary institutions.[29] As with commercialization, however, the basic question of whether the councils could refuse to participate in the government's privatization plans remained.

In the end, the privatization legislation passed by Parliament in July 1990 was a curious document. The Ministry for Ownership Change was given wide powers to sell commercialized firms. The councils, however, were basically given the right to veto state privatization plans.[30] Mass stock distribution schemes were recognized as a possible instrument in the privatization process, but no specific plan was identified. Almost as an afterthought, a paragraph was added that made it possible for councils, with the approval of the Ministry, to legally dissolve their firms and rent, lease, or sell their assets to a new corporation. Significantly, this new corporation could be solely or partly owned by its employees, essentially providing a loophole for employee ownership.

In December 1991, an advocate of stock distribution schemes was made minister of ownership change, and the focus of the privatization program shifted from public offerings to mass privatization. The ministry began to identify 500 large and medium-sized firms that it wanted to include in the first round of the program, and to design the mutual funds whose shares would be given to the public. But if reformers had earlier found that they could not simply use the market to allocate property rights, they now found that the very

28. As the director of commercialized firms at the Ministry of Ownership Change later told us, mass commercialization would "have made me a second Hillary Minc," the economic tsar of Polish Stalinism.

29. In 1988, Lewandowski and Szomburg proposed using a voucher scheme to privatize state assets in Poland. See Lewandowski and Szomburg (1989, 1990). Jeffery Sachs's proposal to combine vouchers with mutual funds came later. See Sachs (1990).

30. In theory, their veto powers could be overturned by a majority vote of the Council of Ministers with the approval of the prime minister, but these powers have yet to be used.

construction of giveaway schemes involved making all sorts of judgments about what kinds of markets each particular scheme would create. As the details of the operation grew hazier, firms declined to participate, while the ministry itself scaled down its ambitions.

What the ministry was able to accomplish was to convince—for one reason or another—about 250 firms to become joint-stock companies of the Treasury by the end of 1991.[31] Elimination of the councils and strengthening management was hoped would improve these firms' performance. Contrary to expectations, however, this has not happened. In fact, the adjustment capacities of commercialized firms may actually have deteriorated.[32] In some firms this seems to be related to the motives that lay behind the decision to commercialize in the first place. Both managers and councils seem to have regarded commercialization as a new way of "hooking onto the plan," expecting that after renationalization they would receive special treatment from the state. Managers, instead of using their new autonomy to pursue reform, generally remained passive, arguing that the unrest produced by change could scare away buyers or that change itself was pointless until the desires of future owners were known. Meanwhile, the newly created boards of directors have neither the authority nor the information to force managers to alter their behavior.

In other firms, managers and councils agreed to commercialization because they were already negotiating with potential buyers. For them commercialization was a necessary legal step toward privatization. At the moment when ownership rights reverted to the state, however, these firms lost control over the choice of buyer and the terms of the sale. Suspicious of sweetheart deals, afraid of sanctioning corruption, and looking to maximize revenues, the ministry almost inevitably tried to involve other parties in the sale. Sometimes earlier negotiations stalled or collapsed, and sometimes the ministry choose buyers that the firms opposed. In a few cases, these choices were clearly ill advised. Finally, in some firms where adjustment efforts had begun, reform ceased after commercialization as both workers and managers waited for ministerial directives. Moreover, industrial relations tended to deteriorate after the normal line of communication between workers and managers—the councils—had been eliminated.

Of all the government's programs to privatize state firms, it is the one that has been least talked about and least invested in organizationally that has proved to be the most successful: the so-called liquidation procedures. Not to be confused with bankruptcy, the procedure allows for the legal dissolution of an enterprise and the lease or sale of all or part of its assets to a new corporation

31. Some firms commercialized expecting to be included in mass privatization. A handful came from the original pool of firms that were to be sold in public offerings. And most were hoping to be bought out by foreign firms in trade sales.

32. The following discussion of commercialization and liquidated state enterprises is based on our own study of 20 privatizing state enterprises. See Dabrowski et al. (1992) and Chelminski and Czynczyk (1991).

created by the existing workforce. So far, more than 1,000 firms have been "privatized" in this way. Despite the fact that most of them were small or medium-sized enterprises, the numbers are impressive given the failure of both public offerings and mass privatization and the fact that little has been done politically or organizationally to promote liquidation.[33]

To begin a liquidation procedure, a firm must have a ministerially recognized consulting firm determine the value of its assets according to three different accounting procedures. At a general meeting of the workforce, it is then determined whether employees are willing to buy at least 20 percent of the book value of the assets. If so, the firm enters into negotiations with the ministry over whether the book value of the assets will be used to determine the value of the firm or whether another price will be set. Firms may also solicit stock commitments from interested outside buyers. Depending on the price that is ultimately arrived at, the willingness of employees to buy shares, and the level of outside commitments, the assets of the enterprise can be purchased outright, rented, or, most frequently, leased for 10 years, after which the formerly state-owned assets become fully privatized. As with the price of the assets, the terms of the lease are the product of intense negotiations, and the ministry can refuse to allow privatization to go forward if it wants to. On average, these procedures take about nine months to a year to complete.

Despite the fact that these privatizations, like all others, legally require the dissolution of the employee councils, councils generally not only agree to them but frequently lead them. Whether the initiative to liquidate a firm came from management or labor, councils virtually always played the principal role in explaining the process to the workforce and a major role in negotiating with consulting firms, provincial authorities, and the ministry. Moreover, unlike in all other privatizations, there is a clear link to efforts to change the structure and functioning of firms before and after the actual legal transformation of the enterprise itself as adjustment efforts begin before privatization and continue after it is completed.

In most firms privatized through liquidation procedures, blue-collar workers purchase 20 to 30 percent of shares. Nonetheless, what is striking about the capital structure of many of these new corporations is the plurality of major shareholders. Typically, the largest group of owners is drawn from white-collar workers, and frequently the managing director is the largest single shareholder. Also, and contrary to expectations, insiders frequently find outside individuals to buy into the firm. Usually these investors come from the network of the firm's suppliers and buyers. Sometimes they acquire a controlling interest. Most frequently, however, they are significant but not dominant shareholders, and generally stocks are more or less evenly divided between managers, workers, and outside investors.

33. Another 534, mostly small, firms have been bankrupted and had their assets sold off by receivers.

Despite the constant accusations of reformers that the councils block privatization, most privatizations are in fact being nursed into the world by them. Moreover, worker-management buyouts do not seem to be creating the immobile capital structures that the government feared. Perhaps most important, firm-led property transformations have not only proceeded faster than public auctions and mass privatization but seem to link legal changes in ownership with economic restructuring of the enterprise itself. If the failure of public offerings demonstrates that the market alone cannot be used to allocate property rights, and if the failure of mass privatization demonstrates that the allocation of property rights cannot be used to create workable markets, the success of liquidation procedures shows that the social reconstruction of property rights and markets not only must be carried out together but is best led by actors closest to the assets and markets at issue.

10.4 The Future of Workplace-Based Representation in Poland

The history of Polish councils can only be understood within a larger comparative context that begins with the widespread application of Taylorist principles of industrial organization in the years just before the First World War. Almost everywhere the adoption of mass production technologies generated resistance on the shop floor and helped spawn movements for the direct control of production by the workforce. And almost everywhere these movements at once sharpened the struggle between labor and capital and helped further fracture the Left between the reformism of the Second International, the etatism of the Third, and the "utopian" socialism of anarchosyndicalism.[34]

In the West, the defeat of the revolutionary Left after the First World War, and the victory of Fordist strategies of production, served to marginalize ideas about workers' control until at least 1968. Tactically, the labor movement seemed better served by organizational forms that linked workers across firms and industries, while strategically, the productive powers of Fordism seemed to legitimate a vision of industrial change that saw its endpoint not so much in the abolition of the division of labor but in its planned regulation. Indeed, between 1945 and 1970 the social democratic combination of Keynesian macroeconomic policies and arm's-length industrial bargaining proved remarkably successful in raising working-class living standards.

For all its success, however, the traditional modalities of social democratic politics began to unravel in the mid-1970s when increasingly volatile international markets turned the rigid organizational structures of Fordism into a competitive liability (Piore and Sabel 1984). The attempt to regain flexibility at the point of production has prompted capital to renew its struggle against unionism. At the same time, this attack has been accompanied by at least verbal

---

34. See chap. 1 in this volume by Joel Rogers and Wolfgang Streeck. See also the extremely useful collection of essays edited by Horvat, Markovic, and Supek (1975).

attempts to replace the adversarial and arm's-length industrial relations of the past with some new, more cooperative modus vivendi.

In countries where the institutions of postwar social democracy never fully crystallized—such as France and the United States—the very weakness of organized labor has allowed capital to behave as if unilateral control over the workplace was a sufficient condition for flexible competitiveness. Attempts to institutionalize more cooperative industrial relations have oscillated between voluntarism and defection, leaving capital's expressed desire for greater worker participation rather hollow. In countries where organized labor remains relatively strong—such as Sweden—or where this strength has been accompanied by the legal and institutional preservation of plant-based forms of worker representation—such as Germany—the effort to find a new, more cooperative system of industrial relations has been more successful.

In Poland, however, not only were plant-based forms of worker representation more prominent throughout most of the postwar period, but ironically their very strength in the past has become a liability for their future. As we have argued, the fusion of Taylorism, central planning, nationalization, and Party-controlled unionism served to transform works councils into one of the principal institutional locations of a larger struggle between state and society. Ideologically, this struggle pushed and pulled the opposition in general, and the labor movement in particular, toward reinventing the anarchosyndicalist vision of industrial organization that elsewhere had been in retreat since the First World War. In practice, it accelerated the decomposition of both state planning and state property, leaving in its wake a highly confused set of relations between economic actors and the industrial assets they inhabited.

The confused nature of these relations, combined with the poor performance of the Polish economy during the 1980s, prompted not only a reappraisal of "market socialism" but also the complete rejection of all ideas that linked positive economic outcomes with worker participation in management. Thus, paradoxically, at precisely the moment when workplace-based forms of worker representation are coming to be seen in the West as institutions necessary for competitive success, they are being rejected in the East as legacies of the past.

This rejection can be seen in virtually all aspects of the neoliberal reform strategy adopted by Poland's post-Communist reformers. Not only was the rapid privatization of state assets understood as the sine non qua of systemic transformation, but the primary strategies of privatization were explicitly designed to eliminate worker influence over the process itself. Moreover, and not surprisingly, there has been no effort to mandate legally a role for workplace-based forms of worker participation either in the emerging private sector or in privatized state enterprises. Worse, while in general working reasonably well with the councils at the local level, the unions have not sought to defend them at the national level. In part, this is because councils are seen as institutional competitors. More important, however, it reflects the unions' belief that they cannot survive politically being party to unpopular restructuring plans when living standards are falling.

Nonetheless, the difficulties that Poland's neoliberal strategy is encountering may ultimately serve to modify the current hostility to plant-based forms of worker representation. As we have argued, the only privatization strategy that has worked to date has been critically dependent on the active support and participation of the employee councils. Despite the fact that the councils stand to lose their legal standing after privatization, there are indications that in many liquidated enterprises former council members are being named to the newly created boards of directors, irrespective of the structure of stock ownership. This suggests that at least in the short term, and in firms that have succeeded in transforming their legal and economic identities on their own, new and old owners have come to recognize the value of plant-based worker representation.

Moreover, the government is increasingly coming to realize that privatization cannot be carried out without the prior or simultaneous restructuring of enterprises. As a result, state actors are beginning to search for local allies in the reform process, trying actively to involve not just management but labor in the discussion of the future of plants, regions, and industries. Increasingly, the massive problems presented by industrial restructuring are forcing the state to look for more cooperative relations with labor, in the same way that market volatility in the West has forced capital to at least partly rethink worker participation.

The informal reproduction of workplace-based forms of worker representation in newly privatized firms and the state's recent attempts to involve the councils in industrial restructuring continue to take place against the background of the reformers' general hostility to worker participation in management and the unions' desire for a "pure and simple" industrial identity. This makes it unlikely that the existing informal structures of worker participation can survive, let alone prosper, without a stronger legal foundation. When negotiations stall, it is all too tempting for both labor and capital (read for the moment: the state) to blame each other for the failure and to defect from future efforts at co-determination. On the other hand, few in Poland have fully realized the degree to which market volatility renders arm's-length industrial relations a competitive liability. Without some state regulations that force labor and capital into permanent negotiations at the plant level, Poland is in danger of replacing the existing institutional foundations for such negotiations with a model of industrial organization that has already lost its competitive edge.

References

Agency for Property Transformation. 1990. *Kierunki prywartzacjiw roku 1990* (Directions of privatization in 1990). Warsaw: Ministry of Finance 4389/90, October.

Balcerowicz, Leszek. 1980. *Alternatywy rozwoju: Reforma gospodarcza—glowne kierunki i sposoby realizacji* (Developmental alternatives: Economic reform—main directions and instruments). Warsaw: Main School of Planning and Statistics.

Beksiak, Janusz, Stefan Kawalec, and Danuta Malczewska. 1990. *Zarzadzanie przedsiebiorstwami, 4: Zachowania uczestnikowzycia gospodarczego* (Enterprise management, 4: The behavior of economic actors). Warsaw: Panstwowe Wydawnictwo Naukowe.

Berg, Andrew. 1992. The logistics of privatization in Poland. Paper presented at NBER conference on Transition in Eastern Europe, Cambridge, Mass., February.

Berliner, Joseph. 1956. A problem in Soviet business administration. *Administrative Science Quarterly* 1:83–101.

Blanchard, Oliver, and Andrew Berg. 1992. Stabilization and transition: Poland 1990–1991. Paper presented at NBER conference on Transition in Eastern Europe, Cambridge, Mass., February.

Bobrowski, Czeslaw. 1983. *Wspomnienia ze stulecia* (Memories of a century). Lublin: Wydawnictwa Lubelski.

Boguszewski, Piotr, Michal Federowicz, Kazimierz Kloc, Wanda Mizielinska, and Tadeusz Smuga. 1993. Banki a przedsiebiorstwa (Banks and enterprises). *Economic Transformations*, no. 37. Gdansk: Gdansk Institute of Market Economics.

Brainard, Lawrence. 1991. Reform in Eastern Europe: Creating a capital market. *Economic Review of the Federal Reserve Bank of Kansas City*, January: 49–58.

Brus, Wlodzimierz. 1986. 1950–1953: The Peak of Stalinism. In *The economic history of Eastern Europe*, vol. 3: *Institutional change within a planned economy*, ed. M. C. Kaser, 3–40. Oxford: Clarendon.

Chelminski, Dariusz, and Andrzej Czynczyk. 1991. Spoleczne bariery prywatyzacji: Prawomocnosc ladu instytucjonalnego w przedsiebiorstwach skomercjalizowanych (The social barriers to privatization: The authority structure of the institutional order of commercialized enterprises). Department of Management, Warsaw University.

Chodorowski, Marcin. 1991. Siec-Rok 1981: Powstanie, struktura, dzialanie (Network 1981: Emergence, structure, activity). M.A. Thesis, University of Warsaw.

Coricelli, Fabrizio, and Anna Revenga. 1992. Wages and unemployment in Poland. Working Paper Series, no. 821. Washington, D.C.: World Bank.

Council of Ministers. 1990. *Program Gospodarczy: Glowne zalozeniai kierunki* (The economic program: Main assumptions and directions). Warsaw, October. Mimeo.

Coutouvidis, John, and Jaime Reynolds. 1986. *Poland 1939–1947.* Leicester: Leicester University Press.

Dabrowski, Janusz, Michal Federowicz, and Anthony Levitas. 1990. Stabilization and state enterprise adjustment: The political economy of state firms after five months of fiscal discipline. Working Paper Series on Central and Eastern Europe, 1–69. Harvard University.

———. 1991a. The collapse of the state sector: The moment of truth? *Economic Transformations*, no. 21. Gdansk: Gdansk Institute of Market Economics.

———. 1991b. Polish state enterprises and the properties of performance. *Politics and Society* 19(4): 403–37.

———. 1991c. State enterprises in 1990: Research results. *Economic Transformations*, no. 11. Gdansk: Gdansk Institute of Market Economics.

Dabrowski, Janusz, Michal Federowicz, Anthony Levitas, and Jan Szomburg. 1992. The privatization process in the Polish economy. *Economic Transformations*, no. 27. Gdansk: Gdansk Institute of Market Economics.

Drenowski, Jan. 1976. *O mysli politycznei* (On political thought). London: Odnowa.

Ellman, Michael. 1979. *Socialist planning.* Cambridge: Cambridge University Press.

Feiwel, George. 1971. *Poland's industrialization policy: A current analysis.* New York: Praeger.

Freeman, Richard. 1992. What direction for labor market institutions in Eastern and Central Europe? Paper presented at NBER conference on Transition in Eastern Europe, Cambridge, Mass., February.

Gesicka, Grazyna. 1989. Zwiazkowa orientacia samorzadowcow (The union orientation of self-management councils). In *Niezalenzne samorzady pracownicze* (Independent employee councils), ed. Szymon Jakubowicz, 304–36. Warsaw: Institute of Sociology, Warsaw University.

Goodwyn, Lawrence. 1991. *Breaking the barrier: The rise of Solidarity in Poland*. New York: Oxford University Press.

Golebowski, Janusz. 1965. *Nacjonalizacja przemyslu w Polsce* (The nationalization of industry in Poland). Warsaw: Ksiazka i Wiedza.

Gruszecki, Tomasz. 1990. Privatization in Poland during 1990. *Working Papers of the Stefan Batory Institute.* Warsaw: Stefan Batory Institute.

Hinds, Manuel. 1990a. *Issues in the introduction of market forces in Eastern European economies.* IDP-0057. Washington, D.C.: World Bank.

———. 1990b. Sequencing problems in reforming socialist economies. Paper presented at the Massachusetts Institute of Technology, November.

Horvat, Branko, Mihailo Markovic, and Rudi Supek, eds. 1975. *Self-governing socialism.* White Plains, N.Y.: International Arts and Sciences Press.

Jakubowicz, Szymon, ed. 1989a. *Niezalenzne samorzady pracownicze* (Independent employee councils). Warsaw: Institute of Sociology, Warsaw University.

———. 1989b. *The struggle over employee councils: 1980–81.* London: Aneks.

Jasinski, Piotr. 1990. Two models of privatization in Poland. *Journal of Communist Economies* 3:373–401.

Jaworski, Tomasz. 1985. Blaski i cienie procesow uspolecznienia zarzaddzania (The ups and downs of socializing management). Paper presented at IOZiDK conference, Warsaw, February.

Jedruszczak, Hanna, ed. 1983. *Wizje gospodarki socjaistycznej w Polsce, 1945–1949: poczatki planowania* (Visions of the socialist economy in Poland). Warsaw: Panstwowe Wydawnictwo Naukowe.

Jezierski, Andrzej, and Barbara Petz. 1988. *Historia gospodarcza Polski Ludowej: 1944–1985* (An economic history of People's Poland: 1944–1985). Warsaw: Panstwowe Wydawnictwo Naukowe.

Johnson, Simon. 1992. The private sector in Poland. Paper presented at the NBER conference on Transition in Eastern Europe, Cambridge, Mass., February.

Kalecki, Michal. 1982. Nie preceniac roll modelu. (Don't overestimate the role of the model). In *Dziela*, vol. 3: *Socjalizm: funkcjonowanie i wieloletnie planowania* (Collected work, vol. 3: Socialism: Its functioning and long-term planning). Warsaw: Panstwowe Wydawnictwo Ekonomiczne.

Kawalec, Stefan. 1989. Zarys programu prywatyzacji polskiej gospodarki (Outline of a privatization program for the Polish economy). In *Propozycje przeksztalcen polskiej gospodarki* (Propositions for the transformation of the Polish economy), 29–53. Warsaw: Polish Economics Association.

Kloc, Kazimierz. 1992. *Historia samorzadu robotniczego w PRL (1944–1980)* (The history of workers self-management in the PRL [1944–1980]). Warsaw: Main School of Trade.

Korbonski, Andrzej. 1965. *The politics of socialist agriculture in Poland: 1945–1960.* New York: Columbia University Press.

Kornai, Janos. 1980. *The Economics of Shortage.* Amsterdam: North-Holland.

———. 1985. The reproduction of shortage. In *Contradictions and dilemmas: Essays in the economics of socialism,* 6–32. Cambridge: MIT Press.

Kowalik, Tadeusz. 1984. *Spory o ustroj spoleczno-gospodarczy Polski, 1944–48* (Struggles over the socio-economic order in Poland, 1944–48). Warsaw: Aneks.

————. 1987. Oscar Lange odczytyany na nowo (Oskar Lange, read again). *Nauka Polska* 3–4:20–42.

————. 1988. Trzy postawy, trzy dramaty (Three figures, three dramas). *Zycie Gospodarcze,* August 21.

Laba, Roman. 1986. Solidarite et les luttes ouvriers en Pologne, 1970–1980. *Actes de la Recherche en Science Sociales* 61:45–73.

Landau, Zbigniew, and Jerzy Tomaszewski. 1985. *The Polish economy in the twentieth century.* London: Croom Helm.

Lavoie, Don. 1985. *Rivalry and central planning: The socialist calculation debate reconsidered.* Cambridge: Cambridge University Press.

Levitas, Anthony. 1992. Rethinking reform: The lessons of Polish privatization. *World Policy Journal* 3–4:779–94.

Levitas, Anthony, and Piotr Strzalkowski. 1990. What does the privatization of the nomenklatura really mean? *Journal of Communist Economies* 3:413–16.

Lewandowski, Janusz, and Jan Szomburg. 1984. *Samorzad w dobie "Solidarnosci"* (Self-government in the hour of "Solidarity"). London: Odnowa.

————. 1989. Uwlaszczenie jako fundament reformy spoleczno-gospodarczej ("Propertization" as a fundamental aspect of socio-economic reform). In *Propozyje przeksztalcen polskiej gospodarki* (Propositions for the transformation of the Polish economy), 63–81. Warsaw: Polish Economics Association.

————. 1990. A Transformation model for the Poland's economy: The strategy for privatization. *Economic Transformations,* no. 2. Gdansk: Gdansk Institute of Market Economics.

Lipinski, Edward. ed. 1957. *Przedsiebiorstwo samodzielne w gospodarce planowej* (Independent enterprises in a planned economy). Warsaw: Panstwowe Wydawnictwo Naukowe.

Lipowski, Adam. 1988. *Mechanizm rynkowy w gospodarce polskiej* (The market mechanism in the Polish economy). Warsaw: Panstwowe Wydawnictwo Naukowe.

Malara, Jean, and Lucienne Key. 1952. *La Pologne: d'une occupation a l'autre, 1944–1952.* Paris: Editions du Fuseau.

Michnik, Adam. 1985. *Letters from prison and other essays.* Berkeley and Los Angeles: University of California Press.

Minc, Bronislaw. 1967. Ekonomiczna teoria przedsiebiorstwa socalistycznego (The economic theory of the socialist enterprise.) In *Przedsiebiorstwo w polskim systemie spoleczno-ekonomicznym* (The enterprise in the Polish socio-economic system), ed. Bronislaw Minc, 3–49. Warsaw: Panstwowy Wydawnictwo Ekonomiczne.

Montias, John Michal. 1962. *Central planning in Poland.* New Haven, Conn.: Yale University Press.

Muller, Alexander, ed. 1988. *U zrodel polskiego kryzysu* (At the roots of the Polish crisis). Warsaw: Panstwowe Wydawnictwo Naukowe.

Najduchowska, Halina. 1964. Dyrektorzy przedsiebiorstw przemys lowych: Dobor na stanowiska dyrektorow na tle oficjalnej koncepcji przedsiebiorstwa przemyslowego (Managers of industrial enterprises: Managerial selection against the background of the official conception of an industrial enterprise). In *Przemysl i spoleczenstwo w Polsce Ludowej* (Industry and society in People's Poland), ed. Jan Szczepanski, 79–103. Wroclaw: Ossolineum.

Norr, Henry. 1984. Self-management in Poland, 1980–81: A hard frog to swallow. M.A. Thesis, Boston University.

Osiatynski, Jerzy. 1982. *Michal Kalecki o gospodarce socjalistycnej* (Michal Kalecki on the socialist economy). Warsaw: Panstwowe Wydawnictwo Naukowe.

Osiatynski, Jerzy, Wlodek Pankow, and Michal Federowicz. 1985. *Self-management in the Polish economy,* vols. 1–5. Bologna: Bibliotca Walter Bigiavi.

Ost, David. 1990. *Solidarity and the politics of anti-politics.* Ithaca, N.Y.: Cornell University Press.

Piore, Michael, and Charles Sabel. 1984. *The second industrial divide: Possibilities for prosperity.* New York: Basic.

Polonsky, Antony, and Boleslaw Drukier, eds. 1980. *The beginnings of Communist rule in Poland: December 1943–June 1945.* London: Routledge and Kegan Paul.

Prokuratura Generala. 1990. *Sprawozdania no. dkI RK 728/89.* Warsaw: Ministry of Justice.

Rostowski, Jacek. 1989. The decay of socialism and the growth of private enterprise in Poland. *Soviet Studies* 2:112–32.

Ruszkowski, Pawel. 1985. *Samorzad pracowniczy w przedsiebiorstwach* (Employee self-management in enterprises). Warsaw: Centrum Badania Opinii Spolecznej.

Sachs, Jeffery. 1989. My plan for Poland. *International Economy* 3(6).

Sachs, Jeffery, and David Lipton. 1990. Creating a market economy in Eastern Europe: The case of Poland. *Brookings Papers on Economic Activity,* 1–38.

Schaffer, Mark. 1992a. The enterprise sector and the emergence of the Polish fiscal crisis 1990–1991. Working Paper no. 280. Center for Economic Performance, London School of Economics.

———. 1992b. The Polish state-owned enterprise sector and the recession in 1990. *Comparative Economic Studies* 34(1): 34–68.

Sturmthal, Adolf. 1964. *Workers councils: A study of workplace organization on both sides of the Iron Curtain.* Cambridge: Harvard University Press.

Ustawa o przedsiebiorstwach panstwowych (Law on state enterprises). 1981. *Dziennik Ustaw* 24:122.

Ustawa o samorzadzie zalogi przedsiebiorstwa panstwowego (Law on workers' self-management in state enterprises). 1981. *Dziennik Ustaw* 24:123.

Ustawa o szczegolnej regulacji prawnej w okresie przezwyciezania kryzysu spoleczno-ekonomicznego i zmianie niektorych ustaw (Law concerning the particular legal regulation in the period of overcoming the socio-economic crisis and changes in a few laws). 1983. *Dziennik Ustaw* 39:176.

Zukowski, Tomasz. 1987. *Zwiazki zawodowe i samorad pracowniczy w polskich zakladach przemyslowych, w latach 1944–1987* (Trade unions and workers councils in Polish industrial plants in the years 1944–1987). Ph.D. Thesis, University of Warsaw.

11 Works Councils in Western Europe: From Consultation to Participation

Wolfgang Streeck

11.1 Introduction

The capital-labor settlement after the Second World War provided for recognition of free, adversarial collective bargaining between unions and employers. But as the papers in this volume show,[1] in most Western European countries it also included arrangements at the workplace for collective consultation between management and workforce, in the form of works councils. Supplementing distributive collective bargaining, and indeed sometimes preceding it, works councils were to concern themselves with production issues and ways of increasing productivity through cooperation in the production sphere. Today the remarkable fact of the almost universal establishment of works councils after 1945 in otherwise very different national contexts, as an integral part of a worldwide recasting of the political economy of capitalism after the economic and political catastrophes of the interwar period, is largely forgotten.

Works councils, to be sure, differed considerably between countries. In some, such as the Netherlands and France, they were chaired by the employer; elsewhere they were worker-only bodies. In Germany, the Netherlands, and France, councils were based on legislation; in Sweden and Italy, by contrast, they were set up through national collective agreement, making councils union-based and defining a pattern that lasts until the present day. More impressive than the differences, however, were the commonalities of the various council systems and the simultaneity of their establishment. In all six countries under study, laws on works councils were passed or national agreements signed

---

Wolfgang Streeck was at the time this was written professor of sociology and industrial relations at the University of Wisconsin-Madison.

1. This chapter draws primarily on chapters 3, 4, 5, 6, 7, and 8 of the present volume. While their authors commented extensively on an earlier draft, responsibility for the factual presentation and the conclusions offered rests exclusively with the author.

almost immediately after the war had ended (table 11.1).[2] West Germany came last with the Betriebsverfassungsgesetz of 1952; but the West German state had been founded only in 1949, and in fact works councils had been running most of what was left of its devastated industry in the first few years after 1945. Even Francoist Spain passed works council legislation in 1947, recognizing a need for some form of collective organization of workers at the workplace even under an authoritarian dictatorship.

Typically postwar works councils were kept strictly separate from collective bargaining. More or less consciously following Sinzheimer's 1920 *Entwurf einer Arbeitsverfassung* for the Weimar Republic, collective bargaining was reserved to unions as their exclusive domain, and indeed to nationally centralized unions negotiating with equally centralized employers' associations.[3] In this way, distributional conflict was moved out of the workplace into a national, political arena, where it could be integrated in a broader context and traded off against Keynesian full-employment policy or a universalist welfare state. In any case, given the destructions of the war and the pressing need to rebuild the Continent's shattered economies, collective bargaining did not and could not play much of a role in the immediate postwar years, and in most countries had yet to develop fully. In Germany, in fact, where works councils were to become particularly important later, unions concentrated on collective wage bargaining only with great hesitation and only during the beginning "economic miracle" of the second half of the 1950s when their original objective, a complete *Neuordnung* of the economy on the basis of a multitiered system of parity co-determination, had finally eluded them. Works councils, of course, although quite different ones from those that were enacted in 1952, had played a central part in German unions' economic democracy (*Wirtschaftsdemokratie*) project—which was one reason why the Works Constitution Act was enacted only against their resistance.[4]

Outside Germany and Spain, in countries where pluralist industrial relations emerged or reemerged earlier, works councils were introduced with union and employer support as a counterbalance to institutionalized adversarialism. Sweden and Italy, where councils were created by collective agreement, are particularly instructive in this respect, but the situation was essentially the same else-

2. In Italy, the first major national agreement on works councils (*commissioni interne*) was reached in already 1943, before the restoration of free unions. Until 1947 the *commissioni* had collective bargaining rights.

3. This was, of course, different in Spain, where there were no unions and where the wage settlements dictated by the government could not be made to stick at the workplace. As a consequence Spanish works councils had to serve as outlets for and mediators in distributional conflict, with "cooperation," as it were, ensured at the national level—the reverse of the normal pattern. The fact that almost 20 years after Franco Spanish works councils still negotiate on wages is another impressive example of the stickiness of institutions and the formative power of original institutional design decisions.

4. Interestingly, this was similar in the Netherlands, where the unions were less than enthusiastic about the 1950 legislation, which they regarded as a watered-down version of previous Social Democratic proposals that had emphasized economic democracy at both the firm and sector levels.

where. In both countries, a powerful union movement coming out of the war was willing, at least for a transition period, to respect managerial prerogative in the organization of production in exchange for employer acceptance of, among other things, nationwide collective bargaining. In Italy, unions and employers had even before the end of the war agreed to work together to build a democratic nation after the devastations of fascism and the German occupation.[5] The dominant spirit was one of centrist moderation in both camps, brought about by the shared experience of the resistance movement and influenced by the same Social-Catholic doctrine that subsequently was to become important in Germany as well. In Sweden, under quite different conditions, employers had in 1945 and 1946 beaten back an attempt by the radical Left to move quickly toward some form of socialism. One result was a shift in the leadership of the labor movement toward more moderate factions willing to pursue their objectives in a gradualistic way through, among other things, collective bargaining.

Remarkably, however, in Sweden just as in Italy and the rest of Europe, neither unions nor employers believed that collective bargaining alone was enough for a socially sustainable and economically productive reorganization of employment relations. Together with collective bargaining, the two sides also agreed, almost as a matter of course, that both the exercise of managerial prerogative at the workplace and the conduct of distributional conflict at the national level needed to be supplemented by workplace-based consultation between management and labor. Underlying this was a shared assumption that unilateral management was unable to provide for an optimal utilization of the forces of production, and that institutionalized conflict was less divisive and more socially benevolent if the resources available for distribution were more plentiful. By taking the edge out of the exercise of managerial discretion and the pursuit of political-distributional conflict, consultation at the workplace was to facilitate both. Like the acceptance of pluralism, this view became a constituent part of an almost universal consensus across class lines and national boundaries in the formative years of the postwar industrial relations system.

The only major exceptions from the general movement toward works councils after 1945 were the United States and, to a lesser extent, the United Kingdom. Several explanations come to mind for this, but clearly more research is required, especially on the British case. As for the United States, a major factor seems to have been the history of the struggle of bona fide unionism against company unions, as reflected in the Wagner Act's emphasis on adversarialism and its strong suspicion of nonadversarial, nonunion, cooperative forms of "labor organization" at the workplace. Moreover, unlike Western Europe, the American economy had not been destroyed in the war, and indeed America

5. To be sure, unlike in Sweden, this period came to an end in 1947 at the latest, when it gave way to two decades of union exclusion and authoritarian or paternalistic management practices.

entered the postwar era as the largest and leading industrial nation, with no need to rebuild its productive base through class cooperation. Also, American employers had not been discredited by cooperation with a dictatorship or a foreign aggressor and came out of the war as strong and as determined as ever to protect their right to manage. Apart from the rapid spread of seniority rules, that right was not much contested by American "business unions," except for a few easily defeated attempts especially by the UAW in the immediate postwar years. Not least, collective bargaining had never been firmly centralized in the United States, where in the unionized sector highly independent union locals occupied the organizational space in which works councils existed in Europe, making it difficult to imagine a stable and mutually supportive division of functions between unions and councils.

The British case is more difficult to understand, given that there was before and after the Second World War some experience with "productivity councils" and other consultative arrangements. On the other hand, Britain was among the winners of the war and took a long time to realize the depth of the economic problems it was facing. British employers therefore saw no urgent need for institutionalized cooperation at the point of production, especially since British unions were not much interested in co-determination themselves. Rather than on participation in managerial decisions, they had placed their hopes on nationalization, and in fact more industrial capacity than anywhere else outside the Communist bloc was expropriated by the post-1945 Labour government. Also, unlike in the United States, there was no tradition in Britain of legislative intervention in industrial relations, with the legal system long and firmly committed to abstentionism and both unions and employers insisting on "voluntarism" as the only adequate way of regulating employment relations. Politics was unlikely to change this. Given the very large number of unions, many of them small, that had little to gain from union-independent, unitary workplace representation, the Labour party saw no reason, and indeed thoroughly lacked the political capacity, to institutionalize works councils by legislation; the Conservative party, for its part, continued to defend the managerial prerogative so dear to its core clientele. Arguably because of the weak legal supports of its industrial relations system, Britain later came to be the first major country in Europe in which the postwar structure of centralized collective bargaining broke down and gave way to workplace bargaining.

Postwar works councils, in the countries where they existed, were consultative bodies. While they sometimes did have paternalistic traits, they were not set up by employers to crowd out unions, and could not have been given the unions' preoccupation with national-level, "political" bargaining. At the same time, councils typically had no and claimed no rights to co-determination and were generally not equipped to perform representational functions. The only, limited exception in this latter respect was West Germany with its Weimar tradition of economic democracy. Everywhere else, the early works councils respected the rights of both unions to represent and management to manage;

their main and sole purpose was to enable employers to consult with their workforces on how to improve economic performance, listen to constructive proposals growing out of workers' everyday work experience, and in the process build consensus for managerial decisions in the pursuit of economic progress.

11.2   Decay of Consultative Councils

During the 1950s and 1960s the consultative works councils of the early postwar years fell into disuse, and again the experience was shared by most European countries with the exception of West Germany and, to some extent, the Netherlands. Since mainstream industrial relations research outside Germany has grossly neglected works councils,[6] little is known about the reasons for this once more astonishingly parallel development. Following the papers in this volume, it would seem that as national economies and industrial relations systems consolidated, both employers and unions lost interest in works councils and in part began to regard them as potentially dangerous to their newly established positions. Not only were councils' economic benefits found increasingly doubtful, but there also seems to have been a growing conviction that the separation of consultation and representation, on the possibility of which the early postwar councils had been premised, was untenable in the longer term and that works councils were bound to undermine either managerial prerogative or national unions' representational monopoly or both.

As to unions, it seems that the more they became established parties to sectoral or national collective bargaining, the more they began to regard works councils as potential agents of *Betriebspatriotismus:* of particularistic interests of employed workers in the economic well-being of their employer, undermining worker solidarity across enterprise lines, potentially replacing it with solidarity between individual employers and their workforces across class lines, and serving as an organizational infrastructure for what has been referred to as "wildcat cooperation." Fears like these were clearly strongest in countries where councils were not union-based. But as distributional conflict became more intense with the return of prosperity, there was a general decline in the confidence of unions that employers would respect the difference between consultation and representation and abstain from using councils to lure their workforces into local alliances undermining national or sectoral unions' conflictual capacities.

6. In part, this may have been because on the European continent industrial relations as a discipline took off only in the late 1960s, when the councils of the early postwar period were no more than a distant memory. Moreover, European students of industrial relations tended to sympathize with the views of the unions, which in the formative years of the discipline were eager to dissociate themselves from the postwar council tradition. Furthermore, in the Anglo-American countries from which the discipline was largely imported, councils were either unknown or almost by definition regarded as paternalistic and antiunion, and not part of "good," i.e., union-inclusive, pluralist industrial relations.

Interestingly, employers seem to have withdrawn from works councils out of exactly the opposite concerns. Having successfully restored legitimacy for their control over the workplace, they increasingly began to view councils, whether union-based or not, as potential entryways for unions and thus as threats to their reestablished right to manage. It is easy to imagine that such fears should have induced employers to use councils paternalistically for building antiunion coalitions with their workforces—confirming unions' worst fears and in turn inducing them to try and capture the councils for themselves, so as to prevent them being captured by the employers. The only way out of this self-reinforcing, escalating "spiral of low trust" (Fox) was to agree, more or less tacitly, on abandoning councils altogether.

Convergence on this solution was made possible by the fact that the early *economic* reasons for employers and unions to seek institutionalized consultation at the workplace seem soon to have fallen by the wayside. The 1950s and 1960s in Europe were a period of rapid advance of Fordist-Taylorist mass production. Consensus for "rationalization" was increasingly procured by firm expectations of continued economic growth, as well as by generally accepted perceptions of technological change as linear, predetermined, and self-propelled, with little if any space for alternatives or choice. Collective consultation with workers seemed of little use where compliance with managerial authority appeared to be assured by, or could easily be bought with, the economic benefits of its aggressive exercise, and where the efficient organization of production was regarded, not just by employers, as a matter of technological expertise beyond the reach and competence of democratic participation. In this environment, just as employers found it easy to renounce their past belief in the productive contribution of collective participation, unions typically abandoned their postwar concern with production and concentrated on the distribution of its results, increasingly refusing to become involved in responsibility for cooperation at the workplace either directly or, by condoning works councils regardless of their potential risks for union solidarity, indirectly.

But as the papers in this volume indicate, the demise of postwar councils outside West Germany and, in part, the Netherlands was also related to more narrowly institutional factors. While works councils typically had no rights to co-determination, they could expect consultation to give them access to privileged information and some, however limited, influence on managerial decisions. To this extent, consultation might have performed minimal representational functions for workers. The problem was, however, that employers were free to decide when and on what to initiate consultation. As decisions did not depend on the results, and sanctions for not consulting were weak or nonexistent, the early council systems entailed an ever-present temptation for employers not to consult if this might cause them discomfort. The sheer presence of this temptation, in turn, was bound to cause suspicions on the part of workers that when they were being consulted, it was only because management perceived consultation to be in its interest; if consultation might be advantageous to workers it would not take place. Lacking representative institutions at the workplace, the temptation for workers then was to try to use consultation as a substitute for workplace collective bargaining. *As long as consultation was voluntary, workers were prone to regard works councils as management tools; while employers were inclined to use them as such, as well as to suspect workers of trying to use them for adversarial purposes.*

11.3   German Exceptionalism

For our further argument, it is crucial to understand why the decay of the postwar council system should not have been replicated in West Germany. Because of the division of Germany, the Communist party, which governed the eastern part of the country, was largely absent in the Federal Republic. Among other things this helped contain the radicalization of the union movement in West Germany's newly prosperous economy during the reconstruction period.[7] Division also contributed importantly to the fact that the postwar political unity of West German unionism did not come apart later, as it did in Italy; with Communist influence weak or nonexistent, neither Social Democratic nor Catholic unionists found it necessary or attractive to break away from the unitary union federation, the Deutscher Gewerkschaftsbund (DGB). One consequence was continued strong influence on national union strategy of Catholic social doctrine, which was far less hostile to interclass cooperation, especially at the workplace, than both socialism and communism.

This is not to say that German unions were not afraid of the paternalistic and syndicalist potential of works councils; in fact they were, and had very good reasons to be. Unlike the works councils of the Weimar Republic, the councils that had been created by a conservative government under the Betriebsverfassungsgesetz of 1952 were not as a matter of course conceived to be union controlled. Important elements in the governing coalition intended the works councils of 1952 to have a potential to serve as union alternatives, *and it was partly for this purpose that,* unlike works councils elsewhere in Europe at the time, *they were endowed with rudimentary rights of representation through co-determination.* But while this might have been reason enough for most other union movements to stay away from the council system and to try to destroy it, postwar German unionism can be understood only against the background of its consuming preoccupation with *Mitbestimmung:* the equal sharing of control over economic decisions between capital and labor at all levels, including the enterprise. This defining project, which incidentally made it also more difficult for German unions than for others to move on to collective bargaining pure and simple, or at least made for a programmatically institutionalized bad conscience about any such tendency, effectively prevented a re-

---

7. A related reason for moderation was the relative weakness of German unions at the time, certainly compared to the Scandinavian countries or France.

jection of works councils even at a time when they might still have been used by employers for antiunion purposes: *even where they were, they somehow also incorporated the promise of worker participation in the management of enterprises,* which German unions stubbornly refused to regard as solely vested in property rights. Withdrawing from existing works councils while calling for extended co-determination would have been perceived as deeply and self-defeatingly contradictory. Here Social Democratic and Social-Catholic thinking converged, further fortifying the cohesion of the unitary union movement and protecting the union productivism of the first postwar years from being superseded by an exclusive concern with distributive politics and wage bargaining.

There were yet other reasons why German unions could not, in the same way as unions elsewhere, walk away from works councils. Among them was the prewar tradition of councils, going back to the revolution of 1918 and the Weimar Reichsverfassung of 1920. But most important, it would seem, was the councils' strong legal foundation that made for quite distinctive and, at the time, unique institutional dynamics. Given the way the 1952 legislation had been written, German unions would have found it impossible to undo the councils in the 1950s and 1960s, even if they had wanted to and even if they had won the support of the employers for this. Not only were councils of the state's and not of their or of the employers' making, forcing unions just as employers to find ways of living with them; more important, unlike works councils in other countries, German councils did after all have some effective representative functions that gave them legitimacy among workers and that neither unions nor employers could circumvent. While in hindsight these may not have amounted to much, they did intrude on managerial prerogative, at least in that they made employers defer certain decisions, especially on personnel matters, until the works council had had an opportunity to offer a counterproposal. In addition, the fact that councils commanded considerable support from workers forced unions to acknowledge that workers had workplace-specific interests which, to be adequately represented, needed decentralized in addition to centralized joint regulation. In the 1950s and 1960s, *German unions thus learned to share their representational functions, and German employers their managerial powers, with legally based works councils,* preparing the ground for the extension of co-determination that was to come in the 1970s.

As has been mentioned, an important factor that made it easier for German unionism to reconcile itself with the 1952 works councils was the survival of its political unity. Absence of political division facilitated the rapprochement between unions and councils not just ideologically but also organizationally: lacking significant competition, the unitary industrial unions affiliated to the DGB were able gradually to grow into the unitary works council system and take it over from the inside, turning legally based works councils into chosen union instruments for representing workers at the workplace. This process, to be sure, went far from smoothly. For a while, the suspicions harbored against councils by external unions and the left wing of the movement were so strong that considerable investments were made in separate union workplace organizations (*Vertrauensleute*), even when the vast majority of council members had long come to be elected from union lists.

Slowly, however, this began to change. As unions saw their workplace leaders take over the councils and *exercise council rights as union rights,* their main problem with the system increasingly became, not its existence as such, but the fact that the rights it provided to workers were so limited. A model of how councils could be more powerful while at the same time remaining firmly under union control was offered by coal and steel co-determination, a regime whose extension to the rest of German industry was the DGB's main demand on the road to full *Mitbestimmung.* Having learned from coal and steel how effectively to *infuse representation in consultation,* German unions came to cherish the many other advantages a well-established, workplace-based council system offers to industrial unions engaged in centralized wage bargaining—such as access to information, protection of external unions' strike monopoly, containment of local wage drift, prevention of fragmentation by occupation or skill, competitive disadvantagement for splinter unions, easy de facto union recognition, assistance in the recruitment of members, effective local implementation of collective agreements, and assured union access to workplace-specific interests that otherwise might seek different outlets. As early as the second half of the 1960s, then, external union opposition to works councils had become largely rhetorical, and in practice, unions and councils had made their peace with each other, the former working closely with and through the latter in serving members and workers at the workplace.

11.4   Rise of Workplace Representation in the 1970s

The Europe-wide wave of unofficial strikes in 1968 and 1969 caused the first major revision in the institutional arrangements that had governed postwar industrial relations for two decades. Again, the parallels between countries are impressive. Most of the literature describes the longer-term results of the strikes as a transformation of both industrial relations and parliamentary democracy toward more institutionalized participation of national unions in broad areas of public policy making, under labels like "neocorporatism" (Schmitter) or "political exchange" (Pizzorno). But while this was certainly a very important part of what happened, no less central to the update of the postwar settlement in the late 1960s and early 1970s was the recognition by governments, employers, and unions of *the workplace as a site for legitimate interest representation* and of a role for unions as vital participants in it.

The reorganization of the workplace to satisfy newly discovered demands for "industrial democracy" and "participation" responded to the fact that the strikes had almost universally been called, not by external national unions, but by local workplace leaders. External unions, just as governments and employers, saw the strikes above all as a very serious warning that centralized union-ism and collective bargaining were about to lose control over the articulation of workplace-specific interests—or, more precisely, had for whatever reason failed to develop capacities to represent powerful worker interests that were left unrepresented only at the risk of industrial disorder and social unrest. In part, the unrepresented interests that were perceived as having caused the crisis had to do with wages and, most important, wage differentials, calling into question the leveling wage policies of national and sectoral unions especially in countries like Sweden. But very clearly, other grievances were also involved, in particular over rationalization, technical change, and working conditions. In this respect, the writing on the wall was that after two decades of Fordist-Taylorist progress, its peace formula—assured growth as a reward for voiceless acquiescence with managerial decisions—was coming apart, with workers de-termined to claim a role in the regulation of their working conditions and refus-ing to leave the management of the workplace to employers and their industrial engineers in return for, supposedly, ever-rising material payoffs.

When the strikes were over, European unions were stronger than ever since the immediate postwar years. National union leaders were courted by govern-ments and employers as the only possible managers of what was seen as deep and threatening discontent. In particular, unions were asked to contribute to the restoration of industrial order in two ways. At the national level, they were urged to help contain the rising inflation so as to enable governments to con-tinue to provide for full employment without having to sacrifice monetary sta-bility: this was the incomes policy part of neocorporatism that came to attract most of the attention of researchers. In addition, however, and partly as an advance reward for their expected collaboration in macroeconomic stabiliza-tion, unions were given, or were able to get for themselves, better access to the workplace and an assured role in the representation of workplace-specific in-terests.

Again, there were differences between countries. In some, "qualitative" de-mands of workers for "industrial democracy" were eagerly attended to and even cultivated in order to divert workers' attention from "quantitative" wage issues, in an attempt simultaneously to shore up national unions' solidaristic wage policies and facilitate government efforts to bring down inflation. Else-where, the reforms that followed the strike wave initiated a decentralization of collective bargaining on the vague and sometimes desperate hope that national unions would somehow be able to impose a measure of discipline on their newly empowered workplace representatives. But the overall tendency was al-ways the same: *to increase the representativeness of workplace industrial rela-tions by making space for effective expression of workplace-specific worker interests,* so as to prevent a recurrence of the breakdown of central governance that had in 1968 and 1969 so fundamentally shaken the industrial and politi-cal order.

It is important to note that there was general consensus, again across nations and classes, that restoration of social peace at the workplace was impossible short of major steps toward genuine representation. Paternalistic solutions, like expanded voluntary consultation, were never seriously considered. Governments and employers all over Europe assumed as a matter of course that union substitutes would not do the job and that the only realistic policy was to allow unions into the workplace lest other forces, less responsible and more difficult to include in macroeconomic stabilization efforts, absorbed the discontent and thrived on it. At the same time, increasing the representativeness of workplace institutions required different approaches and was differently risky in different countries. It was comparatively easy in West Germany, where, given the way industrial relations had developed after the war, the solution that offered itself was to satisfy long-standing union demands for more rights for works councils and, in general, for expansion of co-determination.

Comparative analysis reveals the logic of this approach to deviate significantly from received accounts. In many cases the German strike wave had been led, not by unorganized activists or *Vertrauensleute,* but by works councils, certifying the councils' meanwhile developed status as de facto local unions and demonstrating to national unions and employers that the political capacities of well-organized councils far exceeded what the law had intended them to have. The Works Constitution Act of 1972 was passed by a reform government, led by the Social Democratic party, at the demand of its main political allies, the unions. Far from intending to keep the unions out of the workplace, it actually brought them forcefully into it, albeit in a form that was least threatening to centralized collective bargaining and to the unions themselves. This the act accomplished in three ways: by expanding the rights to information, consultation, and co-determination of the meanwhile thoroughly unionized works councils; by improving the access and strengthening the links of external unions to councils; and by confirming the councils' strict exclusion from wage bargaining, thereby protecting the primacy of external unions in this area, formally over the works councils, but actually and more importantly over the internal unions that German councils had in the meantime become. In this way, the 1972 legislation accomplished the remarkable feat of extending the powers of workplace union organizations vis-à-vis the employer while at the same time stabilizing centralized collective bargaining, and in fact did the latter in part by doing the former.[8]

The German solution to the Europe-wide problem of how to increase the

8. It might be mentioned that at the time even more ambitious projects were pursued by German unionists that remained unrealized in the 1972 legislation. Perhaps because (partly) representative works councils were already an established element in German industrial relations, some union groups had already begun to think beyond the immediate exigencies of the period and developed concepts of more decentralized and direct participation, especially of work groups, in the organization of work (*Mitbestimmung am Arbeitsplatz*). In the early 1970s these were rejected by a majority of union leaders, who were afraid that they might undermine union and works council representation. Today, in the context of post-Taylorism work reform, they have forcefully returned on the agenda.

representativeness of workplace industrial relations without destroying the possibility of macroeconomic concertation—and indeed in order to preserve it—had many facets. But in the main it involved a *merger* of a range of *representative functions* typically performed by unions into the *structure of consultation* between employers and their workforces that had been created after the war to support *cooperation* in production. By enriching consultation with representation—a pattern that, as has been noted, had begun to develop long before the crisis of the late 1960s—the German approach saved consultation from attrition. By including representative bodies in workplace cooperation, it also bridged the cleavage between cooperation and representation and overcame the association of representation with adversarialism that was so characteristic of the initial postwar structure of industrial relations elsewhere. In the process, as they became associated with representation—that is, the expression of interests and the exercise of rights—consultation and cooperation ceased to be merely voluntary and became more reliable and trustworthy for both sides. Merging workplace consultation and representation also, at least for a while, shielded centralized distributive bargaining in Germany from both excessive conflict and excessive cooperation at the workplace.

The genius of this approach, and the advantages it bestowed on German industrial relations and the German economy in the difficult 1970s and 1980s, can best be seen in comparison with other countries. By and large, *the same merger of consultation and representation was to occur there as well,* in response to changed and very demanding economic conditions, but later, less comfortably, and often precariously incomplete. Where, as was the typical case, the postwar council system had withered away or forever lost the respect of the unions, there was in the years following the strikes simply no possibility to integrate the new functions of workplace representation in a preexisting consultative-cooperative structure. A partial exception to this was the Netherlands, where a strong legal foundation had preserved the consultative council system of 1950 in spite of its paternalistic elements. Here the government in 1971 half-heartedly reformed the councils to increase their representational capacity—only to find itself forced to follow up with another law in 1979 finally turning Dutch works councils into worker-only bodies, and in fact making them more similar to their German counterparts than ever.

Everywhere else, the issue on the agenda at the time was not yet to combine representation with consultation, but to enable the unions as the only plausible representative agents of workers and as the lesser evil compared to unorganized workplace activists, to insert themselves in the organizational space of the workplace. Already in 1968, the French state found it advisable to legalize the workplace union sections that had formed during the general strike and to impose legal obligations on intransigent employers not to stand in their way. Not much thought, if any, was given to empowering the 1945 councils as an alternative. The same applied to Italy, where in 1970 the statuto dei lavoratori, rather than strengthening the old internal commissions—which would have appeared patently absurd at the time—created a legal base for union organization at the workplace. And in Sweden, unions and the Social Democratic government bypassed the more or less defunct works councils that had been created under the national agreement of 1946, even though they were exclusively union based, and instead expanded industrial democracy by expanding union rights to collective bargaining, deriving what was referred to with the German word, *Metbestemming,* from the general right of unions to represent their members.

Nota bene that law played a central role in the institutionalization of workplace representation, not only in Germany and the Netherlands, but even in countries where the postwar council system had been founded on collective agreement, and even where the representational mechanisms that were being created were union based, as in Sweden and, certainly formally, in Italy. This is why the unofficial strike wave of the late 1960s was followed by the second postwar wave of legislation on workplace industrial relations, beginning with France in 1968 and arguably ending with the same country in 1982 (table 11.1). Indeed the main events were concentrated in the early 1970s—disregarding the late date of the Spanish legislation which reflected the uncertainties of the transition period, the second Dutch law, and the protracted union-employer negotiations in Sweden subsequent to the co-determination legislation of the 1970s.

The importance of legal intervention for the greater representativeness of workplace industrial relations is shown by its use even in Sweden and Italy, where it immediately raised puzzling questions of how to accommodate non-unionized workers in a system in which unions were to hold exclusive legal rights to collective representation. Different, and differently awkward, solutions were found. While in Sweden the matter was resolved by the sheer force of numbers, nonmembers of unions being a tiny minority, in Italy workplace union organizations were pragmatically opened by the unions themselves to nonmembers,[9] first to absorb and domesticate the radicalism of the spontaneous council movement of the *autunno caldo* and later to ensure that workforces spoke, and cooperated, with the employer with one voice.

As remarkable as the ingenuity with which in particular Italian unions responded to the potential conflict between worker and union representation is the fact that even the strongest unions could not rely on their strength alone in establishing themselves as representatives in the workplace. Employer voluntarism was nowhere seen as a solution. Nor was collective bargaining, mostly because employer resistance, when it came to the crunch, was too strong, and also because workplace representation was to be established as a general right of industrial citizenship regardless of one's place of employment. Where such rights could not be vested in existing nonunion structures, and where the repre-

---

9. This included, e.g., the possibility of unions "legitimating," i.e., awarding formal status as a union workplace representation to, a newly founded works council in a nonunionized plant.

Table 11.1   **Dates of Major Legislation on Workplace Representation**

Year	D	NL	F	E	S	I
1945			1945			1943[a]
1946			1946		1946[a]	
1947				1947		1947[a]
1948						
1949						
1950		1950				
1951						
1952	1952					
1953						(1953)[a]
1954						
1955						
1956						
1957						
1958				(1958)		
1959						
1960						
1961						
1962						
1963						
1964						
1965						
1966						(1966)[a]
1967						
1968			1968			
1969						
1970						1970
1971		1971				
1972	1972				1972	
1973						
1974					(1974)	
1975				[1975][b]		
1976						
1977					1977	
1978						
1979		1979				
1980				1980		
1981		(1981)				
1982			1982		1982[a]	
1983						
1984						
1985				(1985)		
1986						
1987						
1988						
1989	(1989)					
1990				(1990)		

Notes: Country abbreviations are D = Germany, NL = the Netherlands, F = France, E = Spain, S = Sweden, and I = Italy. Parentheses indicate years of minor legislation.

[a]National collective agreement.

[b]Beginning of transition to democracy.

sentativeness of workplace industrial relations could be increased only through an expansion of union rights—the case everywhere outside Germany and the Netherlands—governments agreed to expand union rights by law, whatever the legal and constitutional difficulties, taking into account that unions on their own were unable to gain such rights.[10] And needing urgently to insert themselves in the new representational structures in the workplace, unions were willing to call in the state even where they had traditionally been deeply opposed to legal intervention and, as in Sweden, recourse to legislation was certain to jeopardize established collective bargaining relations with employers.

11.5   Return of Consultation

Where, unlike in Germany and the Netherlands, the legally established representational structures of the 1970s could not be attached to a preexisting system of collective consultation, elements of consultation were gradually infused into them in subsequent years, recreating in a new context features of the first postwar council system that had fallen by the wayside in most of Europe during the reconstruction period, and reproducing in a remarkable case of functional convergence certain key properties of the German and Dutch systems. Again, this happened along very different national trajectories and with very different consequences for unions, employers, and the character of their mutual relations.

The fusion of representation and consultation into what may be called a new, integrated system of *workplace participation* developed least in Spain. Although legally based, the Spanish works council comes closer than any other mechanism of workplace representation in Europe to a workplace union organization pure and simple. In part, this is because Spanish councils have remained agents of wage bargaining. But even more important has been the refusal of the Spanish government in the mid-1980s to continue to support centralized wage settlements through some form of neocorporatist political exchange, together with an economic policy that, perhaps inevitably, made the scrapping of outdated industrial capacity its first priority even at the cost of very high unemployment. In this political environment, Spanish unions and works councils typically find themselves reduced to defending their members' and voters' jobs, using what little power they have to resist industrial change. Constructive participation in joint consultation is further impeded by vigorous interunion competition. Moreover, having become associated with the defense of declining industries and traditional labor market rigidities, Spanish unions and works councils are not regarded by employers or, for that matter, by the Socialist government as useful partners for collective consultation on produc-

---

10. In Spain, given the peculiarities of the country's history, the works council legislation of 1980 was effectively union rights legislation—whereas, e.g., in Italy the union rights legislation of 1970 was effectively the equivalent of works council legislation.

tion, which further reduces the possibility of consultative functions being performed by the council system.

More instructive than the Spanish is the French case. Unlike in Spain where the central objective of employers was to establish and exercise their right to shed labor, French employers felt economic pressures in the 1970s to "involve" their workforces more deeply in production and began to invest heavily in the development of "social relations" at the workplace. In their effort to reduce the distance between management and a traditionally indifferent and suspicious workforce, however, French employers were unable and unwilling to make use of existing institutions. The postwar works councils having largely disappeared, neither the union-dominated personnel delegates nor the new workplace union sections seemed suited to serve as conduits for collective consultation, and indeed neither the unions nor the employers themselves were willing to rebuild them for the purpose. In fact, intent as ever on excluding the unions from the sphere of production, French employers perceived the lack of interest among unions in collective consultation, and the limited capacity of the existing workplace institutions to support it, as an opportunity rather than a liability. In the 1970s, they aggressively began to set up union-independent structures of direct participation controlled by themselves, aimed at both increasing worker involvement and reversing the 1968 advance of unions into the workplace.

As the French country chapter shows, while the strategy was quite successful with regard to its second, more implicit objective, it failed to overcome the limits of unilateral consultation without representation in generating cooperation between employers and employees. The Socialist government after 1981 tried to resolve the impasse with its Auroux legislation, which was an attempt to bring the unions as co-governors into the emerging employer-controlled direct participation system, to shore up both its legitimacy and the unions' representative capacity. In an important sense, this was intended to replicate the German fusion of representation and consultation under French conditions by connecting the enterprise committee, the most works-council–like of the three legally supported institutions in the French workplace, both to the representational functions of unions—through the promotion of enterprise collective bargaining—and to the social policies of the firm—through its new role in regulating workforce "expression."

Many problems persist, however, and indications are that the French attempt in the 1980s to institutionalize workplace participation in law failed to break the impasse of the 1970s. A fundamental difficulty with the French system seems to be that the capacity of enterprise committees to represent worker interests is weak, due to both employer resistance and the occupation of crucial representative functions by older layers of workplace institutions unconnected to collective consultation. Adding to the problems is a rapid decline of unions, which itself seems partly caused by the latter's inability and unwillingness to play a role in workplace consultation and cooperation, forcing them to concede cooperative social relations and the worker interests that enter into them to unilateral employer control. As a result, both the Auroux reforms and the new human resource policies of employers seem to have become stuck halfway, as reflected in a pervasive sense of stagnation and institutional deficiency, a growing "representation gap," and the efficiency gains of worker involvement remaining behind what is regarded as desirable.

A strikingly different situation developed in Italy, where in the 1980s in particular collective consultation through works-council–like bodies returned, often quite unintendedly, under the auspices of the system of institutionalized workplace representation that had developed on the basis of the statuto dei lavoratori. Among the factors that make the Italian case so remarkable is that there is nothing in Italian law that requires union workplace organizations to cooperate with the employer in production matters, or that obliges employers to consult with unions or councils or concede them rights to co-determination. Nevertheless, as the Italian chapter shows, Italian union workplace organizations, encouraged by both employers and unions, have today on a broad scale assumed core participative functions of works councils, testifying to the high incentives for firms and workforces in the 1980s and 1990s to work together to improve productivity and efficiency, and constituting a classic case of the general trend in European industrial relations, after the institutional reforms of the early 1970s, toward functional and structural merger of workplace consultation and representation.

Comparing Italy to France, one cannot escape the conclusion that differences in union power and its legal institutionalization must have contributed importantly to the different outcomes. Unlike their French counterparts, Italian employers typically did not try to introduce new forms of work organization, worker participation, and personnel management against the unions, not to mention using work reorganization to deunionize their workforces. Certainly, in part this was because of the strong productivist traditions of the Italian union movement and because in Italy union participation in production issues was much less likely to become a theme of ideological interunion competition than in France. But even so, Italian employers could not possibly have hoped to break their unions in the same way French employers obviously did. When economic needs for cooperation became more pressing, they therefore did not waste time and energy on predictably fruitless and unproductive efforts to create a "union-free environment" in their plants, but instead constructively and creatively explored the possibility of establishing cooperative relations with their workforces. In this they were highly successful, in part because Italian unions, in turn, felt safe enough to offer themselves as agents of workplace participation without fear of losing their representational status and capacity.

The Swedish case is astonishingly similar to the Italian one, which is all the more remarkable since many of the contextual conditions are radically different. In Sweden, too, the union-controlled representative institutions that had been created by legislation in the 1970s later became the basis for a resumption of cooperative collective consultation in the workplace. When cooperation in production was rediscovered as essential for economic performance, it was consensually grafted onto workplace institutions that had originally been meant as channels for unions representing the interests of their members through collective bargaining rather than as sites of joint deliberation of employers and workers on how to improve efficiency. Just as in Italy, the initiative seems to have come more from the employers than the unions, but it was later fully embraced by the latter. With time, the militant resistance of Swedish employers to the co-determination legislation of the 1970s gave way to the insight that, with unions stronger than anywhere else in the world, work reorganization was possible only if consensually mediated through the same representative institutions that employers had earlier rejected as interfering with their right to manage. And, with an ideological tradition that was arguably even more productivist than in Italy, Swedish unions, firmly established in their positions, were in turn prepared to recognize that representation of workplace-related interests that excludes cooperative interests in economic performance does so only at its own peril.

In Sweden, and even more so in Italy—that is, in the two countries in which workplace representation is based on unions only—whatever limits the new configuration of representation and consultation places on managerial prerogative are typically not formalized in law or collective agreement. This, of course, is quite different from Germany and the Netherlands with their—union-infused—statutory works council systems, in which what management may and may not do tends to be formally regulated in great detail.[11] Compared to the latter two countries, many of the consultation and co-determination rights that Italian and Swedish employers concede to their workforces appear on the surface to have been conceded voluntarily—with Swedish co-determination, for example, often taking place in the absence of a local co-determination agreement and formally regardless of the respective legislation. Further inspection, however, and comparison with a country like France make clear that such "voluntarism" depends vitally on a balance of forces of which strong local and national unions are an essential part. Moreover, there are also reasons to believe that even with considerable union strength, employer voluntarism can provide no more than an unstable base for consultation-cum-representation, mainly because it offers employers more options than worker representatives and considerably more control over workplace cooperation than unions. It is for this reason in particular that, on the one hand, there are strong voices among Italian unionists that argue for some kind of legislation on both industrial democracy and union rights so as to make representative consultation and workplace participation less dependent on the goodwill or enlightened self-interest of employers, and that, on the other hand, many Swed-

---

11. In France and Spain, where unions are weak and works council rights limited, management prerogatives are by and large not interfered with, neither formally nor informally.

ish observers are growing increasingly concerned about an impending "Japanization" of the country's industrial order.

What were the structural forces that brought about the interpenetration of consultation and representation, and the growth of a new kind of workplace participation, that we have observed in so many European industrial relations systems in the 1970s and 1980s? While we have no first-hand observations on this, the papers in this volume unanimously point to certain fundamental changes in the organization of decision making and production that occurred during the period. In the Fordist decades immediately after the war, decision making in most firms was centralized, and consultation served to improve the information available to top management, as well as to prepare the ground for the implementation of managerial decisions. Interest representation was conceived as entirely dissociated from this process, especially since decisions on work organization were supposed to be determined by the progress of technology and industrial engineering. As we have seen, these assumptions contributed to the decay of the first wave of consultative arrangements after the war.

All this began to change in the 1970s. With the broad move from mass production to flexible production, the number of decisions and the speed with which they had to be made increased dramatically—so much so that managerial decision making had to be radically decentralized, altering fundamentally the kind of productive cooperation that was required from workforces. With the new intensity of decision making characteristic of the new, flexible organizational structures, what firms needed were no longer just the experiential knowledge and the passive compliance of workforces, as potentially produced by traditional forms of—nonrepresentative—consultation, but their *consensus:* their willingness to agree to continuous changes in rules and work procedures under high uncertainty, as well as their *involvement* and *commitment:* their willingness themselves to make decisions guided, not by bureaucratic rules or superiors, but by internalized organizational objectives. Consensus, involvement, and commitment, however, require that workers develop an active *interest* in their work and "their" firm—or rather that the interests they have in the firm be activated and redefined so as to make them contribute to the efficient organization of the production process. Worker interests also come into play because of the growing number of alternatives in work organization that result from the high malleability of new technology and work arrangements like teamwork, which inevitably *raise questions of interest whenever questions of efficiency are raised,* and give rise to a need to *settle both kinds of questions simultaneously,* rapidly, and on a day-to-day basis, at all organizational levels and not just at the top of the organization.

In post-Fordist firms, that is, consultation on production needs and representation of worker interests tend to be even less separable than in traditional work organizations. Where under a system of decentralized competence, major production decisions are made, not by "management," but by workers as part of their routine work assignments, *consultation between workers and manage-*

ment on how to increase efficiency becomes impossible to keep apart from ne-gotiations on the mutual accommodation of interests. In flexible work organizations, effective interest representation, be it by works councils or by unions, requires deep technical and managerial knowledge that can only be gained through consultation, as well as day-to-day influence of workforces on the organization of work at all levels through ongoing consultation or, better, co-determination. As a consequence, unions as representative organizations can be expected to develop an interest in becoming involved in consultation over productive cooperation even if they have rejected such involvement in the past. Similarly, *efficient production* in post-Fordist organizations requires integration and accommodation of workforce interests, typically in an "organizational culture" that can substitute for prescriptive bureaucratic rules and centralized decisions. Managements, for their part, are therefore likely to become interested in having partners for consultation *that can also represent the interests of workers and commit the workforce as a collectivity* even if in the past they had been strongly opposed to any collective expression of interests at the workplace.

The observed fusion, then, of consultative functions into representational structures, as in Italy and Sweden, or of representative functions into consultative structures, as in Germany and the Netherlands, would seem to reflect a realization on the part of management of the *importance for consensual production of effective representation,* and on the part of unions of the *importance for effective representation of being involved in productive cooperation.* As we have seen, the new configuration of consultation and representation developed unevenly, depending among other things on existing institutional conditions and ideological worldviews.[12] A country like Germany that, more or less by accident, happened to have the right structures in place when the need arose was economically advantaged by it. In Sweden and Italy, the logic of post-Fordist production requirements asserted itself even against the institutional odds and resulted in a renaissance of consultation within primarily adversarial institutions. In France, on the other hand, and certainly in Spain, employers continued to oppose representative institutions at the workplace, while unions did not see it as their task to become involved in the management of produc-

12. But elements of it are present even in countries where one would not have expected them. As Paul Marginson pointed out in a lecture in December 1993, drawing on two recent, comprehensive surveys of workplace industrial relations in Britain, joint consultative committees of management and labor are present in no more than 25 percent of British workplaces. Where workforces are unionized, however, i.e., *where there is institutionalized interest representation to supplement consultation,* joint consultative committees are twice as common as in nonunionized workplaces. Among large companies, group-level consultative committees exist in 75 percent of firms where unions are recognized at all establishments but only in 45 percent of firms where they are recognized at none. And direct forms of participation, such as team meetings and quality circles, are more common in unionized than in nonunionized settings, and in large companies they are particularly frequent where unions are recognized throughout and where there is in addition a group-level consultative committee.

tion; here the transition to a post-Fordist mode of organization, with the competitive advantages it entails, proceeded less smoothly.

In any case, what happened in the 1970s and 1980s in continental European industrial relations systems was the rise of a new system of *workplace participation,* sustained by either unionized works councils or "councilized" workplace unions, through collective bodies at the plant and enterprise level as well as directly on the job, that differed from postwar consultation in that it included a strong element of worker *interest representation.* But it also differed from the traditional mode of interest representation in industrial relations, collective bargaining, in that it did not extend to and remained carefully insulated from wage setting; operated on the basis of legal or contractual rights to information, consultation, and co-determination rather than the power to strike; and was primarily concerned with *negotiating consensus* on the myriad of qualitative microdecisions required in a flexible, post-Taylorist organization of work. Functionally, the emerging new form of workplace participation, in some countries more and in others less, supported a new kind of *cooperation* between management and labor at the point of production: a kind of cooperation that consists in the mutual accommodation of interests through institutional arrangements for continuous co–decision making and co-determination, as opposed to both the passive acquiescence of workforces to employer decisions under the old, often paternalistic consultation regimes, and distributive conflict over the results of productive cooperation.

11.6   Role of Unions and Wage Bargaining

What institutional conditions favor representative participation at the workplace, and what are the consequences of different forms of workplace industrial relations for unions, employers, and economic performance? Beginning with unions, it would seem that *union strength and unity* are important factors for successful blending of consultation and representation. In France and Spain, where representative consultation is least developed, unions are far weaker and interunion competition is stronger than in the four other countries (table 11.2). In Sweden, by comparison, union strength ensures the representativeness of council-like consultative arrangements, although increasingly competitive multiunionism invites employer attempts to weaken external union influence through "coworker agreements." Near-monolithic union unity in Germany helps compensate for no more than moderate union density, whereas in Italy potentially strong interunion competition would seem to make representative consultation somewhat less stable and effective than in Germany or Sweden.

The impact on the unions of different institutional forms at the workplace is difficult to discern. In Germany as well as Italy, participation in works-council–like structures—legally based in the former and union based in the

Table 11.2   Works Councils and Unions

Country	Union Density (%)	Union Competition	Percentage Nonunion on Councils	Direct Union Delegates on Councils	Separate Union Workplace Organizations?	Wage Bargaining Centralized?	Councils Bargaining on Wages?
D	38	Marginal	21	No	Sometimes	Yes	No, not possible
NL	26	Considerable	36	No	Rarely	Yes, but eroding	Possible but rare
F	10	Very strong	29[a]	Yes, but no voting rights	Frequently	Yes, but decentralizing	No, not possible
E	10–15	Very strong	4[b]	Yes	Normally	Increasingly decentralizing	Yes
S	85	Increasing	Not applicable	Only	Not applicable	Increasingly less	No
I	39	Potentially strong	8	Yes	Rarely but increasingly	Periodically	Yes, sometimes

Note: See table 11.1 for country abbreviations.

[a]Plus 5 percent for unions other than the five main federations.

[b]Plus 12 percent for union other than the three main federations.

latter country—is said to have both increased union density and, to different degrees, helped contain competition. In Sweden, density has recently been growing even further, at a time when unions have become ever more widely and deeply involved in workplace participation. And in France and Spain, density has been rapidly falling, amid sharp interunion conflict and with representative consultation hardly developed. In fact, in Spain the legal institutionalization of works councils may have caused union substitution effects. Union substitution is also suggested in the Netherlands, where, unlike in Spain, workplace industrial relations are relatively cooperative. More important than conflict and cooperation, however, seems to be that in both countries, and in France as well, interunion competition prevents unions from using their positions on works councils for the recruitment of members—which is common, although at best semilegal, in Germany. In Italy and Sweden, of course, the problem does not pose itself because workplace representation is institutionally union based—which regardless of multiunionism gives all major unions an opportunity to benefit organizationally from councils.[13]

Nonmembers of unions are numerically important on works councils in the Netherlands and France, where density is low, competition is strong or very strong, and councils are legally based (table 11.2). Note, however, that the same conditions apply in Spain, where unorganized council members, even including members of small, "nonrepresentative" unions, are much less frequent. The difference may be due to the closer institutional links between councils and unions in Spain, as indicated by the legal provision for direct union delegates to councils, which parallels the Italian situation and generally underlines the de facto character of Spanish works councils as unified—or better: *federated*—union workplace organizations, rather than a "second channel" of representation. With higher union density and less interunion competition, German works councils have fewer nonorganized members than Dutch and French councils, but being genuine second-channel institutions they have more than Spanish councils. In Sweden and Italy, unorganized membership is not a problem because councils are union based, although Italian unions do as a matter of policy accept unorganized workers as works councils members. In all countries, whatever the institutional base, nonmembers of unions are less frequent among works councillors than among the workforce at large, with unions under all institutional arrangements routinely winning a share of council seats that comfortably exceeds their density ratio.

Union workplace organizations distinct from works councils are more likely to exist where the fusion of representation and consultation is least advanced (table 11.2). In France and Spain, competing unions usually have their own workplace branches, low density rates permitting. In the Netherlands, by com-

---

13. In other words, legally based councils seem to benefit unitary union movements but weaken divided unions, and unions in competitive union systems have a greater interest in councils being union based than do unions in unitary systems.

parison, union branches are rare in spite of considerable union competition, probably because legally well-resourced councils absorb and satisfy most representational needs. In Germany, the system of Vertrauensleute has typically evolved into an organizational infrastructure for the works council, to the extent that the latter became more representative and was adopted by the unions as their chosen instrument for workplace interest representation. Swedish unions do have separate workplace branches ("clubs"), but it is exclusively these that control consultation and cooperation, as well as make up any specific bodies created for that purpose. In Italy, separate union branches emerge when interunion competition intensifies, indicating a potential weak spot in the Italian pattern of unified union workplace organizations operating as de facto works councils.

Comparing the six countries, it is less than completely clear whether and to what extent *decentralized wage bargaining* interferes with representative participation (table 11.2). Looking only at Germany and Spain, the conclusion seems to offer itself that works councils can be agents of such participation only if they are not involved in wage bargaining.[14] Until some time ago, the Netherlands and Sweden would have easily confirmed this. Recently, however, wage bargaining has become less centralized in those two countries, and while this may be the beginning of the end of representative consultation, it is far from clear that it must. Note that in Italy, councils sometimes do act as wage bargainers without, apparently, having to give up their role as agents of workplace participation. Also, the French case shows, *e contrario,* that excluding councils from wage bargaining as such does not yet ensure that consultation will become representative. What the six cases would seem to suggest is that the important factor may not be whether councils do or do not act as wage bargainers, but the extent to which wage bargaining is centrally coordinated— as, for example, in Italy, where wage bargaining may be deliberately shifted to the enterprise level by the national union confederations in response to changing political and economic conditions but can be recentralized if required by new circumstances.

External union control over works councils is always precarious and never fully assured, but this applies to union workplace organizations in general, institutionalized as works councils or not. Subtle and less subtle power struggles between external unions and workplace representatives take place even in the two union-based systems, Sweden and Italy. Organized in whatever form, institutions of workplace representation will always give expression to interests that must appear "particularistic" from an external union perspective, especially to the extent that they are not exclusively distributive. Whether Swedish,

---

14. Of course, German works councils do play a role in wage bargaining, but only marginally, tacitly, and mostly illicitly. While that role has recently grown somewhat, the important point is that German councils cannot call strikes over wages, which inevitably makes their activities in this area secondary to those of the unions.

Italian, or German external unions have more control over interest articulation and labor-management cooperation at the workplace is therefore an open question that cannot be decided simply with reference to the three countries' different legal and organizational conditions.

Even where workplace industrial relations are conducted through works councils formally separate from unions, the latter are given a range of privileges inside the council system to ensure its representativeness, to prevent it from obstructing unions as organizations, and perhaps to buy unions' acquiescence to legal intervention. In Germany, the Netherlands, France, and Spain, election rules give large national unions sometimes massive advantage over splinter or nonunion groups. Also, external union officials have legally based rights of access to councils and council meetings, formally to offer advice, but de facto also to influence council policies. Typically, councils are obliged in law to consult and cooperate, not just with the employer, but also with the unions. In most countries, they also have the right as well as the duty to help national unions with the local enforcement of legal regulations and industrial agreements, enabling unions indirectly to define a potentially large part of the councils' agenda.

There also is in general an intense *exchange of material support* between unions and works councils. While works councils differ in size (table 11.3), most of their seats are taken by union members. Council legislation thus creates a large number of legally protected positions (see table 11.4, last column) to which union activists may be elected and in which they may conduct not just council but also union business. In this respect in particular, union-

Table 11.3	**Legal Size of Councils by Size of Establishment**			
	Size of Establishment (number of workers)			
Country	50	100	500	5,000
D	3	5	9	27
NL	3–5[a]	7	11	21
F[b]	3(+3)	5(+5)	6(+6)	12(+12)
E[c]	3	5	13(+1)	31(+4)
S	Subject to collective agreement or informal understanding, under a general legal right of unions to initiate co-determination procedures			
I[d]	3	3	6	42

Note: See table 11.1 for country abbreviations.

[a]Enterprises with between 35 and 100 workers may elect between three and five workforce representatives.

[b]Enterprise committees. Number of substitute members allowed to attend meetings but not to vote is given in parentheses.

[c]Number of additional, directly appointed union representatives is given in parentheses.

[d]Minimum number of union representatives (RSA) under the Workers' Statute, assuming the presence of all three union federations. Actual numbers are often higher as a consequence of industrial agreements and due to inclusion of elected delegates not designated as union representatives.

Table 11.4   Size and Coverage of Council System

Country	Minimum Size of Establishment (number of workers)	Number of Eligible Establishments	Percentage of Workforce Eligible	Percentage of Eligible Establishments Covered	Percentage of Eligible Workforce Covered	Number of Council Members
Dᵃ	20	112,000	70	35	50	183,700
NL	35	11,000	55	44	50	20,000
	100	4,500	18	83	87	34,000
Fᵇ						
PD	11	141,500	74	43	70	285,000
UD	50ᶜ	29,800	50	51	70	42,500
EC	50	29,800	50	79	79	108,000
E	6	212,000	37	45	60	132,000ᵈ
	50	20,000	47	70	75	105,000ᵈ
Iᵉ	16	50,000	64	64	70	206,000

Notes: See Table 11.1 for country abbreviations. No data on Sweden since arrangements are local and informal.

ᵃEstablishments with a workforce between 5 and 19 have a works council that consists of just one member, which has fewer rights than works councils in larger firms.

ᵇPD = personnel delegates; UD = union delegates; EC = enterprise committees.

ᶜFewer if stipulated by industrial agreement, or where personnel delegates have been elected.

ᵈExcluding public administration.

ᵉRSA under the Workers' Statute. Numbers refer to manufacturing and services in the early 1980s, when the system was most extensive.

independent councils are actually not much different from legally protected union workplace organizations. Unions benefit in particular from the legal rights of council members to be released from work at full pay. To the extent that the operating costs of councils are borne by the employer as part of the general costs of workplace governance, council legislation de facto provides for mandatory subsidies from employers to unions, or for a union tax on businesses. For example, where the law gives council members the right to receive training for their functions, employers may have to pay their wages while they attend union training courses, and may even have to pay the course fees.

That unions should benefit from works councils is an inevitable consequence of the de facto unionization of statutory council systems in the 1970s and 1980s, which made consultation more representative and thereby revitalized it. Where councils are not formally union bodies, unions may have to offer them technical assistance, expert advice, training, and so forth, in exchange for being allowed to share in their material or political resources. In Germany, national union headquarters invest considerable effort in maintaining connections with the works councils of large firms; smaller firms are serviced by regional or local union offices. Works councils that can find other sources of support may be less inclined to subsidize the unions and would tend to be more politically independent. In Italy, on the other hand, where council resources are formally union resources, it seems that councils sometimes receive material support from the external union.

It is hard to say in which country's unions derive the highest material benefits from councils. Germany and the Netherlands come to mind where works councils have extensive rights to financial support from the employer. But in both countries the unions must in turn be useful to the councils; otherwise, councils may refuse to share their resources with them. German unions especially are forced to expend vast resources on providing councils with advice and guidance on a current basis. In Spain, and partly in Italy, the large size of councils (table 11.3) may point to certain clientelistic functions of the council system, especially in Spain where during the transition the activists of two large, competing unions seem to have been bought into gradualistic reform by large-scale paid release from work at the expense of the employers. French unions, by comparison, seem to draw relatively little organizational benefit from enterprise committees, but then they may not have to given the existence of the, also legally based, union delegates.

11.7 Role of Legal Intervention

As has been noted, in no country is the institutionalization of workplace representation, either as such or fused into consultative practices, left to employers' self-interest or paternalistic sense of obligation. Works councils in Germany, the Netherlands, France, and Spain, and union workplace branches in France, Sweden, and Italy, are not legally *mandated*, so there may be workplaces where they do not exist. But setting them up is easy as it requires no more than pro forma triggering activities by external unions or a very small proportion of the workforce. What is important is that employers are barred from interfering and indeed play no role at all in the process save an entirely passive one. Typically, employers obstructing the creation of a works council or a union workplace branch are threatened with severe legal sanctions. While all legal systems allow for residual voluntary elements in setting up workplace representation, that voluntarism applies exclusively to labor.

Similarly, once councils or legally protected union branches have come into being, they may fall by the wayside or wither away due to lack of interest among workers or lack of attention and resources on the part of external unions. But there is no way for an employer to demand or bring about their formal disbandment. Once set up, legally protected representational bodies cannot formally be undone, not even by a majority of the workforce since this would deprive the minority of essential rights of industrial citizenship. For all practical purposes, works councils are permanent bodies, very much like city councils, and are viewed as such by both unions and employers. For employers in particular, attempting to make an existing council or union branch go away must seem futile, and in fact such attempts are so rare that they are never even mentioned in any of the country papers.

Another important function of legal intervention is to make representation *universal,* that is, to take it out of economic competition between firms. In all six countries, the percentage of the national workforce that is legally eligible for workplace representation is high (table 11.4). Countries differ most in their ambition to cover not just large but also small firms; often, as in Germany, France, and Spain, very small workplaces come under a somewhat different, less formally regulated regime. Actual coverage varies everywhere with the size of workplaces; as firms or plants get larger, coverage rapidly approaches 100 percent. Given the mixture that has developed in all European countries of voluntary and statutory elements in workplace representation, it is not surprising that actual coverage is affected by union strength, as in France and Spain where weak unions make for less than complete coverage even in the larger firms.

Other typical subjects of legal regulation are the resources that representative bodies are entitled to receive from employers; the rights of unions vis-à-vis legally based works councils where these exist; and the rights and obligations of councils or, where applicable, union workplace organizations in representing the workforce in relation to management, especially with respect to the exercise of managerial prerogative (table 11.5). Note that even in Sweden, the resources that employers have to provide for workplace representation are determined by law, in particular the Shop Stewards Act. Legislation typically sets a minimum to which representative bodies are entitled, allowing additional resources to be negotiated. Legal regulation of the employer's contribution is regarded as desirable by legislatures not only because it, again, helps take the

Table 11.5   **Legal Resources of Works Councils**

Country	D	NL	F	E	S	I
Board representation	Strong	Minor[a]	Weak	None	Weak	None
Legal rights						
Information	X	X	X	X	X	X[b]
Consultation	X	X	X	X	X	X[c]
Co-determination	X	X			X	
Full-time release from work	Yes	Not by law	Not by law	As a legal option	Yes[d]	By workplace agreement
Training	Yes	Yes	Yes, but limited in fact	Not by law	Yes[b]	By workplace agreement
Control over social funds	No	No	Yes	Yes	No	No
Paid expert advice	Yes	Yes	Limited	No	Yes	By workplace agreement

Note: See table 11.1 for country abbreviations.

[a]Councils have limited influence on the selection of newly appointed board members, and may reject co-opted members.

[b]By national agreement.

[c]By workplace agreement, with increasing frequency.

[d]For union workplace representatives under the Shop Stewards Act.

costs of workplace representation out of competition but also because it protects the independence of representative bodies: if resources are received as a matter of right, they cannot be used by the employer to extract concessions. Legal entitlements thus help protect a council's or workplace union's legitimacy. Incidentally, all national systems assume that effective representative consultation is part of the governance of the firm and that its costs are therefore rightly paid by the employer, just as the costs of management. All systems also treat workplace participation as a collective good for the workforce, that is, one that the workforce cannot be expected to finance by voluntary contributions even though the workforce benefits from it.

Second, where the law creates union-independent bodies of workplace consultation or participation, legislators usually find it necessary to regulate in considerable detail their relationship to the unions, that is, the intersection of statutory and voluntary representation. Substantively, these regulations vary between countries, depending on the structure of unionism and the character of legally based institutions. As pointed out, union access to councils and council resources always receives strong legal attention as it concerns directly the way representation through unions is connected to consultation between workforce and employer, and to participation of workers in management.

Third, the law may regulate, more or less specifically, the representational rights and cooperative obligations of participation bodies vis-à-vis the employer. Where legislation lays down only broad principles or limits itself to securing union rights, as in Italy and Sweden, information, consultation, and co-determination rights of workplace bodies may have to be specified by collective agreement; alternatively, interference with managerial prerogative may take place informally depending on local power relations. Where the law is very detailed, as in Germany and the Netherlands, and to some extent in France and Spain, employers tend to refuse negotiations over further participation rights, although at least in Germany expansion of such rights by collective agreement would be legally possible.[15]

The most important difference between national systems seems to be the presence or absence of co-determination rights for works councils (table 11.5). Where there are no such rights, the capacity of councils to veto or delay employer decisions depends entirely on the local or economic conjunctural power balance. In Italy, post-Fordist representation-cum-consultation seems to work without any formal co-determination rights of workplace unions or works councils; note, however, the recent demands by unions for some sort of industrial democracy legislation. The weaker councils of France and Spain have control over the social funds of firms, whereas stronger councils do not.[16] While German works councils can draw on representation on company supervisory boards as an important additional institutional resource, there is no board representation in Italy and Spain, and only weak versions of it in the Netherlands, France, and Sweden, making the relationship between board representation and council strength hard to determine (table 11.5). All councils are in different ways involved in the local enforcement of applicable legislation and collective agreements, from which some draw considerable political and organizational strength.

Legal rights for works councils to information, consultation, and co-determination tend to be coupled with, and conditional on, legal obligations to cooperate with the employer in good faith, for example, to respect business secrets and not to engage in, as the English translation of the German Works Constitution Act puts it, "acts of industrial warfare." Such obligations are to ensure that councils do not become exclusively representative bodies and continue to attend also to functional needs for consultation and cooperation. Union workplace organizations are usually not placed under obligations of this kind, which is why some unions, for example, in Italy or France, prefer them over councils even though councils might give them more influence over the exercise of managerial prerogative. (Swedish unions, to the extent that they draw on their legal right to initiate co-determination procedures, are under a general

---

15. Rather than by collective bargaining, works council rights in Germany, and to some extent the Netherlands, are often extended by councils using legal co-determination rights to extract informal managerial commitments to consultation or de facto co-determination on other, unrelated subjects that the law has left under managerial discretion.

16. German councils do, however, have a legal right to full co-determination over company social policy and sometimes to the dismay of the unions become involved in running the cafeteria or the company's health insurance fund.

obligation to respect the economic needs of the firm, which is further elaborated by the national industrial Agreement on Efficiency and Productivity.)

It should be noted, however, that the absence of a legal "peace obligation" does not necessarily preclude cooperation, as demonstrated by the Italian case. Similarly, a legal obligation for works councils to engage in *vertrauensvolle Zusammenarbeit* (trustful cooperation) does not preclude conflict; most unofficial strikes in Germany are more or less openly led by works council members, with employers usually refraining from invoking the legal sanctions that exist for this. In Germany at least, the real functions of the peace obligation for councils seem to be related, not primarily to the relationship between works council and employer, but to that between the works council, as a de facto union workplace organization, and the union: by barring councils from calling official strikes and making it difficult although not impossible for them to call unofficial strikes, the law helps external unions preserve their strike monopoly. In this respect, the peace obligation serves a similar function as the legal prohibition on works councils engaging in wage bargaining.

11.8   Workplace Participation and Economic Performance

The contribution of representative consultation to economic performance, through works councils or union workplace organizations, is hard to establish quantitatively. There is in European systems no equivalent to the American nonunionized sector with which exact comparison (as, e.g., in Freeman and Medoff 1984) could be attempted: almost all firms in a country have basically the same or similar workplace institutions.[17] Moreover, much of the economically beneficial influence of works councils, if it exists, is very likely to be in the fuzzy area of "X-efficiency" (Leibenstein 1987) where causes and effects are not easily traced.

Lack of quantifiability, however, does not mean that, as Gertrude Stein observed when visiting Oakland, California, "there is no there there." While international comparisons, especially in an age of economic interdependence, are not without considerable problems, one may note the conspicuous absence of representative consultation and effective workplace participation in such countries as Britain and the United States, whose economies have suffered most since the watershed of the 1970s, and its strong presence in Germany, Sweden, and Italy. To the latter list one may add Japan, where consultation, although

17. Econometric studies sometimes try to compare economic performance before and after major pieces of workplace legislation. The problems with this include the inevitably small number of yearly observations and the simultaneous influence of other factors, such as business cycles or exchange rates. Alternatively, one may use as the independent variable variations within one country in specific properties of workplace institutions to look for covariations with performance indicators such as productivity or profitability. One problem here is that the extent to which national systems allow for meaningful interfirm variations itself varies between countries. There also are conceptual difficulties of how exactly to specify the independent variable, as well as practical difficulties of access to reliable performance data.

probably more paternalistic than representative, seems to be standard managerial practice.

At the level of descriptive plausibility, the country studies in this volume suggest several ways in which the parallel evolution of representative consultation in European countries over the last two decades may have virtuously responded to economic needs and may have helped these countries master the challenges of post-Fordism. Such accounts receive some if not conclusive validation from the fact that, where representative participation is strongly established, employers often and typically express their satisfaction with it.[18] One example is the advice given to German employers by their central research institute to consider the works council as a "factor of production" and an essential agent of information and communication within the firm: an institution that cuts transaction costs, improves the working atmosphere, and consolidates social consensus. Similarly, for Sweden it is reported that employers have made their peace with the Co-Determination Act and have come to accept "employee and union representation in the change process," with the—American—CEO of Saab stating after the firm's successful reorganization that "weaker unions would not have helped, to the contrary" (Brulin, chap. 7 in this volume).[19]

Expressions of employer satisfaction are also reported from the Netherlands and Italy. In the latter country, the widespread existence of informal participation arrangements may be interpreted, to quote, as "factual recognition of the importance of institutionalized workforce representation in the management of production"—a recognition that is all the more remarkable since it is "in sharp contrast to the official positions of both the external unions and the employers' associations" (Regalia, chap. 8 in this volume). The confession of an Italian manager that, "if works councils didn't already exist, one should invent them," is reported to have been made in exactly the same words by a German employer and might as well have been heard from Dutch or Swedish employers.

More specifically, the papers in this volume mention a number of ways in which representative consultation contributes to economic performance. First, all papers point out that works councils, or council-like structures, *improve the flow of communication* both from the workforce to management and vice versa. As good communication is vital for modern business enterprises, this is widely regarded as extremely important. Second, especially the Dutch and the German chapters emphasize that councils *improve the quality of decisions,* though sometimes delaying them; as well-resourced councils can ask detailed questions and offer counterproposals, managements must scrutinize their own projects more, making it more likely that flaws are discovered early and that the range of alternatives is enlarged. Third, representative consultation *facilitates*

18. Validation is not conclusive because one must never underestimate the capacity of interviewees for verbal opportunism.

19. Note that the Swedish central agreement of 1982 on the implementation of the Co-Determination Act is called the "Agreement on *Efficiency* and Participation," in this order (emphasis added).

the implementation of decisions, something that is emphasized in the Dutch and Italian country studies especially: a management decision that has been made with representative informational and political input from the workforce is more easily carried out later, and this may more than make up for the longer decision time.

Fourth, councils in all countries, perhaps with the exception of Spain, have been found to place pressure on firms to *rationalize their human resource policies,* expand their time horizon, and emphasize the creation and retention of high and broad skills. In this respect, works councils and unions seem to have been a major source of organizational innovation, something that is perhaps particularly visible in the case of German co-determination. Fifth, the Swedish and Spanish chapters mention a contribution of workplace participation to *reducing absenteeism.* Sixth, apparently participation helps firms *handle worker grievances,* not least by encouraging workers to come forward and speak up without fear of retribution. Apart from its negative impact on social peace, worker dissatisfaction may be indicative of general organizational deficiencies, and by expressing themselves workers may add importantly to the information of top management. Seventh, participation also provides *feedback on its middle management* to the top of the organization, something that is mentioned in the Italian study especially. Eighth, the Dutch study emphasizes the advantages of works councils for a customized and flexible, that is, locally negotiated, implementation of regulatory law, something that is likely also to apply in most other countries.

Representative consultation seems to have been particularly useful to firms that try to move to a *flexible and decentralized organization of work and decision making.* This conclusion is far from trivial since especially well institutionalized works councils have often been expected to object to the delegation of managerial decision rights to the shop floor, for example, to semiautonomous working groups, on the ground that this would reduce the capacity of their management counterparts to negotiate with them. Indications are that at least German works councils in fact did at first resist work groups and "quality circles" for such reasons. In recent years, however, this has dramatically changed, and works councils in Germany, just as in Sweden and Italy, have become forceful and active proponents of, to use the Swedish term, "work development." Especially in Sweden, but also in other countries, decentralization of competence and the introduction of semiautonomous work groups have been found to be easier if they are negotiated with a collective representative of the workforce, instead of unilaterally imposed; see the case of Fiat, where management resumed talking to the union workplace organization at the moment when it began to implement its "total quality" strategy. The Swedish paper in particular shows how strong representation combined with consultative arrangements may sustain a "cooperative culture" within which experimentation with decentralized organizational structures can flourish—structures whose introduction is often embraced by the unions as their own objective.

It is worth noting that the French paper reports, not just union weakness, employer resistance to representation, and an impasse in the development of workplace participation, but also a lag in the post-Fordist transformation of work organization. That there may be a more than accidental association between the two is hinted by the Spanish case, where in a largely outdated industrial structure, employers continue to resist the inclusion of works councils in the governance of the workplace and prefer to rely on their hierarchical powers, while works councils are preoccupied with union business pure and simple and have little confidence in employers. Nevertheless, the French chapter reports that councils have at least helped recast the balance between central and local regulation, especially of working time and technology, and have sometimes been a factor in the modernization of the human resource policies of French companies by impressing on them the need to invest in skills and general adaptability.

None of the West European papers discusses the extent to which works council influence may detract from economic performance by giving rise to joint rent seeking or politically prudent but economically self-destructive avoidance of tough decisions. On the other hand, examples abound in the papers and in the literature at large of firms seeking and receiving the support of a strong union or works council in implementing severe capacity cuts, working-time reductions, or productivity drives in response to a deep economic crisis. The case of the Swedish firm, Saab, is only one among many where representative consultation enabled managements to embark on fundamental change without losing control over it or destroying the allegiance to the firm of the remaining workforce.

As to rent seeking, all of the chapters focus on firms in the internationally highly competitive manufacturing sector. In such firms, difficult global market conditions serve as a powerful constraint on whatever deals management and labor may make with each other.[20] Quite possibly, the economically benevolent effects of strong representative institutions at the workplace may be conditional on competitive markets and a tough competition policy, as has been argued for the German case (Streeck 1989). Strong unions or works councils may have less desirable consequences in the public sector, where there is no or much less competition. But this is a separate subject not covered by this volume.

---

20. Note that Italian, German, and Swedish manufacturing are far more internationally exposed than manufacturing in the United States. In fact, rather than devices for rent seeking, the new representative-consultative arrangements that emerged in European economies in the 1970s and 1980s constitute a nonprotectionist response to intensified international competition, aimed at increasing the performance of national firms through improved cooperation between workers and management, allowing for continuous restructuring of production processes.

11.9 Summary

Postwar industrial relations in Western Europe set out with an institutionalized bifurcation between adversarial collective bargaining through unions at the sectoral or national level and cooperative consultation through works councils at the workplace. Works councils were based either in law or in national collective agreement. However, where they had no representational functions, which was the case almost everywhere outside West Germany and, to some extent, the Netherlands, they tended to fall in disuse during the 1950s and 1960s. Simultaneously, a representation gap opened in European workplaces that was related to the inability of both centralized unions and nonrepresentative councils to take up the growing discontent of workers with Taylorist rationalization.

The explosions of 1968 and 1969 made the development of accountable systems of workplace representation for workers a major concern for public policy as well as for unions and employers. Governments strengthened workplace representation either by legal support for union workplace organizations or by improving the rights of works councils and their links to the unions. In later years, it turned out that the resulting new representative arrangements at the workplace responded fortuitously to the requirements of post-Taylorist industrial restructuring, especially where they were from the beginning connected with still viable structures of cooperative consultation, such as German works councils. Where such structures had dwindled away, they were in subsequent years rebuilt either by well-established unions, as in Sweden and Italy, or by legislation. The outcome was a remarkable convergence of European industrial relations systems on a pattern of representative consultation—or participation—at the workplace, promoted by public policy, infused with union influence, and more or less willingly accepted by employers.

Western European systems of representative consultation are kept strictly apart from collective wage bargaining; otherwise, however, their operation is closely linked to unionism, and such links are encouraged by legislation. Legal intervention is used to take the main parameters of workplace participation out of contention between management and labor, as well as out of competition between individual firms. Major details, however, are left to joint regulation between employers and unions, at the national or at the workplace level. While the economic effects of workplace participation are hard to determine statistically, there are good reasons to believe that participation contributes in a variety of ways to efficient workplace governance and thereby to the dynamic efficiency of firms in uncertain economic, technological, and social conditions.

References

Freeman, Richard B., and James L. Medoff. 1984. *What do unions do?* New York: Basic.

Leibenstein, H. 1987. *Inside the firm.* Cambridge: Harvard University Press.

Streeck, Wolfgang. 1989. Successful adjustment to turbulent markets: The automobile industry. In *Industry and politics in West Germany: Towards the Third Republic,* ed. Peter J. Katzenstein, 113–56. Ithaca, N.Y.: Cornell University Press.

III The North American Experience

12 Canada: Joint Committees on Occupational Health and Safety

Elaine Bernard

12.1 Introduction

For over two decades, governments in various jurisdictions in Canada have been experimenting with mandatory joint worker-management committees. For the most part, these committees have been "limited purpose," with worker representatives mandated to participate on committees with management in an advisory capacity on a specific issue or topic, such as education and training, technological change, or plant closure (Adams 1986). In most instances these committees are confined to organized work sites, although in a limited number of cases they may be required by all firms of a certain size or in a particular industry or sector, such as in mining or forestry. By far the most comprehensive experience in Canada with mandated joint committees is in the area of occupational health and safety. Today, a majority of Canadian jurisdictions require firms to establish joint committees with elected worker representatives as vehicles for worker participation in reducing work-related disease and injury and improving the workplace environment. While these mandated joint health and safety committees (JHSCs) are a far cry from European-type comprehensive works councils, they nevertheless constitute a significant development in North American industrial relations by taking the giant step of legislating worker participation outside of and beyond the framework of traditional collective bargaining.

In this paper, a North American contribution to a comparative study on works councils, we will examine the evolution of mandated occupational health and safety joint committees with respect to the following questions:

How were JHSCs introduced into a North American adversarial industrial relations system?

Elaine Bernard is executive director of the Trade Union Program at Harvard University.

How do they perform?

To what extent do mandatory committees substitute for trade unions and/or government enforcement of regulations?

What is the role of government in assisting and promoting such a system of internal responsibility?

In particular, we will concentrate on the evolution and function of JHSCs in Ontario. While there are common features to the enabling legislation and regulations in most Canadian jurisdictions, Ontario, as Canada's industrial heartland and the most populous province, has had the most instructive and far-reaching experience with JHSCs. Ontario was one of the first jurisdictions to promote joint committees, at first voluntarily, then as mandated since 1978. Today it has the most extensive legislation, which not only requires committees in most workplaces but also mandates worker representatives in work sites with too few employees for a full committee. Ontario has evolved toward an "internal responsibility system" in occupational safety and health. This system seeks to empower both workplace parties through joint committees that take mutual responsibility for reducing hazards and injuries in the workplace. With the most recent amendments to the province's health and safety legislation, Ontario moved beyond the level of the firm and has created a bipartite authority, the Workplace Health and Safety Agency (WHSA), with the power to establish and administer a unique certification process with mandatory training for members of health and safety committees. It has also proposed a yet-to-be-developed accreditation system for employers who operate successful health and safety programs and policies. Ontario's creation of the WHSA represents an attempt to extend the bipartite approach beyond the enterprise level and to promote a cooperative approach to the work environment at the sectoral and provincial levels. In this paper, we will begin with an overview of the evolution of the legal and institutional framework for mandated joint committees throughout Canada. We will then look at the specific case of Ontario and the development of sectoral and provincewide bipartite support entities. We will examine joint committees' relationships with employers, unions, and workers and, in the case of Ontario, with the WHSA. Finally, we will examine the role of government in nurturing bipartite committees and forums at the sectoral and provincial levels as well as at the level of the firm.

12.2 Legal Environment

While there are important differences, Canadian labor law is in many ways similar to the Wagner Act in the United States. That is, the law proceeds from an assumption that the "natural state" of a new enterprise is nonunionized. In order for workers to organize a union and receive the designation of exclusive bargaining agent they must surmount legal barriers constructed to prove that the employees freely chose to form or join a union. It is generally conceded that the organizing and certification process is somewhat easier in Canada than in the United States in that the whole process is much faster and there are stronger legal sanctions against employer interference in the process. But in marked contrast to Western Europe, the general North American industrial relations framework assumes that workers have little or no right outside of collective bargaining to participation in decision making in the workplace.

Although the framework of Canadian labor legislation was originally modeled after the U.S. National Labor Relations Act (NLRA), there are some important differences that affect the policies discussed in this paper. Most significant, Canadian governments at all levels have tended to be more interventionist in their approach to industrial relations. From the Industrial Disputes Investigation Act of 1907 to today, governments in Canadian jurisdictions have assumed a more active role in mediation and conciliation of disputes. Also, Canadian governments have sought to promote labor and management cooperation through funding of training and education and through the establishment of joint labor and management research and education centers such as the Canadian Labour Market and Productivity Centre.

In contrast to the U.S. NLRA, Canada has no single labor code for the entire country. In all, there are 13 different jurisdictions in Canada—ten provinces, two territories, and a federal jurisdiction. The federal jurisdiction accounts for only 10 percent of the workforce (Meltz 1989) covering federal government employees, workers in banks, communications, and interprovincial and international transportation. Most workers fall under their respective provincial or territorial jurisdiction, with each province or territory legislating labor standards, industrial relations, and occupational health and safety standards within its own territory. While there is great potential for interprovincial variation in legislation, for the most part unions have been successful in extending supportive labor legislation from province to province. In recent years, with the election of labor-supported social democratic governments in Ontario, parts of Western Canada, and Quebec, provincial labor legislation has played a leading role in extending rights for workers and in improving standards and procedures.

Until the 1970s, work environment standards in most jurisdictions were a patchwork of divergent statutes and administrations. Some work sites were covered by a variety of conflicting and competing statutes, while others were left without any legislative health and safety protection at all. In Ontario, for example, there were different statutes administered by separate ministries for mining, construction, industrial, and logging enterprises (Dematteo 1991). In all Canadian jurisdictions, the previous norm was state standard setting and enforcement. Worker participation was limited to unionized workers lobbying government agencies on standards and contract negotiations where unions could bargain the "terms and conditions" of employment (Tucker 1990, 20–21).

Since the 1970s, however, there have been substantial changes in the public policy approach to the work environment. These changes can be attributed to an overall increased "awareness of and concern about the relationship between the general environment and human health," an interest in lowering health care costs associated with work-related illness and injury, and increased labor mobilization creating pressure for a greater voice for labor in workplace decision making (Tucker 1990).

Saskatchewan in 1972 passed the first omnibus occupational health and safety statute, creating the model for other Canadian jurisdictions. The Saskatchewan legislation established in North America for the first time the workers *right to know* about hazardous materials, the *right to refuse* dangerous work, and the *right to participate* in decision making concerning the work environment through mandatory worker-management health and safety committees (Bryce and Manga 1985, 272).

In spite of its small population (about one million, constituting one twenty-fifth of the Canadian population), Saskatchewan has often been in the forefront of introducing innovative legislation of national significance. The birthplace of the socialist farm-labor party in Canada, the Cooperative Commonwealth Federation (which later with the Canadian Labour Congress cofounded the New Democratic party [NDP]), Saskatchewan was the first jurisdiction in North America to grant collective bargaining rights to public employees. In 1961 the Saskatchewan NDP government developed a universal, comprehensive health insurance system that became the model for Canada's national health care system introduced less than a decade later.

Losing power to the Liberals between 1964 and 1971, the NDP was returned to power in Saskatchewan in 1971 with strong support from the labor movement. Building on the success of their earlier health care plan, the new Saskatchewan government's initiatives in the area of occupational health and safety complemented both the proworker stance of the NDP government and its concern for health promotion through preventive care.

The 1972 legislation consolidated occupational health and safety activities into the province's Department of Labour, Occupational Health and Safety (OHS) Branch. Joint worker-management committees were made mandatory for most workplaces with 10 or more employees. Within a few years, the OHS Branch was able to report that there were over 2,500 joint committees throughout the province, providing coverage for 80 percent of Saskatchewan's nonagricultural workforce (Sass 1990, 3).

Throughout the late 1970s and 1980s most provincial jurisdictions and the federal government moved to consolidate the various pieces of work environment legislation into "omnibus" statutes. These were administered by a single government department or commission with the power to administer and write regulation in its jurisdiction. While not originally conceived of as deregulation, the move toward an "internal responsibility" regime in the workplace can be seen as both a method of simplifying, consolidating, and streamlining complex regulation as well as a means for shifting the burden of authority and responsibility for improving the work environment onto the parties in the workplace.

Concurrent with this legislative consolidation, workers in most jurisdictions won statutory guarantees of what have come to be known as the three basic rights in the area of occupational health and safety: the right to know about hazards in the work environment, the right to refuse unsafe work, and the right to participate in the detection, evaluation, and reduction of workplace hazards (Sass 1990).

The scope of the new health and safety legislation was similar to labor standards legislation, in that it extended rights to workers whether or not they were unionized. But rather like blanket labor standards, certain groupings of employees were exempted from the health and safety legislation either by the limited number of employees at their work site or by the type of work they were involved in. In most jurisdictions, for example, police, prison guards, firefighters, and retail, agricultural, and construction workers were excluded.

While there is some variation in the specific wording and procedures for exercising these rights, all jurisdictions today have guaranteed in some way the right to refuse dangerous work and the right to know about workplace hazards. The federal and provincial governments' adoption of the Workplace Hazardous Materials Information System (WHMIS), which stipulates requirements for labels on hazardous materials and mandates the availability of uniform material safety sheets and training of employees using hazardous materials, has assured at least a baseline of "the right to know" in all jurisdictions.

In all but four jurisdictions the establishment of committees is required as the normative structure for ensuring workers' "right to participation" (see table 12.1). With the exception of Quebec, in the nine jurisdictions where committees are mandated no worker or union action is required to form a committee and the legislation generally requires the employer to assure that a joint com-

Table 12.1   Health and Safety Regulations by Jurisdiction

Jurisdiction	Mandated JHSC	Right to Know	Right to Participate	Right to Refuse
Canada	X	X	X	X
Yukon	X	X	X	X
Northwest Territories	a	X		X
British Columbia	X	X	X	X
Alberta	a	X		X
Saskatchewan	X	X	X	X
Manitoba	X	X	X	X
Ontario	X	X	X	X
Quebec	b	X	X	X
New Brunswick	X	X	X	X
Nova Scotia	X	X	X	X
Prince Edward Island	a	X		X
Newfoundland	a	X		X

[a]Discretionary.
[b]On union initiative or by request of 10 percent of workers.

mittee is functioning. In Quebec, the following preconditions are sufficient to require management to assure the formation of a joint committee: a demand by the local union, or a request by 10 percent of the employees in an unorganized work site; or a request by at least four workers at a work site of fewer than 40 workers (Quebec National Assembly 1979, section 69). Even in the four jurisdictions where committees are "discretionary," committees may be required by either the minister of labor or a designated government official.

The specific responsibilities, functions, and requirements for committees vary tremendously from jurisdiction to jurisdiction. However, there are a number of features common to most jurisdictions. Generally, the firm-size threshold for requiring the formation of a committee is 20 or more employees (Saskatchewan, with the lowest threshold, requires only 10 or more employees). In a few jurisdictions, such as Ontario, provision is made in smaller work sites (of over five employees but fewer than 20) for the election of a single worker representative with powers similar to that of a joint committee (Ontario Legislature 1990, section 8–1).

There is no general rule for defining what constitutes a "workplace" for the purposes of forming a joint committee. As an Ontario study reports, "a workplace defined as a single workplace for ministry inspection purposes" could be divided by a JHSC into several subareas. Similarly, a single JHSC might serve in what the ministry may define as several "workplaces" (Ontario Advisory Council 1986, 17). In Ontario, where negotiated joint committee structures sometimes preceded the legislation in some industries such as steel and mining, the regulations are purposely silent in order to permit existing negotiated arrangements and to maximize flexibility for committees. Whether by design or oversight, the legislation in most jurisdictions is similarly silent on the issue.

The construction industry presents one of the most difficult workplace organizational problems for joint committees. The temporary transitory nature of the work site, the diversity of trades active on a work site, and the potential for large numbers of contractors and subcontractors coming and going throughout the life of the project make it especially difficult to transfer the general JHSC model into this industry. In many jurisdictions, this problem is avoided by simply exempting construction from the general legislation and by writing special codes and regulations for the industry. In Ontario and Quebec, however, both jurisdictions have included construction in their provisions and have provided for joint committees on large construction sites.

In Quebec, a "job-site" committee is required on work sites "where it is foreseen that activities on a construction site will occupy at least twenty-five construction workers simultaneously at a particular stage of the work" (Quebec National Assembly 1979, section 204). The job-site committee includes representatives from the principal contractor, each employer, one representative of the person in charge of the plans and specifications, and one representative from each of the unions with members on site. This committee is to meet at least once every two weeks, during regular working hours (Quebec National

Assembly 1979, sections 205 and 207). In Ontario, a nonmandated "trades committee" is formed from all the represented trades on a job site, and this committee forwards problems and suggestions to the mandated joint committee.

All mandated JHSCs function as bipartite bodies requiring equal numbers of worker and management members on the committee—with a sharing of chairing duties or some other provision for joint leadership of the committee. Some jurisdictions have a formula for committee size according to the total number of employees in an enterprise, others are silent on maximum or minimum committee size. Most jurisdictions prohibit employer representatives from outnumbering the worker representatives.

As is often the rule in Canada, Quebec is a special case, adding an additional element to the general trend of bipartite committees. Taking advantage of the province's unique system of health care and social service delivery, joint occupational health and safety committees in Quebec have the right to choose a physician approved by a designated hospital center or department of community health to prepare and monitor a work site "health plan" and to be "in charge of health services in the establishment." While the joint committee hires the physician, management is responsible for the costs both of the physician and of implementing the health program (Quebec National Assembly 1979, section 78). The designated physician is a member of the joint committee but does not have a vote in meetings. Quebec is the only jurisdiction in which committees regularly include physicians or other outside experts.

In all jurisdictions, management is expected to select its own committee members. In some legislation, such as in the Ontario act, the law seeks to assure that management representatives be persons who exercise "managerial functions" and "to the extent possible" are employed at the workplace (Ontario Legislature 1990, section 9–9). In unionized work sites, the local union is normally empowered in the legislation to determine the method for selecting the worker representatives. In some instances, where more than one union represents the workers, the unions are "encouraged" to work together to ensure that the interests of all the employees are represented by the work representatives on the committee.

In nonunionized work sites, employees select their own representatives—although in most legislation the exact method of selection is not detailed. In Ontario, for example, the employer has the responsibility at the nonunionized work site to "cause a joint committee to be established" and to assure that "members of the committee who represent workers shall be selected by the workers they are to represent" (Ontario Legislature 1990, section 9–4). In Quebec, the legislation simply states that "the workers' representatives on a committee shall be designated from among the workers of the establishment" (Quebec National Assembly 1979, section 72). The legislation normally stipulates the minimum number of meetings for committees, which varies from four times a year to once a month depending on the jurisdiction. Legislation in most jurisdictions also spells out the general terms, functions, responsibilities, and rights of committee members. Worker committee members, for example, have the right to participate in such areas as regular workplace inspections for hazards, accident and incident investigation, and communications and recommendations to management. They also have the right to be present during an inspection or investigation by a provincial health and safety inspector and to engage in other committee-related work and responsibilities during regular working hours with no loss or reduction in pay. In Quebec, the legislation gives committees the right to select the individual protective devices and equipment "best adapted to the needs of the workers in their establishment," which management is required to purchase for their employees (Quebec National Assembly 1979, section 78).

Most legislation includes language to assure that workers in general, and committee members specifically, are not disciplined, threatened, or subject to reprisals by employers either for exercising their right to refuse or for performing work related to their joint committee responsibilities (Ontario Legislature 1990, section 50). The Ontario legislation also includes an "immunity" clause, prohibiting lawsuits for neglect or default arising from "good faith" actions of committee members (Ontario Legislature 1990, section 65).

The joint committees are usually required to keep and in some cases post minutes of all committee meetings. Beyond very rudimentary instructions about number of meetings, minutes, and size of the committee, most legislation does not detail how committee meetings are to proceed—for example, whether by consensus or by vote. Usually these decisions are left to the committees themselves.

Most legislation is silent on what happens if a committee becomes deadlocked. The exception to this is Quebec, where provisions in the legislation give specific procedures for problem resolution when a committee fails to reach an agreement. The legislation permits either party to appeal to the provincial oversight agency, the Commission, for a binding resolution after both parties have submitted their case in writing (Quebec National Assembly 1979, section 79). The Quebec legislation also assures balanced representation at committee meetings by stating that "workers' representatives as a whole and the employer's representatives as a whole are entitled to only one vote, respectively, on a committee" (Quebec National Assembly 1979, section 73).

In most jurisdictions, the function of the committee is primarily advisory and the legislation (except in Quebec) is vague on what is to happen with a committee recommendation, or what procedure is to be followed in case of a conflict on the committee. The B.C. legislation, for example, states that the committee "shall assist in creating a safe place of work, shall recommend actions which will improve the effectiveness of the industrial health and safety program, and shall promote compliance with these regulations" (Workers' Compensation Board [WCB] of British Columbia 1980, 4.06). In response to criticisms over committee deadlock, recent amendments to the Ontario legislation give a timeline of 21 days for management to respond in writing to a committee recommendation (Ontario Legislature 1990, section 8–12).

In most jurisdictions there appears to be little ongoing monitoring of enterprises to assess whether committees have been established and whether they are functioning as mandated. In British Columbia, for example, while the regulations require employers to forward committee minutes to the WCB, a recent administrative inventory reports that "in practice this is seldom done" (Rest and Ashford 1992). While all jurisdictions have the power to levy fines and other penalties for noncompliance, this is an extremely rare occurrence.

The absence of detailed monitoring has led many observers to speculate on the degree to which there is compliance in forming and maintaining joint committees. An important exception to this lack of empirical data is an extensive survey of joint committees commissioned by the Ontario Advisory Council on Occupational Health and Occupational Safety, a tripartite body set up to advise the minister of labor in Ontario on occupational health and safety matters. This 1986 study, designed to measure the effectiveness of the Ontario internal responsibility system after its first five years of operations, surveyed both worker and management JHSC members in a random sample of over 3,000 Ontario workplaces (Ontario Advisory Council 1986, 178). It concluded that JHSCs were established in 93 percent of the workplaces where required, including 88.4 percent of the nonunionized workplaces and 96 percent of the unionized workplaces (Ontario Advisory Council 1986, 35).

Aside from simply assuring that committees are organized, compliance in most jurisdictions also requires that the committees carry out the many functions specified in the legislation. In this area, the Ontario study reported rather elliptically that "most firms comply fully with *most* features of the act, but few are in full compliance" (Ontario Advisory Council 1986, 107). Overall, it concluded that "compliance with *specific* provisions of the act is poor among workplaces with JHSCs: only some 22% of workplaces with JHSCs appear to be in full compliance with the act" (Ontario Advisory Council 1986, v).

There is wide variation throughout Canada in the role of government in supporting and promoting committees, and in monitoring and enforcing compliance. Aside from differences between jurisdictions, even within a given jurisdiction, such as in the case of Saskatchewan, changes in government or policy can lead to increased or decreased interest in compliance. During the first 10 years of the new health and safety legislation in Saskatchewan, the OHS Branch played a very active role in promoting and monitoring the work of joint committees. With a change in government in the early 1980s, however, the branch ceased to play as active a role in assuring that committees functioned (Parsons 1989).

In the two largest jurisdictions in Canada, Quebec and Ontario, governments have sought to augment and extend the enterprise-based "internal responsibility system" through the creation of bipartite administrative bodies responsible for overseeing occupational health and safety and implementing joint business-labor training and decision making at the provincewide level. The Commission de la Santé et de la Sécurité du Travail (CSST) in Quebec and the WHSA in Ontario have essentially similar functions in their respective provinces, including the right to develop, direct, and fund research, to raise general public awareness of the issue, and to conduct training and education in occupational health and safety (Quebec National Assembly 1979, section 167; Ontario Legislature 1990, section 13).

The creation of the WHSA in Ontario is part of an ambitious program to strengthen the "internal responsibility system." In keeping with the recommendations of the 1986 study of joint committees in Ontario, the WHSA was given an extensive mandate to improve training and support for the estimated 50,000 joint committees in Ontario and to encourage the bipartite approach to health and safety throughout the province. The WHSA was also given the special responsibility to establish and administer a mandatory certification process for committee members throughout the province and to develop an accreditation program for employers. Ontario is the first province to take this further step into mandatory training for committee representatives.

12.3 Training, Certification, and the Evolution of the Internal Responsibility System in Ontario

The Ontario Occupational Health and Safety (OHS) Act of 1978 remained substantially unchanged until the summer of 1990, when the provincial Liberal government under pressure from the labor movement and the NDP opposition introduced Bill 208, an extensive package of amendments to the act. These hotly debated reforms expanded the requirement for joint committees to most work sites in the province with over 20 employees, creating an estimated 30,000 new committees, and required committees in all work sites where designated substances were being used. In addition, the reforms extended the right to refuse to workers previously excluded, such as provincial government employees, police, firefighters, and correctional workers.

Most significant, Bill 208 established the 20–2 member bipartite WHSA, to be chaired by a nonvoting government appointee and to have equal employer and labor cochairs and board members. The WHSA was given a provincewide role in promoting the bipartite approach in health and safety, and its creation constituted an important new vehicle for facilitating worker/employer jointness beyond the enterprise-based JHSCs.

As its first major task, the WHSA was given the power to develop the mandated "certification" program for committee members. Originally, the certification requirement was linked to proposed special powers for JHSC members to be able to "shut down" a job site. While the 1978 OHS Act had recognized an individual worker's right to refuse dangerous work, the early drafts of Bill 208 proposed empowering certified worker representatives on a JHSC with the additional right to unilaterally stop work where there was a violation of the act and where any delay in controlling the hazard might seriously endanger a worker. Under considerable pressure from the business community, which was concerned about the unilateral right to stop work, this provision was dropped from the final version of the bill. As a result, the labor movement and the prolabor NDP opposed the bill in the legislature.

While unilateral work stoppage was limited in the legislation, it was not entirely ruled out. Certified members can gain this authority either through an employer giving the authority (and depositing a letter to this effect with the JHSC) or through an adjudicator extending this right in cases where the adjudicator finds that the bilateral stop-work procedure is not sufficient to protect workers.

In place of the proposed unilateral work stoppage, a bilateral procedure was substituted requiring both the management and worker certified representatives to agree in order to stop work. In cases of a disagreement, work was to proceed (though individual workers retained their right to refuse dangerous work) and an inspector was to be called.

Although the majority Liberal government was able to pass Bill 208, in the election that followed the Liberal government was defeated and replaced by a majority NDP provincial government. The new NDP government committed itself to labor law reform but decided not to make revisions to the recently amended OHS Act. Rather, the NDP decided to support the creation of the new bipartite body, the WHSA, and encourage its educational and administrative role in promoting bipartism and internal responsibility in health and safety.

Although it did not provide labor with the breakthrough that it had hoped for—the unilateral right to stop work—in general the Bill 208 amendments did strengthen the power of joint committees and the "internal responsibility system" in the workplace. Many of the specific changes flowed from the recommendations of the 1986 Ontario Advisory Council's study, which found that while workers' rights and resources had been greatly expanded by the 1978 act, their ability to make a *full* contribution was still limited by lack of information, lack of training, and lack of resources. The study concluded "that unless fully developed through careful legislation *and* implementation, through training and education, and unless fully integrated with the workplace, the JHSC leads not to self-regulation, but rather self-deception" (Ontario Advisory Council 1986, 2:169–70).

With the adoption of Bill 208 and the creation of the WHSA in 1991, the controversy moved from the work stoppage question to the mandatory training requirements for certified representatives. The new provision in the act creating certified representatives required that employers pay for training, instruction materials, and salaries of at least one worker and management member on their respective JHSCs. The specifics of the training and the curriculum were to be worked out by the bipartite WHSA. Specifically, the WHSA needed to resolve who would be trained and who would deliver the course. It also needed to draft a curriculum, set the length of training, and decide on a method for evaluating

competence upon completion. Through consensus, the WHSA was able to resolve almost all of these questions. There was consensus that at least one
worker and one employer representative from every committee in the province
was to be certified. A 300-page Core Certificate Training Program Participant's
Manual was drafted. And the province's existing 12 health and safety delivery
organizations were to be made bipartite and designated as authorized trainers
for the certification curriculum.

The program became stalled on the issue of the length of training. Employer
representatives on the WHSA board felt that one week of training would be
adequate, whereas the labor members were adamant that no less than three
weeks would suffice. Eventually, with no consensus in sight, a majority voted
for a compromise, with three levels of core training (depending on the type of
industry): category I would be one week of training plus two days at the workplace, where candidates would jointly draw up a hazards analysis and health
and safety work plan; category II would be two weeks of training plus two days
in the workplace on the analysis and work plan; and category III would be
three weeks of training plus three days in the workplace devoted to the analysis
and work plan. This majority decision, viewed by some employer representatives as a breach of the commitment to consensus, provoked the resignation of
five of the nine employer board members, who claimed that the compromise
was being forced on the employer community by the NDP provincial government.

Complicating the discussions and contributing to the consensus breakdown
on the WHSA board was the business community's heated campaign against
the NDP provincial government's extensive labor law reform bill that was
passed by the legislature in the fall of 1992. With the WHSA less than two
years old, there was some fear that the employer resignations would lead to the
demise of the bipartite experiment. With four employer representatives remaining on the board, new board members were recruited and a provincewide
certification program was launched in April 1993 with the objective of training
the estimated 100,000 committee members requiring certification.

A second major problem for the WHSA was the resistance of the delivery
organizations to adopting bipartite boards. At the time of the creation of the
WHSA, the WCB funded 12 different organizations charged with the delivery
of occupational health and safety programs. They were: eight sectoral safety
associations, which were traditional management safety associations oriented
to specific sectors; the Workers Health and Safety Centre, which was founded
by the Ontario Federation of Labour (OFL) in the early 1980s to provide
worker-oriented programs; and three programs developed to cover the public
sectors (divided into the municipal sector, the educational sector, and the tour-
ism and hospitality sector). The new legislation placed these organizations under the "authority" of the WHSA and gave it the power to withhold their
grants—amounting to $50 million in 1991—if it judged the organizations not
to "have an equal number of representatives of management and of workers."

Commissioning a report on the delivery organizations, the WHSA was advised that in the short term these organizations could not be supplanted or replaced (SPR Associations, Inc. 1991, 14). With the delivery organizations already offering over 500 programs throughout the province, and with their expertise and links to their respective workplaces and industries, the ambitious certification campaign required the cooperation of the experienced delivery groups.

While a level of cooperation was developed between the employer-oriented safety associations and the union-oriented Workers Health and Safety Centre, there was strong resistance to integrating their boards. A compromise was eventually found with the creation of a new bipartite oversight board—the Council of Ontario Health and Safety Sectoral Organizations. The creation of this special council permitted the worker-oriented Workers Health and Safety Centre and the employer-oriented sectoral safety associations to maintain their unitary boards while at the same time meeting the legislated requirement of jointness.

12.4   Relations with Employers

The resistance by the sectoral safety councils to opening their boards to joint participation by worker representatives reflects the fact that there are still profound differences in philosophy and approach between employers and organized labor on occupational health and safety (SPR Associates, Inc. 1991, 7). Simply put, the traditional employer view of the work environment is that it is a "safety management" problem that along with productivity and quality is a responsibility of management (Industrial Accident Prevention Association [IAPA] 1991, 17). The sectoral safety organizations tended to reflect this "loss control" approach, which assumed that employers would be motivated to prevent accidents if they were held financially responsible for them (OFL 1991, 6). Until the 1970s, regulation throughout Canada also shared the assumption that safety and health were primarily a management responsibility. The sectoral employer safety organizations were established in most Canadian jurisdictions concurrently with workers' compensation legislation—1914 in Ontario, 1917 in British Columbia and Manitoba, 1918 in Alberta, and 1919 in New Brunswick. These organizations, funded by grants from provincial workers' compensation assessments, were staffed by safety professionals and managers, as well as hundreds of volunteers from member organizations. They provided expertise, education, and training on health and safety for businesses. If firms were to be fined and assessed according to their safety records, then management needed to retain control over the workplace and train its managers to reduce hazards and accidents. As management was responsible for workplace safety, it needed the right to organize and design the workplace to meet this responsibility. In this context, the development of the internal responsibility system premised on workers and managers having "equal power to act on health and safety manners" was viewed as a major intrusion into the area of management rights (WHSA 1992b, 11).

Historically, the concept of labor and management as "equal partners" in the workplace was associated almost exclusively with unionization and collective bargaining. Legislated joint committees introduced this concept—at least in health and safety—to workplaces that had rejected or successfully avoided unionization. The most vociferous opposition to the legislation came from non-unionized and smaller firms. Both the quantitative data from the 1986 Ontario Advisory Council's study, which shows that firms with fewer workers were less likely to have a joint committee, and the recent battles in Ontario over certification, which focused on the hardship of lengthy and expensive training programs to small firms with few employees, tend to confirm this trend. Fears by some small business owners that mandated participation in decision making might lead to unionization do not appear to have been realized, however. Neither the labor movement nor the business community have linked JHSCs to union growth or avoidance.

In spite of its initial resistance to joint committees and the subsequent strengthening of the internal responsibility system, management has learned to work with the new regulation. And in the case of Ontario, the large sectoral safety organizations have played an important role in facilitating acceptance among employers. The great majority of the funding for health and safety training has continued to be allocated to the employer-oriented safety associations. Funding for 1991, for example, was allocated as follows: $41.7 million to the eight sectoral safety committees, $6.9 million to the Workers Health and Safety Centre, and $1.8 million to the three public sector programs (WHSA 1992a, 25). By retaining and, indeed, even increasing the role of the safety associations and the funds allocated to them, the Ontario government has avoided a major confrontation with these organizations. Yet, it has tied them to its bipartite approach in the long term, both by demanding the restructuring and integration of their boards and by involving them in the bipartite certification and accreditation programs.

With the certification program only recently launched, it is still too early to assess the degree to which the WHSA and the new legislation will be successful in transforming the safety delivery organizations into genuine bipartite entities. However, the experience from the earlier reforms, when committees were first mandated at the level of the firm, shows that management soon learns to work with the new regime and, in many cases, even view it as a positive change.

After only five years' experience with mandated joint committees in Ontario, for example, the 1986 Ontario Advisory Council's study found that management members on JHSCs were quite positive in their assessment of committee relationships and functioning. Allaying management fears that mandated participation and jointness would introduce confrontation and conflict into work sites, the assessment of management committee members has been overwhelmingly positive. Management committee members described committee relationships as being cooperative (89.4 percent), with good mutual respect (90.2 percent), trusting (89.4 percent), and overall friendly (90.8 percent) (Ontario Advisory Council 1986, 70).

On the crucial measure of the effectiveness of committees in reducing hazards and improving safety, management respondents to the 1986 Ontario study were overwhelmingly positive. On the overall record of improving safety and reducing accidents, 56.2 percent judged their committees to be "more than adequate to excellent." Only 9.2 percent saw the committee's role as "poor to less than adequate" (Ontario Advisory Council 1986, 97).

Experience with joint committees appears to have convinced many employers that these committees can play a useful role in reducing accidents and improving safety—and that management does not lose control of the workplace. The Ontario survey, for example, noted that 66.9 percent of managers and 60.3 percent of workers generally agreed that their committee had achieved the stated goal of "equal" influence by both parties. Nevertheless, it also concluded that managers tended to have more influence on committees than workers. Management ultimately retained the power to implement JHSC recommendations. While management was required to discuss decisions with the joint committees, it also had wide discretion over what decisions it felt were appropriate for committee discussion. The study also noted that management representatives on joint committees had closer links to ministry inspectors and the enforcement agencies. Finally, it was noted that management representatives were, for the most part, better trained and more knowledgeable on health and safety issues and legislation than most worker representatives (Ontario Advisory Council 1986, 69–81). In Ontario, a further positive feature of the internal responsibility system for employers has been its evolution toward self-regulation. While not originally conceived as "deregulatory," the growing emphasis on empowering the workplace parties has been seen as a method of reducing the need for government intervention through monitoring and inspection.

12.5   Relations with Unions

Unions have been generally supportive of mandatory JHSCs. The mandating legislation is viewed as enhancing and complementing rights gained by a minority of unions through collective bargaining and extending those rights to all workers through legislation. In most instances, the legislation is viewed as either labor inspired or minimally supportive of organized labor. However, in spite of union support for bipartite committees, unions in Canada view cooperation with management in occupational health and safety with some ambivalence. In particular, unions reject the notion that health and safety is a "neutral" technical issue. Rather, they see it as an economic and political one—with labor seeking to continually improve safety standards and levels which are socially determined and politically mediated. Because of what labor sees as the "political" nature of health and safety, Canadian unions have jealously guarded their role in the education of their members not simply against management-oriented programs delivered by the sectoral safety associations, but in opposition to many university- and college-based programs (Procenko 1991; Bernard 1991).

Labor fears that occupational health and safety training will focus on the seemingly "neutral" technical issues and not give sufficient attention to the wider economic and political ones. As Bob Sass explains:

> In all "technical" questions pertaining to workplace health and safety is the "social." This refers to the power relations in production—who tells whom to do what and how fast! After all, the machine does not go faster by itself; someone designed the machinery, organized the work, designed the job. . . . The widespread view or notion that both labour and management have equal concerns regarding occupational health and safety because we are dealing with pain and suffering is one of the major myths in industrial relations. The betterment of working conditions costs money and management members on the committee are forever aware of this fact as legal agents of the share-holders who are primarily concerned with optimatizing their return on capital investment. (Sass 1990)

Many of these concerns over the politics of health and safety are at the root of the tensions and maneuvering around the "certification" process in Ontario and especially labor's (as well as management's) resistance to attempts by the newly formed WHSA to force the delivery organizations to adopt bipartite boards. Because Ontario is attempting to develop bipartite and cooperative structures throughout the province and especially beyond the level of the firm, its experience is helpful in shedding light on labor's seemingly ambivalent attitude to bipartism.

At the level of the workplace, health and safety bipartitism has been accepted by labor because it has increased labor's influence, in that the work environment is no longer viewed by government as exclusively management's concern. Mandated joint committees have given added strength to labor's participation in creating a safer and healthier work environment. A key provision in the legislation retained the unions' power to select the worker representatives in organized work sites. This assured that unions would view the joint committees as a complement to their role in the workplace, not as a threat.

Organized labor also came to see the creation of the WHSA as a factor increasing its influence—this time by giving it greater voice in decision making at the level of the provincial authority. As noted earlier, labor at first opposed the reforms that created the WHSA and was even somewhat concerned about its bipartite training role. After lengthy debate and discussion within the OFL, however, labor agreed to participate in the WHSA, announcing that "it was better for labour to participate in order to ensure the highest quality of training materials and delivery systems for all workers in Ontario" (OFL 1991, 3).

The WHSA has considerably more power and financial resources than the old Ontario Advisory Council, which was essentially an advisory board with a very narrow mandate. Labor also has significantly more power in the WHSA, a bipartite organization, than it did on the Advisory Council—a tripartite board. Labor in Canada has long preferred bipartite to tripartite boards, arguing that because government is itself a large employer, tripartism simply represents a two-to-one outnumbering of labor on such boards, as opposed to bipartism where the government plays no direct role and labor and management are equally represented. Establishing a bipartite structure for the WHSA was again viewed as an important gain for labor.

But at the intermediate level in Ontario, that is, with the 12 delivery organizations, labor (and management) have both resisted bipartitism. Part of this can be attributed to the fact that the WHSA was a new entity that labor could help to design from inception. The delivery organizations on the other hand were significantly older than the WHSA and were initiated either by employer safety councils or (in the case of the Workers Health and Safety Centre) by labor. Most were set up long before the adoption of the internal responsibility system in Ontario. While they varied greatly in their understanding of the new philosophy in health and safety, a government study commissioned by the WHSA advised that the delivery organizations could not be supplanted or replaced in the short term without "undesirable dislocation of services" (SPR Associates, Inc. 1991, 14). Although there have been important breakthroughs in moving the delivery organizations toward greater collaboration and cooperation, such as the jointly designed curricula, for the most part the organizations still see their approaches as very different and distinct. The labor-oriented Workers Health and Safety Centre, for example, includes chapters on "strategies for change," "collective bargaining," and "violence in the workplace" in its training manual. All these topics are viewed as "political" by the IAPA and are not part of the jointly authored curriculum for the province's certification program (OFL 1992).

Most unionists recognize that the adoption of the internal responsibility system means a significant rebalancing of worker and management roles, with labor gaining new rights and powers on work environment issues. However, many union health and safety specialists remain critical of the system, arguing that worker representatives are not yet "fully empowered as partners in workplace decision making" and have "responsibility without authority." These critics refer to the system as the *eternal* responsibility system. The term "eternal responsibility" was coined to describe the frequent failure to resolve issues because of the relative powerlessness of the committees. Greater responsibility, argue labor representatives, must be balanced with greater authority—and some labor activists had expected that greater authority to be the right of worker representatives to unilaterally stop work.

Gary Cwitco, director of occupational health and safety with the Communications Workers of Canada, observes that there is tremendous turnover and burnout among worker committee members. Cwitco, a critic of the internal responsibility system, explains that with the adoption of the three rights and the joint committees as vehicles of participation, activists misread the changes and assumed that they would now have real joint authority in work environment matters. But in Cwitco's estimation, the purely advisory role of joint committees has meant, in effect, that management can still choose to ignore committee recommendations. Cwitco argues that "responsibility without authority is meaningless and frustrating" (Cwitco 1992). He admits that while the power of argument alone may be effective with an already cooperative management, there is little that a committee can do in a situation where management chooses to "stonewall" recommendations and gives low priority to the work of the committee. In a similar vein, union health and safety expert Bob Dematteo argues that there is a "need for mechanisms which would provide workers with greater influence over health and safety decisions, and the enhancement of the external system of enforcement" (Dematteo 1991, 15).

While unions remain critical of what they view as the imbalance of power in the internal responsibility system, they are generally supportive of the gains that unions and workers have made with the mandating of committees and the winning of the three rights. There is a recognition that even the relatively weak "right to participate" provisions have provided for ongoing discussions with management—an improvement over the old regime of exclusive management rights with periodic collective bargaining. In one example cited by Cwitco, after a series of studies conducted by joint committees at Bell Canada proved that individual performance monitoring of employees caused harmful stress, the worker representatives on the joint committee were able to persuade the company to eliminated the practice—something the union had sought but was unable to achieve through regular collective bargaining.

12.6   Relations with Workers

There are few quantitative studies that look at joint committees in non-unionized work sites. Indeed, it is often asserted that in a majority of non-unionized work sites the committees simply do not exist, though the lack of detailed studies makes this assertion questionable. An important exception to the lack of studies, however, is the 1986 Ontario Advisory Council's survey. While this study shows that nonunion work sites are less likely than unionized work sites to have a joint committee, it nevertheless found an impressive level of compliance even in nonunionized work sites (see table 12.2).

The Ontario study's historical pattern shows that even before the legislation mandated joint committees, many large work sites and unionized work sites had already established committees. There was a significant increase in committee formation after 1976 with the passage of the Employee Health and

Table 12.2   JHSCs in Ontario (% of workplaces with JHSCs)

Type of Workplace[a]	Size of Workplace[b] (number of workers)			
	20–74	75–249	250–499	500+
Nonunionized with no designated substances	86.3	91.4	92.1	90.9
Unionized with no designated substances	92.5	98.2	99.5	100.0
Nonunionized with designated substances	92.4	96.4	96.9	100.0
Unionized with designated substances	97.5	100.0	99.5	100.0
Total		93.2		

Source: Data from screening survey.

[a]Note that status of workplace with regard to size, unions, and presence of designated substances is always estimated from 1985 status (Ontario Advisory Council 1986, 34).

[b]Workplaces of 20 or more workers, where a JHSC is required by the Occupational Health and Safety Act.

Safety Act of 1976, which encouraged, though did not mandate, the forming of committees. Under the voluntary regime, however, committees in nonunionized work sites were rare. With the passage of the OHS Act in 1978 and the mandating of committees, the smaller work sites and nonunionized firms still tend to lag behind the large unionized firms. By 1984, compliance by nonunionized work sites stood at 88.4 percent compared to unionized worksites at 96 percent (see table 12.3).

Although simply registering the existence of committees is a relatively easy task, registration alone sheds little light on their functioning. The Ontario study did, however, record the assessment of committee members of overall committee functioning and reported a generally favorable attitude among worker members of JHSCs: 59.4 percent rated the record of committees in improving safety and reducing accidents as very positive (Ontario Advisory Council 1986, 95).

In attempting to isolate factors contributing to the success of committees, the report found that when the distribution of influence in the committee was in favor of workers, it was seen as a moderate facilitator of JHSC success in the estimation of *both* manager and worker members of committees (Ontario Advisory Council 1986, 149). While this might appear to run counter to the stated intent of "equal partners," it makes sense in the context of advisory committees where management alone ultimately decides whether to implement a JHSC recommendation. Strong worker representation on these committees, judged as "more worker influenced," increases worker input into the committee. However, only about 10 percent of committees were judged by both management and workers to be more influenced by workers, as opposed to 25 to 35

Table 12.3   Historical Pattern of JHSC Establishment (% of workplaces with JHSCs, by year of JHSC establishment)

Type of Workplace[a]	Pre-1970	1971–76	1977	1978	1979	1980	1981	1982	1983	1984
All workplaces with										
20+ workers	9.2	25.8	29.7	37.4	49.5	65.3	74.6	81.3	88.0	92.9
Workplaces by union status										
Nonunionized	4.2	13.9	16.7	21.8	33.4	51.8	64.0	73.8	81.8	88.4
Unionized	12.7	34.0	38.7	48.2	60.7	74.7	82.0	86.5	92.3	96.0
Workplaces by presence of designated substances										
Not present	7.1	22.1	25.8	33.1	45.7	62.6	71.8	79.0	86.2	91.6
Present	16.5	38.7	43.1	52.2	62.8	74.8	84.4	89.1	94.1	97.6
Workplaces by size (number of workers)										
20–74	5.1	18.3	20.9	28.3	40.3	56.7	67.9	75.3	83.0	90.1
75–249	13.4	32.0	38.3	46.2	57.6	74.9	82.2	88.5	94.3	96.4
250–499	17.7	44.6	51.2	58.8	73.0	82.4	88.7	91.3	95.8	97.9
500+	21.0	52.6	54.5	64.1	79.1	87.6	90.2	96.2	98.2	98.9

Source: Data from screening survey.

[a]Note that the status of workplace with regard to size, unions, and presence of designated substances is always estimated from 1985 status (Ontario 1986, 35).

percent viewed as more influenced by management (Ontario Advisory Council 1986, 71).

The problem of management influence of committees exists at a number of levels. First, there is the imbalance of resources. The right to participate does not usually guarantee workers access to resources, including communications with experts, time for preparation and investigation, and training in the field of health and safety. For example, the recent Ontario OHS Act amendments and certification program includes compulsory training for at least one worker representative per committee and stipulates that work representatives are to be given at least one hour paid "preparation time" before committee meetings. Despite this fact, there is still an imbalance of resources between management and workers on the committees.

At a second level, employer influence can be felt over the selection of worker representatives. The 1986 Ontario study found, for example, that in about one-third (35 percent) of the committees worker members of JHSCs were selected by management either through direct appointment by management or by management overseeing the selection of volunteers. This study found that worker committee representatives were selected by the following means (percentages given in parentheses): appointed by management (19), management acceptance of volunteers (16.2), appointed by union executives (18.1), appointed by employee association executive (2.3), chosen by workers at election (31.7), accepted by workers at a meeting where volunteers come forward (12.7) (Ontario Advisory Council 1986, 47). The recent Ontario legislation included a number of measures to assure worker representatives independence from management influence. However, it did not require a secret ballot election or general meeting of all affected employees.

A final level of management influence is sometimes referred to as "company capture" of the committee, with management ignoring worker representatives' concerns and simply using the committee as a forum to justify its practices and explain why workers' fears are unfounded. This is the most difficult phenomenon to measure. Bryce and Manga, for example, noted in their study of committees in Saskatchewan that worker committee members come to "understand" the financial constraints of the enterprise. Robert Sass, on the other hand, contends that this often-cited "maturing" of a committee, one marked by fewer "disputes" and "concerns," might in fact simply be a result of company capture (Sass 1992). Generally, the problem of company capture has tended to focus on committees in nonunionized work sites, where workers have few resources and where there are fewer assurances of independent selection of worker representatives.

A weakness observed in both the 1986 study and the current legislation is the link between the worker representatives and the workers they represent. While the curriculum for the new certificate program in Ontario emphasizes the importance of worker representatives seeking input from workers and the need for representatives to report back to the workers, this link is still tenuous—with no formal reporting procedures required. The 1986 study found that of JHSCs in nonunionized work sites, 46.5 percent reported to worker meetings at least quarterly (compared to 61 percent in unionized work sites), and 37.9 percent of JHSCs in nonunionized work sites never reported to worker meetings at all (compared with 17.5 percent in unionized work sites) (Ontario Advisory Council 1986, 84).

Through Ontario's provincewide certification program worker representatives will have guaranteed access to some training, and it is expected that they will seek to build an ongoing relationship with the delivery organization that provided their training. A major question for the near future will be who will train and service the worker representatives on committees in nonunionized settings. With 12 delivery organizations to chose from, ranging from the labor-oriented Workers Health and Safety Centre to the management-oriented sectoral safety organizations, and no requirement that management and worker representatives take training from the same organization, it remains to be seen how the worker representatives in nonunionized settings will respond to this opportunity.

12.7   Nurturing Joint Committees

The Canadian experience in mandating joint occupational health and safety committees is still relatively new, with less than 15 years practice in most jurisdictions. It marks an important departure from traditional North American industrial relations, which sees worker self-organization into unions and collective bargaining as the primary (if not sole) vehicle for worker participation in workplace decision making. The experience with the JHSCs shows that the seemingly opposing systems of adversarial collective bargaining and cooperation are able to coexist.

An important factor in making coexistence possible is that neither organized labor nor management views the mandated joint committees as either a substitution for or facilitator of unionism. From the management perspective, experience has demonstrated that these committees do not become incipient organizing committees prompting employees to unionize. At the same time, they provide management with independent worker participation and voice in decision making. From the union side, the legislation does not attempt to circumvent unions and by generally extending worker rights has augmented union influence in organized work sites. Unions, for the most part, do not fear the committees will become substitutes for unions because they believe that the full exercise of workers' rights and empowerment requires both self-organization (and independence from management influence) and resources that only the labor movement can deliver to employee representatives.

For nonunionized employees empowered with the new rights and joint committees, the experience has been at best uneven. Compared to the old regime of health and safety as an exclusive management right and responsibility, the new system constitutes an important breakthrough for workers. But, with little active monitoring of the regulation and few resources available to the nonunionized workers, substantial numbers of employees have not been able to fully exercise these rights.

Ontario's recent attempts to establish self-regulation through an internal responsibility system have demonstrated the crucial role that government must play in facilitating and promoting this system. Working with both the existing delivery organizations (and most especially the employer-based sectoral safety committees which constitute rare multiemployer forums in sectors where employers are otherwise highly decentralized) and creating a new entity, the bipartite WHSA, the provincial government has moved the joint system beyond the level of committees in the workplace to provincewide structures. By continuing to work with the existing delivery organizations, the government enlisted these organizations into accepting bipartitism on behalf of the two most powerful parties, the employers and the unions. Transforming the role of government, the move to self-regulation has meant increased rights for workers, new government regulation that seeks to promote and finance training, and the creation of a new bipartite body to administer and promote the new approach.

It remains to be seen whether the mandated joint committee experience will extend beyond occupational health and safety. Possible areas for mandated joint committees are technological change, training, and restructuring. To date, however, no jurisdiction in Canada has taken the initiative in mandating joint committee participation for the workforce in general on other issues. Neither labor nor management seem particularly inclined to promote the extension of bipartitism into other fields. On the other hand, government, under increasing financial pressures and out of a desire to limit regulation, might find the internal regulation system an attractive alternative to direct intervention. Finally, if there is pressure to introduce new forms of employee representation, the mandated JHSCs could provide an instructive prototype.

References

Adams, R. J. 1986. Two policy approaches to labour-management decision making at the level of the enterprise. In *Labour-Management Cooperation in Canada*, ed. W. W. Craig Riddell, 87–109. Toronto: University of Toronto.

———. 1991. Universal joint regulation: A moral imperative. In *Proceedings of the 43rd annual meeting of the Industrial Relations Research Association*, 319–27. Madison, Wisc.: Industrial Relations Research Association.

Bernard, E. 1991. Labour programmes: A challenging partnership. *Labour/Le Travail* 27:199–207.

Bryce, G. K., and Manga, P. 1985. The effectiveness of health and safety committees. *Relations Industrielles* 40(2): 257–83.

Cohen, D. 1993. Interview with author, March 16.

Confédération Syndicale Nationale. 1989. *Les actes du colloque: Sur la prévention en santé-sécurité dans les secteurs prioritaires*. Quebec: Confédération Syndicale Nationale.

Cwitco, G. 1992. Telephone interview with author, April 1.

Dematteo, B. 1991. Health and safety committees: The Canadian experience. *New Solutions* 1(4): 11–15.

George, K. 1985. Les comités de santé et de sécurité du travail: Tables de concertation ou de négociation? *Relations Industrielles* 40(3): 512–27.

Ham, J. M. 1976. *Report of the Royal Commission on the Health and Safety of Workers in the Mines*, vols. 1–3. Toronto: Government of Ontario.

IAPA (Industrial Accident Prevention Association). 1991. *Annual review*. Toronto: Industrial Accident Prevention Association.

Meltz, N. M. 1989. Interstate vs. interprovincial differences in union density. *Industrial Relations* 28(2): 142–58.

McMurdo, Robert. 1993. Interview with author, March 16.

Ontario Advisory Council on Occupational Health and Occupational Safety. 1986. *Eighth annual report, April 1, 1985 to March 31, 1986*, vols. 2, 3, and 7. Toronto: Government of Ontario.

OFL (Ontario Federation of Labour). 1991. OFL speaker's notes on Bill 208. Toronto: Ontario Federation of Labour.

———. 1992. *Occupational health and safety: A training manual*. Toronto: Copp Clark Pitman.

Ontario Legislature. 1990. *The Occupational Health and Safety Act and the Workers' Compensation Act*. June 19.

Parsons, M. D. 1989. Worker participation in occupational health and safety: Lessons from the Canadian experience. *Labor Studies Journal* 13(4): 22–32.

Procenko, S. 1991. Class conscious labour studies programs. *Our Times*, May 17.

Quebec National Assembly. 1979. *An Act Respecting Occupational Health and Safety.* December 21.

Ramsay, Russ. 1993. Interview with author, March 15.

Rest, K., and Ashford, N. 1992. *Occupational safety and health in British Columbia: An administrative inventory.* Cambridge, Mass.: Ashford Associates.

Sass, R. 1990. Prospects for working life reforms. Typescript.

———. 1992. Telephone interview with author, September 24.

Sentes, R. 1983. Labour Department remodels OH&S policy. *Canadian Occupational Health and Safety News,* March 28.

SPR Associations, Inc. 1991. *Evaluation of the twelve WHSA-funded organizations providing occupational health and safety programs in Ontario.* Toronto: SPR Associates, Inc., June 28.

Summers, C. W. 1980. Worker participation in the U.S. and West Germany: A comparative study from an American perspective. *American Journal of Comparative Law* 28:367–92.

———. 1987. An American perspective on the German model of worker participation. *Comparative Labor Law Journal* 8:333–55.

Tucker, E. 1990. Constructing the conditions of worker participation in occupational health and safety regulation: Sweden and Ontario. Paper presented at meetings of the Canadian Law and Society Association, Laval University, September.

WCB (Workers' Compensation Board of British Columbia). 1980. *Industrial health and safety regulations.* Richmond: Workers' Compensation Board of British Columbia.

Weiler, P. C. 1990. *Governing the workplace: The future of labor and employment law.* Cambridge: Harvard University Press.

WHSA (Workplace Health and Safety Agency). 1992a. *Annual report 1991.* Toronto: Workplace Health and Safety Agency.

———. 1992b. *Core certification training program: Participant's manual.* Toronto: Workplace Health and Safety Agency.

13 United States: Lessons from Abroad and Home

Joel Rogers

13.1 Introduction: A Failed System

Labor, management, and neutrals all agree that the New Deal system of labor relations, codified in the Wagner and Taft-Hartley acts of 1935 and 1947, respectively, no longer works to the good of the American economy. While it may have been well suited to the industrial society of the 1930s to 1950s, when it helped deliver enormous growth in real income and productivity, the New Deal system has not adjusted well to the economic realities of the 1990s.

The New Deal system was designed to allow worker selection of exclusive union bargaining representatives[1] through secret ballot elections free of management interference, and to buttress collective bargaining between such representatives and management as a way of dividing the economic pie between

Joel Rogers is professor of law, political science, and sociology at the University of Wisconsin-Madison, where he directs the Center on Wisconsin Strategy.

In thinking about the subject matter of this essay, the author benefits from ongoing collaborations with Joshua Cohen, Daniel Luria, Wade Rathke, Charles Sabel, and especially Richard Freeman and Wolfgang Streeck. See Cohen and Rogers (1992, 1993, 1995), Luria and Rogers (1993), Rathke and Rogers (1994), Rogers and Sabel (1993), Freeman and Rogers (1993a, 1993b, 1993c, 1994, in progress), and Rogers and Streeck (1994a, 1994b). The following draws freely from this joint work—in particular, from Freeman and Rogers (1993c) and Rogers and Streeck (1994a)—while holding all coauthors blameless for errors that have survived their care.

1. The entire structure of the Labor Management Relations Act (LMRA; the Wagner and Taft-Hartley Acts, as amended) is directed to specifying the rights, obligations, and conditions of emergence and stability of such exclusive representatives. The importance of exclusivity in turn derived from assumptions about the appropriate ambit of negotiated wage and benefit settlements. The LMRA contemplates collective bargaining on a firm rather than industry basis. It also generally does not contemplate use of "extension laws," common in Europe, extending the terms of collective agreements to firms not party to negotiation. Without extension, worker gains from collective bargaining depend on worker strength within particular firms. Exclusivity is the gravamen of such power, and thus the key to stability in collective bargaining. See the discussion below.

labor and capital.[2] At the core of the Wagner Act was the conviction that union representation within firms was not only a moral imperative but an economic and political good. The basic economic idea was that workers, acting collectively, would be able to drive up wages. In a closed economy with unemployed resources, the resulting increase in demand would stimulate private investment and job growth. The basic political idea was that, inside the firm and out, worker organization would help American democracy by providing a "countervailing power" to otherwise overwhelming business domination.

The core ideas of this system—that workers should enjoy associational rights within and without the firm and that collective worker organizations can contribute to the vitality of the American economy—retain currency today. But the particular ways in which these ideas were institutionalized in the New Deal system appear increasingly inapposite to present circumstance. The New Deal system effectively premised: a sharp distinction between production workers, who were assumed to be solely concerned with wages and working conditions, and management, who were assumed to have full competence in running the enterprise;[3] an essentially closed economy, with little international wage competition; the organization of production along "Fordist" and "Taylorist" lines, in which the dominant model of efficient production was a large firm featuring assembly-line mass production of standardized goods by unskilled and semiskilled labor; and the feasibility of providing a family wage and benefit package through lifetime jobs held by single male breadwinners. Put simply, the world described by these premises no longer exists—workers have other interests, management needs more worker involvement, the economy is more open, production is more flexible and quality driven, jobs are less stable, the workforce is more diverse—and the system based on them works poorly in the world that does.

The costs of this institutional mismatch are widely distributed.[4] Unions—the only form of independent collective worker organization contemplated in the system—are effectively denied their right to organize, and escalating em-

2. Such division, of course, is not the only function of collective bargaining, much of which is concerned with nonmaterial benefits (e.g., rules on notice and fair treatment), with transfers among workers (e.g., "solidarity" bargaining), and with the appropriate form material gains should take (e.g., wages vs. benefits). Still, determining the worker share of the production surplus is the key function of collective bargaining, and the one which conditions performance of most others.

3. Reflected in the "adversarialism" that has always defined U.S. industrial relations, acceptance of this distinction was a cardinal principle on both sides of the labor-management relation. Consider the heavily circumscribed vision of George Meany, as expressed shortly after he assumed the presidency of the new AFL-CIO: "Those matters that do not touch a worker directly, a union cannot and will not challenge. These may include investment policy, a decision to make a new product, a desire to erect a new plant so as to be closer to expanding markets, etc. . . . But where management decisions affect a worker directly, a union will intervene" (quoted in Derber 1970, 92).

4. Of course, they are not distributed equally. As indicated in a moment in the text, unions are e.g. threatened with extinction while employers are only constrained in their strategies of nonunion worker "empowerment."

ployer opposition[5] is rapidly "disappearing" them as a presence in national public life.[6] Individual managements, while generally welcoming the decline of unions, are limited in their ability to support advanced forms of worker participation in the nonunionized sector.[7] Workers are denied voice, choice of its form, and protection from economic insecurity. The nation as a whole suffers from lost productivity growth, rising inequality, a failure to block the "low-road" response to rising competition, ineffective enforcement of labor standards, and, less tangible but no less real, the erosion of democratic norms.[8]

For all the reasons so many have to be unhappy with the present system,

5. Increased employer resistance is reflected in the sharp increase in employer unfair labor practice charges issued by the National Labor Relations Board (NLRB) since the early 1970s. The reasons for increased resistance are many, but two bear special note. First, internationalization and the union decline itself put wages and benefits once "taken out of competition" forcefully back in. This provides clear economic incentives for firms to resist unionization. Second, increased product market instability has put a premium on flexibility in workplaces and corporate structure. While the experience of other countries (and selective cooperative programs in the United States) indicates that such flexibility can be achieved under unionization, most managers strongly prefer unilaterally imposed to negotiated flexibility.

6. The United States now approximates the "union-free" environment favored by professional antiunionists. Private sector union density now stands just above 11 percent and on a continuation of current trends should fall to about 5 percent by the end of the decade. Of course, history has not always been kind to predictions of continued union decline. In 1932, the president of the American Economic Association spoke confidently of the "lessening importance of trade unionism in American economic organization" as one of the "fundamental alterations" of American society (Barnett 1933, 1). Without some radical changes in the conditions and strategies of union organizing, however, it seems most unlikely that the coming years will see anything like the burst in union power that made these remarks ridiculous.

7. Section 8(a)(2) of the LMRA makes it unlawful for an employer to "dominate or interfere with the formation of administration of any labor organization or contribute financial or other support to it." Deliberately, "labor organization" is elsewhere defined broadly to include not only labor unions but "any organization of any kind or any agency or employee representation committee or plan" that features (1) employee participation, (2) the representation of some employees by others, in (3) dealings with the employer regarding (4) one or more of six traditional subjects of collective bargaining: grievances, labor disputes, wages, rates of pay, hours of employment, and conditions of work. For at least some nonunion employers, this imposes a restraint on desired innovations in worker participation and "empowerment" in workplace governance. E.g., an employer that set out the purposes and powers of a committee making decisions concerning the terms and conditions of employment (e.g., on health and safety or the use of a new technology), subsidized that committee, or appointed some of its managers to it—even if it permitted workers free choice in selecting their representatives to it—would likely be in violation of section 8(a)(2).

8. While few would blame our obsolete labor relations framework and the denial of collective voice to workers for all the country's economic ills, there is growing consensus that they contribute to a host of problems and at this point pose a real barrier to economic renewal. Union decline accounts for about a fifth of the recent rise in American earnings inequality (Freeman 1989; Card 1991), itself an extreme outlier in comparative terms (Freeman and Katz 1994). It contributes to declining company provision of private social welfare benefits, such as pensions and health care (Rogers 1990; Bloom and Freeman 1992). And it encourages federal regulations and court suits to resolve labor problems and protect workers, which are not as flexible or effective as labor-management negotiation at specific workplaces (Flanagan 1987; Weiler 1990). The more general lack of voice representation mechanisms in the present system depresses the productivity gains that would come of substantive worker involvement in enterprise management and job design (Blinder 1990; Mishel and Voos 1992) and contributes to a "hire and fire" culture that discourages investments in human capital (Aoki 1988; Cole 1989; Kochan and Osterman 1991; Office of Technology Assessment [OTA] 1990). On the relation between democratic performance and the level

however, the path of reform is far from clear. At present, there is no consensus on the elements of reform nor even sense of how consensus might be organized. Organized business and organized labor remain sharply divided over their vision of the role of worker organization in the new economy. However unfairly, both are also generally regarded as self-serving in their proposals for reform. At the same time, each retains the power to block the other's favored agenda, and neither favors wholesale transformation of the present system of the sort that many now think is needed.[9] Not surprising given this background, the present administration—already limited in its ability to move favored legislation by a Republican-dominated Congress—is deeply ambivalent on the topic. While its appointment of a Commission on the Future of Worker/Management Relations (the "Dunlop Commission")[10] has at least formally put labor law reform on the national agenda, few observers rank it such a high administration priority. And among the general public, whose views on the subject are barely known,[11] labor law reform is simply not an issue of great salience. In brief, labor law reform lacks a public constituency and an articulate and credible agent—compounding uncertainty about what a workable framework for reform might be.

It is in this context, for good or ill, that considerable interest has been expressed in importing some version of a council system to the United States.[12] Claiming potential gains to democracy, firm efficiency, and the effectiveness of workplace regulation, proponents argue that councils would: (1) provide at

---

of independent collective worker organization, see Cohen and Rogers (1992, 1993), Freeman and Rogers (1993c), Rogers and Sabel (1993), and Putnam (1992).

9. While perhaps sharing prudential concerns about the unintended consequences of global change, the key parties oppose it for different reasons. Labor fears change because its position is already so tenuous; business does not want change because it can already get much of what it wants outside existing legal constraints.

10. So named because of its chair, former Secretary of Labor John Dunlop. The recommendations of the commission, which postdate this writing if not this volume, will almost surely be limited—some speedup in election process, some greater curbs on employer unfair labor practices, some extension of coverage of existing law, some limited exceptions to current section 8(a)(2) prohibitions, some promotion of alternative dispute resolution systems in disputes about workplace rights. These, even if followed, will not amount to wholesale reform of the system and seem unlikely to set the agenda for whatever reform Congress does consider.

11. Determining such is the major goal of the effort outlined in Freeman and Rogers (1993b), with a preliminary report below.

12. Among those making the argument are Adams (1983, 1985), Freeman and Rogers (1993c), Kochan and Osterman (1991), Wever, Kochan, and Berg (1991), Weiler (1990), and, for some time now, Summers (1979, 1982, 1994).

In the 103d Congress, 2d Session, Senator Pell introduced legislation on the subject (S. 2499). The Pell proposal, described by his office as a "discussion starter," would permit the establishment of labor-management committees to "discuss matters of interest and concern (including but not limited to issues of quality, productivity, improved labor-management relations, job security, organizational efficiency and enhanced economic development" upon "the agreement of both the employer and a majority of employees." The committees would be composed of equal numbers of employees (elected by fellow employees) and management officials chosen by the management.

least some representation to those American workers who want increased voice in firm decision making but who do not desire, or who desire but are not any-time likely to enjoy, the benefits of traditional unionization; (2) improve enter-prise and general market efficiency by improving the flow of information be-tween management and labor on issues of mutual concern and, more specifically, facilitate wider adoption of "high-performance" forms of worker organization associated with greater worker involvement, training, productiv-ity, and, more ambiguously, compensation; (3) improve the effectiveness of government regulation of the workplace, chiefly by providing an additional set of eyes and ears for government regulations—a local means of monitoring and enforcement far exceeding the capacities of any plausibly sized inspectorate.

Apart from notice of political infeasibility or opposition to the norms im-plicit in the above, arguments against councils take the form chiefly of doubts about the magnitude—not general direction[13]—of the above-claimed effects, and concerns about the disruption of existing industrial relations institutions by transplant of this "foreign" one. An allied but distinct objection goes less to the merits of councils per se than to the relative weight they should receive in the portfolio of reform energies. Commonly suggested alternative foci range from a more general "experimental" approach to opening up representation options within firms—itself associated with calls for the formal repeal of the current ban on "company unions"—to facilitating union organization or, above the enterprise level, to reform of current wage regulation.

In what follows I assess these competing claims and concerns in light of comparative experience with works councils and the history of councils and council-like forms in the United States. The assessment has three parts. Against the backdrop of a growing "representation gap" in United States, sec-tion 13.2 summarizes the principal values served by collective workplace or-ganization and the contribution of councils to realizing those values. Section 13.3 considers the history of councilist and council-like forms in the United States and the vitality of alternative nonunion forms of representation. Section 13.4 addresses the transplant issue. Section 13.5 briefly situates suggestions for councilar reform in the broader context of the present system's problems.

13.2   Democracy, Efficiency, and Regulatory Performance

The most immediate motivation for considering works councils as a policy initiative in the United States is straightforward. After a 40-year decline, pri-vate sector union density has fallen to a pre–Wagner Act level of 12 percent (Bureau of Labor Statistics [BLS] 1994). At current rates of new organizing,

13. In all the literature considered in research on this volume, I have yet to find any argument that councils actually weaken workplace democracy, reduce the efficiency of firms, or hamper government regulatory efforts. Negative assessments invariably take the form of questioning the robustness of these positive effects, often relative to alternative means.

density will drop to 5 percent by the turn of the century.[14] Given the absence of formal modes of collective voice in nonunionized firms and U.S. labor law restrictions on company unions, only a few workers will have any form of worker representation within private enterprises.

The United States is hardly the only advanced industrial economy in which union membership fell in the 1980s; decline occurred in most OECD countries. But the United States is a leader in deunionization, and it lacks any structure of worker representation, inside or outside the firm, to compensate for declining union coverage. In Europe, falling union membership in the 1980s followed a decade of increased unionization, with the result that rates of organization were still relatively high at the outset of the 1990s, and comparable to their level in the early 1970s. Moreover, mechanisms to extend collectively bargained wages to nonunionized workers, while weaker than in the past, remain operative. And mandated works councils provide workers with collective voice in nonunionized firms. In Japan, where union declines over the past 20 years have been pronounced, the *shunto* economywide wage adjustment system remains robust. And company unions and other means of consensual decision making, including joint consultation committees, provide some mechanism for worker voice within large enterprises (fig. 13.1).

Setting to the side for a moment the problem of external labor market regulation, the absence of effective mechanisms of intrafirm employee voice occasions several concerns. First, democratic ideals are compromised by the absence of collective representation for workers who want it. Survey data indicate that some 30 to 40 million American workers without union representation desire such and some 80 million workers, many of whom do not approve of unions, desire some independent collective voice in their workplace.[15] These numbers dwarf the 16 million or so members of organized labor and point to a large "representation gap" in the American workplace. Second, there is good evidence that this gap harms the economy. Many studies show the critical role of effective labor relations in economic performance and the dependence of

14. At current rates of new organizing, this would describe a new equilibrium for private sector density. There is, however, no reason to assume current organizing efforts will be sustained by a substantially reduced membership. In 1992, the AFL-CIO estimated that it would lose an additional 500,000 members (*Daily Labor Report* 1992), or approximately 5 percent of its dues-paying base. A continuation of that trend suggests a roughly 40 percent reduction in membership by the end of the decade. The costs of recruiting new members through NLRB elections has also increased: Chaison and Dhavale (1990) estimate that maintenance of current density levels will require unions to make, over and above current organizing budgets, an expenditure of $300 million annually. With rising new-member costs, a shrinking base, and essentially fixed costs for servicing existing members, the 5 percent figure could be simply another point on the line of continuing decline. On the other hand, innovative techniques of organizing, particularly outside NLRB elections, and the shrinkage of unionization to its most supportive core groups could produce a new equilibrium above the 5 percent forecast. In either case, however, we see no signs of a "burst" of unionization to an equilibrium above current rates of density.

15. This claim relies on various polls, including those reported in Gallup Organization (1988), Fingerhut/Powers (1991), Quinn and Staines (1979), Louis Harris and Associates (1984), Davis and Smith (1991), and Farber and Kreuger (1993), and, especially Freeman and Rogers (1994).

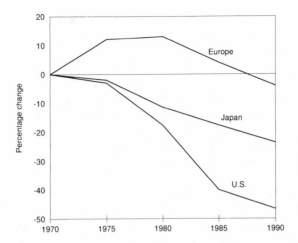

Fig. 13.1 Trends in unionization, 1970–90: Europe, Japan, and the United States

Sources: OECD (1991, 1992); BLS, union membership data gathered from various sources (1992); *The Economist Book of Vital Statistics 1990.*

Notes: Europe includes Austria, Belgium, Denmark, Finland, France, Germany, Italy, Netherlands, Sweden, Switzerland, and the United Kingdom. Union density figures for Europe were weighted using the 1988 labor force size for each country. For 1990, union density rates for Europe and Japan are 1988 figures.

effective labor relations on worker representation. Third, in many areas of public regulatory concern about the workplace—occupational safety and health, wages and hours, and workforce training among them—an effective system of workplace representation appears vital to the achievement of social goals.

13.2.1   Workplace Democracy and Collective Representation

The ideal of democracy is stated simply enough: as moral equals, all persons should be equally free to determine the terms and conditions of social association. As applied to life outside the firm, commitment to the ideal implies limiting inequalities in public life due to ethically irrelevant differences among citizens and guaranteeing equal treatment under law, equal access to public goods, and so on. As applied to the workplace, it implies equalizing power between owners and producers, managers and supervised employees.

The case for workplace democracy can be made on both instrumental and noninstrumental grounds.[16] The instrumental argument is that workplace democracy strengthens democracy in the broader society. Democracy requires some equality in the distribution of material resources, and this is unlikely

---

16. This is a generalization. Elster's (1986) argument for workplace democracy on "self-realization" grounds, e.g., falls into neither category. See Cohen (1989) for a useful inventory of existing arguments.

without some measure of worker representation inside firms (Cohen and Rogers 1983). Also, democracy requires citizens capable and confident in their exercise of deliberative political judgment, and these citizen attributes are unlikely to arise in a society that shows no respect for such attributes at work (Pateman 1970). The noninstrumental argument proceeds by extension of democratic principles beyond formal politics. Democracy might be characterized as the idea that those involved in a socially cooperative activity and bound by its rules have a right to determine those rules. This principle has applicability beyond the state to other sorts of rule-governed cooperative activity, including the cooperative activity of the firm (Dahl 1985, 1989). And this may be particularly so when, as in the case of corporations, the democratic state itself charters and protects the institutions governing such activity.[17]

Thus understood, it is almost definitional that organizations that facilitate effective worker definition and expression of interests inside the firm contribute to workplace democracy. Do councils do this? Certainly. They are arenas of collective deliberation by workers about issues that concern them inside the firm, a partial counterweight to unilateral management decision making, and a check on rival forms of representation.

17. If these sorts of arguments for workplace democracy are familiar, the arguments for qualifying commitments to workplace democracy are equally so. Two objections might be distinguished. The first is that people can more easily avoid autocratic bosses than they can autocratic governments. In a market economy, they can quit their jobs and find a different employer or set up their own business. But it is easy to exaggerate the power of exit. Quitting unsatisfactory conditions is an attractive, even exhilarating prospect if you can rapidly find a job paying comparable compensation elsewhere. But in practice, substantial unemployment, large wage differences across firms and sectors, and many firm-specific, nonportable social benefits, makes exit nonviable for many workers, and potentially least useful to those most in need of protection from autocratic management: the less skilled. Moreover, even where exit options from undemocratic conditions exist, they are not recognized, in formal politics, as compelling arguments against remediation. That it is possible to move from a town that denies its citizens the right to vote, e.g., is never seriously offered as a reason not to reform that town's government. Employing the obverse of the extension argument used above, there is no reason such an argument *not* respected outside the workplace should be respected within it.

A second objection goes to the different functions of formal government and firms. Firms, the argument goes, are designed to produce economic value, not to govern social life, and this implies different criteria of performance. Governments are at least in part judged by representativeness. What firms are judged by is the "market test" of profitability. This objection, which denies any force to the extension argument, might be answered in two ways. First, the distinction between firms and governments is overdrawn. Governments are routinely judged by their success in producing economic value. As a vast literature in comparative politics attests, economic performance is the single best predictor of stability in government (Eulau and Lewis-Beck 1985; Lewis-Beck and Lafay 1991). And firms are routinely judged by standards of conduct more encompassing than profitability. While firms must meet the market test, along the way to doing so they must typically meet other tests, including the recruitment and nondiscriminatory treatment of an adequate labor force. Second and more directly, however, the argument has little practical force. If workplace democracy extracted immense losses in production, we might decide that it was not worth the cost. But while we could undoubtedly devise forms of workplace democracy that are economically costly, the analysis just offered and the practical experience of successful capitalist economies with high levels of worker representation suggest that the opposite is more likely to be true in the real world: a well-designed system of workplace democracy can raise social production.

That councils provide a form of democratic participation attractive to workers themselves is evident from the level of worker participation in them. As the country studies here show, that level is high. In the highly developed German system, for example, councils are elected every four years on a nationwide election day, with opposing slates of candidates in each workplace that has a council, and turnout averaging around 90 percent. During the election campaign unions contend with opposition from competing unions and from nonunion groups, which often try to win votes by distancing themselves from unionism and emphasizing their closeness to the employer. For the largest German union confederation, the Deutscher Gewerkschaftsbund, it has been a source of strength, legitimacy, and pride that the candidates of its affiliates regularly win about 80 percent of works council seats nationwide (more in most large firms). In countries with multiunionism, works council elections force unions to match their policies to the preferences of large numbers of workers, unionized or not, and to measure regularly and publicly their support against that of their competitors. In these ways, a council system promotes a certain accountability of unions to those they purport to serve.

13.2.2   Contributions to Efficiency

Modern economic analysis shows that a well-designed system of intrafirm worker representation can produce economic benefit not just workers, but to firms themselves.

Recognition that information exists at various levels of organizations implies that in many situations it is inefficient for management to make key decisions. Hierarchies tend to work best when there is very low or very high uncertainty at workplaces (so that workplace-specific information provides little guidance on optimal decisions), but at intermediate levels of uncertainty, giving workers the authority to make some workplace decisions is efficient, as they can react better (more quickly, with a response informed by appropriate local knowledge) than centralized management to workplace-specific shocks or unusual circumstances (Aoki 1990, 1988).

The potential for divergent interest groups within firm hierarchies to use information for their own benefit at the expense of the firm implies that there may be payoffs from devising information and incentive structures that link top management to workers outside the standard hierarchy. Diverse principal-agent models make this point in various ways; Tirole (1986) develops it in the context of a three-level firm hierarchy: top management, supervisors, and workers, where a major issue is the possibility for coalitions among the players. Other work focuses on strategies to elicit effort, from incentive pay systems— such as rank-order tournaments (Lazear and Rosen 1981; Lazear 1991), profit sharing (Estrin, Grout, and Wadhwani 1987; Weitzman and Kruse 1990), "gain-sharing" schemes such as the Scanlon, Rucker, and Improshare plans (Eaton and Voos 1992; Kaufman 1992), and employee ownership through employee stock ownership plans (ESOPs) and other mechanisms (Bloom 1986;

Blasi 1988)—to worker participation in management (Levine and Tyson 1990; Eaton and Voos 1992). The major finding is that innovations that give employees substantial decision-making authority ("strategic participation") and a share of resultant productivity increases improve productivity. Weitzman and Kruse report favorably on profit sharing. The General Accounting Office (GAO 1986, 1988) and Conte and Svejnar (1990) find that the productivity effects of ESOPs are substantial and positive when the ESOP links worker stock ownership to substantial participation in daily firm management but not when worker participation is weak or ambiguous. The importance of such linkage finds general support, over a wide range of incentive schemes, in the reviews of Levine and Tyson (1990) and Eaton and Voos (1992).[18]

Labor relations practices based on voice instead of exit also show benefits in training practice. Human capital analyses of investment in firm-specific skills point to the advantages of job rotation and consultation (Koike 1984, 1989; Cole 1979, 1989; Morishima 1991a, 1991b) and highlight the incentive to make investments in training specific to enterprises when workers and firms expect low turnover.[19] This contrasts with studies documenting the limited firm training efforts directed to "frontline" production workers in the United States (Commission on the Skills of the American Workforce 1990; OTA 1990; Osterman 1990).

In chapter 2 of this volume, Freeman and Lazear model the ways in which works councils can produce such happy effects. They stress the virtue of the following: increasing information flows from management to labor, which can lead to worker concessions in difficult economic times, saving troubled enterprises; increasing information flows from workers to management outside the hierarchical chain; providing a forum for both sides to devise new solutions to problems; and motivating workers to make longer-term commitments to the firm. In this analysis, collective voice in the workplace has benefits to the enterprise beyond discouraging strikes due to unmet grievances (a major goal of the Wagner Act) or saving the costs of turnover by reducing quits or giving workers the compensation package they desire (stressed by Freeman and Medoff 1984). It alters the way management and labor operate, creating a more cooperative and informative decision process.

The way it does so, it bears emphasis, and of relevance to our focus on *collective* representation, is by changing the power relations between workers

18. Firm experiments with Quality of Work Life and Total Quality Management programs, discussed in section 13.4, suggest that managers recognize this link but still have problems developing successful participation schemes. Despite the widespread finding that worker participation is key to the success of ESOPs, e.g., the GAO (1986) estimates that only one in four ESOPs includes greater employee input into decision making.

19. In Germany, to take a prominent example, the effect of intrafirm representation is to force management to train more broadly than would otherwise be the case. Since pervasive council representation effectively diffuses this effect across firms, however, no firm is uniquely disadvantaged by training more workers or more broadly than it would otherwise choose. And the economy as a whole benefits from the resulting effort.

and management. On the side of workers, it is their greater control over the use of information they provide to management that leads them to provide it in the first place. Without such control, workers are reluctant to provide the information useful to improving enterprise efficiency for fear that gains in efficiency will come at the expense of their security or compensation. On the side of management, the same increase in the ability of workers to constrain management explains the most commonly observed efficiency effects on management. First, knowing that workers will interrogate decisions that affect their jobs, management must consider more fully the costs and benefits of actions its proposes to take. This limits costly mistakes arising from simple lack of reflection. Second, a management that must discuss its labor decisions with employee representatives will invest more in knowing how workers currently fare, and the likely consequences to them of a change in action, than a management concerned solely with stockholders.[20]

Works councils institutionalize such a power shift inside firms. With strong works councils, employers cannot abolish worker participation unilaterally. Since they know this, they will consider it a waste to try and will direct their efforts to building constructive relations with workers, and the operation of the council itself will not be shadowed (as union relations typically are in the United States) by a prehistory of employer resistance. On the side of workers, knowledge that the employer cannot abolish the council, and therefore will not try, permits workers to be less defensive in their employer dealings than under less safe conditions. The permanence of the council structure, finally, permits both sides to extend their time horizons in mutual dealings through it. A council can extend "credit" to the employer over long periods. And, not having to insure against aggressive short-termism from worker representatives uncertain of their long-term status, management can assume that works councils will keep commitments even in difficult times.

Consultation and co-determination rights vested in representative bodies create space for joint deliberation of decisions between management and worker representatives. Typically, exercise of consultation and co-determination rights delays decisions while at the same time improving their quality; this is the tenor of research on the impact of co-determination on German management. Works councils that provide managers with skillful interlocutors able to interrogate proposals and projects in depth make management consider

---

20. Imagine two interlocutors, A and B, at point X. A wishes to move to point Y; B, with blocking power, must be persuaded of the wisdom of doing so. In seeking to persuade B that a move to Y is in B's interest, A has incentives to familiarize itself intimately with B's present circumstance, if only better to show B that (perhaps contrary to B's initial perception of things) this move is in fact in B's interest, and to learn of the least costly means (to B) of making it. Along the way, A will gain knowledge of how B works and of alternative ways of getting from X to Y. In general, A will become more skilled in making X-to-Y changes in incremental steps and in more routinely spotting opportunities for incremental improvement. In this way, the change in power relations helps underwrite continuous improvement in the organization of production and work— the alleged sine qua non of contemporary business success.

intended decisions more carefully and mobilize extensive information for their justification. Co-determination, which gives works councils temporary veto powers over decisions, may protect managements from narrow, short-term responses to market signals, helping them avoid costly mistakes arising from lack of reflection.

If councils can thus promote efficiency within firms, they also have positive effects on the efficiency of labor markets and multifirm production systems. The way the former happens is straightforward. Increased information flow to employees permits them to adjust to changed circumstances before they directly affect welfare—think of the positive effects of advance notice on plant closings. The latter is more complicated but essentially derives from flows of information and pressures for upgrading mediated by councils themselves.

In successful works councils systems, councils serve liaison functions with the environment outside the firm, often helping the firm perceive and import good practice. In this way councils help diffuse innovations across firm boundaries. In dealing with technical change and its consequences for work organization, for example, councils in several countries may call in experts in ergonomics to advise them and the employer on state-of-the-art solutions. Expert advice helps standardize conditions across firms and draws the attention of firms to advanced solutions that they might have found on their own only with delay and at high cost. In Germany, council members have the right to attend training courses, often organized by unions or employers' associations, on company time and at the employer's expense. Courses deal with questions of new technology, work organization, working-time regimes, health and safety regulations, changes in labor law, and the like. Such courses spread information on high-standard solutions to a large number of workplaces.

Councils can also pressure managers to consider productivity enhancement as opposed to other competitive strategies. By influencing firm decisions, they force managers to consider decisions in light of the interests of employees, to explore alternatives before presenting them for approval, and to learn about their interlocutors (the workers themselves) and the conditions under which they work in arguing for one among these alternatives. This forces a management style that looks closely for the "win win" with employee interest. Moreover, the sheer imposition of demands for the satisfaction of such interests, for example for further training, submits managers to certain productivity-enhancing constraints. Councils cannot bargain over wages, but they can effectively pressure management in ways that can push management toward high-wage strategies, just as would imposition of high wages. These pressures, diffused throughout the economy, exert a cumulative force for restructuring along the path of upgrading labor.

13.2.3   Contributions to Regulatory Performance

Every society regulates some market outcomes, either to remedy market imperfections or externalities, or for reasons of income redistribution. In the United States, government inspectorates usually enforce regulations, often joined by private attorneys pursuing statutory rights through civil actions. In many areas of public concern, however, including the labor market, neither of these means of regulatory enforcement is adequate. Sites of regulated activity are too numerous (six million work sites) for any plausibly sized state inspectorate to monitor, and activity within them is too heterogeneous for a distant state agency to decide the best means of achieving desired outcomes. Private litigation, on the other hand, is a very costly and brittle way to settle disputes about standards of behavior, and its cost makes it least amply supplied to the less skilled who typically are most in need of standard enforcement. The result is often regulatory failure—inadequate performance standards, cumbersome reporting requirements on matters of uncertain relevance to desired ends, inflexibility in adjusting standards to varied or changed circumstance, and weak enforcement.[21] The prominence of regulatory agents and lawyers in the compliance process is widely perceived as a barrier to the intrafirm understandings and practices needed to get desired results.

The example of worker safety and health suffices to carry the general point. U.S. workers rate safe working conditions at the top of their expectations of company performance (National Safe Workplace Institute [NSWI] 1992, 10), and the 1970 Occupational Safety and Health Act (OSHA) commits the government to "assure safe and healthful working conditions for working men and women" (Public Law 91–596). But OSHA enforcement, which relies chiefly on 2,000 federal and state inspectors, falls short of these expectations. Since OSHA's enactment, some 200,000 workers have been killed on the job (about 300 per day), 1.4 million have been permanently disabled, and another 2 million have died from occupationally related diseases. As of the early 1990s, about 9 million workers sustained workplace injuries each year, of which 2.5 million were "serious," 70,000 resulted in permanent disablement, and 10,000 to 11,000 were fatal. Along with pain and suffering, this carnage carries costs in the form of survivor benefits, insurance for hospitalization and other treatment, and days lost in production estimated to run to some $200 billion annually (NSWI 1992).[22] Moreover, while health and safety data are difficult to compare cross-nationally—due to different measurement standards and variations in reporting—comparison of like cases shows poor relative U.S. performance. Comparing the United States to Sweden and Japan, for example, which use the same reporting measures on occupational fatalities, shows death rates in the United States 3.5 times those in Japan and 5.8 times those in Sweden (International Labour Organization [ILO] 1988).[23] Both countries also show

---

21. The resulting regulatory failure is evident in low and uneven compliance with a range of statutory protections—from child labor laws to occupational safety and health rules (GAO 1990, 1991).

22. This estimate includes the costs of deaths, injuries, and occupationally related disease. Deaths alone (calculated on a 7,000 per year basis) are estimated to cost about $40 billion (Moore and Vicusi 1990), and workplace injuries more than $80 billion (Hensler et al. 1991).

23. This comparison reflects adjustment for underreporting, applicable both to the United States and Japan, by the National Safety and Work Institute.

greater improvements in performance over time. In the 1980s, for example, the percentage reduction in Japan's rate of workplace fatalities was better than twice that of the United States.[24]

While many factors contribute to the poor U.S. occupational health and safety record, experts view the U.S. regulatory mechanism as a key factor (Bardach and Kagen 1982; Noble 1986). U.S. reliance on state inspectors to enforce health and safety standards contrasts to Japanese and European (and, increasingly, Canadian) reliance on mandated worker health and safety committees within plants to supplement direct state regulatory efforts. These committees operate with delegated legal powers; they monitor, and in some measure enforce, compliance with regulations, while enjoying more or less broad discretion in bargaining with management (usually also represented on the committee) in choosing the most appropriate local means to achieve regulatory goals.[25] In principle, a system that lodges responsibility for monitoring compliance with health and safety committees, who should be better informed about problems than government inspectors, and that gives those committees some authority to address problems should enlist the knowledge of regulated actors in finding ways in particular settings of satisfying publicly determined standards. That it does so in a context of declared representation rights, moreover, mitigates use of costly litigation. Deputizing workers as local coadministrators of health and safety regulation, of course, carries costs of its own. Worker deputies must be trained and given time off from work to carry out committee responsibilities. Still, most observers believe that the committees provide a more efficient regulatory regime for safety and health than inspectorate and civil liability schemes; this extends to initial experimentation with the approach in the United States itself (Bryce and Manga 1985; Deutsch 1988; U.S. Department of Labor [USDOL] 1988; GAO 1992; Meridian Research, Inc. 1994; Weil 1994).

In Europe, as several of the country studies in this volume show, councils are active in many more areas than health and safety, however. Recurring to the German case, works councils are charged by law to monitor the employer's observance with pertinent labor regulations—including legislation on employment protection or equal employment opportunities. German works councils are also bound by any industrial agreement that unions and employers' associations may negotiate at the sectoral or national level—which, given extension agreements, take on at least the color of more general public regulation—and have the duty to ensure that employers do not pay wages below the industrial agreement. They supervise compliance with statutory or collectively bargained

24. This comparison uses the same ILO series, but without adjustment for underreporting. It shows a 67 percent decline in the rate of workplace fatalities in Japan over 1981–89, as compared to a 29 percent decline in the United States (ILO 1988).

25. For overviews of Europe, see Bagnara, Misiti, and Wintersberger (1985) and Gustavsen and Hunnius (1981); for a review of Japan, see Wokutch (1992); for a report on Ontario, the most developed of the Canadian cases, see Ontario Advisory Council (1986).

working-time regulations and are typically charged with negotiating the details of their local implementation. Finally, they have the rights and obligation to monitor employer compliance with Germany's public-private system of apprenticeship vocational training. They monitor implementation of the nationally standardized curricula for apprentice training at the workplace and are obligated to ensure that apprentices are not unduly used for production and that the skills they are taught are portable and not primarily workplace specific.

In all these areas, the availability of competent enforcement agents, with interests and powers to make regulation "work" in ways respectful of local variation, facilitates the achievement of public goals by facilitating cooperation both between labor and capital and between the private sector and the state. Employers would not have been willing to accept the 1980s German industrial agreements on working-time reduction, for example, had they not known that the enforcement of those agreements through councils would admit flexible adjustment to local preferences and circumstances; unions would not have been content with such enforcement had they not known that "flexibility" would not amount to subversion. And neither unions nor employers would support Germany's fabled apprenticeship-based vocational training system as strongly as they do without the same confidence in council flexibility and powers. Nor could the state plausibly contemplate governing such a system—two-thirds of each age cohort undergoing three and a half years of apprenticeship in one of about four hundred certified occupations—without the contribution of local enforcement agents enjoying the confidence of private parties. And German industrial policy would not be nearly as extensive and sophisticated as it is if the state could not look, as it regularly does, to councils to provide information on emerging needs, worker perspectives, and the effectiveness of past use of government monies and other supports—information of a sort not necessarily provided by employers.

13.3   U.S. Experience with Councils, Shop Committees, and Company Unions

The United States has never mandated nonunion collective worker representation, but American firms have "experimented" at various times with institutions that give elected nonunion employee committees a role in firm governance. Called "employee representation plans," "shop committees," or "company unions" (depending largely on the sympathy of the observer)—or, sometimes, "works councils"[26]—these organizations grew in periods when employers worried about finding tractable forms of employee voice to forestall

---

26. In his superb review of the choice against councils that the Wagner Act represented, David Brody (1994) offers this advice on naming firm-specific joint committees: "The damning term commonly used by historians, and by critics at the time, was the company union, but we will do better to accept the term advanced by employers and one more functionally descriptive—the employee representation plan (ERP), or, in some companies, the works council."

unionization or to reduce labor market strife that threatened wartime production or, most recently, when employers sought to involve workers in responding to international competition. The U.S. experience is valuable because it shows how representation institutions function in a decentralized labor market absent legal or other external mandating.

13.3.1   Early U.S. Experience

U.S. shop committees date back to 1833, and the giant cigarmaker Straiton & Storm developed an elaborate employee representation scheme, including independent arbitration for the resolution of employee-manager disputes, in the late 1870s (Montgomery 1987, 350; Hogler and Grenier 1992). The first great wave of employer representation plans in the United States, however, came during World War I. Introduced to curb wartime strikes (they typically involved explicit renunciation of the strike weapon), and with an eye to inoculating the public against communist agitation, "works councils" or "shop committees" were promoted by various wartime authorities. From virtually zero in 1917, their number grew spectacularly. By 1919, the National Industrial Conference Board (NICB 1919) reported 225 plans covering half a million employees, and by 1922, 725 plans operated throughout the country. Employers reported decreased threats of unionization and reduced grievances as obvious benefits of the plans. With the exception of a small number of plans that provided more or less extensive participation rights, including representation on plant committees, representation on boards of directors, and participation in profits and stock ownership or collective bargaining,[27] however, most of these plans gave workers no real power in decision making.[28]

After the war, some large firms continued their company unions and welfare programs. Many of those who introduced shop committees under pressure from the NLB, however, dropped them (NICB 1919). In the mid-1920s, popularization of the "American plan" open-shop drive to prevent unionization led many smaller firms to introduce representation plans. Over 1919–28, total membership in employer-initiated representation schemes grew from 0.4 to

---

As late as 1934, in announcing a labor settlement for the auto industry that explicitly recognized such forms as legitimate, Franklin Delano Roosevelt expressed hope that it would provide the basis on which "a more comprehensive, a more adequate and a more equitable system of industrial relations may be built than ever before. It is my hope that the this system may develop into a kind of works council in industry in which all groups of employees, whatever may be their choice of organization or form of representation, may participate in joint conferences with their employer" ("Comparison of S. 2926 and S. 1958," *Legislative History of the National Labor Relations Act, 1935,* 2 vols. [Washington, D.C.: Government Printing Office, 1959; reprint 1985], 1, 1347). See as well Douglas (1921).

27. Brandes (1976, 131–32) notes that company unions had some success in wage and hour negotiations at both Kimberly Clarke and the Colorado Fueland Iron Company, and developed wage scales at Standard Oil of New Jersey.

28. These included Filene's, Dutchess Bleacheries, Boston Consolidated Gas, Louisville Railroads, Columbia Conserve Company, Philadelphia Rapid Transit, Dennison, and Nash (see Derber 1970, 267–68).

1.5 million. Along with declining union membership during the 1920s, this dramatically shifted the relative strength of the two representation forms. In 1919, plan membership equaled only 10 percent of union membership; by 1928, the ratio was 45 percent (Millis and Montgomery 1945, 837).

With the coming of the Depression, representation plans ebbed again: membership fell to 1.3 million over 1928–32. But the National Industrial Recovery Act (NIRA) of 1933, which brought about a marked growth in trade union activity and organization, also led to a resurgence in company unions. The NIRA forbade employers from forcing employees to join company unions, but not from encouraging the formation of such bodies (an encouragement that was often tantamount to force). With increased threats of union organizing, the company union movement again grew sharply. NICB and BLS data indicate that, by 1935, over 3,100 companies, with 2.6 million employees, had some significant percentage of their employees covered by representation plans, of which two-thirds had been established since 1933 (Wilcock 1957). The ratio of representation plan membership to trade union membership surged to 60 percent (Millis and Montgomery 1945, 841). In some sectors coverage was even more widespread: for example, after passage of the National Recovery Act, most basic steel companies established employee representation plans, which spread to cover from 90 to 95 percent of the industry workforce (Bernstein 1970). This, however, was the highpoint for representation plans. In the late 1930s the massive organizing drives of the CIO, aided by the prohibition on employer "encouragement" of worker representation in section 8(2) of the NLRA, effectively killed most of them.

During World War II, the government again promoted cooperative workplace relations, this time the form of joint labor-management committees, chiefly in union shops. These flared during the war, growing to cover some seven million workers, but faded immediately thereafter (de Schweinitz 1949). In the early postwar period, again chiefly in the organized portion of the workforce, scattered efforts were made to formalize labor-management cooperation. The best known of these were the Scanlon, Rucker, and other schemes aimed at increasing employee productivity through profit sharing and bonuses. Outside a few specific sites, however, these efforts never caught on in the unionized sector; economywide, their appeal was also limited (Derber 1970, 478–82).[29] One survey found that no company with more than 1,000 employees and no establishment with more than 5,000 employees enjoyed an actively cooperative relationship with its union. With very rare exceptions, the "cooperative" strategy was limited to medium-sized, closely held firms, or to marginal

---

29. Harris (1982, 138–39) also describes efforts at "progressive" firms, notably U.S. Rubber and General Electric, that were allied with the Committee for Economic Development and the National Planning Association, two industry associations that encouraged labor-management cooperation, to raise productivity through labor-management cooperation.

companies; even here, it essentially disappeared in the late 1950s (Harris 1982, 195).[30]

As the prime historic case of employer-initiated works councils operating in a largely nonunionized decentralized labor market, the U.S. experience in the 1920s to 1950s provides valuable insight into the potential for councils in such a setting. It shows, first, that employer-initiated councils were neither a long-lived stable institution nor one that was extended to the majority of the work-force. Even at its peak the council movement covered only a minority of workers, largely in big firms, and the peak came under threat of outside unioniza-tion. Still, this minority was at times higher than the modest private sector unionization rates of the early 1990s. Second, the NICB reports (1919, 1922) and historical investigation (Jacoby 1989; Jacoby and Verma 1992; Nelson 1993) of the operation of councils show considerable diversity. In many cases, company unions were the sham they have come to be widely viewed as, but in some cases they offered significant and meaningful means of worker represen-tation. Taking the NICB studies as valid, absent a guarantee of hard worker rights to such things, or unionism or its immediate threat, "successful" worker representation depended on management commitment—as evidenced in regu-lar meetings, education, and, ideally, concrete payoffs to workers through, for example, a profit-sharing (collective dividend) system (NICB 1922). Not contemplating an actual extension of hard worker rights within the firm, the NICB concluded that "where management is not thoroughly sold to the idea . . . a Works Council should not be formed" (NICB 1922, 10).

13.3.2   Recent U.S. Experience

Renewed interest in employee participation began building in the early 1970s. Focused on Quality of Work Life (QWL) programs, it was initially mo-tivated by concerns about worker alienation (the "blue-collar blues"), which many viewed as responsible for increased militance by assembly-line workers. The National Commission of Productivity and Quality of Working Life and the Ford Foundation sponsored a number of QWL experiments in the early 1970s in both union and nonunion plants. The most widely known included the Rushton Mining Company and the General Motors (GM) Tarrytown plant, which prior to the QWL program had one of the poorest labor relations and production records of all GM plants but within a few years of QWL adoption became one of the company's best-performing assembly plants. But implemen-tation of QWL programs was never widespread, and most of the most-visible experiments faded by the late 1970s—when government funding stopped (Ko-chan, Katz, and Mower 1984, 6–7).

In the 1980s, driven by competitive pressures and management recognition of the need to enlist employee energies to meet them, QWL programs enjoyed

---

30. See Nelson (1989) for an analysis of the historic roots of divergent managerial strategies in the rubber industry.

a resurgence. As noted, some 80 percent of the top 1,000 firms in the United States reported having an employee participation or employee involvement program (EIP), and many smaller firms experimented with one or another form of employee involvement. The more recent programs came under various names[31]—QWL committees, quality circles, autonomous work teams, gain sharing and ESOPs—and varied considerably in structure, representativeness, scope of issues, substantive decision-making power, and links to other changes in work organization. Cutcher-Gershenfeld (1987) estimated that 10 to 15 percent of all American organizations had worker participation programs in the 1980s, covering about 20 percent of the workforce. Cooke (1990) estimated that 40 to 50 percent of the unionized sector is involved with quality circles, QWL programs, or some other form of employee involvement; of these, between one-third and two-thirds are jointly administered; about one-third of the unionized sector has committee-based participation, with health and safety being the most common focus. In a more recent survey of large firms, Osterman (1994) has found wider incidence of teams (54 percent), job rotation (43 percent), quality circles (41 percent), and Total Quality Management programs (34 percent)—although no unique combination of these innovations shows up in more than 5 percent of companies.

Studies of these experiments confirm the 1920s experience. While studies generally indicate positive economic effects from employee involvement, especially at the team level (USDOL 1993; Pfeffer 1994; Jacoby 1994), the economic effects of worker involvement are most likely to be positive when workers are empowered in decision making and receive concrete payoffs to cooperation (Blinder 1990). In unionized settings, where worker power exists independent of management, the evidence shows the greatest gains from cooperation (Eaton and Voos 1992; Kelley and Harrison 1992). In nonunionized settings, where workers have no reserved rights, the performance and stability of the programs depends on management attitudes, which vary widely across firms and over time, and which are subject to an important core ambivalence: even where managers recognize "empowerment" as necessary to productivity gains, they are reluctant to relinquish discretion and control. To guarantee effective empowerment, much more is needed than management will provide on its own.

13.4 A Rejected Transplant? Works Councils and the United States in Comparative Context

Even if the representation gap is real and threatening and works councils are broadly effective and useful in Europe, it does not follow that they can be easily transplanted to the United States. Again leaving aside questions of politi-

---

31. See Eaton and Voos (1992, 208–10) for a comprehensive glossary of terms used to describe contemporary innovations in employee participation and work organization.

cal feasibility, the central issue here is how to get good effect out of a presumptive council system without destroying what little representation currently exists.

Generalizing, the continental European systems in which councils appear most effective have a developed "first channel" of worker representation and labor-management dealings, centered on regional or national wage-setting practices and political bargaining over the social wage and labor market policy, *external* to the firm. In this context, councils provide a useful "second channel" of worker representation *internal* to the firm. Indeed, as we have seen, one of their central functions is to interpret and elaborate, within firms, the terms and conditions of external agreements about how the economy should be run and how the benefits and burdens of economic cooperation should be distributed. Performance of this function often complicates, but seldom directly threatens, the viability of external standard setting and agreements on these more global concerns. The more centralized bodies provide technical assistance, coordination, and economic and political support to intrafirm activities; the councils provide flexibility in achieving general standards and a multiplier on the density of their diffusion and enforcement.

In the United States, however, the first channel barely exists. It generally lacks institutions linking workers in the political system or in wage setting beyond direct collective bargaining. There is of course no labor or labor-dominated party, and American politicians rarely articulate or explicitly direct issues to achieving the aims of workers qua workers. Since the New Deal, unions have been allied with the Democratic party, occasionally dominating local party machines. But labor was a junior partner in the New Deal coalition, and by the late 1970s had become an unfavored one (Ferguson and Rogers 1986). In the 1980s it faced "an indifference bordering on contempt" from party leaders (Trumka 1992, 57). More broadly, unions have had a largely clientelistic relation to the Democrats, looking to the party for patronage, favors, and select program supports, not as a "second arm" to achieve its vision of a good society.

This situation contrasts with Western Europe, where social democratic or labor parties govern countries regularly; with Canada, where unions affiliate with the New Democratic party; and even with Japan, where socialist parties are represented in national and regional government, and where the Rengo union federation has run candidates for political office. In the United States, by contrast, labor's main route of influence in the political system is through special interest lobbying rather than through direct electoral power (fig. 13.2).

The relative weakness of labor in government, itself substantially a function of low union density and centralization, in turn substantially explains why the United States provides less benefits to citizens in the form of universal "social wages" than European countries (fig. 13.3 and table 13.1). On a rank ordering of OECD states by social funding of pensions, health care, unemployment insurance, and the like, the United States is second to last (Esping-Andersen 1990). As a consequence, the well-being of workers depends on market earn-

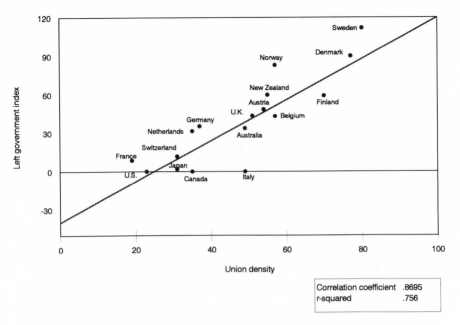

Fig. 13.2   Left government against union density
Sources: Left government index created by Wilensky (1981) and compiled by Wallerstein (1989); union density from Visser (1991).
Notes: Left government index is a cumulative index from 1991 to 1980. Union density is the percentage of total employed that are union members.

ings and employer-provided benefits more in the United States than in most other countries. Moreover, taxes and cash transfers are less redistributive than in other countries. Comparing the effect of tax and transfer programs on poverty among a group of OECD countries, for example, shows an average 79 percent reduction in poverty abroad, and only a 33 percent reduction in the United States (Mishel and Bernstein 1992).

In turn, the greater universalism of nonwage benefits overseas, which takes these benefits "out of competition," has an important consequence both for the incentives and ability of workers to organize unions and for management to oppose such organization. In the United States the onus of providing vacation benefits, parental leave, access to training, health insurance, and so on, falls on collective bargaining or individual employer personnel policy. As a result, union-nonunion differences in these components of compensation as well as in wages are exceptionally great. Large union-nonunion differentials in turn motivate employer opposition to unions: when a union is certain to bargain for greater expenditures on fringe benefits, which will put the firm at a cost disadvantage, management will fight hard against unionization. At the same time, the dependence of important benefits on nonunion personnel policies reduces worker willingness to oppose management.

In terms of wage setting, the United States is the prime example of a decen-

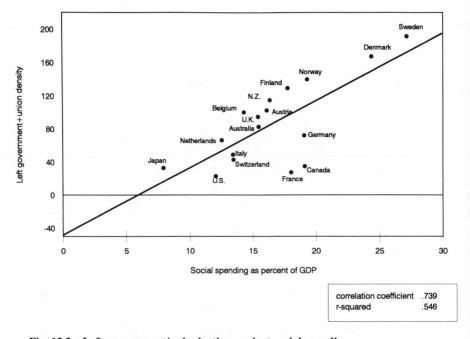

correlation coefficient   .739
r-squared   .546

Fig. 13.3   Left government/unionization against social spending
Sources: Organisation for Economic Co-operation and Development, *OECD National Accounts* (Paris, 1991); OECD (1991); Wallerstein (1989).

Table 13.1   Statutory Regulations Governing Benefits and Rights to Workers in European Countries and the United States, 1991

Benefits and Rights	Europe	United States
Public holidays	12	8–10
Annual vacation	4 weeks	No statute
Sickness leave		
Maximum weeks of leave	54	No statute
Earnings paid during sickness (%)	62	
Maternity leave		
Maximum weeks of leave	18	13
Earnings paid during leave (%)	89	0
Severance pay		
Workers with severance pay (%)	72	No statute
Unemployment insurance		
Months covered	16	6
Earnings paid during unemployment (%)	47	50

Source: Freeman (1994), tabulated from Ehrenberg (1993, tables 2.3–2.5 and 5.1) and from OECD (1991, table 7.2).

tralized system in the developed world. Most collective bargaining and firm wage setting is done on a firm-by-firm, even plant-by-plant, basis. Moreover, except for "prevailing-wage" statutes in government construction (and some procurement), the United States has few mechanisms, particularly in the private sector, for extending the results of union-employer bargaining to non-unionized employees.[32] The government plays little role in wage determination (itself a consequence of the political weakness of labor) and sets the minimum wage at levels that do not affect general wage patterns. Lack of extension of collective bargaining settlements means that coverage by collective contracts is essentially synonymous with union membership; if only 12 percent of private sector workers are unionized, only 13 percent are even covered by some union agreement. This contrasts with Europe, where many governments extend the terms of collective contracts to nonunionized workers in a sector or region, and Japan, where the *shunto* offensive establishes economywide wage patterns. U.S. decentralized wage setting, with rent sharing between prosperous firms and their workers, and limited provision of social wages, puts the country at the top of the developed world in wage inequality (fig. 13.4).[33]

The absence of a labor party and of encompassing wage-setting mechanisms has important implications for the character of representation within firms. In the United States, unions bargain for fringe benefits that are guaranteed by the state elsewhere and bargain for wages that are set outside the firm in other countries. Because higher fringes and wages can put firms at a competitive disadvantage compared to others, confrontation at the bargaining table lies at the heart of labor relations. In Europe—and to some extent even Japan—by contrast, where general welfare benefits and wages are determined outside the firm, there is greater space for the expression of cooperative employee voice and bargaining within the firm. In effect, both sides can "afford" to cooperate because their positions are secured or restrained outside the firm. Workers know that their basic social benefits will remain intact and that their wages will keep pace with those of other workers whatever trade-offs they make within the firm. Management knows that the works council will not place it at a competitive disadvantage through within-firm bargaining. External guarantees— be they social benefit guarantees, centrally determined wages, or rights-based sanctions on job loss—in some measure render moot much intrafirm disagree-

---

32. Pattern bargaining—the copying of a limited set of key bargains such as for steel or auto manufacturing in many other parts of unionized manufacturing—and spillovers of union wage and benefit gains to nonunionized workers due to the threat of unionization produced some implicit institutional coordination in U.S. wage setting. While even at its peak pattern bargaining dominated only a few unionized sectors, some experts believed that patterns spread informally to white-collar workers in unionized firms, and as nonunionized firms raised blue-collar pay to forestall unionization to dominate the overall labor market (Bok and Dunlop 1970).

33. Freeman (1991) and Card (1991) find that declining unionization accounts for one-fifth of the increased variance in male wages over 1973–87. Lemieux (1993) attributes 40 percent of the greater inequality in wages in the United States than in Canada to the difference in the rate of unionization.

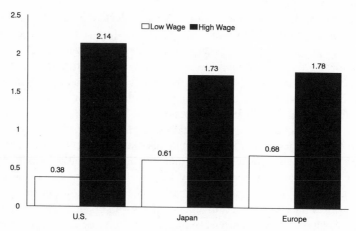

Fig. 13.4   Pay of low-wage and high-wage workers relative to median: United States, Japan, and Europe
Source: Freeman (1994), calculated from OECD (1993, table 5.2)

ment about the division of the surplus. By taking many intrafirm disputes over the surplus "off the table," these guarantees underwrite internal cooperation and flexibility toward the joint goal of increasing firm performance. Standard principles of rational behavior imply that when the share of the pie is exogenous, self-interested parties will cooperate to make a bigger pie, as this is the only way they can benefit themselves. When the share of the pie is "up for grabs," by contrast, there is danger of noncooperative, low-output solutions to prisoner's dilemma problems, including strikes, withholding information that might raise output, and the like.

The implication of this analysis is that all labor relations systems face a fundamental trade-off between external flexibility on one side and internal cooperation and the flexibility that depends on cooperative arrangements on the other. More flexibility in the external market implies less cooperativeness in the internal market. European labor relations systems resolve the tension by a dual channel of labor representation. They provide external guarantees through encompassing collective bargaining and state provision of certain benefits and seek internal cooperative relations through within-firm worker councils.

If external constraints and guarantees thus facilitate internal cooperation and joint dealing, real external organizational power makes that dealing meaningful. As is evident from the country studies, the interaction of unions and councils, the terms of their mutual dependence, are complex and varying. As a general matter, however, it is clear that councils inside the firm work best when they enjoy some relation, however distanced, to a powerful union movement outside it. The latter is a source of residual political support—including, vitally, that needed to extract resources necessary to council functioning from employers or the state—and expertise in issues of council concern, from ergo-nomics to new technologies, work organizations, or whatever.

Where, as in the United States, wage bargaining is decentralized, the social wage is exiguous, and the bargaining parties are not linked systematically to a powerful set of encompassing political organizations; on the other hand, the second channel of local union representation effectively takes on the welfare function and stands alone. Defined by reference to the particulars of individual firms, its preservation is contingent on the preservation of union strength in particular settings. Accordingly, much importance is assigned to the precise terms under which collective bargaining rights would attach within individual firms and to the conditions for maintaining the fruits of organizing success within firms. The arcana of American law regarding the formal certification of bargaining representatives, and the requirement that those representatives be exclusive, were solutions to the problem of contested, decentralized unioniza-tion and wage bargaining. Without a general presumption of unionization, or its equivalent in wage and benefit guarantees, employer assumption of these costs was justified only upon a showing of majority support. Without general-izing support from the state, the welfare of individual workers depended un-usually on their bargaining power vis-à-vis specific individual employers. In relation to those employers, *exclusivity* in representation—a guarantee of a single collective voice—was the gravamen of worker power. Lacking a social mandate, moreover, worker representation in the nonunionized sector de-pended by definition on the will of employers. Given the destabilizing effect of employer-dominated company unions in the 1920s, however, the expression of this will in the form of material support or assistance to representative non-union labor organizations was itself barred.[34]

Translating councils to this setting thus poses a series of nested challenges—particularly threatening to labor, but posing more general threats to the stability and success of a council system. For councils to be effective, the country stud-ies tell us, they are best located within and supported by a broader framework of labor-management dealings external to the firm. Construction and adminis-tration of such a framework, which does not now exist, would require a consid-erable increase in the power of competence of regional and national worker organizations. A precondition of such an increase in power, however, is a strengthening of the labor movement. And given its existing structure and fo-

---

34. For the rationale for such a bar—employer interference with autonomous employee choices about representation—we do no better than to consider the first case decided by the NLRB, *Penn-sylvania Greyhound Lines,* 1 NLRB 1 (1935), enfd. denied in part 91 F.2d 178 (3d Cir. 1937), revd. 303 U.S. 261 (1938); cited in *Electromation Inc.,* 309 NLRB 163 (1992). As the Greyhound manager in charge of the company union challenged there summarized management's goals: "[I]t is to our interest to pick our employees to serve on the committee who will work for the interest of the company and will not be radical. This plan of representation should work out very well providing the proper men are selected, and considerable thought should be given to the men placed on this responsible Committee."

cus, it is far from clear that the introduction of an alternative representative structure, potentially overlapping with many of the functions now performed by local unions, would have a strengthening effect. It seems at least equally plausible that it would lead to substitution away from unions—as is suggested by the Dutch case, and that of France—and a further devolution of the importance of extrafirm structures of mediation and support of the very sort desired. If the above analysis of the sources of labor weakness is correct in its emphasis on the negative effects of decentralization and particularity in bargaining, it raises an obvious question. How would the introduction of further decentralization strengthen labor? Or posed more generally, if councils need external unions to function well, and the introduction of councils would weaken unions as presently organized in the United States, how would the introduction of councils into this already decentralized system do anybody any good?

Identification of this tension does not amount to a convincing argument against councils. It does suggest, however, the need for some care in their potential design in the United States. Several requirements would need to be satisfied. First, premising an interest in not destroying what workplace organization does exist, encouragement of councils as independent forms of representation would seem to need to be limited to nonunionized settings.[35] Second, and whatever the range of issues councils discuss, some bright line would need to be established between them and the wage-bargaining system. This might be done categorically, by restricting council discussion to topics other than wages and benefits. But experience both abroad and at home indicates the difficulty of enforcing such categorical distinctions in practice. A more practical approach, then, would be to limit council *powers* to information and consultation. Third, even within this information-consultation power domain, it appears vital to build in some resource guarantees for their functioning—time off from work, money to hire outside assistance, enforceable rights to elicit information from employers.

Such provisions would work to ensure that councils were in fact a supplement to, rather than detraction from, existing workplace representation. But they would not address the issue of management domination of the committees. In addressing that issue, we distinguish at the outset between the current legal meaning of "domination" and the more precise normative concern with abrogations of employee freedom in selecting representative forms. The current bar on "company unions," deliberately, does not respect this distinction; it treats identically situations that give no offense to the principle of employee free choice in the selection of representative forms and those that do. The reasons for this are many, but all come down finally to doubts among the framers

---

35. And, presumably, settings where unions are not currently engaged in organizing drives.

of the Wagner Act about the stability and usefulness of drawing this distinction too finely. On the one hand, the state's capacity to monitor offensive sorts of domination inside firms was thought to be limited; better to go with institutions whose very powers would provide the needed demonstration of independence. On the other hand, the sorts of powers sought, during a period of deep depression in an essentially closed economy, went directly to wage-setting powers. As Senator Wagner (1934) wrote in the *New York Times* at the time, while nonbargaining or non–independent-bargaining institutions had "improved personal relations, group welfare activities, discipline, and other matters which may be handled on a local basis . . . [they have] failed dismally to standardize or improve wage levels, for the wage question is a general one whose sweep embraces whole industries, or States, or even the nation."

How, in a context in which even unions are incapable of setting wage levels—removing, as Jacoby (1994) notes, at least one reason for not reopening discussion—might the relevant distinction be made? Straightforwardly, it would appear, by carving an "employee free choice" exception to section 8(a)(2). Hyde (1994) and Summers (1994) suggest how this might done. Leaving that section intact and permitting a very expansive definition of "labor organization," "an employer who would otherwise violate that section by establishing or supporting a system of employee representation or communication may defend against unfair labor practice charges by showing: (a) that the system was authorized by a majority of employees in a secret ballot; (b) that before the ballot, employees were specifically advised of their right to oppose the creation of such a plan without reprisal; (c) that such authorization expires in some uniform period of time, perhaps three years, unless reauthorized" (Hyde 1994). To these provisions we might add: (d) that the system may be abolished by a majority of employees in a secret ballot at any time; and (e) that the system cannot at any time be unilaterally abolished by the employer. Were such conditions satisfied, employer "domination" in the sense of "infringing worker independence in choice of representative form" would be effectively extinguished. Of course, the number of employers that would, under such clarification, actually seek nonunion independent worker representation is an open question. How many workers, assuming enactment of the other reforms suggested here, would choose this over rival representative forms is open as well. The real values at stake, however, would be clarified in a way that they are not in the present debate.

Comparative and domestic experience, along with a little creative drafting, suggests how the transplant problem could be overcome. As I read the evidence, it would in theory be possible to graft a "council option" onto the existing U.S. system, despite its obvious differences from European ones, without serious damage to what currently exists. The essential requisite attributes of the system would be powers limited to consultation and information, limitation in independent incidence to the nonunionized sector, direct supports for functioning, and guarantees of employee freedom in opting into the structures in the first place, choosing representatives, and termination.[36]

Finally, we may ask about the form that "encouragement" of council formation might take. It is striking, and instructive, that all functioning council systems involve some degree of state *mandate* of these forms—either direct or the form of *de minimus* expressions of employee interest triggering their formation. Prospects for such in the United States are at the moment vanishingly remote, and the above considerations on design are framed by that fact. But for all sorts of obvious reasons—uncertainty, adverse selection, snowballing effects upon reaching critical mass—a commitment to diffusing councils would appear to require their being mandated strongly (by, e.g., the conditioning of such government benefits as contracts or ESOP tax expenditures on their establishment). The basic point is that there is no good reason to expect that council structures will widely emerge on their own, and good reason to believe that they would not, even if the general presence of councils were preferable to the present state.

13.5 Related Aspects of Reform

Thus far, I have attempted to assess the potential contribution and requirements of council reform considered as a stand-alone reform. This exercise, however, has been doubly artificial: in abstracting from the political realities that make this a very low probability event and in considering councils merely as an add-on to an otherwise unchanged system. Keeping the first abstraction we might ask in closing, what are the sorts of other reforms that would enjoy an "elective affinity" with some council initiative?

Three broad categories of reform seem most relevant:

First, as a widening of employee choice beyond the "all or nothing" choice of majority unions or nothing, while guaranteeing freedom in that choice, council reform might naturally be accompanied and supported by other measures aimed at the same goal.

Recognizing various imperfections in the "market" of associational choice bearing on representation of worker interests, efforts might be made to perfect that market. This means widening the range of employees permitted collective representation, reducing the direct cost of their choosing such, and widening the range of choice itself.

Widening the range of protected employees would mean abolishing most if not all restrictions on the free choice of farm workers, individual contractors, and supervisors, as well as those public employees in that half of the United States that have still not recognized even minimal rights to self-organization. Reducing the direct costs to employees in choosing representation would mean

36. Such guarantees find broad support in the Worker Representation and Participation Survey (Freeman and Rogers 1994).

institutionalizing respect for individual freedom in choice and collective worker deliberation about how it might best be made. At present, as regards the only available form of collective representation—unions—this condition is clearly not satisfied. Whatever one's opinion of unions, current levels and kinds of employer resistance to them clearly impose direct costs on employees and corrupt the process of deliberation.[37] Getting closer to free deliberation would thus appear to require more effective sanctions on such employer behavior, quickly applied,[38] and some expedition of the election process itself. Expansion of the range of representative forms naturally might not be limited to the council option but might be extended to include minority unions, employee caucuses, and other associations below the majority level.[39]

Second, on no account do councils significantly contribute to wage equality. And on all accounts their effective operation requires some external norming of wages and benefits. So, the introduction of councils might naturally be allied with efforts to raise the social wage in the United States, and to move bargaining over wages and benefits beyond the individual firm.[40] Raising social minima is in principle simple enough. Whether administered through firms or not, certain basic benefits would be guaranteed on a societywide basis, much as is currently being promised for health care. The efficiency benefits of doing this are many. As against other means, minima are an efficient way to redistribute income, especially when receipt is conditioned on employment.[41] By raising the base price of labor, minima can also be an important spur to more productive labor use, setting dynamic efficiencies in motion. And, by generalizing certain standards of behavior and performance, minima facilitate flexibility in the deployment of productive resources. As emphasized in recent discussions of health care benefits, socializing benefits promotes greater

37. Apart from repeated documentation of employer violations of the spirit and letter of the LMRA, and the close correlation between such resistance and union failure in representation elections, perhaps the best evidence for the importance of management resistance to current employee choices is provided by the public sector. Controlling for age, income, race, sex, occupation, and all other conceivable individual and group variables, unionization in the public sector—essentially free of management resistance—runs better than three times as high as in the private sector.

38. Sanctions might include such things as outright fines and treble compensatory damages for actual violations of the law, or disqualification from government contract eligibility for repeat offenders. Speed might be achieved by a requirement of hearings and determination of the merit of employer unfair labor practices within 30 days of filing.

39. On their face, sections 9(a) and 8(a)(5) provide no suggestion that employers are *not* obligated to bargain with such "minority unions." Contrary NLRB and court interpretations have stood so long, however, that statutory amendment would now probably be required to establish this obligation. Apart from administrative difficulties in handling the claims of such multiple unions (themselves navigable through threshold representation requirements and rules on their interaction), there seems no reason why it should not be—again, in the absence of an elected majority representative. See Summers (1990).

40. Is this an appropriate topic of labor law reform? It is if that reform is seen as it should be—as an effort aimed at addressing issues not only of worker representation or management prerogative inside the firm but of the appropriate design of a societywide system of production and reward.

41. For a recent argument to this effect, and a more general review of the evidence on minima, see Freeman (1993).

allocative efficiency in the labor market. A firm A employee economically (given skills, taste, whatever) best suited to firm B is more likely to find her way to firm B if firm B does not suffer from a crippling shortfall in benefits compared to those provided by firm A. The most obvious benefit, however, is to the level of equality itself. By removing a chunk of individual welfare from wage competition, minima make it more likely that those less fortunate in that competition will still live a decent life.

While the United States seems unlikely ever to contemplate true peak bargaining between unified union federations and a unified business community, nor even anytime soon to contemplate the full use of extension laws in the unorganized sector,[42] more modest efforts to facilitate wage generalization on a regional or sectoral basis might be considered. The law on multiemployer bargaining might be amended, shifting the presumption away from the voluntariness (and, inevitably, instability) of such arrangements and toward their requirement.[43] And more ambitious schemes of "sectoral bargaining," of the sort now being discussed in Canada, might be usefully considered.[44] In a given area or industry grouping or both, sectors of employees, defined by common occupational positions across different employers, could be defined (e.g., "restaurant workers in New York City"). Unions demonstrating support among members of the sector at different sites would be permitted to bargain jointly with all the employers corresponding to those sites. In subsequent organizing during the term of the resulting contract, union certification at additional sites would automatically accrete their employers to the population covered by the contract, with that employer joining in the multiemployer bargaining in the next round.[45] To make the scheme more palatable to employers and the general public, its application might be limited to traditionally low-wage, underrepresented sectors, characterized by highly uniform conditions of work.

Each of these areas of reform, of course, certainly no less than councilar reform, are subjects of intense conflict. The point here is simply that in thinking about councils, policymakers would do well to consider the natural external supports to their functioning.

References

Adams, Roy J. 1983. The unorganized: A rising force. Paper presented at the 31st annual McGill Relations conference, Montreal.

42. Outside, i.e., their traditionally limited American purview of prevailing-wage statutes.

43. We are speaking of presumptions here. It would be important in any scheme to permit employers a chance to defeat the presumption by showing why the conditions of their enterprise were sufficiently distinct from those with whom they were asked to join.

44. See Baigent, Ready, and Roper (1992); Fudge (1993).

45. Again, it would be important to leave room for some variation due to local circumstance. Authority to make such allowances might be assigned to regional offices of the USDOL, or to the NLRB, or to a more formal, new system of regional labor market boards.

————. 1985. Should works councils be used as industrial relations policy? *Monthly Labor Review* 108:25–29.

Aoki, Masahiko. 1988. *Information, incentives, and bargaining in the Japanese economy.* New York: Cambridge University Press.

————. 1990. Toward an economic model of the Japanese firm. *Journal of Economic Literature* 28(1): 1–27.

Bagnara, Sabastiano, Raffaello Misiti, and Helmut Wintersberger, eds. 1985. *Work and health in the 1980s: Experiences of direct workers' participation in occupational health.* Berlin: Edition Sigma.

Baigent, John, Vince Ready, and Tom Roper. 1992. *Recommendations for labour law reform.* British Columbia: Ministry of Labour.

Bardach, Eugene, and Robert Kagen. 1982. *Going by the book.* Philadelphia: Temple University Press.

Barnett, George E. 1933. American trade unionism and social insurance. *American Economic Review* 23:1–8.

Bernstein, Irving. 1970. *The turbulent years: A history of the American worker, 1933–1945.* Boston: Houghton Mifflin.

Blasi, Joseph R. 1988. *Employee ownership: Revolution or ripoff?* Cambridge, Mass.: Ballinger.

Blinder, Alan S., ed. 1990. *Paying for productivity: A look at the evidence.* Washington, D.C.: Brookings Institution.

Bloom, David, and Richard Freeman. 1992. The fall in private pension coverage in the United States. *American Economic Review* 82 (May): 539–45.

Bloom, Steven. 1986. Employee ownership and firm performance. Ph.D. Thesis, Department of Economics, Harvard University.

BLS (Bureau of Labor Statistics). 1994. *Employment and earnings.* Washington, D.C.: Government Publishing Office.

Bok, Derek C., and John T. Dunlop. 1970. *Labor and American community.* New York: Simon & Schuster.

Brandes, Stuart. 1976. *American welfare capitalism.* Chicago: University of Chicago Press.

Brody, David. 1994. Origins of the Wagner Act. In *Restoring the promise of American labor laws,* ed. Sheldon Friedman, Richard Hurd, Rudy Oswald, and Ronald Seeber. Ithaca, N.Y.: ILR Press.

Bryce, George K., and Pran Manga. 1985. The effectiveness of health and safety committees. *Relations Industrielles* 40(2): 257–82.

Card, David. 1991. The effect of unions on the distribution of wages: redistribution or relabelling? Department of Economics, Princeton University. Mimeograph.

Chaison, Gary N., and Dileep G. Dhavale. 1990. A note on the severity of the decline in union organizing activity. *Industrial and Labor Relations Review* 43(4): 366–73.

Cohen, Joshua. 1989. The economic basis of deliberative democracy. *Social Philosophy and Policy* 6(2): 25–50.

Cohen, Joshua, and Joel Rogers. 1983. *On democracy.* New York: Penguin.

————. 1992. Secondary associations and democratic governance. *Politics and Society* 20 (December): 393–472.

————. 1993. Associations and democracy. *Social Philosophy and Policy* 10 (Summer): 282–312.

————. 1995. *Beyond faction: Associations and democratic governance.* New York: Cambridge University Press. Forthcoming.

Cole, Robert E. 1979. *Work, mobility, and participation: A comparative study of American and Japanese industry.* Berkeley and Los Angeles: University of California Press.

————. 1989. *Strategies for learning: Small group activities in American, Japanese, and Swedish industry.* Berkeley and Los Angeles: University of California Press.

Conte, Michael A., and Jan Svejnar. 1990. The performance effects of employee ownership plans. In *Paying for productivity: A look at the evidence,* ed. Alan S. Blinder.
Washington, D.C.: Brookings Institution.

Cooke, William N. 1990. *Labor-management cooperation: New partnerships or going
in circles?* Kalamazoo, Mich.: W. E. Upjohn Institute for Employment Research.

———. 1990. Factors influencing the effect of joint union-management programs on
employee-supervisor relations. *Industrial and Labor Relations Review* 43(5):
587–603.

Cutcher-Gershenfeld, Joel. 1987. Collective governance of industrial relations. In *Proceedings of the 40th annual meeting of the Industrial Relations Research Association.*
Madison, Wisc.: Industrial Relations Research Association.

Commission on the Skills of the American Workforce. 1990. *America's choice: High
skills or low wages!* Rochester, N.Y.: National Center for Education and the
Economy.

Dahl, Robert. 1985. *A preface to economic democracy.* Berkeley and Los Angeles: University of California Press.

———. 1989. *Democracy and Its critics.* New Haven, Conn.: Yale University Press.

Daily Labor Report. Washington, D.C.: Bureau of National Affairs.

Davis, James Allan, and Tom W. Smith. 1991. *General social surveys, 1972–1991.* Chicago: National Opinion Research Center. Machine-readable Data File.

Derber, Milton. 1970. *The American idea of industrial democracy, 1865–1965.* Urbana:
University of Illinois Press.

de Schweinitz, Dorothea. 1949. *Labor and management in common enterprise.* Cambridge: Harvard University Press.

Deutsch, Steven. 1988. Workplace democracy and worker health: Strategies for implementation. *International Journal of Health Services* 18(4): 647–58.

Douglas, Paul H. 1921. Shop committees: Substitute for, or supplements to trade
unions? *Journal of Political Economy* 29:89–107.

Eaton, Adrienne E., and Paula B. Voos. 1992. Unions and contemporary innovations in
work organization, compensation, and employee participation. In *Unions and economic competitiveness,* ed. Lawrence Mishel and Paula B. Voos, 173–215. Armonk,
N.J.: M. E. Sharpe.

Ehrenberg, Ronald. 1994. *Labor markets and economic integration.* Washington, D.C.:
Brookings Institution.

Elster, Jon. 1986. Self-realisation in work and politics: The Marxist conception of the
good life. *Social Philosophy and Policy* 3(2): 97–126.

Esping-Andersen, Gosta. 1990. *The three worlds of welfare capitalism.* Princeton, N.J.:
Princeton University Press.

Estrin, Saul, Paul Grout, and Sushil Wadhwani. 1987. Profit-sharing and employee
share ownership. *Economic Policy* 2(1): 13–62.

Eulau, Heinz, and Michael Lewis-Beck, eds. 1985. *Economic conditions and electoral
outcomes.* New York: Agathon.

Farber, Henry, and Alan B. Krueger. 1993. Union membership in the United States: The
decline continues. In *Employee representation: Alternatives and future directions,*
ed. Bruce E. Kaufman and Morris M. Kleiner, 105–34. Madison, Wisc.: Industrial
Relations Research Association.

Ferguson, Thomas, and Joel Rogers. 1986. *Right turn: The decline of the Democrats
and the future of American politics.* New York: Hill & Wang.

Fingerhut/Powers. 1991. *National labor poll.* Washington, D.C.: Fingerhut/Granados.

Flanagan, Robert J. 1987. *Labor relations and the litigation explosion.* Washington,
D.C.: Brookings Institution.

Freeman, Richard B. 1989. On the divergence in unionism among developed countries.
NBER Working Paper. Cambridge, Mass.: National Bureau of Economic Research.

————. 1991. Employee councils, worker participation, and other squishy stuff. In *Proceedings of the 43rd annual meeting of the Industrial Relations Research Association*, 328–37. Madison, Wisc.: Industrial Relations Research Association.

————. 1993. Minimum wages—Again! Paper delivered at the conference on Economic Analysis of Base Salaries and Effects of Minimum Wages, Aix en Provence, September 30–October 1.

————. 1994. How labor fares in advanced economies. In *Working under different rules*, ed. Richard B. Freeman, 1–28. New York: Russell Sage Foundation.

Freeman, Richard B. and Lawrence F. Katz. 1994. Rising wage inequality: The United States vs. other advanced countries. In *Working under different rules*, ed. Richard B. Freeman, 29–62. New York: Russell Sage Foundation.

Freeman, Richard B., and James L. Medoff. 1984. *What do unions do?* New York: Basic.

Freeman, Richard B., and Joel Rogers. 1993a. Reforming U.S. labor relations. Manuscript.

————. 1993b. What workplace representation and participation do American workers want? Manuscript.

————. 1993c. Who speaks for us? Employee representation in a non-union labor market. In *Employee representation: Alternatives and future directions,* ed. Bruce Kaufman and Morris M. Kleiner, 13–79. Madison, Wisc.: Industrial Relations Research Association.

————. 1994. Testimony to the Dunlop Commission on the Worker Representation and Participation Survey. Manuscript.

Fudge, Judy. 1993. Labour needs sectoral bargaining now. *Canadian Dimension,* March–April: 33–37.

Gallup Organization. 1988. Public knowledge and opinion concerning the labor movement. Princeton, N.J.: Gallup Organization.

GAO (General Accounting Office). 1986. *Employee stock ownership plans: Benefits and costs of ESOP tax incentives for broadening stock ownership.* GAO/PEMD-87–8. Washington, D.C.: Government Printing Office.

————. 1988. *Employee stock ownership plans: Little evidence of effects on corporate performance.* GAO/PEMD-88–1. Washington, D.C.: Government Printing Office.

————. 1990. *Child labor: Increases in detected child labor violations throughout the United States.* GAO/HRD-90–116. Washington, D.C.: Government Printing Office.

————. 1991. *Occupational safety and health: OSHA action needed to improve compliance with hazard communication standard.* GAO/HRD-92–8. Washington, D.C.: Government Printing Office.

————. 1992. *Occupational safety and health: Worksite safety and health programs show promise.* GAO/T-HRD-92–15. Washington, D.C.: Government Printing Office.

Gustavsen, Bjorn, and Gerry Hunnius, 1981. *New patterns of work reform: The case of Norway.* Oslo: Universitetsforlaget.

Harris, Howell John. 1982. *The right to manage: Industrial relations policies of American business in the 1940s.* Madison, Wisc.: University of Wisconsin Press.

Hensler, Deborah R., et al. 1991. *Compensation for accidental injuries in the United States.* Santa Monica, Calif.: Rand Corporation.

Hogler, Raymond L., and Guillermo J. Grenier. 1992. *Employee participation and labor law in the American workplace.* Westport, Conn.: Quorum.

Hyde, Alan. 1994. Employee caucus: A key institution in the emerging system of employment law. In *The legal future of employee representation,* ed. Matthew W. Finkin, 146–90. Ithaca, N.Y.: ILR.

ILO (International Labour Organization). 1988. *Yearbook of labour statistics.* Geneva: International Labour Organization.

Jacoby, Sanford M. 1989. Reckoning with company unions: The case of Thornton Products, 1934–1964. *Industrial and Labor Relations Review* 43(1): 19–40.

———. 1994. Prospects for employee representation in the United States: Old wine in new bottles? Paper delivered at 89th annual meeting of the American Sociological Association, Los Angeles, August.

Jacoby, Sanford M., and Anil Verma. 1992. Enterprise unions in the U.S. *Industrial Relations* 31(1): 137–58.

Kaufman, Roger T. 1992. The effects of Improshare on productivity. *Industrial and Labor Relations Review* 45(2): 311–22.

Kelley, Maryellen R., and Bennett Harrison. 1992. Unions, technology, and labor management cooperation. In *Unions and economic competitiveness,* ed. Lawrence Mishel and Paula B. Voos. Armonk, N.Y.: M. E. Sharpe.

Kochan, Thomas A., Harry C. Katz, and Nancy R. Mower. 1984. *Worker participation and American unions: Threat or opportunity?* Kalamazoo, Mich.: W. E. Upjohn Institute for Employment Research.

Kochan, Thomas A., and Paul Osterman. 1991. Human resource development and utilization: Is there too little in the U.S.? Paper prepared for the Time Horizons project of the Council on Competitiveness. Sloan School of Management, Massachusetts Institute of Technology.

Koike, Kazuo. 1984. Skill formation systems in the U.S. and Japan: A comparative study. In *The economic analysis of the Japanese firm,* ed. Masahiko Aoki, 44–75. Amsterdam: North-Holland.

———. 1989. Intellectual skill and the role of employees as constituent members of large firms in contemporary Japan. In *The firm as a nexus of contracts,* ed. Masahiko Aoki, Bo Gustafsson, and Oliver Williams, 185–208. London: Sage.

Lazear, Edward P. 1991. Labor economics and the psychology of organizations. *Journal of Economic Perspectives* 5(2): 89–110.

Lazear, Edward P., and S. Rosen. 1981. Rank order tournament as optimum labor contracts. *Journal of Political Economy* 89(5): 841–64.

Lemieux, Thomas. 1993. Union and wage inequality in Canada and in the United States. In *Small differences that matter: Labor markets and income maintenance in Canada and the United States,* ed. David Card and Richard Freeman. Chicago: University of Chicago Press.

Levine, David I., and Laura D'Andrea Tyson. 1990. Participation, productivity, and the firm's environment. In *Paying for productivity: A look at the evidence,* ed. Alan S. Blinder, 183–243. Washington, D.C.: Brookings Institution.

Lewis-Beck, Michael, and Jean-Dominque Lafay. 1991. *Economics and politics: The calculus of support.* Ann Arbor: University of Michigan Press.

Louis Harris and Associates. 1984. *A study on the outlook for trade union organizing.* New York: Louis Harris and Associates.

Luria, Daniel, and Joel Rogers. 1993. Get up and dance! Strategies for high-wage metropolitan economic development. Manuscript.

Meridian Research, Inc. 1994. *Review and analysis of state-mandated and other worker protection programs.* Prepared for Office of Program Evaluation, Directorate of Policy, Occupational Safety and Health Administration. Silver Spring, Md.: Meridian Research, Inc.

Millis, Harry, and Royal Montgomery. 1945. *Organized labor.* New York: McGraw-Hill.

Mishel, Lawrence, and Jared Bernstein. 1992. *The state of working America, 1992–93.* Armonk, N.Y.: M. E. Sharpe.

Mishel, Lawrence, and Paula E. Voos, eds. 1992. *Unions and economic competitiveness.* Armonk, N.Y.: M. E. Sharpe.

Montgomery, David. 1987. *The fall of the house of labor.* Cambridge: Cambridge University Press.

Moore, Michael J., and W. Kip Viscusi. 1990. *Compensation mechanisms for job risks: Wages, workers' compensation and product liability.* Princeton, N.J.: Princeton University Press.

Morishima, Motohiro. 1991a. Information sharing and collective bargaining in Japan: Effects on wage negotiation. *Industrial and Labor Relations Review* 44(3): 469–75.

———. 1991b. Information sharing and firm performance in Japan. *Industrial Relations* 30(1): 37–61.

Nelson, Daniel. 1989. Managers and unions in the rubber industry: Union avoidance strategies in the 1930s. *Industrial Relations Research Review* 43(1): 41–52.

———. 1993. Employee representation in historical perspective. In *Employee representation: Alternatives and future directions,* ed. Morris Kleiner and Bruce Kaufman. Madison, Wisc.: Industrial Relations Research Association.

NICB (National Industrial Conference Board). 1919. *Works councils in the United States.* Boston: National Industrial Conference Board.

———. 1922. *Experience with works councils in the United States.* Research Report no. 50. New York: Century.

NLRB (National Labor Relations Board). 1935. *Pennsylvania Greyhound Lines* 1 NLRB 1.

———. 1992. *Electromation, Inc.* 309 NLRB 163.

Noble, Charles. 1986. *Liberalism at work: The rise and fall of OSHA.* Philadelphia: Temple University Press.

NSWI (National Safe Workplace Institute). 1992. *Basic information on workplace safety and health in the United States, 1992 edition.* Chicago: National Safe Workplace Institute.

OECD (Organisation for Economic Co-operation and Development). 1991. *Employment outlook July 1991.* Paris: Organisation for Economic Co-operation and Development.

———. 1992. *Employment outlook July 1992.* Paris: Organisation for Economic Co-operation and Development.

———. 1993. *Employment outlook July 1993.* Paris: Organisation for Economic Co-operation and Development.

Ontario Advisory Council on Occupational Health and Occupational Safety. 1986. *Eighth annual report, April 1, 1985 to March 31, 1986,* vol. 2. Toronto: Ontario Advisory Council on Occupational Health and Occupational Safety.

Osterman, Paul. 1990. Elements of a national training policy. In *New developments in worker training: A legacy for the 1990s,* ed. Louis A. Ferman et al. Madison, Wisc.: Industrial Relations Research Association.

———. 1994. How common is workplace transformation and who adopts it? *Industrial and Labor Relations Review* 47 (January): 173–88.

OTA (Office of Technology Assessment). 1990. *Worker training: Competing in the international economy.* OTA ITE-457. Washington, D.C.: Government Printing Office.

Pateman, Carole. 1970. *Participation and democratic theory.* New York: Cambridge University Press.

Pfeffer, Jeffrey. 1994. *Competitive advantage through people: Unleashing the power of the American workplace.* Boston: Harvard Business School Press.

Putnam, Robert D. 1992. *Democracy and the civic community: Tradition and change in an Italian experiment.* Princeton, N.J.: Princeton University Press.

Quinn, Robert P., and Graham L. Staines. 1979. *The 1977 Quality of Employment Survey: Descriptive statistics with comparison data from the 1969–70 and 1972–73 surveys.* Ann Arbor, Mich.: Institute for Social Research.

Rathke, Wade, and Joel Rogers. 1994. Labor strategies. Manuscript.

Rogers, Joel. 1990. Divide and conquer: Further "reflections on the distinctive character of American labor laws." *Wisconsin Law Review* 1990:1–147.

Rogers, Joel, and Charles Sabel. 1993. Imagining unions. *Boston Review* 18 (October/November): 10–12.

Rogers, Joel, and Wolfgang Streeck. 1994a. Productive solidarities: Economic strategy and left politics. In *Reinventing the Left,* ed. David Miliband, 128–45. London: Polity.

———. 1994b. Workplace representation overseas: The works councils story. In *Working under different rules,* ed. Richard B. Freeman. New York: Russell Sage Foundation.

Summers, Clyde. W. 1979. Industrial democracy: America's unfulfilled promise. *Cleveland State Law Review* 28: 29.

———. 1982. Past premises, present failures, and future needs in labor legislation. *Buffalo Law Review* 31:9–35.

———. 1990. Unions without majority: A black hole? *Chicago Kent Law Review* 66:531–48.

———. 1994. Employee voice and employer choice: A structured exception to section 8(A)(2). In *The Legal Future of Employee Representation,* ed. Matthew W. Finkin, 126–45. Ithaca, N.Y.: ILR.

Tirole, Jacques. 1986. Hierarchies and bureaucracies: On the role of collusion in organizations. *Journal of Law, Economics, and Organization* 2(2): 181–214.

Trumka, Richard L. 1992. On becoming a movement: Rethinking labor's strategy. *Dissent* 39(1): 57–60.

USDOL (United States Department of Labor). 1988. *The role of labor-management committees in safeguarding worker safety and health.* Washington, D.C.: Government Printing Office.

———. 1993. *Report on high performance work practices and firm performance.* Washington, D.C., July 26.

Visser, Jelle. 1991. Trends in trade union membership. In *Employment outlook July 1991,* 97–134. Paris: Organisation for Economic Co-operation and Development.

Wagner, Robert F. 1934. Company unions: A vast industrial issue. *New York Times,* March 11, sec. 9, 1.

Wallerstein, Michael. 1989. Union organization in advanced industrial democracies. *American Political Science Review* 83(2): 481–501.

Weil, David. 1994. *The impact of safety and health committee mandates on OSHA enforcement: Lessons from Oregon.* Washington, D.C.: Economic Policy Institute.

Weiler, Paul C. 1990. *Governing the workplace: The future of labor and employment law.* Cambridge: Harvard University Press.

Weitzman, Martin L., and Douglas L. Kruse. 1990. Profit sharing and productivity. In *Paying for productivity: A look at the evidence,* ed. Alan S. Blinder. Washington, D.C.: Brookings Institution.

Wever, Kirsten R., Thomas A. Kochan, and Peter Berg. 1991. Worker representation and further training: Comparative case evidence and policy lessons for the United States. August. Manuscript.

Wilcock, Richard C. 1957. Industrial management's policies toward unionism. In *Labor and the New Deal,* ed. Milton Derber and Edwin Young, 275–315. Madison: University of Wisconsin Press.

Wilensky, Harold L. 1981. Leftism, Catholicism, and democratic corporatism: The role of political parties in recent welfare state development. In *The development of welfare states in Europe and America,* ed. Peter Flora and Arnold J. Heidenheimer, 345–82. New Brunswick, N.J.: Transaction.

Wokutch, Richard E. 1992. *Worker protection, Japanese style: Occupational safety and health in the auto industry.* Ithaca, N.Y.: ILR.

Contributors

Elaine Bernard
Harvard Trade Union Program
1350 Massachusetts Avenue, Room 731
Cambridge, MA 02138

Göran Brulin
School of Business
Stockholm University
S-10691 Stockholm
Sweden

Modesto Escobar
Departamento de Sociologia
Universidad de Salamanca
Avenue Campo Charro s/n
E-37007 Salamanca
Spain

Michal Federowicz
Polish Academy of Sciences
Institute of Philosophy and Sociology
Lanceago 4-6
Natolin 02792
Poland

Richard B. Freeman
National Bureau of Economic Research
1050 Massachusetts Avenue
Cambridge, MA 02138

Edward P. Lazear
Graduate School of Business
Stanford University
Stanford, CA 94305

Anthony Levitas
Fundauz Wspolpracy
ul. Zurawia 4A
00-503 Warsaw
Poland

Walther Müller-Jentsch
Ruhr-Universität Bochum
Fakultat fur Sozialwissenschaft
D-44780 Bochum
Germany

Ida Regalia
University of Turin
Department of Social Sciences
via S. Ottavio, 50
I-10124 Turin
Italy

Joel Rogers
University of Wisconsin Law School
Madison, WI 53706

Wolfgang Streeck
Max-Planck-Institut für Gesell-
    schaftsforschung
Lothringer Str. 78
D-50677 Köln
Germany

Robert Tchobanian
Laboratoire d'Economie et de Sociologie
   du Travail
CNRS
35, avenue Jules Ferry
F-13626 Aix-en-Provence CEDEX
France

Jelle Visser
Vakgroep Sociologie
Universiteit von Amsterdam
Oude Hoogstaat 24
NL-1012 CE Amsterdam
The Netherlands

Sigurt Vitols
Wissenschaftszentrum Berlin
Reichpietschufer 50
D-10785 Berlin
Germany

Author Index

Subject Index